3 1336 00117 3765

D0952696

The War for the Union

VOLUME IV . . . *THE ORGANIZED WAR TO VICTORY 1864 • 1865*

by ALLAN NEVINS

CHARLES SCRIBNER'S SONS
New York

A–9.71(H)

Printed in the United States of America
Library of Congress Catalog Card Number 47-11072
SBN 684–10429–6

CONTENTS

ILLUSTRATIONS

ACKNOWLEDGMENT

The author wishes to express his appreciation for material aid given in the preparation of these last volumes of *The War for the Union* to the Guggenheim Foundation, the National Foundation on the Arts and Humanities, and Columbia University. He is deeply indebted to the staffs of the Library of Congress and of the Henry E. Huntington Library at San Marino, California. Without the active support of his colleagues Ray Billington, E. B. Long (a dedicated and most able aide in research), and John Niven, these volumes would never have been completed. The greatest debt is to Lillian K. Bean whose untiring effort can never be repaid. He also acknowledges gratefully the assistance of his daughters Anne Loftis and Meredith Mayer and his wife Mary Nevins. Finally, he would like to express his gratitude to Joseph G. E. Hopkins of Charles Scribner's Sons for his unflagging patience and devotion to the task of editing these volumes.

Allan Nevins

The War for the Union

1

Grant, Meade, and Sherman Take Command

ON HOW MANY FRONTS, as 1864 opened, did the war drag along at a snail's pace and with uncertain outlook for the Union! In Virginia, where the principal news was the ovation that Richmond gave the bold John H. Morgan after his escape from the Ohio penitentiary; at Charleston, where Beauregard held his lines while the Union fleet of ironclad monitors and wooden steamships rode out the winter gales; in northwestern Louisiana, where Kirby-Smith stood firm at Shreveport; in West Tennessee and northwest Mississippi, where Nathan B. Forrest had raised more than four thousand recruits for fresh campaigns; and at Knoxville, where Union troops were watching Longstreet. From Missouri and the Kentucky-Tennessee border had come a stream of dismal reports of men on both sides murdered in cold blood by guerrillas, although by the beginning of 1864 such activities had temporarily slackened. Daily rumors predicted that the Confederates would attempt another invasion of Pennsylvania, or strike at Little Rock, or win a French alliance. The one certainty was stated by Greeley's *Tribune:* "The country expects the war to be resumed with energy the moment it is possible for our armies to move."[1]

That the country's expectations would be met was demonstrated by a ringing summons from Lincoln on February 1: "Ordered, that a draft for five hundred thousand men to serve for three years or during the war will be made on the 10th day of March next, for the military service of the United States." He had called for 300,000 volunteers the previous October, but despite liberal Federal bounties ($402 for veterans, $302 for raw recruits), the response had been unsatisfactory. Recruiting details from field regiments were active in the North all winter, and the new drafts were expected to fill up the lagging State quotas.[2]

1. New York *Times*, January 28, 1864; Swiggett, Howard, *The Rebel Raider, a Life of John Hunt Morgan*, Garden City, 1937, Ch. X; Lytle, Andrew Nelson, *Bedford Forrest and His Critter Company*, New York, 1931, 257ff.
2. Lerwill, Leonard R., *The Personnel Replacement System in the U.S. Army*, Washington, 1954, 100-112.

Suddenly the opening of February brought a flurry of Union activity—partly successful, partly abortive—at half-a-dozen points. Sherman at Nashville had written Admiral D.D. Porter in December, 1863, regarding his plans which included a move up Red River: "I propose to strike at large armies and large interests." He now made good his words. With 20,000 men, he marched directly toward Meridian, Miss., where he ordered General William Sooy Smith with 7,000 cavalry to join him from Memphis. He would seize Meridian, a town of several thousand people near the eastern boundary of Mississippi, destroy the Confederate railroads and supplies about it, and lay waste the country. If successful, he and Smith could press on east to Selma, with its rich manufacturing facilities in the heart of Alabama, or turn south toward Mobile. Sherman later denied he had ever intended to go to Mobile. Beginning his march on February 3, Sherman reached Meridian with little loss, but Smith utterly failed him. He allowed Forrest to head him off at West Point, Mississippi, defeat him near Okolona, Mississippi, and compel him to retreat to Memphis. Sherman had to content himself with tearing up long stretches of railroad about Meridian, and destroying bridges, buildings, supplies, and farmhouses. "He leaves the country perfectly impoverished wherever he has been," declared Richmond papers.[3] Then he, too, returned to the Mississippi, at Vicksburg.

Early in February, Ben Butler planned a sudden descent upon Richmond, but the officer he sent out on this mission, Isaac J. Wistar, found the defensive lines too strong for an attack. Before the month ended, Kilpatrick's cavalry, with Colonel Ulric Dahlgren (son of the admiral) leading five hundred of its best men, launched another raid on the rebel capital, its primary object the release of Union captives in filthy Libby Prison. While Kilpatrick took prisoners on the outer Richmond lines and destroyed railroad property, young Dahlgren and many of his men were killed, and his command was scattered.[4] The gallant Dahlgren was widely mourned.

Much the most unfortunate development early in 1864, however, was the Red River expedition organized and led on land by N.P. Banks, Butler's successor in command of the Department of the Gulf. The genesis and blame for undertaking this expedition has long been a controversial subject among students. Halleck and Banks are usually censured for what became a first-class blunder, although Banks opposed it in the early stages of the planning, and Halleck, although he appeared to support it, was certainly echoing non-mili-

3. Quoted in New York *Tribune*, March 10, 1864; a good summary of the Meridian campaign is in the New Orleans *True Delta*, March 2, 1864. Sherman brought out huge numbers of mules and Negroes. *O.R.N.*, I, 25, 645.

4. Liddell Hart, Basil H., *Sherman, Soldier, Realist, American*, New York, 1929, 224-226; Wistar, Isaac Jones, *Autobiography*, New York, 1914, 1937, Chaps. VIII and IX.

tary considerations in Washington. Lincoln and others apparently favored some such move as the Red River Campaign in 1863 for three reasons: to bulwark Lincoln's new Reconstruction government in Louisiana; to obtain large amounts of cotton; and by possible movements into Louisiana and Texas to present a show of force to the French in Mexico which might discourage adventures in that area.

French troops had impudently entered Mexico City, June 7, 1863.[5] On July 29, 1863, Lincoln wrote Stanton, "Can we not renew the efforts to organize a force to go to Western Texas? . . . I believe no local object is now more desirable. . . ."[6] Welles was writing of July 31, when he said that Seward wanted a meeting with him and Lincoln to discuss a Texas occupation. The idea having been discussed for some weeks, Seward continued to press for a move into Texas at the Cabinet meeting of July 31, and in a later meeting with Stanton and Halleck.[7] On August 5, Lincoln wrote Banks, "Recent events in Mexico, I think, render early action in Texas more important than ever. . . ." The President then turned his attention to Louisiana politics.[8]

Halleck told Banks on August 6, "There are important reasons why our flag should be restored in some point of Texas with the least possible delay. Do this by land at Galveston, at Indianola, or any other point you may deem preferable. . . . There are reasons why the movement should be as prompt as possible. . . ." This message was sent to Banks by direction of Stanton.[9] Halleck enlarged on the subject August 10, writing that the previous dispatch was by order of Stanton, "the only condition imposed being that the flag of the United States should be again raised and sustained somewhere within the limits of that State. That order, as I understood it at the time, was of a diplomatic rather than of a military character, and resulted from some European complications, or, more properly speaking, was intended to prevent such complications. . . ." Halleck now declared that in his opinion Indianola and Galveston were not proper points of attack, but that the move should be up the Red River to Alexandria, Natchitoches, or Shreveport, with military occupation of Northern Texas.[10]

In response to Halleck's message urging a movement into Texas, Banks agreed upon the expediency of moving into so important a part of the country, adding that, "The rebellion in Louisiana is kept alive only by Texas. . . ."[11]

5. Roeder, Ralph, *Juarez and His Mexico*, New York, 1947: II, 512.
6. Lincoln, *Works*, VI, 354.
7. Welles, *Diary*, I, 287-391.
8. Lincoln, *Works*, VI, 364-366.
9. *O.R.* I, xxvi, pt. 1, 672.
10. *Ibid.*, 673.
11. *Ibid.*, 697-698.

The Texas operations were carried out in the fall, but fell short of expectations, for in September, 1863, an expedition to the Sabine was defeated by Dick Dowling and his handful of men at Sabine Pass. In October, the Bayou Teche expedition got to Opelousas and a little beyond. The Union forces landed at Brazos Santiago on November 2, and Brownsville, Rio Grande City, Aransas Pass, and Matagorda Island were occupied, but these small gains did not really constitute a major occupation of Texas. Halleck continued pressing for an advance, writing Grant on September 9 that if Frederick Steele from Arkansas and Banks would succeed, "all the Trans-Mississippi must return to the Union."[12]

In early December, Banks wrote Lincoln that it had been impossible within reasonable time to gain a foothold in Texas that season. He thought he did not have enough strength to march to Texas by either the Sabine or the Red.[13] Halleck maintained his pressure, and Seward congratulated Banks on the utility of his Texas operations.[14] Lincoln, on December 24, also thanked Banks for his "successful and valuable operations in Texas . . . ," urging him "now to give us a free-state reorganization of Louisiana. . . ."[15] The diplomatic objectives with regard to Texas had apparently been satisfied.

Halleck continued to advise Banks on a Red River operation in concert with Steele. Other reinforcements would be found.[16] On January 8, 1864, Halleck told Grant that Banks's campaign against Texas had been less for military than for political reasons. "The President so ordered," he added, "that it might be better to direct Union efforts for the present to the entire dispersion of rebel forces west of the Mississippi rather than to divide the Northern force also operating against Mobile and Alabama. . . ."[17]

Later historians concluded that the plan of operations was Halleck's, and that Lincoln approved it.[18] Halleck wired Banks on February 11, 1864,[19] that the substance of dispatches to him on this subject was given to the President and Secretary of War, and it was understood that, while stating his own views upon operations, Halleck should leave the general free to adopt such plans of campaign as he might deem best.

At any rate, Halleck, in his message of January 8, again had urged Banks to undertake a Red River campaign. Banks had long favored operations against

12. *O.R.* I, xxx, pt. 3, 475.
13. *O.R.* I, xxvi, 833.
14. Johnson, Ludwell, *Red River Campaign*, Baltimore, 1958, 41.
15. Lincoln, *Works*, VII, 89-90.
16. *O.R.* I, xxxiv, pt. 2, 15-16; 29-30.
17. *Ibid.*, 46-47.
18. Randall, James G., and Richard N. Current, *Last Full Measure*, New York, 1955, 145; Nicolay and Hay, *Lincoln*, VIII, 285ff; Williams, T. Harry, *Lincoln and the Radicals*, Madison, 1941, 341.
19. *O.R.* I, xxxiv, pt. 2, 293-294.

Mobile, along with Grant, but in late January he acquiesced. Having finally agreed to try the Red River, Banks sent Halleck a memorandum specifying certain indispensable steps to success. "Not one of these suggestions, so necessary in conquering the inherent difficulties of the expedition, was carried into execution," he later complained.

On March 12, Admiral Porter's fleet of more than twenty ironclads, tinclads, and other vessels entered the Red River and headed toward Alexandria, convoying the three divisions of Brigadier-General A.J. Smith from Sherman's army. Smith's troops captured Fort De Russey near Simsport, La., March 14; the river fleet went on up to Alexandria by March 15. While Banks was detained in New Orleans by the attempts at Union reconstruction of the State, he sent his troops north to Alexandria under William B. Franklin. By March 24, Banks himself was at Alexandria preparing to advance further toward Shreveport, but was now told he would have to return Sherman's troops by April 10. Thus, another obstacle had to be encountered along with low water, inhospitable country, and snipers. Furthermore, Banks really did not have a unified command. Porter and his navy men were quite independent, while A.J. Smith seemed to fancy his troops completely separate from Banks's army. No firm communications were established with Frederick Steele's expedition coming down through Arkansas. The worst impediment of all was the ravenous greed of the naval and the military forces, as well as the speculators, for the seizure of cotton.

The whole force, moving up the Red River, reached the Natchitoches and Grand Ecore area by April 3. At Sabine Crossroads or Mansfield, Louisiana, on April 8, Richard Taylor's Confederates halted Banks and inflicted on him a stunning defeat that ended the whole advance. Banks began to withdraw, and by April 11 he was back at Grand Ecore. He then retreated further down the Red River to Alexandria. According to his own report on the advance from Alexandria and return, including battles, Banks's losses were 289 killed, 1,541 wounded, and 2,150 missing. According to Taylor, the Federals lost 2,500 prisoners, 20 guns, and 250 wagons, but the repulse was conclusive in the general result, coming close to an utter rout.

The gunboats were now in great peril because of falling water in the Red River. Although the Confederates continued to harass the retreat, most of the vessels were brought safely down the river by the masterly construction of dams under the direction of Lt. Col. Joseph Bailey of Wisconsin. These dams permitted the accumulation of sufficient water to keep the gunboats afloat during their passage. By mid-May, the whole enterprise was over. Because neither the Union nor the Confederate forces had conducted themselves with credit, a bitter series of quarrels ensued on both sides. Meanwhile, Steele's

Union column had to return to Little Rock with little if any visible accomplishment.

The moral results were far-reaching, and for the North unhappy. "After the Red River campaign," wrote a participant who became its most effective historian, "no important operation was undertaken by either side in Louisiana. The Confederate forces in that State held out until the end of the war"—the rebel forces, that is, west of the Mississippi.[20] Moreover, the land attack on Mobile upon which Grant had counted so heavily was postponed.

But even as Banks failed, the really important operations of 1864 were about to begin in Virginia and Georgia.

[I]

"When I assumed command of all the armies"—so Grant began a terse chapter of his memoirs. He went on to explain that when he thus took charge, early in 1864, the Union and Confederate forces held much the same Virginia positions as earlier in the war. They stood equidistant between the Northern and Southern capitals, Grant's main forces lying along the northern bank of the Rapidan, Lee's along the southern. Advantage of numbers was with the Army of the Potomac, but advantage of position with the Army of Northern Virginia. Behind Lee the heavily wooded country was intersected by deep streams, difficult to cross until bridged; the roads were narrow and rough, hopelessly miry after rains. Lee was in position to move in response to Grant's expected drive, and back of him had strong defensive lines around Richmond and on the James to which at need he could retreat.

This had been a triumphant winter for Grant. Shortly before Christmas, leaving Thomas in command at Chattanooga, he had moved his headquarters to Nashville, and begun preparing for the spring campaign against Atlanta. Indeed, he took the first step in February, ordering Thomas to march against Dalton, Ga. His home county in Illinois gave him a diamond-hilted sword with a gold scabbard; Congress voted him its thanks for Chattanooga and a gold medal for the victories there and at Vicksburg; and as he rode in bitterly cold weather from Knoxville through Cumberland Gap to Lexington, Ky., he was cheered in every village. Early in 1864, a bill reviving the grade of Lieutenant-General and authorizing the President to confer it upon the Major-General who was most distinguished for courage, skill, and ability, introduced by Grant's patron Elihu Washburne, moved through Congress.

Its passage was by emphatic votes. However, a few critical voices were

20. Irwin, Richard B., "The Red River Campaign," *Battles and Leaders,* IV, 345, 362; cf. Taylor, Richard, *Destruction and Reconstruction,* New York, 1879, Ch. X.

raised: Grimes of Iowa declared that as Grant was already getting $6,000 a year, he was against ramming the hand of Congress into the Treasury to make his pay $13,000 or $14,000. But nearly everybody applauded Fessenden's assertion that if Grant had been at Antietam he would have demolished Lee, and if at Gettysburg the Confederates would never have recrossed the Potomac. The bill passed the House 96 to 41, and the Senate with only six dissenting voices. Lincoln had meanwhile let it be known that he would like to talk with some close friend of Grant. Washburne thereupon had Russell Jones, Federal Marshal in Illinois, call at the White House, where he volunteered an apt remark. "Mr. President," he said, "perhaps you would like to know whether Grant is going to be a candidate for the Presidency." Upon this, he handed Lincoln a letter in which Grant declared that nothing was further from his mind than high political office, and that he meant to support Lincoln in all circumstances and above all other men.[21]

The law providing for the lieutenant-generalship became effective as February ended. Grant was at once nominated, confirmed, and ordered to Washington. At dusk on March 8 he took a room at Willard's Hotel. He was halfway through dinner before guests noted his presence and raised a sudden cheer, for it was easy to overlook the short, slightly-built man with stooping shoulders, brown hair and beard, reddish mustaches, and mild blue eyes. When he went to the White House that evening—a reception evening—he entered the front door through a considerable crowd, the *Republican* having announced that he would attend. The President, gathering from the commotion that he had arrived, said, "This is General Grant, is it?" and received the equally simple reply, "Yes." As they shook hands, the crowd fell back, with no jostling or pushing. After a short conversation, the President turned Grant over to Seward, who took him to pay his respects to Mrs. Lincoln. Then the Secretary and General entered the East Room together, where amid cheer on cheer Grant was compelled to mount a sofa to shake hands with the throng.[22]

Later, Lincoln sat down in the Blue Room with Stanton and Nicolay to give Grant some instructions. "Tomorrow," he said, "at such time as you may arrange with the Secretary of War, I desire to make you a formal presentation of your commission as Lieutenant-General. I shall then make a very short speech, to which I desire you to reply for an object, and that you may be properly prepared to do so, I have written what I shall say, only four sentences

21. *Congressional Globe*, 38th Cong., 1st sess., Pt. I, 431, 798. In the House, James Garfield and Thaddeus Stevens raised objections. For Jones, see Richardson, Albert D., *A Personal History of Ulysses S. Grant*, Hartford, Conn., 1868, 380ff; Jones, George R., *Joseph Russell Jones*, Chicago, 1964, 42-43; Wilson, James Harrison, "Joseph Russell Jones," manuscript in possession of George R. Jones, 12-13.

22. Nicolay, John G., *Ms. Notes*, Nicolay Papers, LC, March 8, 1864.

in all, which I shall read from my manuscript as an example which you may follow and also read your reply; as you are perhaps not so much accustomed to speaking as myself. I therefore give you what I shall say that you may consider it and form your reply. There are two points that I would like to have you make in your answer: first, to say something which shall prevent or obviate any jealousy of you from any of the other generals in the service, and secondly, something which shall put you on as good terms as possible with the Army of the Potomac."[23]

Next day the ceremony took place at one, with the Cabinet, some staff officers, and Grant's oldest son looking on. Grant's speech had been hurriedly written in lead pencil on a half-sheet of note paper, and between his embarrassment and its illegibility, he stumbled badly, making neither of the points Lincoln had mentioned. Nicolay writes that the President had told him he contemplated bringing the general East to see whether he could not "do something with the unfortunate Army of the Potomac." Grant, determined on no account to fix his headquarters in Washington, immediately left to visit Meade's headquarters at Brandy Station.

This journey to the capital was even more important than people supposed. At first Grant had intended to exercise his supreme command from the West, for before his appointment he had written Halleck and others outlining some curious ideas as to the proper operations for 1864. The Western armies, he thought, should push forward from the Chattanooga-Mobile line to Atlanta and beyond, while the Eastern forces assumed a secondary rôle. "I shall recommend," he wrote Thomas from Nashville on January 19, 1864, "that no attempt be made towards Richmond by any of the routes heretofore operated on, but that a moving force of sixty thousand men be thrown into New Bern, or Suffolk, favoring the latter place, and move out destroying the road as far toward Richmond as possible. Then move to Raleigh as rapidly as possible, hold that point, and open communication with New Bern, even Wilmington. From Raleigh the enemy's most inland line would be so threatened as to force them to keep on it a guard that would reduce their armies in the field much below our own." Fortunately this strategy, evidently devised in distrust of the Army of the Potomac and its leaders, was never adopted.[24]

Instead, Grant's initial ideas were quickly revolutionized by pressure from Lincoln and Stanton, acquaintance with Meade and his staff, and a close view of the Eastern battle front. James Harrison Wilson tells us that Grant had intended not only to keep his headquarters in the West, but to make the tall,

23. *Ibid.*

24. *O.R.* I, xxxii, pt. 2, 100-101, 142, 143. Yet the use of a North Carolina bridgehead was not in itself a bad idea.

impressive William Farrar ("Baldy") Smith field-commander of the Army of the Potomac. Wilson ought to have known, for he had sat in conferences with Grant, Smith, and John A. Rawlins in Nashville, but we need more evidence before we accept his story. At any rate, the notion did not last. Grant's national strategy, he wrote Sherman at the beginning of April, was to move all parts of the Army simultaneously in coordinated action—Banks marching as soon as possible upon Mobile; Sigel advancing in the Shenandoah; and Sherman driving against Johnston's army to scatter it, to penetrate the Confederate interior as far as he could, and to do all damage possible to rebel war resources. He did not intend to lay down a plan of operations for Sherman, but to indicate an objective. From the Shenandoah operations Grant did not expect very much, but he borrowed a phrase from Lincoln to say, "if Sigel can't skin himself, he can hold a leg whilst some one else skins. . . ."[25]

Of course, Lincoln clung to his fundamental idea that the prime object of the North was not to close upon Richmond by water, but to close upon Lee's army by land and destroy it. Stanton held the same view. After talking with them, and with Meade and Ben Butler, and reflecting on the situation, Grant decided upon a direct movement from the Rapidan against Richmond. He also decided that Meade should keep command of the Army of the Potomac, while Smith took a lesser role. He would command one corps under Butler in the Department of the James, Q.A. Gillmore taking the other. Butler's force would then be sent from Fortress Monroe up the James in support of the principal army, trying to force the Confederates back along the river and into the entrenchments around Richmond while Meade drove down from the north. This seemed a good plan, but Smith, Gillmore, and Butler—men as ambitious, temperamental, and imperious as Napoleonic marshals—were soon at crippling odds.[26]

In his 1865 final report, Grant was later to say that he believed a continuous and active series of operations on the part of all troops was essential in 1864. He had felt that for far too long the Eastern and Western armies "acted independently and without concert, like a balky team, no two ever pulling together. . . ." Therefore he had determined to keep as coördinated a pressure as possible upon the enemy, now that Federal forces were under his command. He was convinced that the war could not be won "until the military power of the rebellion was entirely broken. . . ."[27]

25. *Ibid*, pt. 3, 245-246.

26. Grant, *Memoirs*, II, 116-117, 129-132; Wilson, James Harrison, *Life and Services of William Farrar Smith*, Wilmington, 1904, 82-83; Dodge, Granville, M., *Personal Recollections of President Abraham Lincoln, General Ulysses S. Grant and General William T. Sherman*, Council Bluffs, Iowa, 1914, 69-70.

27. Grant, U.S., *Report of Lieutenant General U.S. Grant of the Armies of the United States—1864-'65*, no date, no place, Grant's report of July 22, 1865.

Lincoln's exact rôle in setting up this plan is not altogether clear. Grant and Lincoln were conferring frequently, and even before Grant had come to Washington the President had conversed with him by telegraph. Lincoln is quoted as saying he was "powerfully reminded" of his old suggestion to move upon the whole line of the enemy so as to make use of superior Federal numbers.[28]

The simplicity of the plan is deceptive. At its best it was to involve the entire striking force of the Union, and thus keep the enemy more than busy in several widely separated fields. Yet no one part of the plan was dependent directly upon the other. It was not a house-of-cards whereby if one element failed the whole thing failed. It was directed not only against the armies of Lee and Johnston, but, despite later historians, against the inner fortress of the Confederacy combining all military aims, the enemy's armies, his communications, supplies, bases, territory, and people. It was to be a total offensive and the Union had the manpower and the know-how to carry it out.

[II]

Returning West in mid-March, Grant met Sherman, Rawlins, "Baldy" Smith, and other officers in Nashville, turned over his command to Sherman, and made a significant statement. He had accepted the lieutenant-generalship, he told them, on two conditions: that Washington should not interfere with his plans; and that he should control the commissary, quartermaster, ordnance, and other staff men, hitherto largely independent of the line commanders. Lincoln had replied that, while he possessed no legal authority to assign these officers, "nobody but myself can interfere with your orders, and you can rest assured that I will not do that."[29] Grant's news that he would move his headquarters to the Eastern theatre and keep close to Meade in the field must have been a shock to some of the Western group, although he softened it by adding that he intended to take several of the best Western officers with him.

Circumstances made this decision inescapable, as Lincoln and Stanton doubtless pointed out to Grant. The capture of Vicksburg and Port Hudson, the seizure of the whole line of the Mississippi, and the severance of the Confederacy in two, might well be termed the most decisive single operation of the war; but ultimate victory could be achieved only by bringing Lee and the most powerful single army of the South to surrender. The curious fact, if

28. Hay, John, *Lincoln and the Civil War in the Diaries and Letters of John Hay*, ed. Tyler Dennett, New York, 1939, 178-179.

29. Dodge, Grenville, H., Ms. Autobiography, Iowa State Hist. Soc. In his *Memoirs*, II, 123, Grant tells of an occasion when the President submitted some military ideas. Grant listened respectfully, but "I did not communicate my plans to the President, nor did I to the Secretary of War, or to General Halleck."

fact it be, was that Grant should ever have taken a different view. He was now quick to see the true requirements of the situation just as he was quick to perceive the high qualifications of Meade.

What was to become a strong mutual confidence, invaluable in the war effort, was springing up between Grant and Meade. It was the more important because Sheridan, Rawlins, James Harrison Wilson, and "Baldy" Smith all regarded the Pennsylvanian dubiously, and so did many others. The press felt a positive loathing for Meade, who had shown the inability of many professional military men to realize that the war was not their private affair, but a struggle in which the people had a right to full and free information. He was proud, sensitive, and irascible. In his thin-skinned way he had taken offense at a critical paragraph by the Philadelphia journalist Edward Crapsey, given him a humiliating parade through the lines with a placard reading "Libeler of the Press," and sent him off with orders never to return. In retaliation, correspondents had met and resolved to give Meade little publicity and no favor for the rest of the war.[30] The general's ungovernable temper had made countless enemies in the Army; fellow officers spoke of finding him like a bear with a sore head, nobody willing to approach him. Many political leaders had never forgotten his failure to pursue Lee energetically after Gettysburg. Zack Chandler and Ben Wade, the ruling spirits of the Committee on the Conduct of the War, were so hostile that on March 3 they called upon Lincoln, and told him that a sense of duty to the country compelled them to urge Meade's removal.[31]

Grant, however, saw through Meade's pride, touchiness, and irritability to his deeper merits—his mastery of military principles, and a certain cautious, uninspired, but efficient power of Army management that won the reluctant trust of Lincoln, and the readier esteem of Stanton. Grant knew that the man was restrained and safe, whereas "Baldy" Smith, like Hooker, might be impulsively erratic. Before long, in fact, Grant thought so much of him that when Meade was appointed a major-general in the regular Army, the General-in-chief sent a spirited protest to Henry Wilson because Meade's elevation followed that of Sheridan and Thomas instead of preceding theirs.[32] Meade in time came near a place alongside Rawlins as Grant's chief adviser, although he was never so close a friend.

30. Poore, Benjamin Perley, *Reminiscenses of Sixty Years in the National Metropolis*, New York, 1886, II, 126-127. Crapsey was a reputable correspondent, but printed rumors; Andrews, J. Cutler, *The North Reports the Civil War*, Pittsburgh, 1959, 545-548.

31. Patrick, Marsena, *Inside Lincoln's Army, The Diary of Marsena Rudolph Patrick*, ed. David S. Sparks, New York, 1964, and Wainwright, Charles P., *A Diary of Battle*, ed. Allan Nevins, comment on Meade's irascibility. The Committee castigated Meade harshly for the disastrous repulse before Petersburg, on July 30, 1864.

32. Jan. 23, 1865, copy in Meade Papers, Hist. Soc. of Pa.; Wilson was still head of the Senate Military Committee.

The desire of Grant to take able Western officers with him naturally elicited a strong protest from the volatile Sherman. He did not want to be left with second-raters. In the end, Grant had just a few Western stars with him, the chief being Sheridan in command of his cavalry. He also detached James Harrison Wilson, a brilliant topographical engineer by training, who had fought under McClellan and had become a major-general only five years after leaving West Point while head of the cavalry of a key division of Sherman's command. Grant assured Sherman that Wilson would add one-half to the effectiveness of his cavalry. "Baldy" Smith on the James and the ever-faithful Rawlins as heart of his staff were also withdrawn from the West. Sherman kept some of the best officers, of whom two, McPherson and Thomas, could be accounted hosts in themselves, while John M. Schofield, an Illinoisan who had roomed at West Point with McPherson and had seen eventful experience with Lyon in Missouri, possessed administrative gifts of unusual value. (In due course, Schofield and James Harrison Wilson, like Grant and Sherman, were to publish memoirs of exceptional penetration and vigor.)

While still in Nashville, Grant announced to Sherman, Rawlins, and others, that he intended to set all the Northern armies in motion on a given day, and that they must help make certain that Lee could not reinforce Joe Johnston, and that Johnston could not reinforce Lee. His poise and serenity did not fail him as he began preparing orders to his generals. In the East he had studied with concentrated care all the data upon the strength and resources of the chief commands, and had talked with Halleck, who had constantly urged that more troops be raised. Even though we discount somewhat the praise that Sherman later gave to the wonderful precision of Grant's mind and plans,[33] nevertheless, even if the instructions that he gave Sherman in two letters of April 4 and April 19, 1864, were not quite as complete as any of Wellington's to his lieutenants (this was Sherman's comparison), they were remarkably clear and detailed.

On the other side, Lee, who used scouts and spies to keep informed, was perplexed and distressed. "The approach of spring," he wrote Jefferson Davis, "causes me to consider with anxiety the probable action of the enemy and the possible operations of our armies in the ensuing campaign." This was a stiff way of saying, "I am worried about their probable sword-thrust and how we can parry it." He added, "If we could take the initiative and fall upon them unexpectedly, we might damage their plans and embarrass them the whole summer." A big if! The South might strengthen Longstreet in Tennessee for a sudden blow; or—another big if—Lee might draw Longstreet secretly and

33. Sherman, W.T., "The Grand Strategy of the War of the Rebellion," *Century Magazine*, February 1888, XL, No. 4, 591; *O.R.* I, xxxii, pt. 3, 245-246, 409f.

rapidly to his side, and force Meade back to Washington, creating sufficient alarm to weaken any Union offensive. Thus he looked desperately from side to side to escape the coming blow. He had no desire for another Antietam or Gettysburg—"We are not in a position, and never have been in my opinion, to invade the enemy's country with a prospect of permanent benefit."[34]

On March 23, Grant was back in Washington, and three days later made his headquarters at Culpeper Court House. On his passage through the capital the author of *Two Years Before the Mast* glimpsed him, a man with no gait, no manners, no dignity, and a scrubby aspect withal. "He had a cigar in his mouth, and rather the look of a man who did, or once did, take a little too much to drink."[35] Only on closer scrutiny did Richard Henry Dana perceive that the shabby officer, like somebody shelved on half-pay with nothing to do but loaf around Willard's, "had a clear blue eye, and a look of resolution, as if he could not be trifled with, and an entire indifference to the crowd about him." Next morning Dana recorded some fresh impressions. "He gets over the ground queerly. He does not march, nor quite walk, but pitches along as if the next step would bring him on his nose. But his face looks firm and hard. . . ." His air of determination impressed a Yankee colonel, Theodore Lyman, who noted that "he habitually wears an expression as if he had determined to drive his head through a brick wall, and was about to do it." Late in life Grant remarked that a successful general required so much health, resilience, and energy that he would not like to put one in the field past fifty.[36] He was in excellent health, and about forty-two.

[III]

Thus Grant devoted April to his final preparations. In the seventeen different departments under his command he had probably about 535,000 men present for duty. He would have to give direction first of all, of course, to Meade in Virginia, who by conservative estimates at the end of April had in the Army of the Potomac 102,000 present for duty. Burnside's Ninth Corps, operating with this army though for a time not part of it, would participate in the campaign with enough men to give Grant a total of 121,500. Ben Butler's army

34. Lee to Davis, Feb. 3, 1864, A. De Coppet Collection, Princeton Univ. Lee knew that the Army of the Potomac would move in the spring, that it was being reorganized, that every train brought it fresh recruits, that every available regiment at the North was said to be destined to it, and that camps and railroads were guarded with a closeness that pointed to secret preparations. Davis to Lee, *Ibid.*, March 30, 1864.

35. R.H. Dana Jr., to his wife, April 21, 1864, Dana Papers, Mass. Hist. Soc.

36. Lyman, Theodore, *Meade's Headquarters, 1863-1865*, Boston, 1922, 80-83; Young, J.R., *Around the World with General Grant*, New York, 1879, II, 353.

for the advance up the James numbered 53,000.[37] Grant would try to coördinate Butler's movements and those of Franz Sigel's force in the Shenandoah with his own main army. He would have difficulties, for his subordinate generals had their idiosyncrasies.

Butler's abilities were unquestionable, and he was a forcible administrator. He was also a master of quick, clever marches, feints, ruses, and shrewd surprises. He had held difficult posts in Baltimore and New Orleans with great credit, great publicity, and great friction. Nobody ever doubted his energy; nearly everybody doubted his character. He was endlessly useful and endlessly troublesome. Only a Dickens could do justice to his remarkable combination of gifts, faults, and picturesque anfractuosities. Long hampered and limited, he at last rejoiced in an independent and important theatre of action. Compared with him, Sigel, now briefly commander of the Department of West Virginia, was all too simple. This German revolutionary, New York militiaman, and St. Louis school director, journalist, and politician, had two great assets—fiery zeal for high causes, and eloquent power in rallying German-Americans to the Union. He had also two deep-seated defects—bad judgment and general clumsiness. It was not long until Grant pushed him aside for "lack of aggression." As for Burnside of the famous muttonchop whiskers, a handsome failure, an impressive blunderer, he had at last scored his second notable success by capturing Knoxville, the strategic heart of East Tennessee. After this (he entered the city September 2-3, 1863), hardy mountaineers flocked to him in groups of twenty and fifty, with their horses, to enlist. Burnside had then defended the city successfully against Longstreet's thrust later in the fall. It could be said to Burnside's discredit that he was unfit to command an army, and to his credit that he knew it.[38]

Facing Grant stood Lee, with about 62,000 men present for duty after Longstreet rejoined him, and with his unquestioned genius.[39]

In giving some direction to all the armies of the republic, East and West, Grant would have to rely heavily upon the telegraph system as it reached out to all the headquarters. Even with the network that Eckert had established, the task would be difficult, particularly in keeping contact with armies on active operations. Grant would also have to allow a large autonomy to his most trusted generals, especially Sherman, and to work out an amicable *modus ope-*

37. According to *O.R.* I, xxxiii, 1036, 1045, 1053. The figures in Humphreys, A.A., *The Virginia Campaign of 1864 and 1865*, New York, 1879, 14-17, and in Porter, Horace, *Campaigning with Grant*, New York, 1897, 36-41, are essentially the same. See also *O.R.* I, xxxiii, 1297-1298.

38. "Burnside in Knoxville," New York *Tribune*, Sept. 8, 1863. See Grant's verdict in his *Memoirs*, II, 539.

39. Freeman, Douglas Southall, *R.E. Lee*, New York, 1934, III, 270, gives the Confederate numbers most authoritatively.

randi with Meade, yokefellow rather than subordinate on the front against Lee. Would the partnership with so sensitive, hot-tempered a man succeed? It was to the credit of both that it ran almost as smoothly as the yoking of Lee and Stonewall Jackson had run, and with almost the same lubricant of mutual respect—though Grant and Meade could never be called men of complementary genius like Lee and Jackson.

Grant's elevation to the chief command meant almost total extinguishment for Halleck. The lamp that had never burned brightly now gave off waning rays. John Hay had erroneously concluded that Halleck was "badly billious" about the new chief and his steady rise, but he really was not, in part because he knew that he had dropped below all license to jealousy. Lincoln had become contemptuously frank, to intimates, about his incapacity. The President recalled that when the government sent for Halleck after the failure of the Peninsular campaign, the general had stipulated that he be given the responsibility and power of a commander-in-chief. He enjoyed that altitude until his selected army commander Pope collapsed at Second Manassas while the thunder of Lee's guns vibrated in the Washington streets. Then, said Lincoln, Halleck lost all nerve and pluck, so that he became little more than a first-rate clerk, evading all large responsibilities. He had been adroit enough to manoeuvre Hooker, just before Gettysburg, into a position where Hooker felt constrained to resign, but to do this he had needed the help of Stanton and of Hooker's own ineptness. From the moment of Grant's elevation he relapsed, with good grace, into the position of a capable office-manager in Washington for the general. Many officers regarded him as scornfully as did Ben Butler.[40]

The destiny of the country now rested upon two Mid-Westerners, Lincoln and Grant. They had sprung from the common people of the Mississippi Valley; they had scanty background of cultivated homes or communities; a dozen years earlier they had been obscure. In fact, they had long seemed without heroic traits. As Lincoln had entered the Presidency untutored in administration and needing to learn countless lessons as he went, so Grant had entered upon high command ignorant of large-scale war. At Belmont he had been an amateur relying heavily upon luck. At Forts Henry and Donelson his luck held, though some of his movements compared dubiously with those of the older, more experienced Charles F. Smith. At Shiloh he was still amateurish, making dire blunders before the battle just as did Sherman. But he enjoyed three blessings: the opportunity to rise gradually from low rank; the capacity

40. Ben Butler exploded this July: "Now there is General Halleck, what has *he* to do? At a moment when every true man is laboring to his utmost, when the days ought to be forty hours long, General Halleck is translating French books [on strategy] at nine cents a page; and sir, if you should put those nine cents in a box and shake them up, you would form a clear idea of General Halleck's soul!" Lyman, *Meade's Headquarters, 1863-1865*, Boston, 1922, 193.

to learn rapidly from his errors; and the assistance of loyal and discerning men who divined his potentialities. Fellow generals helped him; Elihu Washburne helped him; friendly newspapermen in Chicago and New York helped him—and he justified their faith.

His principal gift was that which English-speaking peoples have always esteemed most, strength of character. Intellectually, he must be ranked below the major strategists of the war; below Joe Johnston, Sherman, and Thomas—far below Stonewall Jackson and Lee. Although his memoirs are justly esteemed to be among the ablest of all military reminiscences, and show in the first volume especially (before illness impaired his powers) much lucidity and penetration, they exhibit more soundness of judgment than strength of reflection. They are as devoid of subtlety or imagination as Caesar's, and their conclusions are sometimes defensive rationalizations, after the event, of lines of action ill-planned at the time. They disclose little of the intellectual power of Napoleon, Wavell, or Bradley.

For the work of the fighter, however, he had better qualities than those of the cerebral gymnast. One was logical vision. He was a clear, simple thinker, with the power of sorting out from many facts the few that were vitally important, of seeing in a complex situation the basic outline. He saw how important it was to seize Paducah in 1861, how Donelson could be taken in 1862, how Vicksburg could be captured in 1863 by a flanking march to the south, and how Chattanooga could be made a gateway to Georgia and the Carolinas in 1864. He saw that when he had established a line in Virginia a little longer than Lee's, a repulse could mean simply a swing to the flank. His staff filled him with facts and theories from which he selected the few that counted. Too much imagination about enemy numbers had paralyzed McClellan; too much pedantry about logistics had ruined Rosecrans; but if Grant was sometimes too simple, as when before Shiloh he thought that one battle might mean final victory, his grasp of essentials rested upon an extremely shrewd faculty of elimination.

His soundness of judgment was supported, like Lee's and Wellington's, by traits that helped make him a great captain. First of these was his decisive promptness. Having made up his mind about a situation, he moved. He did not wait for perfection in training and equipment, an impeccable plan, or overwhelming numerical superiority. He marched—on Paducah, Donelson, Grand Gulf, Jackson, Vicksburg, Petersburg. Second, was his nerve; in tight squeezes he kept his head. At Belmont, he coolly waded his horse out of a Confederate trap. At Donelson, he rallied the line and calmly inspected the Confederate knapsacks. After the first day at Shiloh, he waited unperturbed for dawn, for Buell's arrival, and the wavering of the Confederate onset. A third trait was tenacity. He never knew when he was beaten, for he had the bulldog instinct to hold fast.

With some reservations, we may also say that he had an instinctive ability to distinguish between true and false humanitarianism. A man of gentle ways, never angrier than when he saw a horse maltreated, he tried in the main to spare his troops useless bloodshed. Yet he saw that the truest economy in lives was often a temporary ruthlessness in expending them. He would not have hesitated to follow the Confederate repulse at Gettysburg by firm, unhesitating action.

And another invaluable trait was his strong instinct for obedience to the civil arm. Although naïve in civil affairs, seldom fully grasping them, he knew that when the President and Congress ordered, he must obey. And by the word "obey," as he proved in recruiting Negroes, he meant complete obedience. McClellan, Butler, McClernand, Frémont, Hooker, and Banks played politics with the Army, but never Grant.

Much might also be said about his modesty, contrasting with the strut of other generals; his avoidance of loose language and profanity; his Spartan regimen, a weakness for liquor at relaxed moments excepted; and his generosity to the foe, well illustrated by his letter explaining why he dealt so magnanimously with the prisoners taken at Vicksburg. To be sure, he had his share of faults and shortcomings. Generosity was not evident in his jealous attitude toward his rival McClernand or his perplexing treatment of Thomas. Regard for candor came under eclipse when he deliberately obscured the facts by failing to send in a proper report on Shiloh. Conscientiously vigilant in days of crisis, he marred his record by two deplorable sprees on slack days in loose surroundings. Down to Vicksburg he appeared to many comrades in arms simply a resolute soldier of common abilities and impulses—and some thought much too common.[41]

But he had elemental strength when the republic needed precisely that, and needed it above all else. Lincoln summed up this supreme fact in explaining why he preferred Grant to other generals: "He fights." Then, too, Sherman put his finger on another vital point when he wrote that Grant was "a growing general" throughout the war; he grew all the way from Camp Yates to Appomattox.[42]

Such a man could make mistake after mistake, and still profit by his errors. Military associates of Grant pointed to a variety of blunders. At Belmont, they said, he had mismanaged two brigades, let some of his troops become a rabble

41. See Grant, *Memoirs*, I, 570-572, for his fine position on the Vicksburg prisoners. One spree was reportedly at Vicksburg, another in New Orleans.

42. Sherman to a friend Nov. 18, 1879, in *Century Magazine*, April 1897, 821.

of looters, and almost lost a regiment, the 27th Illinois. After that engagement he should have organized a working staff, but neglected it, and let his time be carelessly devoured by details. When he marched after Fort Henry from the Tennessee to the Cumberland, he permitted excessive dispersion of his troops; and some thought after Donelson that he seemed too confused by his unexpected victory to grasp the rich fruits at hand. For his failure to entrench at Shiloh and throw out scouts he might well have been cashiered. His loss of men and stores at Holly Springs could not be blamed entirely upon a stupid subordinate, and his first bloody assault upon the Confederate lines at Vicksburg was a cruel error. But all generals err, Grant profited more than most from error, and as Lincoln declared: "He fights."[43]

Three comments shed some illumination upon the innermost man. Horace Porter believed that Grant's most extraordinary quality was his simplicity, a simplicity so extreme that many overlooked it. A remark by John M. Schofield reinforces the statement of Hamilton Fish that Grant was the most truthful man he ever knew. "He was incapable of any attempt to deceive anybody except for a legitimate purpose, as in military strategy; and above all, he was incapable of deceiving himself." A mail clerk at Grant's headquarters added another perceptive bit. The general was always perfectly self-possessed, giving the impression that he knew what he meant to do without hesitation or fluster. "He was never in a hurry."[44]

[IV]

On May 3-4, 1864, at the same time that Butler commenced moving his troops up the James River, the Army of the Potomac began moving across the Rapidan, using fords and pontoon bridges, and pressed into the wooded country beyond. Sherman was to advance from Chattanooga two days later with the combined Armies of the Tennessee, the Cumberland, and the Ohio. The grand coordinated sweep had begun. The Army of the Potomac was Meade's army, for any orders Grant gave it were delivered through Meade. It was also an Army of tested corps commanders—Sedgwick, longer with this force than any other high officer; Hancock, supervising most of the trains, in the field for the first time since his Gettysburg wound; Warren, one of the first regular Army officers to ask and receive high volunteer command.[45] But the most important fact was that the days of disjointed action, when the armies of the

43. See criticisms by A.L. Conger, "The Military Education of Grant as a General," *Wisconsin Magazine of History*, (1920-21) IV, 239-260.

44. Porter, *Campaigning with Grant, op. cit;* 13-16, 515 and *passim*. Garland, Hamlin, Interview with Schofield, Garland Papers, UCLA, Box 49; interview with M.H. Strong, *ibid.*

45. Page, C.S., New York *Tribune*, May 6, 1864.

West and of the East had acted independently, with confusing complications, were at an end. The Confederates still had the advantage of interior lines, but the Union possessed the greater advantage of superior numbers, managed with centralized control.[46] Colonel G.F.R. Henderson, who praises as warmly the fighting qualities of the Union soldiers as the wisely planned strategy of Grant, points out that after Grant assumed command, Lincoln ceased his anxious and well-meant but often vexatious and unwise interference with Federal military commanders. The spirit of the troops was high. Many familiar place-names reappeared in dispatches: Ely's Ford, Chancellorsville, Thoroughfare Gap, Germanna Ford. As the first advance, with Warren in the rear, gained distances up to a dozen miles, Stanton expressed a hope of "full and complete success." Grant was elated. Although he had crossed the river just where Lee had expected, the formidable Southern army did little to obstruct him, the first movements of Longstreet, who arrived on the 6th, being dilatory. Some Union divisions might have thrust farther south, but this would have exposed them to a flank attack, left their trains insecure, and tired the men on the eve of heavy fighting.[47] The object was not to take Richmond, but to destroy or paralyze Lee's army—a less costly and arduous operation.

Sunrise on May 5 found the Army of the Potomac pushing deep into the fitly-named Wilderness. This was a district of low sandy soil, worthless for agriculture, but covered, save for scattered open patches and swampy spots, with fairly dense thickets of oak, hickory, and pine, stunted to the size of saplings fifteen to thirty feet tall. The dense bushes and half-formed leaves of the hardwood stands shut off the vision at about fifty yards. When the gray skirmishers of A.P. Hill's corps opened fire on some Union troops under G. W. Getty, they were within easy range, but quite invisible.[48] The fighting immediately became fierce, until in many places the battle-lines grappled at almost pointblank range. Inevitably, as smoke filled the woods, the troops desperately wielding axes to fell trees and bushes became confused. Some regiments lost touch with other units of their division; and the contest swayed back and forth, with sharp losses, but no real advantage on either side. The use of artillery or cavalry was impossible, and any manoeuvering extremely difficult. On the second day of the fighting Longstreet was seriously wounded, a heavy blow to the South, while the North lost James S. Wadsworth. The death

46. Cf. G.F.R. Henderson, *The Science of War*, London, 1910, 255-279.

47. Stanton's phrase is in the dispatch of May 8 to Gen. John A. Dix in New York; New York *Tribune*, May 9. See Law, E.M., "From the Wilderness to Cold Harbor," *Battles and Leaders*, IV, 118, and Wolseley, Garnet Joseph, *The American Civil War*, ed. James A. Rowley, Charlottesville, Va., 1964, 197-199; Grant, *Memoirs*, II, 177ff; Humphreys, *The Virginia Campaigns of 1864 and 1865*, 20ff; and Grant's report in *O.R.* I, xxxvi, pt. 1, 18ff.

48. Lyman, Theodore, *Meade's Headquarters*, *op.cit.*, 89.

of this high-minded, intrepid, and patriotic veteran of Gettysburg, shot in the head while rallying troops and expiring next day within enemy lines, caused great grief in his own area of upper New York State. Impetuous attacks, for both Grant's and Lee's armies had resolved to attack, developed into a stern contest of endurance, not unlike the tenacious fighting about Port Arthur in the Russo-Japanese War, or in front of Stalingrad in the Second World War.

Why did the Union army attack in this Wilderness tangle? Grant told the eight senior members of his staff the night before his offensive that he had weighed the question whether he should assault Lee's left, or his right. A movement against the rebel left offered more decisive results if it succeeded, and would best block any attempt by Lee at a northward thrust, but it would cut off the Union army from easy communication with its bases on the Rappahannock and Potomac, and compel transportation of huge quantities of ammunition and other supplies by heavily guarded wagon-trains. A blow against Lee's right would be facilitated by easy water carriage, for materials could be brought up from the junction of the Rappahannock and Rapidan, while wounded men could be taken out by the same smooth water carriage. Troops fighting on Lee's right would also be nearer Ben Butler's army advancing up the James. Though Meade emphatically disagreed, he was overruled.[49]

Hence Grant and Meade had crossed the Rapidan below the main position of Lee's army, Confederate headquarters being at Orange Court House. They hoped to defeat Lee, or at least push him back into the fortifications about Richmond. Grant had no burning desire to take that city, and no desire whatever to make an assault against troops protected by its defenses. He had always comprehended the possibility that he might have to conduct a siege of Richmond or the Richmond-Petersburg axis. If necessary, he had written Meade on April 17, siege-guns, shells, and general equipment could be rapidly brought from the Washington arsenal and Fortress Monroe. Preparations had been made for all types of water transportation, connecting with land carriage. "The means of moving heavy artillery is always at hand with an army as well as the means of constructing batteries. I will take advantage of Gen. Hunt's

49. A friend of Meade's, Henry Carey Baird, set down some reminiscences in his papers in the E. C. Gardiner Collection of the State Historical Society of Pennsylvania. He quoted Meade as saying that he and Grant had only one sharp disagreement. This was just before the Rapidan crossing. "I wanted," General Meade said, "to move by the right flank, while General Grant wished to move by the left." Grant said, "General Meade, I wish you to understand that this army is not to manoeuvre for position." Meade replied, "General Grant, you will find that you have a consummate general to fight, and that you will have to manoeuvre for position." Meade added that the army never did anything but manoeuvre for position, and never got it. *Newsletter* of Ulysses S. Grant Assoc., Vol. III, No. 3, April 1966.

suggestions as to the number, calibre, etc. of guns necessary for it." Yet he looked forward to open battle, not to siege operations.[50]

Tension rose high in the North. Stanton telegraphed Dix on the 9th that the fighting of the previous days had been the fiercest in modern times. Grave anxiety persisted as news of the two-day battle of the Wilderness trickled in. The struggling armies had been introduced to the area in the Chancellorsville fighting; now they were clasped to its thorny bosom. Tangled trees and brush, uneven ground, and numberless pits and gullies, made it impossible for either side to preserve distinct formations, so that men fought by squads, not companies. Only the roar of rifle-fire, as Hancock later wrote, disclosed the position of the troops to those at a distance, the thud of artillery punctuating it, although in this area cannon could be little used.[51] As fighting began, Ewell and Hill moved forward to meet the Union advance. The Southerners profited somewhat from their superior knowledge of the terrain, the Federal maps being inaccurate and confusing, and from the fact that the inhabitants could tell them about the little woods roads, the clearings, the winding streamlets, the shafts sunk in places for iron ore, and the swampy spots left undrained.

The general direction of the Confederate attack was from the southwest, striking the Union flank as Grant moved southeast; and the rebels struck hard.

Grant's aide Horace Porter gives us graphic vignettes of the general in action. Riding forward on May 5th, he found Meade waiting at the intersection of two highways near the deserted Wilderness Tavern and its weed-grown yard. Here he ordered all forces to seize the initiative and attack vigorously, and then rode on with Warren, Grant slouchy in his plain garb, Warren smart in a fresh blue uniform with yellow sash. The fighting that day left Grant fairly satisfied, though as he said, both sides battled against the forest rather than each other. But the combat on the 6th, when it reached its climax, was quite different in outcome. On their right the Union forces got nowhere, in the center they made little progress, and on their left one brigade after another was thrown back in confusion. At one time late that afternoon word came that the enemy had burst entirely *through* Hancock's line. At headquarters Grant and Meade, their backs to a tree, heard the officer bearing the report, sent reinforcements, and listened impassively to the distant battle clamor. Then Grant said with laconic emphasis, "I don't believe it"—and he was right.[52]

50. For the letter to Meade, see Meade Papers, State Hist. Soc. of Pennsylvania. A little later, April 26, Grant had written Halleck, "The Army of the Potomac is in splendid condition and evidently feels like whipping somebody; I feel much better with this command than I did before seeing it." Ill. State Hist. Soc.

51. Humphreys, *op.cit.*, 44 ftn.; Lyman, *Meade's Headquarters, op.cit.*, 90.

52. Porter, *Campaigning with Grant, op.cit.*, 53-54, 59; C.A. Page in New York *Tribune*, May 10, 1864.

During the afternoon of May 6th, General John B. Gordon's brigades captured two Union generals, Alexander Shaler and Truman Seymour, forced their troops into ragged disarray, and took many prisoners. As twilight deepened the Southerners, struggling through the thickets, themselves became disorganized. It was fortunate, Early writes, that darkness fell to close the affray, for the Northerners might have perceived the disorder and taken advantage of it.[53] That daytime battle had been gloomy enough—gloomy with the shadow of death. Trees riddled by the artillery fell with a crash. Forest fires raged, with ammunition wagons exploding, dead bodies roasting, and wounded crawling frantically to escape the flames.

Yet Grant slept soundly that night, and was up at dawn on the 7th to sit by the campfire in foggy air still darkened by smoke. Porter's hero-worshipping book puts some complacent utterances in Grant's mouth. According to Porter, Grant spoke of the previous day as in one sense a drawn battle, but really an advantage for the North. "We remain in possession of the field, and the forces opposed to us have withdrawn to a distance from our front and taken up a defensive position." This alleged comment, published in 1897, thirty-odd years after the event, does not sound like the modest Grant—and it was not accurate. Lee had been substantially on the defensive from the beginning, and the fact that his numerically inferior army had not smashed the Union lines was nothing to boast about. And what of the price of the battle? Men presently ascertained that the Union losses on the 5th and 6th of May had been fearful. The Army of the Potomac, with Burnside's corps, lost 12,485 men killed and wounded, while lists of the missing brought casualties up to 15,500. The Confederate losses were at most 8,000 killed and wounded, and 3,400 missing.[54]

Once more, long rosters of dead and maimed darkened the pages of newspapers North and South. One of the best Union regiments, the Twentieth Massachusetts, had lost about one-third of its men. Philadelphia had a day of mourning as the brave General James S. Wadsworth's body, delivered to Union troops by the Confederates, was brought through the city to be laid at rest in the Genesee Valley. Many a town and hamlet, many a country farmhouse, were draped in black as thousands of families met the shock of bereavement. And how gloomy the scene of the slaughter! Theodore Lyman wrote that most officers had seen no rebels, only smoke, bushes, and blue-clad men tumbling in all directions. Gone were the days of lines advancing, bands playing, and

53. Early, Jubal A., *Autobiographical Sketch and Narrative of the War Between the States*, Philadelphia, 1912, 346-351. See the anonymous "Recollections of Jubal Early," *Century Magazine*, N.S., XLV, 1905, 311-313.

54. Porter, *Campaigning with Grant*, *op.cit.*, 65-76; Humphreys, *op.cit.*, 53, 54. The figures for Union losses as given in *O.R.* I, xxxvi, pt. 1, 133, are 2,246 killed, 12,037 wounded, and 3,383 missing, a total of 17,666. Freeman, Lee, III, 297, states the Confederate losses in killed and wounded at 7,600.

platoons delivering united volleys. Now the officers bellowed, "Left face—prime—forward!"; the muskets went wrang, wr-r-rang for hours; and as brush fires started, the bleeding wounded streamed to the rear.[55]

It was clear to Union observers on the 7th that continued attempts to force through the Wilderness would be bloody futility, and that the Northern army must be swung to a route where it could attack in open country. As Grant sat under a pine tree stoically pondering on the third day, Colonel Lyman heard him say: "Tonight Lee will be retreating south."[56] Lee had no such intention. He had the use of two good parallel roads in holding on—the Orange and Fredericksburg plank-road and the Orange and Fredericksburg turnpike, running east from Orange directly against Grant's advancing line. On the night of the 4th, the front forces of the two armies had made bivouac in close proximity to each other on the roads just named; and on the morning of the 5th, while the Union columns continued their dogged advance, Ewell on the Confederate side, with equal doggedness, went on marching eastward, so that a lively clash was resumed. The Union men who pretended that they had won a strategic success in Lee's failure to fling back their advance upon Richmond claimed too much. Lee *had* momentarily stopped them. His army was more daring and rapid; it showed a fiercer discipline—in part the discipline of desperation, in part the discipline of tremendous faith in its leaders; it made better use of entrenchments. Only dubious consolation could be found in the losses Hancock and Sedgwick had inflicted, for the larger number of fresh graves lay on the Northern side. The real comfort for Grant was that his vastly stronger army held Lee, not so tightly that he could not manoeuvre, but so firmly that he could never advance.

As the battle closed, a Northern Senator, surveying the frightful carnage, exclaimed: "If that scene could have been presented to me before the war, anxious as I was for the preservation of the Union, I should have said: 'The cost is too great; erring sisters, go in peace.' " A Southern Senator would have said, "Ah, what folly to secede!"[57]

At dawn on the 7th, the initiative seemed to lie with Lee. Would he attack

55. Pearson, H.G., *James Wadsworth of Geneseo*, New York, 1903, 289-290; Lyman, *Meade's Headquarters, op.cit.*, 101.

56. Lyman, *op. cit.*, 102.

57. This statement by Henry Wilson, Senator from Massachusetts and Vice-President, known as "the cobbler of Natick" when he entered public life, was characteristic of his humanitarian attitude toward battle costs—an attitude widely shared North and South by both Union and Confederate leaders witnessing the truly appalling mortality on the battlefield. According to Kirkley, statistician of the War Department, the Union army lost 67,058 men killed, and 43,012 died of wounds received on the battlefield. The Confederate rolls justify Thomas L. Livermore in estimating the Confederate losses as 86,886 killed and died of battle action, which he says "must be much below the full number." Livermore, *Numbers and Losses, in the Civil War in America*, 6.

at the center, lie still behind his fortified line, or launch a flank movement? Union troops quickly ascertained that the Confederate front was so fully intrenched, with powerful artillery at hand, that a charge was impracticable. But Grant had already decided upon a night march southeast to Spotsylvania Court House, between him and Richmond. Detailed orders were issued. Wagon trains were to move at four in advance of the infantry. At dusk they were to park, and let Warren's troops pass them, while Hancock's corps held a screening position. After Warren had gone, Hancock was to follow him. Grant hoped that, containing Lee's right flank, he could move on toward the rebel capital.[58]

But Lee, who knew the importance of Spotsylvania, had anticipated the stroke. In the race for the crossroads he intended to win, again barring Grant's road—and win he did. By dawn of the 8th, two Confederate divisions under General Richard H. Anderson were in position to assist Fitzhugh Lee's cavalry in halting the Union advance. During a morning clash, Northern visions of an easy progress melted away in the reality of another bloody field with a series of uncertain battles beyond it.

[V]

Meanwhile, the restlessly energetic Sherman had put his armies on the march just after Grant's. "We are now moving," he wrote his wife from Chattanooga on May 4, "I will go to Ringgold tomorrow, and will then be within five miles of the enemy."[59] His letter breathed the assurance of Nelson's famous dispatch written "within sight of the combined fleets of France and Spain." Yet he did not underestimate his task, for he knew that it would require a strong army to push into a hostile country along a single railroad, and against his determined opponent, Joseph E. Johnston, leading between 60,000 and 70,000 effective troops. Sherman's three corps commanders, Thomas at Chattanooga with more than 60,000 men, McPherson in northern Alabama with about 30,000, and Schofield in eastern Tennessee with around 17,000, could concentrate in a way to give him more than 100,000 troops. In fact, he soon put his fighting strength at 112,000 including cavalry, and added that he could not possibly supply more. He had capably equipped his force with horses, wagons, ammunition, provisions, and forage, and he felt complete confidence in it. It is a big army and a good one, he wrote his wife, and a little

58. Grant, *Memoirs*, II, 208-212, where Grant asserted that "Lee, by accident, beat us to Spotsylvania;" Meade's Report in *O.R.* I, xxxvi, pt. 1, 189-190.

59. Sherman, William T., *Home Letters of General Sherman*, ed. M.A. DeWolfe Howe, New York, 1909, 288-295.

later, in his exuberant way, he crowed a bit more lustily: "I think I have the best army in the country."[60]

His objectives might be defined as the capture of the vital railway center of Atlanta, the crippling or destruction of Johnston's army, and the further splitting of the Confederacy. He had just told Thomas, "We must whip Joe Johnston wherever he may be."[61] He would have to battle a mountainous country traversed by many streams, its rough, wooded slopes and steeps giving the Confederates many advantages. Johnston had entrenched himself in front of Dalton, a quarter of the way from Chattanooga to Atlanta, and had laid out excellent defensive positions in his rear all the way back. The weather, too, interposed obstacles. At first it was excessively hot; then a fortnight of heavy rains set in. Sherman was certain, however, that he could at least press Johnston close, and prevent his sending any aid to Lee, or to the Confederate defenders of Mobile. Thus he would perform his part in the Grand Plan of the Union high command. Had Banks been able to move against Mobile, this would have prevented Polk from taking strong reinforcements to Johnston in Georgia, where they arrived in time for the Resaca fighting.[62]

The temperamental Sherman, always extreme in opinions and vehement in language, set out on his campaign in a savage frame of mind. The heroic determination that Southerners manifested in fighting on after the loss of kindred, homes, property, and even hope, had given him some harsh convictions. "There is no doubt," he wrote his brother John in Congress, "we have to repeople the country and the sooner we set about it the better. Captured houses and lands must be repeopled by Northern settlers. The whole population of Iowa and Wisconsin should be transferred at once to West Kentucky, Tennessee, Mississippi, and a few hundred thousand settlers should be pushed into South Tennessee." Although such embittered statements were impulsively irrational, the fact that they came from a general leading an armed march into Georgia was ominous. Sherman had been deeply angered by the recent Fort Pillow "massacre" and by the murderous terrorism of irregulars. "You may order all your post and district commanders," he shortly wrote a Kentucky general, "that guerrillas are not soldiers, but wild beasts, unknown to the usages of war."[63]

60. *O.R.* I, xxxii, pt. 3, 468-469; Govan, G.E. and J.W. Livingood, *A Different Valor, the Story of General Joseph E. Johnston, C.S.A.*, Indianapolis, 1956, 250-262; Cox, Jacob D., *Atlanta*, New York, 1882, 26-28.

61. Letter in extra-illustrated copy of *Battles and Leaders*, XIII, HEH.

62. *O.R.* I, xxxii, pt.3, 245ff, 312ff, with Grant-Sherman correspondence; Polk, W.M., *Leonidas Polk, Bishop and General*, New York, 1915, II, Chap. IX.

63. To John Sherman, April 11, 1864, William T. Sherman Papers, LC; to Gen. Stephen G. Burbridge, Cincinnati *Enquirer*, July 12, 1864.

He was resolved to make Southerners *feel* the war. He would shortly write the mayor of Atlanta that it was time for rebels to taste the woes they had inflicted on others. "I myself have seen in Missouri, Kentucky, Tennessee, and Mississippi hundreds and thousands of women and children fleeing from your armies and desperadoes, hungry and with bleeding feet." Army-men were learning that Sherman's mind had more velocity, his emotions a deeper intensity, and his temper a sharper edge than those of any other commander North or South. His nature was a compound of sharply defined and sometimes contradictory traits; if he had the iron will of a Cromwell and the energy of a Hamilton, he had also some of the fierceness of a Tamerlane. When he found some of his foraging troops murdered, he ordered instant reprisals in the shooting of an equal number of prisoners. When he encountered local hostility, his officers were to "enforce a devastation more or less relentless" according to the provocation. His ardor was unquenchable, and his vision far-reaching. But he admitted that his judgment of current situations was faulty. One of his admiring friends made a perceptive observation: "He is a man of immense intellectuality, but his brain is like a splendid piece of machinery with all the screws a little loose."[64]

As the leader of such a military offensive as he now had under way, Sherman was superb, his belief in action, aggressive temper, and impetuosity enabling him to move with a driving vigor that contrasted with the deliberation of his ablest lieutenant, Thomas. He said of himself that he had a "vitality that only yields to absolute death."[65] Endlessly restless and strenuous, vivid in imagination, tireless in talk and gesture, his kinetic qualities expressed his versatility: he was sometimes a dreamer, sometimes a very practical businessman and organizer, and always an intensely combative commander. He did not like fighting and killing. Even success the most brilliant, he wrote, "is over dead and mangled bodies, with the anguish and lamentation of distant families."[66] Yet when aroused he could look upon slaughter, so long as it was for a valid end, with stoic rigor.

He held all his principles fiercely. Fighting for slavery, he said, was fighting against the spirit of the age; to make the navigation of the Mississippi safe, "I would slay millions."[67] And principle distinguished him. Because he had little of Grant's serene equipoise in moments of crisis, or Grant's remarkable self-

64. George W. Morgan, Mt. Vernon, O., to H.V. Boynton, Oct. 8, 1892, Boynton Papers, N.Y. Pub. Lib. Cf. Bradford, Gamaliel, *Union Portraits*, New York, 1916, 131-164, and Liddell Hart's penetrating *Sherman, Soldier, Realist, American*, *op.cit.*, *passim.*

65. *O.R.* I, xlvii, pt. 3, 547.

66. Liddell Hart, *Sherman,op.cit.*, 402.

67. O.R. I, xxxi, pt. 3, 459; also Sherman to Logan, Nashville, Dec. 21, 1863, Logan Family Papers, Yale Univ. Lib.

control, he would never have been suited for the control of all the armies. Where Grant tranquillized friction and jealousies, he might have exacerbated them. Moreover, as Gideon Welles puts it, with a more incisive intelligence than Grant's and a wider range of knowledge, he was too often erratic and uncertain. Grant's friends, as Henry Adams observed, sometimes wondered just what processes of thought he followed. Sherman's friends knew that he often followed no logical processes at all, leaping to his results by intuition, and stating not reasons but conclusions. Principles, however, he did have, and one great principle, frequently reiterated, was especially to his credit. "War is only justified among civilized nations to produce peace," he declared; and again, in the sentence inscribed on his statue in Washington, "The legitimate object of war is a more perfect peace."[68]

A bundle of contradictions, occasionally all too vehement of speech, he could be the most stimulating and delightful of men in his relations with associates, and also one of the most irritating. Grant's *Memoirs* are the product of a clear, accurate mind devoted to the truth; Sherman's *Memoirs* were originally in part so inaccurate that Josiah Royce termed the California chapters a violation not only of sound evidence but of antecedent probability, and Gen. H.V. Boynton, who won a Medal of Honor at Missionary Ridge, called them Sherman's historical raid. Yet the corrected *Memoirs* are fascinating. He ended the war the unrelenting enemy of Stanton, but in their angry controversy the just appraisal of their respective attitudes is difficult, and must be deferred till later in the narrative. He ended it the man whom perhaps the South hated most, vying at times in this dubious distinction with Sheridan, Hunter, and Ben Butler, yet to the general Southern population, especially the poor people and, although no abolitionist, to the Negroes, he was a sympathetic and helpful friend. Altogether, he was the most remarkable combination of virtues and deficiencies produced in the high direction of the Union armies. Many soldiers idolized him while distrusting him a little. Many politicians and journalists admired him while distrusting him a great deal. One student who calls him a typical American in his nervous restlessness, quick ideas, energy, and optimism, adds that he was typical too in lacking a depth proportionate to his splendid breadth and variety—the depth, mystery, and humanity that helped make Lincoln immortal.[69]

We have to think of him in this campaign as a man whose measure the Army and the country were slowly taking. He was not one of the great captains of history, but a very effective general whom Liddell Hart, admiring his grasp of logistics and his daring, calls the first modern general; not a great

68. Liddell Hart, *Sherman, op.cit.*, 425.
69. *Ibid.*, 430.

man, but a great soldier.[70] With advantages of numbers and equipment, he knew how best to use them, as McClellan conspicuously did not, and was intent upon realizing the further advantages of calculated audacity.

The Union soldiers set out in high spirits, confident they could thrust the enemy aside. They built or repaired the Chattanooga-Atlanta railroad as they marched, exultantly cheering the whistling locomotive as it caught up with them. They distributed food and clothing from the cars and wagons to the thousands of Negroes and scores of whites flocking to their camps to ask help. The Confederates had stripped the line of march of as much meat, grain, and vegetables as they could carry off, but a good deal was left for Union seizure. Once crystal waters turned into muddy streams as cohorts of thirsty troops clustered about them. Herds of cattle bellowed wildly as men drove them off to commissary corrals; frantic squealing of pigs rent the air as privates pursued them with bayonets; cackling chickens and quacking ducks disappeared; and troopers cracked their whips over flocks of sheep. Aided at first by a little easily-found whisky, the infantry whooped and sang as they pressed on. And all the while, night and day, there was hardly a minute without the eternal pop —pop—bang—bang of the guns.

70. Bradford, *Union Portraits, op.cit.*, 133, 161-163.

2

Midsummer Frustration, 1864

AS GRANT AND SHERMAN launched their simultaneous attacks upon Lee's Army of Northern Virginia and Johnston's Army of the Tennessee, the anxiety of the Northern people was perhaps more intense and anguished than any they had ever before endured. They knew that the war might well be in its final crisis. What had seemed three stumbling years of carnage, sorrow, and miscarriage lay behind them. Victory had appeared delusively certain until First Bull Run came as a sudden stunning shock in 1861. They had again hoped to win when their splendid army advanced up the Peninsula in 1862, until McClellan's humiliating reverses and retreat to the James had been followed by Pope's defeat in the very gates of Washington, whose people listened in anguish as the sullen thunder of Union guns advanced, paused, and receded. Patriotic people had again hoped to win in 1863 after Vicksburg and Gettysburg—and had tasted apples of Sodom at Mine Run and Chickamauga. As Americans thought of two hundred thousand graves of Northern boys staring at the sky, they were aware that another summer of faltering and defeat might be the last. Meanwhile, dwellers in the cities once more opened their newspapers daily to long lists of the slain and maimed; villagers and townspeople bleakly studied the sheets posted on bulletin boards; farm mothers opened War-Department envelopes with trembling fingers. We shall endure, people said, but—and often they did not complete the sentence.

Day by day, the hammer blows fell, and were parried or returned. Greeley's *Tribune* kept a standing headline—*The Great Contest.* It might also have kept standing the subheads that told of terrific battles and of ever-renewed fighting until night ended the slaughter. On May 12, 1864, such a bulletin announced, "Our Losses So Far 40,000," with some, but all too little, exaggeration. This after the first full week of Virginia battle—the drawn battle of the Wilderness! Next night, Senators Doolittle and Green Clay Smith, Representative Isaac N. Arnold, and Governor Richard Oglesby were to speak for the Union Party in New York City at Cooper Institute. Would the mood of the meeting be fitly heroic? Greeley threw down a disheartening pronouncement in his sometimes Roman-spirited but now faltering editorial page. "Our own conviction is that the opening of the Presidential canvass should have been postponed until after the 4th of July, and that it is advisable for the Union Party to nominate for President some other among its able and true men than Mr. Lincoln. We think the events now transpiring in Virginia and Georgia add force to all that has hitherto been urged in favor of postponement of the Presidential canvass."[1]

Behind uneasy headlines and sour editorials, perceptive men saw that three crucial questions were being decided this summer. Could Grant really operate his Grand Plan for coordinated offensive movements by all the principal Union forces, accurately timed? Could he coordinate the armies in Virginia, Georgia, and the Southwest with such unified precision that Lee could not reinforce Johnston, or Johnston send aid to Lee, or either general send help to Kirby-Smith? In the second place, would the campaign show that Northern recruiting had at last reached the stage where preponderance on the battle lines would enable Grant and Sherman, when checked in a frontal advance, to turn the rebels in that dangerous manoeuvre, a flank march? A preponderance would also enable the Union forces to deploy that array of specialized manpower which just now, in mid-May, was being so efficiently used to rescue Porter's stranded gunboat fleet on the Red River—Maine lumbermen felling trees, Yankee stone-cutters opening an old quarry, Negroes seizing timbers from fences, warehouses, and cotton-gins to build dams.[2] The third question was whether the North had at last equipped its armies with material resources —wagons, horses, mules, ambulances, guns, caissons, uniforms, blankets, tents, medicines, muskets, mortars, repeating rifles—that would give them the decisive fire-power and marching-power they needed. And even though many knew that preponderant material had been provided, yet they still asked themselves, would this preponderance be employed promptly, shrewdly, and with the proficiency of a Caesar?

The answers to these three questions nobody knew in May, 1864. Yet the answers would determine the life or death of the Union, for war-weariness was growing as it had grown in America in 1781, and would grow in France in 1917 and Germany in 1918.

Behind these questions, as fiercely menacing as if written in fire on an inky sky, this election-year posed a larger query. Able and true men, Greeley had

1. New York *Tribune*, May 13, 1864.

2. Harrington, Fred H., *Fighting Politician: N.P. Banks*, Philadelphia, 1948, 130. See Adm. D.D. Porter's vivid account in *O.R.* I, xxxiv, pt. 1, 219-221. Irwin, Richard B., *History of the Nineteenth Army Corps*, New York, 1892, Chs. XX-XXIX, covers the whole Red River subject.

written, must head the nation. If the three questions just named were answered in the negative, and if Lincoln's party repudiated him, what chance would there be of finding leaders staunchly true to the ideas of an indissoluble Union and the maintenance of emancipation measures—and strong enough to hold to them? What if discouragement should overcome the adherents of the patient, indomitable Lincoln, and the men who still stood firm in the Union convictions of Jackson, Webster, Benton, and Douglas?

[I]

The repulse of Du Pont's attack on Charleston on April 7, 1863, the worst naval defeat of the Union thus far, had disheartened multitudes and cast a pall of gloom over the North. Du Pont was relieved of command of the South Atlantic Blockading Squadron, and replaced by Rear-Admiral John A. Dahlgren on July 6, 1863. Du Pont, a brave and conscientious admiral, who had begun his service as midshipman in 1815, and had been given the thanks of Congress for gallantly taking his fleet into Port Royal, naturally chafed under an unwarranted sense of disgrace. For he held the conviction (one which naval colleagues shared) that he had been given improper orders to follow at Charleston, and that Secretary Welles had treated him badly. Lincoln had emphasized the need of remaining before Charleston even if it could not be taken. Before Du Pont resentfully left, however, the Confederate ironclad ram *Atlanta* had been captured in Wassaw Sound by two Federal ships.[3] In mid-June, 1863, Quincy Adams Gillmore, twice brevetted for distinguished service, had succeeded David Hunter in command of the Army Department of the South. On July 10, three thousand Union troops landed on Morris Island and captured works at the southern end. The next day, operations were begun against Battery Wagner farther north on Morris Island. Attack after attack was thrown back with heavy casualties, including many borne by Negro troops; a siege was then undertaken. In mid-August, huge Northern Parrott rifles mounted on Morris Island began a devastating bombardment of Fort Sumter. It was successful in knocking the already damaged fort into rubble, but the guns could do no more and Fort Sumter held on. By the end of August, little was left at Sumter but one gun in operation and a couple of others occasionally serviceable. Slowly the sappers brought their works nearer and nearer Battery

3. Ammen, Daniel, *The Atlantic Coast*, New York, 1883-1885, 121; Du Pont, H.A., *Rear-Admiral Samuel Francis Du Pont*, New York, 1926, 292. Du Pont's resentment is well shown in his correspondence with his friend and protagonist Henry Winter Davis (mss. in Eleutherian Mills Hagley Foundation, Wilmington, Delaware).

Wagner. The warships joined in. Then, on September 6, after a siege of 85 days, the Confederates evacuated Battery Wagner and Morris Island. Questions could well be asked at the North if the prize had been worth the cost. On September 9, a small boat expedition against Fort Sumter proved a fiasco. After a few quiet weeks, the newly built Federal batteries on Morris Island opened up on Fort Sumter again, with heavy and light bombardments which continued for months. Thousands upon thousands of rounds were poured upon the fort. Dahlgren finally gave up any idea of entering Charleston harbor with his ships. The symbolic defense of Fort Sumter against Union guns was a gallant story, while the failure of the overwhelming cannonade and the ironclads was a frustrating story at the North. One outstanding authority puts the total number of Northern projectiles fired against Battery Wagner at 18,491, and the total number of projectiles fired against Fort Sumter from 1863 to 1865 at 46,053, with an estimated weight of 3,500 tons. The fort was said to have been under 117 days of major bombardment, 40 of minor bombardment, and 280 days under either steady or desultory fire, the Union managing to kill only 52 Confederates and wound 267. Thus, by the start of 1864, Charleston Harbor rankled in the hearts of the Northern military and civilian leaders.

Early in that year, action was limited at Charleston to some secondary skirmishing and the continued bombardment of Fort Sumter. After a daring torpedo-boat raid in mid-February sank the Federal gunboat *Housatonic* off Charleston Bar, pressure on Charleston with bombardment and exploratory operations went on into the spring and summer. Plymouth, North Carolina, had been recaptured by Confederates in April, while their formidable ram, the *Albemarle*, was active along the Roanoke River in North Carolina. Although it appeared now that the Union forces were not willing to risk losses even if they could take Charleston, the blockade of the coast went on, and Confederate troops and supplies were being drained away in defending the city of secession.[4]

As we have already seen, the failure of the Red River expedition was equally frustrating to the North; the rescue of Porter's gunboats had been one of that campaign's few bright spots.[5] On May 19, General N. P. Banks was relieved of his military functions by Canby in greater discredit than had overtaken the abler Du Pont. Banks was full of excuses, but his three months

4. Figures on bombardment of Battery Wagner and Fort Sumter are from Johnston, John, *The Defense of Charleston Harbor, including Fort Sumter and the Adjacent Islands, 1863-1865*, Charleston, S.C., 1890, 273. Same source has "Calendar of Events in the Defense of Charleston, South Carolina," Appendix xi-xx.

5. Success was achieved May 13, 1864. See Harrington, *op.cit.*, 158; Knox, Dudley W., *A History of the United States Navy*, New York, 1936, 300; Bailey's concise reports, *O.R.* I, xxxiv, 402-404.

of marching, fighting, and marauding had cost the government needed men, supplies, time, and prestige. The origins of the expedition had been cloudy, apparently lying partly in Lincoln's anxieties over the future course of Emperor Maximilian in Mexico, partly in Halleck's notions of Texas strategy, and partly in the easy acquiescence of Banks, Sherman, and others in badly laid plans. Maximilian landed at Vera Cruz on May 28, resulting in a Congressional investigation, official censure, much quarreling among both Northern and Southern commanders, a well-grounded suspicion of cotton jobbery, some real injury to Lincoln's chances for re-election, and considerable chagrin to the North as a whole.[6] A blow against Mobile, ordered by Sherman, might have accomplished valuable results in 1864; however, such a blow was not struck until after Lincoln had delivered his second inaugural address in 1865.

For more than two years, wrote Grant, he had tried to get the stroke against Mobile launched when it would have been of great advantage, but it was finally undertaken when it had become worthless. Farragut had been eager to undertake a sea expedition against Mobile just after the capture of New Orleans, when land forces did not appear needed, but Washington had given priority to the Mississippi—although advocating an attack on Mobile as well, either after the river was cleared or as a substitute. By the time Banks was sent on the Red River expedition, the strength of the coastal forts had made a coördinated military effort essential, and his absence placed Mobile beyond reach.[7]

Worse still, the North had to accept the immobility of its best naval commander, Farragut. He had returned to his Gulf station in January, 1864, burning to move against Mobile, but for six months he was sentenced to minor duty. "I am *depressed*," he wrote, "by the bad news from every direction."[8] The

6. Cf. Lt.-Col. Richard B. Irwin, "The Red River Campaign," *Battles and Leaders*, IV, 361ff.

7. Grant, *Memoirs*, II, 519. Grant's impatience had also been forcibly expressed over delays in attacking Forrest in April this year. Sherman telegraphed Mason Brayman on April 16: "General Grant is properly offended at the timidity displayed in and about Memphis and has ordered Gen. Hurlbut to be relieved. I have instructed Gen. McPherson as soon as possible to transport his wagons, mules, etc. to Clifton, and make up a force to strike inland from the Tennessee at Forrest." Brayman Papers, Chicago Historical Soc. Washington and the War Department have often been accused of not supporting the idea of a drive on Mobile. Actually, at the time of the capture of New Orleans in April, 1862, Farragut's orders had been to go on up the Mississippi River, but after that, or in place of it, if necessary, "You will also reduce the fortifications which defend Mobile Bay, and turn them over to the army to hold . . ." *O.R.N.*, I, Vol. XVIII, 7-8, Welles to Farragut, Jan. 20, 1862. This idea was repeated several times. The problem had been that the Mississippi Campaign, including Vicksburg, had been more difficult than foreseen, and had taken long to execute. Thus, Mobile had been delayed, and continued to be delayed.

8. Lewis, Charles Lee, *David Glasgow Farragut, Our First Admiral*, Annapolis, 1943, 236-240; Mahan, A.T., *Admiral Farragut*, New York, 1892, 237-252.

bad news which he and the Northern people had to sustain included dispatches concerning Forrest's slashing raids in Tennessee and Kentucky; accounts of the bloody Confederate capture of Fort Pillow on April 12; and the tale of General Frederick Steele's failure to sweep the Confederate columns in Arkansas with their lurking threat to Union movements, away toward the interior of rebeldom. Steele's delays in starting frustrated the intended capture of Shreveport, and his failure added to the gloom over General Banks's reverses. Another sorry item in the catalogue of Union disappointments was the defeat of General Franz Sigel's attack at Newmarket in the Shenandoah, on a field forever immortalized to Southerners by the heroic stand of 147 young cadets of the Virginia Military Institute, a number of whom gallantly gave up their lives before Sigel retreated. At the same time, Ben Butler let himself be bottled up at Bermuda Hundred on the James, in a way that was both too humiliating and too ridiculous for the country ever to forget.

All eyes were turned to Virginia and Georgia, where men recorded heroic deeds in lines as curt as those William Francis Bartlett wrote in the Wilderness on May 6: "It will be a bloody day. I believe I am prepared to die. God bless my friends at home . . . Went into action about eight. Thick woods. Men behaved well. I was struck in head about eleven. Carried to the hospital in rear. Lay there among the wounded and dying until night." This month might well be called "bloody May," the Richmond *Examiner* shortly remarked. Estimating the total killed in all armies at 70,000, it listed seven general officers slain on each side.[9]

Yet it was only gradually that the realities of the situation were grasped by the Northern public, for the official utterances of Stanton deceived both press and people. On Thursday, May 6, the battle of the Wilderness closed, and on the night of the 7th Grant began his losing race with Lee toward Spotsylvania. He had fought a drawn battle with far heavier losses than his opponent and was still far from Richmond. Yet on the 9th the War Department shouted victory! At 4 P.M. Stanton announced: "Dispatches have just reached here from Gen. Grant. They are not fully deciphered yet, but he is 'On to Richmond.' We have taken 2,000 prisoners." In a supplementary dispatch Stanton added that dispatches from Meade showed Lee's army had "commenced falling back Friday night"; that the Union army "commenced the pursuit" on Saturday, the Rebels being "in full retreat for Richmond by the direct road"; that Hancock had passed through Spotsylvania Court-House at daylight on Sunday the 8th; and that Union headquarters at noon on the 8th were twenty miles south

9. Clipped in Selma, Ala., *Daily Reporter*, June 10, 1864. The *Examiner* listed the Union generals Wadsworth, Sedgwick, Haynes, Webb, Taylor, Joshua T. Owens, and James C. Rice; the Southern generals Stuart, Jenkins, Stafford, Jones, Julius Daniel, Gordon, and Perkins.

of the Wilderness battlefield. Another War Department bulletin, May 9, read: "Our army in full pursuit of the enemy toward Richmond."

No wonder that newspapers blazed with exultant headlines on the 10th! "Victory for the Union—The Rebels Fly by Night—Is it a Race for Richmond?" No wonder that Lincoln on May 9 urged people to repair to their homes and churches, to "unite in common thanksgiving" to Almighty God. After confused news from Spotsylvania, the headlines exulted again on Saturday the 14th. "Glorious Successes—Lee Terribly Beaten on Thursday—He Retreats During the Night—His Army Nearly Hemmed In—Occupation of Dalton by Our Forces—'The End Draws Near.' "[10]

The facts of the situation were utterly different from the Stanton bulletins and the silly headlines. Grant had indeed made a momentous decision when, on May 7, instead of turning back to the Rapidan, he had ordered the night march on Spotsylvania. Sherman later called this one of the decisive strokes of the war, and, in his judgment, the supreme moment of Grant's life. The bold movement electrified the Army. Hancock's troops, watching along the road by the light of torches, suddenly saw Grant and Meade pass by, realized that the army was moving southeast upon Lee's flank toward Richmond, and, springing to their feet, gave cheer upon cheer.[11] The drama of the moment was unforgettable. The Army that had suffered endless humiliation since Bull Run at last had a leader determined upon victory.

But morning gunfire showed that victory might yet be far distant. Instead of being "in full retreat for Richmond," the rebels were fiercely barring the road.

The long night tramp had been desperately fatiguing to Union troops who had fought and marched for almost four days and nights; the check at dawn was infuriating. Tempers wore thin as a fierce sun mounted into a dust-choked sky. One division of the hot, dirty, hungry troops broke ranks as its general, John C. Robinson, was carried from the field with a shot in the knee. About noon, an angry quarrel broke out between Meade and Sheridan over responsibility for delays in the advance. Meade, working himself into one of his towering rages, sent for Sheridan to come to his headquarters, and went after him hammer-and-tongs. Sheridan retorted in hot anger, placing all the blame upon Meade for countermanding his first orders. They threw Billingsgate exple-

10. All headlines from New York *Tribune*, but typical of other papers.

11. Porter, Horace, *Campaigning with Grant*, Ch. V; Badeau, Adam, *Military History of Ulysses S. Grant*, II, 235ff. Frank Wilkerson writes in his *Recollections of a Private Soldier in the Army of the Potomac*, New York, 1887, that Grant's standing with the troops hung on the direction he turned. When he moved to the right, a sigh of relief went up. "Our spirits rose. We marched free. The men began to sing." Sherman, William T., "The Grand Strategy of the War of the Rebellion," Century Vol. XXXV, No.4, Feb., 1888, 592.

tives, spiced with profanity, one at the other. "I will not command the cavalry any longer under such circumstances," roared Sheridan.[12] Eventually Meade apologized, but Sheridan thereafter nursed a truculent Irish grudge toward him and Warren. Late that afternoon, renewed attacks by the jaded Union troops broke down under the angry eyes of Grant, watching within bullet range.

All around the Union troops lay reminders of galling hardships and terrible losses. They were still almost as close to Washington as to Richmond, and the map ahead was strewn with tragic names—Mechanicsville, Gaines' Mill, Seven Pines, White Oak Swamp. Would Spotsylvania add another band of crêpe to this dreary list?

The Confederates were now masters of entrenchment. In taking any position they would hastily form a line of defense. They would collect loose stones, small logs, fence rails, and other materials, pile them into a rampart, and use picks, shovels, and bayonets to cover it with dirt from a trench. Within an hour they had sufficient cover for a kneeling man. "It is a rule," wrote Theodore Lyman, "that, when the rebels halt, the first day gives them a good riflepit; the second, a regular infantry parapet with cannon in position; and the third, a parapet with an abattis in front and entrenched batteries behind. Sometimes they put this three-days' work into the first twenty-four hours." The men inside these fortifications matched the veterans of Caesar, Gustavus Adolphus, and Wellington; "sinewy, tawny, formidable looking," they used bullet and blade with terrible effect.[13]

[II]

The approach to Spotsylvania had ended badly; the battle lay ahead. Beginning May 9, it continued more than a week, one bloody encounter following another. The first day was confined to skirmishing and sharpshooting, and

12. Porter, *op.cit.*, 83, 84; Sheridan, Philip, *Personal Memoirs*, New York, 1888, I, 357-369: this is a characteristic report of the unseemly altercation. He writes that Meade "showed a disposition to be unjust, laying blame here and there for the blunders that had been committed. He was particularly severe on the cavalry, saying, among other things, that it had impeded the march of the Fifth Corps by occupying the Spottsylvania road. I replied that if this were true, he himself had ordered it there without my knowledge. I also told him that he had broken up my combinations, exposed Wilson's division to disaster, and kept Gregg unnecessarily idle, and further, repelled his insinuations by saying that such disjointed operations as he had been requiring of the cavalry for the last four days would render the corps inefficient and useless before long. Meade was very much irritated, and I was none the less so. One word brought on another, until, finally, I told him that I could whip Stuart if he (Meade) would only let me, but since he insisted on giving the cavalry directions without consulting or even notifying me, he could henceforth command the Cavalry Corps himself—that I would not give it another order." The acrimonious interview ended with this remark. Cf. Meade, G.G., *Life and Letters of George Gordon Meade*, New York, 1913, II, 220-222.

13. Lyman, *op.cit.*, 100, 106, 115.

Sedgwick was killed when struck in the head by a sharpshooter's bullet. Perhaps the most able corps-commander in the Army of the Potomac, Sedgwick's loss was a serious blow. He was replaced in command of the Sixth Corps by Horatio Wright. Cavalry was useless on a terrain so rough and heavily wooded; furthermore, Sheridan departed on May 9 on a lengthy expedition that penetrated to the suburbs of Richmond, where, at Yellow Tavern on May 11, Jeb Stuart was mortally wounded. Yet Stuart's cavalry and the Richmond defense troops checked Sheridan, so he turned east to the Peninsula, not rejoining Grant until May 24. On May 10, at Spotsylvania, the three corps of Hancock, Warren, and Wright were thrown against the Confederate left and left-center. Little was gained, however; Grant was learning how skillful Lee could be in disposing his smaller force.

On the night of May 11-12, Grant massed about 20,000 men to assault the enemy center, springing forward at the glimmer of dawn. The weather had changed. The 11th had been rainy. A chill downpour continued through the night, the troops lying in wet clothes on wetter ground, without shelter. Morning came with dank fog. The main Union attack was directed at a five-sided salient of the Confederate line held by Ewell, projecting into thick brush in the shape (as farm-boys on both sides noted) of a mule-shoe. Hancock's troops, moving against the salient in dense ranks under heavy fire, at first seemed to be gaining a decisive success. Then, inside the outer works, they encountered a second line. It was a heavy abattis, with rear logs banked with clay, the upper timbers raised just sufficiently to enable the defenders to fire from shelter. Openings in the fortified line gave room here and there for the muzzles of cannon. Some of the artillery faced forward; other pieces were placed at an angle to catch advancing lines in the flank. When Hancock was forced back, Wright and the Sixth Corps came in on his right, assaulting the west face of the salient, particularly at the famous "Bloody Angle." Here some of the hottest fighting of the war took place. Farther to the Union right Warren attacked, and on the Union left Burnside drove in, though the fight was not as severe as at the salient.

"The attempt seemed hopeless," wrote one soldier, "but attack, attack everywhere is the word today; no joint in the enemy's harness must be left unsmitten." His unit, after advancing through heavy underbrush, freed itself from the pine thickets, straightened its line, and faced forward just as the earthworks burst into flame. "A brief dash now across the shot-swept open, no firing, the bayonet only, and with thinned ranks, the abattis is reached. . . . Up now the Fifteenth, what is left of you, up over the logs, inside and hand-to-hand, foot-to-foot in deadly mélée." His regiment forced its way into the earthworks, using the bayonet freely, and took about a hundred prisoners, but too few men were left to hold the place. Moreover, a Southern battery was now sweeping the whole brigade with a flank fire of grapeshot. Like the Light Brigade, they were under fire all the way back. Next morning a roll-call showed that the regiment had lost 116 men.[14]

In his *Memoirs*, Grant stated that two Northern commands, one under Francis C. Barlow and the other under David B. Birney, plunged across the Confederate entrenchments almost simultaneously. Desperate hand-to-hand fighting ensued, the combatants too close to fire, but using bayonets and clubbed rifles. The Union forces, capturing four thousand prisoners and twenty guns, had won such a signal victory that Lee could not afford to leave them in full possession of his works. Bringing up fresh troops, he attacked so furiously that the Northerners under Hancock were compelled to retire. But they retreated slowly, inflicting heavy losses until they stood behind the breastworks they had recently captured. Then they turned, fighting from the new cover, and continued to hold the lines.[15]

"Lee massed heavily from his left flank on the broken point of his lines," wrote Grant. "Five times during the day he assaulted furiously, but without dislodging our troops from their new position. His losses must have been fearful. Sometimes the belligerents would be separated by but a few feet." In one place a tree eighteen inches in diameter was severed and felled by musket balls. All the forest growth between the lines was heavily slashed by artillery and musketry. It was three o'clock next morning before the fighting ceased. "Some [Northern] troops had then been twenty hours under fire." That night Lee took a position in the rear of his former line, fortifying it by breastworks and trenches. On May 13, both exhausted armies rested. That night it again rained heavily, and for nearly a week the general immobility continued, although there was considerable movement and fighting along the battle lines at times. Then, on the 20th, as Lee was inclined to stand fast, Grant ordered a movement toward his left.

The story of the bloody actions that ensued, of Lee's use of interior lines to frustrate Grant, of the stubborn fight on the North Anna in which the armies lost about equal numbers, and of Grant's passage of the Pamunkey River to make a desperate new assault on Lee at Cold Harbor, has long been familiar. Union veterans, in advancing to Cold Harbor, showed an impressive endurance. The New York *Tribune* correspondent C.A. Page wrote that

14. Dodd, Ira S., *The Song of the Rappahannock*, New York, 1898, 245-250.

15. Grant, *Memoirs*, II, 230-232. During a lull at Spotsylvania, Charles Carleton Coffin spent a day in Fredericksburg visiting the hospitals. The city was one vast hospital; churches, public buildings, stores, attics, basements, all full. "There are thousands upon the sidewalk," he wrote. "All day long the ambulances have been arriving from the field." A red flag had been hung out from the Sanitary Commission rooms, a white flag from the Christian Commission. Three hundred volunteer nurses were in attendance, every Northern State having its Relief Committee at work. The Sanitary Commission used fourteen wagons in bringing supplies from Belle Plain. *The Boys of '61*, Boston, 1881, 326, 327.

Wright's Sixth Corps made an especially remarkable showing.[16]

"On Monday [May 30] they marched all day without rations. That night they formed line of battle, and what with the labor of intrenching and several hours of the night getting rations, they obtained no sleep. On Tuesday they were engaged with the enemy more or less all day. That night, on 30 minutes' notice, they marched at midnight, marched till morning, marched till noon, marched till 4 o'clock, and then set to work with all their might intrenching. The day was one of the sultriest I ever knew, and the roads ankle-deep with dust—impalpable Virginia dust, that hung so densely in the air that it became exceedingly palpable. And yet these Corps veterans, hungry for two days, sleepless for three days, fatigued with relentless marching by day and by night, all streaming with perspiration, grim and blear-eyed, their hair dusted to whiteness . . . grasped shovels and axes . . . and sprang to work with never-surpassed vigor, and an hour later exchanged tools for weapons and fought with unequaled spirit and tenacity."

The month of May was one long test of physical fortitude. The men, tired of hard bread and salt meat, craved fresh vegetables so much that one woman, looking at her ravaged garden, exclaimed: "You Yanks don't seem to keer for nothin' but injuns [onions]." Many of the wounded were sent on hospital steamers to Fredericksburg, Washington, or New York, but many suffered in field hospitals. The Topographical Engineers did masterly work in surveying, mapping, and analyzing all the varied pieces of terrain encountered after the crossing of the Pamunkey. One leader, tireless in riding about, questioned Negroes, prisoners, deserters, talked with farmers, and drew sketches of streams, bridges, and roads. This was Captain W.H. Paine, who at Spotsylvania partly found and partly made a road that saved four miles in moving troops. Fifty pioneers improved it for artillery. Nevertheless, the rough country was hard on men and beasts alike. Before Spotsylvania ended, the roads thereabouts were strewn with the carcasses of six thousand horses. Many soldiers were felled by sunstroke. As June began, more than 100,000 of Grant's soldiers had not changed a garment since they started; they had marched, slept, and fought thirty days and thirty nights in the same sweat-stiffened garments. Dense clouds of dust overhung the roads from battlefield to battlefield, filling eyes and lungs. But the fighting spirit of the men never faltered even when they were betrayed by bad generalship.

[III]

For sheer horror of butchery, Cold Harbor, fought June 1-3, can stand beside Fredericksburg. The Union army now faced towards Gaines' Mill, for

16. New York *Tribune*, June 6, 8, et seq., 1864.

it was back near the old battleground of the Seven Days. On the evening of May 31st, Lee made ready to recapture a vital road junction here near the Chickahominy River, for Cold Harbor was not a town or village, but a mere, half-isolated intersection of ways leading to the Pamunkey, York, and Chickahominy fords. A stubborn encounter occurred on June 1, a day of torrid heat. Next day, a heavy downpour fell. Lee, still intent on covering Richmond with his troops, had thoroughly surveyed the familiar terrain and at least partially fortified some of its vital bridges, fords, and other points. Grant, therefore, postponed the general assault he had planned for the late afternoon, but that night orders were given for an attack at 4:30 on the morning of the 3rd, orders that the troops knew would result in terrible loss of life.

The Confederates had entrenched with great energy and efficiency. Before the rain, this had been easy to do for trenches could be dug in the dry, sandy earth with bits of board, tin plates, or any kind of shovel, the dirt heaped alongside; and a few flying axes soon provided enough straight pines to give the breastwork a wall. As dawn broke on the 3rd, a beautiful summer morning, a single cannon pealed the signal for a general assault. The soldiers scanning the area between the armies, an open plain already trampled in many places into fine dust under the baking sun and then turned into a quagmire by the ensuing rain, saw that they had small likelihood of success. Colonel Theodore Lyman, at Meade's headquarters, saw none. "If we could smash them up, the Chickahominy lay behind them," he wrote; "but I had no more hope of it after Spotsylvania, than I had of taking Richmond in two days." Yet, with three corps participating, the men moved staunchly to the charge. Many were so certain of death that they had written their names on slips of paper fastened to their clothes to make identification easier.

This assault, which took place when many officers were out of humor with the costly frontal attacks involved in Grant's strategy, resulted within half an hour in about 7,000 more Union soldiers killed and wounded. "I do think," wrote Theodore Lyman in his journal, "there has been too much assaulting, this campaign. Following our lessons of failure and of success at Spotsylvania, we assault here, after the enemy had taken thirty-six hours to entrench, and that time will cover them over their heads, and give them slashings and traverses besides! The best officers and men are liable, by their greater gallantry, to be first disabled; and of those that are left, the best become demoralized by the failures, and the loss of good leaders; so that, very soon, the men will no longer charge entrenchments, and will only go forward when driven by their officers."[17]

17. Lyman, *op.cit.*, 143-150.

"I am disgusted with the generalship displayed," Peter S. Michie wrote his sister the day after the charge. Michie, a West Pointer of Scottish birth, was a shrewd engineer later brevetted brigadier-general. "Our men have, in many instances, been foolishly and wantonly sacrificed. Assault after assault has been ordered upon the enemy. Thousands of lives might have been spared by the exercise of a little skill." He again wrote his sister on June 5, that the recent assault was murderous. "I say murderous, because we were recklessly ordered to assault the enemy's intrenchments, knowing neither their strength nor position." He went on: "I have seen but little generalship during the campaign. Some of our corps commanders are not fit to be corporals. Lazy and indolent, they will not even ride along the lines; yet, without hesitancy, they will order us to attack the enemy, no matter what their position or numbers. Twenty thousand of our killed and wounded should today be in our ranks."[18] This doubtless paralleled the talk in Nivelle's ranks in 1917, after his grand assault on the fortified German lines from the Aisne Heights was choked in blood. Yet on June 3, almost no Northerner flinched. At the hour prescribed, the men quietly rose from the sloppy trenches they had dug during the night downpour, and moved forward with grim, steady tread. The Confederates were ready for them. "There rang out suddenly on the summer air such a crash of artillery and musketry as is seldom heard in war." All three corps, under Hancock, Wright, and W.F. Smith, were terribly exposed to flank as well as frontal fire, so that each commander complained later to General Meade that the others failed to protect him from an enfilading storm of bullets. The main charge ended in less than half an hour. The ground was soon cumbered with between six and seven thousand Union bodies. Yet so stubborn was the valor of the troops that here and there, where the fire was intolerably heavy and the works in front were plainly impregnable, the men still refused to retreat, lying prone behind some slight ridge and hanging on, though perhaps only two hundred or four hundred feet from the enemy.[19]

After the attack had broken down; after more men had fallen than in any other similar period of brief, intense action in the war; after headquarters in the rear had learned by field telegraph of the opening of deadly enemy fire upon the three corps attacking on diverging lines, new orders came from high command. Orders to retire?—for sharpshooters still swept the field with bullets, and more shells exploded. No. Each corps was directed to attack again, moving directly against the enemy without reference to the action of its fellow corps, thus sacrificing unity. In uneven ranks, troops that had retired to protected areas renewed their plunge forward, as again other detachments, hug-

18. Michie, Peter S., *Life and Letters of Emory Upton*, New York, 1885, 108, 109.
19. McMahon, Martin T., "Cold Harbor," *Battles and Leaders*, IV, 213-220.

ging the muddy ground, loosed ragged but futile volleys. After fresh lines of dead and wounded recorded another total failure, Grant sent his insensate order for a general assault. But this third time not a soldier moved. Everyone knew that a fresh charge would be suicidal. Some volleys were loosed by the prone ranks, but that was all.[20]

Union valor now met the same reward as at Second Manassas and Vicksburg, a callous abandonment of the wounded to hours and days of agony. The field was a horrifying sight, with windrows of the immobile dead and writhing injured marking each stage of the advance. No man on it dared rise to face certain bullets; no stretcher-bearer behind it dared venture into the open.

"When night came on," wrote Martin T. McMahon, the Canadian-born officer who was Wright's chief of staff, "the groans and moaning of the wounded, all our own, who were between the lines, were heartrending." It was like the freezing night of stricken men after Fredericksburg. Morning and noonday brought no relief. "Some were brought in by volunteers from our intrenchments, but many remained three days uncared for beneath the hot summer suns and the unrefreshing dews of the sultry summer nights. The men in the works grew impatient, yet it was against orders and was almost certain death to go beyond our earthworks."[21]

Without care for three days! Without a drop of water, a bandage, a morsel of food, a helping touch—and this fell short of the truth. The troops had begun to fall at dawn on June 3. That hot day passed, and that night; then an equally hot June 4 and its night. The responsibility for action was Grant's; his had been the main losses. An armistice of two hours would have been sufficient. Yet not until June 5 did Grant open with Lee a correspondence which he self-righteously paraded in his *Memoirs.* It is reported to me, he stated, that wounded men "probably of both armies" are lying exposed between the lines. He could see the field of wounded for himself; he knew well that the great majority were Union soldiers—McMahon says "all our own." Grant proposed that each side be authorized to send unarmed litter-bearers out after an action to pick up its dead or wounded. Lee replied this same June 5 that men should be sent "immediately" to collect the dead and wounded, but that a flag of truce should be accepted before such parties were dispatched. Not until June 6 (he does not state the hour) did Grant accede to Lee's demand for use of a flag of truce, and

20. *Ibid.*, 218-219; Swinton, William, *Campaigns of the Army of the Potomac*, New York, 1866, 481-487. Meade in his unrevealing account of Cold Harbor writes: "I had immediate and entire command on the field all day" (Meade, George, *op.cit.*, II, 200). He adds, "Up to this time our success has consisted only in compelling the enemy to draw in toward Richmond; our failure has been that we have not been able to overcome, destroy, or bag his army."

21. McMahon, *op.cit.*, IV, 219.

Union Cavalry Commanders:
second from left, standing, Philip Sheridan;
third from left, seated, Alfred Pleasonton;
seated at right, George Custer.

General Grant and Staff, Spotsylvania, 1864

to his strict limitation of the ground to be covered; for Lee feared that stretcher parties might spy out the strong and weak sections of his line. At 7 P.M. on June 6 Lee then wrote, fixing an immediate time for removal of the casualties. But somehow his message did not reach Union headquarters until 10:45 P.M., when the allotted hour had expired.[22] Thus it was not until June 7 that parties were sent out from the Union lines to collect men who had lain on the field since the morn of the 3rd—more than four days earlier. A hundred hours of burning thirst and agony had intervened!

But it was not so long for most of the casualties. In the interim, as Grant succinctly stated, "all but two of the wounded had died."[23] And what had their lives purchased? Grant gave the answer in his *Memoirs:* "No advantage whatever was gained for the heavy loss we sustained."[24] We may well believe his statement late in life that, "I regret the assault more than any I have ever ordered."[25] Inadequate as this statement seems, it was a greater admission of fault than any that Meade, quick to lose his temper but slow to admit fault, ever made.[26]

[IV]

Grant's Cold Harbor attack, blundering and seemingly callous though it was, had behind it a thoughtful plan and design characteristic of the reflective, studious general. It did not have behind it the egoistic hardness of David Hunter, discarding prudence in Missouri and rules of Army authority in Georgia to better himself, or the blind impetuosity of Hooker at Chancellorsville. Still determined upon erosion of Confederate strength and numbers even by an unequal trading of manpower and positions, Grant looked ahead. He must push inexorably forward against Richmond whatever the cost. He knew that the marshy Chickahominy, often called "a wet ditch, in front of the outer fortifications of the capital," still lay before him. Had he won Cold Harbor, two bridges over it would have lain open, and he could have used the full strength of McClellan's old position, lying secure behind breastworks, as he besieged the city. But he had failed to force the passage of the Chickahominy—and now what? If he persevered in "fighting it out on this line. . . . all summer," his next

22. This Grant-Lee correspondence is in Grant's *Memoirs*, II, 273-275.

23. Why the delay? Because, McMahon declares, "An impression prevails in the popular mind, and with some reason perhaps, that a commander who sends a flag of truce asking permission to bury his dead and bring in his wounded has lost the field of battle. Hence the reluctance on our part to ask a flag of truce." *Battles and Leaders*, IV, 219.

24. Grant, *Memoirs*, II, 276.

25. Cf. *Battles and Leaders*, IV, 220.

26. Cleaves, Freeman, *Meade of Gettysburg*, Norman, Okla., 1960, 151.

advance by the left would carry his army not toward Richmond, but away from it.

His first impulse was to try again to force the Chickahominy line, not by hammer blows, but by the regular approaches of a siege operation. With Lee's army still intact, however, and Lee's genius undimmed, and with strong fortifications available to rebel use, a breach of one line in front of Richmond would simply bring the Union army up against another even more formidable. When a rebel newspaperman suggested that Grant might move down the Chickahominy to try crossing in the vicinity of White Oak Swamp, he found Lee's veterans exultant in the thought of the earthwork defenses the Union troops would have to assail.[27]

Grant, however, had learned his lesson. Long afterward, he admitted in his *Memoirs* that the ghastly Union losses at Cold Harbor had been without "adequate compensation"; he might have said without *any* compensation. He also admitted that the battle had elevated Confederate morale, and depressed the Union army and people. Like Shiloh, mention of Cold Harbor always pained him.[28]

Now he wrote Halleck on June 5 that after thirty days of trial he had decided that "without a greater sacrifice of human life than I am willing to make, all cannot be accomplished that I had designed outside of the city" of Richmond; that is, Lee could not be defeated north of that city. He must embrace the only real alternative, transferring his army south of the James. In the darkness of June 12-13, his frustrated force took up its march from Cold Harbor to the lower reaches of the James, the Harrison's Landing shore where McClellan had once ensconced himself under naval guns. On the 14th, Grant's advance reached the river, and immediately pressed across to march against the defenses of Petersburg beyond. On June 15, when General William Farrar Smith (whose corps had been moved from the Peninsula by water) began an assault on these works, the whole battle front suddenly and dramatically changed.

Well it was for Grant that in the very week of Cold Harbor the Republican National Convention diverted a portion of the nation's attention by opening its sessions in Baltimore. Grant had hoped, nay, had expected, to defeat Lee decisively between the Rapidan and the James, but had failed. Many observers thought that his strategy might be summed up in one word: "Butchery." He had told Meade in the hearing of one press correspondent, "I never manoeuvre," and the result proved it.[29] Various high officers blamed him, and

27. Swinton, *op.cit.*, 481; Tyrone Power in Selma *Dispatch*, June 6, 1864.

28. Grant, *Memoirs*, II, 264-278; here he turned abruptly to discuss the Vicksburg assaults.

29. Note statement of G.F.R. Henderson, *The Science of War*, London, 1910, 7: "Grant knew not only how to command an army, but how to teach an army, how to form skilled leaders, strategists, and technicians . . ." For the remark to Meade, see Swinton, William, *op.cit.*, 440.

Meade, and others including his aide Comstock who was credited with the aphorism "smash them up!", for the fearful loss of life. His inexorable thrust against Lee rested upon the same basic advantage that enabled the Russian armies to move as inexorably in 1944-45 against the Germans: heavily superior numbers, greater length of line, and utterly heedless sacrifice of lives.[30] We may accept an English estimate that the total cost of Grant's attrition policy from the Wilderness through Cold Harbor exceeded 52,000 casualties, the Confederates losing slightly over one-third as many.[31]

Attrition at this rate was too costly. If three Union men died for one Confederate, the North would give up sooner than the South. The patriotic press put the brightest face possible on matters: Grant's overland movement had kept Lee from threatening Washington, he had taken twice as many prisoners as Lee, his wounded and ill would recover more rapidly than Lee's, and after all, it was relative, not positive, losses that counted.[32] Forlorn comfort! The gloom that thickened over a great part of the Union as people read of Cold Harbor and of new exploits by Nathan Bedford Forrest in crushing a raid by General "Sooky" Smith into North Mississippi, mingling with the news of Lincoln's renomination, made Republican victory dubious. The close observer Swinton declares that while the morale of Lee's army now reached its highest point, Northern depression produced "great danger of the collapse of the war."[33]

Yet Grant had accomplished much. He had bled the South to weakness, especially its échelons of command. He had compelled Lee to accept the defensive once and for all. Grant now had a stranglehold on Lee, and by virtue of his tenacity as well as his superior numbers, was firm in maintaining his iron grip. The public at large could not see this; they were more aware of the depressing surface manifestations of failure. Grant had proved the merits of his (and Lincoln's) fundamental plan. If he had taken his army at the outset by water to the James River landings below Richmond, then Lee on the Rapidan might have retained a dangerous freedom to lunge at Washington. Now he could not consider any such advance. Had Grant flanked Lee's army on its left, moving southwestwardly, he would have limited the flow of his

30. In Virginia, Meade's official return of Union casualties for May 5-12 was 29,410, and for May 12-21 was 10,381, a total of 39,791. At Cold Harbor on June 1-3 about 12,000 more were killed or wounded. Official returns for the period May 5 through June 15, including Wilderness, Spotsylvania, North Anna, and Cold Harbor, totaled 52,789 casualties, including 7,407 killed, 37,264 wounded, and 8,118 missing. Confederate total losses are estimated at something around 20,000.

31. *O.R.* I, xxxvi, pt. 3, 598, Grant to Halleck, June 5, 1864. Pt.I, 133, 149, 164, 180, gives a complete return of casualties from the Rapidan to the James. See also Livermore, T.L., *Numbers and Losses in the Civil War in America, 1861-1865*, Boston, 1901, 114-115; Burne, Col. Alfred H. Lee, *Grant and Sherman*, New York, 1939, 50-52; and Long, A.L., *Memoirs of Robert E. Lee*, New York, 1886, 348.

32. New York *Tribune*, July 2, 1864. But Greeley actually was disheartened.

33. Lytle, A.N., *Bedford Forrest and His Critter Company*, New York, 1931, 259ff; Swinton, *op.cit.*, 492.

essential supplies. Instead, he had kept in easy communication with vital sources of transport, arms, food, and forage, and still had moved steadily closer to Richmond.

[V]

Having formed his new plan, Grant stuck to his central aim. In vain had Halleck proposed, just after Cold Harbor, that the army invest Richmond from the north. Grant's superiority in numbers would have made this feasible, and it would have given Washington a continued sense of security; but it would have entailed bloody new assaults on lines of tremendous strength, while leaving Richmond in possession of all the arteries of supply below the James. Grant therefore threw his army across that river. Union engineers chose the vicinity of Wilcox's Landing as the best point, for it was covered on the west by Herring Creek, with eminences at hand to protect the rear. Fortunately, no better military engineers could be found in the world than those of the Army of the Potomac. According to the historian of the Fifth Corps, Lieut.-Col. William H. Powell of the regular Army (an Ohio manufacturer of Welsh birth who won the Medal of Honor, and was wounded at Wytheville, Virginia, and became brigadier-general of volunteers in October, 1864), the engineers of the Fifth Corps built in this campaign no fewer than thirty-eight bridges, aggregating 4,458 feet in length.[34]

"To cross so wide and deep a river with so large an army," writes the ablest Union engineer, A.A. Humphreys, "with all its artillery, together with its ammunition, subsistence, quartermaster, ambulance, and hospital trains, was a difficult operation, and exposed the army to attack under disadvantages while crossing."[35] But Lee could not attack without moving so far from Richmond as to imperil his own line. The building of a great pontoon-bridge over the James, one of the engineering triumphs of the war, the passage of the army, and deployment on the south bank, were swiftly and expertly managed. By June 16, Grant had his main force on the south bank. Whether he completely deceived Lee by his rapidity of movement is a question much debated by strategists. At one moment he seemed to have a decisive victory within his grasp in the capture of ill-defended Petersburg or even Richmond itself. He had been deprived of this triumph, however, by the fumbling of Ben Butler and William Farrar ("Baldy") Smith.

Fumbling is an inadequate word for the failure of Butler and Smith, which had about it more the quality of *opéra bouffe* than of war. It will be remembered

34. *The Fifth Army Corps of the Army of the Potomac*, New York, 1896, 678.
35. Humphreys, *op.cit.*, 199.

that part of the Grand Plan for coordination of the Union drive against Lee's army and Richmond was a movement by Ben Butler and his Army of the James. This force of about 39,000 infantry and cavalry, and 82 guns, was expected to march at the same time that Grant left the Rapidan, occupy City Point on the south bank of the James near the mouth of the Appomattox, and then advance along the river toward Richmond, getting a foothold as far upstream as possible. If the Confederates fell back upon the city, the Army of the Potomac would try to unite with the Army of the James in the area which Butler had reached. Whenever Butler should learn that the Confederates were sustaining an attack by Grant or feared it, he was himself to attack with all possible vigor. Was this a good plan? An officer of the Royal Engineers, Captain E.H. Steward, who watched operations, declared that it was "thrusting in a division between Petersburg and Richmond, before the main Confederate army could fall back to cover the capital, while the garrison at Petersburg was held in check by fear of the advance of the Federal army," and that it "was one of the boldest pieces of Grant's strategy, and deserved success . . . It is possible that, had less reliance been placed on the fleet, the advance on the Confederate capital and its capture when almost denuded of its defenders, might have been effected according to Grant's plan."[36]

On May 5-6, Butler's main force had landed at Bermuda Hundred on the north side of the mouth of the Appomattox, across from City Point, which was seized by Negro troops. At this time, Confederate defences were very thin, but Beauregard was attempting to organize an adequate force. The night of May 5, Butler proposed to take what ship-weary troops had landed, and advance on Richmond! The proposition was turned down by both corps commanders, Smith and Gillmore, because of the darkness, unfamiliar terrain, and confusion natural upon landing. On May 6, Butler sent his army forward toward the important Richmond & Petersburg Railroad and the Richmond-Petersburg road. Despite very light opposition, they did not get there. On May 7 and 9, operations against the railroad were a little more successful, but the line was not held. On May 9, Gillmore and Smith proposed to Butler that they cross the Appomattox and enter Petersburg, but Butler refused, saying that his cavalry was operating against the railroads near Petersburg.

Then on May 12, Butler began an advance northward toward the outer works of Richmond. Painfully slow, the Army of the James invested Drewry's Bluff on the James, the main Confederate defensive position south of Richmond, but a proposed general assault was abandoned. On May 16, the Confederates themselves advanced, and after some furious fighting, Butler's army

36. *O.R.* I, xxxiii, 904-905; Steward, *Royal Engineers Professional Papers,* War Office, London.

retired. A heavy rain fell, and early in the evening the Army of the James withdrew to its Bermuda Hundred lines. Butler was now cooped up tightly by a much inferior force on the narrow peninsula about fifteen miles from Richmond and seven from Petersburg. Grant, learning of the defeat of the Army of the James, ordered Smith's corps to move north in aid of Grant's own efforts. Butler as late as June 9 sent Gillmore and his cavalry to try against Petersburg, but Gillmore soon gave up the effort. At one time or another, Butler, W.F. Smith, Gillmore, cavalry commander August V. Kautz, and Rear-Admiral S.P. Lee, delayed movements, muffed opportunities, and failed miserably. Tempers became ragged, everyone blamed everyone else, and everyone was to blame. The Confederates under Beauregard scraped together troops from here and there and managed, with the help of Federal asininities, to hold Richmond, Petersburg, and the vital communications between, while at the same time penning up the much superior Army of the James. A comedy of errors and general ineptitude combined with a skillful Southern leadership to prevent a Northern success, one that might have obviated ten months of siege at Petersburg.[37]

For the final failure to overrun Petersburg on June 15th, when capture might still have been relatively easy, most observers placed immediate blame upon "Baldy" Smith, a stain upon the record of the short, portly, roundheaded officer that obliterated the memory of all his proud services in the Seven Days, at Antietam, and Chattanooga. The military historian, Colonel Thomas L. Livermore, pronounced Smith's timid inaction at the critical moment quite inexcusable. Others censured Butler for not following orders on June 15, and attacking between Petersburg and Richmond. Then, too, Hancock is also criticized. His Second Corps was slow in arriving at Petersburg from the crossing on the James River pontoon bridge because of poor maps and other handicaps. Many feel that when he did arrive, a night attack in the moonlight would have been effective. Grant, too, has been criticized. Busy supervising the James crossing, he and Meade could not oversee all the operations at Petersburg. In fact, enough faultiness existed for twenty men, and controversy over its distribution proved endless. It was Smith whom Grant shortly cashiered, and his presumed reasons for relieving that officer generated another controversy. No part of a sad campaign was sadder than these delinquencies.[38]

37. Basic correspondence, both Union and Confederate, *O.R.* I, xxxvi, pt. 3, 722-903, for June 10-30, 1864. See *Butler's Book*, Boston, 1892, Chs. XV, XVI: West, Richard S., Jr., *Lincoln's Scapegoat General, Benjamin Butler*, Boston, 1945, Chs. XX, XXI; *Private and Official Correspondence of Gen. Benjamin F. Butler*, Norwood, Mass., 1917, III, 155-452, containing spirited letters by Mrs. Butler.

38. Livermore, Thomas A., *Days and Events*, Boston, 1920, 353-364; Gray, John C., and John Codman Ropes, *War Letters, 1862-1865*, 185, 202ff., 461-490; Francis A. Walker, *History of the Second Army Corps*, New York, 1891, 525-538; Kautz, Gen. A.V., *Battles and Leaders*, IV, 533-535; R.E. Colston and G.T. Beauregard, *ibid.*, 536-544; and Meade, *op.cit.*, II, 198 ff. Smith's defensive letter of July

And alas, on the heels of the blunders of the Bermuda Hundred Campaign and June 15 at Petersburg, ensued the commission of more errors by high commanders. On June 16, General Meade, who had arrived before Petersburg, ordered Hancock, who had now taken command of all the forces facing the city, to attack at six in the evening. In the spirited assault that followed, driving the Confederates back at some points, the Union troops suffered severely. At dawn on the 17th, another assault, delivered so stealthily that the command "Forward!" was passed along the line in whispers, made so much fresh ground that Beauregard withdrew to a shorter, stronger line in his rear. Here, on the 18th, more fighting brought the two sides to another deadlock, but when night fell, Grant at last declared himself satisfied, and ordered his troops under cover for some rest. Their losses for the three desperate days, June 15-18, in killed, wounded, and missing, had aggregated 10,586. Thus ended six weeks of blood-drenched marching from the Rapidan to the James.[39]

The final assaults had proved that it was almost impossible to storm Petersburg, no matter how many men were flung against it. And now that Lee could tighten his grip upon it, storming Gibraltar would be as easy. The Confederate positions from Petersburg to Richmond defied such attacks as had been made. While fortified lines were not impregnable, they were proof against assaults so imperfectly coordinated as those Grant's army could deliver. One officer who vividly described a repulse at Petersburg—"it was beyond human endurance to stand such an iron rain;—our men broke and came back a broken, bleeding, routed body"—emphasized the lack of harmony in troop movement.[40] Besides, the Army of the Potomac was now fairly exhausted. Its almost incessant marches day and night, the close grapples with the enemy for more than six weeks, the repeated attacks on trenches defended by brush entangle-

30, 1864, to Senator H.S. Foote of Vermont is in the *Century Magazine*, XXXII, No. 4, Aug., 1897, 636-638. The Walter Wilgus Collection, private, contains correspondence upon Smith's contention that Butler employed a "hold" upon Grant to get Smith ousted, the "hold" being that Butler had seen Grant in his cups. The New York *Independent*, June 16, 1864, carried a vigorous editorial defense of Butler's strategy. Cyrus Comstock in his Journal (LC) writes on July 17 that "Some time ago Smith criticized in his ex-cathedra way this campaign as having been a series of useless slaughters. The General heard of it and told me he did not know which to do, relieve him or talk to him. . . . Smith has declared he will not serve with Butler, and as Butler is to stay for the present, Smith will probably be relieved." Smith had also criticized Meade harshly, apparently for "useless slaughters." But then Meade got on badly with other officers. "Meade and Burnside managed to quarrel again," writes Comstock on July 30. See also Livermore, Thomas L., "The Failure to Take Petersburg June 15, 1864," *Papers of the Military Historical Society of Massachusetts*, V, 33-74; Smith, William F., "The Movement Against Petersburg," *ibid.*, 75-115.

39. Freeman, *Lee*, IV, 444, footnote, remarks that "the actions of June 15-17 were as much mismanaged as any that Grant ever fought in Virginia"; A.H. Burne writes in *Lee, Grant, and Sherman*, 62, that for these three days Grant had "the best opportunity open to him throughout the campaign of winning a great victory," but missed it. His prestige in the North sensibly declined. Humphreys, *op.cit.*, 216-225.

40. Carter, Robert and Walter, *War Letters from the Battlefront* (Ms. Letters), II, 743-744, HEH.

ments and heavy embankments, the discouragement as ranks wilted under hot musket and artillery fire, had worn it out. A considerable number of the officers, dauntlessly leading the men into battle, had been slain or wounded; great numbers of privates were in their graves or in the hospitals. Rest and reanimation were badly needed.

It was a spent and shaken body of men who, realizing by the opening of July that the campaign from the Rapidan had ended in disillusionment, contrasted their present ragged ranks with the ardent hundred thousand who had plunged into the shades of the Wilderness. They would need time to recuperate, and reinforcements to supply their depletions. At this date, with Lincoln's Presidential battle just beginning, great numbers of voters felt tired and shaken too. As Senator Lyman Trumbull wrote, they "fear he is too undecided and inefficient to put down the rebellion."[41]

When the so-called siege of Petersburg began (not a true siege for the town was never invested, but a beleaguerment, resembling that of Stalingrad in the Second World War), a new phase of Grant's campaign also opened. In reality, the Federals were besieging both Petersburg and Richmond. By midsummer, the lines ran about 26 miles from north of the James to south of Petersburg. Grant had been hammering away incessantly at the enemy; now he would try instead the use of military science and strategic combinations. He had varied his flank marches with frontal assaults; now he would move against the enemy communications at Petersburg—the Richmond & Petersburg, the South-Side Railroad to Lynchburg, the Norfolk & Petersburg which immediately fell, and the Weldon Railroad running south out of Petersburg, thin webs of iron reaching west and south. In his hammering operations, his able quartermaster-general, Rufus Ingalls, had shifted his base of supplies from Aquia Creek to Port Royal on the Rappahannock, then to White House on the Pamunkey, and finally to City Point where the Appomattox River empties into the James. He had done this with such skill and precision that the troops had never lacked food, ammunition, or other essential supplies a single half-day. As new lines were laid out, the men put down their rifles for the axe, spade, and pick with which they rapidly built trenches and covered ways. City Point became an ant-hill humming with activity.

"Steamboats and sailing vessels, transports and lighters of all kinds," wrote one brigade commander, "encumbered the river near the improvised wharves on which they were still working. Higher up, toward Richmond, the eye could

41. White, Horace, *Life of Lyman Trumbull*, Boston, 1913, 218. See Field Marshal Wolseley's judgment that the military balance in 1864 up to and beyond Cold Harbor was with the South; Wolseley, Garnet J., ed. James A. Rawley, *The American Civil War: An English View*, Charlottesville, 1964, 205.

distinguish at a distance the turrets of the monitors, which appeared to stand out of the water, and the gunboats, on which enormous pivot guns were visible. The river bank, rising up high, had been cleared and levelled, so as to make room for storehouses, . . . and for a station for the railroad. All this had sprung out of the earth as if by magic . . . All was activity and movement. Legions of Negroes were discharging the ships, wheeling dirt, sawing the timber, and driving piles. Groups of soldiers crowded around the sutlers' tents; horsemen in squadrons went down to the river to water their horses." On the plateau above the James, a small city of huts and tents leaped into sleepless animation.[42]

While the Army of the Potomac and the Army of the James had been playing the most prominent roles in the Federal advance, the third prong in Grant's thrust had been frustrated in the Shenandoah. On May 9, Sigel left Winchester heading south, or up the Shenandoah Valley. He met little opposition until he arrived near New Market, where, on March 15, outnumbered Confederates under John C. Breckinridge smashed him. This was the battle, relatively small, in which the youths of the Virginia Military Institute won great and enduring fame. A few days later, Sigel was relieved and replaced by the controversial David Hunter. A new Union advance aimed at Charlottesville was begun. Hunter defeated Confederates at Piedmont on June 5, burned the VMI building at Lexington, and spread destruction in the Valley. Grant ordered Sheridan to take his cavalry and operate on the Virginia Central from Hanover Junction to Charlottesville where he was to join Hunter. On June 11-12, Sheridan was defeated by Wade Hampton's Southern cavalry at Trevilian Station, and forced to call off his raid. Jubal Early now took over for the reinforced Confederates in the Shenandoah, and planned to attack Hunter June 19 at Lynchburg, only to find the Federals pulling out. Hunter retreated into the Kanawha Valley of West Virginia, leaving the Shenandoah open to Early who headed north toward the Potomac. Grant's plans for the cooperating movement in the Shenandoah had gone awry.

A war of greater organization, ingenuity, and strategic skill had now commenced in Virginia, but its results could not be immediately registered, and its first heavy stroke continued the disheartening tale of bungling and disaster. On July 30, the great mine under the Confederate works at Petersburg, which had been planned by Lt. Col. Henry Pleasants, a civil engineer commanding a regiment (the 48th Pennsylvania) made up largely of former coal miners, was exploded. In the ensuing Battle of the Crater, Union casualties reached a total of about 3,800 while the Confederate casualties were about 1,200. As Grant

42. De Trobriand, Gen. Regis, *Four Years with the Army of the Potomac*, Boston, 1889, 594.

put it, the effort was "a stupendous failure," adding to the midsummer sense of gloom and frustration.[43]

[VI]

Meanwhile, a livelier kind of history was being written by William Tecumseh Sherman as commander of the military division of the Mississippi, though it too had tragic interludes, and ran into mid-July without decisive result. He and his subordinates, Thomas, McPherson, and Schofield, had to press their campaign from the Tennessee simultaneously with Grant's from the Rapidan. His army of a hundred thousand, with 254 guns, had gotten under way with a promptness that heartened everybody, and, as we have seen, had quickly thrust Johnston's army from its positions at Dalton and Resaca, for it was large enough to outflank its smaller adversary with ease.

Yet the disparity of strength was not as great as it appeared. Johnston might have counted a ratio of three-to-five, far from hopeless for a defensive position in rough and confusing country. Ahead of Sherman lay a mountainous, thickly wooded, ill-roaded district, with three potentially difficult rivers, the Oostenaula, the Etowah, and the Chattahoochee, in his path. Before him also stood a general who was not only a strategist of stubborn skill, but a vivacious, warmhearted, determined leader, most of whose veterans loved him and would follow him to death with implicit confidence.[44]

Mid-May found Sherman's army pushing beyond the Oostenaula, after taking the two strong Dalton-Resaca positions at a cost of only 6,805 casualties compared with Johnston's 5,245. By the 20th, the rapidly advancing flank marches of Sherman had compelled Johnston to retreat across the Etowah, a stream that he later regretted he had not attempted to defend. Johnston had listened to the advice of two of his three corps commanders, Polk and Hood, in making the withdrawal. Sherman was not confident of his future. "I shall

43. See articles on the Crater by W.H. Powell, C.H. Houghton, and H.G. Thomas, *Battles and Leaders*, IV, 540-567. The vigorous account in Munroe, J.P., *Life of Francis Amasa Walker*, New York, 1923, 266-268, emphasizes Hancock's vigilant competence as contrasted with Burnside's incompetence. The story, possessing suspense and drama, but little military significance, has been too often told to require retelling. This may also be said of Jubal Early's foray toward Washington (best recounted in *Jubal's Raid*, New York, 1960, by Frank E. Vandiver), which reached an outer fort of the capital on July 11, but failed in all its main objects and did the Confederacy as much harm as good. It weakened neither Grant's army nor his determination to fight doggedly ahead. For its effect upon Lincoln see Nicolay and Hay, *Lincoln*, *op.cit.*, X, 165-171.

44. Govan, Gilbert E., and James W. Livingood, *A Different Valor, The Story of General Joseph E. Johnston*, New York, 1956, give an appreciative view of Johnston; Foote, Shelby, *The Civil War*, New York, 1963, II, 618ff., 622, 623, 646, 647, is judicious; Bradford, Gamaliel, *Confederate Portraits*, Boston, 1914, Ch.I, is balanced. The best edition of Johnston's *Narrative of Military Operations* is edited by Frank E. Vandiver, Bloomington, 1960.

give two days' rest to replenish and fit up," he telegraphed Washington. "On the 23rd I will cross the Etowah and move on Dallas. This will turn the Allatoona Pass." He had managed his operations with skill, taking advantage of the fact that no matter how far Johnston extended his flanks, he could extend his own farther. In his reminiscences he scoffed at the claim of some Southerners that Johnston had deliberately planned to give up his strong points in order to draw the Union army farther south. On the contrary, he wrote, Johnston evacuated these towns only because it was unsafe to wait another hour lest the Northern pincers close.[45]

While he advanced, scattered troops had to guard the railway lines all the way back to Chattanooga, back to Nashville, back to Louisville—they and the railwaymen shouldering a dangerous task. While they maintained the flow of supplies in heat and dust, or more often in pouring rain and mud, they had to fight off the hornet attacks of cavalry, guerrillas, and snipers. Whenever the Southerners could not set a bridge afire or derail a train, they struck other blows. They burned thousands of tons of munitions and stores on the long lines through Tennessee and Kentucky, and captured thousands more. The Tennessee Unionist, John W. Burgess, later noted as a scholar, declared that after a year of watching, and fighting, he was physically almost ruined.[46]

To ensure the efficiency of the long rear lines, Sherman placed them under iron military control with civilian assistance. He restricted trains, subsequently cutting down forage and camp equipment to a minimum; he impounded locomotives and rolling stock from Northern railroads. Later he recalled his satisfaction in seeing cars from distant lines (such as the Lackawanna) hauling his supplies. When the impoverished inhabitants of East Tennessee clamored for food, especially around Chattanooga, he made them grow vegetables with the energy of hunger.

These measures might have excited violent opposition had Sherman not sternly denied his own soldiers aught but necessities. He ordered that each regiment and battery should be restricted to one wagon, and the officers of each company to one pack-animal, for supplies; that the headquarters of each corps, each division, and each brigade should have only a single wagon apiece; and that all remaining transportation should be organized into ordnance and supply trains, carrying twenty days' rations per man for each command. When

45. *O.R.* I, xxxvii, pt. 4, 533-595, contains Sherman's dispatches of June 20-25, 1864; see also his revised *Memoirs*, 4th ed., Chs. XVI-XVIII, and M.A. DeWolfe Howe, ed., *Home Letters of General Sherman*, New York, 1909, 296-308. Stone, Henry, "The Atlanta Campaign" (Pt.I, *Papers of the Military Historical Society of Mass.*, VIII) covers the opening of the campaign, and gives the casualties noted here.

46. See Grenville M. Dodge, Ms. *Autobiography*, Iowa State Hist. Lib., for railway duty; Burgess, John W., *Reminiscences of an American Scholar*, New York, 1934, 32-33.

practicable, the soldiers were to carry three days' provisions with them. "This made our ordnance and supply trains pretty heavy," wrote General Grenville M. Dodge, "but the rest of the transportation was very light." Troops began the campaign with 140 rounds of infantry ammunition for each man, 100 rounds of artillery ammunition for each gun, and no tents whatever. Most of the officers in the Army of the Tennessee followed this order literally, and when Sherman took the field he himself stuck to it rigidly.[47]

The Confederates defending the craggy passage from Ringgold into Atlanta were also tied to the same single railway line, the old Western & Atlantic, long owned and operated by the State. The country through which they retreated was steadily being drained of able-bodied men, supplies, and horses. It was so rough and hilly, largely covered by thick woods and brush, and channeled by swift streams, that bodies of troops dared not venture far from the rails, and had little room for manoeuvering, so that Sherman, with far superior forces, was able to compel Johnston to make retreat after retreat by simply moving around one flank or the other. Thus, until Kenesaw Mountain, no great battles marked his early progress. Brisk, fierce engagements took place, confined to one or two corps on each side. The Union Army could always extend its line beyond the Confederate positions on one side or both, making any stand by Johnston impossible. Thus, neither Johnston's defensive situation nor his ability to fortify his lines helped him very much.

Sherman summarized his advance to Atlanta in a few sentences. He declared that Johnston, who in time had 62,000 men, was confident that he could draw the Union forces far from their base, and then turn and destroy them. "We were equally confident and not the least alarmed," asserted Sherman. Johnston fell back by June 21 to just west of the vicinity of Marietta, with the bold and striking peak called Kenesaw Mountain marking his center, and his line extending approximately ten miles. As this was too long, he contracted his flanks and concentrated on Kenesaw, repairing the railroad up to his camps, and preparing for the contest. "Not a day, not an hour or minute," wrote Sherman, "was there a cessation of fire."[48]

Finally, on June 27, Sherman made the mistake of ordering a general assault. Thomas had objected to this, suggesting an advance by systematic sapping trenches, but the commander could not be restrained. Word had just come that Forrest, at Brice's Crossroads, Mississippi, had defeated S.D. Sturgis (the incompetent cavalry officer supposed to help protect Sherman's outer com-

47. Dodge, *ut supra;* also *Personal Recollections of President Abraham Lincoln, General Ulysses S. Grant, and General William T. Sherman,* Council Bluffs, Iowa, 1914, 143ff; Perkins, J.R., *Trails, Rails, and War; The Life of General G.M. Dodge,* Indianapolis, 1929, 91-94.

48. Sherman, *Memoirs,* II, Chs. XVI, XVII, XVIII.

munication in Tennessee) and had driven him back into Memphis. This bad news may have contributed to Sherman's impetuosity. At eight in the morning, he began the fighting all along the high, narrow, and extremely steep front of Kenesaw, its three-mile ridge crammed with batteries and rifle-pits. The battle soon became one of the hottest of the war, with nearly 35,000 men engaged on the two sides. "We have no words to describe this awful day," wrote one Middle Westerner engaged. He found the roar of artillery, explosion of shells, crash of small arms, and yells and groans of the combatants, positively sickening.[49]

"The infantry next to us made a splendid charge and partially took a strong line of works, but were driven back with terrible slaughter," he continued. "So the battle raged all along the west side of the mountain, and so it rolls away down to the right along a line of flame and smoke and blood. But on the extreme right our men are more successful and drive the rebels back . . . Our men on the south have taken three lines of the enemy's works and hold two of them, but are driven from the third with fearful slaughter. This has all occurred before ten A.M., and it has become apparent even to Sherman that the assault is a failure." On the hot days following, the stench of corpses, clouds of flies, and hosts of maggots made the Union position almost intolerable. The total Northern losses were put by Sherman himself at 3,000, a rough figure.[50]

At the end, Sherman did what he should have done at the beginning. The night of July 2, he began to move his main forces by the right flank around Johnston. Part of these troops were now armed with Spencer repeaters, which enabled a single company to fire as effectively as a regiment with the old Springfields. The result was inevitable; Johnston had to pull out to new defences near Smyrna Church. Union troops soon marched past line after line of substantial earthworks, now useless and empty, to enter Marietta on July 3. By July 4, Johnston had pulled back to the bridgeheads across the Chattahoochee, and Sherman pushed him fairly beyond that stream by the 10th. The river, he wrote, was "covered and protected by the best line of field entrenchments I have ever seen, prepared long in advance." These flanking movements were spirited and effective. "I begin to regard the death and mangling of a

49. Magee, E.F., *History of the 72d Indiana Volunteer Infantry*, Lafayette, Ind. 1882, 324ff. S.R. Watkins, in his history of the First Tennessee Regiment, *"Co.Aytch," Maury Gray's First Tennessee Regiment*, Nashville, 1882, 151-164, writes that the Southerners shot down "column after column" until weary of killing. Among the dead were Gen. C.S. Harker, half-a-dozen years out of West Point, and Daniel J. McCook, a former law-partner of Sherman's, just thirty, who recited Macaulay's "Horatius at the Bridge" to his men before the attack.

50. Livermore, *Numbers and Losses*, 121, puts the Union killed and missing at 2,051 on the day of the Kenesaw charge, June 27. *O.R.* I, xxxviii, pt. 3, 703, 870, gives Confederate losses as 270 for killed and missing.

couple of thousand men as a small affair, a sort of morning dash," he wrote home. [51]

In this advance upon the Chattahoochee and Atlanta the impatient Sherman had to proceed, as he informed Halleck, by the slow tactics of movement upon a long line of fortified positions. "The whole country is one vast fort, and Johnston must have at least fifty miles of connected trenches, with abattis and finished batteries." Sherman kept his army well in hand, reproving Hooker sharply on June 23 for his tendency to separate his Twentieth Corps from the armies under Thomas, McPherson, and Schofield so that he might win a little special glory for himself. Hooker was jealous of these three commanders, all younger and in his view less experienced and capable.[52]

The loss of perhaps three thousand men at or near Kenesaw Mountain in the last ten days of June, however, remained a sore point in the Northern consciousness. Were the attack and repulse unavoidable?

As his troops were approaching the impregnable slopes, Sherman had declared that "we cannot risk the heavy losses of an assault at this distance from our bases." Yet three days later, he telegraphed Halleck that he had changed his mind and now inclined to thrust at the enemy center, although "it may cost us dear." Why the shift? Sherman explained that the results of a frontal drive "would surpass any attempt to pass around." The sequel proved the opposite. In his report he gave a fuller and franker statement of his reasons for a direct attack. "I perceived that the enemy and our own officers had settled down into a conviction that I would *not* assault fortified lines. All looked to me to outflank. An army, to be efficient, must not settle down to one single mode of offense, but must be prepared to execute any single plan that promises success. I wanted, therefore, for the moral effect, to make a successful assault on the enemy behind his breastworks." The moral effect of uselessly throwing away lives![53]

The soldier-journalist Donn Piatt, who had been made General R.C. Schenck's chief-of-staff, later offered an explanation even less creditable to Sherman. Quoting John A. Logan, he told how on the night before the assault, after reading a newspaper full of news about Grant's fighting, Sherman had looked up from it to say that the whole attention of the country was fixed on the Army of the Potomac, while his army was forgotten. Now *he* would fight; next day he would order the assault. McPherson quietly commented that no necessity existed for this step, since Johnston could again be outflanked. To this Sherman replied that "it was necessary to show that his men could fight

51. Sherman, *Home Letters*, 299.
52. See Sherman's report, *O.R.* I, xxxviii, pt. 1, 61-85.
53. *Ibid.*, also Greeley, Horace, *The American Conflict*, Hartford, Conn, 1879, II, 629.

as well as Grant's." This was hearsay evidence. Yet it was a fact that Sherman had telegraphed Grant the previous week that he was out of patience with Thomas, that the Army of the Cumberland was dreadfully slow, and that "I have again and again tried to impress on Thomas that we must assail and not defend."[54]

The bloodshed at Kenesaw was made harder to bear by the fact that McPherson's subsequent flanking movement on the right (July 2) was an instant success. After reaching the Chattahoochee, Sherman paused. Realizing that his men needed rest, and that Johnston's army was still intact with numbers practically equal to those he had led out of Dalton, Sherman gave the Union forces a breathing-spell to make ready for the next move. He remained quiet until July 16, and on the 17th the main crossing of the Chattahoochee began. Also in July, Farragut was still outside Mobile Bay, its fortifications untested; the national debt was mounting toward two billions of dollars; and the Democrats were preparing for the August Convention that was shortly to nominate McClellan for the Presidency amid cries that the war was a failure.

54. Piatt, Donn, *Memories of Men Who Saved the Union*, New York, 1887, 248-255; Lewis, Lloyd, *Sherman, Fighting Prophet*, New York, 1932, 374-375.

3

Cement of the Union

AS A war becomes rougher, internal politics get rougher too. Throughout the spring and summer of 1864, Lincoln's most anxious efforts, aside from military affairs, were devoted to holding a majority of Northern voters in sufficient harmony to maintain his prestige and moral power. Unity and patience!—these were his fundamental demands. If impatience grew, if men gave way to fear and anger, party disruption would open the gate to national destruction. In June he urged the Yankee journalist Noah Brooks, who sent Washington correspondence to various journals East and West, to do all he could to correct the optimistic delusion that "the war will end right off victoriously." It would not, and people must steel themselves for a cruel endurance of stubborn exertion. Although the North was further ahead than he had anticipated, he stated: "as God is my judge, I shall be satisfied if we are over with the fight in Virginia within a year." As the strain of war increased, he had to meet one domestic crisis after another. Subjected to constant vicissitudes in his relations with the Cabinet, Congressional leaders, editors, governors, and political adventurers, he fought always a central battle for balance, compromise, and an overriding insistence upon unity. If he struck a hard blow here, it was for harmony; if he yielded there, it was for harmony.

[I]

Nobody knew better than Lincoln that the prospect for his reëlection that fall was anxiously uncertain. A democracy always feels the failures of a leader more sharply than his successes. In political sagacity, adherence to principle, and vision of the national future, Lincoln rose superior to his contemporaries. The people of Civil War days, however, saw incomplete lineaments of his wisdom, generosity, and eloquence. What they did see clearly were his deficiencies in executive energy and skill. Some agreed with George Bancroft that he was self-willed and ignorant—ignorant of finance, economic forces, foreign governments, and military necessities. Others thought with Lyman Trumbull that he had drifted when decision was needed. Still others held with Charles

Francis Adams, Sr., that in the storm then raging a stronger hand was needed on the tiller.

Lincoln's prestige had sunk to its nadir after the failure of the Peninsular Campaign and Pope's defeat just outside Washington at Second Manassas. The Democrats were embittered by his decisive removal of McClellan, and Radical Republicans had fallen into the deep depression that inspired fierce demands after Fredericksburg for a reorganization of the Cabinet. Had the United States possessed a government of British type, its Ministry might have fallen. Antietam and the Emancipation Proclamation had lifted the President's standing; Chancellorsville unquestionably depressed it again. Gettysburg and Vicksburg raised it anew; the drama of Missionary Ridge lifted men's hearts like a sudden burst of martial music. Chickamauga hurt Lincoln's prestige but Chattanooga restored it; the first bloody checks of May and June, 1864, sank it once more, and even though Grant was at the gates of the Confederate capital, many in the North did not consider that a victory.

Lincoln and the Administration, knowing the value politically of war news, kept the Baltimore Union Party convention delegates well posted, so that when the news of Hunter's victory at Piedmont (June 5, 1864) came in, there was great cheering. Stanton is credited with having sent these dispatches. Such oscillations of elation and despair were natural and understandable, but they struck many observers as unworthy of a great people with the traditions of the Seven Years' War, the long Revolutionary struggle, and of Valley Forge in its past. Surely Americans had the Spartan valor of their ancestors who had crossed the stormy seas and had subdued a rocky continent to found a nation. It was confidence that he could appeal to the deep, latent tenacity of the American people, complete faith in their chilled-steel devotion to ancient principles, which had inspired Edward Everett Hale to publish in the *Atlantic Monthly* for December, 1863, his unexpected yet clearly inspired tale "The Man Without a Country," which was more than a short story, soon soaring to a mass circulation—which was a trumpet peal lifting the national heart. It was in the same faith that the deep national fealties and convictions of the American people rose superior to the fluctuations of victories and defeats, that another gifted author, the economist and veteran journalist David A. Wells, published *Our Burden and Our Strength* (1864), which was worth as much to the Union cause as a resounding battlefield victory. This book, like Hale's imperishable story, represented the true devotion and tenacity of the Northern people, and helped nerve their arms to strike. So did another telling book of 1864, Charles J. Stillé's *How a Free People Conduct a Long War*, a study of British resolution in combating Napoleon, that helped fortify countless readers. Was this really the spirit of the majority of Northerners?

Lincoln's military missteps, beginning with War Order No. 1 for a general advance on Washington's Birthday in 1862, and his occasionally maladroit interferences with generals, were more evident than the soundness of his basic strategic ideas. Suspension of the habeas corpus, military arrests, and spasms of press censorship offended multitudes who revered the Bill of Rights. As the conflict lengthened, it was saddening to think of the battlefield agonies of tens of thousands of young men, the myriad of bereaved homes, and the coarsening of the national character which were among its effects. Little stories illuminated the popular tension—the story, for example, of a speculator who said exultantly in a crowded car, "Well, I hope the war may last six months longer; in the last six months I've made a hundred thousand dollars." Instantly a woman slapped him, crying "Sir, I had two sons—one was killed at Fredericksburg, the other at Murfreesboro!"; and the indignant spectators hustled him out the door.[1]

Few events of the war aroused such a feeling of mingled anger and anguish in the North as the April "massacre" at Fort Pillow already mentioned. The facts of this occurrence, in which 231 Union soldiers, largely Negroes, were killed while only 14 Confederates fell, have provoked some disputation. Northerners, however, saw only one side. They read headlines announcing "Attack on Fort Pillow—Indiscriminate Slaughter of the Prisoners—Shocking Scenes of Savagery"; dispatches from Sherman's army declaring "there is a general gritting of teeth here"; reports from the Missouri *Democrat* detailing the "fiendishness" of rebel behavior; and editorials like that in the Chicago *Tribune* condemning the "murder" and "butchery." Senator Henry Wilson published in the New York *Tribune* a letter from a lieutenant-colonel in the Army of the Tennessee giving gory particulars, while others poured in from survivors in the Mound City (Ill.) hospital. All this made a heavier impression because of the unquestionable facts that Confederates had previously killed some Negro soldiers after capture, and had exchanged not a single Negro private of the many captured at Battery Wagner, Port Hudson, and Olustee. Was Lincoln doing enough, men asked, to prevent such ebullitions of the barbarism of slavery and to punish them when they took place?[2]

People were now aware that the fast-lengthening casualty-rolls confronted the nation with one of the saddest tragedies of modern history. They had taken

1. Nevins, Allan, *The New York Evening Post*, New York, 1922, 320-321.

2. For Fort Pillow, see files of newspapers April 16-30, 1864; Castel, Albert, "The Fort Pillow Massacre: a Frank Examination of the Evidence," *Civil War History*, IV, No. 1, March, 1958, 37-50, a careful examination which reaches the conclusion that a massacre did occur; and the papers in the Chicago Historical Society of Gen. Mason Brayman, commanding this summer at Natchez, which support the charge of an inhuman massacre. Brooks, Noah, *Washington in Lincoln's Time*, ed. Herbert Mitgang, New York, 1958, 138. There is great conflict between various Confederate reports and the *Report of the Joint Committee on the War*, "Fort Pillow Massacre," Washington, 1964, 39th Cong., 1st Sess., House Report No. 65.

deaths hard when Elmer Ellsworth and Theodore Winthrop fell in the first weeks; they took them still harder as the graves of young men numbered hundreds of thousands. And at last the moral costs were all too evident. The war had so many heroic aspects that at first it had been easy to ignore the moral erosion. But now men comprehended that the conflict was accentuating some of the baser features of a society too full of frontier crudities, too casually addicted to neighborhood violence, and too often ready to let the dollar prove or excuse wrong acts. Civil wars often have a Cain-Abel savagery, and this one had sent large armies trampling across defenseless communities. Guerrilla warfare on both sides sometimes became mass-murder, as in Quantrill's raid on Lawrence, Kansas. All along the indefinite warring fronts, and in tenuously-held Federally-occupied areas, bands of outlaws, often irrespective of North or South, were busy ambushing sentries, slaying householders, and perpetrating outrages that made the blood run cold.

The treatment of prisoners of war on both sides was often a story of neglect. Financial corruption spread like some valley fog along ill-cleared waterways —graft in illicit cotton traffic, contracts, appointments to office, bounty-jumping, and tax-evasion. It was small wonder that, while the nation's sacrifices were sullied by so much rascality, sensitive men, anxious to protect the nation's character, sometimes lost heart. Some criticism of Lincoln was healthy, but the danger was that licentious criticism might lead a majority to falter in the war. "Jefferson Davis is perhaps in some respects superior to our President," Charles Francis Adams wrote from the London legation in the spring of 1863. When a perceptive man, snobbishly class-conscious, could write this, public sentiment might take any turn. James Gordon Bennett, who had little education or insight, but a good deal of hard Scotch common sense, was arguing in the *Herald* that Lincoln's vacillations had already gravely prolonged the war, and "will cause it to be interminable if another sort of man, independent of political factions and true to the Constitution, is not soon placed in the President's chair."[3]

A majority of Republicans not only saw that the party must stand or fall with Lincoln, as governors like Andrew, Morton, Curtin, and Yates of Illinois did, but admired his record and personality. Yet a powerful body of the Radicals, who had supported Frémont's emancipationist ideas, were so dissatisfied with Lincoln's conciliation of Border settlement and ten-percent plan for Reconstruction, that they were ready to revolt.[4] Among the War Demo-

3. New York *Herald*, quoted in Detroit *Free Press*, Jan. 7, 1864, C.F. Adams to R.H. Dana, Jr., Apr. 8, 1863, R.H. Dana Papers, Mass. Hist. Soc.

4. Welles, Gideon, "The Opposition to Lincoln in 1864," *Atlantic Monthly*, March, 1878, No. CCXLV, Vol. XLI, 366-376.

crats, indispensable to a Union Party, a large number adhered to Lincoln. They shrank from the Copperheads, respected the President's abilities, and rejoiced over his charitable attitude toward conquered Southerners. Yet here, too, some would prefer another man. They parroted the cry: "The Constitution as it is and the Union as it was," which sounded patriotic and was actually defeatist. They accepted the argument, pleasing to Lincoln-haters, that the principle of one-term Presidencies ought to be firmly established. Nobody since Andrew Jackson had served two terms, and eight men in succession had held the White House four years or less.

The Radical opposition to Lincoln might have been less formidable if he had treated members of Congress, who now included more than the usual proportion of vain, jealous, and fanatical men, with greater tact. He never concealed his contempt for "politicians" and their "sophisms." In conversation he sometimes gave the names, with biting comment, of men he thought foolish or rascally. He took pains, to be sure, to maintain his friendship with Charles Sumner, Thaddeus Stevens, Henry Wilson, Lot M. Morrill, James W. Grimes, Galusha Grow, and other influential figures. He tried to handle a few men he really despised, such as coarse Ben Wade and serpentine Henry Winter Davis, with gloves. He was ready to give Congressional leaders the patronage they wanted. But he could be as hostile to enemies like the New York Peace Democrat Ben Wood as they were to him; and, having sat in Congress himself, he had no awe of it. He was no more disposed to let Congress manage the war than when he had refused to call a special session after Fort Sumter, and he was still less willing to let it manage the peace.

He had been aloof in his relations with some of his Cabinet. To the two principal departments, State and War, he gave close attention, but Welles, Chase, Montgomery Blair, Caleb Smith, and Bates were expected to run their machines to suit themselves. His Administration remained a loose coalition, never unified, seldom harmonious. Chase still complained to friends that no coordination of the departments existed, and so little consultation that when he wished to know how the war was getting on he had to consult newspapermen. While the Cabinet is not historically a consultative body, Lincoln might have made fuller use of it for the exchange of information; it was important for Welles to know what moneys Chase could provide for ships, and for Blair to know what naval vessels might carry mail. Lincoln visited Stanton every day, saw Seward frequently, and sometimes consulted Montgomery Blair, but neglected the others. The fact was that the country did not wish a highly centralized government, and he could make no greater error than to strive to give it one.

Gideon Welles, grumbling that he had little of Lincoln's confidence, thought that Seward and Stanton got too much of it. He suspected that Seward, by his devious ways and loose talk, risked pushing some States into the Democratic column. He was equally distrustful of acid-tongued Senators like Lyman Trumbull and William Pitt Fessenden, who seemed trying to destroy confidence in the President. Their criticisms too often reached critical editors like Greeley, Medill, and Bennett. "If, therefore, the reëlection of Mr. Lincoln is not defeated, it will not be owing to them."[5] When Welles wrote this, Greeley believed that Rosecrans might be a more popular Presidential candidate than Lincoln.[6]

Secretary Chase held no stronger position in the Administration than that of financial specialist. Yet he was not only an able fiscal administrator, the creator of the national banking system and a military organizer of some limited experience within his State, but also the ambitious head of one fairly numerous wing or faction of the Republican Party in the Middle West. Chase believed that Lincoln's conception of the Executive was too constricted, but Lincoln's instinct in this matter was sound. Nevertheless, some careful enlargement of the Administration to include a bureau of transportation and supplies, the partial equivalent of the War Industries Board in the the first World War, and a bureau for the freedmen, might have strengthened it immediately, and helped it cope with the grave problems of 1864-1866. Other men agreed with Chase that Lincoln's gifts simply did not include distinction as an administrator.[7] In political acumen he was unexcelled; his sense of timing—his patient instinct for the occasion, or as Nicolay and Hay put it, his *opportunism*—was remarkable; his breadth of view was statesmanlike. But his haphazard, unsystematic ways were sometimes the despair of associates.

All spring, visitors found Lincoln painfully altered in looks and manner; as April ended, the Ohio Congressman A.G. Riddle found him worn and harassed.[8] The almost endless war, the grief and anxiety were proving an intolerable burden. Others in and outside Congress were equally worried, and nerves were growing taut. Washington, no longer close enough to battlefields to hear the guns, was still a huge receiving-station for the wounded. As boatloads of casualties steadily arrived on the Potomac waterfront, and trainloads rumbled in by rail, cohorts of ambulances jolted through the streets to the twenty-one hospitals. People from the North and West, betraying hurry, anxiety, and grief, thronged through the city on their way to hospitals in Freder-

5. Welles, *Diary*, II, 130-131.

6. Gilmore, James Robert, *Personal Recollections of Abraham Lincoln and the Civil War*, London, 1899, Chs. X-XII, especially 103, 145-46.

7. See Maurice, Sir Frederick, *Statesmen and Soldiers of the Civil War*, Boston, 1926, Ch.V, on the penalties Great Britain and the United States have both paid for lack of system in war.

8. Riddle, Albert G., *Recollections of War Times*, New York, 1895, 266-267.

icksburg or Culpeper. Details of clerks from government departments who had volunteered for half-month duty as nurses and orderlies came back with tales of the suffering they had seen. Night after night, men with anguished faces, and women who wilted at the sight of bloody forms, viewed the changing procession. Those watchers in the May or June moonlight who saw two or three thousand casualties landed at a time on the Sixth-Street Wharf never forgot the ghastly lines of shattered men, the clumps of tearful spectators, and the rigid shapes of those who had died in transit, outlined against the flowing river and distinct shores. Meanwhile, letters written in the midst of amputations, hemorrhages, and death were scattered far and wide across the country.

"There are many very bad now in hospital," ran one letter signed Walt Whitman, "so many of our soldiers are getting broke down after two years, or two and a half, exposure and bad diet, pork, hard biscuit, bad water or none at all, etc., etc., so we have them brought up here. Oh, it is terrible, and getting worse, worse, worse. I thought it was bad; to see these I sometimes think is more pitiful still."[9]

[II]

The cement of the nation had been furnished since Federalist-Republican allegiances by its political parties; what if the cement began to crumble? In the spring of 1864, it seemed to be disintegrating, for the two main parties were both more deeply riven than ever. Peace Democrats were willing to end the war even without saving the Union; War Democrats were determined to end the war on a full restoration of the Union and on no other fixed condition whatever. In opposition to them the Moderate Republicans stood for the Union, Emancipation, and a rapid Reconstruction on mild terms; the Radical Republicans demanded Union, Emancipation, and a delayed Reconstruction on steel-hard terms or rather penalties. A variety of shades of opinion might be distinguished under these four areas, but they suffice for a broad classification. If the Peace Democrats ever gained overwhelming strength in the North and Northwest, the Union was lost. If the Radical Republicans conquered majority opinion, they would insist upon nominal union in spiritual disunion.

Lincoln, the chieftain and animating spirit of the Moderate Republicans, provided by his moral leadership the truest national cement of all. He stood for a party of the Center, uniting the War Democrats and Moderate Republicans in the new Union Party. Clearly, he had two battles to fight. In the first,

9. Walt Whitman to his mother, Washington, Apr. 5, 1864; *The Wound Dresser*, New York, 1949, 160-161.

he must enforce sufficient harmony within this Union Party to gain and hold the nomination with a strong chance of election. This did not appear easy in April, and looked still harder in August, when many discontented members clamored for a new convention. In his second battle he must defeat the Democrats, who were expected to nominate McClellan. All the while the war would be a mighty tide bearing the ship of state and the several parties in unpredictable directions. Waves of hope would lift the vessel forward. Waves of dejection would stop it, spin it into eddies, or throw it upon the rocks. Was shipwreck a real danger? Very real, indeed, for a few more defeats in late summer might possibly have swept the country into an irrational demand for peace at almost any price. All spring, all summer, Lincoln and his adherents had to confront ever fluctuating difficulties and perils, while the dragging, wearisome war itself, with its inevitable drain upon national morale, was a far more important factor than the changing ideologies of the stormy time.

The Administration, though numbering old Jacksonian leaders like Welles and Blair, could do little for the Democratic rank-and-file. It offered a haven in the Union Party for staunchly individualistic War Democrats like John A. Dix and Andrew Johnson, and that was about all. To Peace Democrats it could only assert a defiant, unremitting opposition. Lincoln expressed this defiance in an April address at the Sanitary Fair in Baltimore, drawing a line between liberty as defined by wolves and defined by sheep, and coupling his use of colored troops with the general advance of emancipation.[10] On the Republican side the Moderate Republicans presented no problems of grave perplexity, but the Radical Republicans offered Lincoln nearly as much hostility as the Peace Democrats, and were as refractory and treacherous.

These Radicals showed no lack of resolution. Initially their movement had possessed four principal objects. They meant, first, to insist on a more energetic prosecution of the war; second, to require that no great army be entrusted to a general who did not believe in complete victory and emancipation; third, to persuade the President to get rid of lukewarm Cabinet members like Montgomery Blair; and fourth, to induce him to make more efficient use of his Cabinet. Later, they added another object, governmental adoption of a Reconstruction policy that would keep the South subjugated until all roots of rebellion were dead, and this they soon regarded as the most important of all. Radical critics made some mistaken assumptions. They thought that Seward and the Blairs led while Lincoln followed, when the opposite was the fact. They believed that Ben Butler would make a better military adviser than Halleck or Stanton. Nevertheless, they held a few correct ideas upon the need

10. Lincoln, *Works*, VII, 301-303.

for such firm war leadership as Grant and Sherman and Farragut were soon to supply.[11]

Lincoln never lacked humility, and this spring gave it emphatic expression. His political difficulties were brought home to him when Governor Thomas E. Bramlette of Kentucky faced a tempest over the compulsory enrollment of male slaves of twenty to forty-five for military draft. As Border State slaveholders saw Federal officers take down names, they trembled for their property. The governor hurried to Washington to talk with Lincoln, and the President thereupon explained in a letter to the Frankfort *Commonwealth* why he believed that Negro enlistments were a necessity. These enlistments, he wrote, had cost the government nothing in foreign embarrassments or in popular strength at home; they had helped the freedmen; and they had given the nation fully 130,000 soldiers, seamen and laborers. To this he added a characteristic comment. "I claim not to have controlled events, but confess plainly that events have controlled me. Now, at the end of three years struggle the nation's condition is not what either party, or any man devised, or expected. God alone can claim it. Whither it is tending seems plain. If God now wills the removal of a great wrong, and wills also that we of the North, as well as you of the South, shall pay fairly for our complicity in that wrong, impartial history will find therein new cause to attest and revere the justice and goodness of God."[12]

Feeling in Kentucky nevertheless remained so inimical to a slave-arming Administration that the self-styled Unionists there shortly took action which made it certain that the State in the fall would cast her electoral vote against Lincoln. Provost Marshals meanwhile enlisted Negroes in large numbers, for Kentuckians, seething with discontent and hatred, refused to fill the State quotas with volunteers.[13]

Beyond doubt, the astute young Maine politician, James G. Blaine, was right in believing that the prevailing judgment of the Union-Republican Party pointed to Lincoln's renomination. The party would fatally cripple itself if it repudiated the Administration. Moreover, the President's faith had fortified the national heart, for he saw as nobody else the American Idea. But would the party battle for him in a fervent or a lukewarm spirit?

Among the men whose jealous ambition impaired party harmony, the able, self-righteous Salmon P. Chase held a conspicuous place. Although he maintained with Chadband rhetoric that he never used the Treasury to build a personal machine, its staff supplied active workers on his behalf. Friendly with

11. See the exchange of opinion among Stanton, Chase, and Welles in Oct. 1862, on Lincoln's deficiencies, Welles, *Diary*, I, 160-169.

12. Lincoln, *Works*, 281-283; to Albert G. Hodges.

13. Coulter, E.M., *The Civil War and Readjustment in Kentucky*, Chapel Hill, 1926, 198-207.

all Radicals, he had given them energetic assistance in the State elections of 1862 in the hope of winning their support. In his financial labors he had taken pains to conciliate such leaders of industry and banking as Erastus Corning, George S. Coe, W. M. Vermilye, and George Opdyke, at the same time wooing the principal Republican editors and officers of the Union League. While pretending throughout 1863 that he was not anxious for the Presidency, he was actually burning for the office.[14]

When Lincoln at the close of 1863 announced his liberal plan of Reconstruction, Chase did not need to warn his friends that the hour for action had struck. His diary tells us nothing. But an impetuous Kansas politician of erratic judgment, Senator Samuel Clarke Pomeroy, a former Amherst student full of New England Radicalism, helped form a "national committee". Pomeroy and his Radical associates dealt just one blow—but it proved a fatal blow to Chase's aspirations. They issued a pamphlet entitled "The Next Presidential Election", and a shorter statement soon known as the Pomeroy Circular. These were at once summarized by the press and franked widely over the country by Radical Congressmen, so that Washington's Birthday in 1864 found the entire North acquainted with them. They offered an offensively phrased argument that aroused widespread irritation and derision. The reëlection of Lincoln, they declared, would be a national calamity; only an advanced thinker, versed in political and economic science, could guide the ship of state through the rapids ahead; and fortunately this advanced thinker was at hand—nobody needed to be told that Secretary Chase was the man; he even was named. Chase assured Lincoln on February 22 that he had known nothing about the circular or a formal committee, although he admitted he had consented to the use of his name to "several gentlemen" who had called on him. Ten years later, his statement that he had no prior knowledge of the circular was contradicted by its author, James M. Winchell, who declared flatly that Chase had been informed of the proposed action and approved it fully.[15]

14. Lincoln, *Works*, VII, 200-201; Schuckers, J.W., *The Life and Public Services of Salmon P. Chase*, New York, 1874, 356-489; Donald, David, ed. *Inside Lincoln's Cabinet*, New York, 1954, 179, 190, 208-209. Chase esteemed Lincoln, but personal uneasiness tinged his attitude, for he suspected that the virulent attack that Frank Blair made upon him in the House at the end of April might have had Lincoln's sanction. It did not; Lincoln was distressed to learn that Blair had kicked over another beehive. But the circumstances of the attack, made as Blair departed to resume his commission as major-general with the 17th Corps in the Atlanta campaign, were highly irritating; and Blair's charges, impugning Chase's honesty, were so outrageous that the Secretary's Radical friends had advised an immediate and abrupt resignation. Much annoyed, Lincoln considered cancelling his orders restoring Blair to the army. Chase accepted the President's disclaimer of any connection with the attacks, brought to him by two Ohio politicians (Riddle, *Recollections of War Times*, Chs. XXXVII, XXXVIII), but he and his friends resented more than ever Lincoln's friendliness to the Blair clan. Congressional Globe, 38th Cong., 1st Session, Appendix, 50, 51, and Pt. II, 1829.

15. New York *Times*, Sept. 15, 1874; Schuckers, *Chase, op.cit.*, 497, 499-501.

This movement was so premature and ill-supported that John Sherman, one of Pomeroy's helpers, instantly retreated.[16] The country, in fact, received the circular with general hostility. Moderate Republicans, War Democrats, and most uncommitted voters, however critical of Lincoln, regarded him as decidedly preferable to Chase. "The Pomeroy Circular has helped Lincoln more than all other things together," wrote one of John Sherman's friends.[17] As Welles put it, the Chase gun had been far more dangerous in its recoil than its discharge. Lincoln kept a dignified silence.[18] How little strength Chase possessed was demonstrated when the Ohio legislature passed a resolution in favor of Lincoln's reëlection.

But although this first Radical foray against Lincoln quickly collapsed, an alarming amount of ill-humor was evident in the country. The New York *Times*, declaring the House had done nothing for nineteen weeks but dawdle over empty speechmaking with an utter neglect of urgent financial legislation, accused Congress of "flagrant unfaithfulness."[19] Sensible men were aghast at the Senate's passage of a bill against speculation in gold, a measure certain to defeat its object by raising the price of gold. When it did rise on June 23 to 208 in greenbacks, Congress saw that the new law must be repealed. Publication of the President's letter to Montgomery Blair, suggesting that his brother Frank let his commission as major-general lie dormant while he returned to the House, and have it revived when he wished to rejoin the army, seemed to many a flagrant evasion of the Constitutional provision that "no person holding any office under the United States shall be a member of either House of Congress during his continuance in office," and repugnant to a sentiment that in English-speaking lands went back to the "Self-Denying Ordinance" of Puritan Commonwealth days.[20]

In May, Henry Winter Davis carried through the House a Reconstruction Bill that was designed to make mincemeat out of Lincoln's policy as laid down in his annual message. Much talk was meanwhile heard about the "rotten boroughs" that might figure in Lincoln's reëlection—Arkansas, Delaware, Louisiana, Maryland, West Virginia, statehood for Nevada, and so on—and the possible perversion of democracy by manipulation of their votes.

At the same time, a sinister interpretation was placed on the government's impetuous suppression of two New York newspapers, the *World* and *Journal*

16. Details in Schuckers' *Chase*, 497-500; Zornow, W.F., "The Kansas Senators and the Reëlection of Lincoln," *Kansas Historical Quarterly*, May, 1951; letters of Philip Speed and J. Gibson to Lincoln, Feb. 22, 1864, Lincoln Mss., LC.

17. Zornow, *op.cit.*, 137.

18. Welles, *Diary*, I, 525, 533.

19. As cited in New York *World*, May 5, 1864.

20. Lincoln, *Works*, VI, 554-555; New York *World*, May 5, 1864.

of Commerce, on what turned out to be no grounds at all. In mid-May they had been hoaxed into publication of a fictitious Presidential proclamation appointing a day of national fasting, humiliation, and prayer, and announcing an imminent draft of 400,000 more men. This was the work of a would-be stock-market manipulator, whose forged proclamation, foisted upon the two newspapers in the dead of night, was quickly repudiated. Sales of papers were stopped, and bulletins announcing the imposture were posted. A dispatch boat that was hurried down New York Bay caught the *Scotia* before she cleared the Narrows for Europe with the forgery. Although in the temporary excitement gold shot up ten percent, little real harm was done. The suppression was indefensibly abrupt and harsh. Democratic spokesmen wildly asserted that civil liberties were dead, and lamented that the United States had no Thiers who dared denounce its despot. The editors of the two injured newspapers, when these dailies were restored to their owners on May 22, were left boiling with anger, and denouncing the Administration for both its arbitrary action and its tardiness of release. Gideon Welles agreed that the suppression, for which he correctly blamed Seward and Stanton, had been "hasty, rash, inconsiderate, and wrong."

This suppression gave Horatio Seymour an opportunity to attack the Administration afresh, and to instigate legal proceedings in the local courts against General Dix and his subordinates, all of which only deepened the general conviction that Seward lacked judgment. Worst of all, it reminded the country of numerous other instances in which editors had been disciplined and their papers stopped on charges that they were interfering with enlistments or otherwise hampering the war effort. And the fact that three of the ablest newspapermen of the country, Henry Villard, Adam Hill, and Horace White, were needlessly harassed—Villard ordered under arrest by Stanton, and White sharply questioned—added to the general feeling of uneasiness.[21]

John G. Nicolay, talking with Thurlow Weed at the end of March, had found him gloomy. "His only solicitude," Nicolay wrote the President, "was for yourself. He thought if you were not strong enough to hold the Union men together through the next Presidential election . . . the country was in the utmost danger of going to ruin." Actually, Weed doubted that Lincoln *could* hold the Union men together. The Cabinet, he pointed out, was so notoriously discordant and jangling that it gave the President little support and set the

21. The New York *World, Herald, Tribune*, offer full accounts in late May issues. For general studies, see Randall, James G., *Constitutional Problems under Lincoln*, Urbana, 1951 pp. 396-499; Nicolay and Hay, *Lincoln*, IX, 47-50; Rosewater, Victor, *History of Cooperative News-Gathering in the United States*, New York, 1930, pp.104-105. The man guilty of the forgery, Joseph Howard, then city editor of the Brooklyn *Eagle*, was quickly run down, but Henry Ward Beecher pleaded for him with Lincoln, and he escaped lightly. Welles, *Diary*, II, 37-38.

nation a bad example. "Welles is a cipher, Bates a fogy, and Blair at best a dangerous friend."[22] This lack of harmony was all too obvious. Seward and Stanton were openly gleeful over Chase's discomfiture, laughing about it in a corner chat at a Cabinet meeting, while Montgomery Blair frankly delighted in every buffet that Stanton took. Judicious men feared that even though Chase and Frémont were weak candidates, their fractious followers might disrupt the party and cripple the national war effort.[23]

Everybody knew, as spring advanced, that Lincoln would be renominated by the national Convention to meet in Baltimore on June 7. Decisive majorities in both houses of the Maryland, Minnesota, Kansas, and California legislatures had called for him; so had most Union and Republican members of the New Jersey, New York, Connecticut, and New Hampshire legislatures. Republicans of diverse views knew that, all in all, he was the best candidate available.[24] But this was not the important point: the danger was that he would be named without deep conviction, and that factional quarrels would then defeat him and weaken the battle power of the North. Greeley had offered a fresh demonstration of folly in a rumbling editorial declaring that Chase, Frémont, Butler, or Grant would be better.[25] Chase made it plain in letters to friends that, while he was ready to withdraw his own name, he was far from ready to advocate the reëlection of an indecisive President subject to the influence of such political schemers as Thurlow Weed and Montgomery Blair, and leaning toward a soft Reconstruction policy.[26]

Factionalism rode higher and higher in the party. It was astonishing how much sordid greed and personal malice pervaded the organization that had seemed so happily idealistic four years earlier. Gideon Welles, resentful of stinging attacks on the Navy Department that he ascribed to contractors, claim agents, corrupt newspapermen, and such unprincipled members of Congress as John P. Hale, thought that Chase abetted his harassment. They exchanged blistering letters, and glared at each other in Cabinet meetings.[27] Blair, Chase, and Stanton, indeed, hardly concealed their mutual detestation. When Montgomery Blair wrote later that he believed Chase was the only man Lincoln ever really hated, he spoke for himself; it was Blair who nursed the hatred, for Lincoln based hatreds only on principle, not on personal feeling.[28] As for Frémont, few people except his wife Jessie and the extreme Abolitionists

22. Nicolay to Lincoln, Mar. 30, 1864, Nicolay Papers, LC.
23. Welles, *Diary*, I, 536.
24. New York *Tribune*, Feb. 23, 1864.
25. *Ibid.*, Feb. 2, 1864; he used the one-term argument.
26. Chase, Feb. 29, 1864, to James A. Hamilton, *Chase Papers*, New York Public Library.
27. Welles, *Diary*, I, Chs. XV, XVI.
28. Blair to Samuel J. Tilden, June 5, 1868; *Letters and Literary Memorials of Samuel J. Tilden*, ed. John Bigelow, New York, 1908, I, 232-233.

thought him really fit for the presidency. Yet when the Missouri House rejected 46 to 33 a resolution endorsing the Administration, the St. Louis press explained that most Republicans of German blood favored the election of Frémont.[29]

"Stanton has a cabinet and is a power in his own Department," growled Welles. "He deceives the President and Seward, makes confidants of certain leading men, and is content to have matters move on without being compelled to show his exact position. He is not on good terms with Blair, nor is Chase, which is partly attributable to that want of concert which frequent assemblages and mutual counselling on public measures would secure. At such a time the country should have the combined wisdom of all." In May, 1864, R.H. Dana, Jr., wrote his wife, "The cabinet is disjointed. There is more hate, more censure uttered by members of the cabinet against each other than I supposed possible. I speak for what is said directly to me." In another letter, to Motley, Dana said: "The cabinet is at sixes and sevens . . . They say dreadful things about one another. . . ." Blair was quite critical of Welles, for example, but not of Seward.[30]

While the Union Leagues rallied to Lincoln's side, and Henry J. Raymond brought the New York *Times* into a supporting position, two of the most powerful Republican editors, Bryant and Greeley, refused to endorse him; independent-spirited governors like John A. Andrew and Oliver P. Morton, and critical-tempered Senators like Sumner and Fessenden stood coldly aloof. Wisely, Lincoln refused to antagonize the doubtful ones by aggressive measures in his own behalf. He was receptive, but avoided any grasping eagerness. He discouraged Carl Schurz from leaving the army to work for him,[31] and evinced no anxious uneasiness lest Grant might seek the White House. Though glad to hear from Rufus Jones that Grant spurned politics, he remarked with philosophic magnanimity that, if Grant took Richmond, we should let him have the office.[32] Whatever men talked about in politics interested Lincoln keenly, but he lifted himself above appetite or animosity. As Noah Brooks told California readers, he took almost no thought of his own future. "But, patient, patriotic, persevering, and single-hearted, he goes right on with his duty, pegging away just as though, as he has said to me, his own life was to end with

29. Among Frémont's supporters were some Radical Republicans, some Abolitionists, some Germans, and some War Democrats; 350 to 400 all told.

30. Welles, *Diary*, II, 17-18; Dana to his wife, May 3, 1864 and to Motley, May 7, 1864, Dana Papers, Mass. Hist. Soc.

31. Nicolay and Hay, *Abraham Lincoln*, IX, 56, 59, 60.

32. Grant was simply not interested. He wrote from Nashville, Jan. 20, 1864, to a politician who tried to tempt him (I.N. Morris) that election as the next President was the last thing in the world he desired. "I would regard such a consummation as being highly unfortunate for myself, if not for the country." Grant Papers, Illinois State Hist. Library.

his official life, content to leave his earnest labors and conscientious discharge of duty to the disposal of God and country." To which Brooks added: "A nobler and purer nature than his never animated man."[33]

Frémont was the first possible nominee pushed into the arena. A "people's provisional committee" of Radical origin invited like-minded lovers of freedom to gather in Cleveland on May 31, and about 350 self-chosen men from fifteen states and the District of Columbia met that day in Cosmopolitan Hall.[34] Since the really important Radicals like Henry Winter Davis, Zach Chandler, and Ben Wade had stood coldly aloof, the calls were signed by such relatively obscure Missouri politicians as B. Gratz Brown, Emil Preetorius, Friedrich Kapp, and James Redpath. Although some observers believed the movement had the covert sympathy of John A. Andrew, Schuyler Colfax, and David Dudley Field, they had sense enough to keep quiet.[35] Wendell Phillips, Frederick Douglass, and Elizabeth Cady Stanton were the principal personages of some national renown to stand up for the Pathfinder, or to support the call for a convention. The proceedings were short and businesslike, for everyone present agreed that Frémont should be nominated, and everyone believed that more emphasis should be thrown upon repudiation of Administration policies than upon condemnation of the rebellion.

The brief platform, Radical from beginning to end, promised a sweeping reversal of Lincoln's policies, and an acceleration of government action against slavery. One resolution, insinuating Administration indifference to governmental integrity and economy, promised strict regard to both. It contained a forcible assertion that as the war had destroyed slavery, the Federal Constitution should now be amended to prohibit its reëstablishment, and "to secure to all men absolute equality before the law." Another plank demanded that civil liberties be protected against infringement outside of areas under martial law. A third called for a constitutional amendment restricting Presidents to a single term. The most important resolutions declared that control of Reconstruction

33. Letter dated Oct. 6, 1863, in Sacramento *Daily News.*

34. Blaine, James G., *Twenty Years of Congress,* Norwich, Conn., 1886, I, 516, says *150. American Annual Cyclopaedia,* 1864, 786, says *500.*

35. Nevins, Allan, *Frémont,* New York, 1955, 574-575. Frémont later wrote: "The Cleveland Convention was to have been the open avowal of that condemnation which men had been freely expressing to each other for the past two years, and which had been fully made known to the President. But in the uncertain condition of affairs, leading men were not found willing to make public a dissatisfaction and condemnation which could have rendered Mr. Lincoln's nomination impossible; and their continued silence and support established for him a character among the people which leaves now no choice." The New York *World* commented Sept. 20: "Frémont alone of all the recognized leaders of the Republican Party dared to stand forth as the public opponent of a man who has been for two years the object of their freely expressed private scorn. . . ." McPherson, Edward, *The Political History of the United States of America During the Great Rebellion,* Washington, 1865, 410-415.

belonged to the people through their representatives in Congress, not the Executive, and asked that the lands of rebels be confiscated and distributed among soldiers and actual settlers. Clearly, the document was not a practical program of action, but an extremist manifesto. This tiny splinter-party hoped not to elect any man, but to ally itself with malcontent Republicans in defeating Lincoln and his moderate aims. The vital question to most members was the adoption of a Radical plan of Reconstruction. Others were actuated by devotion to the Pathfinder, memories of Administration hesitancy in Kentucky and Missouri, sympathy for the freedmen, and disgust with the protracted war effort.

Frémont, now fifty-one, restless, ambitious, and erratic as ever, had neither liking nor aptitude for politics. Living in New York surrounded by Radical antislavery men who had bitterly resented his removal from command in Missouri, influenced by his impatient wife, and bruised by what that judicious corps-commander Jacob D. Cox believed to be the Administration's negligent treatment of himself and his soldiers in the West Virginia campaign, he had longed for restoration to military authority. If nearly everybody mistrusted the calculating Blairs, he had special reason for dislike in their enmity and the malicious stories they had circulated about him; if the Wades, Sumners, and Chandlers criticized Lincoln, Frémont was still more critical when he heard that Lincoln had called him a "bespattered hero." When nominated for President by acclamation, he felt reluctance, for he knew he was a mere figurehead. To his discredit, his letter of acceptance on June 4 betrayed personal animus toward the Administration, being full of shopworn Radical phrases about military dictation, usurpation, executive feebleness, incapacity, and imminent bankruptcy. But to his credit, he repudiated the platform declaration upon the confiscation of Confederate lands, and with more promptness than McClellan showed this summer, resigned his army commission.

John Cochrane, chosen for Vice-President, was neither stronger nor weaker than most such nominees. A graduate of Hamilton College, a hard-working Congressman in Buchanan's time, a former State-Rights Democrat, a patriotic brigadier-general who had himself raised a regiment, he had been elected Attorney-General of New York State on the Union-Republican platform in 1863. He had been an early advocate of the enlistment and arming of Negro troops. So astute an observer as Gideon Welles pronounced him a leader of ability and principle.

The Cleveland nominations utterly failed to impress the country. While most Moderate Republicans thought the convention a motley assemblage of weak and erratic political vagrants, the War Democrats and Peace Democrats for quite divergent reasons disdained it and its choice. Lincoln packed his condemnation into a neat quotation from the Old Testament (II Samuel, 22) about the four hundred Adullamites who withdrew from Gath into a cave. Lincoln is said to have read these words; "And every one that was in distress, and every one that was in debt, and every one that was discontented, gathered themselves unto him, and he became a captain over them; and there were with him about four hundred men."[36] Yet the Convention could not be lightly dismissed. Although in May nobody would have given a copper cent for Frémont's chances of a substantial presidential vote, in a close contest even a small poll might prove as important as James G. Birney's Liberty Party vote had been in 1844; and the full story of his rôle in the election was yet to be written.

[III]

So certain was it that Lincoln would be nominated at Baltimore and control the platform that David Davis, the President's closest Illinois friend, did not deem it worthwhile to leave his Bloomington home for the Convention. The opposition was utterly routed, he assured Lincoln, and if a spokesman for their State was needed, Leonard Swett would suffice.[37] Most of the party, indeed, demanded the renomination. As Bryant wrote, the plain people believed Lincoln honest, the rich people believed him safe, the soldiers believed him their friend, the religious people believed him God's choice, and even the scoundrels believed it profitable to use his cloak.[38] When the Convention opened on June 7 with ex-Governor William Dennison of Ohio as permanent chairman (tactfully selected as a prominent friend of Chase), more than 500 delegates were present. Louisiana, Tennessee, and Arkansas had sent representatives who were unconditionally admitted, while Virginia and Florida men were seated without a right to vote, and South Carolina was rejected.[39]

The gathering met in the Front Street Theatre, festooned with flags and soon densely packed. At the outset, a rugged Kentucky parson, Dr. Robert J. Breckenridge of a ruling border-family, made a speech awesomely Radical in temper. Fortunately, few took him seriously when he said that the government must use all its powers to "exterminate" the rebellion, and that the cement of free institutions was "the blood of traitors." Former Governor Morgan of New York called for a constitutional amendment abolishing slavery. The platform, which received perhaps less note or discussion than usual, called upon citizens

36. Nicolay and Hay, *Abraham Lincoln*, IX, 40.
37. Davis to Lincoln, June 2, 1864, David Davis Papers, Chicago Hist. Soc. (photocopies).
38. New York *Evening Post*, June 3, 1864.
39. *American Annual Cyclopaedia*, 1864, 788.

to discard political differences and center their attention upon "quelling by force of arms the Rebellion now raging." No compromise must be made with Rebels and the demand was laid down for unconditional surrender of "their hostility and a return to their just allegiance . . ." Slavery was the cause of the rebellion and thus there should be an amendment to the Constitution ending slavery. In addition to usual platitudes, harmony in national councils was called for. Discrimination in the armies was to be ended; there was to be speedy construction of the Pacific Railroad; and, of course, there was to be economy and responsibility by the Administration. Then came the ballot for President. Only Missouri voted for General Grant, and Lincoln received a renomination on the first ballot by a vote of 506 to 22. A Missourian moved that the nomination be made unanimous. Then, suffering fearfully from heat, humidity, and overcrowded hotels, the politicians concentrated their attention upon the one undetermined question—the Vice-Presidency.[40]

"Things are going off in the best possible style," Nicolay had written John Hay from Baltimore on the 6th. With only a shadow of opposition to Lincoln visible except for the Missouri Radicals, the Convention seemed too docile under Administration leadership to be exciting. When Nicolay added that Hannibal Hamlin would in all probability be renominated, he might be forgiven his bad guess, for there were as many opinions about the proper selection as factions.[41] Hannibal Hamlin, Joseph Holt, Ben Butler, Simon Cameron, John A. Dix, W.S. Hancock, Edwin D. Morgan, Andrew Curtin, and William S. Rosecrans all had advocates. Even the sixty-three-year-old War Democrat, Daniel S. Dickinson, who had done so much to rally New York after Sumter, was lustily supported by Middle State Radicals, and more slyly by Sumner and some New Englanders who saw that, if Dickinson were elected, Lincoln would

40. McPherson, *op.cit.*, 406-407. Talk about the Vice-Presidency had been going on all spring. Ben Butler later asserted that he had been approached by emissaries professing to speak for Chase and Lincoln, as they inquired whether he would accept a vice-presidential nomination. "Vice Presidential Politics in '64," *North American Review*, Vol. CXLI, No.3, Oct. 1885. He doubtless heard random questions from slandering busybodies, but his story concerning Lincoln is certainly untrue.

41. A.K. McClure says in *Abraham Lincoln and Men of War Times*, Philadelphia, 1892, 444, that Lincoln discreetly but earnestly favored Andrew Johnson's nomination. George Jones, owner of the *Times* and one of Raymond's closest friends, says Raymond was influenced by Lincoln, as McClure was. Nicolay states that, on the contrary, Lincoln's personal feelings were for the renomination of Hamlin, but he persistently withheld any opinion calculated to influence the convention. Nicolay and Hay declare: (*Abraham Lincoln, op.cit.*, Vol. IX, 72-73): "It was with minds absolutely untrammeled by even any knowledge of the President's wishes that the convention went about its work of selecting his associate on the ticket."

Out of these statements grew a controversy to which McClure gives an appendix of nearly fifty pages in his *Lincoln and Men of War Times*. It offers much personal vituperation on both sides; a few statements of historical significance; and, on the whole, a substantiation of Nicolay. McClure's recollections in 1891 of what happened in 1863 are not impressive. Nicolay, Helen, *Lincoln's Secretary, a Biography of John G. Nicolay*, New York, 1949, 207-208.

have to drop Seward from the Cabinet. Sumner was in fact suspected of being a general marplot. He would rejoice if he could get Seward out of the Cabinet by the election of Andrew Johnson. At the same time, Seward, consistently filled with a desire to protect the rights of the freedmen, and in favor of a reorganization of parties that would attract the support of both Southerners and Northern Democrats, also showed a leaning toward Johnson.[42] If the shelving of Hamlin resulted in his running against Fessenden for the Senate in Maine's next Senatorial contest, Sumner would rejoice again, for he hated Fessenden. Seeing a plain threat to Seward, the latter's friends vehemently opposed Dickinson.[43] Hence, the situation became highly confused.

Many men who would really have preferred Hamlin conceded that, as the Republican Party, a sectional organization in 1860, now claimed to possess a national character, a Southern man would better befit it than a Maine down-easter.

Hamlin deserved renomination, for he had been a dignified, salty, right-minded Vice-President, and if he had given little impression of force or stature, his office made it almost impossible to make any impression at all. The son of a poor farmer, deprived of a college education, he had steadily grown as he rose from a law office through legislature, House, and Senate. A gentleman of the old school, a six-footer of blandly courteous manners, he had clung to a stock and black swallow-tailed coat after most men abandoned them. He was punctilious in the discharge of duty; his speech had terse Yankee pungency, but also judgment and tact; and he held some firm convictions—one that amnesty ought to be granted all Southerners sincerely converted to loyalty, and another that the Negro could be developed into a useful citizen just as surely as he had been developed into a soldier.[44]

Lincoln, declared Welles, would have liked Hamlin renominated, despite his personal fondness for Andrew Johnson. But he kept his hands off, and a curious combination of circumstances gave Johnson the victory. For one, Sumner rallied most of New England against Hamlin.[45] For another, the day before

42. Cox, Lawanda and John H., *Politics, Principle and Prejudice*, 1865-1866, London, 1963, 220-223.

43. Glonek, James F., "Lincoln, Johnson and the Baltimore Ticket," *Abraham Lincoln Quarterly*, Vol.VI, No.5, Mar., 1951, 261 and *passim;* Hamlin, Charles E., *The Life and Times of Hannibal Hamlin*, Cambridge, 1899, 462-466.

44. Hamlin, *Hamlin, ut supra*, 461ff., and Jellison, Charles A., *Fessenden of Maine*, Syracuse, N.Y., 1962, 178ff., offer full materials.

45. Simon Cameron wrote Senator Fessenden after the convention: "I strove hard to renominate Hamlin, as well for his own sake as yours, but failed only because New England, especially Massachusetts, did not adhere to him." Lot M. Morrill bore the same testimony that the hostility of Massachusetts (i.e. Sumner) had crushed his own efforts for Hamlin. See Hamlin, *Hamlin, op.cit.*, 461-488; Noah Brooks, letter of June 7 from Baltimore in Sacramento *Union;* Charles A. Dana, Jr., in his Journal of a Trip to Washington in January, 1862, has a good characterization of Hamlin, Dana Papers, Mass. Hist. Soc.

the Convention met, the Illinois delegates conferred in Barnum's Hotel upon the attitude they should take toward two rival Missouri groups that were asking admission—a body of Radicals hotly opposed to the Blairs and hence to Lincoln, and some Conservative Republicans who would join everybody else in making the nomination of Lincoln unanimous. The Illinois men were about to vote to debar the anti-Blair contestants, an action which other States would reluctantly ratify, when suddenly a slight, thin-visaged young man arose, and announced that he wished to say a word for himself alone. In his opinion, he went on, Illinois had better favor the admission of the Missouri Radicals. He was John G. Nicolay, Lincoln's secretary! He gave no argument; it was not necessary. Next day Illinois voted as Nicolay suggested. Delegations hostile to the Blair faction joyously took their seats and, as we have noted, the 22 votes of Missouri went on the first ballot to Grant.[46]

This action reflected Lincoln's sagacity, for if the Radicals had been excluded they would have raised a damaging cry of tyranny. But the admission of Missouri Radicals had to be balanced by letting in Lincoln Moderates from Louisiana, Tennessee, and Arkansas. When Tennessee was admitted, Johnson became available. Henry J. Raymond, head of the national committee, had for months argued that a War Democrat should be nominated, and had come to Baltimore convinced that Johnson, with his record as a hot opponent of secession, an effective military governor, and a Radical with some Lincolnian ideas, was the right man. When men whispered that Lincoln must have told Raymond to take this position, the editor said nothing to dispel the idea. It was in such clever management of political movements and manoeuvres that Lincoln excelled.[47]

The Grand National Council of the Union League held a meeting on June 8, and adopted a declaration of principles or quasi-platform, pledging the Union League to vigorous prosecution of the war, to the backing of an antislavery amendment, support of the Monroe Doctrine, and championship of the principle that every person bearing arms in defense of the flag is "entitled, without distinction of color or nationality, to the protection of the government . . ." But the Union League's statement of principles differed from the Union platform in declaring "that the confiscation acts of Congress should be promptly and vigorously enforced, and that homesteads on the lands confiscated under it should be granted to our soldiers and others who have been made indigent by the acts of traitors and rebels."[48]

46. Carr, Clark E., *My Day and Generation*, Chicago, 1908, 133-144; Hume, John F., *The Abolitionists*, New York, 1905, Ch. XXI, tells how he cast the votes.

47. Brown, Francis E., *Raymond of the Times*, New York, 1951, 252-253. Cf. George H. Mayer, *The Republican Party, 1854-1964*, New York, 1964, 518, 519.

48. McPherson, Edward, *The Political History of the United States*, Washington, 1864, 410.

The first ballot showed Johnson, Hamlin, and Dickinson far in the lead—Johnson 200, Hamlin 150, Dickinson 108. Instantly Iowa shifted its vote to Johnson, and the avalanche began. For the credit or discredit of this decision we must turn primarily to honest Raymond, who some thought at the time had read Lincoln's mind, but more probably had just followed his own. Hamlin accepted the result with good humor, ready to work hard for both candidates.

The day after the Convention, a committee under Dennison called on Lincoln to inform him of what had been done, and hand him the first copy of the resolutions that he had seen. "I know no reason to doubt that I shall accept the nomination tendered," he replied, "and yet, perhaps, I should not declare definitely before reading and considering what is called the platform." This definite answer he delivered in writing on June 27, sounding a note of warning to the French Emperor in the remark that he would sustain the positions of the State Department and the Republican Convention respecting Mexican affairs. Andrew Johnson's acceptance carried some foolish rhetoric to the effect that treason was "worthy of the punishment of death."[49]

[IV]

As the last delegates from Baltimore reached their distant homes, a thunderbolt fell upon the Radical wing of the party in the resignation of Chase from the Treasury. Washington was dismayed by the announcement (June 30) that he had stepped down, and still more by the news that Lincoln would nominate David Tod, first war governor of Ohio, as his successor. Tod was a notorious dunderhead. When the Senate met in executive session on July 1, Chase's admirers were livid with wrath, asserting that he had been driven out by the machinations of the Blair family, that Tod was unfit, and that the quarrel would cost Lincoln his reëlection.[50] Old Francis P. Blair was jubilant. Chase, he wrote his son Frank, had first tried to bully Lincoln, and then astonished himself and everybody else by dropping off like a rotten pear.[51] This analysis was shrewd and sound. The Secretary had gone too far, for the President must control executive appointments; and once more Lincoln's shrewd managerial tactics had triumphed.

The head of the Sub-Treasury in New York, John J. Cisco, had offered his resignation several weeks earlier, to take effect July 1. Chase, after vainly inviting several others, told Maunsell B. Field, a Yale graduate and literary

49. Seward, Frederick W., *Seward at Washington*, 1861-1872, New York, 1891, III, 226; Stryker, Lloyd Paul, *Andrew Johnson, a Study in Courage*, New York, 1929, XI; Hamlin, *Hamlin, op.cit.*, XXXVI; Lincoln, *Works*, VII, 380-382.

50. Noah Brooks, letter dated July 1, 1864, Sacramento *Daily Union*.

51. Smith, William E., *The Francis Preston Blair Family in Politics*, New York, 1933, II, 271.

figure of some small note, then Assistant-Secretary in Washington, that he would get him transferred to the office, which was only less important in the Treasury than Chase's own. The Secretary lobbied for Field among Senators, and was assured that he could easily be confirmed. But Lincoln objected. The New York Republicans were deeply divided, and he dared not offend the Moderates under ex-Governor (and now Senator) Edwin D. Morgan by naming Chase's protégé to the vacancy. This, he later told Field, "would have been another Radical triumph, and I could not afford one." In correspondence with Chase, the President made it plain in his considerate way that, after offending the New York Moderates by keeping Hiram Barney in control of the Custom House, and making John T. Hogeboom general appraiser there—that is, giving Radicals control of two vital patronage centers—he could not put Field into a high metropolitan post without outraging many friends.[52]

But Chase was obdurate. As Field himself wrote, it was his nature to command, not obey.[53] Chase had refused to consider three other names for the New York post. Instead of yielding graciously, he told the President that he had recommended Field as the best-qualified man willing to take the place, and for that reason alone. "This, especially in these times, should be a controlling reason."[54] With this lecture to his superior, he enclosed a note. Lincoln did not at first see it, for he was hurried that day. Then, after forgetting lunch until three o'clock, he seized Chase's letter to read it in full before answering. "I took it out of the envelope for that purpose," he later wrote, "and, as I did so, another enclosure fell from it upon the floor. I picked it up, read it, and said to myself, 'Halloo, this is a horse of another color!' It was his resignation. I put my pen into my mouth, and *grit my teeth* upon it. I did not long reflect. I very soon decided to accept it."[55] This, he noted, was the fourth time that the irritating Mr. Chase had offered to resign.

Another consideration played its part in the affair. The House Ways and Means Committee had refused to support Chase's request that Congress, soon to adjourn, should pass a supplemental tax law for a hundred million to meet various appropriations which had already been authorized, but which the estimates of the Treasury Department had failed to cover. Lincoln declined to send a special request to Congress for this tax bill. Presumably, the President's patience with the much-demanding Secretary was exhausted.

Chase retired in the self-righteous mood so characteristic of him. "No man

52. Lincoln, *Works*, VII, 413-414. Barney, a man of character, had lost public confidence by letting the unscrupulous J.F. Bailey, special Treasury agent in New York, usurp many of his powers; *op.cit.*, VII, 181.

53. Field, Maunsell, *Memories of Many Men and of Some Women*, London, 1874, 305.

54. Lincoln, *Works*, VII, 414 ftn., Chase to Lincoln, June 29, 1864.

55. Field, *ut supra*, 302.

has labored more earnestly to promote the welfare of the country than I have," he wrote an old Ohio friend,[56] "and I cannot see, on looking back, that I could have done better than I have. I . . . felt sure that if I could have the full support of Congress and the hearty sympathy of the President I could carry the country safely through the financial embarrassments of the present as I did through those which attended the adjournment of Congress last year. Unfortunately, I had neither . . . But what was really wanting was the sympathy and good will of Mr. Lincoln. We have never seen public duties through exactly the same glasses; and within the last year he has allowed Mr. Blair, without the least grounds that I am aware of, to assail me in the most shameful manner, when a Jacksonian command from him would have silenced him. But all this alone would not have moved me." He further complained of the rebuff to Maunsell B. Field, and Lincoln's implied demand that Chase accept the necessity of placating New York Moderates. "It was impossible to hold office with this understanding. It would be degrading to me and dangerous to the country."

Chase did not reflect that it might be degrading to Lincoln, whose view embraced facts and interests not seen by the Secretary, to ignore the fourth resignation and submit to Chase's demand for full control of Treasury appointments. "Of all I have said in commendation of your ability and fidelity, I have nothing to unsay," Lincoln wrote him June 30; "and yet you and I have reached a point of mutual embarrassment in our official relation which it seems can not be overcome, or longer sustained consistently with the public interest."[57]

Nearly everybody squirmed at the name of Tod. Happily, he alleged uncertain health and business cares, and declined the appointment.[58] Lincoln, after vainly offering the Treasury to the able and popular Governor John Brough of Ohio, who was in Washington,[59] resolved upon appointing William Pitt Fessenden, Chairman of the Senate Finance Committee. Early on July 3, the President prepared the nomination and handed it to his secretary, John Hay. When told that Fessenden was then waiting in the anteroom, Lincoln made a quick, shrewd decision.

"Start at once for the Senate," he ordered, "and then let Fessenden come in." The gray-whiskered, thin-faced Yankee, on entering, launched into a discussion of the vacancy and suggested Hugh McCulloch, only to be met by Lincoln's reply that it was too late—he had just sent Fessenden's own name to the Senate. "You must withdraw it," exclaimed Fessenden, leaping to his

56. Chase to W.T. Coggeshall, July 8, 1864, Illinois State Hist. Libr.

57. Cisco on June 28 offered "temporary withdrawal" of his resignation; Lincoln, *Works*, VII, 414.

58. Lincoln, *Works*, VII, 419; Wright, G.B., "Hon. David Tod," *Ohio Archeological and Historical Publications*, Columbus, 1900, Vol.III, 107-131.

59. Reid, Whitelaw, *Ohio in the War*, Cincinnati, 1868, I, Chs. XIV-XIX.

feet. But when Lincoln explained that he would not, Fessenden thereupon softened his refusal, and as news that the Senate had instantly confirmed the nomination was followed by the entrance of happy friends, he saw that he must yield. After extracting from Chase a promise of help and advice, he accepted.[60]

First, however, Fessenden and Lincoln came to a clear understanding.[61] Its tenor indicates that the President had learned something from his recent collision with Chase. They agreed that Lincoln would keep no officer in the Treasury against the Secretary's express will, and also that in filling Treasury vacancies the Secretary would bow to Lincoln's wishes whenever they were made known. Lincoln further explained, in a memorandum for Fessenden, his ideas upon proper Cabinet procedure: that questions affecting the whole country should be given full and frequent consultations, and that no action particularly affecting any department should be taken until after a consultation with its head. Fessenden obviously knew all about Chase's complaints, and Lincoln plainly was trying to satisfy him that due heed would be given to their substance. The President would retain control over his appointments, but would recognize the desire of Cabinet members for fuller information, explanation, and consultation.[62]

Chase returned by way of New England to Ohio, licking his wounds, and showing resentment over the treatment he had received. This was resentment partly of Lincoln's acts, but more largely of the malignant course of the Blairs, the attacks of Thurlow Weed, and the inability of many people to understand his financial policies. He was in a dangerous mood. He did not head an open revolt against the Administration, for he lacked the strength. But he did temporarily support the idea of a new Republican Convention, refusing to drop it until it was clearly doomed to failure. Later he wrote that as soon as he learned

60. Jellison, *Fessenden of Maine*, *op.cit.*, 181-182. He faced a difficult Treasury situation, for at least fifty millions of money were urgently needed to meet demands on the government, and he had to hurry to New York to try unsuccessfully to get bankers to loan him the funds. *Ibid.*, 184.

61. Fessenden had criticized Lincoln freely. He had been part of the Senate caucus committee that tried to force Seward out of the Cabinet. Later he had written J.S. Pike; "Unhappily the President began by thinking Seward and Wood the great wise men of the nation and the delusion still continues." Still more recently he assured Pike that he felt no faith in the men in charge of affairs—he thought Ben Butler more the man of the hour than anybody else—but he believed the weight of the North would crush the South. Fessenden, April 5, 1863, March 4, 1864, to J.S. Pike, Fessenden Papers, Bowdoin College. One reason for Fessenden's reluctance was that he suffered from dyspepsia and irritability; Jellison, *op.cit.*, Ch.XIII. Fessenden had arraigned the Administration in Congress on Dec. 21, 1863, for hamstringing the Conscription Act of March by excessively liberal exemptions, and by continuing and increasing bounties for volunteers. Stanton had taken offense and protested. Fessenden had also attacked Lincoln's amnesty proclamation of Dec. 8, 1863, grumbling: "Think of telling the rebels that they may fight as long as they can, and take a pardon when they have had enough of it." He criticized Lincoln's Reconstruction policy, and had voted against admitting Fishback and Baxter to Senate seats.

62. Lincoln, *Works*, VII, 423; mem. dated July 4, in Fessenden Papers, Bowdoin College.

of the nominations and platform of the Democrats, he devoted all his energies to Lincoln's reëlection. In stating this he exaggerated. He did belatedly take the stump, perhaps realizing that party loyalty might later help him gain the post of Chief Justice in succession to Taney. The final verdict upon his devious path must be that given by the candid Ohio journalist William H. Smith:

> "When the true history of the differences between President Lincoln and Secretary of the Treasury Chase shall be written, it will not redound to the credit of the Secretary or his indiscreet and ambitious friends. The persistent effort of these men to break down the President during a great civil war were discreditable in the extreme."[63]

As the Convention ended, observers could truly say that its delegates, fresh from the people, had expressed one central sentiment. The speeches, the platform, the hotel talk had all breathed patriotic devotion to the Union, a determination to crush the foes attempting its disruption, and an intention to rebuild it on the rock of universal freedom. The harmony of the assemblage had been almost complete; its avowed aims had been lofty beyond cavil. Nevertheless, under the florid speeches of those early summer days, and the professions of harmony, lurked the serpents of dissension. Lincoln had been named with apparent unanimity. Yet, as the members caught outgoing trains, they read not only new accounts of futile assaults north of the Chickahominy, but acrid comments by Democratic politicians and recriminations among Republicans that boded ill for the election.

"The life of the republic is still in imminent peril," declared Horace Greeley, "and its bitterest enemies are of its own household." He pointed to a formidable party in the loyal States who were at heart enemies to the national cause. Saying this, Greeley understated the peril. Several such parties existed and he himself headed one; his editorial vacillation and defeatism played into the hands of the Confederates as much as Montgomery Blair's gift for sowing dissension, or Seward's naive idea that traitors could be coaxed back, or Vallandigham's fondness for playing with fire. All the divisive factions, continued Greeley, make their assaults under cover of hostility to the Administration. "And the renomination of Mr. Lincoln will inevitably intensify their efforts and rebarb their arrows. A Presidential election implies dissent, difference, criticism—nay, license, assault, and open hostility. . . . These charges will often convert passive into active and efficient hostility to the prosecution of the war."[64]

This was all too true. And the first heavy spear launched at Lincoln and

63. Undated note, W.H. Smith Papers, Ohio Hist. Soc. Smith was a friend of Whitelaw Reid.
64. New York *Tribune*, June 9, 1864.

at united effort for the Union came from two champions of a Radical Reconstruction policy.

[V]

During the spring of 1864 Lincoln's program for Southern Reconstruction had made progress in Louisiana and Arkansas, and as it moved forward, had evoked violent dissent from the Radical wing of Congress. When Arkansas sent William M. Fishback and Elisha Baxter to apply for admission to the Senate, the door was slammed in their faces. After some delay, the Senate asserted 27 to 6 that the rebellion had not been so far suppressed in Arkansas as to entitle the State to representation in Congress. Sumner would have gone further. He offered a resolution that any State in arms against the Union must be regarded as subject to military occupation, and without right of representation until readmitted by vote of both Houses. Although this motion was shelved, both Chambers were clearly ready to do battle with the President.

A momentous conflict over national policy impended, recalling the historic combats of Hamilton and Jefferson, Jackson and Clay, Buchanan and Douglas, but weightier far than the old struggles over Jay's Treaty, the Bank, and Lecompton. The President was coolly, tactfully adamant. He had not settled the details of his Reconstruction program; he was ready to modify them as time and circumstance dictated; but he was determined to do everything in his power to restore a fraternal Union, never stooping to vengeance or malice. Far different was the stand of the Radical leaders, athirst for party advantage, sectional domination, and the sating of old hatreds and new economic greeds. They turned from their Arkansas decision to throw down the gage of battle to the White House.

Three preliminary demands for Reconstruction must be met, they declared in a bill which Ben Wade and Henry Winter Davis, as chairmen of the Senate and House Committees on the Rebellious States, pressed through both Chambers. First, the President should appoint a provisional governor for each State declared to be in rebellion. Second, as soon as military resistance ended, the governor should enroll the white male citizens and offer them an oath to support the United States Constitution. Finally, when a majority of registrants had signed the oath, the governor should arrange the election of a State constitutional convention. This was perhaps a reasonable program, although Lincoln thought of inaugurating Reconstruction on a ten-percent basis rather than a majority basis. But the Wade-Davis legislation proceeded to lay down additional tests of penalizing character.

One, a requirement that the new constitutions cancel all debts incurred in aid of the rebellion, was perfectly equitable. It would impoverish some Southerners, but they deserved their losses. Quite different was a Draconian stipulation that the constitutions should forbid all men who had held high civil office under the Confederacy, or military rank above a colonelcy, to vote for a legislator or governor, or occupy these positions. No former office-holder or person who had voluntarily borne arms against the United States could take the oath, and no one who did not take the oath could vote for the constitutional convention. This would proscribe the ablest and most experienced leaders in the South. Worse still, in theory and practise, was a demand that the constitutions abolish slavery. This was plainly unconstitutional, for Congress had no power to deal with slavery inside the States. It was also unwise, for if slavery were thus abolished by national action, the nation might be expected to take steps to aid and protect the freedmen for which it had made no preparatory study, and possessed no adequate machinery. The Wade-Davis bill provided that, whenever a State constitution embodying these iron provisions had been adopted by a majority of the registered voters, the President, with prior Congressional assent, should recognize the government so established as competent to send men to Congress and choose Presidential electors.[65]

This legislation had originally been prepared by Henry Winter Davis, an active Marylander whose emotional instability reflected his intense ambition for national prominence and personal advancement. He had allied himself in succession with the Whigs, Know-Nothings, Republicans, Bell-Everett men, and Radical Republicans, consistent only in seeking to further his own career. He had never failed to cherish the dream that he might ultimately become President. Why not? He came of aristocratic parents, his father a president of St. John's College in Annapolis; he had gained a good education at Kenyon College and the University of Virginia; tall, handsome, eloquent, he had a flair for bold action. Sitting in Congress since 1855, except for one term 1861-63, he had inspired powerful friendships and hatreds. He had come to detest Montgomery Blair, idolize Thaddeus Stevens, and distrust Lincoln, his feeling about the President being tinged by disappointment that he was not appointed to Lincoln's Cabinet in 1861. Left out of Congress by the Maryland election of 1861, Davis employed the next two years in delivering anti-Administration speeches all over the East. He resumed his diatribes as soon as he reëntered the House in 1863. It was not the Blairs and Lincoln alone that he attacked, for he indicted Seward, Gideon Welles, and all moderate editors, governors, and Congressmen as hotly.[66]

Davis had persuaded John Sherman to introduce his first bill on Re-

65. Blaine, *Twenty Years*, II, 41-42, gives an account of the bill; *Congressional Globe*, 38th Cong., 1st Sess., Pt.4, 3448-3449.

66. Steiner, B.C., *Life of Henry Winter Davis*, Baltimore, 1916, *passim;* Welles, *Diary*, I, 505, 531; II, 30, 95ff. Gideon Welles characterized him as a man of cultivation who was eccentric, unreliable, and given to intrigue—"restless and active, but not useful"; *Diary*, II, 408-409.

construction just before he returned to Congress, when it was blocked by a counter proposal. Now he offered it anew, with Wade as sponsor in the Senate.[67] Davis was riding the wave of Radical feeling, and riding high.

To this Wade-Davis bill, supported by Sumner and opposed by Thaddeus Stevens only on the ground that it was insufficiently severe, Lincoln had invincible objections. It practically scrapped all the work of Reconstruction he had done under his fluid ten-percent plan proclamation the previous December, and showed a hard retaliatory spirit which he believed altogether the wrong attitude toward the defeated and humbled South. He would have accepted Winston Churchill's dictum on the proper approach of a victorious nation to a vanquished enemy. We should help the foe to his feet, said Churchill, and we should remember only so much of the past as is useful for the future. Lincoln believed that to see the hopeful governments already created in Arkansas and Louisiana roughly flung aside would inevitably discourage loyal men in other States. Looking to the early destruction of slavery by constitutional amendment, he was unwilling to repudiate his oft-stated contention that Congress had at the present no power to touch the institution within the States. Of course, he would let any State adopt the Wade-Davis plan if it liked, but he would not close the gate on milder plans.

The bill came to Lincoln in the anxious hour before Congress adjourned on July 4, 1864. Rejecting heavy pressure to sign it, he put it to death by a pocket veto.

The scene, as the President thus squarely confronted the Radicals who intended to destroy his Reconstruction program, was one of the most dramatic in wartime history. The House had occupied its last minutes with a reading of the Declaration of Independence. Sitting in the President's room in the Capitol, Lincoln had been signing final bills. Sumner entered with characteristic vehemence, his fanatic mind centered on the measure. George S. Boutwell, equally nervous and angry, raised a voice of lamentation. Zach Chandler made a scene by buttonholing the President, threatening him with the prospect that loss of the Wade-Davis Bill would cost the Republicans Ohio and Michigan in the fall election, and denouncing his constitutional objections. Secretary Fessenden reminded the excited group that Republicans had always agreed that Congress had no power over slavery inside the States. With his manifest approval and the support of Seward and Usher who looked on, Lincoln then delivered a pointed speech.

"This bill and this position of these gentlemen," he said, "seems to me to make the fatal admission (in asserting that the insurrectionary States are no longer in the Union) that States whenever they please may of their own motion

67. Sherman, John, *John Sherman's Recollections of Forty Years in the House, Senate, and Cabinet*, Chicago, 1895, I, 359-360.

dissolve their connection with the Union. Now we cannot survive that admission, I am convinced. If it be true, I am not President, these gentlemen are not Congress. I have laboriously endeavored to avoid that question ever since it first began to be mooted. . . . I thought it much better, if it were possible, to restore the Union without the necessity of a violent quarrel among its friends as to whether certain States have been in or out of the Union during the war: a merely metaphysical question and one unnecessary to be forced into discussion." John Hay stated that Lincoln, after they left the Capitol, said: "If they choose to make a point upon this, I do not doubt that they can do harm. They have never been friendly to me and I don't know that this makes any special difference as to that. At all events, I must keep some consciousness of being somewhere near right; I must keep some standard of principle fixed with myself." He was concerned about the constitutional issue, and still more deeply concerned over a harshly vengeful formula of Reconstruction. If it were adopted, farewell to his dream of a fraternal Union! The Wade-Davis Bill was in effect a stinging censure of his course. Lincoln admitted no right of Congress to censure him, or to thwart his settled policy by last-minute legislation. He was determined to maintain all the dignities and powers of the Presidency.[68]

We may well believe the assertion of contemporaries that Henry Winter Davis was beside himself with rage that afternoon, for his boiling-point was low.[69] But we must reject both the statement of young James G. Blaine that Republican members of Congress almost unanimously dissented from Lincoln, and Sumner's preposterous assertion that Lincoln later expressed regret that he had not signed the Wade-Davis Bill.[70] In disregard of precedent, Lincoln on July 8 issued an explanatory proclamation giving with brevity and point his main reasons for refusing his assent.[71] Some members of Congress sided with him and Seward and Fessenden. More rallied to him later when Henry Winter Davis wrote a caustic arraignment which, signed also by Wade and published in the newspapers, became famous as the Wade-Davis Manifesto. Its averment that the Presidential veto was a blow at the rights of humanity and the principles of republican government could be dismissed as sophomoric rhetoric. But it went beyond rhetoric; it was a chal-

68. Lincoln, *Works*, VII, 433-434; Hay, John, *Lincoln and the Civil War in the Diaries and Letters of John Hay, op.cit.*, 204-206.

69. *Ibid.*; W.E. Dodd's article on Henry Winter Davis in *Dictionary of American Biography*, Vol. V, 119-121.

70. Blaine, *Twenty Years, op.cit.*, II, 42; Sherman, *Recollections*, I, 361. Blaine had entered Congress in 1863 and as yet knew its membership imperfectly; while the speedy dispersal of members all over the North after the veto forbade any systematic inquiry into sentiment. Sumner's alleged assertion is a bit of stale hearsay contradicted by the facts.

71. Lincoln, *Works*, VII, 433-434; July 8, 1864.

lenge of force and power, the most direct that Republican leaders ever gave Lincoln.

Lincoln's proclamation and the Wade-Davis Manifesto at once transformed the Republican campaign; it became in great part a referendum upon the issue of Reconstruction. The Manifesto, addressed to supporters of the government, declared it their duty "to check the encroachments of the Executive on the authority of Congress and to require it to confine itself to its proper sphere." English Tories had never been more emphatic in assailing the aggressions of Whig Ministries, followers of Adams and Clay never so bitter in resisting Andrew Jackson. The President, declared the Manifesto, "must understand that our support is of a cause and not of a man; that *the authority of Congress is paramount* and must be respected; that the whole body of Union men in Congress will not submit to be impeached by him of rash and unconstitutional legislation; and if he wishes our support, he must confine himself to his executive duties—*to obey and to execute,* not to make the laws—to suppress by arms armed rebellion, and leave political reorganization to Congress." In conclusion, it implored citizens to "consider the remedy of these usurpations and, having found it, fearlessly to execute it."[72] This was flat defiance! It asserted the doctrine of the Radicals that Congress held paramount authority in rebuilding the nation, and it laid down principles which reached their logical conclusion within four years in the impeachment of a President.

Such declarations suggested a possible disruption of the government and the whole Union effort, but fortunately the authors overshot their mark. Their paper, as Blaine observes, was so extreme that it recoiled upon itself, and its indictment of Lincoln "rallied his friends to his support with that intense form of energy which springs from the instinct of self-preservation."[73] It helped defeat Winter Davis's efforts for a renomination, so that soon he was once more out of Congress.

Reconstruction was now a subject for national debate in which the Radical Republicans were outnumbered and outgunned by the combined forces of the Moderate Republicans and War Democrats. Simultaneously the position of the War Democrats was well defined by James W. Sheehan's Chicago *Post,* the oldtime organ of Stephen A. Douglas. It maintained that, as the government had always denied the right of any State to leave the Union, the ordinances of secession were null. No State can commit treason, it argued, and no State can give its citizens authority to commit treason. The war was therefore a struggle not to reduce States to submission, but to compel the obedience of rebellious individuals. While War Democrats took a variety of constitutional

72. *American Annual Cyclopaedia,* 1864, 307-310.
73. Blaine, *op.cit.,* II, 44.

views, they would all stand with Lincoln in battling the Wade-Davis extremists.

As for Moderate Republicans, the feelings of a majority were tartly expressed by the Maine newspaperman, now Washington correspondent of the Sacramento *Union*, Noah Brooks. "It is a matter of regret," he declared, "that a man of so much oratorical ability and legal sharpness as Henry Winter Davis should be so much of a political charlatan as he is; but he is, like the Blairs, insatiate in his hates, mischievous in his schemes, and hollow-hearted and coldblooded." Most Republican newspapers agreed. So did *Harper's Weekly*, which had remarked of Lincoln's letter of acceptance that, "like all he says and does," it would appeal "to the heart of the people whom he serves so faithfully and well." George William Curtis, editor of this now powerful organ, growled: "We have read with pain the manifesto of Messrs. Wade and Winter Davis, not because of its envenomed hostility to the President, but because of its ill-tempered spirit, which proves conclusively the unfitness of either of the gentlemen for grave counselors in a time of national peril."[74] Most people refused as yet to grow excited about Reconstruction. Let's win the war for the Union first, and talk about its rehabilitation later, they said. Meanwhile, Lincoln's mild attitude, tentative and pragmatic, offended few and satisfied many. It had ambiguities, but then the situation was ambiguous.

Meanwhile, although the heavy Virginia carnage darkened men's spirits, now and then a ray of light glimmered along the horizon as possible augury of coming dawn.

The Union commander in West Virginia, David Hunter, who had taken control after Sigel's defeat in May at New Market, had the task of holding down the ebullient Jubal A. Early, who headed an aggressive segment of Lee's army in the Shenandoah Valley. Hunter was a stodgy, ill-tempered man with a passion for assisting the Negro, but little military skill. When he retreated into West Virginia to reorganize and refit, he left the Shenandoah wide open. At the beginning of July, Early seized the opportunity to throw his veterans northward in the Valley and into Maryland behind Washington. Had not Lew Wallace gallantly delayed him for a few days on the Monocacy (July 9), he might conceivably have penetrated the city's fortifications. As it was, he destroyed part of the Philadelphia, Wilmington & Baltimore Railroad, did some damage to the Baltimore & Ohio, and Northern Central, and sent his troops within sight of the Capitol dome, killing men of the city garrison.[75] Public anxiety rose high in Washington on the 10th. Then, in the nick of time, it was relieved on the 11th, as cheering crowds gathered by the Potomac shore to

74. See Chicago *Post*, July 10-25, 1864, for Sheehan's view; *Harper's Weekly*, July 9, 30, August 20, for Curtis; and Noah Brooks's letter, July 1, 1864, in Sacramento *Union*.
75. Vandiver, Frank E., *Jubal's Raid*, New York, 1960, 122-179.

watch transports discharging long lines of blue-coat reinforcements. These troops headed for Fort Stevens, where on both July 11 and 12 Lincoln himself mounted the ramparts to see rebel sharpshooters firing in his direction, and hear Captain Oliver Wendell Holmes shout, "Get down, you fool!"—Holmes not recognizing the President.[76]

Great if brief excitement had seized both Baltimore and Washington as they realized that they were momentarily cut off from the North except by sea; no trains, no Northern newspapers, no fresh food, prices soaring, and courage dropping! As Early's men pulled back, people were left fuming with rage and humiliation. That at this late date it should be possible for more than 12,000 rebels to swarm across the Potomac, capture trains, force Stanton to send a carriage in haste to bring the President's family back from the Soldier's Home, and take south great stocks of horses, cattle, and general supplies, was outrageous. Some secession sympathizers displayed impudent delight in Washington streets, crying "At last, at last! Thank God." In Maryland, disloyalists plundered many houses, including that of one of the governors, and the Blair family home in Silver Spring. Early had gathered part of the Shenandoah harvest for Lee's army. He had lifted the sagging Confederate prestige abroad.[77]

But at last he had been repelled! And his gains were offset by losses and disappointments so important that the Richmond press gave his raid as much criticism as praise.

While the disturbance over Early was at its height, a refreshing breeze blew in from the English Channel. On July 6 came news that the United States sloop-of-war *Kearsarge* had fought a short naval duel June 19 with the *Alabama* off Cherbourg, and destroyed that world-famous cruiser. No vessel under the Confederate flag was so hated by Northerners as Raphael Semmes's "pirate." Moreover, this battle seemed as much an encounter between Britain and America as between South and North. The *Alabama* had been built in England, manned largely by Englishmen and Irishmen, armed with British guns, and driven by British coal. It refreshed Americans, smarting under Tory gibes, to hear how completely she had been vanquished.

Considerable advantages, to be sure, had lain with Captain John A. Winslow's *Kearsarge*. She had a makeshift armor of sheet-chains which her adversary lacked, and the merits of which are disputed; she had held frequent target practises which a shortage of ammunition had denied the Confederates; she carried a heavier armament—two 11-inch Dahlgrens together with other guns.

76. Howe, M.A. DeWolfe, *Justice Oliver Wendell Holmes: The Shaping Years, 1841-1870*, Cambridge, Mass., 1957, 168-169.

77. Early, Jubal, *Autobiographical Sketches and Narratives of the War Between the States*, ed. Frank E. Vandiver, Bloomington, Ind., 1960, 455-456, for his boastful account of his achievements; Riddle, *op.cit.*, 291.

The action lasted sixty-two minutes, during which the *Kearsarge* was but slightly injured by the twenty-eight shots she received.[78] At the end, Semmes, with thirty men killed and wounded, vainly tried to regain the French shore. He charged in his official report to the Confederate agent, J.M. Mason in London, that the *Kearsarge* had been deplorably slow in sending boats to save lives after the *Alabama* went down. He himself was picked up, with others, by the English yacht *Deerhound.*[79] Nevertheless, Winslow paroled more than sixty prisoners. At news of the battle, Americans exultantly recalled the days of the *Constitution* and the *Guerrière.* The seas were now freer for American shipping.

The *Alabama*, no privateer but a properly commissioned naval vessel, was to become a brilliant part of Confederate legend, and Semmes unquestionably had gallant traits. When the ship's log was published in London, however, readers found that the seemingly heroic cruise had not really been "glorious." The story had little interest and less dignity.[80] From the time *Sumter* (her original name) first sailed out of the Mississippi until she was sunk as the *Alabama*, not a speck of real danger enlivened the narrative. Hunting and fleeing, fleeing and hunting, made up the monotonous tale. It recorded mainly a series of efficient chases of helpless prey, stained by unscrupulous but not unprecedented or unusual use of the flags of the United States and of neutral nations. Only once did the *Alabama* get involved in a true sea-fight, and then her superiority over the *Hatteras* lifted her so far above peril that but two men were slightly wounded. The story had no touch of Marryat or Cooper or Conrad.[81]

For Northerners, Winslow's exploit was a much-needed ray of sunshine in a dark hour. It was particularly welcomed by merchants, for Semmes had spread ruin far and wide, capturing sixty-five vessels worth more than six million dollars, Confederate raiding was one factor, though a relatively short-lived one, influencing and affecting the long decline of the American carrying-trade.

[VI]

But alas for Lincoln in this hot, bloody, and gloomy summer! The resignation of Chase and the Wade-Davis insurrection were heavy shocks. So far as

78. Captain Winslow in London *Daily News*, June 27, 1864.

79. John Lancaster, the owner, acted at Winslow's request, saving Semmes, thirteen officers, and twenty-six men; see London *Daily News*, June 24, July 2-22, for the ensuing controversy. Also *O.R.N.* I, iii, 649-651.

80. For the log, see *Cruises of the Sumter and the Alabama*, London, 1864; Roberts, Walter Adolphe, *Semmes of the Alabama*, Indianapolis, 1938, *passim.*

81. The story is best told in Semmes, Raphael, *Memoirs of Service Afloat*, Baltimore, 1869.

we can judge, public sentiment sustained them well, while they gave many Republicans a desperate sense that they must close their ranks or be ruined. Yet they deepened the general impression of political disorganization and Administration uncertainty, and helped convince weak-kneed men that if military defeats continued the party would face disaster. The seven weeks from Independence Day until late August, weeks with Atlanta still untaken and Lee's army still formidable, saw the spirits of Republican fainthearts at their lowest point. Whitelaw Reid, war correspondent of the Cincinnati *Gazette* and librarian of the House, travelling in these weeks from Cincinnati through Washington to Kennebunk, Maine, gathered from available reports that Lincoln's reëlection under existing circumstances was an impossibility. Attorney-General Bates was telling friends that the prime need of the country was a competent leader.[82]

When ex-Mayor George Opdyke of New York signed letters in mid-August inviting Republican leaders to a meeting to discuss the withdrawal of Lincoln in favor of a stronger candidate, he met a remarkable body of support. This honest but commonplace clothing merchant was of course merely a catspaw. The real movers, of whom Winter Davis was the most determined, stood behind him.

His letters went out to Lyman Trumbull, Zach Chandler, Charles Sumner, Jacob Collamer, Ben Wade, and other Senators, to War Democrats like Daniel S. Dickinson, to various governors, and to leading party editors.[83] The meeting, originally fixed at Opdyke's house on August 19th, was soon postponed until early September with David Dudley Field as host. The responses to Opdyke struck a sullen chord. Chase, of course, warmly approved the proposed gathering, writing that the Republicans were never more in need of wise counsel and fearless action. Dickinson, a compromiser by nature, long wavering between men and parties, expressed his belief that if Lincoln were fully advised of the dismal state of party affairs, he might withdraw. "Mr. Lincoln is already beaten," declared Horace Greeley. "He cannot be elected. And we must have another ticket to save us from utter overthrow. If we had such a ticket as could be made by naming Grant, Butler, or Sherman for President, we could make a fight yet." John Jay proposed a letter asking Lincoln to cancel his acceptance of the Baltimore nomination. Ben Wade, as Winter Davis ascertained, was hopeful of getting a stronger candidate, but wished to wait—like other men whom Davis called "snails."[84]

82. Reid to Chase, Aug. 22, 1864, Chase Papers, Hist. Soc. of Pennsylvania; Bates to Orville H. Browning, *Diary of Orville Hickman Browning*, ed. T.C. Pease and James G. Randall, Springfield, Ill., 1925-33, I, 676.

83. All this correspondence is printed in New York *Sun*, June 30, 1889.

84. Brown, Francis, *op.cit.*, 260ff.

Word of this letter-writing quickly got around. It contributed to an atmosphere in high party circles as chill and clammy as a Labrador fog. When the Republican National Committee met at the Astor House on August 22, the chairman, Henry J. Raymond, exuded the sepia gloom of a cuttlefish. Despair, he reported, glowered from every corner of the horizon. As editor of the *Times*, he possessed information that seemed decisive—information that men everywhere had a deep longing for peace and a conviction that Lincoln could not or would not furnish it. Other committeemen shared his impression. In despair, he wrote Lincoln that all seemed lost, for Elihu Washburne had told him that if an election were held immediately in Illinois, the Republicans would be worsted. Cameron had sent word that Pennsylvania would go Democratic, and Oliver P. Morton had declared that only the most strenuous fighting could save Indiana. As for New York, Raymond thought that in an early election Lincoln would lose the State by 50,000.[85] Such pessimism had seized some party leaders that Raymond, usually clearheaded and determined, persuaded the National Committee to support him in laying a preposterous suggestion before the President.

This suggestion was that Lincoln should send a commission to propose peace to Jefferson Davis on the sole condition that the South give up its demand for independence and accept the Constitution, all other questions—including slavery—to be settled in a national convention![86] Davis would reject this, argued Raymond, and Northerners would thus be aroused to a new passion of loyalty. It did not occur to him that millions might be aroused to a new sense of bewilderment, disgust, and discouragement.

And what of Lincoln while defeatism and hostile conspiracy swirled about the White House? He knew of the general pessimism. Thurlow Weed and others had assured him that his reëlection was impossible.[87] When Raymond came to Washington to tell him that all seemed lost, and his close friend Leonard Swett offered the same opinion, the President felt that McClellan (for the Democrats would certainly nominate him) would be the next occupant of the White House. At a Cabinet meeting on August 23 he therefore asked the members to endorse the back of a memorandum which he did not show them, but sealed and laid away.

"This morning, as for some days past," he had written, "it seems exceedingly probable that this Administration will not be reëlected. Then it will be

85. Seward, F.W., *op.cit.*, 244, for Seward's admission that as late as August 29 the American people "seemed vacillating and despondent."

86. Brown, Francis, *op.cit.*, 260-261; cf. Nicolay and Hay, IX, 218-219; Raymond to Lincoln, Aug. 22, 1864, Robert Todd Lincoln Papers, LC.

87. Lincoln, *Works*, VII, 515-516; Weed so recalls in a letter to Seward Aug. 22.

Executive Mansion

Washington, Aug. 23. 1864.

This morning, as for some days past,
it seems exceedingly probable that
this Administration will not be re-
elected. Then it will be my duty
to so co-operate with the President
elect, as to save the Union between
the election and the inauguration;
as he will have secured his election on such ground that he can not
possibly save it afterwards.

A. Lincoln

William H. Seward
W. P. Fessenden
Edwin M Stanton
Gideon Welles
Edw. Bates
M Blair
J. P. Usher

August 23. 1864.

Pledge Signed by President Lincoln and his Cabinet, Prior to the 1864 Election

my duty to so coöperate with the President-elect as to save the Union between the election and the inauguration; as he will have secured the election on such grounds that he cannot possibly save it afterward."[88] The plan on which Lincoln had solemnly resolved was to confer with President-elect McClellan, and ask him to raise as many troops as he possibly could for a final effort to save the Union before March 4, 1865.

Raymond's recommendation of a peace offer requiring the return of the South to the Union, but omitting any stipulation respecting emancipation, was certain not only to dismay Lincoln, but to fill him with mingled chagrin and resentment. The idea that he might repudiate his slavery policy was worse than insulting; it was odious. It meant that he would surrender all claim to principle. Such a course would break national faith with the host of Negroes serving under the Union flag; it would antagonize all Radicals and most moderate Republicans; it would disgrace the nation in the eyes of the world. Lincoln told Judge Joseph T. Mills on August 19 how deeply he felt on the subject. "There have been men who proposed to me to return to slavery the black warriors of Port Hudson and Olustee to conciliate the South. I should be damned in time and eternity for so doing. The world shall know that I will keep faith to friends and enemies, come what will."[89] His enemies said he was fighting an Abolition war. It would be carried on, as long as he was President, for the sole purpose of restoring the Union, but no human power would subdue the rebellion without using the weapon of emancipation. "Freedom has given us control of 200,000 able-bodied men, born and raised on Southern soil. It will give us more yet."[90]

Charles A. Dana, then in the War Department, had made an emphatic statement in connection with some recent delusive negotiations at Niagara with professed Confederate agents exploring a possible peace. The President had made no pronouncement suggesting a relinquishment of his measures against slavery in connection with these peace talks, said Dana. If he had, he would have done irreparable harm to his party; he would have convicted himself of insincerity upon a supreme issue of the war; and he would have shown readiness to let Southern leaders return to Washington with all their former power.[91] In short, he would not have been Lincoln had he done this, for, as Dana wrote long afterward: "His strongest point was judgment—soundness of judgment—not making any mistakes as to the nature of the thing he had to deal with. . . . The great thing about him was a great, wide and solid

88. Lincoln, *Works*, VII, 514, 515.

89. Lincoln, *Works*, VII, 506-508, gives this same note from the Mills Diary in correct form; see also *Conversations with Lincoln*, ed. Charles M. Segal, 338-339, quoting from Mills's Diary.

90. *Ibid.*

91. Undated letter to Raymond cited in Brown, *Raymond*, 260.

judgment."[92] Ever since his Cooper Union speech he had proved how effectively he had trained himself to think—to think problems through with precision and clarity, keeping his thought on a high and disinterested plane.[93]

While doubt still reigned, Lincoln took a step to placate the Moderate Republicans in New York under Thurlow Weed's leadership. He was well aware that the Albany editor, wielding tremendous political influence upstate, felt irritated by Hiram Barney's continued tenure of the Collectorship of the Port of New York. For months the President had worried about it. He did not wish to offend Chase, long a protector of Barney, or to be unjust to a hardworking, honest official not at all responsible for the corruption that plagued the Custom House. Yet he knew that Barney was running the place in the interest of the Radicals. His initial plan for getting Seward to transfer the Collector to a diplomatic post had been balked by Chase. Finally, a few weeks after Fessenden took Chase's place (August 31), the President asked for the resignation of Barney, who gave way to one of Weed's oldest friends, Simeon Draper.[94] The choice was sound, for Draper was able and independent, but it left the Radical wing more convinced than ever that Weed, Seward, Montgomery Blair, and Senator James Dixon of Connecticut held what Zach Chandler fatuously called full possession of Lincoln.[95]

Nobody less intemperate and abusive than Zach Chandler would have accused Lincoln of letting himself fall into the possession of one faction. His independence and impartiality never wavered. Aware that he must reconcile disparate groups, keep the party balanced, and shut the door against extremism, he knew that in accepting Chase's resignation he had not completed the task of remodelling his Cabinet. The Radicals who hated Montgomery Blair were quite as numerous as the Moderates who hated Chase, and their detestation was quite as fervent. The judicious Fessenden had fairly well represented the idea of party harmony. Could Lincoln find a replacement for Blair who would equally typify restraint and unity? The President felt liking and respect for Blair, just as he felt respect (though not liking) for Chase, but he did not approve the man's quarrelsome and malignant streak. Once when Blair was

92. Dictated Memorandum in Tarbell Collection, Allegheny College.

93. In the "Miscellaneous Mss. Civil War 1861-1865" in the New-York Historical Society is a sheet of note-paper headed "Executive Mansion" on which are pencilled figures in Lincoln's handwriting, allotting the electoral vote in the contest of 1864 to himself and McClellan. The memorandum is not signed, but is indubitably Lincoln's. The date is uncertain, but must have been at a time when the probable result seemed very close, and when three crucial Northern States could be assigned to the Democrats. In McClellan's column Lincoln put New York 33; Pennsylvania 26; Illinois 16; Missouri and Kentucky 11 each; New Jersey and Ohio 21; Indiana 13; Michigan, Wisconsin, and Iowa eight each; and five other States to bring the total to 117. This was a dangerously close result.

94. Barney Papers, HEH.

95. Chandler Papers, LC; undated scrap on Dixon.

denouncing the Radicals as selfish and vindictive, Lincoln rebuked him: "It is much better not to be led from the region of reason into that of hot blood, by imputing to public men motives which they do not avow."[96]

In late summer a Damoclean sword hung over Blair's head, and it was certain that Lincoln, in his deep concern for party and Union harmony, would soon sever the thread holding it.

As the first half of August wore on, the military outlook continued discouraging for the North, with Grant immobile at Petersburg and Sherman's progress checked by such equivocal battles as Kenesaw Mountain. The front of domestic affairs was equally gloomy, as published in a summary of the situation by Greeley in the *Tribune* of July 7, with news that gold had risen to 270. "Gold goes up like a balloon; so that $4,000 of it will buy $10,000 of United States six percents, payable principal and interest in coin! The business of the country is all but fatally deranged; all nominal values are so inflated and unsettled that no one knows what to ask or how to trade; the Laboring Class are stinted in spite of ample work and large wages; and there is danger of Social Convulsion from the artful, inflammatory incitements addressed to Ignorance by Treason. . . . Avarice and Gambling, engineered by Disloyalty, ride the whirlwind and direct the storm. . . . Every necessity of life grows hourly dearer; and the congregated Traitors who burrow in this city here scheme and struggle to paralyze the raised right arm of the nation." Nor did the political outlook seem happier.

When mid-August came, the Republican Party had not yet pulled itself together, or made a final decision upon its candidate, and the Democratic Party had made no decision whatever. All seemed confusion. Militant Radicals might yet force Lincoln to retire in favor of a stronger nominee; copperish elements might yet set McClellan aside for a wilder man. Connecticut Democrats were proposing a demagogic defeatist in Thomas H. Seymour of Hartford, who had come near gaining the governorship on a negotiated-peace platform, and who steadily denounced efforts to restore the Union as atrocious and abominable. Lincoln, in view of the deepening calamities and perils, designated August 4 as a Day of Fasting, Humiliation and Prayer. Friendly editors pronounced this very fitting; the public burdens were fearful, the taxes enormous, the debts, State and national, almost crushing. Conscription and volunteering were

96. This characteristic utterance of Lincoln's is too general in terms to be directly identified with any specific date or political episode. Lincoln consistently emphasized the unity in Republican or Union Party ranks, and deplored the schismatic personal denunciations of conservative or moderate Republicans by associates and followers of Thaddeus Stevens or Charles Sumner, along with the vendetta that some of the Jacobins waged against Secretary Seward as a spineless "moral and physical coward." In such intemperate language Lincoln saw national division and ruin. Randall, J.G., *Lincoln, the President*, New York, 1945, Vol.III, 241, 242.

more and more painful, discontent and sedition increasingly flagrant.

But, courage countrymen!, cried the ablest editors, Bryant, Raymond, and even Greeley; "the darkest hour is just before the dawn!" It was even so.

[VII]

In this crisis—"this great trouble," as the President called it—the cement of the Union was furnished from three main sources besides the nation's historic memories, traditions, and principles. It came from Lincoln's tact, sagacity, and patience; from such victories as the preponderant Northern armaments could now win; and from the nation's party system, which bound Americans together in adherence generally to patriotic clarification of political principles as laid down in the exalted arguments of Hamilton, Jefferson, Jackson, Clay, and Webster. The American party system ever pitches and sways like a wagon traversing rough ground. It gives forth ominous cracks and groans, and threatens to crash on the rocky hillside. Nevertheless, as the generations struggle forward, it endures. It must remain a viable wagon to reach its goal and deliver its straining load of offices, honors, and power. Whatever the rude strains and torsions, all the main groupings, the radicals, moderates, and conservatives, must consent to be held in one fabric; it must not give way to the far right, the far left, or the sudden ideological eruption. Keeping crazily, illogically intact, one party cannot differ too sharply from the opposite party, which feels the same stresses but responds to the same demand for a working degree of unity. Thus holding groups of varying opinions and interests together, the parties become a strong ark and essential chariot of national unity. Americans in 1864 had fresh in mind the catastrophic results of the temporary disintegration of one party by extremist demands in 1860.

The Presidential campaign would really begin when the Democrats made their nomination in the final days of August. Actually, the Republicans came up to that point with fair unity; a battalion of shortsighted dissenters might clamor for a new chieftain, but the main army marched forward unperturbed behind Lincoln. If the Democratic Party made a strong campaign, it too would have to conquer its divisions, show a workable unity, and convince the North that it was safe. As delegates began to flock to the Chicago Convention, the chances were two to one that it would do this. Meanwhile, the other essential source of cement for the Union was at last, after harrowing delays, coming into play. Sherman was moving forward. Grant was holding on like a bulldog. On Tuesday, August 16, 1864, the front page of the New York *Tribune* blazed with a huge map, taking up two-thirds of its space, labelled: "Map of the Bay of Mobile——THE SCENE OF FARRAGUT'S VICTORY."

Victory at last, on a tide that was just beginning to swell!

4

Lincoln, McClellan, and the Presidential Battle

ON SEPTEMBER 3, 1864, every steeple throughout the North was clangorous with bells. From every staff and window rippled the stars-and-stripes; in city squares, batteries of guns set the hills echoing, and on every village green a brass nine-pounder barked its joy. Every face wore a look of happy triumph. Atlanta had fallen; the news had reached Washington on the first day of the month. Yet amid these exultant scenes, posters, handbills, and newspaper columns reminded the public that the Democratic Party had just been bewailing "four years of failure to restore the Union by the experiment of war," and had just called for "a cessation of hostilities, with a view to an ultimate convention of the States." Four years of struggle, according to the Democratic chieftains, had resulted in failure and ignominy.

How was it that the great party of Jefferson, Jackson, and Polk had put itself in so abysmal a posture? How could it possibly extricate itself?

By the beginning of September, other resounding victories had been won.

"I am going into Mobile in the morning, if God is my leader," Farragut had written his wife on August 4 from his flagship *Hartford.* At daybreak he had quietly remarked to the captain, "Well, Drayton, we might as well get under way." By a few minutes after seven on August 5 his fleet of four monitors and fourteen wooden warships was engaged with Fort Morgan and other defensive works on Mobile Bay. At 7:40 the leading monitor in the starboard column, *Tecumseh,* hit a torpedo (or mine) and almost immediately sank. *Hartford* now took the lead by passing *Brooklyn,* while Farragut himself, aloft in the rigging to keep a better watch through the billows of smoke, was lashed fast there by subordinates who feared he might fall. By ten o'clock the battle was substantially ended when the rebel ironclad *Tennessee,* formidably gunned but with weak engines, struck her flag. At a critical moment, warned that mines strewed the channel ahead, Farragut is said to have uttered his historic exclamation, "Damn the torpedoes! Four bells!"—the signal for high speed ahead. The three-hour action had given the Union fleet the mastery of the most important port left to the Confederacy on the Gulf coast, although the city of Mobile itself remained in Confederate hands. Casualties were heavy, the Union fleet losing about 315 men killed or wounded, including 93 lost on the *Tecumseh*, but the glory won was great. How much Farragut had done to lift the Northern heart was made evident when he returned soon afterward to one of the most enthusiastic welcomes New York had ever given a popular hero.[1]

Meanwhile, the beleaguerment of Petersburg dragged its slow way along with a tardiness that tried Northern patience, but was not without its dramatic gains. In the battle of Globe Tavern or Weldon Railroad in mid-August, for example, a bloody four-day engagement, Warren's Fifth Corps bit deeper than before into the vital rail and road communications of Petersburg and Richmond with the south and southwest, and held firm under the most ferocious attacks that Lee and A. P. Hill could launch. Late in September, Federals pushed west of the Weldon Railroad at Peebles' Farm, while on October 27 at Burgess Mill a Federal advance against the Southside Railroad was repulsed.

[I]

The Democratic Convention had opened on August 29 in Chicago amid tumultuous and meaningless enthusiasm. Eleven railroads had poured delegations and excitement-seekers into the city, until it housed a hundred-thousand strangers; parades with bands of music filled the streets and fired salutes at intersections; hotel lobbies and barrooms were choked. Everyone knew that McClellan would be nominated, behind whom stood a half-dozen influential New Yorkers—S.L.M. Barlow, Samuel J. Tilden, Dean Richmond, August Belmont, Peter Cagger, Manton Marble. They were reinforced by such veteran leaders as S. S. Cox of Ohio, James Guthrie of Kentucky, and Ex-Governor William Bigler of Pennsylvania.

The two opening speeches were floridly rhetorical. August Belmont, national chairman, predicted that Lincoln's reëlection would mean "the utter disintegration of our whole political and social system," while Bigler lamented that the land was "literally drenched in fraternal blood." Then Horatio Seymour seized the gavel of permanent chairman for another burst of sound and fury.[2]

1. Lewis, Charles Lee, *David Glasgow Farragut, Our First Admiral*, Annapolis, 1943, Chs. XXII and XXIII; Farragut Papers, Huntington Library; *Official Records, Navy*, Ser. I, Vol.XXI, 405-407, 422-423; Farragut, Loyall, *The Life of David Glasgow Farragut*, New York, 1879, 422-423.

2. New York *World*, Aug. 29, 30, 31, 1864. The men named had dignity and ability, and deserved kindlier descriptions than Noah Brooks gave them. He contrasted August Belmont, "pale, sleek-headed, dapper and smooth," with Dean Richmond, who had done much to create the New York Central system, and this year succeeded Erastus Corning as president, "a tall, potbellied, bottle-nosed man, austere and arbitrary." He spoke ill of Fernando Wood, sour because he hated McClel-

The delegates had braced themselves for a deadly struggle between War Democrats who would keep on fighting for Union and emancipation, and Peace Democrats who would compromise. One side talked of McClellan as a leader who would give fresh energy to the war; the other talked of a speedy arrangement with Jefferson Davis to end the bloody struggle. McClellan's strength lay chiefly in the New England, New York, and Pennsylvania delegations, while peace sentiment ran highest among men of the Middle West and Border. Yet it was a curious fact that, although the principal champion of peace by submission was Vallandigham, his staunchest allies came from the raffish element in New York City, where Fernando Wood and Ben Wood led the unwashed myrmidons of Tammany Hall; and it was another curious fact that, although New England was full of wartime zeal, the handsome, ever-popular Thomas Hart Seymour of Connecticut—a talented reactionary of exhibitionist tendencies, often called traitor by Republicans—held views as disloyal as Vallandigham's.

In this situation, with the two wings of the party sternly hostile to each other but with a measure of unity essential for success, talk sprang up of mixing oil and vinegar on a simple formula—the War Democrats to name the candidate and the Peace Democrats to write the platform. The compromisers would have liked to nominate T. H. Seymour, but McClellan's fame was so great that they were abruptly stopped in their tracks. Moreover, Seymour protested that he did not want the post. The Peace Democrats, seeing that they had to accept McClellan, helped nominate him on August 31 by a moderately greater vote than that given Seymour. They resolved, however, to control the Convention in every other respect.

They managed this so smoothly that hardly a ripple disturbed the surface harmony as the oil blended with the vinegar. Men who had predicted a fierce battle could hardly believe their eyes and ears when nobody objected to McClellan except two delegates who accused him of measures unfriendly to civil liberties in Maryland early in the war. George H. Pendleton was unanimously nominated for the Vice-Presidency, and the defeatist platform was adopted with but four dissenting votes. Observers guessed that all this was done by clever pre-arrangement, and the advantages lay so clearly with the Peace Democrats that cynical men surmised that Vallandigham had dominated those who had made the pre-arrangement.

Perhaps this was true, perhaps not. But it was apparent that when the

lan and knew he would be nominated, but was more respectful of Horatio Seymour, "smooth, oily, dignified, and serene," who came in with a knot of small politicians "over whom he towers head and shoulders mentally and physically." De Alva Stanwood Alexander, in *A Political History of the State of New York*, New York, 1906-1909, III, *passim*, treats these leaders accurately.

platform spoke of "four years of failure" in the war effort and the prostration of "public liberty and private right," it took a submissionist view. Men realized that when the platform called for cessation of hostilities "with a view to an ultimate convention," it was suggesting unconditional surrender of the main differences between North and South. The platform did not come out directly for Confederate independence, but for restoration of the Union and rights of the States unimpaired. The Democrats also opposed alleged interference by military authorities in elections in Kentucky, Maryland, Missouri, and Delaware; opposed subversion of the civil law by military law in States not in insurrection; condemned arbitrary military arrests; arraigned suppression of speech and press; and defied employment of "unusual test oaths." The word slavery was not mentioned in the platform. It was rumored that at one of the secret meetings Dean Richmond had waged a desperate battle for a plank proposing an attempt at negotiation first, and then if necessary a war to the knife, but Vallandigham fought so angrily to strike it out that nobody dared interfere.[3] Actually Vallandigham had much to do with drafting the vital planks of the platform, and it was generally known that Pendleton was one of the most unyielding Copperheads in the country. Inheriting the prestige and opinions of a great Virginia family, although a native of Ohio, he had opposed the war from the beginning, voted against supplies to carry it on, and denounced all Northern leaders involved. He had in fact never concealed his desire to see the South gain its independence.

Nor did anyone lose sight of the fact that McClellan's nomination received the enthusiastic adherence of Vallandigham, Pendleton, Fernando Wood, T.H. Seymour, and other politicians of equivocal loyalty.[4] It was also noted that Manton Marble's New York *World* and other Copperhead publications took immediate pains to republish McClellan's letter to Lincoln in June, 1862, from Harrison's Landing. They repeated, as being still his views, his protests against

3. The War Democrat, Amasa J. Parker, wrote S.L.M. Barlow on Sept. 5: "You have seen the platform adopted at Chicago; but you do not know what difficulty we had in modifying it to its present shape, and how fain were our efforts to still more improve its phraseology." Barlow Papers, HEH. The platform asserted "that, after four years of failure to restore the Union by the experiment of war, during which. . . . the Constitution itself has been disregarded in every part, and public liberty and private right alike trodden down. . . . justice, humanity, liberty, and the public welfare demand that immediate efforts be made for a cessation of hostilities, with a view to an ultimate convention of the States . . ." Stanwood, Edward A., *History of the Presidency from 1788 to 1897*, Boston, 1912, I, 304-305; McPherson, Edward, *The Political History of the United States of America During the Great Rebellion*, Washington, 1865, 423.

4. Men disloyal to Jackson's principle, "Our Federal Union: It Must be Preserved." Senator James A. Bayard's views about the struggle had not changed since 1860, he wrote S.L.M. Barlow on Feb. 4, 1864. "I cannot but look upon the idea of many Democrats that a govt. such as ours can be restored by war, as a sheer hallucination." He had stayed in the Senate wishing to be of public use. "I have however lost all hope and look forward to a far more disastrous condition of affairs than the people dream of." They would see tyranny, then revolution, and then entire disintegration of the Union, all largely the fault of New England. Barlow Papers, HEH.

attacks upon slavery, and against any confiscations of property, any territorial reorganization of States, or any military arrests outside the area of actual hostilities. They readvertised his belief of 1862 that any declaration of radical attitudes toward slavery would "rapidly disintegrate" the Union armies.

It was also noted that Pendleton said nothing to modify his old position that the government should allow the erring sisters to go in peace. In the Congressional session beginning in July, 1861, he had declared, "I will heartily, zealously, gladly support any honest effort to maintain the Union and reinvigorate the ties which bind these States together." But somehow he had then found every practical Union effort dishonest. He had voted against increasing the regular Army, against the draft, against the Legal Tender Act, and against the important revenue bills; he would later propose to redeem United States bonds, not in gold but in greenbacks—thus combining inflationary ideas and financial dishonesty in a single measure. In short, men of conviction found him to be a gentleman of unstained private reputation, but untrustworthy in principles respecting the Union.[5]

The Richmond *Examiner* accurately estimated the situation. Reporting that Peace Democrats and War Democrats had compromised on McClellan, it commented that the platform "is half peace and half war; it floats between peace and war, being constructed in such a way as to drift to either side, and settle down next March in a war or peace policy as circumstances may require. Armistice will certainly be a feature in the new policy; armistice with a view to negotiation." If Washington should negotiate under McClellan with Richmond, Confederate independence might be safe, but if Washington should negotiate separately with the several States, Southern independence would be imperilled. In either event, thought E. A. Pollard's *Examiner*, negotiations for peace under the Constitution would mean the preservation of slavery.[6]

But the Democratic position, in view of recent events at Atlanta and Mobile, was asinine. If the party went before the voters with asseverations that the war was a failure while every week loosed fresh jubilations over victory, its own defeat was certain. If the Democratic Party stood for negotiations with the Confederacy embracing possible disunion and the certain restoration of slavery, angry desertions from the Democratic ranks would become general. Some people supposed that McClellan had given clear intimations of the kind of platform he wished built for him, and had promised to stand squarely upon it.[7] They thought that Vallandigham was aware of this when he told a crowd on reaching home from Chicago: "That convention has met every expectation

5. See New York *World*, Sept. 6, 1861, for summary and comment. Horace Greeley, in his *Tribune*, shared this opinion of Pendleton.

6. Richmond *Examiner*, Sept. 1, 1864.

7. See New York correspondence dated Sept. 13, London *Daily News*, Sept. 27, 1864.

of mine; the promises have all been realized." Others thought that the Peace Democrats were merely counting on McClellan's well-understood malleability. Whatever Little Mac's intentions, whatever the expectations of spineless peace-men, the storm of disgust and anger that met the platform gave intelligent and patriotic Democrats a shock they could not mistake.

"The whole thing can be put right with McClellan's letter of acceptance," the New York jurist Amasa J. Parker wrote Barlow,[8] meaning that McClellan must repudiate the "failure" plank and sound anew the slogan of Union. McClellan's letter of acceptance, which Barlow helped him write, was blazoned throughout the North on September 9. In spite of this brilliant opportunity given him to rebuke defeatism, he was, instead, weakly equivocal. To be sure, he rejected the idea that the war could be called a failure. "I could not look in the face my gallant comrades of the army and navy, who have survived so many bloody battles, and tell them that their labor and the sacrifice of so many of our slain and wounded brethren had been in vain. . . ." But he cravenly yielded to the platform in asserting that whenever the South showed a disposition to reënter the Union on any terms, he would negotiate. After Chancellorsville, Gettysburg, and the Wilderness, he would return to Buchanan and to the Union of 1859! No unity! He surrendered to the defeatists again in emphasizing the national longing for peace, and to the compromisers by declaring that if "any one State is willing to return to the Union, it should be received at once, with a full guarantee of all its constitutional rights."[9]

A chorus of approval from many leading War Democrats which greeted McClellan's rejection of the plank declaring the war a failure drowned out resentful growls from Ben Wood's semi-traitorous New York *Daily News* and Washington McLean's Cincinnati *Enquirer*. Yet the damage done the Democratic Party by the platform could not be undone. Its silly and evil stigmatization of the heroic war effort as worthless gave the Northern millions an image of the Democratic Party they could never forget. That phrase upon the failure of the war was to echo down the coming decades as the pronouncements of the Hartford Convention had echoed for decades, and would cost the party votes for a generation.

The issues were now crystal clear. Lincoln would entertain no proposal for a return to the Union by the rebellious States which did not include the abandonment of slavery by the whole Confederacy. McClellan would receive into the Union any State, restoring immediately all its constitutional rights, including the right to hold slaves, while other States yet remained in rebellion.

8. London *Daily News, ut supra;* Parker was a founder of the Albany Law School.

9. The Barlow Papers, HEH, contain both a rough draft of the letter in Barlow's handwriting, and a final draft; McClellan to Barlow, June 17, 1864.

Yet, ever since the days of Van Buren and Wilmot, a host of Northern Democrats had been antislavery men, and they still recoiled from the idea of embracing the foul hag slavery, even if paired with the beautiful maiden peace.

Thus, as the wind of sentiment shifted to favor Lincoln, McClellan's letter gave his party only the slenderest chance of success. To Peace Democrats, it promised almost nothing, to War Democrats nothing that the moderate Lincoln did not offer. In experience, Lincoln's four years in the White House gave him an overwhelming advantage. In personal popularity, he held a better place than McClellan in most towns and cities outside New York, while in rural areas his strength was unconquerable. The acute correspondent of the London *Daily News* pointed out that while country folk cared nothing about his defects of dress and manners, "his logic and his English, his jokes, his plain common sense, his shrewdness, his unbounded reliance on their honesty and straightforwardness, go right to their hearts." No important peace party really existed, the correspondent declared, and now that a brief interval of national weariness and depression was being overcome, no Administration would dare to cease fighting as long as the Confederacy was in existence.

"I think of Lincoln's chances at this moment," wrote the correspondent on September 10, "as five to three."

[II]

Although the voting was yet to come, by the end of September the campaign was indeed over. The wave of popular disgust with Vallandigham's platform flung tens of thousands of Democrats out of their party, and hundreds of thousands of wavering Republicans back within their own. Seldom has so swift a change occurred in the political situation of the great republic. No sooner did the country learn of the Chicago platform than Bryant, Greeley, Charles Sumner, John A. Andrew, Richard Yates, Lyman Trumbull, and other influential Republican dissidents, one by one, fell in behind Lincoln, declaring they would put every ounce of strength into the fight against McClellan. After Mobile Bay and Atlanta, gold came down with a rush, easing the pressure on national finances and prices. Volunteers pressed forward. Seward, delivering his annual address to his fellow townsmen of Auburn on September 3, made the welcome announcement: "We shall have no draft, because the army is being reinforced at the rate of five to ten thousand men a day."[10]

More significant still, Washington dispatches early in September included news that informed Republican circles expected Frémont to withdraw in the next ten days, and Ben Wade to take the stump immediately. Uneasiness would

10. Seward, Annual Address, Sept. 3, 1864.

persist until the Frémont splinter and the Chase factions disappeared completely. And the echoes of earlier successes had not ceased when the press carried jubilant new headlines late in September: "Victory! Another Glorious Triumph in the Shenandoah Valley!" Sheridan had smashed Early's forces at Fisher's Hill, capturing twenty guns and eleven hundred prisoners. This thrilling news of victory reached the public together with intelligence of the third battle of Winchester (September, 1864) in which Sheridan's forces drove Early's army in full retreat up the Shenandoah Valley, with substantial losses. General James A. Garfield wrote his wife from Cincinnati, September 23, 1864, that Sheridan had just made a speech in the Shenandoah more powerful and helpful to the Union cause than all the speeches the Union stump-orators could make; "our prospects are everywhere brightening."[11]

Lincoln had been unfortunate early that summer in that the war had moved so tardily, defeats appeared to outnumber victories, and Grant's losses had proved so poignant. What tragedies from the Wilderness to the Crater were registered in the Northern memory! Yet he had been politically fortunate in that no victorious chieftain had arisen in the North. What if the handsome, plausible Hooker had defeated Lee at Chancellorsville?—what if he had pressed on to destroy the Confederate army at Gettysburg? He might have been politically invincible. The efforts of men like Greeley to galvanize the unfit Rosecrans and Ben Butler into political leadership in the spring of 1864 indicate the perils that might have existed. Happily for Lincoln and the nation, inept generals possessed no appeal. As has been seen, a successful general like Grant had taken himself out of the picture. Now it was fortunate that Democratic blunders, recent military and naval victories, and the dissipation of the last foreign threats coincided to furnish a background for Lincoln's climactic efforts to unify the party and nerve the nation for the final critical months.

The last dangerous breaches in Republican ranks were healed when a sudden Radical assault upon Montgomery Blair accomplished his downfall. Chase and his friends regarded the retention of Blair in the Cabinet as an affront, for (as Lincoln told Gideon Welles) they considered it a condemnation of themselves and an endorsement of the whole Blair clan. Stanton's hostility had deepened as he heard stories about Montgomery's aspersions on his character, and a special incident had fanned the coals of his anger into flame. When Early's troops, in their raid north of Washington, burned Blair's mansion "Falkland" at Silver Spring, the postmaster-general had been stung into a bitter comment: "Nothing better could be expected while politicians and cowards have the conduct of military affairs." He termed the commanders

11. Freeman, Douglas S., *Lee's Lieutenants*, III, 577ff.; Garfield to his wife, Cincinnati, Sept. 23, 1864, Garfield Papers, LC.

about Washington "poltroons." Halleck wrote Stanton that if this accusation could be substantiated, the commanders should be cashiered; if not, the slanderer should be dismissed from the Cabinet. Stanton laid the letter before Lincoln. Meanwhile Gideon Welles was irritated by Blair's efforts to get the navy yards made cogs in the Republican machine.[12]

Beyond question the multifariously malicious Blair family was imperiling party unity and Northern cohesion. Montgomery was distrusted by Moderate Republicans, hated by such Radicals as Schuyler Colfax and Thaddeus Stevens. Henry Wilson, who thought his Rockville speech an insult to the Administration, told Lincoln that Montgomery Blair would cost the Administration tens of thousands of votes. The Union League and Loyal Legion refused him membership. A host of German-Americans in the Middle West, adhering to Frémont and recalling that all three Blairs had been Democrats, disliked him. Such Radical Congressmen as George S. Boutwell and John Covode urged Lincoln to dismiss him, and as September wore on, men anxious for success in November—Washburne, Senator James Harlan of Iowa, James M. Edmunds of the Union League, and Zach Chandler—became active in a two-headed undertaking. By getting Montgomery Blair ousted they would placate Chase and his allies, and at the same time persuade Frémont to withdraw his third ticket. Frémont flatly denied, with every evidence of sincerity, that he had made a political bargain in return for an assurance that Blair would be dropped, and although any final statement on the subject is impossible, we may well accept his statement. The final dénouement came with startling swiftness. On September 23, Blair astonished Gideon Welles and Edward Bates as they left a Cabinet meeting by announcing: "I suppose you are both aware that my head is decapitated—that I am no longer a member of the Cabinet." Lincoln had reminded him that morning of an earlier promise to keep his resignation available. "The time has come," wrote the President.

Since this followed by one day the withdrawal of Frémont, many people erroneously connected it with that event. The connection was tenuous. Frémont, a lifelong Abolitionist at heart, had withdrawn primarily because he thought that McClellan's candidacy on a platform which offered longer life to slavery must at all cost be defeated. "The Chicago platform is simply separation," he wrote. "General McClellan's letter of acceptance is re-establishment with slavery." Both were intolerable. "The Republican candidate, on the contrary, is pledged to the re-establishment of the Union without slavery . . ." Frémont would do what he could to prevent a Democratic victory, and he

12. Seward, Frederick W., *Seward at Washington, op.cit.*, 243; Riddle, A.G., *Recollections of War Times*, New York, 1895, Chs. XXXVII, XXXVIII; Welles, Gideon, *Diary*, New York, 1960, II, 136ff; Nevins, *Frémont* (1961 ed.), 581.

realized that Republican unity was a paramount necessity. In saying this, he did not yield his conviction that the Lincoln Administration had been "politically, militarily, and financially a failure," and that, "its necessary continuance is a cause of regret for the country." Years later Frémont was to write in his own hand: "I resigned [from the army] when I entered the political contest against Mr. Lincoln himself. In that contest I was strongly supported by the West, and the North East. So strongly that it became evident that Mr. Lincoln could not be elected if I remained in the field. In order therefore to save the Republican party, as they alleged, an appeal was made to me by Mr. Lincoln and his friends to withdraw. A council was held at the President's house and a committee appointed to wait upon me in New York for this purpose. Upon our meeting, which was at the office of a lawyer . . . in New York I took a week to consider the appeal. At a second meeting, in the same place, I had concluded to withdraw and so informed the Committee and withdrew accordingly. By this act I offended and alienated many friends, especially in the West. The Com. brought me offers, of patronage for my friends, and of disfavor to my enemies. I refused both; my only consideration was the welfare of the Republican party. I cannot permit my withdrawal to be placed otherwise than upon the sole ground—as it was alleged by the Com., 'vital to the party.' "[13]

In the complicated talks that preceded his retirement, Frémont had heard directly or indirectly from spokesmen for Seward, Weed, Chase, Ben Wade, Zach Chandler, and others. He later said he had been promised that if he withdrew he would get rewards for himself and punishment for his foes, the rewards apparently being reinstatement in active military command or a Cabinet appointment, the punishment Blair's dismissal; and he had refused both as insulting. This statement may be accepted as quite honest. Zach Chandler in particular was frantically zealous to bring all Radicals back to the flock.[14]

13. Lincoln, *Collected Works*, VIII, 18; New York *Herald*, *Tribune*, *Times*, Sept. 23, 1864; Nevins, *Frémont* (1961 ed.), 659ff; Frémont Papers, Bancroft Library, Univ. of Calif. Berkeley, manuscript corrections in Frémont's hand of his memoirs, written largely by his wife and sons.

14. Nevins, *Frémont*, *op.cit.*, 578-582, 659-661. Zach had a blunt way of shouldering himself into any office, even Stanton's, to demand action. According to the Detroit *Post* and *Tribune*, he went first to see Ben Wade, then Lincoln and Henry Winter Davis, and then "the leaders of the Frémont organization." Before seeing Lincoln a second time, about mid-September, while at the Astor House in New York, he learned that William Cullen Bryant was about to publish an editorial urging Lincoln's withdrawal and the assembling of a convention to name a new candidate. It was in type, but "by instant and earnest efforts, he obtained its withholding until the result of his labor could be known." (Detroit *Post* and *Tribune*), *Zachariah Chandler*, New York, 1880, 275.

Winter Davis, in a letter of Sept. 28 to Admiral DuPont, gives a more sensational story of Chandler's machinations to get rid of Montgomery Blair. "Chandler says he began when things looked very hopeless four or five weeks ago, everybody telling him success was hopeless. He did not go to Lincoln, but found out who his boon companions are, the men who crack jokes Sunday night till 1 A.M.—not politicians or Cabinet members, but the President's *familiar spirits*. [He] imbued them with the darkest views of Lincoln's prospects and sent them night after night to regale him with some new tale of defection or threatened disaster, never appearing himself for eight days till Lincoln was in the condition of a child frightened by ghost stories and ready to take

"If Montgomery Blair left the Cabinet, Chase and his friends would be satisfied, and this the President thought would reconcile all parties, and rid the Administration of irritating bickerings." So Lincoln later explained his course to Welles.[15] He did not bargain directly with Chase; he did not bargain directly with Frémont. When he threw Blair overboard he pleased not only both of them but Stanton and Halleck, Greeley and Bryant, Sumner and Wade, and a thousand other leading Republicans. Chase said nothing. Frémont should have said less, for his diatribe against Lincoln showed a poor spirit and poor taste. But Frémont, who might have reached for benefits by bargaining, had lost much. And there was real truth in the remark of Bennett's *Herald* as it recalled how recently leading Republicans had abused Lincoln as "a tyrant," "a failure," and "imbecile." "He (Frémont) does not act the cowardly, treacherous, and hypocritical part of Greeley, Chase, Pomeroy, Wade, Opdyke, and the rest. He does not deny his principles and eat his words."[16]

The hypocrisy of various Republican politicians and editors had in fact been unconcealed until the very opening of the Democratic Convention. The meeting that the hastily-assembled Opdyke political camarilla called to discuss a possible new convention had duly taken place at the house of David Dudley Field on August 30. This snake-cold attorney, aggressive in temper and sometimes careless of ethics in conducting dubious legal cases, had been chairman of the New York delegation to the Peace Conference of 1861, had since leaned toward a compromise peace, and would yet rejoin the Democrats. He was no friend to Lincoln. Henry Winter Davis had come to distil his poison into the discussion, and George Wilkes, a conservative newspaperman, had asserted that Grant alone could be elected. Francis Lieber had sent Charles Sumner a

refuge anywhere. . . . Next morning Chandler called and Lincoln said if Frémont could be induced to withdraw by giving up Blair, he would do it. Chandler went to New York; no Wade. He went to Massachusetts [and] saw Frémont, who was told the condition on which Lincoln would remove Blair. Frémont took time to consult his friends, met Chandler: 'But I wish a conditional one to get Blair out.' Fremont: 'I will make no conditions; my letter is written and will appear tomorrow!'

"So Chandler jumped into the cars, was in Washington next morning, saw Lincoln, and told him the condition on which he had promised to remove Blair had been complied with, and he claimed the performance of his promise. Lincoln: 'Well, but I must do it in my own way to soften it.' Chandler: 'Any way so it be done.' Exit Chandler. In the evening he called to see if it were done, when lo! Frémont's letter was before the President, who was excited at the form of it, and showed symptoms of flying from the bargain. Chandler recalled to him that the form of the withdrawal was not a condition, and offensive as it was, still it was a substantial advice to support Lincoln. So Lincoln yielded and wrote to Blair, 'The time has come.' Sic transit Blair! Stanton knew nothing of it yesterday when it was done!" H. W. Davis's Letters to S.F. DuPont, Eleutherian Mills, Hagley Foundation, Wilmington, Delaware.

For a modern analysis, see Trefousse, H.L., "Zachariah Chandler and the Withdrawal of Frémont in 1864; New Answers to an Old Riddle," *Lincoln Herald*, Winter, 1968, Vol. 70, No. 4, 181-187. Trefousse concludes that Frémont did act independently, but "it also becomes manifest that Chandler played an important part in the negotiations. . . ." Trefousse feels the evidence shows Chandler prevailed upon Lincoln to carry out the bargain when the President hesitated.

15. Welles, *Diary*, *op.cit.*, II, 158.

16. New York *Herald*, Editorial, Sept. 23, 1864.

report. Numerous States were represented, he wrote: "All agreed that Lincoln cannot be re-elected, unless great victories can be attained soon, which is next to impossible on account of the worn-out state of the armies of the Potomac." Henry Winter Davis told Admiral DuPont about the meeting, adding, with a note of sour Radical vindictiveness, "Those who think Lincoln came down from Heaven will soon be convinced he was on his way lower down and was not intended to stop here much longer and having been found out he will be sent on his way rejoicing. There was but one opinion among *all* the persons consulted—that the Chicago nominee must be selected unless Lincoln be withdrawn; and we hope people enough will act on that opinion to make it effectual. . . ."[17]

This was just before the Chicago platform and the capture of Atlanta put a new face on affairs. Three editors—Greeley, Parke Godwin of the *Evening Post*, and Theodore Tilton of the *Independent*—had undertaken to sound the opinion of other Republican leaders. In the swiftly changing situation they obtained answers that set them running to board the Lincoln wagon—an ignoble but edifying spectacle.

By October, as we have seen, the Presidential battle was virtually over. On September 29-30, Federal troops on the Petersburg front pushed west and north once more beyond the Weldon Railroad at the battle of Peebles' Farm. At the same time, north of the James, Grant's men captured Fort Harrison on September 29, and other ground, forcing Lee to pull back, build new intrenchments, and actually extend his already lengthy lines. Most spectacular of all had been the aforementioned movements of Sheridan in the Shenandoah where, after victories at Third Winchester September 19, Fisher's Hill September 22, and Tom's Brook October 9, Federal forces continued to press Early farther southward in the Valley.

By this time Phil Sheridan had become one of the best-loved Northern leaders, his picture and exploits familiar to all. Driving the defeated, ill-equipped Confederates before him, he began, it seemed to sanguine Northerners, to threaten Lee's lines from the Northwest. The many-fronted Union advances had several noteworthy results. Lincoln's reputation being inextricably bound up with the success or failure of the armed forces, the gains burnished his reputation as war leader to new lustre. They helped men peer through the battle-smoke in expectation of a sunrise of cheerful postwar activites. Meanwhile, so intense was the suspense over daily dispatches headed "The Gulf," "Atlanta," or "The Valley," that everybody forgot about ordinary issues. No national task stood paramount but one—the grim task of war.

17. Wilkes to Elihu Washburne, Aug. 31, 1864, Washburne Papers, LC.; H.W. Davis to S.F. DuPont Letters, Aug. 31, 1864, Eleutherian Mills-Hagley Foundation, Wilmington, Del.

The battle news now wrote an increasingly sardonic commentary upon the phrase "four years of failure," which Bennett's *Herald*, after long standing cynically on the sidelines, now called the most stupid, impudent, and detestable phrase coined by any conclave since Valmy had ended one of the severest defeats of the French revolutionary wars.[18] On October 21-22, Northern newspapers blazed again with the news of Cedar Creek, fought on October 19. Stanton's bulletin curtly summarized one of the most dramatic encounters of the war, long to be celebrated and translated into legend in prose, poetry, and drama. "Another great battle was fought yesterday at Cedar Creek, threatening at first a great disaster," he wrote, "but finally resulting in a victory for the Union forces under General Sheridan more splendid than any heretofore achieved."

Fuller accounts told how the Confederates under Early had been the assailants; how they intended, as Longstreet wrote Early, to "crush Sheridan out of the Valley at once and at all hazards"; how they struck when Sheridan had been called to Washington for a consultation with Stanton and was returning; how, at dawn in Winchester where he had unaccountably delayed over night, he heard the boom of cannon in the distance; how he galloped out of Winchester at seven-thirty, and how two hours later he reached the field of battle twenty miles away. Actually an officer reported hearing firing about 7:00 A.M., but Sheridan later admitted he paid no attention to it and "was unconscious of the true condition of affairs until about 9:00, when having ridden through the town of Winchester, the sound of the artillery made a battle unmistakable. . . ."[19] Furthermore, the distance was under the legendary 20 miles to the battlefront. Here the incipient panic caused by Early's stunningly effective surprise attack had already been checked by General H. G. Wright, but Sheridan's dramatic entrance made the Union recovery quick and complete. To Northern observers it seemed that from the jaws of defeat, like Napoleon at Marengo, he had snatched means to parry a desperate Confederate stroke that might have altered the entire face of the war in Virginia in favor of Lee, and to convert it into a stunning blow to the South. The stampede of the rebel troops was followed by another stampede of the gold gamblers and the supporters of McClellan.[20]

The Richmond press was carrying material of quite different import. It made room for letters written by Alexander H. Stephens, Governor Joseph E.

18. New York *Herald*, Oct. 20, 1864. Lincoln reputedly offered Bennett about this time the post of minister to France; Harper, Robert S., *Lincoln and the Press*, New York, 1951, 320-321.

19. *O.R.* I, xliii, pt. 1, p.52.

20. Merritt, Wesley, "Sheridan in the Shenandoah Valley," *Battles and Leaders*, IV, 500-521; Early, Jubal A., "Winchester, Fisher's Hill, and Cedar Creek," *Battles and Leaders*, IV, 522-530; *O.R.*, I, xliii, pt. 1, 52, 561.

Brown of Georgia, James P. Boyce of South Carolina, and Herschel V. Johnson, which caught eagerly at the idea of a national convention, Johnson sagaciously and courageously writing that the sooner the issue could be transferred from the field of blood to the forum of rational discussion the better for both sides.[21]

[III]

Both parties were deficient in organization. But the veteran editor Henry J. Raymond as the Republican national chairman was more resourceful and dexterous than the Democratic national chairman, the capitalist-politician August Belmont, and the fact that the Republicans were in power gave him a clear advantage. In 1862 the Democratic organization had been stronger in most States than the Republican; now the Republican was as good, if not better. In raising money for speakers, pamphlets, and a thousand other purposes, the Republicans fell back upon the well-established process of assessing Federal officeholders for contributions. With some exertion Raymond obtained the assistance of the War Department, Treasury, and Post Office, but the Navy under the stern moralist Gideon Welles remained impregnable. Regarding Raymond as a journalistic mercenary, Welles was disgusted by his attempt to use navy yards to elect candidates instead of build ships. He stigmatized the collectors of assessments as harpies who put into their own pockets much of the money they extorted. Nevertheless, Raymond finally succeeded in getting the Brooklyn navy yard to dismiss men because they supported McClellan. He collected money so brazenly in the New York Post Office and (after Hiram Barney left) the Custom House, that the *Herald* and *World* emitted indignant growls. When Phelps, Dodge, the metal dealers, gave him $3,000, and he tightened the screws on other contractors, the *World* snorted that every man who sold the government a pound of pork or bottle of quinine was expected to walk into the National Committee offices and plank down his greenbacks.[22]

Welles was the only cabinet member who objected to the general levy upon officeholders, five percent being the accepted amount. A committee under Senator James Harlan of Iowa looked after this shabby screw-tightening. Montgomery Blair had given $500 to the campaign fund, and when workers in the New York post office objected to paying tribute, his successor William Dennison told them he thought the levy was right. Lincoln had a hard-headed sense of the importance of parties and elections, but also a hard-headed conviction that party demands must not pervert the standards of honesty and effi-

21. Summary in Richmond *Whig*, Oct. 18, 1864.
22. Brown, Francis, *Raymond of the Times*, New York, 1951, 362-364.

ciency in government. He took no position on assessments except to refuse to permit coercive pressures on officeholders. He rejected the request of a Congressman that he bring official influence to bear to compel assistance from a reluctant postmaster, and rebuked the Philadelphia postmaster because his employees displayed a suspiciously Republican unanimity. In August and September the party was straitened for funds,[23] but by October the prospect of victory had loosened purse strings.

Some dubious methods of rallying the party were well illustrated even in distant California. "I went to the Navy Yard today," wrote Richard Chenery of the Naval Agent's office in San Francisco on September 22, "to induce the commandant to put in 200 more men, that we may carry that county and assist in saving the district, but he is timid and feared he might be censured if he did so. . . . I told him that the Administration expected him to do such a thing." The subject of politics was dominant in Presidential councils. Attorney-General Bates was at an October 28 cabinet meeting "and was not a little surprised to hear nothing talked of but election matters, and those minor points. Neither great *principles*—nor great *facts* seem, at present to have any chance for a fair consideration. . . . I wish the election was over. . . ."[24]

On the Democratic side, Manton Marble of the New York *World* was put in charge of publicity by August Belmont and Dean Richmond, gathering funds and paying speakers, publishers of pamphlets, and distributors of government documents. On one September day, five men contributed a thousand dollars apiece for his work, one of them that shrewd businessman, collector, and party-indefatigable, Sam Barlow. Yet he found his task arduous. "It looks ugly," the sensible Congressman "Sunset" Cox wrote him from Ohio on October 12. "The Vallandigham men have done just enough for us to damn us. Medary's paper put up McClellan's name—a little bit—and damned him with faint praise." At the end Marble referred bitterly to the difficulties of a contest "against an administration disbursing millions daily, employing one-third of the active industries of the whole population, and directing the interested energies of a whole army of stipendiaries scattered through every city, town, and village in the land. . . ."[25]

Each party had its loyal phalanx of speakers and writers, the Republicans leading. To be sure, the Democrats could call upon such intelligent stalwarts as William R. Morison of Illinois, Thomas A. Hendricks of Indiana, John V.L. Pruyn of New York, Reverdy Johnson of Maryland, S. S. Cox of Ohio, Samuel

23. Fowler, Dorothy Canfield, *The Cabinet Politician: The Postmasters-General, 1829-1909*, New York, 1943, 119-122; Brown, *Raymond of the Times*, *op.cit.*, 264.

24. Chenery to Senator Cornelius Cole, Cole Papers, UCLA Library; Bates, *Diary*, *op.cit.*, 422.

25. Cox in Manton Marble Papers, LC. Samuel Medary's *Crisis* was so obnoxious to Union men that an angry mob had wrecked its press in 1863; he died that fall. Marble in New York *World*, Nov. 10, 1864.

J. Randall of Pennsylvania; men who had served in Congress, made their mark in debate, and begun careers that would later be noteworthy. But how many seats in Congress once filled by eloquent Southern members were now marked "vacant"! And how many prominent Democrats would do the party more harm than good by public speeches! To place Bayard of Delaware, Voorhees of Indiana, or Ben Wood of New York upon a platform would be to invite a disastrous bolt of lightning, or cause a vast secession of honest men from the party. They would attract mobs more quickly than adherents. Among editors, such figures as Wilbur F. Storey of the Chicago *Times*, William Wright of the Newark *Journal*, and Washington McLean of the Cincinnati *Enquirer* wielded two-edged swords, as dangerous to friend as to foe. The manly activities of James Sheehan of the Chicago *Post*, George Lunt of the Boston *Courier*, Manton Marble of the *World*, and James C. Welling of the *National Intelligencer*, undaunted champions of civil liberties and political moderation, suffered heavy damage from wild party associates.[26]

Greatest of all was the disparity of literary strength in this party contest. Had Nathaniel Hawthorne, the devoted friend of Franklin Pierce, not died this spring, he might possibly have raised a voice for consideration of the Democratic position, though his single essay on wartime affairs had irritated many by his neutralism.[27] Some writers were as little concerned with politics as Herman Melville or Walt Whitman. A few were as inefficiently on the Democratic side as George Ticknor Curtis, the biographer of Webster and Buchanan. A staunch phalanx of authors, however, with the most famous names in America—Lowell, Longfellow, Whittier, Holmes, Emerson, Mrs. Stowe—took the field for Lincoln. When Bryant's seventieth birthday practically coincided with election day, it evoked from Lowell one of his happiest war poems, vibrant with the feeling of the Republican host behind the President. His spirited lines, beginning "Our ship lay tumbling in an angry sea," rose to a climax in his tribute to the much revered poet-editor:

> But now he sang of faith to things unseen,
> Of freedom's birthright given to us in trust;
> And words of doughty cheer he spoke between,
> That made all earthly fortunes seem as dust,
> Matched with that duty, old as time and new,
> Of being brave and true.

26. The Boston attorney, George S. Hillard, friend of Hawthorne and Sumner, esteemed Lunt highly. "Lunt wants tact, discretion, and temper," he wrote Manton Marble on May 4, 1864, "but on the other hand, he has dauntless courage, and that fidelity to conviction which is the rarest quality in our people, and for want of which the country is going to the devil." Manton Marble Papers, LC.

27. Hawthorne, Nathaniel, "Chiefly About War Matters," *Atlantic Monthly*, July, 1862.

Undoubtedly Lowell was the most effective literary champion of Lincoln. He made embattled America seem greater, just as Milton and Wordsworth had once made embattled Britain rise to higher grandeur. He was contemptuous of the Democrats, who in his opinion had not a single principle on which to keep afloat the great party of Jefferson and Jackson. His article in the *Atlantic* of October, 1864, "McClellan or Lincoln?" not only proved that McClellan was committed to an untenable policy of conciliation, but provided a summary of the President's traits. "Mr. Lincoln, in our judgment, has shown from the first the considerate wisdom of a practical statesman. If he has been sometimes slow in making up his mind, it has saved him the necessity of being hasty to change it."[28] A message from Whittier to Frémont, "There is a time to *do* and a time to *stand* aside," helped influence the explorer to withdraw from his race.[29] Some young writers showed especial zeal. A young clerk in Washington named John Burroughs, who often glimpsed Lincoln from his Treasury window, went to vote this fall. Hearing some disparaging comments on Lincoln from a farmer who gave him a ride, he angrily leaped from the wagon, shook his fist, and declared that he would be damned if he rode farther with such a damned Copperhead.[30]

The young French journalist August Laugel, visiting Boston in the last stages of the campaign, found Sumner and Henry Wilson aroused, and Edward Everett, Josiah Quincy, George Ticknor, John G. Palfrey, and Longfellow exerting all their influence. The two Abolitionist leaders, Garrison and Wendell Phillips, were at odds, for though Garrison spoke and wrote for Lincoln, Phillips stubbornly refused his aid. The President's reëlection was certain, he said, but it would make the task of friends of the slaves hard. "We have constantly to be pushing him from behind."[31] But otherwise all was unity.

Not all the pamphlets, speeches, and other writings were on such a high plane by any means. The 1864 election was little different from previous ones in its fulminations, except that the war lent a somewhat unusual context. For instance, *Harper's Weekly* in late September printed a list of terms which were said to be applied by the friends of General McClellan to the President: "Filthy Story-Teller, Despot, Big Secessionist, Liar, Thief, Braggart, Buffoon, Usurper, Monster, Ignoramus Abe, Old Scoundrel, Perjurer, Robber, Swindler, Tyrant, Fiend, Butcher, Land Pirate, A Long, Lean, Lank, Lantern-Jawed, High-Cheek-Boned-Spavined-Rail-Splitting Stallion."

28. Scudder, H.E., *James Russell Lowell*, Boston, 1901, 56-57.
29. Pickard, A. T., *Life and Letters of John Greenleaf Whittier*, Boston, 1907, II, 487.
30. Barrus, Clara, *Life and Letters of John Burroughs*, Boston, 1925, I, 99-100.
31. Laugel, Auguste, *The United States During the Civil War*, ed. Allan Nevins, Bloomington, Ind., 1961, 311-325.

Pamphlets played their usual important role. For the Democrats there were such as "The Future of the Country by a Patriot," "Corruptions and Frauds of Lincoln's Administration," "The Lincoln Catechism whereby the eccentricities and beauties of despotism are fully set forth," "Lincoln's Treatment of Grant, with Lincoln's Treatment of McClellan and The Taint of Disunion," "Mr. Lincoln's Arbitrary Arrests." From the Republican side came Isaac N. Arnold's "Reconstruction; Liberty the corner stone, Lincoln the architect," "The Chicago Copperhead Convention: The Treasonable and Revolutionary Utterances of the Men Who Composed It," D. S. Coddington's "The Crisis and the Man," "The Copperhead's Prayer, containing remarkable confessions by a degenerate Yankee," the Chicago *Tribune*'s "Issues of the Campaign, Shall the North Vote for a Disunion Peace?" "Proofs for the Workingman of the Monarchial and Aristocratic Design of the Southern Conspirators and Their Northern Allies," "Spirit of the Chicago Convention—a surrender to the rebels advocated—a disgraceful and pusillanimous peace demanded—the Federal government savagely denounced and shamefully vilified and not a word said about the crime of treason and rebellion," "Letters of Loyal Soldiers," "How Douglas Democrats will vote." Many others of a like nature, along with speeches and campaign biographies, clog the archives of that time.

A few quotes suffice. "Corruptions and Frauds of Lincoln's Administrations," claimed that there had been fraud after fraud, and described "the wretched schemes of speculation and plunder into which the prominent partisans of Mr. Lincoln have embarked." Charges are based on the New York Custom House case and alleged corruptions in selling of cargo of captured blockade runners. "The Lincoln Catechism," one of the most vicious, has a devilish-looking colored face on a bright yellow cover. The publisher advertises such songs as "Ballads of Freedom and Abraham Africanus I." The text of the Catechism goes, "What is the Constitution? A compact with hell—now obsolete. By whom hath the Constitution been made obsolete? By Abraham Africanus the First. To What end? That his days may be long in office—and that he may make himself and his people the equal of the negroes. . . . What is the meaning of the word 'patriot?' A man who loves his country less, and the Negro more. What is the meaning of the word 'traitor?' One who is a stickler for the Constitution and the laws. What is the meaning of the word 'Copperhead?' A man who believes in the Union as it was, the Constitution as it is, and who cannot be bribed with greenbacks, nor frightened by a bastille. . . ."

The Republicans were not far behind, if behind at all, in such trash. From "The Copperhead's Prayer", we quote: "To the great and the mighty, the terribly feared, and the wonderfully adored Jefferson Davis, . . . Thou who are exalted so high above the common people—thou more than mortal whom we delight to deify, and worship as a God—knowing thou art DEVIL! Thou Aristocrat, professing Democracy—thou who hatest the poor white man, and whose mission it is to establish the only slave government the world ever saw. . . . It is not so much for the consideration of any natural affection which we have for you personally, O, immaculate Davis! but because we know that we are necessary to each other's political salvation. . . . It has been our prayer by day and our comfort by night that the time is not far distant when we shall be permitted to greet you as conqueror—and as the head of a great, independent, and glorious SLAVE CONFEDERACY. . . . I have joined the enemies of my country, and I must go with my party."

On a somewhat different level, Francis Lieber and his Loyal Publication Society distributed widely: "Report of the Judge Advocate General, on the 'Order of American Knights,' or 'Sons of Liberty'—A Western Conspiracy in Aid of the Southern Rebellion." This report of Judge Advocate General Joseph Holt presented a series of wild and exaggerated stories on the Copperhead menace.[32]

It was truly a Union Party in great parts of the North that faced the Democrats, a coalition of War Democrats and Republicans. A Union Convention was held in New York; the Union Party in Indiana took strength from the fact that Governor Oliver P. Morton had appointed Joseph A. Wright, a Democrat, to a Senatorship; Governor Buckingham in Connecticut called himself a Union Party man, and owed his spring victory largely to the support of Ex-Governor James T. Pratt, long a loyal Democrat. In Maine, town and county tickets uniting Republicans and Democrats were placed in nomination, and in Wisconsin the same procedure was followed. This alliance made it easier for Raymond's helpers to collect money, for by placing their pleas on a Union Party basis they could appeal to contributors of former Democratic allegiance. John Hay used White House stationery in acknowledging the receipt of a non-partisan contribution from a Federal attorney.[33] When Nicolay spent a mid-October week in Missouri he did it to obtain a full and harmonious combination of Union voters there and wrote Lincoln that "with the exception of very few impracticables, the Union men will cast their votes for you."[34]

The last weeks found the tide setting in one direction. "I have just had a conversation with a prominent New York politician and McClellan man,"

32. The Chicago Historical Society possesses an outstanding collection of these campaign documents, from which we have mentioned or quoted only a few. For a more readily available selection see Freidel, Frank, ed., *Union Pamphlets of the Civil War*, Cambridge, Mass., 1967, particularly Vol. II.

33. Hay to Raymond, Oct. 17, 1864, George E. Jones Papers, NYPL.

34. Oct. 18, 1864; Hay Papers, Illinois State Hist. Library.

Halleck wrote Lieber on October 22. "He says they expect to carry New York, New Jersey, Delaware, and Kentucky, and hope to get Pennsylvania and Missouri, but have given up all hope of electing McClellan. What they now want is to roll up as large a vote against Lincoln as possible, so as to preserve their party organization for the next election." Here and there a nervous Congressman like Schuyler Colfax feared local defeat, but the State elections on October 11 revealed an unmistakable trend. In Indiana Morton was reëlected governor for four years by nearly 21,000 majority over Joseph E. Macdonald, and Ohio also registered large Union Party gains. In Pennsylvania the result was at first in doubt. Democratic leaders had made heroic efforts in McClellan's former home State, where irritation had been excited by frauds connected with the recruiting system. But after several days of uncertainty the soldier vote gave the Union Party a clear majority.[35]

In an astonishingly close election, the voters of Maryland meanwhile approved 30,174 to 29,799 a new Constitution which provided for the emancipation of all slaves, without compensation to owners. Vehement opposition was made to this destruction of a property right that some citizens declared existed by divine authority as well as laws passed in accordance with the national Constitution. Voters were required to take an oath that they had never given aid or countenance to the rebellion, and nearly a hundred men refused it; as they would have voted against emancipation, the real majority for it was only about 270. But this margin gratified Lincoln, who made a special plea for approval two days before the election. "I desire it on every consideration," he wrote. "I wish all men to be free. I wish the material prosperity of the already free, which I feel sure the extinction of slavery would bring. I wish to see in process of disappearing that only thing which ever could bring this nation to civil war."[36]

35. Halleck in Lieber Papers, HEH; Colfax to Raymond, Oct. 8, 1864, Jones Papers, NYPL; New York *Herald*, *Times*, Oct. 11-16, 1864; *American Annual Cyclopaedia*, 1864, 436-438, 629-632, 648-652.

36. Lincoln to Henry W. Hoffman, Oct. 10, 1864, *Collected Works*, VIII, 41.

5

The Triumph of Lincoln

AS MEN of the Union Party read the encouraging State returns in October, 1864, Lincoln had a new opportunity to augment the strength and unity of his followers. On October 12 Roger B. Taney died, scion of an old Roman Catholic family of Maryland, graduate of Dickinson College in 1795, cabinet member under his friend Andrew Jackson, and successor of John Marshall in the Chief Justiceship. Even those who most detested his part in the odious Dred Scott decision could not deny his erudition and courage, nor the dignity and impartiality, apart from a pro-slavery bias, with which he had conducted the business of the tribunal. For years he had been a walking skeleton, kept alive, said some, by his annual visits to White Sulphur Springs, and by his determination, said others, to maintain a judicial citadel against Republican policies. Ben Wade had made a rough joke about him: during Buchanan's Administration he was fearful that Taney would die any day and "Old Buck" name his successor, but after Lincoln came in his fear was that Taney would manage to hang on into a new Democratic regime.[1]

The Supreme Court needed a firm hand, for peace was certain to bring before it important questions of finance, State rights, and the new status of the freedmen. For a time after taking office, Lincoln had hesitated to fill three vacancies. Two of the outgoing justices had been residents of seceded States. Appointments from the same area, even if possible, could not serve the vacated circuits; and he did not like to make all selections from the North, thus impeding justice to the South when peace was won. Early in 1862, however, he named Noah H. Swayne, a Virginia-born Ohioan, to one vacancy, and later that year appointed Samuel F. Miller of Iowa, and his old friend David Davis of Illinois. In 1863, Stephen J. Field of California was appointed, making a total of ten justices. This move was made by the Administration and Congress primarily to insure a "safe," strongly pro-Union Court. Now, who would guide the vessel thus partially remanned and enlarged?

1. Nicolay and Hay, *Lincoln*, New York, 1890, IX, 386.

The week after Taney's death, well-informed newspapers predicted that Salmon P. Chase would probably be made his successor.[2] Great was his friends' rejoicing—and great the anxious chagrin of Montgomery Blair, then conducting a characteristically devious movement to obtain the office. Instigated by the Blair family, William Cullen Bryant, John M. Forbes, and other men of influence had written Lincoln in Blair's behalf, while editors like Joseph Medill had made representations for him. When Mrs. Lincoln mentioned to Francis P. Blair, Sr., that the pressure of lawyers was giving Chase the advantage, the old politician hurried to the White House to lobby for his son. Montgomery himself tried to enlist Senator E. D. Morgan. "There is one consideration which I hope you will bring to the President's attention to prevent Chase's appointment," he wrote. "He is known to be so vindictive towards me for supporting the President, that no one would employ me as counsel to the Court if he were Chief Justice. Now the President cannot consent not only to turn me out of his Cabinet, but to drive me from the bar for life, because I supported him for the Presidency."[3]

Lincoln, however, had his own ideas about the Chief Justiceship. He told old Blair that he could not resist the general will of the bar. "Although I may be stronger as an authority, if all the rest oppose I must give way." He knew that Montgomery Blair's promotion would be politically divisive. When Chase's appointment was finally announced on December 6, Charles A. Dana astutely appraised Lincoln's reasons: "That appointment was not made by the President with entire willingness. He is a man who keeps a grudge as faithfully as any other living Christian, and consented to Chase's elevation only when the pressure became very general and very urgent. The Senate especially were resolved that no second-rate man should be appointed to that office, and if Mr. Montgomery Blair had succeeded in presenting his programme to that body, I have no doubt it would have been smashed to pieces in a moment. Mr. Blair's idea was that one of the existing justices, as for instance Judge Swayne, should be appointed Chief Justice, and that he himself should be made an Associate Justice . . ." Later he could step up. It was

2. Lincoln had repeatedly told friends earlier of his willingness to appoint Chase if a vacancy occurred; Nicolay and Hay, *Lincoln, op.cit.*, IX, 387. Chase's advice to him on constitutional questions like West Virginia, emancipation, and Negro enlistment, had been careful and weighty; Schuckers, *Chase*, New York, 1874, 459-464. For Lincoln's judicial appointments see King, Willard L., *Lincoln's Manager David Davis*, Cambridge, Mass., 1960, 192ff.; Silver, David, *Lincoln's Supreme Court*, Urbana, Ill., 1957, 83-93.

3. F.P. Blair, Sr., to John A. Andrew, *Massachusetts Historical Society Proceedings*, 1930, 88-89; Blair to E.D. Morgan, Nov. 20, 1864, Morgan Papers, New-York Hist. Soc.; J.M. Forbes to Bryant, Nov. 21, 1864, Bryant-Godwin Papers, NYPL. Montgomery Blair's wire-pulling was neither honest nor dignified.

fortunate for the country that this seat-warming arrangement for Blair never eventuated.[4]

It was still more fortunate that the opportunity for service went to Chase. Though regarded by the bar with some doubt as to the completeness of his professional training (graduating from Dartmouth without distinction, he had studied law sketchily under William Wirt before being admitted to practice), Chase had such eminent gifts that in due course he took rank among the great American jurists. Nobody could foresee that he would have to deal with the proposed trial of Jefferson Davis for treason, and the impeachment of an American President, but everyone knew that he would have to meet critical tests. William M. Evarts, who was delighted by his nomination, lived to deliver a judicious, if eschatological, judgment upon him. He compared Chase, as a financial statesman, with Alexander Hamilton. He laid emphasis upon Chase's deep religious convictions and his stern sense of duty, but most of all he praised his vision as a jurist intent upon making the government of the republic one not of men, but of laws.[5] Lincoln, faced with one of his weightiest decisions, had disregarded personal feeling and unwise counsel to choose aright. No other man suggested—Blair, Bates, David Davis, Stanton, Swayne, or William M. Evarts—had the stature of Chase. Lincoln appointed him with butone apprehension, that in his exalted new seat he might still look covetously at the Presidency.[6]

[I]

The main issue of the Presidential contest as it moved into its final month had little to do with the party platforms, for after McClellan published his letter of acceptance both candidates stood on the same central demand, the maintenance of the Union at all costs. The question was which man and which party could best assure this goal. Some voters doubted McClellan's sincerity in asserting that "reëstablishment of the Union in all its integrity is and must be the indispensable condition in any settlement." They were relatively few

4. Segal, Charles M., editor, *Conversations with Lincoln,* New York, 1961, 360-361; Dana to James S. Pike, Dec. 12, 1864, Pike Papers, Columbia Univ. Lib. The unscrupulous Montgomery Blair, meeting Senator Henry Wilson, told him that, unless Blair got the place, it would go to "one of the old fogies on the supreme bench, and so he ought to help Blair." Nicolay Papers, Illinois State Hist. Lib.

5. *Arguments and Speeches of William Maxwell Evarts,* edited by his son Sherman Evarts, New York, 1919, Vol.III, Ch.III, "Eulogy on Chief Justice Chase," 59-92.

6. *Ibid.,* 78-82. Lincoln told Henry Wilson: "I fear if I make him C.J. he will simply become more uneasy and neglect the place in his strife and intrigue to make himself President. He has got the presidential maggot in his head, and it will wiggle there as long as it is warm." Nicolay Papers, Illinois State Hist. Lib.

in number, however, for the Democrats now stood no possible chance of winning the election except on such firm pledges. As Bennett's *Herald* said on September 24, the salvation of the Union was the all-absorbing issue with the masses of both parties in all the loyal States. They might elect Lincoln or elect McClellan, but only as a Union man. This meant war to complete victory, for not only Davis, Lee, and Toombs, but the six Southern governors who met at Augusta on October 17 were still stubbornly demanding Confederate independence.[7]

With every passing day, moreover, the question of slavery retention became more unreal. The institution had been too far mutilated and undermined to recover. John J. Crittenden had said it would go out like a candle, and it was now guttering. Missouri was on the point of abolishing it as Maryland did. The only question was whether emancipation there should be gradual, as the State convention of 1863 had provided, or immediate, as the so-called Radicals, demanding a new convention, urged. Farther South, hundreds of thousands more who had heard Sherman's bugles and Farragut's cannon would tolerate slavery no longer. If McClellan were elected, it would be by the votes of men who knew that slavery was moribund, but would try to write into the peace arrangements a few mild stipulations on the subject. If Lincoln were elected, it would be by the votes of men who knew that slavery was dead and would write into constitutional amendments steel-clad guarantees of a new political and social order. Which man, which party, could best be trusted with a future certain to be utterly different from the past?

A new spirit was in the air which made platform declarations, and such vague assurances as those in McClellan's acceptance letter, quite meaningless. McClellan promised economy without saying when or where; "a more vigorous nationality" in foreign affairs without telling how it would be gained; "a return to a sound financial system" without defining "sound." The new spirit appeared when a crowd serenading Seward in Washington rose enthusiastically to his assertion that Sherman and Farragut had knocked the bottom out of the Chicago nominations, and somebody recited lines from Thomas Buchanan Read's poem "Sheridan's Ride."[8]

On nearly every front the conditions we have listed as precedent to victory were now being fulfilled. Was the coordinated and unified command of all the armies operating so efficiently that it interdicted Confederate attempts at exchanging army reinforcement on interior lines? Lee, aware of how desperately

7. McPherson, Edward, *The Political History of the United States of America During the Great Rebellion*, Washington, 1864, 421. Some governors possibly came in subversive mood: Coulter, E.M., *Confederate States*, Baton Rouge, 1950, 400.

8. Shotwell, W.G., *The Civil War in America*, London, 1923, II, 300.

the Western armies and other forces of the Confederacy needed men, was helpless to aid them. He was pinned down, with his hands overtaxed in Virginia. Did the Northern commanders at last have such heavy superiority in numbers and fire-power as permitted a steady outflanking of the enemy and continual pressure in lieu of costly frontal assaults? Grant's movements since before Cold Harbor and nearly all Sherman's movements answered this query affirmatively. Their strategy anticipated that of the Russian leaders in driving back the German armies in 1944-45. Finally, did the superiority of the North in medicines, equipment, transportation, artillery, and cavalry lend force to truly shattering blows and give the fighters irresistible confidence in the future? Nearly every week some engagement proved it did.

The superior power of the Union forces was being used, in the last weeks before election, to tighten the noose about Petersbrug, or rather to extend the beleaguerment of the little city. Hancock, who had been sent to the north bank of the James to harass Lee's lines before Richmond, and prevent Lee from sending further reinforcements to Early in the Shenandoah, remained there until August 20, when he was recalled. Warren, as has been mentioned at the start of the preceding chapter, had been ordered on August 16 to move against the Weldon Railroad, to cut it, and to renew the pressure upon Lee. This vital line, only three miles from Grant's flank, was obviously a prize of the first importance—the road running straight south through Weldon to Wilmington, with a lateral connection in North Carolina to Raleigh, and in South Carolina to Florence. The tracks, locomotives, and cars on this cluttered artery were in deplorable condition, but it and the Southside Railroad running to Danville and the North Carolina Piedmont still carried indispensable supplies and men. By noon on August 18 Warren had reached the railroad. Sharp battles filled several days, Henry Heth and A. P. Hill fighting hard to keep control of the lines. But Warren held tenaciously to his position, permanently ousting the Confederates, and compelling Lee to haul his supplies thirty miles by wagon around the break.[9]

This was a telling Union gain although made at high cost. A few days later in a separate operation, Hancock enlarged the Northern hold, although the Confederacy was temporarily successful in an attack on the Federals at Ream's Station, August 25. Cyrus Comstock of Grant's staff wrote in his diary on August 27 that he had visited the new line. "Hancock has destroyed the road for five miles below Ream's Station, but lost 9 guns and 2,000 prisoners. He says Gibbon's division behaved disgracefully . . . It is disgusting—Warren lost 3,000 the other day and now Hancock 2,000." Official figures were a total of 4,279

9. Freeman, Douglas S., *R.E. Lee*, New York, 1934, III, Ch.XXVII; Humphreys, Andrew A., *Virginia Campaign*, New York, 1883, 273-279.

Federal total casualties for Weldon Railroad and 2,742 for Ream's Station. Comstock added later, on September 10, that the Union position has been further improved. "Our line now runs across the Weldon R. R., then down its western side, then across it again on a line nearly parallel to the front, giving a large entrenched camp. A railroad is nearly completed in rear of our line from the City Point to the Weldon R. R. . . . Meade returned today and his staff report the feeling of the North very much improved by the successes at Atlanta, Mobile, and the Weldon R. R."[10]

On September 29, in conjunction with the Union attack on Fort Harrison north of the James, Federals moved out against Petersburg once more. The battle of Peebles' Farm, September 29 to October 1, failed to take the Southside Railroad, but did extend the lines three miles westward. Losses were again heavy, totaling 2,889. On October 27, Grant made another thrust to the left in an effort to outflank Lee and seize the now indispensable Southside Railroad. The drive known as Burgess' Mill, Boydton Plank Road, or Hatcher's Run failed, but the Union nevertheless had made considerable fall gains in the Petersburg fighting. As election day impended, a long lull began at Petersburg, a lull that meant enhanced strength to the North and growing weakness to the South. The winter about to begin proved a season of unusual severity. The Confederate soldiers, poorly clad, meagrely fed, and scantily sheltered, suffered terribly, having almost no meat, little bread, and no coffee, tea, or sugar. Rickety railway cars and wagons could not haul sufficient rations to the front. "Ten days ago the last meat ration was issued and not a pound remained in Richmond," Robert G. H. Kean was soon writing in his diary. An emergency supply had to be borrowed from the navy. "The truth is we are prostrated in all our energies and resources." Men shivering in bitter winds, living mainly on coarse corn-bread, and receiving piteous appeals from wives and children, were deserting in large numbers.[11]

These last weeks of the Presidential campaign found the situation in Georgia and Tennessee also in rapid transformation. The familiar events that led up to the capture of Atlanta will not be recounted here, save to note that they included President Davis's transfer of the Western army from Joseph E. Johnston to John B. Hood, a Kentucky West Pointer. Hood, who had taken command of the "Texas Brigade" early in 1862, had proved himself an aggressive fighter in engagement after engagement, from the Seven Days through

10. *O.R.* I, xlii, pt. 1, 128, 131; Comstock Papers, LC; cf. Willcox, O.D., "Actions on the Weldon Railroad," *Battles and Leaders,* IV, 568ff.

11. *O.R.* I, *ut supra,* 143; Humphreys, *Virginia Campaign, op.cit.,* 290-292; 294-303; Kean, *Inside the Confederate Government, op.cit.,* 181; Taylor, Walter H., *Four Years with General Lee,* ed. J.I. Robertson, Bloomington, Ind., 1962, 141-144.

Chickamauga, and during the campaign and siege of Atlanta, where he failed to drive back Sherman's forces. Then followed a Confederate repulse at Jonesboro (August 31 and September 1, 1864), demonstrating that Hood's troops would be enveloped if he did not evacuate the place, and his retreat a few miles south of Jonesboro to Lovejoy's Station on the railroad that connected Atlanta with Macon. Hardly a week after the Union entry into Atlanta, Sherman issued his edict that the whole population must remove; those who preferred it going South, and the others North. And on the day after the occupation General W. J. Hardee, at Hood's suggestion, sent President Davis a piteous telegram:

"Unless this army is speedily and heavily reinforced, Georgia and Alabama will be overrun. I see no other means to arrest this calamity. Never, in my opinion, were our liberties in such danger. What can you do for us?"[12]

The story of the Atlanta campaign, if narrated in detail, is an engrossing story, but it has been told too often to bear full review except in works primarily military. The important facts are that Davis made one of his worst mistakes when he removed the wary Johnston, who was following the only strategy that offered his weaker army a vague chance of success against Sherman's host, in favor of the rashly impetuous Hood; that in the final fighting around Atlanta the Union troops managed for the most part to take advantage of entrenched lines while the Confederates did the assaulting; that the loss of General James B. McPherson on July 22 at the Battle of Atlanta, a vigorous, able, and lovable leader only thirty-five years old, was one of the worst blows in leadership the Union army suffered; and that Sherman's removal of the people of Atlanta, while naturally assailed by Southerners as cruel, was justified by the situation and the laws of war. After taking Atlanta, Sherman rested his men for a time. He held not only an important rail center but a cluster of manufactories that had given the Confederacy a goodly stock of munitions. He had finished a considerable amount of the work of again cutting the Confederacy in twain, this time by a line from Memphis through Chattanooga and Atlanta to Mobile. Little military resistance southwest of this line was henceforth feasible.

Whither now should Sherman march? Forward! Forward into new eastern areas! The decision to go was his own, and one he conditionally made soon after taking Atlanta. While Sherman made the decision, the idea had been prevalent for some time, and was obvious to anyone who glanced at a map. Apparently Thomas had been urging a campaign south from Atlanta with his own army. Grant had wired Sherman as early as September 10, "As soon as

12. September 4, 1864; Hood, John Bell, *Advance and Retreat*, New Orleans, 1880, 245.

your men are sufficiently rested and preparations can be made, it is desirable that another campaign should be commenced. We want to keep the enemy constantly pressed to the end of the war. If we give him no peace while the war lasts, the end cannot be distant. Now that we have all of Mobile Bay that is valuable, I do not know but it will be the best move to transfer Canby's troops to act upon Savannah, whilst you move on Augusta. . . ."

Thus began a lengthy correspondence. At first Sherman favored moving if he could find provisions at Augusta or Columbus, Ga. He felt he could make such a march if another Federal force would take Savannah and move up the Savannah River as high as Augusta or up the Chattahoochee as far as Columbus. Otherwise, the risk would be too great. This line of thought continued with variations until early October when Hood moved north and westward. It could not be a final decision, of course, until he knew more about Hood's intentions, and about Grant's wishes. But he sent Grant his plan for destroying Atlanta as a base, and that part of its rail connections with Chattanooga that might be perilous to Union forces in the future. When this work was done, he suggested, he might push on through the heart of Georgia. The Confederacy would thus be dissevered not only to the Gulf but to the Atlantic. While Sherman rested and made plans, Jefferson Davis was visiting Hood's army, and making speeches to the disheartened troops and the people of several cities. Frankly admitting that the loss of Atlanta had been a heavy blow and that gloom enshrouded the future, he bade no one despond. "If one half the men now absent without leave will return to the front, we can defeat the enemy." When he added in Montgomery, "Let us win battles," Sherman knew that Hood would undertake a new offensive.[13] He was convinced of this six weeks before election day.

As early as September 18, in fact, Hood was shifting his army from the Macon Railroad and his base at Lovejoy's Station westward to the West Point Railroad, obviously hoping to cut Sherman's communications with the bases behind him. That is, he moved his forces from interior Georgia toward the western boundary. This backward movement was in effect, as Sherman later wrote, "stepping aside and opening wide the door for us to enter Central Georgia." Grant in his City Point headquarters far away saw the situation somewhat differently. He thought on September 26 that the next logical step for Sherman would be to turn back to Middle Tennessee in order to drive out the troublesome Forrest, who had just won a smart new victory at Athens in Northern Alabama. Sherman, however, had few fears about enemy forces at

13. Van Horne, Thomas B., *The Life of Major-General George H. Thomas*, New York, 1882, 255; *O.R.* I, xxxix, pt. 2, 355-356, 364-365, 411, 432, 464; Strode, Hudson, *Jefferson Davis, Tragic Hero*, New York, 1964, III, 94.

the rear. He knew that it would be safe if he were to send Thomas back to Tennessee, reinforced by an extra division, and by reserves which Grant had ordered to be sent him. Much of this movement was accomplished by rail and march by early October; whereupon, Sherman telegraphed Grant on October 1 an all-important question. As Hood had moved behind Atlanta, would it not be best to leave Thomas to cope with him, set fire to the city, "and march across Georgia to Savannah and Charleston, breaking roads and doing irreparable damage?" Receiving no immediate assent, on October 9 he telegraphed Grant more insistently. He must move forward to the sea. "I propose that we break up the railroad from Chattanooga forward, and that we strike out with our wagons for Milledgeville, Millen, and Savannah. Until we can repopulate Georgia, it is useless for us to occupy it; but the utter destruction of its roads, houses, and people will cripple their military resources . . . I can make this march, and make Georgia howl!" Grant still demurred, thinking it best to destroy Hood's army first. But by November 2 he had decided that Thomas could take care of Hood, and that Sherman would lose valuable territory by pursuing him. "I say, then, go on as you propose."

Hood, having reached Sherman's rear early in October on the railroad between Atlanta and Chattanooga, occupied several points, and on October 5 attacked a fortified Union post at Allatoona Pass. Sherman pulled part of his force out of Atlanta to go after Hood. From this movement rose the legend about Sherman sending a dispatch by signal to John M. Corse, defending Allatoona, "Hold the fort for I am coming." The courageous defense of Allatoona captured the imagination of the nation. Hood swung westward and then hit the railroad again, taking Dalton on October 13 before moving over to Gadsden, Alabama, October 22. By the 31st, he was at Tuscumbia preparing for his move into Tennessee. Then came Grant's decision of November 2 to let Thomas handle Hood.

Public attention had also been called to the Trans-Mississippi area once again, where Sterling Price had invaded Missouri from Arkansas, swinging up through Pilot Knob to the outer environs of St. Louis, and then westward across the State. General Samuel R. Curtis gathered what forces were available at Kansas City and Westport, while a force under Pleasonton was following Price. After several preliminary actions at Lexington and the Little Blue River, Curtis's troops defeated Price's Confederates in the battle of Westport, just south of Kansas City, on Sunday, October 23, 1864. Price was forced into a somewhat headlong and disastrous retreat southward.

These events took place only a few days before the election. The stir of preparations in Georgia for a lusty new stroke—guns and wagon-trains being readied, munitions collected, and sick and wounded sent back to Chattanooga

—was known throughout the North as men prepared to vote. It heartened everybody. The day before election, Bennett's *Herald* summarized the situation in an inaccurate but influential editorial note. "General Hood has been defeated with considerable loss in his first attempt to cross the Tennessee River. . . . It appears from our correspondence that General Sherman has sent the Fourth Corps to Decatur to operate against Hood, while, with the remaining five corps of his army, he has moved to Atlanta, and is, in all probability, about to inaugurate an offensive campaign from that point."

Meanwhile, did national questions which looked beyond the restoration of the Union without slavery receive the attention they needed in the Presidential contest? Far from it. The war obliterated every other topic, and men on both sides skirted every controversial subject that risked votes. Wendell Phillips complained that even the pending Thirteenth Amendment received no attention; "it is avoided as a subject which, too freely handled, may endanger the election." The exigent social, economic, and legal issues plainly lying ahead were ignored.[14]

Reconstruction was too prickly a subject to be gripped. The President having declared his tentative policy, and Wade, Sumner, and Winter Davis having momentarily retreated from their defiance, most Republicans were content to let that tiger doze. War Democrats and Peace Democrats were also sharply divided on the advisability of imposing probationary tests upon the rebel States, and content to hold their tongues.

Bennett's *Herald*, ostensibly neutral between McClellan and Lincoln, supported the kind of straddle that appealed to every corner-grocery loafer with bellicose prejudices. Smash the Confederate armies completely; hold seats in both Houses ready for the return, no questions asked, of any Senators and Representatives whom the Southerners chose to elect; hold a friendly national convention later; demand that France instantly vacate Mexico, and Britain instantly foot the bill for her "piratical depredations"—these were Bennett's terms.[15] A Peace Democrat from Boston, Robert C. Winthrop, one of the old money-minded cotton Yankees, his long, bony bespectacled face owlishly shortsighted, had an even easier formula of evasion. Elect McClellan to arrange a peace with restoration of the Union the only object; drop not only all attacks on slavery but all tests for Reconstruction as well; pass a sponge over the secession folly, and swing the door wide for return of the South, its staples, and its markets—these were his dollar-hungry conditions. Should they treat the Southern sisters as subjugated provinces? "Are we deliberately bent on having an American Poland?"

14. Cooper Institute speech October 26, 1864, New York *Herald, Tribune, Times;* Bartlett, Irving H., *Wendell Phillips*, Boston, 1961, Ch. XV; *O.R.*I, xxxix, pt. 2, 48; pt. 3, 3, 162, 594.
15. New York *Herald*, October 25, 1864.

For making speeches of this tenor in Massachusetts, Connecticut, and New York, Winthrop was angrily assailed by various journals and hooted at the Harvard Commencement. Some wealthy Yankees like William Amory and William H. Gardiner, and rich New Yorkers like William B. Astor, James T. Brady, and James Gallatin, agreed in part with him, but not many. Such other important business and professional men as R. B. Roosevelt, Moses Taylor, Henry G. Stebbins, and the Stewarts and Wadsworths, calling themselves War Democrats or Jacksonian Democrats, stood for enduring safeguards of the Union. At a mass-meeting in Wall Street just before election, wealthy men like Moses H. Grinnell, Hiram Walbridge (head of the Produce Exchange), and even David Dudley Field, who was at last reconciled, spoke for Lincoln.[16] The rich were feeling the income tax, which this year rose to five-percent on incomes above $600. But of real discussion upon either Reconstruction in the South, or long-term fiscal measures in the North, little as yet emerged.

The fact was that the country could not debate Reconstruction intensively until it made perfectly certain of defeating the Confederacy; until it knew more about the Negroes, their masters, and economic prospects North and South; until the temper of the people and the new Thirty-ninth Congress was more clearly defined; and until certain Cabinet changes now being adumbrated took reality. The best time and place for debating Reconstruction were doubtful, but certainly the hustings in a heated Presidential campaign were the worst. Sensible men realized that McClellan had good reasons for omitting the platform demand for a national convention from his acceptance speech. They knew that Winthrop's notion of blotting out secession with a sponge of forgiveness was asinine. If they had any insight, they knew that the groping country could best trust to Lincoln's fluid, experimental approach to Reconstruction.

Nor was the issue of civil liberties discussed with proper vigor, although Democratic spokesmen gave it noisy partisan treatment. Lincoln had proclaimed on September 15, 1863, that the privileges of the writ of habeas corpus should be suspended throughout the United States in cases where persons were held under the authority of the government as spies, prisoners of war, aiders and abettors of the enemy, or as soldiers or deserters, or for offenses against the military service. This proclamation remained in effect during the remainder of the war. Under it, officers in various departments created military commissions from time to time to try persons who fell under government suspicion. They did not necessarily deal with specific offences or charges, and their purpose was not necessarily to judge and convict. The suspicions they explored might be vague. They might find it more important to amass evidence

16. New York *Herald*, October 28-Nov. 5, 1864; Boston *Advertiser*, September 21, 1864; New York *Times*, November 5, 1864; Winthrop, Robert C. Jr., *Memoir of Robert C. Winthrop*, Boston, 1897, 235-262.

by inquiry, and develop the outlines of a situation, than to prove anybody guilty of a crime. These commissions were quite different from courts martial, which tried military personnel alone, and only for specific offences under strict rules fixed by law and precedent.[17]

This sweeping proclamation, as we have said, was one of Lincoln's most unfortunate acts. Under it, numerous men were arrested and tried during 1864, in circumstances imperiling the basic civil liberties long held sacred in Anglo-American tradition and law. The editor of the Newark *Evening Journal* was prosecuted before a military commission for an article on the draft; the editor of the Bangor *Republican Journal* for a similar offense; the editor of the New York *Metropolitan Record* for advising resistance to conscription; and the editor of the Indianapolis *Daily Sentinel* for criticizing a Mid-Western military commission. Arbitrary arrests, according to the New York *Journal of Commerce*, became so numerous that a mere list would fill eighteen columns of the paper. No one will ever be able, probably, to come up with a narrowly accurate figure on the number of political arrests at the North or the total number of papers suppressed. Figures as to arrests range from 38,000 as a top to 13,535 which may be too low. Many of these persons were held for short terms. Perhaps a good estimate of the number of papers suppressed for any period is 300.

As the campaign drew to a close, many men were jailed on charges of cheating soldiers out of their votes, or making false returns of soldier votes. Kentucky witnessed particularly flagrant violations of civil liberties on the scantiest evidence, the lieutenant-governor and chief justice being imprisoned, and the former temporarily banished beyond Union lines. In Missouri, Congressman William A. Hall was arrested for his denunciation of the President.[18]

Although Lincoln's secretaries later defended his course vigorously, declaring that he took the greatest care to restrain officers from abusive acts,[19] he and his subordinates were repeatedly open to grave criticism. Attorney-General Bates said so emphatically. He remained in office, he wrote his friend James O. Broadhead in August, to perform a painful and almost hopeless duty. "When the nation wakes up from its present revolutionary delirium, and begins to remember that it once had principles and laws, I do not mean that it shall be truly said, that *all* of us were guilty of that disloyalty which consists in trampling down the law. I am resolved that the records of my office shall

17. See the able article, "Habeas Corpus," *American Annual Cyclopaedia*, 1864, 421ff.

18. All this is summarized in the *American Annual Cyclopaedia*, 1864, 422-423; Rhodes, James Ford, *History of the Civil War*, New York, 1917, IV, 230-232; Randall, James G., *Constitutional Problems under Lincoln*, Urbana, Ill., 1951, 152; Eaton, Clement, *A History of the Southern Confederacy*, New York, 1954, 231; Thomas, Benjamin P., and Harold Hyman, *Stanton, The Life and Times of Lincoln's Secretary-of-War*, New York, 1962, 375-377.

19. Nicolay and Hay, *Lincoln*, *op.cit.*, VIII, Chs. I and II.

bear testimony that at least *one* member of the government did sometimes resist capricious power and the arbitrary domination of armed forces." Lincoln, he continued, saw clearly the good of the nation. "O! that he could *act* as well as *see!*" His intentions were upright, but he "lacked the faculty to control—the will to punish the abuses of his power, which rampant and unrebuked, are rapidly bringing him and this good cause to sorrow and shame."[20]

Lincoln's own defense of his general course in the long, careful letter which he had sent to Erastus Corning and other agitated New Yorkers on June 12, 1863 (first reading it to the Cabinet), included his arguments for the constitutionality of his acts, his prediction that he might yet be censured for having made too few arrests instead of too many, and his agonized question, "Must I shoot a simple-minded soldier who deserts, while I must not touch a hair of a wiley [*sic*] agitator who induces him to desert?" This and other papers from his pen offered an able and earnest plea for his precautionary measures. The men who abused him for "executive usurpations" and called him "another Genghis Khan" deserved no attention.[21] With reason, he sometimes felt that he sat on a powder-barrel. Francis Lieber, for example, wrote Halleck in the spring of 1864 that it was the universal conviction of the best citizens of New York that new riots of the worst kind were certain if any military disaster occurred.[22] Two Ohioans warned Governor Dennison early that year: "Camp Dennison is surrounded with perhaps the most violent Butternut population in Southern Ohio, and in several localities it was, during the summer, unsafe for Union people to hold public meetings for the promulgation of loyal sentiments. This subtle disloyalty entered into camps and the hospital. . . ."[23] Honest officers of the law, and the President in particular, had to walk a razor's edge between rigorous severity and culpable laxity. With the nation's life at stake, they preferred to err on the side of safety.

Stanton in particular, who had been given military control of state prisoners, leaned to severity, for he regarded the judiciary as exasperatingly indifferent to his security measures. In 1863, asking Seward to urge the Federal district attorney in New York City to help enforce the law, he complained: "There never has been any assistance rendered by civil officers of the government in this war where they could get a tolerable pretext for withholding it."[24] We may suspect that Stanton had the least judicial mind in the Cabinet, and that he was

20. Bates to Broadhead, Aug. 13, 1864, Broadhead Papers, Missouri Hist. Soc.

21. Lincoln, *Collected Works,* VI, 260-269. These phrases are from the Hon. Levi Bishop's pamphlet, "Mission of the Democracy, An Address, Cincinnati, Feb. 4, 1864."

22. April 20, 1864, Lieber Papers, HEH.

23. J. C. Dunleavy and G.R. Sage, Lebanon, O., Jan. 21, 1864, Mason Brayman Papers, Chicago Hist. Soc.

24. Flower, Frank A., *Edwin McMasters Stanton,* Akron, Ohio, 1905, 135.

much too tardy in laying down explicit lines of policy. An overburdened man, ill-tempered and abrupt, he allowed confusion to envelop the subject. Excessive zeal by officers who based arrests on flimsy tale-bearing was sometimes followed by carelessness in getting cases scrutinized, and too much buck-passing when a final decision was sought. Thus when Dennis A. Mahony of the Dubuque *Herald* was jailed, the buck went from hand to hand until the fall elections of 1862 halted it and gave Mahony justice. Although Stanton eventually introduced more order into procedures and moderated their rigor, because of great and dangerous provocations some harshness persisted.[25]

It is not strange that the Cincinnati *Enquirer*, edited by a Peace Democrat, burst out during the summer of 1864 in fierce denunciation. How, it asked, can men celebrate Independence Day "with the habeas corpus suspended by fiat of the President—with our prisons and dungeons filled with men guilty of no offense except holding opinions different from the Administration—punished without trial and without law, simply because the President so willed it—the press existing only by sufferance of the government, and under a censorship as rigid as that of Austria or France—with elections carried by the bayonet, and the whole civil power prostrated at the foot of the military?" Nor is it strange that Edward Bates later lamented to Gideon Welles the subversion of ancient principles. "You and I were taught in our youth to respect and honor the Revolutionary fathers. . . . because they were brave, wise, and good enough to establish for themselves and for us a just Government of Law—a government—all of whose powers and duties are specified by law." The Constitution and laws, he concluded, must be obligatory upon all officials, civil and military.[26]

Many Americans, however ill-schooled in literature, science, and economics, were well versed in the principles of liberty and equality before the law that they had inherited from vigilant forebears. They could trace them back to the Bill of Rights penned by George Mason, the Petition of Right, and Magna Carta, and felt an instinctive reverence for every line of them. The embattled Democrats of 1864 neglected a plain opportunity in not making a more spirited appeal against infractions of these principles. Why didn't they? Because they would at once be placed in a defensive position. The troublesome Vallandigham, who had returned to Ohio in time to make speeches denouncing "King Lincoln," did far more harm to the Democratic Party than to the Union, but he was a standing menace to the Northern cause nonetheless.

The safety of the nation was the primary consideration to be kept in view.

25. Cf. the treatment of this subject in Nevins, *War Becomes Revolution, 1862-63*, New York, 1960, 309-318.

26. Bates to Welles, Oct. 23, 1866, Welles Papers, Claremont Graduate School.

During the summer of battle-thunder on the Georgia hills and of blood-soaked fields and trenches along the Rapidan, the James, and the Appomattox, while fresh cohorts of volunteers pressed forward to drill-grounds throughout the North, every patriot knew that the temporary humiliation, hardship, and suffering of a few thousand men suspected of sedition and disloyalty was a small price to pay for the assured preservation of the republic. A few traitors, left to perfect their plots, might cost tens of thousands of lives; they might endanger the future of tens of millions. The traitors were there. The question was, how numerous were they, and how effective were their operations. Brigadier-General Henry B. Carrington, a Yale-trained Abolitionist, spoke simple truth when he said of the Knights of the Golden Circle: "Their oaths are disloyal. They have used their influence to protect deserters. They have passed resolutions to defy United States law."[27] Carrington, whose management of a military commission was sharply criticized, and who was accused of making political capital, was upheld not only by Lincoln, but by public sentiment, and certainly deserved warm commendation for the protection he gave to Indiana citizens threatened with Copperhead incendiarism and violence.

[II]

During the summer and fall, reports and rumors of sinister conspiracies in the Middle West filled the air, becoming more alarming after the Democratic Party had adopted the Chicago platform, and more definite in character when various officers and members of the new Copperhead organization called "Sons of Liberty" were put on trial before a military commission in Indianapolis, set for September 22. The wide-spread despondency that seized the North in the summer months of defeat and deadlock seemed especially acute in the Great Valley, so long and closely tied to the South by the Mississippi River. Currency inflation, protective tariffs, rising railroad rates, and high farm-mortgage charges fed popular resentment over conscription, and fears of a suffocating influx of freedmen kept apprehensions of the future keyed high.

Panicky governors like Oliver P. Morton demanded troops to forestall armed outbreaks, Copperhead businessmen like Cyrus McCormick talked wildly of a union of the South and Northwest, and the nervously anxious Joseph Medill of the Chicago *Tribune* even told Congressman Elihu Washburne that the last desperate expedient might be to concentrate all Union armies to clear the Mississippi as a prelude to a ten-year armistice with the Confederacy! Fright and folly stalked abroad. Most people were above such

27. General Order No. 6, April 9, 1863, HQ District of Indiana.

panic—nevertheless, violent draft-resistance and deserter-protection remained endemic diseases in southern Indiana and Illinois. Copperhead zealots like Lambdin P. Milligan would gladly turn foxes with flaming tails (and skunks and weasels) into inflammable areas, and rebel agents lurked and schemed along the Canadian boundary. Plotters faced plotters, spies faced spies, and officers ready to hang traitors confronted fifth columnists ready to murder their opponents.[28]

It was a tangled, murky situation, full of darkness and prowling bogeys. The summer gloom of 1864 had shrouded dangerous subversives, scheming politicians, blundering Dogberries, rumor-mongers, lovers of disorder, conceited paranoiacs, sensational journalists and irresponsible crackpots as well as the mass of sincere patriots. It in fact affected all manner of men—from Dr. Samuel Bowles, chief of the Copperheads' Military Department of Indiana, laboring to drill his followers in minuteman tactics, to the patriotic General Carrington, who dispersed the "Sons of Liberty" in time to rejoin the army before Nashville.

The two centers of genuine peril were Chicago and lower Indiana. Lieutenant-Governor William Bross of Illinois later published a melodramatic and doubtless weirdly exaggerated story of the Camp Douglas plot.[29] Going east early in August to retrieve the body of a brother killed in the battle of the Crater, he had told Lincoln of the deep Western depression and its purplish hues of subversion. "Well," responded Lincoln sadly, "they want success and they haven't got it; but we are all doing the best we can. For my part, I shall stay right here and do my duty." Bross had learned of a newly hatched Copperhead conspiracy for liberating eight or nine thousand rebel prisoners in Camp Douglas, arming them, and seizing the city of Chicago. He learned also that the Copperheads had secreted ten thousand stand of arms downtown near the Tremont House. He and Colonel Benjamin Sweet, commander of Camp Douglas, a sharp, incisive young man, searched and found the arms. Colonel Sweet then placed his spies adroitly in various conclaves of the Knights of the Golden Circle or the Sons of Liberty, had every leading rebel who came from the South or Canada spotted and trailed, and took steps to cope with the uprising which, according to serpentinely devious rumors, they had arranged to coincide with the Democratic Convention.

On Saturday, August 26, the politicians began to arrive, and among them, according to Bross, milled numerous thugs and desperadoes. "As day after day

28. See the studies of disloyal activities in Milton, George Fort, *Abraham Lincoln and the Civil War*, New York, 1942; Gray, Wood, *The Hidden Civil War: The Story of the Copperheads*, New York, 1942; and Klement, Frank L., *The Copperheads in the Middle West*, Chicago, 1960.

29. Bross, William, pamphlet, "Biographical Sketch of the Late B.J. Sweet, and History of Camp Douglas," Chicago, 1878.

passed, the crowd increased till the whole city seemed alive with a motley crew of big-shouldered, blear-eyed, bottle-nosed, whisky-blotched vagabonds, the very excrescence and sweepings of slums and sinks of all the cities in the nation. I sat often at my window on Michigan Avenue, and saw the filthy stream of degraded humanity swagger along to the Wigwam on the lake shore, and wondered how the city could be saved from burning and plunder . . ."[30] Then on Monday morning the authorities heard that the danger was over. The New York leaders, Seymour, Dean Richmond, and Tilden, had arrived, taken counsel together, and put their feet down. They declared that if any riot or disorder took place, it would ruin the party—and the convention proved one of the most sedate in history. The humiliated conspirators left Chicago, their whole elaborate effort a pitiful debacle.

A new presumption of peril to the Union Government raised its dragon-head when a second conspiracy was formed to mature on election day. The plan this time was to release the Camp Douglas prisoners, seize the polls, stuff the ballot boxes, and then sack the city. Only about 800 Union troops guarded the 60-acre camp. Knights of the Golden Circle began to arrive from Fayette and Christian Counties, two Copperhead centers of Illinois. But when reckless men filtered in from Missouri and Kentucky, Southern sympathizers from Indiana, and Confederate officers from Canada, Colonel Sweet was ready. Two days before election he arrested Colonel G. St. Leger Grenfell, who had been adjutant to the Confederate raider John H. Morgan; Vincent Marmaduke, brother of General John S. Marmaduke; Captain George E. Cantrill of the Confederate Army; Charles Walsh of the Sons of Liberty, at whose house 349 revolvers, 189 shotguns, 30 carbines, powder, and cartridges were found, and others. Twenty-seven well-armed plotters were seized in one hotel, while others brought the total to a hundred. The conspiracy, which in great part reflected Confederate desperation, collapsed.[31] How much of this whole baleful story was a gin-bottle miasma, how much of it was an emanation of the Sunday Supplement sensationalism of the period, and how much of it had some slippery bases in fact, we shall never know. Probably little of the huge concocted fable can ever be substantiated, and that little inextricably mingled a few facts with a barrage of wild inventions. Plots and conspiracies may have had some transient political utility to various party irresponsibles, but in

30. *O.R.* I, xlv, pt. 1, 1077-1080. There are many conflicts in the several accounts, and what actually transpired is hard to pin down in details. For instance, Bross's and Sweet's accounts differ considerably from Ayer, Col. I. Winslow, *The Great Treason Plot in the North During the War*, Chicago, 1895. In this, Ayer gets most of the credit as "The Preserver of the City of Chicago." Among secondary accounts, Klement, *The Copperheads in the Middle West*, 199-202, deprecates the whole plot.

31. Gray, Wood, *op.cit.*, 206-222; Milton, *op.cit.*, Chs. XI-XV; Bross, *Sweet*, *op.cit.*, *passim*.

general they had never done the Confederacy, the Copperhead movements, or the valid Democratic organizations aught but harm. Some plotting of course did take place at the time, covert, clumsy, and ineffective; the so-called "Lake Erie Conspiracy", supposedly organized to seize "strategic points on or in the Erie", is one of the best-known instances.

Indiana, where the Indianapolis *Sentinel* cheered on the Copperheads, where the temperamental and voluble "Sycamore of the Wabash," Daniel Voorhees, preached peace at any price, and where the Sons of Liberty organized members in forty counties, had possessed seditious areas ever since Jesse D. Bright had been expelled from the Senate for disloyal activities. The vigilant Carrington, with headquarters in Indianapolis, found a resourceful aide in an energetic and imaginative young infantryman named Felix Grundy Stidger. It is probable that Stidger exaggerated his rôle and the strength of the Indiana Copperheads. Many of his recounted details are suspect. But he did organize an elaborately efficient system of espionage which soon put him in possession of seditious plans and secrets in Kentucky and Indiana, and undoubtedly he enlarged upon them in reports. Worming his way into the heart of the conspiracy, Stidger said he found the leading Knights communicating by two direct lines with Confederate leaders, experimenting with Greek fire and hand grenades, planning assassinations, and using Southern money channeled through Canada for a variety of violent purposes. The true facts probably will never be known.

Thanks largely to Stidger, Carrington soon laid the so-called Northwest Conspiracy in ruins, seized large caches of arms and piles of treasonable materials, and haled the leading plotters to trial before a military commission. Three of the accused, of whom the most notorious was Lambdin P. Milligan, a Copperhead who liked to talk about the "pecuniary vassalage" of the agrarian West to the industrial East, were found guilty and sentenced to be hanged, but appealed to the Federal Courts, and after the famous decision in *ex parte Milligan*, were released on the ground that military commissions were unconstitutional in peaceful districts. This was right and proper, but it cast no shadow upon the achievement of the four unsleeping watchers, Bross, Sweet, Carrington, and Stidger, who had brought the miscreants to bay.

In addition to the Chicago plot and activities in Indiana there was also the Lake Erie Conspiracy, perhaps the most sensational of all. The basic idea was for Confederate agents operating out of Canada to free prisoners at Johnson's Island in Lake Erie off Sandusky and at Camp Chase, Columbus, Ohio. To do this it would be necessary first to capture the Federal gunboat *Michigan* and then release the Johnson's Island prisoners. A train would be commandeered to go to Columbus for the prisoners there. Sandusky would be captured and the released prisoners would set up a Confederate army and department on the shores of Lake Erie. Main agents for this wild scheme were Charles H. Cole of Forrest's cavalry and Captain John Yates Beall of the Confederate Navy. Cole visited Sandusky, making plans and enlisting help, while Beall gathered men in groups at several Canadian ports. On September 19, Beall and his followers seized the steamer *Philo Parsons*, and also took possession of another vessel, the *Island Queen*, which they later scuttled. The *Philo Parsons* moved to a point near Johnson's Island and the U.S.S. *Michigan*. Cole, who had carefully ingratiated himself with the officers, was aboard the gunboat. During the evening, *Michigan* received word that Cole was a spy and he was arrested before he could give any signal to the *Philo Parsons*. Beall's crew, becoming apprehensive, mutinied and Beall had to steam away and destroy the vessel. Beall was later captured and hanged; but Cole was later pardoned.[32]

It was military men who blighted these budding conspiracies. Military commissions, however, contributed little to the work, and the conspirators might better have been haled before civil courts of law. The so-called Northwest Conspiracy had benefited neither the Confederacy nor the Peace Democrats, had injured McClellan's candidacy, and had ruined various circles of unknightly Knights. Republicans made good use of the conspiracies and rumors of conspiracies, exaggerating them considerably. The Democrats involved (as previously noted) would have done more for their party if they had spent time and energy in a reasoned indictment of the Administration infringements of civil liberties. The issue, however, like those presented by the tariff, inflation, inadequate taxes, and the excessive wartime profits of manufacturers, was fumbled. On this subject McClellan in particular exhibited what the diarist George Templeton Strong called "his uncommon faculty of brilliant silence."[33]

[III]

Much was heard, as election day approached, of the soldier's vote. Republicans had been hostile early in the war to the proposal that soldiers be allowed the ballot in national elections. The three leading Union generals at the opening of the war—McClellan, Halleck, and Buell—were Democrats, and McClellan achieved a remarkable popularity with the Eastern troops. In January, 1863, the Republican Congressional caucus decided against supporting soldier enfranchisement. Then, however, came the emergence of Grant, Sherman, Rosecrans, and Meade, who clearly supported Lincoln, while the President himself

32. See the report of Adj.-Gen. W.H.H. Terrell of Indiana (1869), in 1890 reissue, 288-393.
33. Strong, George Templeton, *A Diary of the Civil War*, ed. Allan Nevins, New York, 1962, 297.

gained an ever-larger place in the volunteers' hearts. By the beginning of 1864 the Republican leaders were exerting themselves to give fighters the ballot. The rising Republican Speaker of the New Hampshire House, William E. Chandler, indeed, published a pamphlet in which he not only claimed party credit for this, but accused the Democrats of selfish opposition.[34]

Some states had made provision before the war for the votes of soldiers absent on military duty. Others now made due arrangements, until eleven in all (out of twenty-five) allowed participation by the troops. The list did not include New York, where Horatio Seymour had vetoed a suffrage bill and impromptu alternative measures proved cumbrous and uncertain. Both parties devoted much time and effort to courtship of the soldiers. In this the Union Party gained a lead, for Secretary Stanton barred practically all Democratic campaign material from the camps until a month before the election. Moreover, Union men had the larger campaign funds, and the distributor of their campaign circulars, George T. Brown, showed special enterprise, boasting later that he had sent nearly a million documents to the troops.[35] Influential men of both parties visited all the larger camps, and badges for the candidates were sold at many sutlers' stores.

In Sheridan's command at Cedar Creek an old ambulance was outfitted as a polling place, and a thousand-ball cartridge box was set up as receptacle for the ballots.[36] Other arrangements were as crudely efficient. They were not always impartial. Brigadier-General Clinton B. Fisk in Missouri issued General Order No. 195, directing officers to see that "no rebel, traitor, bushwacker, or Southern sympathizer touches the sacred ark of our liberties," and the commander in the Hannibal district specially charged field officers to see that this order was in the hands of all officers at the polls when they opened. Theodore Lyman noted that in Meade's command Lieut.-Col. Martin T. McMahon, who had talked openly and strongly in favor of McClellan, was mustered out of the service in October without warning. "You would scarcely credit the number of such cases as this," he added.[37]

In October, eyes were turned upon the three States, Pennsylvania, Ohio, and Indiana, which held elections that month for State offices. In Pennsylvania the result was at first in doubt, but was eventually turned in favor of the Republicans by the soldier vote. This had been McClellan's home State. The

34. Chandler, William E., "The Soldier's Right to Vote," Washington, 1864.

35. Zornow, William F., "Lincoln Voters Among the Boys in Blue," *Lincoln Herald*, Vol. LIV, No. 3 (Fall issue, 1952).

36. Taylor, James E., Ms. Diary, "An Artist with Sheridan in the Shenandoah Campaign, 1864," Palmer Coll., Western Reserve Hist. Soc.

37. Fisk's order was dated St. Joseph, Nov. 5, 1864; copy in Broadhead Papers, Missouri Hist. Soc. Cf. Greeley, Horace, *American Conflict*, Hartford, 1867, II, 671; Lyman, Theodore, *Meade's Headquarters*, Boston, 1922, 247-248.

bounty system had painfully strained the resources of some counties, and the draft was unpopular among laboring folk; hence the narrowness of the majority. In Ohio and Indiana, however, the Republicans won sweeping victories, a portent of the November result. Ohio elected 17 Republicans and two Democrats to Congress in comparison to the old lineup of 14 Democrats and five Republicans. Pennsylvania was now 15 Republicans to nine Democrats, compared to the previous 12 and 12. Lincoln's role is shown by his message of September 19 to Sherman stating, "The State election of Indiana occurs on the 11th of October, and the loss of it to the friends of the Government would go far towards losing the whole Union cause. . . . Any thing you can safely do to let her soldiers, or any part of them, go home and vote at the State election, will be greatly in point. They need not remain for the Presidential election, but may return to you at once. This is, in no sense, an order, but is merely intended to impress you with the importance, to the army itself, of your doing all you safely can. . . ."

For various good reasons Lincoln remained apprehensive until the end. He vividly recalled the cold douche he and his party had received in 1862, when the Democrats had elected legislatures in Illinois, Indiana, and Pennsylvania, and a governor in New York. Next year, to be sure, Brough had defeated Vallandigham in Ohio, and Curtin had beaten Woodward in Pennsylvania. Still, few if any could see that these two States had then passed from a generation of Democratic ascendancy into a long generation of Republican dominance. Lincoln knew that many of his own party deeply resented his refusal to give effective enforcement to the Confiscation Act. If he opened a newspaper it was likely to be the New York *Herald*, and on October 26 he could read a *Herald* editorial declaring: "The imbecility of Old Abe, his mismanagement of the war and total incompetency exhibited at almost every stage of the present struggle, have alienated many whose sympathies are with the Republican Party." He knew that some officers in his own camp were as uncertain supporters as the double-tongued Speaker, Schuyler Colfax, who could be flatterer and obstructor at the same time, or the House overlord, Thaddeus Stevens, of imperious will.[38]

As campaign excitement mounted to a climax on November 7 and 8, a host of voters scurried home to cast their ballots. Many Pennsylvania regiments

38. Lincoln, *Works*, VIII, 11; or Ben Wade to Zach Chandler, October 2: "As for the election of Lincoln, I never had a doubt of our ability to reëlect him by an overwhelming majority. I only wish we could do as well for a better man. . . . Were it not for the country there would be a poetical justice in his being beaten by that stupid ass McClellan, whom he persisted in keeping in the service. . . . That stupid wilfulness cost this nation more than a hundred thousand men, as you well know, and when I think of these things, I can but wish the devil had Old Abe." Chandler Papers, LC.

were sent back on furlough, and New York troops, distrusting the machinery for casting their ballots by proxy, also got leaves. Hospitals and convalescent quarters in and about Washington discharged thousands more into the homeward-bound throng, and a swarm of civilians from government departments swelled the ranks. "The railroad is blocked up with trains going north," wrote Noah Brooks on the 7th, "and more than once during the past week there were not cars enough to make up the regular train for Baltimore." This stream angered the Democrats, who knew that a great majority of the men would vote for Lincoln. Since Indiana had no provision for letting soldiers vote in the field, the War Department specially favored the return of her troops. Schuyler Colfax had written Lincoln that the State might be lost unless whole regiments were sent back, and one Hoosier commented sarcastically upon the fearful "sickliness" of the men, crowds of whom flocked home on invalid leave. Charles A. Dana long afterward recalled how busy he was kept in the War Department responding to telegrams asking that soldiers on detached service be sent home.[39]

Everywhere, as the final returns showed, the soldiers stood ready to vote in overwhelming strength for Lincoln; everywhere except in Kentucky, where his stand on slavery was resented. In California and Iowa, the soldier vote was more than ten to one for Lincoln, and in Wisconsin, Vermont, Maine, Maryland, and Ohio nearly five to one; yet in not a single State was it the decisive factor in the result. Countless soldiers were of course too busy or preoccupied to vote.

Election Day was filled with anxiety and tension in the largest cities, especially in New York, where memories of riots mingled with warnings of coming incendiarism that Secretary Seward helped circulate. This incendiarism would become a reality on November 25-26, when eight men sent by Jacob Thompson, that egregiously unprincipled member of Buchanan's cabinet now plotting in Canada, made a futile effort to start blazes in the St. Nicholas, Fifth Avenue, Metropolitan, St. James, and Belmont Hotels, the Astor House, and four others; their mixtures of camphene and phosphorus smoldering feebly and going out while firebells clanged. Barnum's Museum had a fire and there were alarms in two theaters. But on November 8, fog and rain beset the long

39. Colfax to Lincoln, July 25, 1864, Nicolay Papers, LC; Dana, Charles A., *Recollections of the Civil War*, New York, 1898, Ch.XVIII. Democratic leaders in States like Illinois and Indiana, which did not permit voting in the field, sent agents to the South to see that convalescent soldiers in the hospitals were returned to the front lines; Republican agents meanwhile acted to get them invalided or furloughed home! Because the uproar interfered with military duty, Grant ordered all electioneers out of his army. In the West, Col. James T. Davidson of the 73d Illinois wrote that the politicians were manipulating surgeons, who in turn manipulated the soldiers—especially on Lincoln's side. "One lot passed through Nashville this morning of several hundred, and others are coming." Davidson to his wife, Oct. 27, Davidson Papers, Alabama State Archives.

lines that waited patiently in the streets to deposit their ballots. The grog-shops were tightly closed, and disorder was unknown, save for a little street-fight in one ward. Hardly a soldier could be seen, and the police kept a quiet mien. General Dix, commanding the department, had of course taken full precautions. The Hudson and the East River were lined with vessels full of troops which could be landed at any point if needed, and the armories held detachments armed with bayonets. August Belmont's vote was challenged on the ground that he had laid bets upon the election! When night fell people began thronging to the hotels and newspaper offices, still quiet and orderly.[40]

In Washington, only two members of Lincoln's official family attended the Cabinet meeting that dull, gloomy, rainy day. Stanton was sick abed with chills and fever, Seward, Usher, and Dennison were voting at home, and Fessenden was consulting with New York financiers, leaving Welles and Bates on duty. The President showed manifest anxiety. He had said before the session: "I am just enough of a politician to know that there was not much doubt about the result of the Baltimore Convention, but about this thing I am far from certain."

First returns came from Indianapolis at half-past six. Lincoln had made a gain of 1,500 votes in that city. At seven he went with a friend to the War Department to listen to telegrams, but it was nearly nine before he had definite news. Then Baltimore reported that he had a majority of more than 10,000, and Massachusetts a majority of 75,000. After a long interval New Jersey sent news of a Union gain of one Congressman. As the President was telling a story about this Congressman, a family friend, he was interrupted by a New York dispatch stating that he had carried the State by 10,000. He expressed doubt, and when Greeley presently reported that he should have a margin of 4,000, he accepted that as more reasonable. By midnight he was sure of Pennsylvania, the New England States, Ohio, Indiana, Michigan, Wisconsin, and Maryland, while it appeared he would also have Delaware, which he eventually lost in a close vote. He was especially concerned to hear from his own State, and was cheered about one o'clock by a New York dispatch stating that he had carried Illinois by 10,000. A bad storm then shut off further news from the West.[41]

Later intelligence from Missouri revealed that Lincoln had defeated McClellan there by more than two to one, that the Radical Union candidate for governor had triumphed, and that a great majority had approved a constitutional convention certain to decree the immediate abolition of slavery. Francis Lieber said he hoped the event would go down in history as the Great and Good Election of 1864. The President, happy that both Maryland and Missouri

40. The *London Illustrated News*, Dec. 3, 1864, has a good account.
41. Noah Brooks's letter, Nov. 11, 1864, in Sacramento *Union*.

were "secure to Liberty and Union for all the future," turned his thoughts to further steps in Reconstruction, which he would announce in his Annual Message the next month, and to plans for implementing the Constitutional amendment abolishing slavery. McClellan wrote his friend S.L.M. Barlow: "I suppose I must make up my mind now to shake the dust off my shoes and go elsewhere. So be it." He was soon in Italy. Horace Greeley packed into a letter of December to the elder Blair more wisdom than he had lately shown: "There is yet much work before us, and we are in great danger of being betrayed by divisions. I look to you, as the oldest in political experience of our men at Washington, to mediate and moderate and bring about a good understanding among all our true men. I am sure you realize that we cannot afford to have such true men as Sumner, Wade, and Julian alienated from the Administration, and yet there is danger of it if you do not interpose to calm the fury of faction."[42]

In a total vote counted of about 4,175,000 Lincoln's majority was in excess of 500,000. He had an electoral vote of 212 against 21 for McClellan, who had carried only Kentucky, New Jersey, and (rather narrowly) Delaware. Out of slightly more than 154,000 soldiers' votes Lincoln received 119,754. The Union Party victory was decisive. The two States of Louisiana and Tennessee, which had held elections deemed valid by the President but invalid by Congress, offered their votes when the electoral college met, but Vice-President Hamlin, who presided, declined to present them.[43]

[IV]

The election of 1864 was not so great and refreshing but that it left the country many lessons to ponder, and some to take deeply to heart. It was perfectly true that, as Lincoln told his serenaders on the day his confirmation in office was announced, the people of the North had proved the strength of democracy by holding a free election, with an untrammeled discussion of a still new party's principles, in the midst of a terrible civil conflict.[44] They had demonstrated that a people's government could sustain and renew itself; had

42. McClellan, Nov. 18, 1864, in Barlow Papers, HEH; Horace Greeley in Blair-Lee Papers, Princeton Univ. According to Thomas D. Drake of Missouri, the magnitude of the victory of Lincoln and the Radical element in that State could be ascribed to Rosecrans's Order No.135 for using troops at the polls "to prevent illegal voting." Gates wrote this order and Rosecrans issued it after Gates had written Lincoln an urgent letter on the necessity of the step, and Nicolay had paid a special visit to Rosecrans. What Gates called "military interposition" thus helped assure the immediate eradication of slavery in Missouri—and eleven electoral votes for Lincoln. Gates, Ms. Autobiography, Ch. XXXVII, Missouri State Hist. Soc.

43. Stanwood, Edward, *A History of the Presidency*, Boston, 1912, I, 307-312.

44. Lincoln, *Collected Works*, VIII, 100-102, Nov. 10, 1864.

shown how sound and how strong they were; and had found that they possessed more men—"living, brave, patriotic men"—than when the war began. The orderliness with which a decisive verdict had been rendered did much to prove to the world, as Lincoln said in his December message this year, a quiet firmness of purpose that was highly creditable to the much-suffering people.

Some considerations far less happy, however, had to be weighed. The Republican hesitations early in the year, the willingness of many governors, senators, and editors to cast Lincoln aside and seek another candidate, and the tentative approaches to Grant and Rosecrans, showed how fortunate the country was that no military hero had gained wide popular acclaim by the summer of 1864. A victorious general of strong political ambitions could have unseated the President. The vacillations of many of the Republican as well as Democratic chieftains proved that the political leaders of the North were much too erratically responsive to the tides of victory and defeat. Had the record of bloody repulse and lost battles continued into the autumn, McClellan might have won after all, while Union resolution might have grown flabby and uncertain. The defeatism rife in New York, Philadelphia, parts of the Middle West, and the Borderland was the spirit of the Hartford Convention, not Valley Forge. It seemed to contrast shamefully with the devotion of soldiers who at Gettysburg and Cold Harbor exulted in giving an eye, a leg, or life itself for their cause.

We do not know how widespread that spirit was, for not even the crudest modes of appraising public opinion existed. We can only trust that it was not really pervasive; that the politicians and editors had underrated the courage and tenacity of the plain folk of the land. We can only trust that Greeley may have been right when he had exhorted Lincoln, much earlier, to "lean upon the mighty heart of the people," and that the correspondent of the London *Daily News* may have been correct when he wrote in September that great as was the credit he had given to Northern fortitude, he believed that he had underestimated it.

"I have always scouted the idea," this correspondent wrote, "that there was any large class of people at the North, outside the scum of the towns, who were prepared to make any peace with the South which would divide the United States into two nations; but I have always acknowledged that I see limits to this devotion. Today I do not think I can see any. I am astonished the more I see and hear of the extent and depth of the determination which seems to pervade the farmers to fight to the last. . . . The men may be infatuated, but they are in earnest in a way the like of which the world never saw before, silently, calmly, but desperately in earnest; and they will fight on, in my opinion, as long as they have men, muskets, powder, and corn and wool, and would fight on, though the grass were growing in Wall Street, and there was not a gold dollar on this side of the Atlantic."[45]

Henry Winter Davis commented in his usual serpentine way on the reelection of Lincoln—"that the people now know Lincoln and voted for him to keep out worse people—keeping their hands on the pit of the stomach the while! No act of wise self-control—no such subordination of disgust to the necessities of a crisis and the dictates of cool judgment has ever before been exhibited by any people in history. . . ."

Confederate comments varied from disgust to the belief that Lincoln's election would strengthen the Southern will to resist. The Richmond *Sentinel* stated: "It is the official declaration of a great people, that they will not only have war against us, but war in its most barbarous and malignant form. . . . We say it is sad that the evil design entertained against us should be marked by such deliberate depravity in the attempted execution. But perhaps this, also, is for good. It deepens and widens the gulf between us, and renders our success more certain by rendering failure more dreadful and intolerable. . . ." The Richmond *Dispatch*, just before the election: "Give us Lincoln with his brutalities—those inhuman measures and persecutions which have united our people, given vigor to our resistance, and must finally establish our independence. . . ." After the election, the *Dispatch* stated that the victory of Lincoln had done away with any hesitation. "Had McClellan been elected, our danger would have been much greater than it is likely to be under the rule of Lincoln. . . ." Various observers agreed that the election was a confirmation that the war would go on until the subjugation of the Confederacy.[46]

The time came when people would recall with shame the responsiveness of so many of the strong men of the republic, even Charles Sumner and William Cullen Bryant, to the call for arranging a new convention and the selection of a new candidate; when Chase's bid for power would seem pitiably eccentric and unrealistic; when Henry J. Raymond would blush to remember that he had told Lincoln his reëlection was impossible, and had thus stung Lincoln into writing a secret memorandum on the course to be pursued after his defeat. The time came when the distrust and dissension so rife in the Cabinet during the summer of 1864 would seem a bad dream, and the utterances of Winter Davis as foully malign as those of Vallandigham. These unhappy episodes of a deeply troubled time could not be forgotten. They would

45. London *Daily News*, Sept. 27, 1864; a paper as admirable as the *Times* was wretched.

46. Henry Winter Davis-S.F. DuPont Letters, Eleutherian Mills-Hagley Foundation, Nov. 1864, no date, but after election; Richmond *Sentinel*, Nov. 12, 1864; Richmond *Dispatch*, Nov. 7 and Nov. 10, 1864; Kean, *Inside the Confederate Government*, *op.cit.*, 177; Jones, *Rebel War Clerk's Diary*, Philadelphia, 1866, 448; Gorgas, Josiah, *The Civil War Diary of General Josiah Gorgas*, ed. Frank Vandiver, University, Ala., 1947, 150.

have to be pondered even when final victory helped people to conclude, with that acute observer from England whom we have previously quoted, that the fighters and toilers of the North were in earnest in a way which the world had never seen before, and would battle on to the last cartridge and last drop of blood to save the Union of their fathers, and to save it purged of the foul blot of slavery.

6

Sherman's March to the Sea: The Disruption of the South

DURING THE second half of 1863, the Union forces had for the first time definitely seized a winning strategic position in the war. In great part, the way had been opened for a final advance against Southern forces by the capture of Vicksburg, and the stunning checkmate administered to Lee's bold Confederate invaders at Gettysburg. The tenacity with which the Union army under Banks maintained the bloody struggle (after Vicksburg's surrender) to capture Port Hudson was also of cardinal importance, although disappointing use was made of that capture. Grant would have preferred to turn the entire army against Mobile just after the fall of Port Hudson, thus completing the clearance of the Mississippi. Banks also favored this movement, but Halleck once more made the inept blunder of dispersing the Union armaments which might have been kept concentrated for use against an important objective. Then, too, Lincoln was filled with such lurking suspicions of Napoleon III that he desired a stronger grip upon Texas; and to the dismay of Grant, who saw that Union sea-power at Brownsville would adequately protect Texas from the French, the newly-released Union strength was squandered without permanent result. Happily for the North, however, the Confederates also made mistakes, so that at Chattanooga (as we have seen) Rosecrans was able for a time to out-general Bragg, who had equal or even superior forces. The spectacular Union victories at Lookout Mountain and Missionary Ridge that followed freed Grant and Sherman to move forward upon Atlanta, Dalton, and other industrial towns of Georgia. The North had suffered a humiliating defeat at Chickamauga, but it had placed its armies in a situation where they could sweep into the heart of the South, and if they took bold decisions, even farther still.

The achievement of a decisive strategic advantage by the North was attributable also in part to non-territorial gains—to progress unconnected with the full control of the Mississippi, the Gulf Coast, the vital rail center of Chattanooga, and the mountains looking down on central Tennessee, the

Tennessee River, North Alabama and North Georgia. These great and important advantages were now safe. But the Union had achieved advances of equal importance in the experience and skill of its generals, in the recruiting and organization of its armies, and in the contributions of invention, technology, and growing industrial resourcefulness to the power of its now seasoned and determined ranks of fighting men.

Lincoln's proclamation calling out a half-million more men (the draft to take place on March 10) had been a measure of obvious necessity; and it was one of the vital facts of the war that Washington by late 1863 had comprehended this necessity.

"To secure the permanence of our conquests in Tennessee," declared *The Army and Navy Journal* on February 5, 1864, "our army under General Grant should be doubled." The heavy losses in the Wilderness, at Spotsylvania, Cold Harbor, and before Petersburg, emphasized the need thus stated for more recruits. The country had the men—and difficult though it was to enforce the vague, loosely-worded draft law of 1863; distressing as were the endless instances of fraud, bribery, and evasion; costly as was the gigantic bounty system erected by national, State, and local governments to cajole civilians into uniform; and undemocratic as was the substitute system,[1]—the men steadily if unevenly, and not altogether reluctantly, moved into the armies. Conscription stimulated volunteering. Provost-Marshal General James Barnet Fry, a brave field officer and an efficient administrator, served ably as director of the drafts. Struggling against political pressures, the incompetence or dishonesty of his subordinates, and the shifting winds of public sentiment, this Illinoisan product of West Point training, despite inevitable errors, carried through an admirable piece of work for his country. He also helped arrest and return to their commands many thousands of deserters and other absentees.[2]

The draft riots in New York, the scandals of the substitute-brokerage system, and the crimes of the bounty-jumpers stained the shield of the nation in a way that could never be erased. But Fry's courageous activities helped fill the depleted ranks, and kept on filling them. The draft of 1863 had furnished 35,850 men; the draft calls of February and March, 1864, furnished 12,321; and that of July, 1864, yielded 37,577.[3] The early drafted men, with very few exceptions, were sent to existing regiments as replacements for lost manpower, and thus the draft law became immediately beneficial.[4] But conscription did not provide enough men by far—it did not come anywhere near maintenance of

1. Murdock, Eugene C., *Patriotism Limited, 1862-1865,* Ms., Ohio Hist. Soc., 1-172.
2. Williams, Kenneth P., *Lincoln Finds a General,* New York, 1959, II, 557. states that more than 76,325 were returned.
3. *O.R.*, III, iv, 927, 928; v, 486-487.
4. Lerwill, Leonard L., *The Personnel Replacement System in the United States Army,* 97.

existing units at effective strength. In consequence, volunteering furnished most of the replacements in the two last years of the war.[5] The War Department followed faulty policies of placement. It could have insisted that the State governments assign all volunteers, as they enlisted, to regiments then in being. Instead, it gave governors permission to raise new regiments—fifteen at first in Pennsylvania, and then others until forty in all had been authorized—regiments largely of green troops, often ill-officered. Happily, however, the veteran regiments themselves prosecuted effective recruiting activities, not only by sending agents back to home areas, but by inviting loyal men in such occupied districts as East Tennessee and Western North Carolina, to join.[6]

Meanwhile, the effectiveness of the troops was enhanced by closer attention to drill and instruction. The institution of training camps can be traced back to a camp that was ordered established at Annapolis in June, 1862, under General John E. Wool, who had learned military skill in Taylor's campaigns against Mexico, and exhibited his shrewdness and celerity at Buena Vista. General Wool was given facilities for fifty thousand men or more.[7] The pressing need for elementary instruction was emphasized in Charles S. Wainwright's fascinating *Diary of Battle.*[8] To pitch shelter tents; to march steadily under the burden of heavy knapsacks, blankets, and accoutrements; to make meals of fat pork, molasses, and cornmeal, and to keep watch vigilantly—all required training and experience. The high command, however, found it more convenient to send new recruits, along with drafted men and substitutes, directly to regiments in the field, expecting that they would master the craft and bearing of the soldier most effectively in simple association with veteran troops and experienced officers. As General Thomas wrote, "Recruits added to old regiments are at once under the hand of discipline, learning how to take care of themselves, and by mingling with their comrades who have seen service, readily learn their duties, and in a short time become almost as efficient and reliable as the old troops."[9]

The main failures of the Union armies in 1862 had arisen from deficiencies of leadership in Washington and also in the field, the quality of the brains, character, experience, and training of commissioned officers and non-coms being lower in the Union armies than the Confederate, and too low for a conflict so unexpectedly fierce and trying. Many of the failures in 1863 had resulted from want of adequate numbers, organization, and discipline.

5. Lerwill, *Ibid.*, 97.
6. Lerwill, *Ibid.*, 99, 100.
7. *O.R.*, III, ii. 108.
8. *A Diary of Battle: The Personal Journals of Col. Charles S. Wainwright, 1861-1865*, ed. Allan Nevins, New York, 1962, viiff.
9. *O.R.*, I, xlv, pt. 2, 344-345, quoted in Lerwill, *op.cit.*, 102.

The system of regimental recruiting instituted in the summer of 1863—that is, the dispatch of details from existing regiments to bring back from home communities as many veterans as possible—was continued during the winter of 1863-64 with enhanced effectiveness.[10] Distribution of troops according to Army needs was also improved by the creation of well-managed depôt camps or pools for recruits of all kinds. Thus, in the latter part of 1864, young Middle-Westerners who were wanted in the Department of the Gulf or in one of Sherman's armies were collected at Cairo, to be sent by steamboat down the Mississippi or up the Tennessee. Those marked for the Army of the Mississippi were likely to arrive at a training camp established at Nashville. Large contingents, however, were sent to the Army of the Ohio, and the Army of the Tennessee.[11]

In short, the Federal government had at last taken measures for enlisting, organizing, distributing, and training troops which met the urgent necessities of the military situation. Armies that were too small, armies constantly reduced by battle casualties, sickness, and (most deplorably of all) by desertions and absences without leave, were now being built to formidable strength. More and more commands were being "veteranized" by the recall of experienced soldiers, subalterns and officers to serve alongside raw volunteers, drafted men, and substitutes. An army of accomplished and tenacious fighters was coming into being, an army ready for any hardship, any ordeal of fire and steel, any sacrifice. The importance of able, careful, efficient officers to good training and effective fighting is noted in many regimental histories. Captain Thomas H. Parker, for example, tells how Major Edwin Schall trained his men under the scorching Carolina sun until they were able to make a hot dusty march of forty-two miles and fight a long battle under murderous grape, canister and musket fire at Currituck Court House until victorious. Later, Schall (now a Colonel) and many of his men were killed charging dauntlessly at Cold Harbor.[12]

Could a supreme Western commander be found, as Lincoln thought he had at last found one in Grant for the East, of high skill, relentless determination, endless patience and courage, and deep resourcefulness—one worthy of the new legions, better armed, better organized, better officered—one who would not fail the national government and his armies of brave men as John Pope had failed at Second Manassas, who would not be found lacking in vigilance at a critical moment as even Grant had lacked vigilance at Shiloh, and who would not hesitate in the pursuit of an undoubted advantage as Meade had hesitated

10. Lerwill, *op.cit.*, 104.
11. *O.R.*, I, xxxiii, pt. 3, 488ff., cited in Lerwill, *op.cit.*, 105.
12. Parker, Thomas H., *51st Pennsylvania Volunteers*, Philadelphia, 1869, 542-569.

after Gettysburg? This was a critical question asked by every high official in Washington, every corps commander in his camp, and every plain citizen sitting distressed and worried beside his fireside.

Nobody knew the answer. It was encouraging, however, to read the thoughtful encomium upon William Tecumseh Sherman that William Conant Church, founder and editor of the *Army and Navy Journal*, penned at this moment—September 10, 1864—under the title "Atlanta Ours." He wrote that a leader of remarkable ability and strategic skill had suddenly emerged.

"The progress and result of the Georgia campaign, in our judgment, stamp Sherman as a thorough soldier . . . That his plan at the outset was good, success, the final criterion, has demonstrated. His combinations have been sound, and he has been fertile in expedients. The country he traversed was unfriendly to military manoeuvres. Arduous and abrupt mountains, hazardous ravines and ridges, were constantly interposed across the path of the army into central Georgia. His march, nevertheless, had been steady, without a single retrograde. Sherman has fought his campaign, in some respects unlike any of his others, displaying more maturity, greater power, skill learned from experience, observation, and history, and no little coolness, method, and deliberation. Heretofore promptness, rapidity, and brilliancy were the chief qualities the majority of the American people saw in him. Now he has exhibited caution, sound judgment, and pertinacity." In one assault, Kenesaw Mountain, Church added, Sherman had revealed his impetuosity, but he had then turned to flanking.

One very noticeable trait in the campaign was the skill with which Sherman's line of communications had been protected. This long line was not a little precarious, and more than once aroused the anxiety of the nation.

"His base was, in one sense, not at Chattanooga, but at Nashville, with the former railway center as the secondary base. The rebels did their best not only to break the line Atlanta-Ringgold, but to raid the road from Chattanooga back to Nashville. From Atlanta to Nashville the railroad is 145 miles long, from Chattanooga to Nashville only a little less. With this line of 250 miles stretched across the great Allegheny chain from flank to flank, in a disputed country filled with guerrillas and hostile inhabitants, with nooks and eyries in the mountainous region apt for the assemblage and protection of marauding bands, with that attenuated line infested by many squadrons of the best cavalry in the Confederacy, long accustomed to be victorious everywhere, under such bold and skilful leaders as Morgan, Forrest, Wheeler, Stephen Lee, and James Chalmers. In spite of all, Sherman has been able to keep his line strong and clear."[13]

13. *Army and Navy Journal*, "Atlanta Ours", Sept. 10, 1864.

But Sherman did not stand alone. Around him in the West stood other Union generals of elevated intellectual and moral qualities, a band who recalled, if not Napoleon's resplendent marshals, at least the type of keen and steadfast officers who were assembled about Wellington in the Peninsular and Belgian campaigns.[14]

[I]

To understand the memorable march that Sherman, as the foremost Union leader in the West, was now about to begin from Atlanta across the State of Georgia to Savannah—from the rugged Appalachians to the heaving Atlantic—readers should keep in mind a number of basic facts.

We start with the fact that he was attempting not a raid, but a much more important strategic movement—a new bisection of the Confederacy, supplementing the north-south bisection on the line of the Mississippi, and involving an eventual exchange of his inland base for a more secure base on the ocean, commanded and supplied by Northern sea-power. His object was not primarily the capture of a great city, although he did capture several; it was not primarily the destruction of a powerful army, though his campaign did encompass such a destruction. It was the disruption of the Confederacy by a great march, leaving ruined farms, shattered factories, and uptorn and severed railroads and highways behind it. It was a demonstration of the validity of a belief increasingly held by Northern war-leaders, that the South was to a great extent an empty shell, which could be seized and broken by bold Federal strokes.

A second important fact is that he commanded not a single relatively compact army, like that which Grant had thrust down and across the Mississippi, or like Meade's Army of the Potomac, but a great loosely composite force, really three or four armies linked together, under as many comradely leaders, for the North now had that many able and experienced commanders.

Three or four armies? The list is readily summarized.

On succeeding Grant as prime military commander in the West, Sherman had combined the Eleventh and Twelfth Corps to form a new Twentieth Corps. This was under the athletic, red-faced, rather seedily handsome Joseph Hooker, who bore (along with his wounds from Antietam, and his letter of thanks from Congress for his defense of the capital) a sense of humiliation for

14. Sherman tells us that in Thomas, McPherson, and Schofield he had three officers of education and experience, admirably qualified for the work before them. Each, he adds, possessed special qualities of mind and character which fitted him in the highest degree for his tasks. *Memoirs*, II, 15ff.

his share in several costly defeats and for bad conduct that had drawn from Lincoln early in 1863 such a letter of mingled kindliness and severity as Lincoln seldom penned. History would long remember Lincoln's reproach of overcautiousness,[15] yet thousands still admired Hooker. Sherman had also arranged for the respected Oliver Otis Howard, who had lost an arm at Fair Oaks but continued to serve with gallantry through subsequent campaigns, to command the Fourth Corps. Grant, in addition, had seen to the formation of a new cavalry corps.

Under Sherman now stood likewise the Army of the Cumberland, led by George H. Thomas, the Virginia-born patriot who had fought well at Mill Springs in the dawn of 1862, and in Buell's advance across difficult country to Pittsburgh Landing. Thomas had been made a major-general in the spring of 1862 over forty-two of the fifty-five brigadiers senior to him, had fought ably at Murfreesboro, and had especially distinguished himself at Chickamauga where he had held the battle-line with an immovable corps while less steely troops were routed. He had then risen to command the Army of the Cumberland, with its recent infusion of veteran fighters from Potomac ranks, and had been in general charge of Union forces when they pinned the glory of Lookout Mountain and Missionary Ridge to their banners. Thomas had conspicuously displayed his qualities of poise, coolness, and imperturbable tenacity, which Grant came in time (though some thought tardily) to appreciate. Some observers thought that Grant might have given Thomas the Western command that he assigned to Sherman.[16]

Beside these contingents, Sherman numbered among his forces the Army of the Tennessee with its brilliant but ill-fated leader James B. McPherson, a clean-cut West Pointer who had aided Grant in the Tennessee campaign of 1862, playing a sturdy part in the operations that raised the national colors over Vicksburg. In the spring of 1864 McPherson would take energetic charge of the Army of the Tennessee, which included one able Illinoisan, John A. Logan, a histrionic figure with flowing hair and bellowing voice, who remembered standing with Lincoln to hear Douglas address a Chicago crowd. Defying the Copperhead elements in southern Illinois, Logan had helped rally that region to support the North. He had played a determined part in taking Donelson, and later had distinguished himself in the fighting before Atlanta.

Finally, Sherman's officers included John M. Schofield of the Army of the Ohio, another West Pointer who, after long and difficult service in Missouri, had become a corps commander early in 1864, just in time to take part in

15. *O.R.*, I, xix, pt. 1, 13.

16. Livermore, Col. Thomas L., *Sketches of Some of the Federal and Confederate Commanders*, Boston, 1895, 238-243, does not agree on this.

Sherman's victorious Atlanta campaign. He was a more mature officer than McPherson, though only thirty-three years old in the summer of 1864. Sherman, born in 1820, was much his senior—"old Uncle Billy," who had not reached his forty-fifth birthday!

"What a a galaxy of commanders!" men later said.[17]

Another cardinal fact to be remembered in following Western movements is that the rough, ill-roaded terrain of Sherman's operations played a dominant role in affairs, laying down stern topographical laws that he had to obey. South of Chattanooga, the Allegheny range ran in a great diagonal roughly NNE and SSW, throwing out lower ranges eastwardly, ending in an expanse of chaotically broken country.

It is equally important to remember that the railroads were an essential factor in Sherman's activities—in this first great railroad war of world history. He was tied to them, their iron bands vital to his operations. If he ever attempted to make any point north of central Ohio his base, he would leave the vital State of Tennessee uncovered and open to a rebel thrust. Thomas's protective Army of the Cumberland had its natural base on the Ohio, just as Schofield's Army of the Ohio found its natural base in Cincinnati.

This being so, the most important railroad of the area to Sherman and Thomas was the Louisville & Nashville, running down from the Ohio River to the capital and central city of Tennessee, 135 to 140 miles from Chattanooga. Sherman, with the support of James Guthrie, the loyal president of the L & N, had boldly taken control of the railroads of the area himself in April, 1864, and had soon brought together enough rolling stock to carry his campaign against Johnston to the gates of Atlanta. Within a short time (as previously noted), the Union forces had equipment from almost every line north of the Ohio, and were amused to see far down in Georgia cars marked "Pittsburgh & Fort Wayne," "Delaware & Lackawanna," or "Baltimore & Ohio." "I have always felt grateful to Mr. Guthrie," Sherman wrote, "who had sense enough and patriotism enough to subordinate the interests of his railroad company to the cause of his country."[18] The usefulness of railroads in the war (and far greater use was being made of them than ever before in any conflict) was just being grasped by American and foreign observers. They drew their value from the great distances of the shaggy, unkempt continent, the slovenly marking of the highways and byways, and the rapidity with which rain and summer dust made roads a horror to man and beast. They could be quickly destroyed, as Sherman had demonstrated, but even more quickly repaired if needed materials were at hand. A single railroad in good order, with sidings, rolling stock,

17. Sherman, *Memoirs*, II, 15.
18. *Ibid.*, II, 11, 12.

and junctions, was sufficient for the ordinary supply of an army in the field. Sherman, assuming the strength of the army with which he moved from Chattanooga into Georgia to be a hundred thousand men, with 35,000 animals for cavalry and transport to be fed, while beef cattle were driven on the hoof, had calculated his resources shrewdly. He had decided that even a daily movement of 130 cars of ten tons each into Chattanooga would not meet the army's needs unless he dispensed with a normal amount of hay, oats, and corn for his horses and mules, but that he could do this by feeding his livestock in large part from growing crops.[19]

A British observer, Captain H.W. Tyler of the Royal Engineers, laid down shrewd military rules based on his American observations.[20] He declared that railroads built for strategic purposes and intended for troop conveyance should be given a double row of rails. Every soldier should be trained both to destroy and repair railroads; the officers must remember that railroads were of much greater advantage in defensive than offensive warfare. A commander should in no instance rely upon a railroad for communication in a hostile country, and should not rely too much upon a long railroad, subject to enemy attack, in any country. He praised Sherman for the fact that the establishment of depots of supplies in his immediate rear was part of his plan for any forward movement, thus making himself in large degree independent of communications.

The grand disruptive movement began, inevitably from Atlanta. But first, Sherman had to deal with the Confederate commander and forces there.

[II]

The battle of Atlanta had been fought on July 22, 1864, with General Hood, who had succeeded Johnston by order of Jefferson Davis, observing it from the Confederate entrenchments.

As the Union army approached Atlanta, Sherman had placed the troops of Thomas on the right, moving southward toward it, while McPherson's command on the left drove against the city from the east. Schofield's command was in the center, approaching from the northeast. Sherman, McPherson, and Schofield had talked together on the climactic morning about the prospects of a battle—both McPherson and Schofield having been in the same class with Hood at West Point, their class also including Sheridan. They had agreed that they should be prepared for sharp Confederate thrusts from the defensive lines about Atlanta, for Hood was by temperament a bold, aggressive leader, and

19. Sherman, *Memoirs*, II, 23.
20. *Army & Navy Journal*, June 11, 1864.

everybody knew that he had been given his command because the Confederate government was out of patience with Johnston's caution and his repeated Fabian retreats.[21] It was true that Hood had given orders for an attack, which opened about noon on July 22nd, falling upon the left wing of the Union advance. At this point, McPherson, riding intrepidly along his lines without escort, was shot dead, a heavy loss to the Army and the nation. The battle developed so fiercely that Sherman himself felt it necessary to visit his endangered left wing, but his guidance and a timely use of part of Schofield's artillery retrieved the position, and the battle of Atlanta turned decisively against the South.[22] The skillful maneuvering of Sherman was the principal factor in this Union victory, but Hood later attempted to throw the blame upon his subordinates Cheatham and Hardee. In his book, *Advance and Retreat,* he placed his finger upon what he wished identified as the fatal moment in the battle.

> A considerable time had elapsed when I discovered, to my astonishment and bitter disappointment, a line of battle composed of one of Hardee's divisions advancing directly against the entrenched flank of the enemy. I at once perceived that Hardee had not only failed to turn McPherson's left, according to positive orders, but had thrown his men against the enemy's breastworks, thereby occasioning unnecessary loss to us, and rendering doubtful the great result desired. In lieu of completely turning the Federal left, and taking the entrenched line of the enemy in reverse, he attacked the retiring wing of their flank . . . I then began to fear that his disregard of the rule in war that one danger in rear is more to be feared than ten in front—in other words that one thousand men in rear are equal to ten thousand in front—would cause us much embarrassment and place his corps at a great disadvantage.[23]

Immediately thereafter, Sherman executed one of the masterly strokes which gave justification to the high praise by Church in the *Army and Navy Journal.* He struck the railroad above Jonesboro and was thus able to interpose his forces between Hardee and Atlanta, placing the Union army between two main parts of a divided rebel army. It was necessary for the Confederates to give up both Jonesboro and Atlanta. Hardee retired in confusion. Early next day, Hood, destroying his munitions and stores, fled from Atlanta which Sherman at once entered.

The effect of this achievement upon the Northern people was tremendous. Lincoln had ardently desired Sherman's success, for he knew well that it would decisively affect the Presidential election, then hanging in the balance.

But Sherman himself was by no means completely satisfied. He had not

21. Sherman, *Memoirs* (old edition), II, 74, 75.
22. Hoehling, A.A., *Last Train from Atlanta,* New York, 1958, 125-145.
23. Hood, *Advance and Retreat,* New Orleans, 1880, 179ff.

accomplished all he desired, for Hood's army, his principal objective, had eluded him.

In moving from Chattanooga to Atlanta he had expertly directed one of the great campaigns of the war. His loss, to be sure, had been about 30,000 men; but the Confederates had lost about 40,000. Hood as always had his excuses. The fault was Joseph E. Johnston's. "My failure on the 20th and 22nd to bring about a general battle," he wrote later, "arose from the unfortunate policy pursued from Dalton to Atlanta, and which had wrought such demoralization amid rank and file as to render the men unreliable in battle."[24]

On September 21, Hood shifted his forces from Lovejoy's Station on the Macon Railroad, to the West Point road at Palmetto Station, seemingly toward the Alabama line. Here he made systematic preparations for an aggressive campaign against Sherman's communications, hoping that he might thus compel the Union leader to abandon Atlanta. Here, too, at Palmetto Station, President Jefferson Davis paid Hood another visit, in the course of which he delivered a speech, assuring the Confederate army and the Southern people that their troops would soon compel Sherman's army to begin a retreat from Georgia which would prove more disastrous to them than Napoleon's retreat from Moscow had proved to the French armies. This gave Sherman the information he needed, and spurred him to take vigorous action. "Forewarned," wrote Sherman later, "I took immediate measures to thwart his plans. One division was sent back to Rome, another to Chattanooga, and the guards along our railroad were reinforced and warned of the coming blow. General Thomas was sent back to the headquarters of his department at Nashville, Schofield to his at Knoxville, and I remained in Atlanta to await Hood's initiative. This followed soon."[25]

Hood had the cooperation of the indomitable and enterprising cavalry leader, Forrest, who began playing havoc with the Union forces and lines in West Tennessee, raiding all the way from the Mississippi border north to Kentucky. Both the Davis Administration and public sentiment in the South brought the heaviest pressure to bear upon Hood, to see that all his available forces took determined offensive action early in September, Davis had written Hood that he had exhausted his resources for reinforcing Hood's army. It was also essential that all Confederate absentees be brought back into the ranks, and that the means at hand be used with an energy proportioned to the needs of the country.[26] Hood, therefore, weighing the situation carefully with his force of only 40,000 men, decided to continue operating in Sherman's rear. By

24. Hood, *Advance and Retreat*, 123.
25. Sherman, *Memoirs*, II, 144-155.
26. Hood, *op.cit.*, *passim.*

effectively threatening his communications, he believed he could draw Sherman after him into Tennessee, and eventually into Kentucky, or could force the Union army back into the mountains of North Georgia as General Lee had on two different occasions transferred the fighting from Virginia into Maryland, and on northward.[27]

Hood's whole plan to halt Sherman's march into central Georgia and southward was a desperate gamble, as he well knew. He made some changes in the organization of his forces to improve their efficiency, while Sherman was sending General Thomas back to Chattanooga and Nashville to keep the situation in his Department under control, and to prepare to meet Hood's expected invasion. Receiving information that Sherman had gathered large supplies of stores at Allatoona, Hood sent General Samuel Gibbs French with his division to seize the place and the stores—French beginning his attack on October 5, but meeting stiff resistance from General Corse and his Union veterans. On October 7, Hood telegraphed General Richard Taylor to send Forrest at once to operate in Tennessee, and on the 11th Hood's army crossed the Coosa, marching directly towards Rosecrans and Dalton. In his *Memoirs*, Hood wrote: "If Sherman would cut loose and march south, as I believed he would do after I left his front without previously worsting him in battle, I would occupy Richmond, Kentucky," and as this was a position of great advantage, Sherman would have to take defensive action for the rescue of Kentucky and Ohio. He might follow Hood directly into Tennessee and Kentucky. Alternatively, Sherman might choose to march directly to the support of Grant in Virginia. If he did take this bold step, stated Hood, "I could pass through the Cumberland gaps to Petersburg, and attack Grant in rear at least two weeks before he, Sherman, could render him assistance. This move, I believed, would defeat Grant, and allow General Lee, in command of our armies, to march upon Washington, or to turn upon and annihilate Sherman. Such was the plan which, during the 15th and 16th (October), as we lay in bivouac near Lafayette, I maturely considered and determined to carry out."[28] It will be seen that Hood looked at the situation in a large, loose way, and laid his plans with more of wishful thinking than of a sober study of possibilities.

There were others, too, who took a large and reckless view of the possibilities of the situation for the Confederacy. Benjamin H. Hill, for example, thought that Davis's removal of Joseph E. Johnston had been right and that this drastic step should have been taken a month earlier. He wrote his friend Herschel V. Johnson that the appointment of Hood had been quite a venturesome experiment, but that he did not see how, under all the circumstances,

27. See John P. Dyer, *The Gallant Hood*, Indianapolis, 1950, 272.
28. Cf. *Battles and Leaders*, IV, 425ff.

President Davis could have done otherwise. Atlanta had virtually been lost when Hood took command, but it had been important to delay the final fall of the city so as to discourage Sherman from attempting any further progress into Georgia that season. Hill added:

> Hood's new movement is more than was originally anticipated and thus far is most promising. I warmly approved it from the beginning, and have great hopes of the result. I am now a little afraid Hood will go back too fast and too far. It is now intimated he is going directly to Nashville. It is urged by some that he can go on *to the Ohio.* The idea is that he will get 50,000 soldiers in Tennessee and Kentucky. I think he may get these men if Lincoln should be elected, and in that event also the appearance of our army, strong and increasing, in Kentucky, may encourage a revolution in the North itself.
>
> *All these ideas are in the calculations.* Price seems to be helping the movement in poor Missouri—I mean 'poor' because of her sufferings.

Hill wished to find a safe place for his family; but what place nowadays was really safe?

The way was now open for the culminating battles which were to wreck Hood's elaborate Tennessee campaign, and would not only bring all his ambitious plans to naught, but would leave his armies in so shattered a condition that Sherman need feel no further anxiety respecting his movements and might lay secure plans for his own southward thrusts. October 5 found Sherman near Marietta, with Atlanta still securely in Union hands. General Schofield, who held a position at the rear where he might delay Hood's movements, and had been chafing over what he regarded as lost opportunities to achieve the grand goal of the destruction of Hood's army, was deeply disappointed. Jonesboro seemed to him the place to deliver the final decisive blow. "So anxious was I that this be attempted that I offered to go with two corps, or even with one, to intercept Hood's retreat on the McDonough road, and hold him until Sherman could dispose of Hardee."[29] Schofield remained near Marietta until a smart action at Spring Hill enabled him to move his troops to Franklin, Tennessee, ready to defend that position against any further advance by Hood. This was just south of the Harpeth River. He decided to stay there with his 32,000 men and organize a strong defense against Confederate attack.

Hood had telegraphed President Davis early in September that the soldiers were much in need of rest. His men had since endured even further trials. Not only were they wearied out by their efforts to maintain a fighting front against Sherman; they were deeply discouraged after their defeats, retreats, and evasive movements to avoid outflanking, and disheartened by what they knew of

29. Schofield, John M., *Forty-Six Years in the Army*, New York, 1897, 159.

General William Tecumseh Sherman

General John Bell Hood

the quarrels within the Confederacy itself. They were in large part ragged, shoeless or ill-shod, and without money to send their families, not having been paid for ten months.[30] The Confederate Army was being weakened as steadily by desertions as the Union Army was being strengthened by drafting and volunteering.

But Sherman also had his perplexities. He had suffered from some of the attacks the Confederates under Forrest and others had launched at him and his lines of communication. Deep in hostile territory, exposed to cavalry thrusts, his army of about 82,000 had to deal with Hood from its precarious position at the end of the long line of rails running back to Chattanooga and thence to Nashville. He could not sit still while enemy forces manoeuvered recklessly behind him, and he soon recognized that but one course was really open to him. In his march from Chattanooga into north Georgia he had discovered that his large army, carrying with it all necessary stores and baggage, could actually overtake and bring to bay an inferior enemy force in its own country. He saw that with an army, including communications forces, of nearly a hundred thousand men and 254 guns, he could not safely hold the long supply line from Louisville to his troops if he advanced into Tennessee in pursuit of Hood, while at the same time trying to protect middle Tennessee from invasion. The safest course would therefore be to turn not northeast, but southwest. He would divide his forces into two parts, using one to take the offensive, while with the other he would act on the defensive and invite the enemy to attack him. Thus it was that a curious military situation suddenly revealed itself to the country. Almost immediately upon the capture of Atlanta by the Union forces, the main armies, which had been battling each other at close quarters, had separated and moved in opposite directions. Sherman was now well on his way through the wide, fertile tract between Atlanta and Waynesboro, the garden of Georgia. Down from the mountainous and hill country of north Georgia the army moved into the area of the rivers, all flowing toward the sea.

The great March to the Sea began in a spectacular and memorable scene on November 16, 1864. That day Sherman sat astride his horse on a small eminence just outside Atlanta, and with stern mien but exultant heart watched the foremost detachments of his army, some 60,000 fighting veterans, encumbered by as little impedimenta as possible, swing past, some shouting exultantly, and some chorusing "Glory, Glory, Hallelujah!" They were on their way to the sea—perhaps even to be first into Richmond and to achieve a junction with Grant.[31]

Sherman's intrepid decision to transfer his army to Savannah and the

30. Dyer, *The Gallant Hood*, 272.
31. Liddell Hart, B.H. *Sherman, Soldier, Realist, American*, New York, 1929, 308ff.

seacoast made many Northerners catch their breath. General Thomas, commanding one wing of Sherman's army, advised against it. Lincoln was dubious, and even apprehensive. General Grant thought that the safest course would be to destroy Hood before pushing the army farther to the south. But Sherman believed that it might be impossible to destroy Hood—that no single army could catch him.[32] He was determined that he would not let himself be manoeuvered out of Georgia.

A half-dozen objectives dawned upon Sherman at once. Cutting his army free from his communications with Tennessee, he would march through the country, living upon it as he went. He would create a new base on the coast, with a shorter supply line, protected in part by the Navy as Nelson's fleet had protected Wellington's fast-moving columns in Spain after Trafalgar. In slicing across Georgia, he would strip that State of its summer crops, so that Hood's army would lack sustenance until the next harvest-time. He was confident that he could entrust the defense against Hood to Thomas. By shrewd and systematic retreats, Thomas could draw Hood well up into Tennessee, meanwhile concentrating on strengthening his own army until the moment when he could turn decisively about and destroy or fatally cripple Hood.[33]

"I was thereby left," wrote Sherman in his final report to the War Department, "with a well-appointed army, to cut the enemy's only remaining rail communications eastward and westward."

[III]

The Federal army that moved out of Atlanta in mid-November numbered some 60,000 infantry and 5,500 cavalry, and they were stripped down for action. Quantities of necessary supplies had been gathered, and all needless baggage eliminated. This elimination was generally easy, for by this time the veterans had learned how to travel light, carrying only a well-packed knapsack, tightly rolled blankets, and arms. They usually bore with them rations for two days, had supplies in wagons for a longer period, and drove cattle before them; but their main dependence for food, and particularly for forage, was to be upon the countryside.

In bare figures the Union army lost in the great movement at least 103 men killed, 428 wounded, and 278 missing for a remarkably low total of 809.[34] As Sherman put it, his men and animals "consumed the corn and fodder in the region of the country thirty miles on either side of a line from Atlanta to

32. Sherman, *Memoirs,* II, 165.
33. *O.R.*, I, xliv, 13.
34. *Ibid.*, 15, and Sherman, *Memoirs,* 221.

Savannah, and also the sweet potatoes, cattle, hogs, sheep and poultry, and have carried away more than 10,000 horses and mules, as well as countless numbers of their slaves." He declared that several hundred miles of railroad were destroyed and that the damage inflicted upon the State of Georgia aggregated a hundred million dollars—"at least, $20,000,000 of which has inured to our advantage, and the remainder is simple waste and destruction." This, he commented, ". . . may seem a hard species of warfare, but it brings the sad realities of war home to those who have been directly or indirectly instrumental in involving us in its attendant calamities."[35] For one instance, for the four infantry corps which had 3,476 cattle on hand at Atlanta when the march started, 13,294 more were captured en route, and 6,861 were available when they reached Savannah.[36] Sherman had indeed carried out his threat to make Georgia howl, or as he wrote General Schofield as early as October 17, "I will then make the interior of Georgia feel the weight of War."[37]

In the actual march, Sherman's object was not to capture important strategic towns, but to place his army between Macon and Augusta, the two towns where he was likely to encounter strong defensive forces. Thus he would force the Confederates to defend both cities, along with the sorry hamlet of Millen where lay a noisome Southern prison-camp almost directly south of Augusta in the Savannah River valley; the Confederates, meanwhile, would have also to maintain a tight grip upon Savannah and Charleston. Kilpatrick, with grim eyes, hawk nose, and bristling side-whiskers, marshalled his cavalry with Howard's right wing, moving against the Oconee. He carried out his orders to make a feint against Macon, keeping on the right flank of the main force until it passed that city, and cutting a swath of destruction as he moved on. At Griswoldville the Northern infantry and cavalry had to fight a sharp battle, Kilpatrick losing about 2,000 men, according to hurried reports. Then Slocum's left wing, which included troops under Gen. A.S. Williams and Gen. Jefferson C. Davis, moved on against the capital of the state, Milledgeville, and the crossing of the Oconee.

On November 22, Slocum occupied Milledgeville, from which the legislature had fled precipitately a few days earlier on learning of the Union army's proximity, revealing panic that quickly infected the people as they evacuated their shops, factories, and houses to join outgoing vehicles. But a few Union soldiers entered the city. Factories, warehouses, and depots were burned, but few private dwellings were touched, and civilians were treated with courteous respect. Sherman, who had marched with the left wing, occupied the executive

35. *O.R.* I, xliv, 7-14, Sherman's report.
36. *Ibid.*, 65.
37. Sherman, William T., *Sherman's Home Letters*, New York, 1909, 300.

mansion of Governor Brown, protecting its contents. Slocum then pushed on over the Oconee, dispersing some Confederate horsemen under General Joseph Wheeler. Kilpatrick paused in his progress to break the railway from Augusta to Millen, and Northern journals soon carried ghastly pictures of emaciated prisoners just released, and of the clay mounds in the prison-pen under which they had crawled to find refuge from burning sun and beating rains. Some unburied corpses lay near the graves of 700 dead.[38]

The only organized opposition had come from Joe Wheeler's cavalry, G.W. Smith's 3,000 Georgia militia (made up of exempts from Confederate enlistments), scattered groups of men not in rebel military service,[39] and a few local volunteers at various points. Generals were plentiful, with Beauregard, Richard Taylor, Toombs, Cobb and Hardee figuring prominently in the operation. But generals were not enough. Delaying and harassing operations were all that were possible, and even these were not telling except in nuisance value. After Milledgeville, Sherman in person moved to Howard's right wing. Now the whole force was marching southeasterly between the Savannah river on the left and the Ogeechee River on the right, although one corps was south of the Ogeechee. Destruction of railroads and bridges was continued under light opposition. Wheeler hung around the edges and occasionally attacked isolated elements, but could deal no substantial blows.

By December 3, Sherman's main forces were in the Millen area and thereabouts. Orders were given to march on toward Savannah. As they approached the sea, the country became lower and more marshy; marching difficult. Additional obstructions were presented by trees chopped down across the roads, particularly near creek, swamp and causeway crossings, but Sherman's able workers, under the skilled engineer Col. Orlando M. Poe, a West Pointer (1856) of frontier experience, rapidly removed them. By the time the army was within fifteen miles of Savannah, opposition thickened and so did the barricades, while supplies became shorter. By December 10, the Confederates were forced back into the fortifications of Savannah. Here Hardee was protected by swamps, creeks, and flooded rice fields. In investing the city, Slocum's columns were supported by Davis's corps on the left on the Savannah River, while other troops on the right extended the siege line toward the sea where Admiral Dahlgren's fleet was awaiting Sherman.

Five narrow causeways ran through formidable swamps into the city—two carrying railways and the others mere dirt roads; these were all well defended. So Sherman wisely turned his attention to the necessary opening of communication and supply lines with the warships waiting off shore in the sounds south

38. *Harper's Pictorial History of the Rebellion*, New York, 1866, 687.
39. Confederate Records of Georgia, III, 647ff.

of Savannah. Hardee himself was partially trapped in the city, with railroad connections cut both north to Charleston and to the south.

Sherman determined that the mouth of the Ogeechee River south of the city was the proper place to establish communications with the supply fleet. The river was well defended by a huge earthwork, Fort McAllister, with 200 men, 23 guns, and one mortar, but its main defences were toward the river and the sea rather than on the land side. Late on the afternoon of December 13, Hazen's division stormed the works at three points and was everywhere successful. Sherman watched the storm from a neighboring rice mill. Soon afterward he went out in a small boat to the tug *Dandelion*. After talking with Dahlgren about opening supply lines, he returned to the siege to prepare for an assault, aided now by improved bases on the Ogeechee.

To the north in South Carolina, General Foster from his position at Port Royal had failed to break the railroad from Savannah to Charleston, though he had placed guns to command it. The Confederates, therefore, continued to run trains to Savannah.

On December 17, Sherman demanded Hardee's surrender with his 10,000 men. But Hardee had decided against surrender and was planning an escape by way of the one causeway still open across the Savannah. Realizing that he could no longer delay evacuation, he completed the movement on the 20th. At daybreak next day, the Twentieth Corps entered Savannah. Sherman himself followed on the 22nd, and he wrote: "I was very much disappointed that Hardee had escaped with his garrison, and had to content myself with the material fruits of victory without the cost of life which would have attended a general assault." [40]

Sherman comprehended the full import of his dramatic triumph and electrified the nation with his famous telegram from Savannah, December 22: "His Excellency President Lincoln: I beg to present you, as a Christmas gift, the city of Savannah, with 150 heavy guns and plenty of ammunition, and also about 25,000 bales of cotton."[41]

We may take as typical of the exultation felt by Union soldiers that Christmas season in 1864, a report made by Brigadier-General William B. Hazen, commander of the Second Division of the Fifteenth Corps, at the beginning of 1865. He recalled that on November 15, "every preparation being completed," his division had broken camp at Atlanta and set out on its march through Georgia. It had an effective strength of 4,426 officers and men, and comprised 17 regimental organizations. He recalled how the troops moved

40. *O.R.*, I, xliv, 7-14, Sherman's report. Cox, Jacob D., *The March to the Sea: Franklin and Nashville*, New York, 1882, 21, 61; and Gibson, John M., *Those 163 Days*, New York, 1961, *passim*.
41. *O.R.*, I, xliv, 783.

forward rapidly, crossing the Ocmulgee River on November 19, and reaching Clinton, Ga., on the 21st. He related how they left a brigade here to cover the Macon roads, and had engaged in some skirmishing with a few casualties. On November 22, the Macon and Augusta Railroad was crossed, and the march continued past the Oconee River and Bell's Ferry on the 25th. Here the column encountered the enemy, but pressed on through continuous pine forests, crossing low, marshy branches of another river, and reaching Summerville on November 30. He followed this with a typical entry: "On Dec. 1 the march was resumed in the direction of Statesborough along the right branch of the Ogeechee River. The remainder of the march was impeded by low, broad marshes which it was invariably found necessary to corduroy." From Summerville to the Canauchee River, which they reached on December 7, the Second and Third Divisions formed a separate column under Hazen's command which, he writes, was "somewhat exposed to annoyances from the enemy," endeavoring to reach Savannah before the Union army could get there. On December 3, the Fifty-third Ohio lost twenty-seven men captured and eight wounded.

This narrative is characteristic of the record of many organizations which participated in the march. They executed a long, wearying, military advance, diversified seldom by battles, but often by adventurous incidents, with the constant possibility that a soldier or officer would be killed, wounded, or captured, if he strayed far off the main path or was involved in the numerous small skirmishes, clashes, and impromptu duels that occurred. But the bare facts convey only a fragmentary and inadequate impression of the great martial feat accomplished by Sherman and his veterans, and only a partial intimation of the tremendous consequences, some of them physical and material, but others of far larger significance, spiritual and moral, which sprang from this exhibition of national planning, daring, and determination in one of the most spectacular enterprises of modern war. The unconquerable industrial and military strength of the Union, and the surpassing skill of its most experienced commanders, were at last plain. A new confidence had entered the American spirit, and a fresh and brightly-colored panel of pictures had been impressed upon the national consciousness. The pictorial sweep and color of Sherman's march across Georgia to the Atlantic at Savannah worked upon the national imagination in a way which, while obscuring his grand strategic purpose of disrupting Southern railroads, roadways, and other communications, emphasized his ability to cut a swath of ruin across the granary of the South, while proving that his army could subsist and move at will upon the wide countryside.

Before the Federal army left Atlanta, it had been treated to a scene which was at once dramatic, uplifting, and terrible. All the while that Sherman's men were setting the torch to the "workshop of the Confederacy," the band of the Thirty-third Massachusetts rendered "John Brown," heard even above the din. "The men took up the words wedded to the music, and, high above the roaring flames, above the crash of falling walls, above the fierce crackling of thousands of small-arm cartridges in the burning buildings, rose the triumphant refrain, 'His truth is marching on!' "[42]

The following description of a typical marcher by one who made the march has a convincing vigor: "He was fertile of resources, and his confidence was unbounded. His careless, swinging gait when on the march was the impersonation of a determination to 'get there,' although he knew absolutely nothing of his destination. Of that he was careless. His confidence in the longheadedness of the 'old-man' was such that he did not disturb himself on that score. He was heading south instead of north, and this was ample assurance that Thomas was taking care of Hood, and that Grant was 'holding Lee down.' He went into action as unconcernedly as he took the road in the morning for a day's march; or, if not ordered into the conflict, he would sit on a fence, or lie down in the road, the image of peaceful contentment, within hearing of a fierce engagement, apparently wholly indifferent as to the result. . . . He waded swamps, made corduroy roads, and pulled wagons and cannon out of ruts from which the bottom had seemingly dropped. But there was one thing he did not know, that in all this magnificent effort he was making immense drafts upon his reserve energy, and that the day was sure to come when he would find himself far older than his years by reason thereof. . . ."[43]

The real achievement of Sherman in this march across Georgia to Savannah did not lie in the physical endurance shown, nor in the show of arms which accompanied it, although all such feats were recorded. His achievement was primarily moral, not physical. It is not to be compared with such a heroic march as that of Field Marshal Hugh Henry Rose (Baron Strathnairn) across India during the Great Mutiny of 1858, storming cities and engaging formidable forces as he went; or with some of the fighting marches of the Russian armies or of Field Marshal Wavell during the Second World War. Sherman defeated the enemy by strength of will, dexterity of movement, and unconquerable fixity upon a few grand purposes, culminating in the achievement of important goals. Seldom have the soldierly virtues of foresight, determination, patience and skill been better illustrated in a single campaign. To comprehend the value of Sherman's stroke, we must realize that it had been, in his own phrase, long contemplated. As we have already seen, during the campaign for

42. Hedley, F.Y., *Marching Through Georgia, Pen-Pictures of Every-day Life in General Sherman's Army, from the Beginning of the Atlanta Campaign Until the Close of the War*, Chicago, 1890, 257-258.
43. *Ibid.*, 259-263.

Atlanta he, and others, had realized two great facts: first, that a hostile force operating over long distances and a rugged terrain had endless capacities for delaying and diverting an invading army; and second, that in a State rich enough to support such a population as Georgia's the invaders could never really be threatened with starvation unless they tarried too long in one location. We must realize, too, that the Atlanta campaign had also taught him the great value of elasticity of operation, and the possibility of adapting his plans to ever-changing circumstances.[44]

While dismemberment of the Confederacy had been a part of the Federal strategy since near the beginning of the war, the cardinal questions were always *where*, *when*, and *how* to invade the inner fortress of the South. Grant had been unable to get his proposed campaign against Mobile effectively launched. Undoubtedly many men had hit upon the general idea of invading Georgia. Its advantages were clear to anyone who glanced at a map, but implementing the idea was far more difficult. For instance, early in May, 1864, Sherman had told the Inspector-General of the Union army of his plan for seizing Atlanta. That officer was nonplused for, as he pointed out to Sherman, when he reached Atlanta he would be 450 miles from his base of supplies and dependent upon a single precarious railroad. To keep his communications open and well protected would absorb all his military strength. How could he solve the problem of further movement? Sherman snapped out a concise reply in the words: "Salt water!" He obviously meant that he would exchange his Chattanooga base for one at Savannah or possibly Charleston. He would cross Georgia to the Atlantic, living on the country as he went, without worrying about his own base of communications. But until October it was not clear what Hood and his army would do. The Confederate army had to move, for the morale of the Army of Tennessee was declining, and the Southern people expected it to act.

We have already noted the part that the defiant speech which Jefferson Davis delivered at Macon, Georgia, played in shaping Sherman's purposes. The angry Davis served rash notice that the Rebel generals would do their utmost to force Sherman to quit Atlanta, and would then try to visit upon his retreating army the same fate that had overtaken the French during Napoleon's retreat from Moscow. This was nonsense, for Sherman's movement from Atlanta would be in reality anything but a "retreat". He would leave the city and push boldly to the sea and new supply lines, and in doing so his withdrawal would in reality be carefully planned and a well-organized offensive.

Sherman had not been the only leader anxious to deliver so clearly effective

44. Liddell Hart, B.H., *Sherman*, *op.cit.*, 317.

a stroke at the heart of the South. Early in September, General Thomas reportedly asked Sherman to allow him to move to Andersonville, Georgia, to release the prisoners there and go on to the sea coast, while Sherman looked after the Confederate army in the area. Thomas is said to have proposed to Sherman: "Now you have no more use for me, let me take my little command and go eastward to the sea." Sherman replied that he would take it up with Grant, but nothing more was heard until Thomas was ordered to face the Confederate armies in the neighborhood of the Georgia capital, while Sherman himself set out for the Atlantic.[45]

But Sherman might well have had hesitations, especially at first. In late September he wrote Silas F. Miller: "I've got my wedge pretty deep and must look out that I don't get my fingers pinched." [46] About the same time he wrote: "I fear elevation, as a fall would be the harder." If the draft is successful, "we should make big strikes to that end for which I know the loudest Peace men of the land do not yearn with more solicitude than you and I." "When this only question of sovereignty is settled by war and nothing else can settle it, all else is easy." For himself, although pained to undertake it, Sherman had "warmed to the work."[47]

Confederate Joshua Hill, who had several interviews with Sherman in September, quoted Sherman as expressing regret over the inhumanities of war, but "I shall be forced to march to the sea, touching it somewhere in Georgia or South Carolina. Hood keeps cutting my communications with Chattanooga, endangering my supplies, and I shall be forced to move."[48]

On September 10, Sherman wrote Grant: "I am perfectly alive to the importance of pushing our advantage to the utmost. I do not think we can afford to operate farther, dependent on the railroad. . . ." If he could be sure of finding provisions and ammunition at Augusta, or Columbus, Georgia, he could march on Milledgeville, the capital, and compel Hood to give up Augusta or Macon. He was aware of the major problem of any march. "The country will afford forage and many supplies, but not enough in any one place to admit of a delay." So he proposed, "If you can manage to take the Savannah River as high as Augusta, or the Chattahoochee as far as Columbus, I can sweep the whole State of Georgia. Otherwise, I would risk our whole army by going too far from Atlanta."[49] For some weeks Sherman continued to propose to march from

45. Chicago *Tribune*, Dec. 24, 1894, from Gen. Fullerton in St. Louis *Globe-Democrat;* Van Horne, Thomas B., *The Life of Major-General George H. Thomas*, New York, 1882, 255, and footnote quoting Thomas in letter of Gen. W.F. Smith to Van Horne.

46. Letter from Sherman to Silas F. Miller, Filson Club, Louisville.

47. Sherman to Theodore S. Bell, Sept. 18, 1864, Sherman Papers, HEH.

48. Hill, Joshua, article in Atlanta *Daily Herald*, Feb. 28, 1875, typed copy in W.T. Sherman Papers, Ohio State Museum, Columbus.

49. *O.R.*, I, xxxix, pt. 2, 335, Sherman to Grant, Sept. 10, 1864.

Atlanta, providing he could be met by a column coming in from the coast, probably from the Hilton Head, South Carolina, area, held by Federal forces since the fall of 1861.

Sherman had other problems too. There had been furores over his evacuation of the civilian population of Atlanta, a policy for which he was violently condemned by General Hood, by other Confederate leaders, and the citizens themselves, Further, he felt that with his old troops "I have never felt a waver of doubt," but he was opposed to having Negro troops with him. There had been some talk of Sherman for President: "If forced to choose between the penitentiary and the White House for four years, I would say the penitentiary. . . ."[50] Through many of his letters there shows, though subtly, a doubt of his own ability, a wonder that he was where he was.

But at the same time, he was forthright as to war. In a statement that was to reverberate for more than a century in a somewhat different and stronger form, Sherman wrote Halleck, September 4; "If the people raise a howl against my barbarity and cruelty, I will answer war is war, and not popularity seeking. If they want peace, they and their relatives must stop war."[51] In answer to a protest by the Mayor of Atlanta regarding the evacuation order, Sherman replied: "War is cruelty, and you cannot refine it; and those who brought war into our Country deserve all the Curses and Maledictions a people can pour out."[52]

Grant wrote Sherman concerning future plans as early as September 12, showing that he understood his subordinate's position and difficulties. He had hoped to have sent him more men, but Price's raid in force in Missouri had prevented it. Grant had felt that these extra troops should have been sent half to Mobile and half to Savannah. The latter group would then have tried to come up and meet Sherman as he moved down from Atlanta.[53]

By September 20, Sherman was still thinking of having Savannah taken from the sea, and "if once in our possession, and the river open to us, I would not hesitate to cross the State of Georgia with 60,000 men, hauling some stores and depending on the country for the balance. . . . But the more I study the game, the more am I convinced that it would be wrong for me to penetrate much farther into Georgia without an objective beyond. . . . If you can whip Lee and I can march to the Atlantic, I think Uncle Abe will give us twenty days' leave of absence to see the young folks."[54]

50. *O.R.*, I, xxxviii, pt. 5, 791-794, Sherman to Halleck, Sept. 4, 1864.
51. *Ibid.*, 794, Sherman to Halleck, Sept. 4, 1864.
52. Sherman's reply to the Mayor of Atlanta, Sept. 12, 1864, ms. Houghton Library, Harvard Univ., Cambridge, Mass.
53. *O.R.*, I, xxxix, pt. 2, 364-365, Grant to Sherman, City Point, Va., Sept. 12, 1864.
54. *Ibid.*, 411-413, Sherman to Grant, Sept. 20, 1864.

In October, however, Sherman had his hands full diverting Hood's offensive movement between Chattanooga and Atlanta, and trying to keep his lines of supply and communication open.[55]

Grant was never opposed to Sherman's march. He left its development to the field commander in large part, but he wanted to make sure what the objectives were and that they could be kept as targets of action. On October 13, he wrote Stanton: "On mature reflection I believe Sherman's proposition is the best that can be adopted. With the long line of railroad in rear of Atlanta Sherman cannot maintain his position. If he cuts loose, destroying the road from Chattanooga forward, he leaves a wide and destitute country for the rebels to pass over before reaching territory now held by us. . . . Such an Army as Sherman has, (and with such a commander) is hard to corner or capture. . . ."[56]

Any intelligent professional officer might well have conceived of such a move as the March to the Sea, although he would have wisely asked questions during the planning stage. That able soldier and keen observer, Jacob D. Cox, felt that the march had been commonly misunderstood: "There has been a singular tendency to treat the conception of a march from Atlanta to the Gulf or to the ocean as if that were an invention or a discovery. People have disputed the priority of the idea, as if it were a patent right. . . ." Cox felt that Sherman's final decision and plan were highly creditable. A weak general might have followed Hood, but Sherman had the determination to take the opposite course. Cox added that "Grant's sympathies were never lacking for a bold and decided course, but in this instance he had less faith than Sherman that all would go well in Tennessee." Lincoln, too, was "anxious, if not fearful."[57] Grant confirmed the apprehensions of Lincoln, and there was certainly a momentary bit of hesitation in Washington, though never any basic disagreement.[58]

In his letters Grant wrote: "I was in favor of Sherman's plan from the time it was first submitted to me."[59] Sherman was later to identify November 2 as the first date on which General Grant assented to 'march to the sea.' . . ."[60] Sherman also asserted that he "saw" the move in his "mind's eye," when after the fall of Atlanta Hood shifted from Lovejoy's Station to Palmetto, and he was more positive in his determination after President Davis's speeches. The ques-

55. Sherman, *Memoirs,* II, 157ff.

56. Grant to Stanton, Oct. 13, 1864, City Point, Va., Ulysses S. Grant Letters and Papers, Illinois State Hist. Libr.

57. Cox, Jacob D., *The March to the Sea: Franklin and Nashville,* New York, 1882, 2-6.

58. Grant, *Memoirs,* II, 374-376.

59. *Ibid.*

60. Sherman, *Memoirs,* II, 166.

tion was time and manner. We have evidence, however, that as early as September 10 Grant told Sherman that, after rest and preparation, "it is desirable that another campaign [against the Confederate leader] should be commenced . . . If we give him no peace while the war lasts, the end cannot be distant." Grant thought it best to send Canby's men to advance upon Savannah while Sherman moved on Augusta.[61] Sherman replied, as we have seen, that if a force could be pushed up from Savannah, he could come southeast and meet it.[62] A lengthy correspondence shows that the overall planning did not spring into existence at once, or from any one person. It developed slowly and steadily, although the basic aim and conception remained the same.

Sherman kept pressing for help from the coast.[63] By October 1, he was proposing to send Thomas to Nashville and to undertake his march, if Hood would go over toward Alabama, for "We cannot remain on the defensive."[64] Sherman's famous message of October 9 spelled out his plans in greater detail and dropped the idea that Savannah should be taken first. He felt that it would be "a physical impossibility to protect the roads, now that Hood, Forrest, and Wheeler, and the whole batch of devils, are turned loose without home or habitation." He proposed breaking up the line from Chattanooga to Atlanta, abandoning it and then marching directly on Savannah. "Until we can repopulate Georgia, it is useless to occupy it, but the utter destruction of its roads, houses, and people will cripple their military resources . . . I can make the march, and make Georgia howl. . . ."[65] Grant foresaw that Hood would go north of the Tennessee, and wrote Sherman, "If there is any way of getting at Hood's army, I would prefer that, but I must trust to your own judgment." Grant also declared he could not send a force to act against Savannah in concert with Sherman.[66] The same day, Sherman, who was now at Kingston, Georgia, informed Grant of Hood's manoeuver to the north, adding, "but I believe he will be forced to follow me. Instead of being on the defensive, I would [then] be on the offensive; instead of guessing at what he means to do, he would have to guess at my plans. The difference in war is full 25 per cent. . . ."[67] Immediately thereafter, shortly before midnight on October 11, Grant replied: "If you are satisfied the trip to the sea-coast can be made, holding the line of the Tennessee firmly, you may make it, and destroy all the railroad south of Dalton or Chattanooga, as you think best. . . ."[68]

61. *O.R.*, I, xxxix, pt. 2, 355, Grant to Sherman, City Point, Sept. 10, 1864.
62. *Ibid.*, 355-356, Sherman to Grant, Atlanta, Sept. 10, 1864.
63. *Ibid.*, 464, Sherman to Halleck, Sept. 25, 1864, and *passim*.
64. *O.R.*, I, xxxix, pt. 3, 3, Sherman to Grant, Atlanta, Oct. 1, 1864.
65. *Ibid.*, 162, Sherman to Grant, Atlanta, Oct.9, 1864.
66. *Ibid.*, 202, Grant to Sherman, City Point, Oct. 11, 1864.
67. *Ibid.*, Sherman to Grant.
68. *Ibid.*, Grant to Sherman, Oct. 11, 1864.

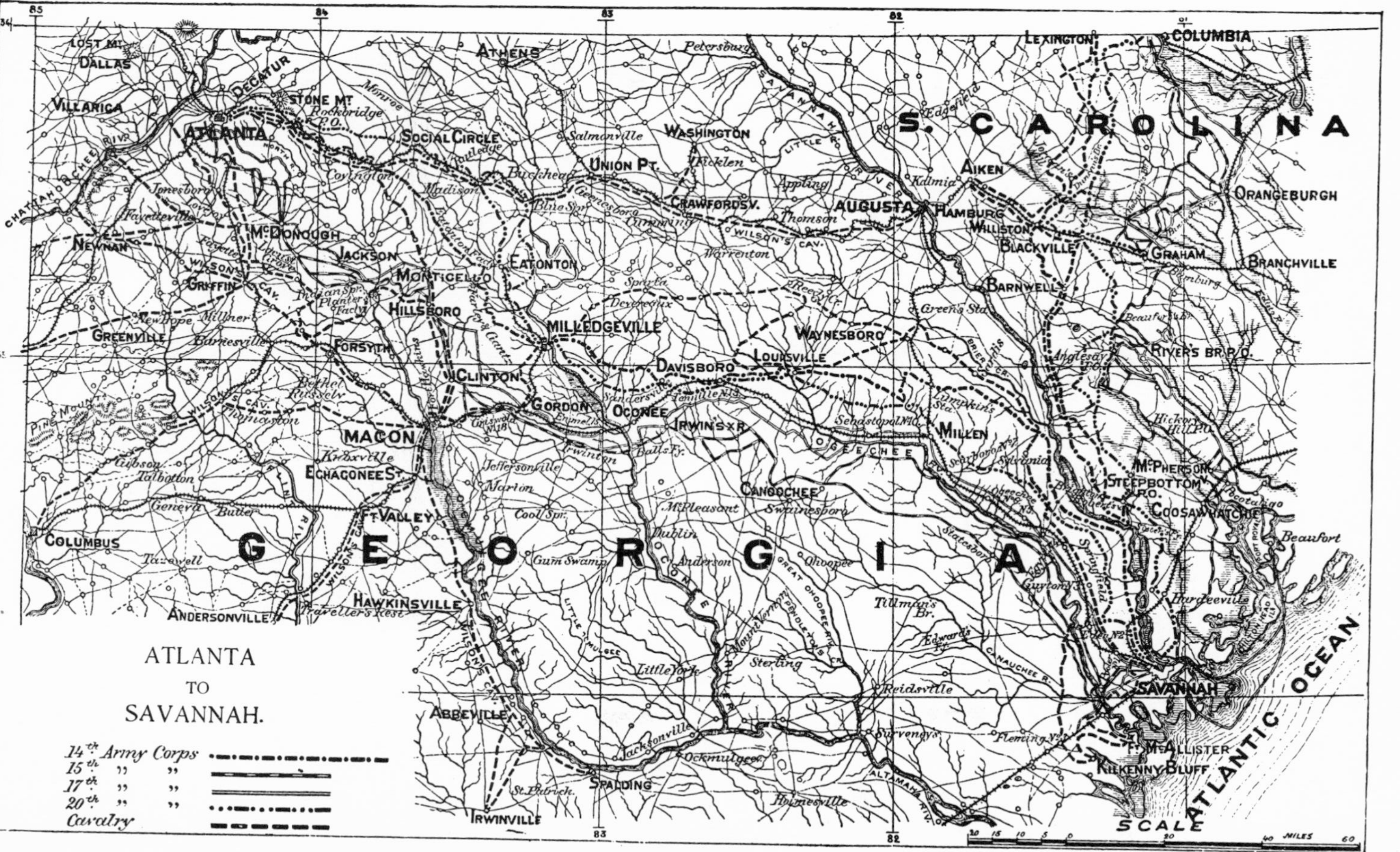

Map of Sherman's March from Atlanta to Savannah

Thus the two generals had worked out a program together by use of the telegraph, and Grant had fully approved the specific plan. Still, the President felt some additional "solicitude" and Grant had again to give his approval.[69] Grant had to understand what the manoeuver was intended to accomplish; in addition to giving his approval, he had to ship south stores and vessels ready to meet Sherman when he should break out upon the coast.

Even then, however, certain doubts seemed to have arisen in Sherman's mind, for as late as November 2, he telegraphed Grant from Rome, Georgia: "If I could hope to overhaul Hood, I would turn against him with my whole force . . . If he ventures north of the Tennessee I may turn in that direction and endeavor to get between him and his line of retreat . . ." But the same day he also wired: "I am clearly of the opinion that the best results will follow me if I hold to my contemplated movement through Georgia."[70] Grant, in fact, had to embolden Sherman, writing: "I see no present reason for changing your plan . . ."[71] Very soon Northern papers outlined Sherman's plans despite War Department efforts to keep them secret.[72] One source of information on these plans was furnished by officers who went North before the campaign. A number actually resigned and others tried to. One officer commented on these absentees: "They are being laughed at by the whole army here . . . I can't see why they are so much afraid of this campaign, for I regard it as one of the easiest campaigns I have engaged in. . . ."[73]

[IV]

The essentially triumphant character of Sherman's march, producing a tremendous popular effect upon both the North and the South, would have been shattered and its moral effects would have been reversed had it encountered any staggering check, compelling it to retreat, and resulting in an augmentation of Confederate confidence. This would have been sweeping in nature and consequences if Hood's Tennessee campaign had succeeded, and if he had occupied Nashville and the surrounding mid-South and crushed Thomas's army. Tennessee and Kentucky would then have lain open to the Confederacy with little immediate opposition in front of its columns, while Hood's army could have been supplied from the region. Conceivably, he could have pushed even to the Ohio, and the moral encouragement given to the

69. *Ibid.*, 222, Stanton to Grant, Oct.12, 1864, and Grant to Sherman, Oct.12, 1864.
70. *Ibid.*, pt. 3, 594-595, Sherman to Grant, Nov. 2, 1864.
71. *Ibid.*, 679, Grant to Sherman, Nov. 7, 1864.
72. *Ibid.*, 740, Grant to Stanton, and Stanton to Grant, Nov. 11, 1864.
73. Connolly, Major James Austin, Major Connolly's Letters to His Wife, 1862-1865, *Transactions of the Illinois State Hist. Soc., 1928,* Springfield, 1928, 370, Nov. 11, 1864.

Confederacy thereby would have been even greater than the North experienced through Sherman's successful march. While the outcome of the war itself would probably not have been jeopardized, unquestionably the history of 1865 would have been drastically changed if Hood had succeeded in Tennessee. But this is one of the colossal and unprofitable "ifs" of history, along with "if Napoleon had taken a winning stand against Wellington." Nothing of the kind happened because Hood and his army possessed weaknesses that even on the first glance appeared disabling compared with the strength possessed by Sherman and his veterans; because a courageous, although heedlessly impetuous Confederate commander led an army which fatigue and losses were rendering impotent; because the great industrial strength of the North was growing more and more overwhelming, and because the incalculable fortunes of war always favor the better-prepared, better-trained, and more thoughtfully directed forces.

Even before the threat delivered by Hood and his army, Sherman worried about the safety of the middle South and the area to his rear at Atlanta. In fact, besides trying to bring Forrest to bay, he even suggested that the guerrillas and malcontents in Kentucky and elsewhere be put aboard troop-ships and exiled to Honduras, British or French Guiana, or San Domingo, or even Madagascar or Lower California would do. "But one thing is certain," he declared, "there is a class of people, men, women, and children, who must be killed or banished before you can hope for peace and order, even as far south as Tennessee."[74] Stanton seemed to approve this flint-hearted scheme, but nothing came of it.[75]

In addition to the guerrillas, and Wheeler's cavalry operations in Sherman's neighborhood, the Union troops had repeatedly encountered Forrest, all summer and on into the fall. Forrest at Brice's Crossroads and Tupelo; Forrest raiding even into the Federal stronghold of Memphis itself in late August; Forrest moving up from Mississippi to Pulaski, Tenn., and back into Alabama and Mississippi in late September and early October. In this exploit, the brilliant Confederate master of raiding operations reported that in sixteen days he captured 86 Yankee officers, 67 government employees, 1,174 noncommissioned officers and privates, 933 Negroes, and killed a thousand others of the enemy. He captured 800 horses, 7 guns, 2,000 small arms, 50 wagons and ambulances, several hundred saddles, medical, commissary, and quartermaster's stores. In addition, Union forces had to bear the destruction of the Duck River railroad bridge in Tennessee and other depredations. Forrest's army was now well supplied with boots, shoes, hats, blankets, overcoats, and other kinds of equipment.[76]

74. *O.R.*, I, xxxix, pt. 2, 131-132, Sherman to Stanton, June 21, 1864.
75. *Ibid.*, 157, Stanton to Sherman, July 1, 1864.
76. *O.R.*, I, xxxix, pt. 1, Forrest's report, 542-549.

Forrest was not yet through. Fortunately for the North, when Hood's army marched west and north from the vicinity of Atlanta, eventually reaching northern Alabama, Forrest was not on the scene to meet him and to augment immediately the Army of Tennessee. Indeed Forrest was some 300 miles away from Hood at the time Hood most needed him, executing a raid into Tennessee that was spectacular but by no means necessary to the Confederacy. Cavalry under Forrest had moved to the Tennessee River, capturing a gunboat and several transports. He manned some of them with crews, fought a river gunboat battle, burned and sank nineteen vessels at the wharf at Johnsonville, Tenn.; he also destroyed immense Union stores. All this was in late October and early November. Of course, Thomas had to send troops to Johnsonville. Sherman angrily wrote that "that devil Forrest was down about Johnsonville and was making havoc among the gun-boats and transports . . ."[77]

By October 21, Hood was at Gadsden, Alabama, some 30 miles southwest of Sherman's pursuing forces who were at Gaylesville on the Georgia-Alabama line. By this time Hood had abandoned his campaign against the Chattanooga-Atlanta railroad and was formulating other plans. This new scheme was to cross the Tennessee at or near Guntersville, Alabama, drive first toward Stevenson and Bridgeport, Alabama, and then against Thomas and Schofield, hoping to beat them before they could fall back to Nashville. He would then take Nashville and operate from that city, boldly threatening Cincinnati.[78] Hood moved on, threatening Decatur, Ala., then withdrawing to the west to Tuscumbia. Sherman continued to send troops to Thomas in Tennessee, and to make plans for the Great March. Thomas had been quite weak before the 9th of November when he received Schofield's 10,000-man Twenty-third Corps to add to the Fourth Corps of David S. Stanley. With a strong field force now, Thomas was in a good position to shift his troops and defend Tennessee against Hood's promised advance. Previously he had been handicapped by the necessity of garrisoning a number of important posts with inferior or raw troops.

By early November, Hood had already failed in his main effort. Unable to move north promptly, because of deficient supplies and the absence of Forrest who was away at Johnsonville, Hood had lost the opportunity to strike into Tennessee against Thomas's garrisons, a move that quite possibly would have forced Sherman to give up his own plans for the grand march.[79] Thomas now sent Schofield down to Pulaski, Tenn., and on November 14 the thoughtful careful Schofield took over command of the major Union field force of about

77. *Ibid.*, 859-60, Thomas to Sherman, Nov. 4, 1864; *O.R.*, I, xxxix, pt. 3, 658-661, Sherman to Grant, Nov. 6, 1864.

78. Hood, John Bell, *Advance and Retreat*, New Orleans, 1880, 267; and Stone, Henry, *The Battle of Franklin, Tennessee, Nov. 30, 1864*, MHSM, Vol. VII, 435-437.

79. Stone, *op.cit.*, 439.

17,000. By the time Hood crossed the Tennessee, Thomas's available force totaled about 29,000, in addition to various garrisons.[80]

One military critic, it may be noted, feels that Sherman misrepresented to Grant the large numbers Thomas had, and that he actually neglected Thomas while taking more than 60,000 on "a holiday march."[81] Sherman did at least order A.J. Smith's corps to Nashville from the Mississippi, but this force was delayed by the advance of Price's impetuous expedition into Missouri during October, essentially a great raid against that Northern area.

Altogether, Thomas as of November 20 had 54,240 infantry present for duty, and an aggregate strength of 65,615 foot-soldiers. To this might be added 17,563 cavalry, making a total of 71,803. But garrison duties and detachments employed more than half of this. So, as far as field forces are concerned, Hood actually outnumbered Thomas at the start. Thomas had about 29,000 in the field, whereas Hood's aggregate effective force was about 35,000, with some more than 40,000 total present.[82] Hood did not begin his northward advance into Tennessee from Tuscumbia until November 21, nearly a week after Sherman left Atlanta for the sea. He maintained that the failure of Forrest to join him caused the long delay in Alabama.[83] Beauregard, who conferred with Hood, later claimed that if his ideas of the campaign had been followed "without undue delay and modifications and with vigor and skill, Sherman most probably would have been compelled to return to Middle Tennessee to repair and protect his line of communications . . ." and that the disasters of Franklin and Nashville would not have occurred.[84] It is quite possible that Sherman would have been forced to make new decisions if Hood had crossed the Tennessee before the Federals left Atlanta, and before Sherman gave up his communications with the North.

When he did move, Hood hoped to place his army between the Union field force at Pulaski, Tenn., and Nashville. He attributed his failure to reach Columbia, Tenn., before the Federals to deep mud and lack of maps.[85] Actually, however, the Union troops themselves frustrated Hood's first move. Hearing of Hood's movement, Schofield sent Jacob D. Cox with two divisions towards Columbia. Despite the rain, Cox moved rapidly, arriving within ten miles of that town the night of November 23. On the 24th, he reached Columbia just in time to frustrate Forrest's move. One critic surmises that in another

80. Stone, *op.cit.*, 440; *O.R.*, I, xlv, pt. 1, 590.
81. Stone, *op.cit.*, 441-442.
82. *O.R.*, I, xlv, pt. 1, 590. Important Article on Comparative Union and Confederate Strength in New York, *Nation*, February 23, 1905, 149, 150.
83. *O.R.*, I, xxxix, pt. 1, 801-803, Hood's Report
84. *O.R.*, I, xlv, pt. 1, 649-651, Beauregard's Report.
85. *Ibid.*, 652-653, Hood's Report.

half-hour the Confederates would have taken lightly garrisoned Columbia, and the crossings of the Duck River.[86] Skirmishing was frequent until the night of November 27 when Schofield's force was pulled north of the Duck River, and the bridges destroyed. That same night, Hood was making plans with Forrest to seize Spring Hill, about halfway between Columbia and Franklin, the possession of which was vital to any Federal withdrawal toward Franklin.

Forrest started out on the 28th but was encountered by Federal cavalryman James Harrison Wilson, who informed Schofield that Forrest was moving toward Spring Hill, having pushed aside feeble defenders. Schofield at Columbia was in close touch by telegraph with Thomas at Nashville. Thomas told Schofield that if Wilson's Federal cavalry could not hold off Forrest, the Union infantry would have to withdraw from their Duck River position and fall back to Franklin behind Harpeth River. But Schofield was reluctant to pull out. Early on the morning of November 29, Thomas again wired Schofield to fall back to Franklin, leaving forces at Spring Hill to deter the enemy advance.[87] Schofield delayed a few hours more before his army was sent back up the road from Columbia to Spring Hill.

The scene was being set for one of the most controversial and mystifying events of the war in the West—the Spring Hill affair. Students have long debated the events of that November night in 1864 when Schofield's army managed to go right up the road from Columbia to Franklin through Spring Hill, even though the Confederate Army of Tennessee had beaten them to the area and was encamped along the Franklin Pike. The incident has been so thoroughly investigated that it is doubtful that any new material will now appear to give a definitive answer to the puzzle. But the vital fact is that Thomas's field force was not cut off from Franklin and Nashville. It did get back to defend the approaches to the Tennessee capital while Thomas was building his defences and awaiting the arrival of A.J. Smith's corps from Missouri.

The fact that it accomplished its return by a thin margin was certainly the second of the major events that frustrated Hood, the first having been his failure to seize Columbia before its occupation in strength by the Federals. Schofield's duty was to impede Hood, avoid imperilling his own force, and keep in touch with Nashville, where Thomas was directing the general defense of Tennessee and preparing his army to repulse Hood's moves against obvious objectives. Schofield's delay for a few days at Columbia could have resulted in Union disaster.[88]

86. Stone, *op.cit.*, 444-445.
87. *Ibid.*, 450-451.
88. Wilson, James Harrison, *Under the Old Flag*, New York, 1912, 39-40.

Forrest and his horsemen arrived at Spring Hill at about the same time as Stanley's Union infantry from Columbia. Sharp fighting ensued as more Confederates came in, but Stanley's men succeeded in holding the main highway. That night, the 29th, Schofield's entire force passed through Spring Hill and on up to Franklin.[89] In discussing this question of the true blame for failures on either side, the shrewd General Jacob D. Cox, who acquitted himself very ably in this campaign, later asserted that Hood was wrong in trying to shift the blame for the escape of Schofield to the shoulders of B.F. Cheatham, and adds: "Had his own confidence not wavered, and had he not begun to yield to the belief that much more than one division stood facing him, [Hood's] own energy would have carried his subordinates with him, and [they] would have made the assault," unavoidably desperate though it was, the next day. Cox felt that Hood lacked the grasp of mind and will to seize upon the situation, despite his earlier record of quick, vigorous action.[90] Another critic feels it was not until about 3:00 on the afternoon of November 29 that Schofield realized Hood was trying to cut him off, and even then he also failed in energy.[91] This same observer describes the confusion in Hood's army as to which officer should have taken some undefined action during the 29th, and then attributes this confusion to the alleged fact that there "was music and dancing and feasting [in Hood's ranks] and other Gods than Mars were worshipped."[92]

One Union soldier describes the night with grateful relief; "Straight past a thousand gleaming fires, around which were bivouacked the soldiers of Hood's army, had marched the Federal column, and those two gallant corps were saved. When it was known that the peril was past, a hearty 'Thank God!' escaped from many lips unused to prayer. The star of 'good-luck' twinkled upon Schofield's army out of the midnight sky!"[93]

Hood later maintained that if Cheatham had carried out his instructions, "there is no doubt that we should have possessed ourselves of the road . . ."[94] The Confederate general does not explain why he did not see to it that the orders were carried out. He writes a simple admission of the disastrous Southern failure: "The enemy continued to move along the road in hurry and confusion, within hearing nearly all the night." Thus was lost a great opportunity of "striking the enemy for which we had labored so long—the greatest this campaign had offered, and one of the greatest during the war . . . The fruits

89. For a good account, see Cox, Jacob D., *The Battle of Franklin, Tennessee*, New York, 1897, Ch.II, 21-36.

90. *Ibid.*, 79.

91. Stone, *op.cit.*, 455.

92. *Ibid.*, 462.

93. Hinman, Wilbur F., *The Story of the Sherman Brigade*, privately published, 1897, 643-644.

94. *O.R.*, I, xlv, pt. 1, 652-653, Hood's report.

ought to have been gathered at that point . . ."[95] Hood's report was dated February 15, 1865. In it and other reports,[96] he seemed correct in attaching great importance to the Spring Hill fiasco, but he persisted in shifting the responsibility to others, as was too often his wont. Each of Hood's accounts varied a little.[97] In fact, the narratives of Hood, when compared with Cheatham and others, are not easily reconciled with each other.[98]

Some, or many, in the Confederate high command, had blundered. One recent writer lays the Confederate failure to the lack of "a definite and well-organized plan of action." He writes that Hood either failed to work out a plan, or, if he had one, "he failed to brief adequately his subordinate commanders." Hood at the time seemed "to have failed to grasp the full significance of the situation as it developed at Spring Hill." Furthermore, the "entire group of Confederate generals seems to have been permeated with a paralyzing lack of initiative. . . ."[99] These reasons certainly are part of the explanation, although they seem somewhat superficial. Whatever the reasons, the fact remains that "the Yankees lit their pipes by the campfires of the Rebs. . . ."[100]

When Schofield with most of his national troops arrived at Franklin and the south bank of the Harpeth River in the early morning of November 30, following their escape at Spring Hill, the Union commander found that the pontoons he had ordered had not arrived. Busying himself with repair of bridges and improvement of fords, Schofield turned over his corps to General Jacob D. Cox, who organized an infantry line south of the Harpeth, facing down the road to Spring Hill. The line ran in a rough semi-circle from the river above the town to the river below. Quickly the tired and hungry infantrymen began to dig. In half-an-hour they expected to have an earthwork behind which they could at least rest a bit. By noon, the two-mile line was nearing completion.

Meanwhile, a chagrined and angry Hood had ordered his whole army to move in pursuit from Spring Hill. When, about four miles south of Franklin, Hood came upon the Yankee rearguard, he attempted to outflank them, but the Federals retired. This retreat caused some delay, and it was about 3:30 P.M. when the seven Confederate divisions of the Army of Tennessee formed along

95. *Ibid.*, 653-655.

96. *O.R.*, I, xlv, pt. 1, 652-654, Hood's Report, Feb. 15, 1865.

97. See also Hood, J.B., "The Invasion of Tennessee," *Battles and Leaders*, IV, 425-37, in comparison with his reports in *O.R.*, I, xlv, and also in Hood, John Bell, *Advance and Retreat*, 284-291.

98. See Campbell Brown Books, Southern Historical Collection, Univ. of N.C. Library, interview of Brown with Gov. Isham G. Harris of Tenn., May, 1868; Cheatham, B.F. "General Cheatham at Spring Hill," *Battles and Leaders*, IV, 438-439.

99. Crawford, W.T., "The Mystery of Spring Hill," *Civil War History*, Vol.I, No.II, June, 1955, 101-126.

100. Buck, Irving, *Cleburne and His Command*, Jackson, Tenn., 1959, 269.

the Winstead Hills south of Franklin. As the gray line swung forward two-and-a-half miles to Cox's main position, the whole advance being in full sight, Schofield occupied a fort north of the river, overlooking the entire field. An advanced Union position was overrun as the retiring Federals and advancing Confederates poured into the main works at about the same time. At first it appeared that the hot Confederate upsurge made Union disaster imminent, but Colonel Emerson Updycke saw the emergency and, according to at least one critic, "saved the army from the threatened destruction" by the quick deployment of his brigade.[101] In a few moments, the Confederates who had entered the works were killed, captured, or forced back. Thirty-two battle flags were taken. Around the Carter House and the Columbia Pike the fighting became sanguinary in the extreme. A locust grove was almost cut down by rifle fire. At sunset, the field was "lighted up to redness" by the hot exchange of fire.[102]

Hood, his commanders, and his army had delivered a blow expressing their desperate frustration in a hot fury of anger and determination, but it was a blow struck in passion without sufficient serious consideration of the defenses to be met. By midnight, the battle of Franklin was over, and Schofield, withdrawing his troops across the river, urged them on their way to Nashville. Out of some nearly 28,000 troops possibly engaged, the Yankees lost only 189 killed, 1,033 wounded, and 1,104 missing—a total of 2,326. The effective Confederate strength employed in the action was a matter of dispute, but it probably was well over 20,000 infantry. Of this force, a staggering casualty-roll had to be reported: 1,750 killed, 3,800 wounded, and 702 missing, to make a total of 6,252.[103]

We must ask, first of all, should such a dreadful blood-bath as Franklin ever have stained the pages of history. Schofield felt that he was protecting his transportation by keeping his infantry south of the Harpeth, but in fact his transportation was over the river before 1 P.M. It would seem that Schofield made his mistake in ordering Cox to prepare and maintain an unnecessarily exposed and dangerous position with his back to a river because of a misunderstanding of the situation, perhaps deepened by sheer fatigue.[104] If he had placed himself on the high ground north of the Harpeth, Hood could not have attacked.

At the same time, most authorities feel that Hood should never have attacked such a formidable position, or at least not so directly as he did. Little or no strategic skill or tactical ability was exhibited on the part of the Confeder-

101. Stone, *op.cit.*, 469-470.
102. *Ibid.*, 471.
103. *O.R.*, I, xlv, pt. 1, 343; Livermore, *Numbers and Losses*, 131-132; Hood, *Advance and Retreat*, 298; Crownover, Sims, *The Battle of Franklin*, reprinted from Tennessee Hist. Quarterly, Vol.XIV, No.4, December, 1955, 26; Cox, *op.cit.*, 96.
104. LeDuc, William G., *Memoirs*, ms., HEH.

ates. Lower commanders on both sides shone in the fighting—Jacob D. Cox, Stanley and Updycke for the Federals; Cleburne, Forrest, and others for the Confederates. On Hood's side, the defeat was not only a lamentable display of rashness, but costly both in manpower and morale. The Federals sustained losses, and drew off, but they had achieved their object in impeding Hood. For the third time within a few days, the Confederate army had been frustrated.[105]

Personal recollections of the conflict were many and vivid. A Wisconsin soldier wrote: "It is impossible to exaggerate the fierce energy with which the Confederate soldiers, that short November afternoon, threw themselves against the works, fighting with what seemed the very madness of despair." He spoke of thirteen assaults including one in which he saw General Patrick Cleburne with his staff ride up onto the works, until "horse and rider and some of his Staff went down to death."[106] The stark, deadly simplicity of the Battle of Franklin impressed those who participated. Many of them could see it all from the Winstead Hills to the Carter House; and one can survey the tragic and memorable field today, virtually unchanged without the intrusion of monuments or modern memorials.

As Schofield moved on up toward Nashville and the Confederates who survived sullenly followed, post-mortem analyses were volunteered, particularly on the Confederate side. Cheatham, Cleburne, and Forrest, among others, had opposed the attack, and now Cleburne, with five other general officers, was dead.[107] Hood was once more full of excuses, including a plea that Schofield had been instructed to hold Franklin, and for this reason he wished to attack before the Federals were solidly intrenched.[108] In his book *Advance and Retreat*, Hood makes much of the Confederate disappointment at Spring Hill as an impelling motive for the bloody charge at Franklin. He says nothing about opposition to the attack from his generals,[109] maintaining that the attack "became a necessity as imperative as that which impelled General Lee to order the assault at Gaines's Mills."[110] On the other hand, Confederate Lieut. Gen. A.P. Stewart wrote: "To assault was a terrible proposition to troops who, during Johnston's long retreat, had been trained to avoid charging breastworks."[111] Another officer commented: "The truth is, the failure at Spring Hill was General Hood's own failure. . . . The loss at Spring Hill could have been fully

105. Cox, *op.cit.*, 81-98; Horn, Stanley, *The Army of Tennessee*, 394-404; Van Horne, T.B., *History of the Army of the Cumberland*, II, 198 and *passim;* Hood, J.B., *Advance and Retreat*, 292-300; Hay, Thomas Robson, *Hood's Tennessee Campaign*, New York, 1929, 119ff.

106. Atwater, M.B., *Reminiscences*, ms. State Hist. Soc. of Wisconsin.

107. Hay, *op.cit.*, 120-121.

108. *O.R.*, I, xlv, pt. 1, 652, Hood's report.

109. Hood, *Advance and Retreat*, *op.cit.*, 292-300.

110. *Ibid.*, 294.

111. Quoted in Buck, *Cleburne and His Command*, *op.cit.*, 287.

retrieved at Franklin by crossing the Harpeth River by fords above Franklin and getting a strong position among the Brentwood hills in the rear of the enemy."[112] One Southern eyewitness frankly declared: "Our men were flushed with hope and pride and all thought they fought for Tennessee. They felt that the eyes of the men and women all over our country as well as in Tennessee were upon them, and the Yankee army which they had followed so long was before them. . . . The chivalry of the South did charge. . . ."[113] But despite the courage of that charge and the frightful carnage, Hood had lost the battle, a battle that probably should never have been fought.

By the second day of December, Hood had approached Nashville. He found the handsome city ready to meet his onset. Strong Union lines ran from the Cumberland River on the west, or right, around the south side of the city to the river on the left, or east. There were three Union corps under Thomas along with an extra division, and the cavalry under James H. Wilson. Hood placed his own troops on high ground, but they actually circled less than half the city. Forrest, of course, commanded the cavalry. There they stood, adamantly waiting. This waiting was extended when, for the entire half-month ending December 14th, the two armies were icebound. Cox tells us that from the 7th to the 13th, "the slopes in front of the lines were a continuous glare of ice, so that movements away from the roads and broken paths could be only with the greatest difficulty and at a snail's pace. Men and horses were seen falling whenever they attempted to move across country. A man slipping on the hillside had no choice but to sit down and slide to the bottom."[114] Rain, snow, and sleet had begun on the 8th and prevented any action whatsoever. One officer later said that the ice problem "was so exceptional that it was not appreciated or fully understood at the East."[115] The weather did not improve until December 14, when Thomas was able to issue afternoon orders to his corps commanders for an advance. His 50,000 men, now fully in hand, were impatient to go. Hood, for his part, felt confident of the result if the Union army took the offensive. "I felt," he wrote in his official reports, that if Thomas attacked him in his works, "I would defeat him and thus gain possession of Nashville, with abundant supplies for the army. This would give me possession of Tennessee." Meanwhile, the leaders in Washington and Virginia did not share Thomas's hopefulness, for as time passed the situation appeared more and more anxious. Sherman and his 60,000 troops were busy somewhere in Georgia. Grant and Meade were held fast at Petersburg, while Hood had

112. *Ibid.*, 287.

113. William D. Gale to his wife, Jan. 14, 1865, in Gale-Polk Papers, Southern Historical Collection, Univ. of N.C.

114. Cox, Jacob D., *Military Reminiscences of the Civil War*, II, New York, 1900, 352-353.

115. *Ibid.*, 354.

marched into central Tennessee to Nashville. And it was about Hood that they were deeply concerned.

For his part, Thomas, by noon of December 1, had Schofield's two somewhat battered corps back from Franklin, along with Wilson's cavalry. A.J. Smith's veteran corps had come in from Missouri, so by the tenth of December Thomas's total force was 70,272 present for duty, many in garrison duty rather than at Nashville.[116] That city had been strongly fortified since early in the war, and the defenses several times enlarged until a formidable series of forts and entrenchments encircled its southern half and guarded the eight primary pikes that led into the place. Nashville had served since 1862 as a major, if not the major, base of the Union in the West. The eight miles of new lines held 44,000 infantry and there were 10,000 more men of the post garrison and quartermaster's department. They were ready but they continued to improve their defensive positions. Thomas still had a lot to do when the inclement weather set in.

Hood was up to Nashville and in position by December 3, with about 37,000 infantry present for duty although he maintained that he had but 22,000.[117] The Army of Tennessee was very well posted as were their opponents; Hood had a string of detached, self-supporting redoubts helping him hold an extremely strong position. So secure did Hood feel that he sent Forrest out toward Murfreesboro with a considerable part of his cavalry and an infantry division which the inexperienced Federal garrison ably repelled. Meanwhile he made a strong position stronger by fortifying Montgomery Hill near the Union center and other lines paralleling the northern exposures. He could do little with his left, however, which, widely separated from the swollen river, remained weak enough to be easily flanked. The central question remains whether he should have entrenched at all! Might it not have been possible for him to move around Nashville and head north, weather permitting? This would have forced Thomas into action, a different action than was taken at Nashville.

But the Southern idea was that if Hood forced Thomas out of Nashville, the Confederates could resist and repulse the attack. At a council of war with his generals, Hood exclaimed that Thomas's strength had been exaggerated, and "that we must take Nashville and we *shall* take it! And then, gentlemen, how we shall feast off the rich Yankee spoils!"[118]

Meanwhile, Thomas's problems mounted—problems that for the most part should never have arisen. He had not wanted to go back to Tennessee and felt

116. Stone, *op.cit.*, 483.
117. *Ibid.*, 487-489.
118. N.Y. *Herald*, Dec. 22, 1864, dispatch of D.P. Conyngham.

that he was not liked by Grant (as was Sherman), though at the same time he did not know why he should not be equally trusted.[119] Smith's troops and others had reached Nashville lacking transport, and the horses and mules of the other two corps, like those of the cavalry, were in bad shape after the fighting withdrawal from Pulaski to Nashville. While men, arms, ammunition, and rations were sufficient, many other needed items were in very short supply. Furthermore, this was not an Army in the best sense; it was a command put together in a hurry and needed shaking-down. The Union leader did his utmost. As an officer who was there put it, Thomas knew what his job was, and "he realized too keenly the importance of victory to allow anything that might help secure it to be neglected."[120] Nashville became a busy workshop of preparation, day and night. Every draft animal within many miles was gathered in, and even those of a storm-bound circus were appropriated.

But an anxious Washington was growing more and more impatient. Grant, far distant and unaware of the biting cold that impeded Thomas's ill-clad troops, on December 6 peremptorily ordered an attack. Thomas called in his corps commanders, but they decided it would be impossible before the 10th. Grant tells us in his official report that before the battle of Nashville he grew restive over what he thought of as the unnecessary Union delay. This impatience was increased upon learning that the enemy had sent a force of cavalry across the Cumberland into Kentucky, for he feared that Hood might cross with his whole army, and create a vexatious situation there. He was ready to start west himself to take general command in person, but when he arrived in Washington from Petersburg, he found there a dispatch from Thomas announcing his attack upon the Confederates and its initial progress. "I was delighted," his report recalls. "All fears and apprehensions were dispelled." He still thought that Thomas should have moved out earlier as soon as Hood approached Nashville, but now he realized that Thomas had made his plans and completed his preparations with a quiet, consummate skill stamped by the deliberate, tenacious genius he had shown at Chickamauga.

Grant had heard nothing in Virginia of the attack, so he had wired Stanton recommending that Thomas be replaced with Schofield! A very observant officer called this attempt to displace Thomas an "unprecedented and unmerited indignity."[121] In retrospect, it is difficult to regard it otherwise. On the other hand, Lincoln, Stanton, and Grant were seeing the situation from the East, in Washington and Petersburg, and affairs did hold a different aspect from that distance and at that time. Still, the doubts respecting Thomas and

119. Stone, *op.cit.*, 492.
120. *Ibid.*, 496.
121. *Ibid.*, 500.

the movement toward his replacement were in many ways puzzling.

Defenders of Thomas feel that he had been left by Sherman with an inferior army to accomplish a huge task, given scattered detachments of troops from which to create an adequate force, ordered to hold a position which he did not seek, given promises of support which were never fulfilled—and then on the eve of the crucial battle was threatened with the loss of his command to a subordinate whose actions in the campaign up to that time had been somewhat questionable.

Actually, larger elements entered the situation than the natural and not altogether impulsive (though excessively hasty) anxiety shown by Grant. The President himself felt the deepest uneasiness. Secretary Stanton had telegraphed Grant as early as December 2 that "The President feels solicitous about the disposition of Gen. Thomas to lay in fortifications for an indefinite period 'until Wilson gets equipments.' This looks like the McClellan and Rosecrans strategy of do nothing and let the rebels raid the country. The President wishes you to consider the matter."[122] It may seem strange that Washington could not perceive the difference between a McClellan or a Rosecrans and Thomas! But Washington received only bits of authentic intelligence from the front mingled with conclusions and guesses. Little was known about the weather and other logistical impediments, and the indifference shown by Thomas to any success less than decisive had naturally reawakened Lincoln's mistrust of commanders with the "slows". That same December 2, Grant told Thomas that he should attack because if the Federals did not, Hood could inflict "incalculable injury upon your railroads . . ."[123] Thomas retorted that Smith had just arrived along with another division, that he lacked cavalry and "it must be remembered that my command was made up of the two weakest corps of General Sherman's army and all the dismounted cavalry except one brigade, and the task of reorganizing and equipping has met with many delays, which have enabled Hood to take advantage of my crippled condition. I earnestly hope, however, that in a few more days I shall be able to give him a fight."[124] Grant continued to bait Thomas who replied that he would possibly attack on the 7th.[125] Then came the order of December 6 at 4 P.M., "Attack Hood at once, and wait no longer for a remount of your cavalry. There is great danger of delay resulting in a campaign back to the Ohio River."[126] At 9 P.M. on the 6th, Thomas replied: "I will make the necessary dispositions and attack Hood at once, agreeably to your order, though I believe it will be hazardous

122. *O.R.*, I, xlv, pt. 2, 15-16.
123. *Ibid.*, 17, Grant to Thomas, Dec. 2, 1864, City Point, Va.
124. *Ibid.*, 17.
125. *Ibid.*, 29, 55.
126. *Ibid.*, 70.

with the small force of cavalry now at my service."[127] The next day, the 7th, Stanton continued to bring pressure upon Grant, writing: "Thomas seems unwilling to attack because it is hazardous, as if all war were anything but hazardous. If he waits for Wilson to get ready, Gabriel will be blowing his last horn."[128] Then, at 1:30 P.M. the chafing Grant informed Stanton that if Thomas did not attack promptly, "I would recommend superseding him by Schofield, leaving Thomas subordinate . . ."[129] Late in the afternoon of the 8th, Grant burst out to Halleck: "If Thomas has not struck yet, he ought to be ordered to hand over his command to Schofield. There is no better man to repel an attack than Thomas, but I fear he is too cautious ever to take the initiative." Grant was completely out of patience, and adding that he feared Hood would reach the Ohio, he asked if it was not advisable "to call on Ohio, Indiana, and Illinois for 60,000 men for thirty days."[130]

Then and even later, Thomas was regarded as a defensive general addicted to a type of Fabian warfare at which he had excelled. At the same time, it was and still is too often forgotten that he had repeatedly shown capacities for the offence, both in action and in planning. But Halleck now entered the situation. He reluctantly told Grant—at 9 o'clock in the evening of December 8—"If you wish General Thomas relieved from command, give the order. No one here will, I think, interfere. The responsibility, however, will be yours, as no one here, so far as I am informed, wishes General Thomas's removal."[131] Grant now retreated a little, telling Halleck he wished Thomas "reminded of the importance of immediate action," but he would not say relieve the general until he heard further from him.[132]

More messages were exchanged, and then on December 9, through presidential instructions and by direction of the Secretary of War, orders were given to relieve Thomas.[133]

But Halleck delayed transmitting them, apparently because of news of the bad ice storm.[134] Grant had even repeated his order for removal. Yet, on the evening of December 9, in a message to Halleck, he stated: "I am very unwilling to do injustice to an officer who has done so much good service as General Thomas has, and will, therefore, suspend the order relieving him until it is seen whether he will do anything."[135] This was judicious. Halleck, then, by his advice and by his delay in acting had prevented Thomas's supercession.

127. *Ibid.*, 70.
128. *Ibid.*, 84, Stanton to Grant, 10:20 A.M., Dec. 7, 1864.
129. *Ibid.*, 84, Grant to Stanton, Dec. 7, 1864.
130. *Ibid.*, 96.
131. *Ibid.*, 96.
132. *Ibid.*, 96.
133. *Ibid.*, 114.
134. *Ibid.*, 97, 114, 115, 116.
135. *Ibid.*, 116, Grant to Halleck 5:30 p.m., Dec. 9.

Meanwhile, that General was keeping Washington informed of the hazardous state of the weather and the impossibility of moving over the icy hills. By the 11th, however, Grant's impatience once more burst out: "If you delay attack longer the mortifying spectacle will be witnessed of a rebel army moving for the Ohio River, and you will be forced to act, accepting such weather as you find. Let there be no further delay. . . . I am in hopes of receiving a dispatch from you today announcing that you have moved. Delay no longer for weather or reenforcements."[136] Of course, Hood's army would slip and slide about on the ice just as much as Thomas's so that nobody was moving, and Thomas was quite aware of the possibility of Hood's heading north. He replied to Grant late on the 11th that he would obey the order promptly "however much I may regret it, as the attack will have to be made under every disadvantage. The whole country is covered with a perfect sheet of ice and sleet, and it is with difficulty the troops are able to move about on level ground. It was my intention to attack Hood as soon as the ice melted, and would have done so yesterday had it not been for the storm."[137] On the 12th, Thomas sent Halleck word that he was ready as soon as the ice melted sufficiently.[138]

But it seemed almost too late, for on December 13 Grant sent orders from City Point that General Logan should proceed immediately to Nashville, reporting by telegraph his arrival at Louisville, and also his arrival at Nashville.[139] Halleck, in a less strenuous way, urged Thomas to act. He replied on the evening of December 14 that, the ice having melted away that day, "the enemy will be attacked tomorrow morning. Much as I regret the apparent delay in attacking the enemy, it could not have been done before with any reasonable hope of success."

Grant himself then rushed up to Washington, bound for Nashville, but he was still in the capital city when he heard the news of the Union success on December 15.[140] Logan stopped at Louisville and went no further. Students must study pages of official dispatches and other material to analyze satisfactorily this seeming crisis in Union command, which was actually but a transiently dramatic episode. The telegrapher David Homer Bates tells us that Grant wrote three orders removing Thomas, and that Lincoln suspended the first, that Logan did not deliver the second because of the attack, and that Eckert suppressed the third.[141] Bates believed that Halleck intensified Grant's doubts respecting Thomas, but the official dispatches indicate rather that Halleck softened the removal order. Bates asserts that the order made out in the

136. *Ibid.*, 143, 4 P.M., Dec. 11.
137. *Ibid.*, 143, Dec. 11, 10:30 P.M.
138. *Ibid.*, 155.
139. *Ibid.*, 171.
140. *Ibid.*, 195.
141. Bates, David Homer, *Lincoln in the Telegraph Office*, New York, 1907, 310.

name of the President was not sent because Lincoln halted it. Bates also reports a conference in the War Department on the evening of December 15 with Lincoln, Stanton, Grant, and Halleck present. Grant then wrote his third order although Lincoln and Stanton were opposed. Telegraph director Eckert delayed sending it more than an hour, and by that time news of the first day's battle came. Lincoln and Stanton quickly approved Eckert's action.[142]

Lincoln's secretaries emphasize the tension in Washington, adding that Grant exhibited his impatience much more strongly than the civil authorities.[143] But we must not overlook the second message of Stanton to Grant, noting that the President "feels solicitous about the disposition of General Thomas to lay in fortifications for an indefinite period . . ."[144] The secretaries also criticized Grant for sending Logan west to relieve Thomas and in starting for Nashville himself.[145] But they recognized that Halleck's delays saved Thomas for a few vital days.[146] Cavalry commander James Harrison Wilson writes that Thomas told him with deep emotion on the night of Dec. 10: "Wilson, they [meaning General Grant and the War Department] treat me as though I were a boy and incapable of planning a campaign or fighting a battle. If they will let me alone I will fight this battle just as soon as it can be done, and will surely win it; but I will not throw the victory away nor sacrifice the brave men of this army by moving till the thaw begins. I will surrender my command without a murmur, if they wish it; but I will not act against my judgment when I know I am right, and in such a grave emergency."[147]

Grant in his *Memoirs* is unduly critical of Thomas, employing such phrases as: "Thomas made no effort to reinforce Schofield at Franklin . . ." and "Hood was allowed to move upon Nashville and to invest that place almost without interference . . ."[148] Neither statement is accurate and both are distortions. Hood did not "invest" Nashville, the word "allowed" is inaccurate, and how could Thomas have reinforced Schofield at Franklin when he did not know that Hood would attack and had already properly ordered Schofield back to Nashville? The Tennessee capital was the only place for Thomas to organize and watch and prepare to oppose Hood. Grant admits the weather was bad, writing, "But I was afraid that the enemy would find means of moving, elude Thomas and manage to get north of the Cumberland River . . ."[149] Perhaps

142. *Ibid.*, 315-317.
143. Nicolay and Hay, *Lincoln*, X, 23.
144. *O.R.*, I, xlv, pt. 2, 15-16.
145. Nicolay and Hay, *Lincoln*, X, 28.
146. *Ibid.*, 24.
147. Wilson, James Harrison, "The Union Cavalry in the Hood Campaign", *Battles and Leaders*, IV, 467.
148. Grant, *Memoirs*, II, 379.
149. *Ibid.*, 380.

Hood, as we have said, should have moved north, but Thomas was watching and would have undoubtedly taken action if the Confederates had done so. Grant gives the traditional picture of Thomas's slowness (another distortion at least at Nashville) and he does not mention the orders for Schofield to take over.[150] He does mention sending Logan west and his own going to Washington, and he is very critical of the follow-up after the victory at Nashville. It is difficult to defend Grant in his actions at the time, and even more difficult to justify the comments in the *Memoirs* which were written after a lapse of time sufficient to have provided a clearer recollection of the facts.

Schofield states that no anxiety was felt at Nashville, that Hood's operations were closely watched every day, and that the Federals awaited the attack with confidence. "The anxiety felt elsewhere, especially by General Grant, was probably due to some doubt of the wisdom of Sherman's plan of going off with his main army before disposing of Hood . . . as well as to lack of confidence in General Thomas on account of his well-known deliberation of thought and action. . . ."[151]

The ice was gone on the 15th of December (although the weather was foggy and drizzly, but fairly warm) when the guns boomed out from Fort Negley and other points, awakening the people of Nashville to the fact that a great battle was going on to the south of their city. The Union troops were in line of battle waiting for the offensive to begin. On the Federal left, General James B. Steedman's troops including two brigades of black soldiers advanced against Cheatham, an operation to conceal the real attack which would be on the Confederate left. A reporter found one black warrior who made light of a seeming injury: "Oh, Lor, cannon struck me right on the breast and rolled me over." [152] Steedman's men did well, making the proper simulation of an assault. But the principal action was on the Federal right, where Union troops overlapped the Confederate line on a slanting advance. A.J. Smith's corps moved into position, and by the time the fog lifted, Wilson's cavalry was also ready for battle. The Confederate left was driven back and several redoubts fell. Schofield's corps and then Wilson's cavalry advanced further around Hood's left. Montgomery Hill was captured. Once when the charge seemed to falter, a timely burst of cheering heartened the assailants. "That is the voice of the American people," exclaimed Thomas.[153] About four o'clock in the afternoon,

150. *Ibid.*, 380-382.
151. Schofield, *op.cit.*, 236-237.
152. New York *Herald*, Dec. 22, 1864, dispatch by D.P. Conyngham.
153. Stone, *op.cit.*, 517.

another general charge was made with success, until further progress was halted by the early December darkness. Thomas's plan of attack against the weak Confederate left flank was paying off. Meanwhile, Steedman threatened Hood's right, holding new troops in that quarter.

Hood could have retired, but he did not; he simply withdrew his battered troops into a shorter two-mile position, well entrenched. Meanwhile, Thomas and his generals conferred and determined to continue the conflict.

The 16th was warmer and cloudy, with some gleams of sunlight followed later by showers. The Federal hosts were ready for the fight and moved forward. The plan was much the same, to hit Hood's left, but now the Union army could operate more as a single force, the enemy line being much shorter. In the great assault on Shy's Hill the Federals were more than successful. Beset in front and rear, "the rebels broke out of the works at a bound and ran down the steep hill toward their right and rear as fast as their legs could carry them. It was more like a scene in a spectacular drama than anything in real life. The steep hill, its top crowned with trees through which the enemy's works and movements could be dimly seen, and its sides still green with patches of moist grass—the waving flags, the smoke slowly rising through the leafless branches, the wonderful outburst of musketry, the still more ecstatic cheers, the multitude racing for life, the eager and rapid pursuit—so exciting was it all the lookers-on involuntarily clapped their hands as at a splendid and successful transformation scene; as indeed it was just that, for in those few minutes the whole elaborate structure of the rebellion in the Southwest was utterly overrun by one crash, and even its very foundations destroyed."[154]

As Thomas rode with his staff to the crown of Overton's Hill at the battle's end, he lifted his hat and said, "Oh, what a grand army I have! God bless each member of it."[155] As for the victorious General himself, he had planned well, struck when ready, and struck hard with great skill. Later he was to confess what he called a "grave error of judgment," remarking that at the close of the first day he should have detached a force and sent it round to Hood's rear to cut off his retirement. Had he done so, he might have captured nearly or quite the whole of Hood's army. Instead Hood was enabled to effect his retreat, with the help of Forrest, who made a timely appearance upon the scene, throwing a large body of cavalry westward at the rear of the defeated Confederates, and shielding them from J. H. Wilson's force. Thereafter, Forrest, together with some infantry reinforcements, protected Hood's final retreat to the Tennessee, and his successful crossing of that river on December 27th. The really important charge against Thomas, however, remained that of excessive caution in

154. *Ibid.*, 531.
155. Johnson, Richard W., *Memoir of Maj. Gen. George H. Thomas*, Philadelphia, 1881, 195.

forming a concentration against Hood, with consequent risks to the Union army.[156]

Thomas probably had a force in the field of approximately 50,000, which lost 387 killed, 2,562 wounded, and 112 missing, or total casualties of 3,061. Confederate statistics are much more difficult to ascertain because the demoralization of Hood's army made accurate returns impossible. Hood probably had nearly 23,000 men engaged.[157]

Hood's broken army fled southward in the December darkness. Units were split into fragments, nobody quite sure where they were going. A heavy rain added to the misery and confusion. The night bivouac was sorrowful and painful, but a small semblance of order was restored.

The total character of Hood's defeat has been exaggerated. His army had suffered heavily, and its fighting power was shattered for at least the moment. But the commander, the staff, and part of the manpower were still in the field. Wilson's dismounted cavalry were not in condition or position to pursue the Confederates on the evening of December 16, and not ready for action until the morning of the 17th.

A Confederate effectively described one good reason for the Southern defeat. "We could see the whole line in our front, every move, advance, attack, and retreat. It was magnificent, if our men had only fought. I could see the Capitol all day and the churches. What a grand sight it was! The Yankees had three lines of battle everywhere I could see, and parks of artillery playing upon us and raining shot and shell for eight mortal hours . . ." This mighty force broke and routed the Confederate defenders. " 'Tis impossible to give you any idea of an army frightened and routed. Some brave effort was made to rally the men and make a stand, but all control over them was gone, and they flatly refused to stop, two out of three throwing away their guns, and, indeed, everything that impeded their flight, and fled every man for himself. 'Sauve qui peut' actuated and urged all officers and men, who poured over the fields and hills in wild confusion, all trying to be first towards Franklin."[158]

A few Federals pursued the fugitives down the Franklin Pike on the night of December 16, taking prisoners by whole squads; the darkness, however, prevented more effective pursuit at the moment.[159] In fact, on the 17th, Hood found himself able to march rapidly with the forces he still possessed, unhampered by artillery, wagon trains, or wounded. As they passed safely through

156. Van Horne, *Life of Gen. George H. Thomas, op.cit.*, 344, 345; Formby, John, *The American Civil War*, London, 1910, 365, 366.

157. Livermore, *op.cit.*, 132-133; *O.R.*, I, xlv, pt. 1, 105, 679.

158. Gale-Polk Papers, So. Hist. Coll., Univ. of N.C. Library, William D. Gale to his wife, Jan. 29, 1865.

159. New York *Herald*, Dec. 22, 1865.

Franklin behind Wilson's cavalry, Stephen D. Lee's men held off attacks as a rearguard. By nightfall of December 17, they were around Spring Hill, of bitter memory, and on the 18th were concentrating near Columbia, delayed by high water in the streams. But these adverse conditions also impeded the pursuing Federal cavalry and foot-soldiers. By the 19th, Hood was fleeing across the Duck River, rejoined by Forrest, who now furnished cover. The main forces crossed the Tennessee at Bainbridge, December 26-28. The sufferings of the army had been deplorable, but at least a remnant still existed. The heavy rains, more cold, mud in the atrocious roads, added to the difficulties of both sides. Everyone was exhausted. The Federals wisely halted their advance and Hood's sullen army limped on westward through Tuscumbia toward Iuka.[160] The Confederate army concentrated January 3, 1865, at Tupelo, Mississippi. On January 17, Richard Taylor was ordered to replace a now useless Hood, who resigned. As one historian puts it, "The once powerful army of Tennessee was all but a mere memory."[161]

Jacob D. Cox vividly sums up the campaign: "Hood's retreat from Nashville to the Tennessee and Thomas's pursuit were almost equally arduous for their armies, though very different in their effect upon the spirits of the troops. The roads were in horrible condition, even those which had been macadamized being almost impassable. The ordinary country roads were much worse, and after passing Pulaski, till the Tennessee was reached, the wrecks of wagons and carcasses of animals filled the way. . . ."[162] One writer states that the men captured in the battle and pursuit included one major-general, seven brigadier-generals, 14 colonels, and many lesser officers, with more than 8,600 fighting men in all. In engagements preceding Nashville, some 75 field guns, over 60 colors, more than 300 wagons, a thousand mules, and countless amounts of equipment were captured by the Union forces.

[V]

In the view of the government, the Atlantic coast, from Fortress Monroe to Florida, was never really a secondary front, and it was in the news almost constantly. During most of the war the Federals had held a lodgment on the North Carolina coast around Roanoke Island and New Bern. This back door to Virginia had not been sufficiently utilized, but it remained ajar. Now, after Nashville, late in 1864, the time had come for the North to turn belated attention to the last major port of the South open to blockade runners—Wilming-

160. For a good summary, see Hay, *op.cit.*, 171-178.
161. *Ibid.*, 181.
162. Cox, *The March to the Sea*, *op.cit.*, 124-130.

ton. There was another reason for coastal action. If Sherman was to come north from Savannah and the Georgia coast, he certainly would need help from an operational Federal base at Wilmington.

The key to Wilmington was Fort Fisher, a typical wartime coastal defense, largely of sand, erected on the right or west bank of the Cape Fear River south of Wilmington. From the summer of 1862 until December, 1864, Colonel William Lamb had been strengthening Fort Fisher to the point where he hoped "it could withstand the heaviest fire of any guns in the American Navy. . . ."[163] That he did not make an effective defense was not his fault. He certainly made a gallant effort. The fort had been built with the sole view of receiving naval fire, and it withstood, uninjured except for its armament, two of the fiercest bombardments the world had thus far known.[164]

In the end, Fort Fisher was to fall, like Fort McAllister, to an attack by land. Up to that time it had ably protected Wilmington and the blockade runners, proving that a sand fort was difficult if not impossible for naval guns to destroy completely, while at the same time revealing once more the vulnerability of any fort when attacked by mobile columns. By 1864 Union officers referred to Fort Fisher as the "Malakoff of the South." Strong works supported heavy coast defense guns, though there was no moat with scarp and counterscarp. These defences against storming were nullified by shifting sands. Bomb proofs, magazines, passageways, traverses and other military engineering construction added to the strength of the fort as did land mines across the peninsula and a palisade of sharpened logs, both intended to stave off land assaults.

Slowly the blockade around the mouth of Cape Fear tightened, but despite some 65 captures and destructions of vessels, numerous runners got through. New Inlet, protected by Fort Fisher, soon became the major gateway to the port.

In the fall of 1864, Bragg took over comprehensive command of the North Carolina defense, with General W.H.C. Whiting as second. On the morning of December 20 the Federal fleet was seen off Fort Fisher. The garrison had been cut to not more than 500 men. A severe gale impeded the fleet, however, and by the 23rd reinforcements came in; the defenders now mustered 900 men and boys.

Colonel Lamb reported that on the night of December 23 he was awakened by a gentle sway of his small brick house followed by a slight explosion. No one took it very seriously, on the Confederate side at least.[165] On the 24th,

163. Lamb, William, "Defence of Fort Fisher, North Carolina," *Operations on the Atlantic Coast, 1861-1865*, Vol.IX, Papers of the Military Hist. Soc. of Mass., Boston, 1912, 350. See also: Lamb's article in *Battles and Leaders*, IV, 642-654.

164. *Ibid.*, 350.

165. *Ibid.*, 361.

Porter's great armada approached the fort. His bombardment was soon at thunderous height, the "most terrific bombardment from the fleet," declared Lamb, "which war had ever witnessed."[166] Many Union shots fell in the parade ground without harming the garrison. After two hours the flag was shot away, but despite the rain of shot and shell, no casualties occurred. Damage was slight and by 5:30 the fleet withdrew. The warships had not tried to get inside the bar where they could have taken the fort in reverse. Colonel Lamb estimates the Federals fired 10,000 shot to his 672. Probably never, since the invention of gunpowder, had so much of it been so harmlessly expended as in this first day's attack on Fort Fisher.[167]

On Christmas day, the Yankee fleet moved in to mount another heavy bombardment. Lamb, losing two 7-inch rifles by explosion, maintained a slow, deliberate, economical return-fire. Some quarters were destroyed and earthworks penetrated, but damage remained trivial. By now, Lamb had 1,371 men, including 450 Junior Reserves. Late in the afternoon, a heavy fire against the land-face commenced, and skirmishers advanced upon the fort. Lamb opened upon them with grape and canister. But no real assault was undertaken, and casualties for the day continued light. The Federal landing party avoided capture.

The project of a Union attack upon Wilmington and Fisher had long been considered. Gideon Welles had told Farragut that fall that the Navy Department had desired an amphibious attack on the Cape Fear defences since the winter of 1862, but the Army had refused. Welles believed that Grant was now ready to spare troops and that Farragut could command the naval forces. But Farragut rejected the assignment because of deficient health.[168] Rear-Admiral David Dixon Porter was then given the task, and the command of the North Atlantic Blockading Squadron. Grant named Major General Godfrey Weitzel, one of Butler's officers, to the Army command; but, to the annoyance of Grant and Porter, Butler took over the land forces in person.[169]

Butler had heard of a tremendous accidental explosion near London which had destroyed buildings, and he wished to try such an explosion before Fort Fisher. An old hulk filled with two or three hundred tons of gunpowder would be towed near the fort, run aground, and detonated, and the troops sent ashore without further preparation. Porter finally took the old powder-ship *Louisiana* and exploded her early on the morning of December 24 (about 1:00 A.M.) in one of the most ludicrous fiascoes of the war. "It was terrible," exclaimed one defender later. "It woke up nearly everybody in the fort!" Only a slight shak-

166. *Ibid.*, 362.
167. *Ibid.*, 364-365.
168. Farragut to Welles, no date, Farragut Papers, HEH.
169. King, Capt. Joseph E., *The Fort Fisher Campaigns, 1864-1865*, U.S. Naval Institute Proceedings, August, 1951.

ing was felt on the walls at Fort Fisher. On December 24-25 the naval expedition opened another immense cannonade, and helped land some 2,000 troops. When, on approaching within about fifty yards of the palisades, they were met with a heavy burst of canister, the Yankees withdrew to their lines! Porter tried to get Butler to try again, but he sullenly took his men and sailed northward to Virginia. Grant was chagrined; Washington was mortified. This was Butler's last explosion, however, for on January 7, 1865, he was relieved.[170] Grant told Lincoln on the 28th: "The Wilmington expedition has proven a gross and culpable failure . . ."[171]

The powder-ship experiment had been absurd enough, but Grant and others were more critical of Butler's failure to sustain the assault. In the end, Fort Fisher remained in Confederate hands, and Wilmington was still open to blockade runners. To the Federals, it was clear they could not let this blot on their military-naval record stand. Besides, Wilmington was needed.

Hence, in January, about two weeks after the first expedition had failed, Porter's fleet was again off Fort Fisher, with 8,000 troops under Major General Alfred H. Terry, an unspectacular soldier up to now, but a sound one. On January 13 the bombardment began, and expeditionary forces were landed. On January 14, the attack continued from land and sea, and on January 15 the fort was assaulted and captured. The Army put 4,700 men ashore in entrenchments to watch for an attack by Bragg from the north, or Wilmington. Terry took 3,300 men against Fort Fisher itself. When the land attack was launched in mid-afternoon of January 15, some 400 marines and 1,600 sailors assailed the fort from the beachside, despite heavy fire. The sailors and marines were forced to retreat in disorder, but their charge served as a decoy, and the Federal infantry fought their way into the fort. The combat was hand-to-hand, and fighting continued well into the evening until the Confederates surrendered at ten o'clock. The Union army lost 955 men killed, and about 1,700 wounded or missing. Bragg with 6,000 men to the north did not get involved.[172]

Confederate Colonel Lamb, still in command of the fort, had been aware the Yankees would return. As soon as the lights of the armada were seen, he had prepared for action. Daylight of the 13th had "disclosed the return of the most formidable fleet that ever floated on the sea," shortly raining upon the fort and beach a storm of shot and shell which, he wrote, "caused both earth and sea to tremble." When the naval bombardment ceased, suddenly the steam whistles of the fleet sounded a charge by the Federal army and the sailors and marines. Lamb's men held and repelled the naval force, but shouts of triumph

170. King, *op.cit.*, 844-848, Grant's *Memoirs*, II, 387-395; *O.R.*, I, xlii, pt.3, 1085, Butler to Grant, Dec. 27, 1864.

171. *Ibid.*, 1087; Report of the Joint Committee on Conduct of the War, Vol.II, 1865, Fort Fisher Expedition, 51-56.

172. *Battles and Leaders*, IV, 661-662.

arose, and Lamb espied Federal flags upon the land-side ramparts. The naval guns continued to aid the Union land attack, driving the defenders from the parapets. The scene in the galleries "was indescribably horrible. Great cannon broke in two, their carriages wrecked, and among their ruins the mutilated bodies of my dead and dying comrades. Still no tidings from Bragg! . . ."[173] Lamb was wounded, but the fight continued until there was nothing to do but surrender.

Bragg was to say that, "To have assaulted the enemy behind his intrenchments, covered by his fleet, with inferior numbers, would have exhausted our means to aid the fort, and thereby not only have insured its ultimate fall, but have opened the country behind it."[174] General William H.C. Whiting, who was mortally wounded, in his report while a prisoner wrote: "I think that the result might have been avoided, and Fort Fisher still held, if the commanding general had done his duty. I charge him with this loss . . ."[175] Bragg had still more to say in his own defense: "Believing myself that Grant's army could not storm and carry the fort if it was defended, I felt perfect confidence that the enemy had assumed a most precarious position, from which he would escape with great difficulty . . ." But "such was the configuration of the country and the obstacles, that he would have accomplished his object with the force he had. Our only safe reliance was in his repulse . . . The defense of the fort ought to have been successful against *this* attack, but it had to fall eventually. The expedition brought against it was able to reduce it in spite of all that I could do. . . ."[176] One naval officer called the Fort Fisher operation and landings the most important and most instructive of the Civil War.[177] Cooperation of a high degree was achieved between Porter and Terry, an important factor.[178]

With the fall of Fort Fisher and the end of Wilmington as a sanctuary for blockade runners, the city itself remained intact, waiting to be opened to the Federals. On January 14, Schofield's Twenty-third Corps was ordered east from Tennessee. Down the Tennessee, up the Ohio, and by rail to Washington and Alexandria, they went, and before February 1st were ready to sail. Bad weather delayed them until February 4 when they were well started.[179] Gales off Hatteras hampered progress, but the new force landed safely at Fort Fisher

173. Lamb, *op.cit.*, 370-382.

174. *O.R.*, I, xlvi, pt. 1, 433.

175. *Ibid.*, 441.

176. Bragg, Braxton, Letter to His Brother, Southern Hist. Soc. Papers, X, 346, Jan. 21, 1865. Terry's report, *O.R.*, I, xlvi, pt. 1, 396-397; Ames, Adelbert, "The Capture of Fort Fisher, Jan. 15, 1865," Papers of the Military Historical Society of Mass., Vol. IX, 402-407.

177. Soley, John C., "The Naval Brigade," Papers of the Mil. Hist. Soc. of Mass., Vol.XII, 247.

178. Harkness, Edson J., "The Expeditions Against Fort Fisher and Wilmington," *Military Essays and Recollections, Illinois Commandary*, Chicago, 1894, II, 163; *O.R.*, I, xlvi, pt. 2, 155-156, Stanton to Lincoln, Fort Monroe, Jan. 17, 1865.

179. Cox, Jacob D., *The March to the Sea, op.cit.*, 147-162.

on February 9, joining Terry's men. The intention was that, after Wilmington surrendered, Schofield would open a route from Wilmington and New Bern to Goldsboro in time to meet Sherman coming north from Savannah. This was a wise plan, reminiscent of Sherman's original idea at Atlanta that he might be met by a force from the coast.

The Union campaign against the city of Wilmington was complicated by the wildness of the area, which included inlets, sands, swamps, ponds, lakes, and numerous other water deposits.[180] Yet the indefatigable General Jacob D. Cox led two brigades on a by-pass, forcing the Confederates to abandon their strong positions. The Union troops moved up both the left and right banks of the Cape Fear River, and despite stubborn opposition the two-pronged Union attack made a steady successful advance. By February 21, the Federals saw huge columns of smoke arising from the city of Wilmington, and on the morning of Washington's birthday, the Northern army entered it. In the long run, however, New Bern proved more valuable as a base for Sherman than Wilmington. Its adjacent harbors were better, and its rail facilities more efficient.

The Confederates had found their defensive efforts fruitless. Once Fort Fisher fell, Wilmington was of little use. One analyst of the evidence believes that the Southern troops should have been evacuated from the city sooner, with all forces concentrated and made available in the Carolinas and Georgia nearer the Savannah River. "Bragg, with the independent command of North Carolina, remained in Wilmington . . . until he was pushed out, frittering away his strength in skirmishes and letting the dry rot of desertion unchecked by vigorous action gnaw into his army, until in a few weeks he had no troops left but Hoke's division and a regiment of cavalry. . . ."[181]

It is doubtful that such concentration against Sherman would have been successful, but certainly it would have been a far more promising military policy than an inert submission to the dissipation of the discouraged, ill-supplied, and more and more desperate Confederate forces that remained. To be sure, a confessed failure to resist Federal invasions would have had its own debilitating effects on the Army and the population. Either way, by February 1865, little hope could be found in the Carolinas except in adherence to the policy of grimly hanging on.

[VI]

The bare statistics of miles marched, days and weeks spent, and men killed and wounded on both sides, convey only a fragmentary and inadequate impression of the great martial feat accomplished by Sherman and his veterans. Long

180. *Ibid.*
181. Hagood, Johnson, *Memoirs of the War of Secession*, Columbia, S.C., 1910, 329-331.

columns of statistics give us only a partial and hazy intimation of the tremendous consequences, some of them physical and material, but others of far larger significance, spiritual and moral, which sprang from this exhibition of national planning, daring, and determination in one of the most spectacular enterprises recorded in the history of modern war. For generations to come, Americans would view the feat with all the accompaniments of color and drama to be found in a great historical narrative by Thucydides, or in a romanticized and poetic canvas by J. M. W. Turner when he was most chromatic and imaginative. They would see again Sherman's serried lines of bayonets and snake-like files of covered wagons, his foam-flecked cavalry pressing southward along the yellow-clay roads, past pine-clad hills, while Atlanta flamed behind them. Their vision would pursue the march as the blue-clad soldiers met ragged battlers in gray, as they moved past forlorn groups of refugees, black and white, male and female, fleeing with bellowing cattle and squealing pigs in front of Yankee squads which fired farmhouses and whole towns as they drove inexorably on—toward the State House of Milledgeville, toward the long bridges which betokened the approach to the seacoast. Accompanying this vision would be the flash of flags flying, the sound of bands playing, or the sullen boom of artillery as a new action was begun against the unpredictable Hood or the dashing Forrest.

The country would never forget Sherman's fierce determination, his repeated demands for total war against a section that he described as "simply one big fort." It would never lose its memory of the grim tenacity of Thomas, the gallant immovability of the "hold-the-fort" course, nor the dash and velocity of Kilpatrick's bodies of cavalry. The march had effected many pragmatic results, but by no means its least gifts were those it had given the American vision and imagination. It had imparted to the sodden, bloody, exhausting and immeasurably depressing conflict some touches of rhetoric, of a grim poetry that would linger in the popular mind of the republic long after the gallant leaders had died, long after the phrase "Sherman's bummers" had lost its undertones of meaning for North and South alike, long after men ceased to feel the thrill that so long nerved millions on hearing the bands strike up clangorously the strains of "Marching Through Georgia."

[VII]

Elsewhere the war continued, but at a much more diminished pace. After the battle of Burgess Mill, October 27, 1864, little movement of any importance was undertaken on the Petersburg front until February. Intermittent sniping took place. Grant and Meade sustained their unwearied pressure. Lee was forced to defend a front of roughly thirty-five miles, from east of Richmond down to Hatcher's Run lying southwest of Petersburg, his effective force reduced to a mere 57,000 men.

On February 5, Meade's men, two corps, moved out toward Hatcher's Run and took the Boydton Plank Road. The Confederates fought back but were unable to dislodge the enemy. Although the road itself proved none too important, the action did extend the Federal line to the west, and once more Lee was forced to defend a longer line, now up to thirty-seven miles. Furthermore, his army was steadily draining away.

In the Shenandoah Valley, Sheridan was reaping the rewards of the October victory at Cedar Creek. There were numerous small raids and actions, and Early had to send a good portion of his troops to Richmond. Late in February, Sheridan left Winchester in the direction of Staunton, forcing Early back to Waynesborough. On March 2, Sheridan easily defeated the mere 1,800 men Early had left at Waynesborough, dispersing and capturing them. Destruction and devastation were rife in the Valley, and Sheridan was free to rejoin Grant at Petersburg.

A great deal had happened in the field since the reëlection of Lincoln in November. Sherman had completed his destructive march across Georgia and taken Savannah. Hood's offensive movement into Tennessee, the last major campaign by any Confederate army, had been frustrated, and his forces no longer required primary consideration. The last principal port for blockade-runners had been closed by capture and occupied, giving the Union an enlarged foothold in North Carolina. The Shenandoah Valley was at last placed completely at the mercy of the North, and Lee's army could not move at Petersburg, but remained stretched out upon a rack that steadily grew more agonizing.

Leadership had shown growing proficiency under Sherman, Thomas, Grant, Schofield, Porter, and Terry. Only once had a high commander really failed—Butler, in the first attempt upon Wilmington. The leadership had profited more and more from the experienced and vigorously supplied body of troops with which it could operate. The North could take the initiative freely now while the Confederacy had to respond. And it was even growing late for any vigorous response. By February it was plain on every front that the springtide would bring more than mild showers and lilacs and breezes.

7

The Second Administration Opens

"IT HAS long been a grave question whether any government, not *too* strong for the liberties of its people, can be strong *enough* to maintain its own existence in great emergencies." The President-elect thus began his response to the jubilant serenade given him by Lincoln and Johnson Clubs of Washington the day after the election of 1864.

He frankly told John Hay, his secretary, that his comments were "not very graceful," adding, "but I am growing old enough not to care much for the manner of doing things." No extempore response by a tired man to an excited audience is likely to be graceful, and Lincoln may well have felt that, after election night, propriety counselled him to speak with modest restraint. He did not attempt to approach the literary achievement of Gettysburg, and with an instinctive sense that he spoke to a nation above and beyond any section, merely refused to sound the strident notes of national triumph or victory that might have wounded many. Indeed, he said just the fitting words with a suitable combination of gravity and sober decorum. He told his hearers and the waiting country that the rebellion had placed the republic under wholly unprecedented tensions, and the presidential contest had added not a little to the strain. Nevertheless, "the election was a necessity. We cannot have free government without elections; and if the rebellion could force us to forego or postpone a national election, it might fairly claim to have already conquered and ruined us." He urged men to study the incidents of the election as examples of human nature and "as philosophy to learn wisdom from," rather than to be corrected or "prevented."

Furthermore, he continued, the election "had demonstrated that a people's government can sustain a national election in the midst of a great civil war." This had not previously been certain. The contest at the polls, added the President, had shaken the country, but "it shows also how *sound*, and how strong we still are." Evidences a-plenty appeared of that strength. And now that the election was over, he asked, "May not all, having a common interest, be re-united in an effort to save our common country?" With three cheers for the soldiers, seamen, and commanders, the brief speech was over. Perhaps Lincoln's ideas were not then sufficiently comprehended; perhaps they have not since been sufficiently studied.[1]

The festive campaign clubs listened in an atmosphere curiously unattuned to so serious a pronouncement as the President's. Gay banners lit with lanterns and transparencies danced over the huge crowd in front of the main entrance of the White House. Cannon roared, bands played, and Tad Lincoln ran from room to room lighting his own "illuminations." As the concourse thickened, a few windows were broken by the sweeping movements of the crowd. When the President did appear, it was many minutes before he could speak. "And then," wrote Noah Brooks, "in all probability the listeners were more entranced with the event they were celebrating than the words of the successful candidate."[2]

The Northern press, for the most part, applauded the victory, though some stubbornly partisan journals accepted the decision reluctantly. The widely read *Harper's Weekly*, for instance, spoke for many when its editor, George William Curtis, declared exultantly: "This result is the proclamation of the American people that they are not conquered; that the rebellion is not successful; and that, deeply as they deplore war and its inevitable suffering and loss, yet they have no choice between war and national ruin, and must therefore fight on. . . . One other of the most significant lessons of the election is that the people are conscious of the power and force of their own Government. . . . Yet the grandest lesson of the result is its vindication of the American system of free popular government. No system in history was ever exposed to such a strain directly along the fibre as that which ours has endured in the war and the political campaign, and no other could possibly have endured it successfully. The result is due to the general intelligence of the people, and to the security of perfectly free discussion. . . . Thank God and the people, we are a nation which comprehends its priceless importance to human progress and civilization, and which recognizes that law is the indispensable condition of Liberty."[3]

The happy military leader, Henry Wager Halleck, in one of his thoughtful letters to Francis Lieber, wrote on November 13, "Besides its general effect upon the country, its effect upon our armies in the field will be most excellent. Had the Marshal of Salt River been elected, the tone of the army would have rapidly changed through the influence of his military partisans, and we should

1. Lincoln, *Collected Works*, VIII, 100-102.
2. Brooks, Noah, "Lincoln's Reelection," *Century*, Vol. XLIX, No.6, Apr. 1895, 866-867.
3. *Harper's Weekly*, Nov. 19, 1864.

have had no more victories under this administration. . . ."[4] In this, he greatly exaggerated McClellan's possible influence.

Yet while the opposition had to lie quiescent perforce for the moment, scattered malcontents and resentful individuals were quick to express disappointment and pessimism over the election. S.L.M. Barlow, for instance, burst out to McClellan, "I see little prospect of anything, but fruitless war, disgraceful peace, and ruinous bankruptcy. . . . The fearful responsibility to be assumed by a President next March, with an empty treasury, a wasted army, and a defiant and apparently ill-united people in rebellion, is enough to appall anyone. . . ." Barlow and perhaps, indeed, McClellan were relieved that the general did not have to accept what Barlow termed a burden "greater than ever before borne by any man. . . ."[5]

Manton Marble, editor of the Democratic *World*, wrote McClellan, "I never have despaired of a constitutional restoration of things at the South; the election shows that we had more reason to despair of a constitutional restoration of things at the North. The coming calamities will teach even the North their bitter lessons; suffering pierces at last the most obdurate heart and finds some secret access at length to the most pervert understanding . . . the North in its secret soul is still stubborn and stiff—in its refusal of constitutional right to those who saw its temper and sought a lawless and wicked remedy, therefore the time is not ripe for our success. . . . We must never despair of the Republic; yet how impossible it is to hope. . . ."[6]

To a sympathetic friend in Washington, T. J. Barnett, Barlow declared that though the President's words had sometimes been smooth, no proof existed that Lincoln would be anything but "a radical fanatic." Barlow predicted that the results of the election would enable the Confederates to unite and "divide the people of the North as they have never been divided since the war began."[7]

In the capital of the Confederacy, press comment following the election was about what well-informed men expected. After all, Lincoln's re-election proclaimed with thunderous emphasis that the policies of the Northern government would remain adamant. Any misty expectation that he might give way to a new President vanished. All the heady dreams of a friendly armistice or of some vague arrangement for putting Southern independence into a magic pill that credulous Yankees might swallow in a coma, vanished. The Richmond *Sentinel*, as noted earlier, acknowledged the realities confronting the Southern people when it raised a Pecksniffian lament that ". . . perhaps this, also, is for

4. Lieber Papers, HEH.
5. Barlow to McClellan, Nov. 9, 1864, Barlow Papers, HEH.
6. Marble to McClellan, Nov. 13, 1864, Manton Marble Papers, LC.
7. Barlow to Barnett, Nov. 15, 1864, Barlow Papers, HEH.

our good. It deepens and widens the gulf between us, and renders our success more certain by rendering failure more dreadful and intolerable. Every charred homestead is a fresh warning to our people that they must never be conquered, but must rather fight forever. . . ."[8]

The Richmond *Dispatch* was still more hypocritically abusive: "What other men on the habitable globe would have chosen an ignorant and vulgar backwoods pettifogger for their Chief Magistrate: or having incurred the loss of the richest portion of their territory, more than a million of men, and two billions of money, in penalty of their folly, would have worked for his re-election with every energy of soul and body? What other men would expect anything else from another four year's experiment but a double amount of debt and dead men! What other men would find occasion for thanksgiving in such a past and such a future! . . ."[9] The *Dispatch* also pretended to think that the danger would have been greater to the Confederacy had McClellan been elected: "He would have insisted on conducting the war in a spirit more humane and more nearly approaching the rules recognized and binding among Christian and civilized communities."[10]

Such a perceptive Confederate as Josiah Gorgas saw the bitter truth, and exclaimed, "Lincoln has been reëlected President of the United States by overwhelming majorities. There is no use in disguising the fact that our subjugation is popular at the North, and that the War must go on until this hope is crushed out and replaced by desire for peace at any cost."[11] Robert Kean of the Confederate War Department, to his credit, made an honest entry in his diary. "The Yankee election," he wrote, "was evidently a damper on the spirits of many of our people, and is said to have depressed the army a good deal. Lincoln's triumph was more complete than most of us expected."[12] The rebel war-clerk Jones also admitted, "This makes many of our croaking people despondent. . . . The large majorities for Lincoln in the United States clearly indicate a purpose to make renewed efforts to accomplish our destruction."[13]

While he felt obvious personal satisfaction over his re-election, Lincoln continued to pursue his routine tasks unemotionally, following his laborious daily round of interviews, correspondence, and frequent inquiries respecting military and naval progress, and exchanges with the South. Many of the

8. Richmond *Sentinel*, Nov. 12, 1864, Virginia State Library.

9. Richmond *Dispatch*, Nov. 10, 1864, Virginia State Library.

10. *Ibid.*

11. Gorgas, Josiah, *Civil War Diary*, ed. Frank E. Vandiver, University, Alabama, 1947, entry of Nov. 17, 1864, 150.

12. Kean, Robert Garlick Hill, *Inside the Confederate Government*, ed. Edward Younger, New York, 1957, 177, Nov. 20, 1864.

13. Jones, John B., *A Rebel War Clerk's Diary*, ed. Earl Schenck Miers, New York, 1958, 448, Nov. 14, 15, 1864.

applications made to him had political as well as military and economic undertones, while other interruptions might be regarded as trivial. For instance, the day after election, Lincoln sent Secretary Stanton a request that Ella E. Gibson be appointed Chaplain of the First Wisconsin Heavy Artillery; but, perhaps wisely, because of her sex, Stanton rejected the proposal.[14]

At the first Cabinet meeting after the election, on November 11, the President did astonish his associates. In the midst of the Presidential campaign, on August 23, he had asked Cabinet members to sign a document which they had not read, and which had since remained sealed. "Gentlemen," he asked, "do you remember last summer I asked you all to sign your names to the back of a paper of which I did not show you the inside? This is it. Now, Mr. Hay, see if you can get this open without tearing it." Lincoln then read the memorandum.

"This morning, as for some days past, it seems exceedingly probable that this Administration will not be reëlected. Then it will be my duty to so cooperate with the President-elect as to save the Union between the election and the inauguration; as he will have secured the election on such grounds that he cannot possibly save it afterward." This incident shows not only the despondency of the President for a time regarding his re-election, but also his conviction that the Democrats and McClellan, pursuing their probable policies after election day, could not or would not win the war.[15]

At the meeting on November 11, the President remarked, after reading the memorandum, "You will remember that this was written at a time six days before the Chicago nominating Convention, when as yet we had no adversary, and seemed to have no friends. . . ." He added that he had resolved, if McClellan were elected, to see him and talk things over and try to reach an agreement on a policy intended to bring a rapid termination of the war. Seward caustically interposed: "And the General would answer you 'Yes, Yes'; and the next day when you saw him again and pressed these views upon him, he would say, 'Yes, Yes'; and so on forever, and would have done nothing at all." Lincoln, however, retorted: "At least, I should have done my duty, and have stood clear before my own conscience. . . ."[16] Probably we shall never know whether additional facts going beyond the limited information which this account provides were then revealed. Although there is clear evidence that in August, 1864, Lincoln did entertain grave doubts about the election, many people will still ask what was the precise character of these doubts, and how deep was his

14. Lincoln, *Collected Works*, VIII, 102-103; for day-to-day activities a useful summary is presented in Miers, E.S., *Lincoln Day by Day; A Chronology*, Washington, D.C., 1960.

15. Hay, John, *Lincoln and the Civil War in the Diaries and Letters of John Hay*, ed. Tyler Dennett, New York, 1939, 237; Lincoln, *Collected Works*, VII, 514.

16. Hay, *op.cit.*, 237-238.

apprehension that he would not be elected, and how seriously did he fear that the policies of his successor would involve the defeat of the Union and the ruin of its previous constitutional principles.

Amid all the excitement of the election and its results, the routine occupations and duties of life continued in Washington, on the battle fronts, and at home. As November waned, Sherman, as we have seen, had begun his thrust into the half mysterious terrain from Atlanta to the sea; Hood's Confederate Army of Tennessee was moving northward into Tennessee; and Grant was still stubbornly gripping Lee's forces before Richmond and Petersburg. In the Trans-Mississippi area, operations had become quieter after the October defeat of Sterling Price at Westport, Missouri. Troops exchanged shots and fought minor engagements all along the Army fronts, while the blockade tightened its silent but deadly hold upon the Gulf and Atlantic coasts of the Confederacy.

In Northern homes the majority of the war-worn people could glimpse more and more tokens of hope. The wistful longing that throbbed in the bars of "When This Cruel War Is Over," seemed ever closer to fulfillment. More and more confidently the press, politicians and people began discussing the great practical questions of the future. What new course would public and private life follow after the silencing of the guns and bugles? Might the war possibly go beyond the summer of 1865? Mr. Lincoln, now elected for four more years, had been the patient, sagacious leader in war. What would he do to meet the even more perplexing problems of peace?

[I]

As congratulations upon the election came to Washington, there came also a communication from General McClellan. He was resigning from the army! While a decision undoubtedly motivated by a feeling of defeat, pique and purely personal chagrin, the resignation, accepted November 14, did at least remove the controversial Democratic leader from the public scene. McClellan spent the next three years abroad, quite aloof from the political and military conflicts in which he had so conspicuously been a participant. In 1878, he was elected governor of New Jersey, but he never again assumed the stature of a national figure. His polemical and defensive memoirs, *McClellan's Own Story*, published after his death, provoked a controversial renewal of various old disputes which have never quite died,[17] but the man himself remained impotent and, ere many years, became totally disregarded.

17. The literature, all of it exuding heat both for and against McClellan, is vast and continuing. A full unbiassed biography is badly needed.

On November 21, in the course of his usual attention to individual matters, the President wrote a letter to a Mrs. Lydia Bixby which was printed in the Boston *Transcript* of November 25, 1864, a beautiful tribute to the mother of five sons "who have died gloriously on the field of battle." Celebrated thereafter, reprinted and anthologized as the Bixby letter, the manuscript original has never been found. Some historians have conjectured that John Hay may have written this miniature masterpiece, while others maintain that it is Lincoln's own, and forged facsimiles have continued to be numerous. It may be noted that Lincoln was given inaccurate information regarding Mrs. Bixby's sons by the Adjutant General's Office. Two sons only were killed, another was captured and reported to have deserted to the enemy, a fourth was listed as a deserter, and the fifth was honorably discharged December 17, 1864, after this letter was written. But even the official records are not completely certain. The whole matter has been blown up into a mystery of Lincolniana.[18]

Re-election would also require readjustments in the cast of characters, both major and secondary. The Chief Justiceship had been an object of fervent competition among men and parties since the death of Roger Taney in mid-October. Several Cabinet posts would undoubtedly be open; lesser posts would be available as well; and a new flood of office-seekers would base their claims on tasks performed or assertedly performed during the recent campaign.

Since the opening of the Lincoln Administration in 1861, four of the seven Cabinet positions had changed hands; only Secretary of State Seward, Secretary of the Navy Welles, and Attorney-General Bates remained. The incompetent Cameron, the colorless Caleb Smith, the ambitious Chase and the contriving, though astute, Montgomery Blair were gone. Now it was time for the conservative Missouri lawyer Bates to step down. Long a target of the Radicals, accused then and later of being stuffy and pedestrian, Bates had brought a following to the Administration, and had shown himself to be a solid bulwark of Union policies and of social justice in the Cabinet, particularly during the early years of the war. Slowly his influence had lessened, and Bates had, himself, felt unhappy in opposing some of the Administration's policies. He had never been congenial with Stanton, Seward, or Chase. Back home in Missouri, the political struggles of State factions, won eventually by the Radicals, had undermined his prestige and influence. Government by sound legal principles, as he conceived them, had been for Bates an unchanging ideal, a difficult ideal to pursue.[19]

18. Bullard, F. Lauriston, *Abraham Lincoln and the Widow Bixby*, New Brunswick, N.J., 1946, *passim*.

19. Cain, Marvin R., *Lincoln's Attorney-General, Edward Bates of Missouri*, Columbia, Mo., 1965, is the only modern biography of this neglected public figure.

Dejected over the course which plans for Reconstruction were following, and believing the Radicals were gaining an unfortunate control in the nation, Bates had indicated to the President early in October his desire to resign. Upon the death of Chief Justice Taney, he sent Lincoln a request for appointment to the post. Nothing came of this application, for Bates was no longer close to the President. By November 1, he had determined to leave, and on the 24th, sent a formal letter of resignation to Lincoln, quitting his office December 1.[20]

Seeking an able attorney to replace him, the President asked Judge-Advocate-General Joseph Holt, a former member of Buchanan's cabinet, to take his place as Attorney-General. Holt refused in a letter of November 30,[21] and suggested the appointment of James Speed of Kentucky. Lincoln therefore telegraphed Speed on December 1: "I appoint you to be Attorney-General. Please come on at once." Speed promptly arrived.[22] From the same western State as Holt, Speed had been prominent in politics and law and had turned into a strong Lincoln supporter after (in 1861) favoring the Union though anxious to avoid war. Speed, a brother of the President's close friend Joshua Fry Speed, who had often advised Lincoln on Kentucky affairs, was deemed a worthy successor to Bates. In the Johnson Administration, he soon fell out with the new President and moved closer and closer to the Radicals, until he stood in violent opposition to Johnson and became a leader of the Kentucky Radicals. By appointing him to office, the President kept a Cabinet seat for a western Border State man, border politics being never far from his attention.

The cardinal question was that of the next Chief Justice of the United States. Although the decision to appoint Chase has been already discussed in Chapter 5, it will be reviewed here more particularly from the point of view of Lincoln's reasons for making the appointment. Taney had died October 12, but Lincoln had waited until after the election to name a successor. The list of those who sought the post, or had friends urging their elevation, was formidable. The former Treasury Secretary, Chase, cherished ambitions from the outset, even before Taney's death. Attorney-General Bates had forthrightly and promptly asked for the appointment. Two justices, Noah H. Swayne and Lincoln's close Illinois friend David Davis, were seriously considered. Other men duly scrutinized were Postmaster-General Dennison, Secretary Stanton, Judge William Strong of Pennsylvania, and the eloquent attorney, William M. Evarts. The Blair family was urging the President not to overlook former Postmaster-General Montgomery Blair. The vacancy occurred as the Presi-

20. Summation and details in Cain, *op.cit.*, 310-315. Also see Robert Todd Lincoln Papers, LC, Bates to Lincoln, Nov. 24, 1864; Bates, Edward, *Diary*, ed. Howard K. Beale, Washington, 1933, 428.
21. Robert Todd Lincoln Papers, LC, Nov. 30, 1864.
22. Lincoln, *Works*, VIII, 126-127.

dential contest coincided with the last phases of war, and the opening of the struggle over Reconstruction. It was therefore regarded in a partisan rather than a judicial or really national light.[23]

We have some evidence (although secondhand) confirming the supposition that the President had thought of naming Chase as Chief Justice some time before Taney's death. According to Orville H. Browning, Secretary of the Treasury Fessenden told him on the morning after Taney died that he knew the post would be Chase's. Fessenden tells us that after Chase resigned, Lincoln refused to reinstate him in the Cabinet despite Fessenden's plea that he do so. Lincoln spoke of his respect for Chase, adding that if the Chief Justiceship was now vacant, he would appoint him to that place.[24] When, a few days later, Browning called on Mrs. Stanton, she asked him to see the President about naming the Secretary of War as Chief Justice. Browning wrote in his diary that he feared the appointment of Chase, and was anxious to prevent it.[25]

Chase himself recorded in his diary at the end of June that the President had spoken of intending to appoint him Chief Justice if a vacancy occurred. Chase had learned this from Congressman Samuel Hooper of Massachusetts, who received the intelligence from Lincoln in the midst of the Cabinet crisis.[26]

Thus, it seems that by the middle of 1864, Chase was the foremost candidate for Chief Justice, while all Washington was engaging in a political death-vigil over Taney. And Lincoln's comments upon the matter had certainly not been kept secret. The scramble of various men to seize the position at the time of Taney's death was inspired both by personal ambition and by a desire to keep Chase out of an office which was certain to be powerful during Reconstruction and later. Montgomery Blair's activities can be attributed without question to his wish to keep the conservatives stronger than the Radicals.

Hard upon the demise of the old Chief Justice, Sumner led the Radical movement in behalf of Chase. He immediately wrote Lincoln an argument for Chase's appointment.[27] It may be asked why, if Chase had had assurances in mid-1864 from the President, did he take part in the late-summer plotting to overturn Mr. Lincoln as a Presidential candidate. To be sure, Taney was still alive, and the Radicals might turn to Chase to replace Lincoln. It could be that

23. Little primary research has been done upon the true motives of Lincoln in making the appointment, or the pressures exerted upon him. Estimable secondary narratives include Randall, J.G., and Richard N. Current, *Lincoln the President, Last Full Measure*, 270-276; Carman, Harry J., and Reinhard H. Luthin, *Lincoln and the Patronage*, New York, 1943, 315-320; and Silver, David M., *The Supreme Court During the Civil War*, Urbana, 1956, *passim*.

24. Browning, Orville Hickman, *Diary*, ed. Theodore Calvin Pease, Springfield, Ill., 1925, 686-687.

25. *Ibid.*, 687-688.

26. Schuckers, J.W., *The Life and Public Services of Salmon Portland Chase*, New York, 1874, 509-510. Also, Hay, *Lincoln and the Civil War*, 203.

27. Robert Todd Lincoln Papers, LC, Sumner to Lincoln, Oct. 12, 1864.

Chase was simply playing all horses, or that the rumors of his becoming Chief Justice were exaggerated. A few days later, the President let Chase know through Fessenden that, while he had not forgotten what he had earlier said, he thought it best to delay action until after the election.[28] Chase, meanwhile, was campaigning in Ohio for Lincoln. Whether this helped him gain the appointment is uncertain, but it certainly did him no injury; indeed, rumors of a bargain soon cropped out, although no specific evidence of one has been found. After the election, Sumner and other Radicals evinced pique over the delay.

How inevitable was the appointment, and how nearly had it ever been certain? We can never know, for the secret lay with the President. Gideon Welles was not sure that Chase would obtain the place—but then, Welles did not always possess authentic information. As of November 26, he wrote: "I have not much idea that the President will appoint him, nor is it advisable that he should." Lincoln had told Welles that he would delay a choice until Congress met, and he also spoke of Evarts. Welles, who vainly championed Montgomery Blair, wrote of the "host of candidates."[29] He concluded that Chase would obtain the post, although he confided to his diary a wry comment on the possibility: "The President sometimes does strange things, but this would be a singular mistake, in my opinion, for one who is so shrewd and honest,—an appointment that he would soon regret. . . ."

On the same day that his message went to Congress, Lincoln sent a two-line nomination of Chase to the Senate, where he was at once and unanimously confirmed.[30] Welles reported that not a word had been spoken in the Cabinet about it. He continued to feel "apprehensions" about the appointment of Chase, and feared that the man would use it for "political advantage." He set down a caustic estimate of Chase, pronouncing him "selfishly stubborn at times, and wanting in moral courage and frankness, fond of adulation, and, with official superiors, inclined to play the sycophant."[31]

Historians may still inquire why Lincoln selected Chase. Did he have some perception that Chase would, as he did, make a more than distinguished record in the post? Did he feel the Radicals needed appeasing? Was this selection part of the old manoeuvre, used so often and so effectively to reward and keep in official posts those who had been replaced or those who might be more troublesome as political enemies, if kept outside of the government? The answers elude us.

28. Randall-Current, *op.cit.*, 271, from Fessenden to Chase, Oct. 20, 1864, Chase Mss., Historical Society of Pennsylvania.

29. Welles, *Diary*, II, 181-184.

30. Lincoln, *Collected Works*, VIII, 154.

31. Welles, *Diary*, II, 192-193.

According to Congressman George S. Boutwell, of Massachusetts (a Radical), Lincoln appointed Chase because he was a prominent leader with impressive backing, because he would uphold the Administration, and because the office required a man whose opinions were known. Furthermore, although Lincoln realized that the former Secretary of the Treasury nursed most irritating and discreditable ambitions to grasp the Presidency, this did not prevent the appointment.[32] Lincoln might have felt that the appointment would put an end to such ambitions. However, it did not.

Other men possessed high qualifications, equalling Chase's by Lincoln's severe standards. Blair, in particular, had great gifts and merits, but his appointment to the Chief Justiceship would have produced a revolt among the Radicals. Lincoln had given this important subject careful study, had patiently considered the rivalries of the men who guessed, contrived, and schemed, had waited until their emotions and appetites cooled, and had at last named the man most acceptable to the Radical Republicans. Who can doubt that once more Lincoln had exhibited consummate political skill, and in the end had given the country a Chief Justice whom history would accord high rank as a jurist and statesman.

He had again proved, moreover, his majestic qualities of balance. His annual message, which comprehended much of his legislative programme for 1865 on controversial and sensitive subjects, received more patient attention from the Radicals than would otherwise have been accorded it. As might be expected, the abolitionist voice of Henry Ward Beecher was raised in the New York *Independent*, expressing raptures over the naming of Chase.[33] A voice from the past even approved. In a private letter, James Buchanan, rusticating at Wheatland near Lancaster, Pa., wrote: "I think Mr. Lincoln made the best selection from his party for the office of Chief Justice. Mr. Chase is a gentleman; and although extreme in his views on the abolition question, I have no doubt he will worthily fill the place of his eminent predecessors. . . ."[34]

The second session of the Thirty-eighth Congress met in Washington on December 5, 1864—the same Congress that had witnessed the rise of Radical antagonism to Lincoln, that still held a little anti-war group, along with many supporters of the President. The election could not prevent the gathering of this rather out-of-date assemblage. The new Congress would not meet until the following December, more than a year after election, unless called in special session. This new Congress would have a heavily preponderant majority of Republicans and Unionists, two-thirds of the members. Meanwhile, results of

32. Boutwell, George S., *Reminiscences*, II, 29.
33. New York *Independent*, Dec. 15, 1864, E.B. Long Collection, Oak Park, Ill.
34. Buchanan Papers, Hist. Soc. of Penn., Philadelphia, Buchanan to Joseph C. G. Kennedy, Dec. 23, 1864.

the election in November, 1864, would certainly be felt, albeit indirectly, in the fresh session of the old Congress, now beginning.

As was customary, the President's Secretary, this time John G. Nicolay, appeared before the Senate and the House (separately) on December 6th, to deliver the written Presidential message. It was a longer and more factual message than Lincoln usually wrote, devoid of the inspiring and thoughtful passages of his greater documents. Nevertheless, the message expressed his firmness of purpose, fixity of policy, comprehension of the profound importance of the long-continued struggle for the Union. These all-important aspects of the document were only partially concealed by the fact that the President plunged at once into a rehearsal, not of the state of the war or wartime policies, but of foreign affairs which he termed "reasonably satisfactory." Relations with Mexico, Costa Rica, Nicaragua, Colombia, Venezuela, Peru, Chile, all received treatment. In every instance, except the comment on Mexico, the exposition dealt with matters of distinctly secondary or tertiary importance. Lincoln then turned to Liberia, and to the proposed overland telegraph between America and Europe by way of the Bering Straits. Covering developments the world over, he even discussed at length affairs in Egypt, China, and Japan.

After this rather dull review, Lincoln turned to trade, mentioning that Norfolk, Fernandina, and Pensacola had been opened as ports by proclamation November 19, and that it was hoped foreign merchants would trade there to avoid the blockade. Because of the series of disturbances on the Canadian line, and particularly the raid upon St. Albans, Vermont, by Confederates in October, the President felt constrained to notify Canada that it would be necessary to increase naval armaments on the Great Lakes, although this, by no means, implied any unfriendliness towards Canadians.

Turning to finances, the President said that they had been so successfully administered that on July 1, 1864, the Treasury balance reached $96,739,905.73. The War Department was spending $690,791,842.97, while the Navy was costing $85,723,292.77. This came out to well over two million dollars a day in Federal operating expenditures. The public debt was $1,740,690,489.49, and was undoubtedly increasing. He asked Congress to turn its attention to increased taxation, but made no specific recommendations. By November 25, the United States had 584 national banks, and the President found that the system was proving acceptable to capitalists and to the people.

As usual the reports of the various secretaries were submitted as accompanying documents. Lincoln gave special attention to the Navy, however, outlining the great increase in the number of vessels, praising their construction, and in general paying tribute to the efficiency of naval operations.

It was noteworthy, he wrote, that the steady expansion of population, improvement and governmental institutions over the unoccupied new parts of the country had scarcely been arrested, much less impeded or halted by the war, which at first glance might seem to have absorbed almost the entire energies of the nation. As was being proved in many fields, the Federal Union could fight a civil war while the normal progress of social and economic life was largely maintained. The message touched on the Western States and territories, public lands, the transcontinental railroad, noted discoveries of precious metals, recommended revision of the Indian Administration, a grant of pensions to invalid soldiers and sailors with their families, and the work of the new Agriculture Department.

Somewhat lost in the laconic array of facts was a statement that, despite economy of words, displayed a strength that proved well for the years to come. "The war," said Lincoln, "continues."

The advance of the Federal armies did not have to be recorded in detail, but the President happily declared that the liberation of Missouri, Kentucky, Tennessee, and other areas, gave the promise of fair crops. He called the "attempted march" of Sherman from Atlanta to the sea "the most remarkable feature of the military operations" but did not mention Grant's campaign to the gates of Richmond. Two brief paragraphs were all that were devoted to the land military operations!

The strongest emphasis in the message was in the last pages dealing with "important movements (that) have also occurred during the year, to the effect of moulding society for durability in the Union." He emphasized, in this regard, the organization of loyal State governments in Louisiana and Arkansas, and similar movements in Missouri, Kentucky and Tennessee. He held up Maryland as the happiest example of all, now "secure to Liberty and Union for all the future."

The crux of the policy for the future, however, was the "proposed amendment of the Constitution abolishing slavery throughout the United States." He pointed out that the amendment had passed the Senate but failed of the two-thirds needed in the House. Even though this was the same Congress, the President said he recommended reconsideration and passage of the measure at the current session, stating that while the abstract question had not changed, the election had decisively shown that the new Congress would pass the measure. "And, as it is to so go," he asked, "may we not agree that the sooner the better?" He reasserted that the voice of the people, as expressed in the election, had unmistakably declared for passage of the amendment.

Even the opposition, he urged, had not been in favor of giving up the Union. And so, although means and modes of action had been argued with

The Union Army Entering Richmond

heat, the election had been of tremendous value in proving once and for all that no popular division existed on the issue of union or disunion.

Coming back to the theme of Western advance, Lincoln found that the recent political campaign had taught people the enormous importance of the fact that America had not been drained of its most important resource—manpower. While the grave and casualty lists had been melancholy, indeed, "it is some relief to know that, compared with the surviving, the fallen have been so few." The soldier vote had proved that the nation had more men in 1861 than in 1865; that we were not exhausted, "nor in the process of exhaustion; that we were *gaining* strength," and might, if necessary, maintain the contest indefinitely. Material resources, too, he believed, were "more complete and abundant than ever," even inexhaustible. Only the manner of continuing the national effort remained to be chosen.

The President specified some of the courses desirable, and some he then rejected. For instance, he wrote, "no attempt at negotiation with the insurgent leader could result in any good," (although within two months he would try such negotiations at Hampton Roads), for nothing less than severance of the Union would satisfy the Southern leader—"precisely what we will not and cannot give. . . . He cannot voluntarily reaccept the Union; we cannot voluntarily yield it." This issue was "distinct, simple and inflexible."

But while the Southerners in revolt could not yield, wrote Lincoln, "some of them, we know, already desire peace and reunion." He hoped this number would increase and said, "They can, at any moment, have peace simply . . . by laying down their arms and submitting to the national authority under the Constitution." If any questions remained, they should be adjusted by legislation, conferences, courts and votes. In view of the bitter realities, this idea seems naïve. However, the President did admit that some questions such as admission of members to Congress or appropriation of money would not be for him to decide; indeed, he foresaw that executive power would be "greatly diminished by the cession of actual war." Pardons and remissions of forfeitures would remain within Presidential power, nonetheless, and the temper controlling the exercise of this power might be fairly adjudged by past history. The difficulty was that, although Lincoln regarded past policies as lenient, the people of the South did not!

The door of general pardon and amnesty had been open for a year. "It is still so open to all," stated the President. "But the time may come—probably will come—when public duty shall demand that it be closed; and that, in lieu, more rigorous measures than heretofore shall be adopted." In declaring that abandonment of armed resistance was the only indispensable condition to ending the war, Lincoln added, "I retract nothing heretofore said as to slavery." He would plainly maintain the Emancipation Proclamation and the Acts of Congress. And, in conclusion, he mildly stated that the government's peace condition was simple: ". . . the war will cease on the part of the government, whenever it shall have ceased on the part of those who began it."[35]

No comprehensive new policy was defined in the speech, which rather combined a somewhat curious recital of the state of the Union with some indications of future action. That Lincoln keenly desired to incorporate the Thirteenth Amendment in the Constitution was no secret, but he now made it absolutely clear. The extinction of slavery in the United States had not been in doubt for some time, but it was well to have it once more made a fundamental object. The plan of appealing to influential individuals and groups in the South, rather than to the oldtime Confederate leaders, had also been given careful trial for a year. The threat of ending the period of moderation in the South was now given firmer statement. All those loyal to Confederate ideas and authority were still summoned by Lincoln to absolute surrender. His emphasis upon foreign relations at a time when such relations were in no critical state, struck some as odd, but was perhaps useful in warning Paris and Madrid to be watchful. The attention he gave to westward development encouraged many people by reminding them of our untapped wealth, and drew the attention of others to the organization of railroads, mining ventures, and cattle-ranching; it was also a refreshing diversion from political squabbles and sectional dissensions.

Open Confederate comment on the message was what might be expected. The Richmond *Dispatch* noted that Southerners, determined to have peace on any terms, must now realize that they could have it only by unconditional submission. The editor tried some feeble sarcasm. If they so yielded, people without a record of active disloyalty would be allowed to breathe, but after acquiescing in all the legislation of the Yankee Congress and proclamations of President Lincoln, they would be left no property of any kind whatever. "Their estates, real and personal,—the whole vast territory of the Confederate States has been declared confiscated, and Congress is called on to abolish slavery. . . ."[36] The Richmond *Sentinel* took the same attitude, angrily telling peacemen that they faced "absolute, unqualified submission, to be followed by spoliation of our property and the Africanization of our country, all this superciliously laid down as the only terms of 'peace' . . ."[37]

The rebel Chief of Ordnance, Gorgas, felt much the same, "Lincoln's

35. Lincoln, *Works*, VIII, 136-152.
36. Richmond *Dispatch*, Dec. 10, 1864, Virginia State Library.
37. Richmond *Sentinel*, Dec. 10, 1864, Virginia State Library.

message spawns nothing but subjugation."[38] War-clerk Jones recorded that "President Lincoln's message to the Congress . . . produced no marked effect. His adherence to a purpose of emancipation of the slaves, and his employment of them in his armies, will suffice for an indefinite prolongation of the war, and perhaps result in the employment of hundreds of thousands of slaves in our armies. The intimation, however, that all applications for 'pardon,' etc., have been and are still favorably entertained, will certainly cause some of our croakers who fall into the lines of the United States forces to submit . . ."[39]

On the Union side, *Harper's Weekly* was enthusiastic about the message, terming it a "calm, simple, concise statement of public affairs—this firm, manly expression of the noblest national aspiration for equal justice. . . . The prospects of peace as set forth by the President are exactly what every faithful citizen supposed them to be. When the men who began this war upon the Government lay down arms, and yield to the Constitution and the laws and acts in accordance with it, the war will end. . . ."[40] Seward found the statement of the President "generally satisfactory."[41]

In the House, however, a long debate arose over the message. Representative James Brooks of New York brought up the subject on December 14 in true Copperhead vein, by denouncing Lincoln's policies and making Biblical references to the tolerance of slavery. When George S. Boutwell of Massachusetts interrupted him, asking if he really understood that the institution of slavery was dead, Brooks replied, "Why should you try to kill a dead body?" In a customarily tart retort, Thaddeus Stevens drily advised him, "we ought to bury it lest it become noxious." Brooks, by now ferocious, cried: "The whole country has become intoxicated on this subject of slavery, and in the midst of the intoxication, this civil war is kept up. . . . Centralization and consolidation is nothing but unlimited despotism. There is no freedom for the people, no self-government, no municipal government, no household government, under such a system."[42]

Representative Hiram Price of Iowa thought that the entire aim and intent of Brooks's speech and the desire of the man himself were to aid the enemies of our country. Amos Myers of Pennsylvania hotly declared: "We are told that we must have an armistice, negotiation, must exhaust all the arts of statesmanship and have a national convention. Sir, we *have* peace Commissioners. They are Grant, Sherman, Sheridan, Thomas, and Farragut. We have our national convention, and the delegates to it are the invincible soldiers and sailors of the

38. Gorgas, *Diary, op.cit.*, 155.
39. Jones, *A Rebel War Clerk's Diary, op.cit.*, 458.
40. *Harper's Weekly*, Dec. 24, 1864.
41. Seward, Frederick W., *Seward at Washington*, III, 253.
42. *Congressional Globe*, Second Session, 38th Cong., Pt.I, 38, 39, 42.

Union, clothed in the royal purple of the nation, the Union blues; and they are now debating that question. . . ." Debate followed on the issue of calling a national convention and setting up an armistice. For the moment, it was obvious that argument would be the order of the hour. The issues were too deep, too intertwined with personal ambition and politics to permit agreement.

[II]

For approximately two years, the Emancipation Proclamation had been in effect; for two-and-a-half years the Second Confiscation Act had been a law. Other measures had contributed to the disintegration of slavery, yet the issue as a permanent national question had not been met! It could not be met clearly except by means of a constitutional amendment. The slavery issue was so completely involved with the fabric of the war in all its phases that it was almost a sentient part of it. At the same time, extending above and beyond the war itself, and far beyond slavery, was the question of what to do about the Negro. But perhaps, as many thought at the time, the truly supreme issue was that of local government versus Federal. Desirable as the end of slavery might be to many, what would a constitutional amendment do to the rights of States, local governments and the people? Could the Federal Union rule on property, could it intrude into the field of social reform? What was done about all this, or was not done, would clearly decide the principles of national action for long decades to come.

It was an issue not properly to be decided in the heat of a Civil War, nor with an eye to partisan politics and personal gain, nor in the give-and-take of economic life, but on the loftier level of philosophic principle. Few men considered it in that light.

The climactic issue of the disposition of slavery, however, had arisen. What would be the scope of the decision; how much would it solve? Few, regardless of their feelings, were really clear on this issue. Slavery was, indeed, moribund —it could not be restored—nevertheless, it was not yet dead. "The rebellion, instigated and carried on by the slaveholders, has been the death-knell of the institution." Representative James A. Rollins of Missouri, a former slaveholder himself, deprecated the refusal of Border State men to accept compensated emancipation, and further said that the "American sentiment is decidedly anti-slavery," and, "we never can have an entire peace in this country as long as the institution of slavery remains as one of the recognized institutions of the country."[43]

43. *Congressional Globe*, 38th Cong., 1st Sess., Vol.I, 259-260.

Resolved by the Senate and House of Representatives of the United States of America in Congress assembled, (two-thirds of both Houses concurring), that the following article be proposed to the legislatures of the several States as an amendment to the Constitution of the United States, which, when ratified by three-fourths of said legislatures, shall be valid, to all intents and purposes, as a part of the said Constitution, namely: Article XIII, Section 1. Neither slavery nor involuntary servitude, except as a punishment for crime whereof the party shall have been duly convicted, shall exist within the United States or any place subject to their jurisdiction. Section 2. Congress shall have the power to enforce this article by appropriate legislation.

So read the proposed new "Amendment"—the first to be added to the Constitution since the Twelfth Amendment of 1803, ratified in 1804. Nor was this an amendment in the strictest sense of the word. It was, in a larger sense, an expansion of the Constitution, permitting entrance into a new field of social control and reform by the Federal government.

That Lincoln perceived the larger implications of the action now to be taken we cannot doubt. Some Radicals thought he was too deliberate in dealing doom to the institution, as some Democrats declared that he was an intemperate abolitionist. Not only was he convinced that, even if emancipation had become "an indispensable necessity," events had not conferred upon him "an unrestricted right" to act in accordance with his feelings;[44] he felt a firm though still unformulated conviction that the North had entered upon a course of enlarging social and racial equality that would require cautious if courageous definition.[45]

On the last day of January, 1865, the Thirteenth Amendment came before the House for vote. After debating throughout the morning, the vote was taken that afternoon—the result being 119 "aye", 56 "no", 8 not voting.[46]

One publication declared that even up to noon the issue had been in doubt.[47] The direction of the wind was indicated when applause greeted the Democrats, James English of Connecticut, and John Ganson of New York as they voted "aye." The four Democrats who had previously voted in favor did so again, to be joined now by thirteen others. In addition, eight Democrats were reported absent without pairs, a result which Lincoln's secretaries admit was "perhaps not altogether by accident."[48]

Leading Democrat S.S. Cox of Ohio later wrote of a "fund which was said

44. Randall, J. and Richard N. Current, *Lincoln the President, Last Full Measure*, New York, 1955, 298.
45. Quarles, Benjamin, *The Negro in the Civil War*, Boston, 1953, 255ff.
46. *Congressional Globe*, 38th Cong., 1st Sess., Pt.I, 531.
47. Nicolay and Hay, *Lincoln*, *op.cit.*, X, 85, from Report of Special Committee of the Union League Clubs of New York.
48. *Ibid.*, X, 83.

to be ready and freely used for corrupting members. Can anything be conceived more monstrous than this attempt to amend the Constitution upon such a humane and glorious theme, by the aid of the lucre of office-holders?"[49] As is usual in such cases, proof of corruption is lacking, but rumors abounded. Cox clearly believed it, and had personal experience. Other Congressmen made allusions to job deals as well.[50]

The *Congressional Globe*, which seldom reveals strong feeling, states that, "The Speaker called repeatedly to order, and asked that the members should set a better example to spectators in the gallery . . ." Finally, the Speaker announced that the constitutional majority of two-thirds having voted in the affirmative, the joint resolution was passed. The announcement was received by the House and by the spectators with an outburst of enthusiasm. "The members on the Republican side of the House instantly sprang to their feet, and, regardless of parliamentary rules, applauded with cheers and clapping of hands. The example was followed by the male spectators in the galleries, which were crowded to excess, who waved their hats and cheered long and loud, while the ladies, hundreds of whom were present, rose in their seats and waved their handkerchiefs, participating in adding to the general excitement and intense interest of the scene. This lasted for several minutes."[51]

Carl Schurz, who was present, wrote his wife, "The scene that followed the announcement of the result of the vote was worthy of the great event. . . . All arose as at a word of command . . . they embraced, they shook hands, and ten minutes passed before the hurrahing and the enthusiastic racket ceased. The House immediately adjourned and the news of the action spread through the city. Cannon were brought out to greet with their thunder this great step on Freedom's path. It is worth while to live in these days. . . ."[52]

[III]

The election, the reaction to it, the appointment of Chase, the Cabinet changes, the message to Congress outlining policy, the fight for and final passage of the Thirteenth Amendment, the various peace efforts, were all events of the fall and winter of 1864-1865 in which the role of the military was intermingled.

At the Christmas season, General Ben Butler had once again occasioned embarrassment (as we have seen) by a defeat in his blundering effort to take Wilmington. In January, after pressure by Grant, he was removed, thus alter-

49. Cox, S.S., *Three Decades of Federal Legislation*, San Francisco, 1885, 329.
50. Riddle, Albert Gallatin, *Recollections of War Times*, New York, 1895, 324-325.
51. *Congressional Globe*, 38th Cong., 2nd Sess., Pt.I, 531.
52. Carl Schurz to his wife, Feb. 1, 1865, Carl Schurz Papers, State Hist. Soc. of Wis.

ing the temporary relationship between Lincoln and the Radicals. Once more, Lincoln had bided his time and then, at the most opportune moment, had removed one of his most troublesome thorns.[53]

The President, still watching the military movements at Petersburg, Wilmington, and elsewhere, sent Stanton down to Savannah to confer with Sherman. Lincoln, who had been worried about the march to the sea in December, was now anxious that Sherman should move forward as "the enemy is wavering," going down hill, and he should be kept going that way.[54]

Legislative action between December, 1864, and March 4, 1865, reflected the war and the peace to come. Early in the session, among other bills, Congress passed and the President approved an act to establish the highest naval rank, that of Vice-Admiral, to honor Rear-Admiral Farragut. An act of February 25, 1865, made it unlawful for Army and naval officers to have troops at election places unless necessary to repel armed enemies or keep the peace. There was also a bill to aid Western railroads financially, several measures relating to Indian affairs, and a measure to end any disqualification by reason of color in carrying the mails, as well as a resolution providing that wives and children of any person in the military or naval service should be free.[55]

But the major legislation of the session was "an act to establish a Bureau to serve one year for the Relief of Freedmen and Refugees." Abandoned lands and, indeed, all subjects relating to refugees and freedmen were to be handled by this Bureau.[56]

In the Senate, Sumner said that to end slavery was not enough. "The debt of justice will not be paid if we do not take them by the hand in their passage from the house of bondage to the house of freedom; and this is what is proposed by the present measure. The temporary care of the freedmen is the complement of emancipation; but the general welfare is involved in the performance of this duty. . . ."[57] And so, appropriately enough, the Congress began debate on the most crucial aspect of national Reconstruction—the status of the soon-to-be-free black man—as Washington prepared for the second inauguration of Abraham Lincoln.

[IV]

On March 4, 1865, the great bronze statue of freedom by Thomas Crawford, crowning the Capitol dome, looked down upon a murky, muddy, confused scene. According to Welles, "All was confusion and without order—a

53. See Chapters I, II, and IX, this volume.
54. Lincoln, *Works*, VIII, 201, Jan. 5, 1865.
55. *Congressional Globe*, 38th Cong., 2nd Sess., Vol.II, Appendix, Laws of the United States, 113ff.
56. *Ibid.*, Vol.II, 141; Vol.I, 988.
57. *Ibid.*, Vol.I, 768.

jumble."[58] The mud in the streets was worse than usual, and the atmosphere warm and smoky, while from dun-colored clouds there broke occasional light showers. About 11 A.M. a curious celestial phenomenon occurred whereby a small, sharp, pointed diamond or star of light could be seen directly at the zenith.[59]

Mud hampered the procession on its way to the Capitol, where the President labored over last-minute business. There were the usual "bands of music". Two regiments of the Invalid Corps, a squadron of cavalry, a battery of artillery, and four companies of black troops were in the military escort, as well as visiting dignitaries, firemen of Washington and Philadelphia, groups of Odd Fellows and Masons, including members of a Negro Masonic Lodge.[60]

As General Halleck wrote later: "The Inauguration passed off well. Thanks to abundant preventions we had no disturbances, no fires, no raids, or robberies. I was out on the *qui vive* all day and night and consequently did not join in the proceedings. There were a large number of rebel deserters here who excited some suspicion of wrong intentions, but they were closely watched. New York and Philadelphia also sent their quotas of roughs and rowdies, but they were completely overawed."[61]

Lincoln and Johnson had been declared elected by 212 votes, with 21 for McClellan. Thus the first order of the day was the swearing-in of the new Vice-President in the Senate Chamber, an unfortunate occasion, later much belabored by his political opponents. Johnson, having suffered from a severe illness, had arrived late in Washington, where, indisposed because of restoratives he had been obliged to take, he indulged in rambling talk punctuated with maudlin, ill-timed, and inappropriate comments. The brilliant gathering was dutifully shocked, believing him to be intoxicated; Lincoln waited patiently for it to be over, while others were not so patient. Consequently, reports, which ignored Johnson's illness, were exaggerated by those who were already his political enemies.[62]

After Johnson's speech, everyone proceeded from the Senate Chamber to the portico for the swearing-in of the re-elected President. About the time of the ceremonies the sun came out, to give a feeling of hope to the assembled throng. One free Negro wrote in his diary ". . . and on the fourth of March 1865 on Saturday the hon Abraham Lincoln taken his Seat. Before he came out on the porch to take his the wind blew and it rained with out intermission and as soon as Mr. Lincoln came out the wind ceas blowing an the rain ceased

58. Welles, *Diary*, II, 251.
59. Riddle, Albert Gallatin, *Recollections of War Times*, New York, 1895, 229-230.
60. New York *Times*, March 5, 1865.
61. Halleck to Francis Lieber, Mar. 5, 1865, Lieber Papers, HEH.
62. Thomas, Lately, *The First President Johnson*, New York, 1968, Chap. I, 268-269, 289, 295-303.

raining and the Sun came out and wear as clar as it could be and calm and at the mean time there near a Star made its apperence west rite over the Capitol and it Shined just as bright as it could be. . . ."[63]

This Inauguration Day was vastly different from that of March 4, 1861, when people awaited the words of the newly elected President on the crisis momentarily descending on the nation. Now a tremendous shout, "prolonged and loud, arose from the surging sea of humanity" that spread in waves from the specially built platform on the east front of the Capitol, out to the foliage of the Capitol grounds.[64] With few preliminaries, Lincoln, "rising tall and gaunt among the groups about him," advanced with a single sheet of paper in his hand. A roar of applause greeted him and at this moment the sun burst forth in full splendor.

This second Inaugural was very brief; one of the shortest on record. In his opening words, the President admitted that little new could be presented. The progress of arms was well known and, "I trust, reasonably satisfactory and encouraging to all. . . . Both parties deprecated war; but one of them would *make* war rather than let the nation survive; and the other would *accept* war rather than let it perish. And the war came. . . . Neither party expected for the war, the magnitude, or the duration, which it has already attained. Neither anticipated that the *cause* of the conflict might cease with, or even before, the conflict itself should cease. Each looked for an easier triumph, and a result less fundamental and astounding. Both read the same Bible, and pray to the same God; and each invokes His aid against the other . . . but let us judge not that we be not judged. The prayers of both could not be answered; that of neither has been answered fully. The Almighty has His own purposes. . . . If we shall suppose that American Slavery is one of those offences which, in the providence of God, must needs come, but which having continued through His appointed time, He now wills to remove, and that He gives to both North and South, this terrible war, as the woe due to those by whom the offence came, shall we discern therein any departure from those divine attributes which the believers in a Living God always ascribe to Him? Fondly do we hope—fervently do we pray—that this mighty scourge of war may speedily pass away. Yet, if God wills that it continue, until all the wealth piled by the bond-man's two hundred and fifty years of unrequited toil shall be sunk, and until every drop of blood drawn with the lash, shall be paid by another drawn with the sword, as was said three thousand years ago, so still it must be said 'the judgments of the Lord, are true and righteous altogether.' With malice toward none; with charity for all; with firmness in the right, as God gives us to see

63. Shiner, Michael, *Diary*, LC. (Spelling is his own.)
64. Brooks, *Washington in Lincoln's Time*, *op.cit.*, 212-213.

the right, let us strive on to finish the work we are in; to bind up the nation's wounds; to care for him who shall have borne the battle, and for his widow, and his orphan—to do all which may achieve and cherish a just, and a lasting peace, among ourselves, and with all nations."[65]

The crowd listening to the President's "ringing and somewhat shrill tones," broke in with applause several times, interrupting the continuity. At the close, cheers burst forth from many who had been moved, accompanied even by the tears of those who had grasped the solemn impact of the most religious of American state papers.[66]

The youthful-looking Chief-Justice Chase, almost as tall as Lincoln himself, delivered the oath; the President kissed the Bible; the artillery boomed, and Lincoln retired. But in that vast concourse of people stood a sullen group of men, their minds closed to the moving eloquence of the President, the simple pageantry of the scene, intent only on dark thoughts of revenge.

Harper's Weekly termed the address "characteristically simple and solemn. He neither speculates, nor prophesies, nor sentimentalizes. . . ."[67] Others called it "noble," and one Congressman pronounced it "most masterly, and regarded by some as the best of his many remarkable utterances. . . ."[68]

In contrast to the loud applause, the New York *Herald* ventured to comment, "It was not strictly an inaugural address. . . . It was more like a valedictory. . . . Negroes ejaculated 'bress de Lord' in a low murmur at the end of the almost every sentence. Beyond this there was no cheering of any consequence. Even the soldiers did not hurrah much." But the Boston *Evening Transcript* said, two days later, "The President's Inaugural is a singular State paper—made so by the times. No similar document has ever been published to the world. . . . The President was lifted above the level upon which political rulers usually stand, and felt himself 'in the very presence of the very mystery of Providence.' " Charles Francis Adams, Jr., wrote his father, "That rail-splitting lawyer is one of the wonders of the day. . . . This inaugural strikes me in its grand simplicity and directness as being for all time the historic keynote of this war. . . ." The London *Times* called it, "an address full of a kind of Cromwellian diction and breathing a spirit very different from the usual unearnest utterances of successful politicians." Gladstone said, "Mr. Lincoln's words show that upon him anxiety and sorrow wrought their true effect. The address gives evidence of a moral elevation most rare in a statesman, or indeed in any man." According to James Grant Wilson, "Emerson said he thought it

65. Lincoln, *Works*, VIII, 332-333.
66. Brooks, *op.cit.*, 213-214.
67. *Harper's Weekly*, March 18, 1865.
68. Brooks, *op.cit.*, 213-214; Riddle, Albert G., *op.cit.*, 329-330.

was likely to outlive anything now in print in the English language."[69]

"The Last Inaugural" was at once seen to breathe an elevation of soul worthy of a great people in a climactic moment of its history. Its influence upon the events in 1865 which closely followed it was slight. But this immortal admonition was designed for the decades and the ages, not for the immediate moment, for many men were still far from ready to forget their hot malice or adopt the golden maxim of charity for all in a land so long rent by resentments and hatreds. The nobility of Lincoln's words, however, gripped the national consciousness with a force that moulded thought and action as nothing had done since Washington's Farewell Address—a force that still lifts and shapes the American purpose.

69. Lincoln Lore, Fort Wayne, Ind., No.1212, June 30, 1952.

8

Net and Trident: The Growth of Southern Desperation

IN THE Punic Wars, the Seven Years' War, and the Napoleonic Wars, a time came when the vital question was not which of the combatants would win the next victory, but which nation would exhibit the sterner resolution and grimmer persistence. Commanders could do little without the support of their embattled people. Would the Romans, in the discouraging days before Cannae, continue harassing Hannibal's seemingly unhaltable army, and would they, in the yet darker hours after Cannae, rally their men as unflinchingly as ever to the standard of Scipio? The brilliant younger Pitt saw one coalition after another wrecked by Napoleon's genius. Would he again set indomitably to work, people and Parliament behind him, to build new bulwarks? Much later, in 1918, a year of alternate victories and defeats on each side, would the reeling Allies or the reeling Central Powers first give way?

The familiar drama was playing itself out on the American stage in 1864. By late summer the test of endurance, the ordeal of fortitude North and South, was the same risk that so many leaders from Pericles to Churchill have had to run. Not the next battle, but the last battle, would be decisive, and skill in arms would count less than dogged persistence behind the fighting lines. At the same time the fact that the Confederacy was besieged and that it was fighting a war of desperation had to be considered. In courage, tenacity, and resourcefulness, the North and the South were well matched. Nobody could say which was superior. On the other hand, the disparity in material resources constantly intruded into the picture. Since circumstances tried the combatants unequally, the fortunes of war swayed back and forth; and down to Lincoln's reëlection few could feel sure which antagonist would win.

The South was of necessity the more daring fighter, armed with the swifter sword—the sword of Lee and earlier that of Jackson, now dead, but inspiring millions from his grave. The North was a slow, cool battler, a gladiator armed with the net of blockade and the trident of three powerful armies in Virginia, in Georgia, and in the Mississippi Valley. Nerve and endurance must ultimately fail somewhere; but on which side?

Late in August, 1864, William E. Dodge, Jr. sent Greeley's *Tribune* a letter by Brigadier-General Truman Seymour, a veteran of the Mexican and Seminole Wars who, after being taken prisoner in the Wilderness, had just returned from Charleston. Having talked with old Army friends there, he set down an honest impression. "The rebel cause is failing fast from exhaustion," he wrote. "Their two grand armies have been reinforced this summer from the last resources of the South. From every corner of the land every old man and every boy capable of bearing a rifle has been impressed. . . . Lee's army was the first to be strengthened; it was at the expense of Hood's. Governor Brown told the truth with a plainness that was very bitter, but it was nonetheless the truth."[1] Blunt Joseph E. Brown, whose devotion to the Confederate cause was surpassed only by his devotion to State Rights, had told his Georgians before the fall of Atlanta that Jefferson Davis was giving all his energies to the protection of Virginia; that he would leave to Georgia itself the main task of saving Atlanta and Johnston's army; and that their hopes lay in themselves alone. Governor Brown added ominously: "If General Johnston's army is destroyed, the Gulf States are thrown open to the enemy, and we are ruined."[2] General Seymour added that the Southern people realized the desperate weakness of a government that could not reinforce Lee and Johnston at the same time. He had copied a letter by one leading Georgian, which he gave in an apparently authentic text.

"Very few persons are preparing to obey the call of the Governor," it ran. "His summons will meet with no response here. The people are soul-sick and heartily tired of the hateful, hopeless strife. They would end it if they could, but our would-be rulers will take good care that no opportunity is given the people to vote against it. . . . We have had enough of want and woe, of cruelty and carnage, enough of cripples and corpses. There is an abundance of weeping parents, bereaved widows, and orphaned children in the land."

It was perhaps Herschel V. Johnson, a State Rights Unionist, who wrote thus from Georgia. He had feared disaster and defeat from the beginning, and he informed several Georgians about this time that he longed for peace as the hart pants for the cooling waterbrooks.[3] In Richmond, Mary Boykin Chesnut noted in her diary late in July, 1864, that talk of defeat had been rife for weeks. "How they dump the obloquy on Jeff Davis now, for no fault of his but because

1. New York *Tribune*, Aug. 22, 1864.
2. Fielder, Herbert, *A Sketch of the Life and Times and Speeches of Joseph E. Brown*, Springfield, Mass., 1883, 255-334.
3. Flippin, Percy S., *Herschel V. Johnson of Georgia*, Richmond, 1931, 261-263.

the cause is failing. A ruined country! Who can bear it?" Another observer who scrutinized the whole South closely, the soldier-journalist T. C. DeLeon, declares that as early as the fall of 1863 the people were utterly losing faith for a variety of reasons. The government was hopelessly divided, for the weak Congress which President Davis had once led by the nose had turned dead against him. The blockade had become so thoroughly effective that blankets and shoes had almost given out, and a large proportion of the army was barefoot, with old rugs cut up by patriotic women for overcoats.[4] At every point the North was superior, its armies stronger, its navy in command of the seas, its artillery more powerful, its supplies seemingly inexhaustible. All the old Southern illusions were dying: the illusion that France and Britain would intervene; the illusion that Union finances would utterly break down; the illusion that a seditious Northwest would break away from the selfish, canting New Englanders.

The American correspondent of the London *Daily News*, who kept a close eye on the South, wrote on August 21 that he saw "the apparent commencement of the debacle in the Confederacy—the signs of it in Mississippi and North Carolina are very strong."[5] They were in fact overwhelming. Governor Zebulon Vance had written President Davis as 1864 began that after a careful examination of all the sources of discontent in North Carolina, he had concluded that the people wanted peace, and that some effort at negotiation with the North was desirable. Offering of terms without retreat from principles would strengthen the Southern cause, Vance believed.[6] Davis replied with his usual defiance, but with a significant admission that he comprehended the danger of a revolt in the State. He feared from the news he received "that an attempt will be made by some bad men to inaugurate movements . . . which all patriots should combine to put down at any cost. You may count on my aid in every effort to spare your State the scenes of civil warfare which will devastate its homes if the designs of these traitors be suffered to make head."[7] He urged Vance, a former Whig of the Henry Clay school who had stubbornly opposed disunion until Lincoln's call for troops, to avoid conciliating malcontents, for otherwise "you will be driven to the use of force to repress treason." Efforts to communicate with the North had failed, Davis added.

As for once-fiery Mississippi, which out of her 92,000 white males aged sixteen to sixty-five in 1861 had put about 78,000 into uniform by 1865, even her

4. DeLeon, Thomas Cooper, *Four Years in Rebel Capitals*, Mobile, Ala., 1892, 316-319, 341, 348; Chesnut, Mary Boykin, *A Diary from Dixie*, New York, 1905, 424, July 26, 1864.

5. London *Daily News*, Sept. 5, 1863.

6. Vance, Gov. Zebulon, Dec. 30, 1863, a letter Davis received early in 1864; Rowland, Dunbar, *Jefferson Davis Constitutionalist*, Jackson, Miss., 1923, VI, 141-142.

7. *Ibid.*, 143-146, January 8, 1864.

military ardor was chilled after Vicksburg and paralyzed after Atlanta. The northwestern district from the upper waters of the Big Black and Pearl to the Alabama boundary, an area of pineland and hills where much of the land was poor, the farms very small, and slaves but few, became by 1863 a "disloyal country"—disloyal to the Confederacy. One county that year had so many absentee soldiers that runaway slaves found themselves crowded out of their refuges by runaway white men. Other counties were "deluged with deserters."[8] When the people grew hungry, many women openly encouraged sedition. They danced at news of the fall of Vicksburg, they urged men in the army to return and join the "swamp service." Union sympathizers of Attala County, denouncing the Confederate demagogues who were ruining the land, began to escape to the Yankee lines. In the prevalent discontent, a story sprang up that men of the piney woods in Jones County had seceded from Mississippi as the "republic of Jones."[9] In October, Senator James Phelan wrote Davis that only a Spartan band retained their firm loyalty, "whilst the timid, the traitor, and the time-server are legion."[10]

Yet if evidences of defeatism were most obvious in Mississippi, so heavily invaded, and in North Carolina, so reluctant to secede, so little attached to slavery, and so sorely stricken by battle losses, they could be found everywhere by the autumn of 1864. In Richmond gloom grew thick during September. That month had barely begun when loud cheers from the Union lines around the city heralded the fall of Atlanta. This calamity created general Southern dismay. Angry denunciation fell upon the head of Joe Johnston, and bitter reproaches were heaped upon Jefferson Davis for not removing him sooner. The discontent was naturally greatest in the Confederate capital. "You could hear the loungers growl as you pass along the street," writes one Richmond annalist.[11] Everyone knew that the capture of the vital railroad center of Atlanta with its invaluable machine shops and foundries was a sore blow to the Confederacy and provided an open portal for possible further invasion of Georgia. At the same time, some in the South were hopeful and others in the North fearful that Sherman's army was over-extended and that he could or would be cut off from his tenuous supply lines running clear back through Chattanooga to Nashville. Sherman's ensuing march across the State to Savannah seemed to Pollard of the Richmond *Enquirer* an annunciation of the end.[12] Already bisected north and south and ringed by fire, the Confederacy would now be cloven east and west.

8. Bettersworth, John K., *Confederate Mississippi*, Baton Rouge, 1943, 218ff.
9. *Ibid.*, 226-227.
10. *O.R.*, IV, pt. 3, 707-710.
11. Bill, A.H., *The Beleaguered City: Richmond, 1861-1865*, New York, 1946, 234.
12. Pollard, Edward A., *The Lost Cause*, New York, 1967, 645-646.

Everywhere in the South, in fact, discontent boiled to the surface as people lost their last shreds of confidence in the Davis Administration. Many, anguished by their mounting deprivations and losses, felt that since defeat was now inevitable, the sooner it came the better. Congress made some clumsy efforts to allay the general despondency, but these simply revealed that it had neither a plan nor determination enough to meet the crisis. People began to look desperately for any way out. "Now, for the first time," wrote T. C. De Leon, "they began to speculate upon the loss of their beloved capital. It was rumored in Richmond that General Lee had told the President that the lines were longer than he could hold; that the sole hope was to evacuate them and collect the armies at some interior point for a final struggle. . . . And the rumor added that Mr. Davis peremptorily and definitely rejected this counsel; declaring that he would hold the city at any cost and any risk." However, "even now there was no weak relaxation—no despairing cry among the Southern people."[13] Where was the interior point, the fortress, to use for a last stand? Chattanooga? It was gone. Montgomery? It was surrounded. Lynchburg? It was too weak. And what was the use of throwing lives away in a last stand?

One index of Southern desperation was the preposterous character of some of the last-minute expedients proposed. Robert G. H. Kean of the War Department thought that the government might well try to obtain the help of a foreign power even at the expense of its pride and independence. Why not sound out Napoleon III upon his willingness to come to the aid of the Confederacy? It might be made a French protectorate, with French control of its foreign policy, special French access to its cotton, ship timber, and naval stores, and French security in the occupation of Mexico. Of course the South would retain complete autonomy in domestic affairs. Kean embodied this harebrained idea in a memorandum to Secretary Seddon, in July, 1863, who gave it with a grimace to the Secretary of State![14]

[I]

The Southern will to resist was heroic; it had such iron strength that well into the last year of the war it still seemed almost unconquerable. The hardships of the Southern people, taken alone, would perhaps never have fatally sapped it. Whatever their sufferings, they might well have fought on. It was the interaction of three principal forces that brought Southerners to the point where they began to accept the idea of defeat. These forces were the heavier and heavier loss of life—the drawing of an ever-deeper stream of blood from

13. DeLeon, Thomas Cooper, *op.cit.*, 348.
14. Kean, Robert G.H., *Diary*, New York, 1957, 82, July 12, 1863.

veins that could not be replenished; the ever sharper bite of a hundred steel teeth of internal privation; and the growing conviction that all the Southern losses would be in vain, that no matter what the struggles of the people or the feats of the armies, superior Northern strength and organization would ultimately win.

For Southern leaders knew that as the spirits of the Confederacy fell, the spirits of the North rose. They learned from stray Yankee newspapers after Atlanta fell that Grant had recently telegraphed Lincoln (July 19, 1864) suggesting a draft of 300,000 more men because the Confederacy "now have their last men in the field. Every depletion of their army is an irreparable loss—desertions from it are now rapid." They learned that the day before Grant telegraphed, Lincoln had anticipated him by calling for a full half-million recruits. And if at all well informed, Southern leaders knew that although the total raised under this call was not large, a steady current of fresh soldiers did flow into all the Northern armies from August onward.[15]

Grant reiterated on August 16, 1864, his conviction that the Southern armies were becoming disastrously weaker. "The rebels have now in their ranks their last men. The little boys and old men are guarding prisoners, railroad bridges, and forming a good part of their garrisons for intrenched positions. . . . They are now losing from desertions and other causes at least one regiment per day."[16] A great body of Southerners must have guessed that such statements were being made by Northern generals. They may even have suspected that Lee was making statements that tallied with Grant's. "Unless some measure can be devised to replace our losses," Lee wrote Seddon on August 23,[17] "the consequences may be disastrous. Without some increase of strength, I cannot see how we are to escape the natural military consequences of the enemy's numerical superiority." And early in September he wrote President Davis that immediate measures must be taken to reinforce the Army of Northern Virginia. "The necessity is now great, and will soon be augmented by the results of the coming draft in the United States. As matters now stand, we have no troops disposable to meet movements of the enemy . . . without taking them from the trenches and exposing some important point."[18]

The death's head of defeat grinned and grimaced at dejected Southerners, while a spectral hand wrote under every death-roll the burning question: "To what end?"

And what black rolls these were! The deepest grief of the South, the pro-

15. Lerwill, L.L., *The Personnel Replacement System in the United States Army*, Washington, 1954, 165.
16. To Elihu Washburne, *Grant Papers*, Illinois State Hist. Libr.
17. *O.R.*, I, xlii, pt. 2, 1199-1200.
18. *Ibid.*, 1228.

foundest source of disheartenment, sprang from the continuous losses by death, mutilation, and sickness, and the harsh measures taken to repair them. Even more than in the North, every town and village shuddered at the long casualty lists posted in public places. The slow, jolting trains brought home anguished huddles of the sick, exhausted, and maimed, crowding ever more thickly alongside piles of officers' coffins; then bore away the reluctant conscripts. "It was not unusual to see at the railroad stations long lines of squalid men, with scraps of blankets in their hands, or small pine boxes of provisions, or whatever else they might snatch in their hurried departure from their homes, leaving for training camps."[19] These recruits were what a British observer termed "poor old Dixie's bottom dollar." They could never fill up the depleted ranks. At every point the Northern strength was now vastly superior. Even the Yankee cavalry was now stronger. The days when the Stuarts, Wade Hamptons, Forrests, and Fitzhugh Lees had outridden and outfought the Pleasontons and Griersons were gone forever. Southern horses were worn out, and Southern horsemen had lost some of their dash and pride; that the Yankees had learned to fight was comprehensible, but that they had also learned to ride was a fact harder to grasp.[20]

The scanty Southern successes were meanwhile won upon the same old costly terms as at Chickamauga; once more a terrible exertion, a ghastly loss of life—more than 2,300 men killed, 14,600 wounded,[21] and nearly 1,500 missing. Once more a merely nominal victory, and a disheartening failure to grasp its fruits. Like Sisyphus, the South toiled up hill after hill to meet exhausting defeats or equally exhausting triumphs that dissolved into new chagrins. In the bloody shambles of the Wilderness, Lee's army of just over 61,000 effectives was believed to have lost about 7,750 men slain and wounded. The Union loss was much greater, but it could be repaired; the Confederate casualties could not. In the heavy combat at Spotsylvania on May 8-12, Confederate losses were placed by Generals Hancock and Humphreys at 5,000 to 6,000. In the fighting at Petersburg on June 15-18, Humphreys pronounced the Southern losses "severe." The battling along the Weldon Railroad on August 18-25 cost the Confederates 1,200 killed and wounded. Meanwhile, Hood's futile assault at Atlanta on July 22, when the South threw 37,000 men into what Hardee termed one of the most desperate and bloody encounters of the war, left about 7,000 Confederates killed or wounded.[22]

19. Pollard, *op.cit.*, 646-647.

20. DeLeon, *op.cit.*, 318-319.

21. Livermore, Thomas L., *Numbers and Losses in the Civil War in America*, Boston, 1901, 106.

22. *Ibid.*, 111, 113, 118, 123; Humphreys, A.A., *The Virginia Campaign of 1864 and 1865*, 106, 225; *O.R.*, I, xxxvi, pt. 1, 337; *O.R.*,I, xxxviii, pt. 3, 75, 699. As usual, such casualty figures are subject to much dispute as to accuracy, particularly on the Confederate side.

What a wealth of talent these and other similar cold figures represent, what a load of grief they laid upon Southern homes, and how terribly the losses crippled coming generations! Longstreet, badly wounded in the Wilderness, mentions in his memoirs that Micah Jenkins, son of a leading planter family in South Carolina, was slain the same day: "intelligent, quick, untiring, attentive, truly faithful to official obligations, abreast of the foremost in battle." He was but one of a thousand; and as the Southern historian Douglas Freeman notes, in all the commands fewer and fewer brilliant juniors were left to fill gaps.[23] One man who was promoted from a captaincy to a brigadiership in a single jump was killed before he had served a fortnight in his new rank. As this gory summer of 1864 wore on, Southern officers took more desperate personal risks to stiffen wavering troops against Union soldiers who fought better and better. Valor endured, but frequently inexperienced troops had to be placed under incompetent captains and colonels, and untested generals.[24]

While bloodshed had a limited effect upon Grant, it grieved Lee so intensely that Pollard and others accused him of excessive tenderness.[25] When Pemberton proposed a useless charge against the Yankee lines before Richmond, Lee silenced him with cutting words.[26] It seems clear that by the last weeks of 1864, he realized that further fighting would be hopeless. After the war a Southern woman, finding him pensive and depressed, asked the reason. He was thinking, he replied, of the men who had died under the Confederate banner after all prospect of victory had vanished. "Why didn't you tell them?" asked his questioner. "They had to find it out for themselves," he responded. Unquestionably, however, many Southerners knew after Lincoln's reëlection, after the terrible carnage of Franklin left 1,750 Confederates dead and around 3,800 wounded on the field, and after Sherman's army approached the defenses of Savannah, that the lives thereafter lost were a senseless sacrifice to Moloch. Many a devoted Southern officer reproached himself as he gave fatal orders. Yet still a Spartan sense of duty bound the President, the high civil officers, and the generals as in bands of steel.

"It is agonizing to see and hear the cases daily brought into the War Office," wrote Kean as the screws of the conscription were tightened; "appeal after appeal, and *all* disallowed. Women come there and weep, wring their hands, scold, entreat, beg—and almost drive me mad. The iron is gone deep into the heart of society."

Countless Southerners felt, during this last year of the war, as if they were

23. Longstreet, James, *From Manassas to Appomattox*, Philadelphia, 1896, 566; Freeman, Douglas S., *Lee's Lieutenants*, New York, 1955, III, 546-548.
24. *Ibid.*, 556.
25. Bradford, Gamaliel, *Lee the American*, Boston, 1927, 176.
26. Sorrel, G. Moxley, *Recollections of a Confederate Staff Officer*, New York, 1905, 265.

walking in a nightmare. And yet, busy people might momentarily forget the almost universal grief over the extinction of bright young lives; they might put out of mind for an hour other sources of anxiety and anguish. Many gradually became accustomed to the abnormal situation. They had interludes of reconciliation with fate, exhilaration over good fortune, and even bursts of gaiety. The churches were flower-trimmed for bridals; dining-rooms were now and then lighted for school-commencement suppers of fruits, ices, and cakes. Judith McGuire, returning from a hospital where she had seen a young girl mourn by her dying brother, passed a house bright with music and dancing, and thought of the ball in Brussels the night before Waterloo.[27] Some young people held "starvation parties" to laugh at their privations; some crippled soldiers went courting with a jest over "Cupid on Crutches." Yet the sword seemed to flash in the lamplight of parlors, the whine of shells seemed to pierce bars of the lightest music, and the tramp of distant battalions echoed through wedding marches. The iron pressures of a hundred deprivations never relaxed their grip; if the throbbing pain was eased at one point, it struck at another.

The phrase "a hundred deprivations" could be taken literally. The young wife with market-basket on her arm felt that the growing inflation was beyond human tolerance; how could people endure such costs? Sewing ugly frocks of unbleached Macon calico in place of wornout gowns, nursing children without medicines, or learning that a son's amputation had been without benefit of anaesthetics, older women writhed in the grip of the blockade. A hardworking farmer who saw the steel ploughshare of invasion rip through his plantation, his buildings burned, his cotton seized, his poultry, cattle, and pigs butchered, his slaves urged to flee, realized that war must mean utter impoverishment. And if this was only individual tragedy, the long lines of smashed railroads, the wrecked bridges, the dilapidated public buildings, the sacked stores, the decaying factories, meant the ruin of whole communities. Everywhere in northern Virginia, western Mississippi, Tennessee, half of Georgia, and much of Alabama and Louisiana, such sights had become familiar. The loss of lives, the loss of property; who did not know their ruth and pang? And whenever men glimpsed a gutted library, a shattered college, or a ruined church like St. Finbar's Cathedral in Charleston, they realized how deadly a blow the war had struck at cultural and moral progress.

Was inflation worse than invasion and devastation? Who could answer such an inquiry? Some would have said that the steady breakdown of the Southern railroads was more painful in its social and economic consequences than the blockade, but the imponderables in such an equation defy measurement. The

27. Freeman, *Lee, op.cit.*, III, 496; McGuire, Judith White, *Diary of a Southern Refugee*, New York, 1867, 328, and *passim.*; Kean, *Diary, op.cit.*, 174.

shortages of salt, medicines, and cutlery, of tea, coffee, and sugar, of silverware, china, and fine textiles, and of a thousand luxuries that had become almost necessities, were galling in the extreme. So were the demands of the impressment system, which placed as inexorable a hand upon all war-needed commodities as conscription laid upon the able-bodied men of the land. Was the problem of refugee-crowding in some areas worse than the problem of loneliness in others when all wonted modes of communication and intercourse failed? Nobody could say. The important fact was that the South suffered from all these ills. By the autumn of 1864 it was an aching void, and the typical Southerner regarded himself at times as but a hungry aggregation of bruises, aches, and unsatisfied wants.

"It is impossible to say precisely when the conviction became general in the South that we were to be beaten. . . . It was a part of our soldierly and patriotic duty to believe that ultimate success was to be ours, and Stuart only uttered the common thought of army and people, when he said, 'We are bound to believe that, anyhow.' We were convinced, beyond the possibility of a doubt, of the absolute righteousness of our cause, and in spite of history we persuaded ourselves that a people battling for the right could not fail in the end. And so our hearts went on hoping for success long after our heads had learned to expect failure. . . . It was our religion to believe in the triumph of our cause, . . ."[28] Take away the Southerner's belief in ultimate victory and substitute a gnawing anxiety for the welfare of family and friends, and his valor grew steadily staler and limper.

It was not the hardships of war-bound life in a hundred socio-economic respects, not the widening devastation, not even the steady splash of blood of multitudes of young men, that sapped the Southern spirit. The people would have fought on despite all this as their grandfathers had fought on under Washington. It was, we repeat, the combination of a sickening conviction of ultimate defeat along with such adversities and losses that broke down the will to endure.

[II]

Then and later many were willing to say that the greatest single cause of demoralization lay in inflation—in the flood of paper currency choking the Confederacy. Treasury Secretary Memminger and his associates had really possessed no choice. They had been compelled to finance the war on credit. It was impossible to obtain a sufficient revenue from tariffs, the blockade

28. Eggleston, George Cary, *A Rebel's Recollections*, Bloomington, Ind., 1959, 172.

shutting off imports and exports more and more completely; from taxation, no considerable collections being possible; or from the sale of lands, there being no cash customers. The monetary resources of the South had been slender. No stocks of gold and silver existed, and no Confederate coins could be minted. After secession about twenty million dollars in United States coins, it was estimated, remained in the possession of the people, who in considerable part jealously hoarded the money. The only basis for borrowing lay in the staple crops, which could not be exported in any appreciable quantity, and lay increasingly at the mercy of invading armies.[29]

The history of Confederate finance is a record of prolonged failure, but failure attributable far more to hard circumstances than human short-sightedness or error. Tariffs, taxes, produce loans (that is, contributions in cotton, tobacco, sugar and the like in exchange for bonds), tax-in-kind or tithe, loans floated abroad—all were tried, and all proved false lights; will-o'-the-wisps glimmering over the depths of a fiscal quagmire. The story of the tariffs can be briefly dismissed. At the very outset (February 9, 1861) the Confederate Congress voted temporary adoption of the tariff of 1857; the next month it erected the first distinctly Confederate tariff; and within two months more it voted the second—a low tariff devoid of protective duties, which were in fact prohibited by both the temporary and permanent Constitutions. But the tariffs on imports amounted to very little. All told, the customs receipts of the Confederacy came to less than $3,481,000, for the whole war period.[30] As for export duties, which were permissible under the Confederate Constitution, they yielded practically nothing. The total amount collected on shipments of cotton, tobacco, and naval stores came to just over $39,000![31]

Taxes also proved a frail support. Secretary Memminger realized perfectly well that theoretically they were much better means of gathering resources for government use than the floating of loans; but practically, he faced mounting and almost insuperable difficulties. The first $15,000,000 loan, authorized nearly a fortnight before the firing on Fort Sumter, and bearing eight per cent interest payable in specie, was a success. This was because the banks gave it full support, throwing their resources into the effort so loyally that they lost control of a great part of the specie held in the South; much of it went abroad for the purchase of munitions and satisfaction of other needs. Almost at once in the spring of 1861 Congress had to authorize the Secretary to issue another $50,000,000 bond issue, payment this time coming not from the banks in specie,

29. Todd, Richard C., *A History of Confederate Finances*, Athens, Ga., 1954, Ch. I.

30. Reports of Secretary of the Treasury to Congress, Mar. 14, 1862-Nov.7, 1864; Summary, Todd, R.C., *op.cit.*, 121-130.

31. Todd, R.C., *op.cit.*, 127.

but from the agricultural population in salable produce. Then issue followed issue, Memminger perforce turning to sales of bonds as the main source of revenue.

Although the exchange of government paper for produce was the logical expedient of an agricultural society for paying its way, vexatious problems of storage and marketing arose, and acrimonious controversy followed. As the blockade tightened, many subscribers to loans complained that the stipulation that crops be turned over on a fixed day carried the seeds of their ruin. The government could compel a sale on that date even though prices had fallen abysmally low.[32] When Congress refused to guarantee the growers any relief, various States followed Mississippi in issuing notes and bonds for cotton; and the States thus drifted into speculations in cotton in competition with the Richmond government. These activities, carried on abroad as well as at home, led to embarrassing conflicts between State and Confederate authorities.

Efforts to raise money abroad were of little avail. Obtaining title to large quantities of cotton, the Treasury issued 1,500 Cotton Certificates valued at $1,000 each, which Secretary Memminger regarded as the most hopeful implement for obtaining funds from abroad. The results were very far below those he anticipated. The certificates sold so slowly on a reluctant market that the field soon had to be cleared to give sole possession to the Erlanger Loan. As we have seen previously, the house of Emile Erlanger & Co. agreed, under a contract with the Confederacy signed October 28, 1862, and perfected on January 8, 1863, to market $15,000,000 worth of cotton-secured bonds. James Spence of Liverpool, who had been authorized to sell as many of the Cotton Certificates as he could, had to stand aside. By the time that the Confederacy began to collapse, the Erlanger loan had slumped lower and lower. Henry Hotze wrote Judah P. Benjamin on August 17, 1863, that "the slightest causes affect it sensibly without adequate reasons"—as if Vicksburg and Gettysburg were trivial matters! When the Confederate financial authorities submitted a final report (February 11, 1865), it showed total receipts of about seven-and-one-half millions, a little more than half the face value of the loan.[33] Actually, the true net figure is not known.

The failure of tariffs, taxes, and foreign borrowings, with the emission of greater and greater quantities of paper money, meant a rapid drop into the abyss of inflation. By midsummer of 1863 a gold dollar would buy $10 in Confederate notes; by August it would buy $12; and by November it would purchase $15, so swift was the descent into the financial Avernus! Peering

32. See letters in *Correspondence of the Treasurer CSA*, IV, V, *passim*.

33. Report on the Erlanger Loan, showing receipts to Oct. 1, 1864; *Confederate Treasury Reports*, III, 435, 436. For further details see Nevins, *War for the Union* (Vol. 7, Chap. 13), "Foreign Relations."

ahead, people could wonder whether even $25 in Confederate notes would obtain a gold dollar a year later. As a matter of fact, in the month of Lincoln's reëlection, about $35 in rebel money was asked for one dollar in gold, or $150 for a sovereign.[34] As Pollard bitterly wrote, a soldier's monthly pay (if he received it) would hardly buy him a pair of socks as Christmas of 1864 approached. When hostilities began, the amount of Federal currency circulating in the Confederacy had been estimated at $85,500,000. By the beginning of 1863, however, about $290,000,000 in Confederate Treasury notes not bearing interest were circulating; $121,500,000 in interest-bearing notes; and at least $20,000,000 in States notes and banknotes.[35] The consequences were inevitable.

As in the North, the premium on gold in exchange for paper money bore no close relationship to the amount of paper in circulation. It was governed rather by popular hopes and fears, expectations and disappointments, over the probable outcome of the war. The amount of Union greenbacks in circulation did not rise greatly after midsummer in 1863, and not at all after midsummer in 1864, yet the gold valuation assigned to greenbacks fluctuated sharply in value even while increasing in volume. It is significant that Union credit rose and Confederate credit fell decidedly in the summer of Vicksburg and Gettysburg; that quotations on Northern greenbacks fell in the militarily anxious weeks preceding and following Chancellorsville, but rose that fall and winter while Treasury notes of the Confederacy slumped; and that from May through August, 1864, as Grant's army suffered heavy losses, greenbacks were again low. But, beginning in October, Confederate credit sank, and in January, February and March of 1865 it dropped tragically lower. By February, indeed, it took $58 in Confederate Treasury notes to buy a dollar in gold.[36]

It would be tiresome and pointless to recapitulate the list of Confederate funding acts and their amendments; to repeat the oft-told story of the growing Southern demand for Union greenbacks; or to rehearse the tale of Southern speculation in gold, and of the chorus of opprobrious epithets rained upon the speculators. Gambling in specie ran parallel with gambling in cotton. The search for scapegoats, as usual in such situations, was hotly pursued. They were found in certain Army officers—and indeed, Lee aimed some general orders against soldiers who bought supplies for a speedy resale;[37] in certain Jews whom the diarist Jones accused of profiteering on shoes, and of buying real estate because they had no faith in Confederate money; in turncoat Yan-

34. Schwab, J.C., *The Confederate States of America, 1861-1865; A Financial and Industrial History*, New York, 1901, 167. This gives a full wartime table.

35. Pollard, *Lost Cause, op.cit.*, 647; *Confederate Treasury Reports*, III, 59-70; 90-115.

36. Schwab, *op.cit.*, 167.

37. General Orders, Department of Northern Virginia, Nov. 14, 1862.

kees; and in blockade runners.[38] Trade with the enemy across the lines, nominally illegal but winked at even by the Secretary of War,[39] profited the Confederacy by bringing in supplies; it profited the speculators by bringing in foreign money. Such speculation had a demoralizing effect which invited the condemnation of Lee and other leaders, and of the press. But the opinion of some of the ablest generals was a bit more moderate; they said that it was essentially outrageous,[40] but that it could not be stopped.

The excessive paper money issues, the appalling rise in the cost of living as measured by paper, and the destruction of all confidence in the future value of paper money, government securities, bank deposits, and industrial shares, meant much more than a decay of normal financial standards. That would have been bad enough in the feeling of helplessness, and sometimes even despair, which it often created. But far worse was an accompanying degeneration in the moral tone of the Southern people. When money changed its value overnight, men used it in reckless speculation. As in France during the Revolution, and much later in inflation-riddled Germany after the First World War, rising markets led people to turn money into goods with frenzied haste. And as in various countries at numerous times, many observers blamed gamblers for the speculation, when actually speculation bred the gamblers. Extravagance was a natural consequence of inflation. Holding fortunes real or fictitious, the *nouveaux riches* used them in fast living; they seized on all available luxuries—gay dress, handsome houses, fine carriages, and glittering fêtes. Gambling halls, which rose overnight in Richmond, Charleston, and other cities, were crowded with men. Soldiers gambled because they did not know whether they would live another month, government contractors gambled because they could not be sure of next week's orders, and bankers, lawyers, and merchants because their money was fairy gold.[41] "Speculation is running wild in this city," wrote the Rebel War Clerk in April of 1863. From gambling and extravagant spending sprang crime. Cupidity became general, so that one observer remarked: "Every man in the community is swindling everybody else."[42]

Currency inflation, in fact, was a contributory agency in the breakdown of social discipline and self-control which became so marked as the war continued, and which we had a glimpse of previously in 1863. It helped bathe much of the South in an atmosphere of laxity, self-indulgence, and blind resignation. The section had always displayed an excessive fondness for whisky and rum, toddies, and juleps; now drunkenness became frequent inside and outside the

38. Jones, John B., *A Rebel War Clerk's Diary*, Philadelphia, 1866, I, 150, 289ff.
39. Schwab, *op.cit.*, 264.
40. *Ibid.*, 264ff.
41. Jones, *A Rebel War Clerk's Diary*, *op.cit.*, I, 288.
42. Quoted in Schwab, *op.cit.*, 230.

Army—until after 1863 the scarcity of intoxicants cut it down. The South had always been too much addicted to duelling, street affrays, and rural feuds of the kind described in *Huckleberry Finn;* now violence, sanctioned in battle, grew familiar behind the lines. "With the imposing and grand displays of war," writes Pollard in describing Richmond life, "came flocks of villains, adventurers, gamblers, harlots, thieves in uniform, thugs, tigers, and nondescripts. The city was soon overrun with rowdyism."[43] Statements of the same kind can be found in all newspapers. It was with good reason that, a quarter-century after the war, the principal historian of Confederate finance included in his book a section headed, "The Moral Decadence of the South."[44]

Many were the wails that arose from impoverished Southerners as they saw not only their property but their pride in character and principle vanishing in the smoke of inflation, speculation, and extravagance. It was not the Richmond government alone that was responsible. States, cities, and smaller local units issued notes; the total became at the end purely conjectural, but it must have approached if it did not exceed a billion dollars.[45] Private businesses added their petty shinplasters valued at from five to fifty cents. "Virginia is flooded with trash," exclaimed one irate citizen of the Old Dominion, while a Mississippi editor cried out against the financial mismanagement that cursed the people with 250 different kinds of paper promises, and not one silver dime to give them weight. The Confederacy itself printed fifty-cent notes. As the currency became debased, a resort to barter (as in the exchange of corn for nails, cotton for cloth) became general. Payments were made in kind, just as taxes were collected in crops.

Counterfeiting of the badly executed Confederate notes soon became rampant. Some unscrupulous Southerners engaged in it, though scarcity of paper and rarity of engraving tools and skills limited their nefarious activities, but most of it was the work of Northern hands, the notes being smuggled from New York, Philadelphia, and Louisville into the Confederacy. Near the end of the war some counterfeits were made in Cuba, and slipped through the blockade to Mobile or Texas ports. Although the Confederacy established a detective bureau in Atlanta,[46] efforts to identify the counterfeits were largely abortive, and when persons who passed them were arrested, they could usually plead ignorance. The most famous of the Northern counterfeiters, Samuel Upham of Philadelphia, later boasted that he had printed, in all, twenty-eight

43. Pollard, Edward A., *Life of Jefferson Davis,* Philadelphia, 1869, 152-153.

44. Schwab, *op.cit.*, Ch. XII; cf. material on Southern morale in Nevins, *War for the Union: The Organized War,* Ch. 10.

45. Schwab, *op.cit.*, 165.

46. *Correspondence of C.S.A. Treasury,* IV, 381; Col. G.W. Lee was head of the bureau; Todd, *op.cit.*, 99; Schwab, *op.cit.*, 159-161.

different facsimiles of Confederate notes and shinplasters; that Senator Foote had credited him with doing more to injure the Confederate effort than McClellan's army; and that President Davis had offered a reward of $10,000 for him dead or alive.[47] But it was not until late in the war that the government engaged a London firm to prepare plates of new design, with "chemiograph" engraving hard to counterfeit; and then some if not all the plates were intercepted by the blockade, passing into the hands of Northerners who cheerfully used them.[48]

[III]

Only less painful than the conscription of men, and well-nigh as strong a contributor to general demoralization as the growing rottenness of the currency, was the military seizure of all manner of goods and supplies. Impressment had swiftly become a dread word in the Confederacy. By 1864 it fell on men's ears like a pronouncement of doom. Early in the conflict army officers had begun to distrain commodities, and they expanded their grabbing as necessity or convenience prompted them. As it was not until March, 1863, that the Confederate Congress voted some systematic regulations for the collection of materials, arbitrary action long held full sway and set unhappy precedents. Military men attached crops, meat, flour, salt, hardware, horses, and wagons on the simple plea that necessity knew no law. Nor did the new law introduce evenhanded justice or really judicious procedures. It provided that, in every State, President Davis and the governor were each to appoint a commissioner, and these two were to try to agree on fair prices for goods impounded. If they disagreed they were to call in an umpire. In fixing the general scale, producers or men who kept supplies for their own consumption were to get preferential treatment over those who kept them for sale. The farmer and householder, that is, fared better than the merchant or speculator. If any holder disputed the price given him, he might appeal to two citizens of the neighborhood or an arbiter of their choice. This was a hit-or-miss procedure, full of holes. It had to be applied in a loosely organized society undergoing rapid deterioration, by army men acting under more and more desperate strain.

It worked wretchedly. Neither in theory nor in practise can much be said at any time for military impressment of the goods of a people carrying on a war. Efforts to seize supplies during the Revolution, in an effort to thwart "forestallers," speculators, and monopolists, and to help ragged veterans, had

47. Lee, William, *The Currency of the Confederate States of America*, Washington, 1875, 24-25; Todd, *op.cit.*, 100-101.

48. Chase, Philip H., *Confederate Treasury Notes*, Philadelphia, 1947, 123ff.

done more harm than good. Now, in the Confederacy, even the conscription of young men was hardly more detested, for *that* was acknowledged a necessity, at least by some. The system would have been regarded as abusive in the hands of men as honest as Lee and as conscientious as Stonewall Jackson, whereas the impressment officials were in fact sometimes knavish, often incompetent, and always under shaky supervision. Impressment reached deep into the rural areas and hamlets where the war had not been quite directly felt, and where any government supervision was generally resented. No other single exercise of power, declares a thorough investigator, produced such sullen discontent and sharp resentment.[49]

At first the general complaint was that the prices fixed were too low; later in 1863-64, that they were lifted too high.[50] Efforts by State commissioners to agree on a uniform scale east of the Mississippi broke down. Six States met in Montgomery in September of 1863 for the purpose, but got nowhere. The various impositions and abuses suffered by the people in the name of impressment authority aroused a rebellious temper and created an angry confusion that had no counterpart in the North. The activities of well-accredited agents were irritating enough. In addition, false officers appeared, brandishing their weapons before farmers and shopkeepers, signing worthless receipts, and filling their wagons by barefaced imposture. Various States passed laws to punish these cheats. The Louisiana legislature, for example, instructed Governor Henry W. Allen early in 1864 to call on Confederate troops to assist him in stopping illegal seizures, recovering unlawful confiscations, and making impostors suffer proper penalties.[51] In Georgia the Supreme Court pronounced a portion of the Impressment Act unconstitutional, and Governor Brown tried to make rascals who had taken property under false pretences subject to thirty-nine lashes and ten years' imprisonment.[52]

The interminable losses and harassments, in fact, aroused bitter antagonism throughout the whole South. When impressment officers lost good corn in the mud, and let bacon spoil in the sun, whole countrysides grew angry. Lack of planning accentuated local and regional disparities of supply, so that while one district had an excess, another sixty miles distant felt painful want. Farmers found it hard enough at best, what with lack of horses, broken-down railways, and uncertain steamboat service, to get their crops to market; they were rebellious when, on reaching town, they had their produce impressed at prices flagrantly below market rates. Indeed, as the governors of Virginia and

49. Ramsdell, Charles William, *Behind the Lines in the Southern Confederacy*, Baton Rouge, 1944, 117.
50. Coulter, Ellis M., *The Confederate States of America, 1861-1865*, Baton Rouge, 1950, 252.
51. Bragg, J.D., *Louisiana in the Confederacy*, Baton Rouge, 1941, 268.
52. Bryan, Thomas Conn, *Confederate Georgia*, Athens, Ga., 1953, 92.

the Carolinas complained, military detachments often seized commodities on the roads to market.[53] And what tremendous volume the seizures attained! During 1863, as Seddon admitted, the government was compelled to rely almost exclusively on impressment to meet its needs.[54] As 1864 began, this was "its only reliance." It has been estimated that at the end of the war the Confederacy owed half-a-billion dollars to citizens whose goods it had taken with promises to pay; and much more had been taken with fraudulent promises or none. Seddon gave Jefferson Davis a frank view of the matter.

"Impressment is evidently a harsh, unequal, and odious mode of supply," he wrote. "With the utmost forbearance and consideration even its occasional exercise is harassing and irritating; but when it has to prevail as a general practise, to be exercised inquisitorially and summarily in almost every private domain, by a multitude of subordinate officers, it becomes beyond measure offensive and repugnant to the sense of justice and prevalent sentiment of our people. It has been, perhaps, the sorest test of their patriotism and self-sacrificing spirit afforded by the war, and no other people, it is believed, would have endured it without . . . resistance. It has caused much murmuring and dissatisfaction, but a knowledge of the necessities which alone justified it has caused the outcry to be directed rather to the mode and . . . occasional excesses of its exercise than against the system itself."[55]

The universal hatred of impressment became commingled with the widespread hostility to President Davis, and the fear of a military despotism headed by the Secretary of War and leading generals. The personal resentments of some Confederate chieftains gained depth from the property seizures. When Senator A. G. Brown asserted that in Mississippi impressment was sheer robbery, when Governor Vance of North Carolina made the same charge, and Governor Brown of Georgia issued a proclamation in the fall of 1864 warning the people against rascals who made impressment a veil for robbery, they accentuated the feeling of an unbridgeable gap between State and Confederate governments. Impressment seemed part of the centralizing tendency that excited the wrath of Toombs and Stephens, and the waspish Richmond *Examiner* dwelt on the theme no more acridly than the moderate Richmond *Whig*.[56]

Property seizures of course extended to slaves, and the impressment of Negroes became more and more general in 1863-64, as we have seen in an earlier volume of this work. Here too, sporadic irregular activity gave way to a clumsy approach to system under legislation of March, 1863. Congress required that

53. Schwab, *op.cit.*, 208.
54. *O.R.*, IV, ii, 1009; Report Nov. 26, 1863.
55. *Ibid.*
56. Owsley, Frank Lawrence, *State Rights in the Confederacy*, Gloucester, Mass., 1961, 112ff.; Schwab, *op.cit.*, 208-213.

appropriations of slave labor must conform to State laws, or if none existed, to regulations laid down by the Secretary of War. Although these regulations were fairly simple, public necessities made their application steadily harsher. The paucity of labor in the South by 1863 was painful, and such workers as were available—over-age men, free Negroes, men unfit for fighting but able to do limited manual labor—demanded excessive wages. They were reluctant to leave home to go to distant mines, saltpeter caves, or factories.[57] Owners of slaves resisted hiring them to the government. They feared they would be exposed to battle, enemy seductions, or temptations to vagrancy if sent away from personal supervision. Congress had provided in 1862 for the use of Negroes as teamsters, cooks, and other camp employees, but here also the opposition of owners forbade hiring. Impressment had become a necessity.[58]

By 1864, indeed, the labor shortage became truly desperate. The Tredegar Iron Works in Richmond wanted a thousand men whom it would pay $25 a month with keep; the government shoe factory in Columbus, Georgia, wanted 200 cobblers; armories, salt works, and lumber mills needed help at once in large numbers. The cotton manufacturer William Gregg maintained a twelve-hour day in his workshops, and offered double wages to those who would toil fourteen hours.[59] Efforts to attract workers from Europe were largely fruitless; the hardships of inflation, and the threat of conscription, repelled foreigners, and of the few who came a great many soon departed. Inside the Confederacy the adaptability of labor to new conditions and environments was slight. It was noted that among the multitudinous refugees, many tilled the soil for the first time, buying or renting farms. But comparatively few farmers and planters could enter mechanic or mercantile employment with satisfaction or profit.

The Confederate government tried to be fair to owners in impressing slaves. It paid an agreed wage, or, failing agreement, $30 a month; it cared for the slaves in illness, and offered full compensation for those who died. But, above all other forms of property, this was the one whose impressment hurt. On December 30, 1863, Wigfall spoke in the Senate contrasting the early willingness of Southerners to make heavy sacrifices with their subsequent angry reluctance. In 1861 an appeal by Beauregard for corn and provisions to feed his army at Manassas had been read in every church on Sunday, and next day sixty wagonloads had been delivered to him without charge. But now farmers burned their wheat rather than sell it to the government at $5 a bushel, and haggled about the price of pork while their sons in the army went hungry. It was the refusal of owners to lend their slaves to the cause, however, that most

57. Seddon, in *O.R.*,IV, ii, 998, 999.
58. *Ibid.*
59. Coulter, *op.cit.*, 235-236.

irked Wigfall. "Singular to say, they think a great deal more of their negroes than of their sons and brothers." A friend had encountered a slave on a train to Richmond who reported that his master had felt worse to give him up than to have his five sons enlist. The planters, said Wigfall, would willingly put their own flesh and blood into the army, but asking for a Negro was like drawing an eyetooth.[60]

Such was the pressure for slave labor that in February, 1864, Congress made all male Negroes between 18 and 50 liable for work upon fortifications, in factories, or in army hospitals. This included freed Negroes. It further authorized the War Department to employ not more than 20,000 male Negro slaves. Owners were to receive compensation in case of death or escape to the enemy. If the Secretary of War should be unable to procure sufficient slaves for service then he was authorized to impress slaves not to exceed 20,000. This measure warned the South of more severe action impending! Sure enough, in the last desperate days of the war the States were required to furnish more Negroes (but not more than one in every five male slaves from a single owner) for rear service, while some officers talked of giving them front-line action. This, too, came about, for in the act approved March 13, 1865, the use of slaves as soldiers was authorized. If sufficient troops were not raised through request the President was authorized to call on each State for a quota, though not more than a fourth of the male slaves should be called. Although the act did not grant the slave his freedom if he served in the army, there appeared to be that tacit understanding. A few Negro troops were organized in Richmond, but time ran out before they could see any real action.[61]

To invest government officers with authority to seize supplies and labor was to give them power of economic life and death over whole communities. The South, which had taken up arms to achieve a larger liberty, was falling under the most arbitrary tyranny. It was becoming, in large areas, a police state. War has always been arbitrary, and always increasingly harsh. Southerners were finding that it poured its heaviest broadsides into individual freedom and local independence. They were learning what Napoleon's marshal had meant when he growled to a Franconian town: "We battle for liberty and equality—and the first person who moves without permission will be shot!"[62] The worst scars of the conflict, moreover, were not physical, but moral and psychological.

This fact was illustrated in the vein of callous inhumanity that by 1863-64 streaked the refugee life now becoming a broader and broader part of Southern

60. *American Annual Cyclopaedia*, 1863, 231-232.
61. Schwab, *Confederate States*, *op.cit.*, 193-195; *O.R.*, IV, iii, 208, 1114-1116, 1161.
62. Montross, Lynn, *War Through the Ages*, New York, 1944, 509.

existence. Just how many of the four million Southerners became wartime fugitives nobody can say, but it is certain that they finally numbered in hundreds of thousands. All Southern States passed laws to provide relief for indigent dependents of soldiers, and in many these laws applied to families on the run from the foe.[63] Their need was often pitiful. Old men, women, children, abandoning their homes all the way from Galveston and Memphis to Atlanta and St. Augustine, found the refugee camps ugly, crowded, and comfortless; the shelters offered by friends dreary and chill; the bankruptcy they carried with them a grievous burden to ruined communities. When they came into countrysides dotted with burned homes and desolated fields, they looked in vain for a cabin or an onion. To travel in dilapidated buggies behind skeleton horses, to beg a slave for some hoe cakes, and to take refuge in roofless walls covered with canvas, or even in caves, was a depressing experience.

A grandniece of Jefferson Davis, who found a dreary haven in Tuscaloosa, wrote bitterly: "What mockery to call this home! We are poor refugees. How suggestive that word refugee is to my poor heart of sorrows past, present anxieties, and future misery." Her grandfather, Joseph Davis, had lost all—his handsome mansion burned, his plantation confiscated; and he never returned home again, for he had none.[64]

Many refugees were forced to exchange their most prized personal possessions, including family heirlooms, for subsistence. They saw their children go with random education or none. Sensitive ladies learned to beg for help from men wearing ragged overalls with homemade galluses, and women able to expectorate tobacco juice ten feet. They met rudeness, insult, and occasional violence along with kindness and aid—the extremes of generosity and meanness. Many of them showed remarkable resourcefulness and courage in hewing out new pursuits; but many encountered suspicion and jealousy, finding that Virginians looked down upon Alabamians, and South Carolinians upon Georgians. When Dr. Joseph LeConte of South Carolina College sent off his carefully packed laboratory equipment for safe-keeping, it got only as far as Greensboro before it disappeared forever; whether into Southern or Northern hands nobody knew.

Yet these distressed folk, who showed so much courage, devotion to duty, and patriotism, got far less sympathy and aid than they deserved. High Confederate officials said little in their behalf, and did less; well-to-do people closed their hearts and purses so tightly that Kate Stone of Louisiana laid down an accurate generalization: "it is not the rich who are most generous." Charleston newspapers with reason denounced residents of the interior who leeched coastal refugees by steep rents and commodity prices; people of North Georgia

63. Massey, Mary Elizabeth, *Refugee Life in the Confederacy*, Baton Rouge, 1964, 244-246.
64. *Ibid.*, 269-270.

assailed the residents of Augusta and other southern towns for their greedy exactions. Those who plundered refugees, wrote an Atlanta editor, might yet meet "*their* day of tribulation." Pollard called the dispossessed Tennesseeans who came to Richmond for assistance "vultures who are now preying upon the community." The pressures of the time, in short, made inhumanity, ill-will, and selfishness familiar in all communities. It was a rare citizen who showed the spirit of Thomas Dabney, publishing in the Vicksburg press a notice that any and all citizens quitting the city might take refuge on his estate.[65] Much more common were the people who regarded refugees first as a nuisance, and then as foes.

The woes of displacement, the gloom of homelessness, the frictions of exile, were a cancer that ate into not merely the endurance of Southerners, but their very soul. Hundreds of thousands were never the same afterward. By the final winter of their struggle they felt the price they were paying for its maintenance almost unendurable, and knew that it would leave marks they would carry to the grave.

[IV]

Inevitably, the rising Southern discouragement and desperation found outlets in two fatal movements: an organized demand for peace among the civilians, and a spasmodic impulse toward desertion among the soldiers. A rough logic lay behind both impulses. On every side stretched a stormy sea of confusion and disorder. Look at the commissary service under the hated Northrop, so clear a failure in collecting and storing indispensable supplies! Look at the quartermaster department under that unstable South Carolinian, Abraham C. Myers—by no means so generally disliked, but somehow never truly effective in allotting and distributing supplies until he gave way in August, 1863, to an equally hampered West Point graduate, General Alexander R. Lawton. Look at the railroads! The flagging circulatory system of the Confederacy was managed first by William S. Ashe, an attorney and planter who had become a Congressman, and then a railroad president; later by William M. Wadley, a burly, self-made man of New Hampshire birth; and later still by a Georgian named F. W. Sims—all three floundering in a swamp of difficulties. Had the Confederacy established a railway dictatorship under an autocrat ruling all the lines, he might have delivered the South from its worst transportation troubles for a short time; but he also might have created new difficulties, and such a dictatorship was for many reasons impossible.

Month by month, year by year, the tracks, the rolling stock, the mechanical

65. *Ibid.*, 152.

facilities for overhaul, and the railroad force decayed. Even a vitally needed forty-mile stretch of rails between Greensboro, North Carolina, and Danville, Virginia, which Davis urged early in the war, remained unlaid until the spring of 1864. Railway companies were so jealous that they balked at uniform gauges. And worse than that, they refused to join their lines at junction points like Petersburg even when gauges were uniform. The Southern railroads had found that when Northern workers went home, they were left with employees so inexperienced that they wrecked trains and ruined locomotives; they learned that when they applied to the Tredegar works, the Atlanta rolling mills, and the Macon machine-shops for iron materials, these facilities had been preëmpted by more urgent demands. Under Sims, the most dynamic action and the most stubborn defiance of red tape were of but trifling and transient value in relieving the railroad system from the unrelenting pressures of Northern military effort and the demon decay. Destruction from without and wastage from within left the South with but a feeble, halting, much-interrupted, and precarious service.

An example of the way in which ruin overtook service is afforded in a page from the records of the eastern Mississippi railroads early in 1864. W. T. Sherman ordered a detachment of 7,000 cavalry under William Sooy Smith south from Tennessee along the Mobile & Ohio toward Meridian, Miss., where he was to meet Sherman's main army of 20,000 infantry. This presumably swift and secret stroke miscarried. Smith barely got across the Mississippi boundary before Forrest stopped him. Sherman's columns did penetrate to Meridian, but made so much noise in the process that the Confederates under Leonidas Polk, with Major George Whitfield as chief of transportation, promptly parried the stroke. Whitfield frenziedly used all the resources of the Mobile & Ohio and the Alabama & Mississippi Rivers line to evacuate a large amount of government stores and rolling stock from Meridian. But Sherman settled down then in Meridian for a full week while his troops roamed the surrounding districts and played havoc with railroad property.

They smashed and burned all the bridges and trestles on fifty miles of Mobile & Ohio track, tearing up twenty miles of rails. They destroyed tracks, bridges, and other facilities on the Alabama & Mississippi Rivers and smashed nineteen locomotives, many cars, and a great stock of car-wheels in the region of Jackson on the Mississippi Central. It was necessary for Whitfield, as soon as Sherman retired, to gather gangs of laborers, obtain rails, ties, and bridge timbers (collecting from other roads whatever materials they could spare) and set frantically to work to restore communications.

"Thereafter, the railroads serving Jackson operated upon a day-to-day basis only," writes the historian of Confederate railroads. "Military supply routine had been broken asunder. As late as May, quantities of bacon were stranded in both north-central and southwestern Mississippi, while heavy shipments of salt, just arrived from Virginia, could find no satisfactory places of storage." Any substantial Union force could now occupy Mississippi at its leisure. Sherman did not attempt this, for he was busy farther east, but other men did.

Evidences that the railroads were falling deeper and deeper into exhaustion multiplied. During 1864, their ability to meet emergency demands for trains of troops at one point, and trains of corn and bacon at another, became more and more dubious. When in May, some Federal troops briefly seized and tore up a short stretch of the Richmond & Petersburg Railroad, Confederate officials tore their hair in anxiety. It required weeks to repair this indispensable link.[66] Already, early in May, the creaky lines south of Richmond had been strained to their utmost as Lee strove to bring troops from Florida and South Carolina up to Petersburg. It took eight days to get about 300 men of the 21st South Carolina to the defenses.[67] In June, the command under Jubal Early had to be brought from Charlottesville to Lynchburg, sixty miles, to reinforce General John C. Breckinridge. The trains were delayed in starting; their average speed was twelve miles an hour; and they arrived in time to save Lynchburg, but not to stage a counterattack that might have staggered David Hunter's army.

By Christmas that year the situation had worsened until the railways were in a pitiable state. When a Union raid created a new emergency in the Shenandoah Valley, Longstreet met the greatest difficulty in moving two brigades from Richmond to repulse it, and the troops were exhausted before they were thrown into the battleline.[68] A tragic occurrence in Georgia late that summer illustrated both the deplorable condition of the railroads and the mismanagement in operation. General Hood's chief-of-staff had noted that the rickety line from Atlanta southeast into central Georgia caused great suffering and loss of life among the casualties it carried. Trains took seventy hours from Atlanta to Macon. Yet the men had to be transported. On September 1, a large number of wounded men were sent off on jammed cars. Part way down to Macon the train collided with another coming north with commissary supplies. Both engines were smashed, cars were demolished, many men were seriously injured, and thirty were killed.[69]

Everything was running down. Even before the capture of Saltville, Va.,

66. Freeman, *Lee's Lieutenants, op.cit.*, III, 464-466; Black, Robert C., III, *The Railroads of the Confederacy*, Chapel Hill, 1952, 238-244; *O.R.*,I, li, pt. 2, 899-900.

67. Black, *op.cit.*, 244-245.

68. *Ibid.*,247; Eckenrode, H.J., and Bryan Conrad, *James Longstreet, Lee's War Horse*, Chapel Hill, 1936, 324-325.

69. Black, *op.cit.*, 253.

with its invaluable mines, late in 1864, the shortage of this indispensable commodity was alarming. The preservation of meat without it was impossible; the boiling of sea-water was a slow process; inland sources were few; and salt, heavy to carry at best, deteriorated rapidly in quality and became useless when wet. A shudder ran through the Confederacy when Saltville fell. Only less distressing was the want of drugs. Quinine and calomel were needed to conquer malaria. The cruel Northern embargo upon shipments of chloroform meant needless anguish not only for Southerners in and outside armed service, but for many Northern prisoners-of-war as well. Everywhere, necessities as well as luxuries were disappearing. And as want strode through half the Southern communities, robbery and marauding strode alongside it. In all parts of the land, trustworthy Confederate officers reported that bogus impressment officers, undisciplined squads of cavalry or mounted militia, and bands of outlaws were roaming the roads, sowing terror and disloyalty with the same hand. Two letters to Governor Vance of North Carolina in 1863 sounded the same note.[70] One from the northern area ran: "There is a degree of Penury & Want in this county, and others no doubt that is truly distressing, & under existing circumstances I do contend that our Government and Legislature should interfere. . . . Now just let the news reach our Soldiers in the Army whose families are thus oppressed, & I should not be surprised to hear any day that many of them had laid by their arms and marched off home." And one from the southern area declared: "the time has come that we the common people has to hav bread or blood & we are bound boath men and women to hav it or die in the attempt. . . . We are willing to give . . . two Dollars a bushel but no more for the idea is that the Slave oner has the plantations & the hands to rais the brad stufs & the common people is drove off in the war to fight for the big mans negro. . . . if there is not steps taken soon necessity may drive us into measure that may proove awful. . . ." Men who wrote thus were near the end of the tether—the breaking point of desperation.

Civilians reached the end of the tether when they joined an organized agitation for peace; soldiers reached it when they deserted. To some extent the two evidences of desperation stood in the relation of cause and effect. Pacifism and defeatism at home, conveyed to soldiers by letters or grapevine telegraph, led to desertion in the field.

The rise of scattered but increasingly large and determined peace organizations in the South in 1864-65 registered forever the fact that, while the people of the Confederacy were able to build a highly effective military machine, they failed to solve the problem of sustaining the welfare and morale of the entire

70. Quoted in Ramsdell, Charles W., *Behind the Lines in the Southern Confederacy*, Baton Rouge, 1944, 46-48.

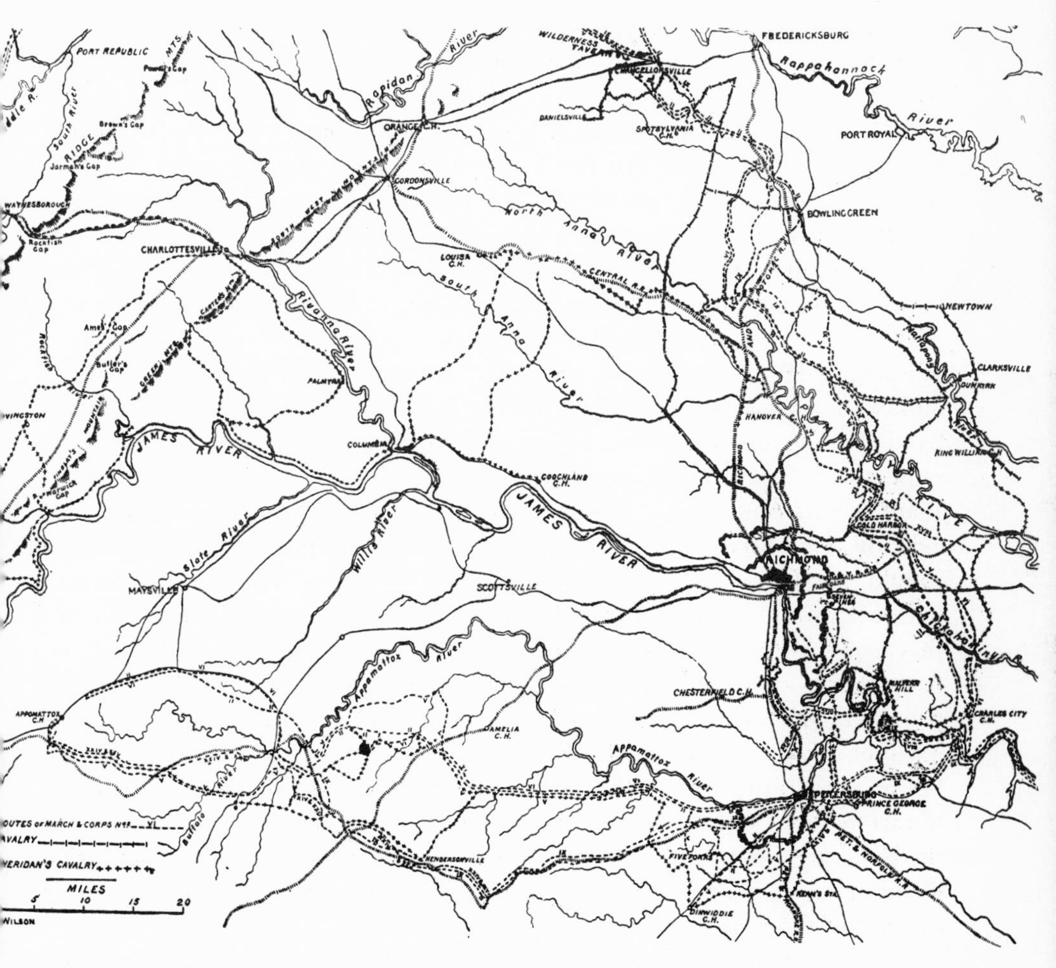

Map of Grant's Campaign against Richmond, 1864-1865

civil population. Governor Vance declared early in the autumn of 1864 that the heart of the people had never been in the war; that it was an attempted "revolution of the politicians, not the people."[71] War-weariness made the defects of public spirit plainly evident. Napoleon's observation that morale is three-fourths of battle-power found larger and larger illustration. President Davis did his utmost to rally the people, making three long speaking and inspection tours of the country east of the Mississippi, during which he held numerous conferences with military and political leaders. Some governors lent him assistance. As late as March 9, 1865, General Lee wrote: "While the military situation is not favorable, it is not worse than the superior numbers and resources of the enemy justified us in expecting from the beginning. Indeed, the legitimate military consequences of that superiority have been postponed longer than we had reason to anticipate. Everything, in my opinion, has depended and still depends upon the disposition and feelings of the people. Their representatives can best decide how they will bear the difficulties and sufferings of their condition and how they will respond to the demands which the public safety requires."[72] But all was in vain.

The hard core of peace movements within the Confederacy was inevitably found in the many thousands of Union men of the South who felt that they had been betrayed into a detestable and disastrous war.[73] Amid its first heady enthusiasms, its swirling banners, thumping drums, and squealing fifes, they had dumbly hoped for a negotiated peace and a restoration of the oldtime republic. As Southern blood was poured out like wine spilling from some mighty press, as defeat followed defeat from Shiloh to Gettysburg, as half the Carolina coast was occupied and starry flags blossomed deep in Georgia, clandestine organizations appeared wherever men kept the memory of the day on which a Southern President of the United States had risen at a dinner in honor of Jefferson to propose the immortal toast: "Our Federal Union: it must be preserved." Their names, as they arose in different parts of Dixie, were various—The Heroes of America; the Peace and Constitutional Society; the Peace Society. But their objects were everywhere the same: to aid each other in passive or active resistance; to impede enlistments; to send information to Union forces; to encourage desertion from the Confederate ranks; to help men get into the Union Army, and assist that Army wherever it invaded the South. Some were pacifists. Some were malcontents. But others were men of iron

71. Quoted in Silver, James W., "Propaganda in the Confederacy," *Journal of Southern History*, XI, No. 4, Nov., 1945, 487-503.

72. Dowdey, Clifford, and Louis H. Manarin, *The Wartime Papers of Robert E. Lee*, Boston, 1961, 913. (See Lee to John C. Breckinridge, Sec. of War.)

73. *O.R.*, I, xlvi, 1295; see Tatum, Georgia Lee, *Disloyalty in the Confederacy*, Chapel Hill, 1934, *passim*.

conviction, who meant to be in at the death of the Blatant Beast—the death of Disunion.

The earliest body to achieve a strong organization, the Peace and Constitutional Society, emerged in the hilly northwestern counties of Arkansas, where slaves were few and nationalist sentiment had true Western strength. It was a natural growth in a section of Arkansas that had voted almost solidly against secession.[74] Stronger and more widely diffused was the Peace Society, which arose in 1862 in two other areas full of Union feeling, East Tennessee and North Alabama—the valley of the Tennessee as it flows down from Knoxville into the Huntsville district, and the Cumberland Gap country. Here Federal agents lent a hand as it grew in vigor, penetrating Georgia and Alabama, and even "contaminating" some Confederate regiments. Strongest of all was the Order of the Heroes of America, which grew lusty enough in North Carolina, southwestern Virginia, and East Tennessee to interfere materially with the Southern war effort. A Confederate agent who reported on it in the fall of 1864 summarized the inducements to membership in a sentence: exemptions from military service, protection to persons and property during the war, and at the end, participation in a division of captured property.[75]

It was with good reason that North Carolina became a center of disaffection. The heroic commonwealth sent into the war about one-fifth of all the Confederate fighters, though it had only a ninth of the Southern population, and it contributed about one-fourth of those killed in action—some 40,000 men. Lee wrote Seddon at the opening of 1863: "I have relied much on the troops of that State." But throughout 1863 resentment grew. A statement issued anonymously complained that conscription and the tithe law were stripping Old North bare; that they took all the fighting men and a great part of the production. "Seizures of persons and property have become as common as they are in France and Russia."[76] The writer added: "Our patient, uncomplaining, heroic soldiers have been placed in the van of every battle and in the rear of almost every retreat." Most of the State held firm. But riotous disturbances by hungry people took place at several points, most conspicuously Salisbury, where a mob of soldiers' wives armed with hatchets assailed warehouses and carried away flour, molasses, and salt. The boldly intransigent editor, W. W. Holden, whose press, the Raleigh *Standard*, was destroyed by soldiers in 1863, was a born fighter whose State Rights feeling made him sternly hostile to the Confederate cause. Early in 1864 he suspended the *Standard* for several months, and ran for governor. It was understood that if elected he would open direct

74. *American Annual Cyclopaedia, 1861*, 25.
75. *O.R.*,IV, iii, 814-815; N.F. Bocock to Secretary Seddon.
76. *American Annual Cyclopaedia*, 1863, 691-692.

negotiations with Washington, or call a convention to leave the Confederacy, or both. But he lost.[77]

"The one great demand of the people in this part of the State," wrote one leader, "is peace—peace upon any terms that will not enslave and degrade us." Most people wanted Southern independence, but if it could not be obtained, "then they are for any terms that are honorable." Throughout 1863-64 a revolt against the authority of Richmond simmered just under the surface in North Carolina. One bloody occurrence filled people with horror. After a raid by Unionists on the mountain town of Marshall, a band of alleged disloyalists was seized in the Laurel area by Lt.-Col. James A. Keith and his Confederate command. Crime and violence had become common along the French Broad. A judicial officer reported to Governor Vance that thirteen captives had been shot, that other men had been seized unarmed in their homes, and that women had been whipped. Vance asked Secretary Seddon to cashier Keith for his brutality. "This heartless execution," writes one chronicler, "aroused the whole section to white heat."[78]

Thus the virus spread. We are not astonished to learn that so many North Carolina soldiers received letters from home urging them to desert, especially after Chief Justice William Mumford Pearson pronounced the conscription law unconstitutional, that they began quitting the ranks in squads.[79]

The peace movements and desertion, it is clear, were firmly linked. Toward the end of the struggle losses in battle, heavy as they became, were more than matched by losses from absenteeism. Soldiers had all too many reasons for leaving the colors anyway. The excitements of battle were rare. Ill-fed, ill-clothed, unpaid for long stretches, alternating weary hours of marching with wearier hours of drill, verminous, enduring fierce summer heat, sharp winter cold, and soaking rains, they suffered from loneliness, homesickness, and above all boredom. The thought in spring of fields to be seeded, in summer of harvests spoiling for want of labor, in winter of pinched wives and crying children, became insupportable. Desertion sometimes seemed an overpowering duty, not an offense. When the fighting spirit ebbed away among the old people, the wives, sisters, sweethearts, and neighbors left at home, and when letters begged not for heroism but for an end of the hopeless carnage, then hearts sank and desertion, always endemic among both Northern and Southern troops, became epidemic.

Statistics of desertion in areas of the Mississippi Valley were highly de-

77. Dowd, Clement, *Life of Zebulon B. Vance*, Charlotte, N.C., 1897, 447ff; Tucker, Glenn, *Zeb Vance, Champion of Personal Freedom*, Indianapolis, 1966, Chap. XXIII.

78. Tatum, *op.cit.*, 11ff; *O.R.* I, xviii, 881; Tucker, Vance, *op.cit.*, 307-311.

79. *O.R.*, IV, iii, 975-979, H.W. Walter of Inspector-General's Dept. to J.W.C. Watson, Dec. 29, 1864.

pressing. In 1863, two hundred men marching to Arkansas left one regiment. All but forty dropped out of an Arkansas regiment within ten days; the First Alabama lost almost a hundred men; and sixty Texans abandoned the colors. For one reason, Vicksburg had filled the troops with a deep distrust of their commanding general, Pemberton. "I have seen a great many of the officers and men who were under him at Vicksburg and have conversed freely with them," Governor Joseph E. Brown wrote Secretary Seddon on August 10, 1863, "and have never yet found one of them who has confidence in him. . . . Without some change to inspire the troops with confidence, General Pillow or anyone else who attempts to carry them back will need a heavy and an active force."[80]

The shock of Gettysburg to army morale, if less serious than Vicksburg, was great; so was Chattanooga. In Virginia in midsummer of 1863, deserters daily tramped the roads homeward, almost invariably bearing their arms. If asked for papers authorizing absence, they patted their guns, saying defiantly: "This is my furlough." When garrison troops of General Samuel Jones, a West Pointer, were sent to reinforce Lee after Gettysburg, desertions were heavy because they felt the new duty a breach of implied contract.[81] Some of John Daniel Imboden's troops deserted for the same reason. Moreover, the general attitude toward desertion was changing. At first it had been regarded as a crime almost equivalent to treason, but in the late summer of 1863 an officer in Columbia, South Carolina, reported that disaffection had reached such a height that all sense of shame was lost. Many recruits in upland counties came from poor, ignorant backgrounds; the mountain coverts furnished them concealment; the success of the boldest in gaining immunity encouraged others, until scarcely a family did not have a deserter husband, son, brother, or cousin hiding in the mountains. "The tone of the people is lost; it is no longer a reproach to be known as a deserter; all are ready to encourage and aid the efforts of those who are avoiding duty."[82]

Six weeks after Gettysburg, Lee wrote President Davis that the number of desertions had become so great that unless they could be checked, "I fear success in the field will be seriously endangered." He had hopes that an amnesty granted to absentees would bring many of them back. After all, it was impossible to define the term deserter with accuracy; men might be absent from illness, exhaustion, imperative family duties, or simple negligence about dates. Americans North and South in Civil War days, like Australians in the First World War, were too individualistic to accept discipline tamely. Self-

80. *O.R.*, IV, ii, 753.
81. Freeman, *Lee*, *op.cit.*, III, 254; *O.R.*, IV, ii, 721.
82. C.D. Melton, Aug. 25, 1863, to Col. John S. Preston, Supt. of Conscription in South Carolina; *O.R.*, IV, ii, 769.

assertion was so general, the line between straggling and desertion was so thin, and the difficulty of keeping commands intact in the wide shaggy American countrysides was so pronounced, that it was impossible to maintain a harsh attitude.[83] On both sides, moreover, political leaders realized that harshness would defeat itself. People who heard that their boys were dying at the hands of martinets in charge of firing squads would refuse to support the struggle.

The Southern army had to be more severe than the Northern. Furloughs were less frequent in the South than the North. Homesick soldiers got little chance of seeing parents, wives, and children unless they strayed when the fortunes of war took them near their hearths. Hence it was that about 4,000 men absented themselves after Shiloh,[84] and large numbers after Vicksburg and Chattanooga. Inferior in manpower, Southern leaders had to strain every nerve to keep their echelons strong. Yet even so, they inflicted the death penalty with reluctance. A table submitted by the Second Corps in the last months of the war tells its own story: tried for desertion, 29; found guilty, 6; shot, 1.[85] Men were too precious to be executed. Sometimes, the array of deserters was so great, running into several thousands, that death sentences were unthinkable, although some executions did take place.[86]

Davis had expected much from his offer on August 1, 1863, of an amnesty to deserters and others absent without leave if they returned within twenty days, provided they were not second offenders.[87] Instead, his gesture encouraged many to remain at home, or to join some partisan corps. General Imboden wrote Lee that many deserters in the Shenandoah successfully hid from the squads sent to arrest them. Lee had to inform President Davis that as the amnesty offer had not borne fruit, he had changed his mind. He believed that all the requirements of mercy and forbearance had been met; and he was now convinced that he must exact a "rigid enforcement of the death penalty in future cases of conviction."[88] His subordinates learned of his views and executions duly took place—without avail.

Early in 1864 Congress passed a law for the punishment of anyone who advised or aided desertion,[89] but the penalties were mild, and it was difficult to enforce them. A wife might write: "The children are hungry, and crying for bread. If only you could come home!" Who would punish her for the

83. Cf. Stephen Crane, *The Red Badge of Courage;* Dowdey, Clifford, and Louis Manarin, eds., *The Wartime Papers of R.E. Lee,* Boston, 1961, 591.

84. Coulter, *Confederates States, op.cit.,* 463.

85. Lonn, Ella, *Desertion During the Civil War,* New York, 1928, 60.

86. *Ibid.,* 57.

87. Coulter, *op.cit.,* 468; it extended to men under punishment; *O.R.,* IV, ii, 687-688.

88. Dowdey and Manarin, *op.cit.,* 591.

89. Coulter, *op.cit.,* 466.

poignant statement? In February, 1864, Congress tried to reward soldiers for resisting the temptation to straggle, desert, or otherwise go absent without leave. If they stuck grimly to the post of duty for six months from April 1, each of them would be given a hundred-dollar bond. When Davis visited Georgia and Alabama in the autumn to hearten the people, he urged men and women alike to persuade deserters to return to the Army of the Tennessee. "Can they see the banished, can they hear the wail of their suffering countrywomen and children, and not come?"[90] "If one-half the men now absent without leave will return to duty," he added, "we can defeat the enemy." When he got back to Richmond on a bright, warm October day, he found the capital depressed, conscription lagging, and desertion increasing. "The dead come in, and the living do not get out so fast,"[91] wrote Varina Davis. By the beginning of 1865 desertions were more alarming than ever. "I have endeavored to ascertain the causes," Lee wrote Seddon, "and think that the insufficiency of food and nonpayment of the troops have more to do with the dissatisfaction. . . . than anything else."[92] But the causes were many—and imperative.

On February 11, 1865, Lee renewed the offer of an amnesty to all absent soldiers who would return within twenty days. It was a final gesture, reinforced by a last appeal to patriotism. Brave men with arms in their hands, he declared, could never barter manhood for peace, nor the right of self-government for life or property.[93]

By the latter half of 1864 great numbers of deserters and draft-evaders had gathered in countless safe refuges in the Southern mountains, swamps, and forests. The fastnesses of Eastern Tennessee, the hills and caverns of North Carolina, the swampy sections of Virginia and Florida, were full of pockets where concealment was easy, escape rapid, and defensible nooks abundant. Lawless men banded to protect themselves from scouting parties, to secrete cotton, and to prey at will upon farms and hamlets. Unionists throughout the lower Appalachians had always been ready to shelter escaped Northern prisoners, help runaway Negroes, and resist Confederate authorities. Some units, like the Independent Union Rangers of Florida, grew to a strength of several hundred.[94] In the West and Southwest, crews of deserters, jayhawkers, and guerrillas, along with mere robbers and desperadoes, terrorized whole counties, seized horses, food, and clothing wherever they could, and became—as

90. Strode, Hudson, *Jefferson Davis*, III, New York, 1964, 93-94; Rowland, *Jefferson Davis Constitutionalist*, *op.cit.*, VI, 342-344.

91. Strode, *op.cit.*, III, 106; to Mrs. Chesnut.

92. Dowdey and Manarin, *op.cit.*, 886-887.

93. *O.R.* I, xlvi, pt. 2, 1230-1231.

94. Lonn, *Desertion*, *op.cit.*, 65-66.

General Gideon Pillow said of some Alabama gangs—as vicious as rattlesnakes.

It added to the distress and discouragement of Southerners to realize that in spite of all their efforts to enforce the conscription laws, to encourage volunteering, to bring deserters back into the ranks, and to heal the sick and lightly wounded, the strength of their armies steadily fell. This fact had been emphatically pointed out to them in Secretary Seddon's report of November 26, 1863. The whole able-bodied male population from 18 to 45 had been made liable to military service although exemptions were numerous during most of the war. Substitution had been repealed by the Act of December 28, 1863. It was difficult to state accurately the number brought into the service, and the number who might still be called into the field. The law gave men the privilege, before being enrolled for conscription, of volunteering, and it was supposed that three volunteers had entered the army to every conscript. Seddon believed that, in the year just ending, about 20,000 volunteers and conscripts had entered the army from Virginia, and 80,000 men from the whole South. "Yet with so serious an addition our armies have not fully maintained their strength in numbers. This affords a startling, but, it is feared, not an incorrect view of the waste by sickness, casualties of battle, captures, desertions, and discharges."[95] Still less did the Confederate armies maintain their strength during 1864. By 1865 the last sands were running out.

[V]

The South was paying the penalty for its involvement in total war. War was its single all-engrossing occupation; war caught up the energies not only of its half-million white men but its boys, its women, its Negroes, its aged. The North looked to many objects—industry, trade, speculation, pleasure; the South had but one, the war. In the North the seashore and mountain resorts were crowded, the theatres, bookshops, and racetracks kept their votaries, and the Western rails and steamboats carried throngs to new homes. In the South people had but one business, war. The South held a small and diminishing number of fighters, and it used nearly the whole, putting into the field beside them beardless youths and white-haired elders. The South was poor, but the Confederate authorities seized whatever they could find; pork, flour, forage, cloth, leather, corn, sugar, tobacco—all were taken by the government, receipted for in worthless paper, and used or sold, no excuse being heard, no

95. *O.R.*, IV, ii, 995.

grumbling tolerated. At the same time there had been considerable amounts of material voluntarily contributed at various times and places.

"Look at this war; it has come to everybody," wrote the tempestuously brilliant South Carolinian, Lawrence Keitt, soon to lay down his life. "States, towns, villages, firesides—all feel it and share in it."[96] Total mobilization and total war, something new in the world, was to mean in the end almost total ruin.

The epic struggle, the war of brother against brother, was not a quadrille in a drawing room; it was a chronicle of endless personal tragedies, many of them enacted far behind the battle-lines and in dim obscurity. "Its interior history," wrote Walt Whitman, "will not only never be written—its practicality, minutiae of deeds and passions, will never be even suggested." True, and truest of all to those who looked within. To Whitman it was the illustrations of character and fortitude on the battlefield and in the hospitals that were most impressive. "The actual soldier of 1862-65, North and South, with all his ways, his incredible dauntlessness, habits, practises, tastes, languages, his fierce friendship, his appetite, rankness, his superb strength and animality, lawless gait, and a hundred unnamed lights and shades of camp, I say, will never be written. . . ." But this was less than half the story. Behind the camps and exploding shells, in caravans of refugees, in desolated homes, at gravesides of mothers and wives just as truly killed by the war as if struck down by a bullet, were found exhibitions of character and devotion as impressive as any in the field. The wide Southern land from the Virginia sounds and Florida beaches to Galveston Bay and Eagle Pass had become, indeed, a land of multi-faceted drama, and it was the domestic drama that was most poignant.

Yet the dragon of desolation that ravaged the South in the last year of war carried, like Shakespeare's ugly and venomous toad, a precious jewel in its head. It cleared a field for new tillage; it did a work of transformation that, however brutal, had to be done. The Northern columns brought torch and sword, but they also brought fresh ideas wherever they tarried. The thousands of refugees who wearily trailed their way from lodging to lodging suffered much, but they gave galvanic activity to a section that had been all too largely torpid. Half of the land under the flail of war had needed a flail to awaken it; it was the land where Frederick Law Olmsted had found houses without a book or paper, and people who were not sure whether New York was a free State or not, or whether Iowa was beyond "the Texies." The tale of wartime destruction was shocking, yet less agonizing when we recall that Olmsted had

96. Sullivan's Island, Feb. 11, 1864, to his wife; Keitt Papers, Duke Univ. Libr.

found in Virginia itself "an essentially frontier condition," with beasts, birds of prey, forests, and marshes increasing while, in areas where slavery had existed longest, bridges, shops, schools, and churches were diminishing.[97] Much was being destroyed in the South, but much had to be destroyed if a better land, with better institutions and ideas, was to be born.

97. Olmsted, Frederick Law, *A Journey in the Back Country*, New York, 1860, Chs. VII, VIII, IX, X; Whitman, Walt, *Walt Whitman's Civil War*, ed. Walter Lowenfels, New York, 1960, 293-294.

9

Final Triumph of Union Arms

AN ARMY of more than 600,000 men present for duty, and with more than half as many more in reserve, making a total Union force of nearly 960,000, stood poised and ready after exceptionally heavy winter snows and rains for what was clearly going to be the last campaigning of the war. Optimism had marked each of the preceding four springs, but confidence was greater in 1865. A million men exerting the tremendous economic and logistical energy of the North simply could not be halted, especially now that the opposing forces had dwindled to an aggregate army of about 160,000 men present for duty in a total force of 358,000.[1]

Not only were the manpower odds three or four to one against the South and the odds in war materiel many times greater still, but the Federal armies were deep in the heart of the Confederacy, chopping the hostile country into smaller and smaller bits, while at the same time the Army of the Potomac held fast, pinning the main Confederate force down tight in the Richmond-Petersburg area. The Union now had the advantage of movement. No longer could Confederate armies strike out suddenly in a bold attempt to throw their opponents off balance. They could only hang on—and for what? Many Southerners were still courageous, but knowledge of practical realities could not but affect the total morale.

First of all, the strongest Southern army, that of Northern Virginia led by Lee, could now do nothing but stand the long watches in the trenches of Petersburg and wait, chilled by the inclement winter and the steady approach of impending doom. In Georgia it was well known that the drenching rains and swollen streams would not long halt Sherman in his well-planned northward sweep into the Carolinas, a march that would be like the irresistible point of a sword thrusting its antagonist back against the high wall of Grant's forces. There was no logical escape.

The western legionaries of the Union had just completed the most success-

1. Troop figures are approximate.

ful march of the war, Sherman meeting little opposition from Atlanta to the sea.

[I]

In less than a month from the time his troops entered Savannah, Sherman had worked out and put into effect an efficient yet humane plan of occupation for the city. As he later wrote, not without pride in his achievement: "No city was ever occupied with less disorder or more system than this of Savannah, and it is a subject of universal comment that though an army of 60,000 men lay camped around it, women and children of an hostile people walk its streets with as much security as they do in Philadelphia. I attach much importance to these little matters. . . ."[2] But he placed major emphasis on the push northward from Georgia into the Carolinas. This would be quite a feat, and vastly different from the march through Georgia. Lengthy and laborious preliminaries had gone into the assembly of the fleet off shore; arms and ammunition had been gathered, food stocks accumulated, horses fattened, men rested, and accoutrements of all kinds readied. At Savannah, in January, supply problems still persisted. One officer felt that his men were being less well fed than at any time during the war. For lack of fodder horses were on short rations too. It took time to organize new supply routes from the north via ships; the area around Savannah, unlike the richer areas of inner Georgia, simply could not support the army. In time, however, the problem was conquered, but much suffering was endured, perhaps more so than on the march through Georgia.[3]

The four corps of Sherman's field force still numbered around 60,000, including cavalry and artillery, and in addition, the Union had in John G. Foster's Department of the South nearly 23,000 troops.[4] To oppose this host of battle-tempered veterans, the estimated enemy strength available was put at a little over 33,000 soldiers of all service branches, and with some units greatly scattered. Even this estimate was much too high.[5] Confederate generals P. G.

2. Sherman, William T., *Home Letters*, ed. M.A. DeWolfe Howe, New York, 1909, 319-322, letter Dec. 31, 1864, to Thomas Ewing. At Savannah Sherman received an official visit of Secretary of War Stanton, and believed at the time that Stanton was pleased with what he saw. Later, however, after the imbroglio with Stanton over the Johnston surrender, Sherman wrote: "The Great War Secretary came to Savannah to 'betray me.' Of this I am more than convinced—I admire his great qualities, but despise his mean ones." Sherman, *Home Letters*, *op.cit.*, 327, Jan. 15, to his wife; also Sherman's handwritten comments in his copy of Boynton, H.V., *Sherman's Historical Raid*, Sherman Collection, Northwestern Univ. Library.

3. Williams, Alpheus S., *From the Cannon's Mouth, The Civil War Letters of Gen. Alpheus S. Williams*, Detroit, 1959, 335.

4. *O.R.*, I, xlvii, pt.2, 192-193; Cox, Jacob D., *The March to the Sea*, New York, 1897, 239.

5. Cox, *op.cit.*, 239-240; Barrett, John G., *Sherman's March Through the Carolinas*, Chapel Hill, N.C., 1956, 49-50.

Beauregard, Hardee, D.H. Hill, G.W. Smith, and others met in a somewhat bleak atmosphere near Augusta to try to see what force they had and what could be done with it. Remnants from the Army of Tennessee were being brought east from Mississippi in bits and pieces. New recruits were scarce, the militia of little use. An ailing Beauregard had to take command over what force remained, but faced a discouraging outlook. Sherman's route north was uncertain to the Confederates, rendering the use of their depleted troops even more dubious. It was finally decided that probably Hardee should not attempt to defend Charleston if pressed strongly, as that would take 20,000 men, and the assembling of such numbers was out of the question. Beauregard, however, continued to oppose abandoning Charleston.[6] Hardee told President Davis in late January that "The people of Charleston, though in many respects to be admired, are so entirely wrapped up in their own State and city as to be unmindful of the wants of other portions of our country—to them Charleston is the Confederacy, and to save Charleston they are willing that Lee should give up Richmond, or any other section of the Confederacy so that their selfish ambition might be gratified. . . ."[7]

There were increased calls for the reassignment of Joseph E. Johnston to command. Johnston himself was reluctant in view of his long-standing disagreements with President Davis.[8] The truth was, and the generals were aware of it, that mere leadership was not enough. They simply lacked the troops, the materiel, the transportation, to oppose Sherman or even effectively to delay him.

By January 15, Sherman had sent Howard by sea with the right wing up to Beaufort, S.C., to make a lodgment on the railroad from Charleston to Savannah. Slocum with the left wing and the cavalry of Kilpatrick were to cross the Savannah River on a pontoon bridge and the Union causeway into the swamps and rice fields north of Savannah. Slocum's move was seriously delayed by the heavy January rains which overflowed the bottom lands, flooded the causeway, and swept away part of the pontoon bridge. It was not until the first week of February that he could cross three miles up the Savannah River from his previously planned transits, which were now flooded land. On January 18, Sherman turned Savannah over to Foster, while he himself went to Hilton Head and Beaufort. From Beaufort he made a demonstration toward Charleston, but later said he never had any intention of actually approaching that city.[9]

6. Roman, Alfred, *Military Operations of General Beauregard*, New York, 1884, II, 336-340, including notes on meeting.

7. Hardee to Davis, Jan. 29, 1865, Davis Papers, Duke Univ. Library.

8. Johnston to Mackall, Jan. 26, 1865, Columbia, S.C., Mackall Papers, Southern Historical Collection, Univ. of N.C.

9. *O.R.*, I, xlvii, pt.1, 17-18, Sherman's report.

In the march straight north from Savannah toward Columbia the army at times moved in four columns, and other times in three, so as to keep the Confederates off balance and inhibit their concentration.

However, the main obstacle was not the rebel forces but the natural geography of the area, made even more difficult by the excessive downpours, the felling of trees along the route, and the removal of obstructions set up by Wheeler's Confederate cavalry. The Union pioneer battalions performed yeoman service in clearing roads, rebuilding bridges, and replacing causeways over the almost continuous lowlands and waterways of southeastern South Carolina. By February 11, the army was fairly close together, occupying a position dividing the enemy, who were thus forced to watch both Charleston on the coast and Augusta to the northwest.

Something of a change came over Sherman's army when it sensed it was heading northward in the general direction of home in what must be its last major campaign. "It now seemed as if every soldier felt he was in the heart of the enemies' country, and it was a portion of his duty to do all the damage possible to the enemy. There were fires in every direction, many times houses were fired so near the road we were marching on that it became so hot in the road that our ammunition trains were obliged to go out in the fields to pass. If we halted to rest in a little town it would be but a short time before houses all about seemed to be in flames. . . . These fires were kept up all across the state. No one had orders to do this work of destruction; but on the contrary, it was strictly forbidden. But in a large family it is always difficult to keep all members on the right track. At any house where the inhabitants had remained, neither they nor their property was molested."[10] Countless eyewitnesses agree that burning, looting, and bumming increased sharply as the Yankees moved en masse into South Carolina, which they regarded as the heart of rebellion and secession.

One member of the 195th Illinois wrote his mother of "the treasonable soil of South Carolina." In one instance a whole brigade rushed pell mell upon a few houses grouped together, and within half-an-hour "not a vestige of them remained save the chimneys and one house for head-quarters. They made us excellent fires and warmed us thoroughly. Such was our entrance into the state. . . ."[11] An officer proclaimed, "We must go, for there are rebel flags flying and rebel guns between us and our Nation's capital, and we must cut our way through to where our banner waves over our war-worn comrades on the James; . . . I want to see the long deferred chastisement begin. If we don't purify

10. Memoirs of Richard Edward May, ms., HEH.

11. Letter from Loring Armstrong, Elmhurst, Ill., Jan. 5, 1865, George F. Cram letters, Loring Armstrong Private Collection, Oak Park, Ill.

South Carolina it will be because we *can't get a light. . . .*"[12] This same major said in March that, "The army burned everything it came near in the State of South Carolina, not under orders, but in spite of orders. The men 'had it in' for the State and they took it out in their own way. Our track through the State is a desert waste. Since entering North Carolina the wanton destruction has stopped." At the same time he was sickened by the "frightful devastation our army was spreading on every hand. OH! it was absolutely terrible! Every house except the church and the negro cabin was burned to the ground; women, children and old men turned out into the mud and rain and their houses and furniture first plundered then burned. I knew it would be so before we entered the State, but I had no idea how frightful the reality would be. . . ."[13]

At first, part of Sherman's army, fearing the new march would be more dangerous, expressed concern lest Lee should confront them. But that did not stop them in their march of destruction. One eyewitness of the columns of black smoke meeting their gaze, stated, "South Carolina has commenced to pay an instalment, long overdue, on her debt to justice and humanity. With the help of God, we will have principal and interest before we leave her borders. There is a terrible gladness in the realization of so many hopes and wishes."[14] Building materials were to be long in demand along the path of Sherman's army. Fire, ashes, and desolation followed the army, but a goodly portion of the army felt South Carolina was only meeting with the fate she deserved.[15] Some soldiers stated that in Georgia few homes had been burned, but in South Carolina few escaped. "The middle of the finest day looked black and gloomy, for a dense smoke arose on all sides, clouding the very heavens. At night the tall pine trees seemed so many huge pillars of fire. . . . Vandalism of this kind, though not encouraged, was seldom punished. . . . Foragers and bummers heralded the advance of the army, eating up the country like so many locusts. . . ."[16] Even the generals were aware of it all. General Alpheus S. Williams wrote to his daughter, "We swept through South Carolina, the fountainhead of rebellion, in a broad, semi-circular belt, sixty miles wide, the arch of which was the capital of the state, Columbia. Our people, impressed with the idea that every South Carolinian was an errant Rebel, spared nothing but the old men, women, and children. . . . The soldiers quietly took the matter into their own

12. Connolly, Major James Austin, *Diary*, *Transactions of the Illinois State Historical Society*, Springfield, 1928, 375.
13. *Ibid.*, Letters of March 12 and 21, 379, 381.
14. Nichols, George W., *The Story of the Great March*, New York, 1865, 131.
15. *Ibid.*, 140.
16. Conyngham, Capt. David P., *Sherman's March Through the South*, New York, 1865, 310-311.

hands. Orders to respect houses and private property not necessary for the subsistence of the army were not greatly heeded. Indeed, not heeded at all. . . ."[17]

When Confederate military leaders protested, Sherman wrote the Southern cavalry officer, Joe Wheeler, on February 8, that "I hope you will burn all cotton and save us the trouble . . . All you don't burn I will. As to private houses occupied by peaceful families, my orders are not to molest or disturb them, and I think my orders are obeyed. Vacant houses being of no use to anybody, I care little about, . . . I don't want them destroyed, but do not take much care to preserve them. . . ."[18] Earlier, Sherman had told Halleck that he realized "the whole army is burning with an insatiable desire to wreak vengeance upon South Carolina. I almost tremble at her fate, but feel that she deserves all that seems in store for her."[19] Halleck, too, in Washington, had written Sherman thus: "Should you capture Charleston, I hope that by some accident the place may be destroyed, and if a little salt should be sown upon its site it may prevent the growth of future crops of nullification and secession . . ."[20]

Sherman charged the Confederates with what he termed the murder of several foragers and threatened severe reprisals.[21] Wade Hampton replied he knew nothing of the cases, but did say he had ordered his men "to shoot down all of your men who are caught burning houses. This order shall remain in force so long as you disgrace the profession of arms by allowing your men to destroy private dwellings. . . ."[22] Yes, in many ways it was a more devastating march than that through Georgia, at least for those still at home in the Confederacy.

Sherman had given his marching orders as of January 19 with the goal of reaching Goldsborough, N.C., about March 15. Much preliminary movement and fortification took place in the latter half of January, but the real march began February 1, when Slocum was able to cross the flooded Savannah. Northward the four corps moved toward the state capital of South Carolina at Columbia, a route that really detoured Charleston, leaving it stranded. After crossing the Savannah, they reached the Salkehatchie where the right wing fought to control the bridges, part of the troops wallowing through a three-mile swamp sometimes in water up to their shoulders. In weather turning steadily colder, after numerous skirmishes along the way, the Fifteenth Corps

17. Williams, Alpheus S., *op.cit.*, 373, Mar. 12, 1865.
18. *O.R.*, I, xlvii, pt. 2, 342, Sherman to Wheeler, Feb. 8, 1865.
19. *O.R.*, I, xliv, 798-800, Sherman to Halleck, Dec. 24, 1864.
20. *Ibid.*, 741, Halleck to Sherman, Dec. 18, 1864.
21. *O.R.*, I, xlvii, pt. 2, 546, Sherman to Wade Hampton, Feb. 24, 1865.
22. *Ibid.*, 596-597.

reached the south bank of the Congaree opposite Columbia on February 16, but were unable to capture the bridges before they burned.[23]

The men were proud of their "semi-amphibian" march to Columbia, and discussed with professional intelligence the decisive moves of the campaign.[24] Once more, pioneers and engineers alike were operating superbly.

At the same time, the capital city, Columbia, South Carolina, was paying the penalties of the State's recalcitrance. As Federal troops arrived on the south bank of the Congaree on February 16, people could be seen excitedly thronging the streets of Columbia and occasional groups of Southern cavalry boldly emerged. The next day Sherman himself was at the newly laid pontoon bridge when a Confederate major drove up in a carriage and formally surrendered to the Twenty-fifth Iowa. Soon a few Union soldiers of the Seventeenth Corps arrived. Sherman had ordered that troops were to destroy all arsenals and public property not needed for Federal use, and all railroads, stations and useful machinery, but that dwellings, colleges, schools and "harmless private property" should be spared. Sherman rode rapidly into the city, where, he reported later, a "perfect tempest of wind was raging."[25] A brigade of Northern men was vigilantly posted. Some heaps of cotton in the street were said to be on fire and blowing loosely around, their flames only partially extinguished. Most of the Federal troops were bivouacked outside the city.

Under circumstances like these, a catastrophe was inevitable. That night the handsome capital of South Carolina burned with a completeness more total than the destruction of any other city during the war. And even more furious than the flames was the resentment felt by the people of the South in widening circles about the ruined city. During the decades since then, scholars and angry or lurid Southern writers have chanted "Who burned Columbia?" until it has become a stale refrain like "Who sank the Maine?" No answer can be given that seems completely convincing. Masses of evidence have been assembled, but still the problem remains insoluble. Three main theories have found support: first, the fires spreading from burning cotton were ignited by irresponsible vagabonds and some drunken, retreating troopers;[26] second, that Sherman willfully ordered the city burned, an allegation that he sternly denied and that seems incredible; third, that released prisoners, emancipated slaves, and/or intoxicated Union soldiers or vagrant Southerners were responsible. For each hypothesis some circumstances can be found to offer partial support except the

23. *Ibid.*, pt. 1, 18-21, Sherman's report; *Sherman Letters, Correspondence between General and Senator Sherman from 1837 to 1891*, ed. Rachel Sherman Thorndike, London, 1894, 245-246.

24. Nourse, Henry, "The Burning of Columbia," *Military Historical Society of Massachusetts Papers*, IX, 440-441.

25. *O.R.*, I, xlvii, pt. 1, 20-21, Sherman's report.

26. Wade Hampton strongly denied such fires.

allegation that Sherman deliberately fired the city. Some observers reported fires breaking out in homes in widely scattered sections of Columbia at about the same time, indicating incendiarism. Others told of drunken soldiers and Negroes breaking into homes and setting blazes.[27]

About two-thirds of Columbia was in ashes when the sun rose on February 18. The homeless gathered in the suburbs, or in open parks or lots around vestiges of furniture and household goods.[28] During the night, a large majority of the city's population, swelled by war from its normal 8,000 to about 20,000, were driven into the streets or engaged in combatting fires and looters. The worn-out fire apparatus was ineffective, hoses often being chopped to pieces by riotous marauders. Wade Hampton's splendid residence was among the first to go. By morning blackened chimneys and an occasional half-ruined building marked the sky-line of Columbia. The new state capitol building itself was razed, as well as the entire business district. Looting of shops had been extensive, particularly the liquor stores. The ringing cheers and martial music of the entry into Columbia were silenced. The neat, little city with its upland Southern charm of frame and brick buildings was a wreck. While mothers sought terrified children among the ruins, and invalids lay exposed in the streets, shots frequently rang out. The Federal guards proved too few or impotent, a lack cf responsibility that may be charged to Sherman.

A Federal captain wrote later that the fires could have been kept under control but for "the folly of its inhabitants and military rules."[29] This captain recorded as one tragic instance of loss that the home and library of the novelist William Gilmore Simms, though intact when he and other Federals left, were burned the following day, and blamed the Negro servants. Simms himself bitterly blamed the Yankees for the destruction of his home and library of eight to nine thousand volumes, many of them autographed, along with volumes of manuscript letters from many distinguished personages.[30]

For the Confederates the situation was desperate, if not hopeless. But Lee, now General-in-Chief, had to try. On February 19, from Petersburg, he wrote Secretary of War Breckinridge that "General Beauregard does not say what he proposes or what he can do. I do not know where his troops are, or on what lines they are moving. . . . He has a difficult task to perform under present circumstances, and one of his best officers (General Hardee) is incapacitated by sickness. I have also heard that his own health is indifferent, though he has never so stated. . . . General J.E. Johnston is the only officer whom I know who

27. *O.R.* I, xlvii, pt. 1, 22, Sherman's report; Sherman, *Memoirs*, II, 286-288.
28. *Ibid.*, 191-199, 242-244; Hedley, Fenwick Y., *Marching Through Georgia*, Chicago, 1890, 389.
29. Nourse, Henry, *op.cit.*, IX, 435-437.
30. *Ibid.*, 445-446.

has the confidence of the army and people, and if he was ordered to report to me I would place him there on duty. It is necessary to bring out all our strength, and, I fear, to unite our armies, as separately they do not seem able to make head against the enemy. Everything should be destroyed that cannot be removed out of the reach of Generals Sherman and Schofield. . . . I fear it may be necessary to abandon all our cities, and preparation should be made for this contingency. . . ."[31]

Although Beauregard was undoubtedly humiliated by the move, he agreed to serve under Johnston; thereafter, however, his duties were primarily routine. As a matter of fact, the Confederacy in the Carolinas now had a surplus of generals, when they really needed soldiers with guns.

Johnston said he took command "with a full consciousness on my part, however, that we could have no other object, in continuing the war, than to obtain fair terms of peace; for the Southern cause must have appeared hopeless then, to all intelligent and dispassionate Southern men. I therefore resumed the duties of my military trade with no hope beyond that of contributing to obtain peace on such conditions as, under the circumstances, ought to satify the Southern people and their Government. . . ."[32] Johnston estimated his available troops to number about 17,000 including cavalry,[33] but the figures kept changing, and no one was ever sure just how many Confederates were available. Believing, with Lee, that the remaining Confederate forces should be concentrated, if possible, to strike Sherman, Johnston even suggested that Lee send him half of his army so Sherman could be crushed near Roanoke, thus enabling them to turn on Grant together.[34] However, Lee was unable to reduce his force and still hold the Petersburg-Richmond axis. The General-in-Chief told Johnston, "If you are forced back from Raleigh, and we be deprived of the supplies from East North Carolina, I do not know how this army can be supported. Yet a disaster to your army will not improve my condition, and while I would urge upon you to neglect no opportunity of delivering the enemy a successful blow, I would not recommend you to engage in a general battle without a reasonable prospect of success. . . ."[35] Lee continued, "I shall maintain my position as long as it appears advisable, both from the moral and material advantages of holding Richmond and Virginia. If obliged to abandon it, so far as I can now see I shall be compelled to fall back to the Danville road for subsistence, . . ." But he felt there could be no fixed rules or plans, for too much clearly depended on the enemy; the Yankees were in control.

31. *O.R.*, I, xlvii, pt. 1, 1044, Lee to Breckinridge.
32. Johnston, J.E., *Narrative*, 371-373.
33. *O.R.*, I, xlvii, pt. 1, 150.
34. *Ibid.*, 1051; pt. 2, 1256-57.
35. *Ibid.*, pt. 2, 1395-96, Lee to Johnston, March 15.

At Raleigh on March 14, Johnston was slowly concentrating the troops of Bragg, of Hardee, and of the Army of Tennessee.

Sherman, realizing full well that Johnston would have to try something, ordered Kilpatrick's cavalry out in front. Slocum on the left was traveling light with four divisions; Howard, on the right, with another four divisions, was ready to give support to the left if attacked. Sherman was with Slocum. Schofield at New Bern, and Terry at Wilmington, were to move towards Goldsboro. The rains continued and the mud increased, but on the morning of March 16, Sherman moved toward the troubled area.

The road to Goldsboro ran through a narrow, swampy neck between the Cape Fear and South Rivers, where Hardee had set up a blockade. The skirmish which followed at Averysboro was not a major engagement, but it was sharp and hard while it lasted. Furthermore, it showed that the Confederates, even though weak, could still be dangerous.

In letters home, Sherman gave rein to just a modicum of emotion late in March: "Soldiers have a wonderful idea of my knowledge and attach much of our continued success in it. . . . I don't believe anything had tended more to break the pride of the South than my steady, persistent progress. My army is dirty, ragged, and saucy. . . . I would like to march this army through New York just as it appears today, with its wagons, pack mules, cattle, niggers and bummers, and I think they would make a more attractive show than your fair. . . ."[36] Later, on April 5, he told his wife, "I will challenge the world to exhibit a finer-looking set of men, brawny, strong, swarthy, a contrast to the weak and sickly fellows that came to me in Kentucky three years ago. . . . Whilst wading through mud and water, and heaving at mired wagons, the soldiers did not indulge a single groan, but always said and felt that the Old Man would bring them out all right; . . . If we can force Lee to abandon Richmond and can whip him in open fight, I think I can come home and rest and leave others to follow up the fragments. . . ."[37] Many felt that the Carolina campaign was much more arduous than that in Georgia. General Alpheus Williams, for example, said that the labor and fatigue were far greater.[38]

Sherman was proud of the job he had done, proud of the adulation he was receiving, but at the same time, he was still the same Sherman who had probably not changed much except perhaps for being more confident than ever. The statement of one observer that Sherman's brain was "a splendid piece of machinery with all the screws loose" is familiar.[39] What such critics

36. Sherman to his wife, Mar. 23, 1865, Goldsboro, N.C., *Home Letters*, 334-336.
37. *Ibid.*, 339-341.
38. Williams, *From the Cannon's Mouth*, *op.cit.*, 377.
39. George W. Morgan, Mt. Vernon, to Boynton, Oct. 8, 1892, H.B. Boynton Papers, N.Y.P.L.

did not realize was that during these months in Georgia and the Carolinas all of the screws had been tightened.

After the capture of Fort Fisher, the high command decided that New Bern was a more useful base of supply for Sherman than Wilmington. Harbors were better, there were some usable railroads that could be repaired toward Kinston through the Dover Swamp. Schofield undertook the task of setting up the lines from New Bern toward Goldsboro with Wilmington as a secondary base.[40]

At first, Schofield's advance encountered little opposition, but from March 8-10, his men were forced to fight for control of the slight ridge that carried the roads through this swampy area. Confederates under Bragg did achieve some element of surprise at the battle of Kinston, but Federals under Cox came up and easily repulsed additional attacks. After some severe fighting, Bragg withdrew to Goldsboro on the night of March 10.[41] Schofield's troops pressed on, occupying Kinston on March 14, while Terry was also advancing toward Goldsboro from Wilmington. The men in this "Campaign of the Carolinas" could hear the dull pounding of distant cannonading from Bentonville as they hurried on, building bridges and removing obstructions in the Neuse River. Schofield's well-organized force reached Goldsboro on March 21, within one day of the time indicated by Sherman.[42]

[II]

A vastly different war was fought in Virginia, ever since the preceding June. Critics were to say that Grant was doing nothing with his huge armies of the Potomac and of the James.

The Union forces on the Petersburg-Richmond front were squeezing as in a slowly-closing vise the last major army of the Confederacy, led by the greatest of the South's leaders. This never-ending pressure even increased in February, 1865, when the Federals extended their lines farther westward. Heading toward Hatcher's Run, two Union corps gained the Boydton Plank Road where the resistance was ineffective, though fighting endured for three days. After taking the Boydton Plank Road, the Union troops decided not to hold it as it was no longer a vital supply route. However, they did set up new lines to Hatcher's Run, thus extending their front a distance of 37 miles if men counted the irregularities in the entrenchments. Furthermore, by March 1, Lee's army had

40. Cox, J.D., *The March to the Sea, Franklin and Nashville*, New York, 1882, 154-156. This is really first-hand as Cox was in the North Carolina operations.

41. *Ibid.*, 156-160.

42. Schofield, John M., *Forty-six Years in the Army*, New York, 1897, *passim.*

been reduced to 46,398 men present for duty, of an aggregate of soldiers present of 56,895.[43]

It was an extremely severe winter for Virginia, and still cold at the time of the February action. Despite snow and frozen ground, the Confederates continued to dig and build their entrenchments. Immobile defense alone remained—no longer the dashing offensive-defensive movements of past years. Earthworks would help compensate for lack of manpower and materiel.

Lee was perhaps not so much concerned with the extension of Federal lines in early February as with the condition of his own army. "If some change is not made and the commissary department reorganized, I apprehend dire results. The physical strength of the men, if their courage survives, must fail under this treatment. Our cavalry has to be dispersed for want of forage . . ."[44] Earlier, Lee had told the Secretary of War, "There is nothing within reach of this army to be impressed. The country is swept clear. Our only reliance is upon the railroads. We have but two days' supplies."[45] Appeals were made to farmers for supplies.

The manpower problem was manifest in Lee's inability to send troops from Virginia to South Carolina. "I do not know where to obtain the troops," he wrote.[46] Desertion was increasing, and Lee's discouragement was contagious.

Despair in countless long-tried homes, and disaffection in the government offices of Southern Congressmen and the State legislatures, was strengthened by the steady flow of reports upon diminishing supplies, failing transportation, and an inadequate supply of employable men and women for households, farms, or factories. Worst of all, the boundaries of the Confederacy were constantly diminishing, as was the population, so that by the closing days of March, 1865, but one army truly worthy of the name existed to defend the various fronts. The rising crisis seemed beyond all the resources of the leaders.

More and more, Lee kept emphasizing the debilities of the Confederate forces and issuing warnings. He predicted dire results if rations were not improved. In one of many such messages, he wrote Secretary of War Seddon on February 8 that in view of these facts of general exhaustion in connection with the paucity of their numbers, the public must not be surprised "if calamity befalls us. . . ."[47]

Lee's assumption of the rank of General-in-Chief on February 9 made no

43. *O.R.*, I, xlvi, pt. 1, 390; Humphreys, Andrew A., *The Virginia Campaign of '64 and '65*, New York, 1883, 310.

44. *O.R.*, I,xlvi, pt. 1, 381-382.

45. Lee, R.E., *The Wartime Papers of R.E. Lee*, ed. Clifford Dowdey and Louis H. Manarin, Boston, 1961, 881, Lee to Seddon, Jan. 11, 1865.

46. *Ibid.*, 885-886, Lee to William P. Miles, Jan. 19, 1865.

47. *Ibid.*, 890.

real difference. By February 21 he gave warning that he expected Grant to move within a week, "and no man can tell what may be the result." Sherman and Schofield, he wrote his wife, "are both advancing, and seem to have everything their own way, but trusting in a merciful God who does not always give the battle to the strong, I pray we may not be overwhelmed. I shall, however, endeavor to do my duty and fight to the last. Should it be necessary to abandon our position to prevent being surrounded, what will you do?" He added, with more anguish than resignation, "It is a fearful condition . . ."[48] Repeatedly, he told correspondents that Richmond might have to be given up and that the most important duty was to save the army. It took no great insight to predict that Grant was going to advance, although the time and exact character of his movements could not be divined. These honest comments upon the growing crisis were not like the frightened outcries of the generals who were easily thrown into panic, and who lacked courageous determination. They were the candid appraisals of an almost hopeless situation by a leader of iron persistence and restrained utterance. To the Secretary of War (now Breckinridge), Lee felt constrained to write: "I fear it may be necessary to abandon all our cities, and preparation should be made for this contingency."[49] While the North was celebrating recent successes on Washington's birthday, Lee was informing Longstreet of the difficulties of resisting both Sherman and Grant. He felt that the Confederate line of defenses was already excessively long and that a point for concentration should be picked if retreat became necessary. He and his aides were already devising plans for specific moves to be taken as circumstances dictated and permitted.[50]

As the war in Virginia wore on, Lee became more deeply alarmed, in his taciturn, unemotional, and resolute way. By March 9 he felt obliged to tell Breckinridge, sadly but with a sense that unity, and the Spartan temper of Fabius after Cannae, must be preserved, that the time was "full of peril and requires prompt action," meaning action to hold on with bulldog tenacity. He added a philosophic tribute to the unyielding valor with which the Confederate nation and fighters had confronted the superior strength of the well-equipped Northern hosts. The consequences of that superiority "have been postponed longer than we had reason to anticipate. . . ."[51]

One illustration of the fatal postponement of much-needed practical reforms lay in the replacement early in February of Commissary-General Northrop by the more competent Capt. I.M. St. John. St. John proved able to

48. To his wife, Feb. 21, 1865, Papers of R.E. Lee, LC.
49. Dowdey, *Wartime Papers of R.E. Lee*, *op.cit.*, 904, Feb. 19, 1865.
50. *Ibid.*, 907-909.
51. *Ibid.*, 913.

augment the supplies sent to the Army of Virginia, and to place increased reserves in subsistence depots.[52] Quartermaster-General F.W. Sims reported that just where transportation was most badly needed, in Virginia and North Carolina, "the roads are least able to furnish it."[53] The number of railroads available to the Confederacy had been so reduced that the fragile facilities remaining had to carry an intolerable load to deliver even the barest minimum of supplies. Sims also reported that, like everyone else, he had to deal with insoluble shortages of manpower. "Not a single bar of railroad iron has been rolled in the Confederacy since the war, nor can we hope to do any better during its continuance." The main lines were robbing the tributary lines of their rails and rolling stock.[54]

[III]

As the winter approached its end, Southern discontent inevitably increased in the gravest degree, though no one can measure it precisely. The War Clerk Jones formed the opinion that "the disaffection is intense," but thought that all the leadership in the world would not have produced a difference by 1864 or 1865 in delaying the final termination of the struggle.[55]

The familiar dreary tale of rising prices, painful shortages on every hand, and what seemed to be blundering in the government's measures, is conclusive, and need not be detailed at length here. President Davis's letters show that he was groping to find a way out of the Confederate difficulties, and to enlarge his supply of men and workers. But what little reinforcement he could obtain for the army was by this time necessarily drained away from some essential industry; at the same time, to assist industry he had to rob the army of some of its troops.

Various people were propounding possible methods of assisting the Confederacy, none of them practical. Governor A.G. Magrath of South Carolina sounded other Southern governors upon a shadowy plan to invigorate the Confederate Constitution, and along with it the dignity and efficiency of the State governments.[56] Howell Cobb wrote Davis lamenting the "deep despondency of the people," which too often extended to disloyalty. He wished to have Joseph E. Johnston restored to command, as countless others did, and

52. St. John, Gen. I.M., *Resources of the Confederacy in 1865*, Southern Historical Society Papers, III, No.3, Mar., 1877, 98-100; Coulter, E.M., *The Confederate States*, Austin, 1950, Ch.XVIII, "Progress and Decay," *passim.*

53. St. John, *ut supra*, report of Sims, 121-122.

54. *Ibid.*

55. Jones, J.B., *A Rebel War Clerk's Diary*, Philadelphia, 1866, 471-472.

56. A.G. Magrath to Gov. Brown of Georgia, Jan. 26, 1865, LC.

more of the zeal of volunteers imparted to an army more and more filled with conscience.[57] One soldier urged Davis to take the field command in the West.[58]

John A. Campbell, in the War Department, seemed to see the situation more clearly, but even his suggestions proved impossible. In early March he sent Breckinridge a long report full of sorry details upon the condition of the forces and the Confederacy as a whole: "The armies in the field in North Carolina and Virginia," he declared, "do not afford encouragement to prolong resistence. . . . The political situation is not more favorable. Georgia . . . may properly be called insurrectionary against the Confederate authorities . . ." In other areas the situation was equally deplorable. "Virginia will have to be abandoned when Richmond is evacuated and the war will cease to be a national one from that time." He concluded that the South might succumb, "but it is not necessary that she should be destroyed. I do not regard reconstruction as involving destruction . . ."[59]

Late in January, James Seddon resigned as Secretary of War, after serving as capably as any man could have under the restrictions of President Davis, and in the face of the nation's many limitations and adversities. His successor was John C. Breckinridge, who had served as a general during much of the war. Davis accepted the retirement of the never-vigorous Seddon, but deprecated Seddon's acceptance of the view of the Virginia Congressional delegation that the Cabinet could not then be completely reorganized.[60]

Lincoln, unwavering in his purpose of preserving the Union, and restoring the authority of the United States Government in the rebellious States, had little faith in "peace movements," for he was familiar with Jefferson Davis's grim determination not to surrender.[61] However, in spite of several abortive efforts between 1862 and 1865, a peace mission did materialize early in 1865, through the unofficial efforts of Francis Preston Blair, Sr., 73-year old patriarch of the politically-minded Blair family. On the pretext of searching for some missing papers, lost when his home in Maryland had been burned by General Early's men in July, 1864, Blair received a pass to go South in January, 1865. Lincoln was unaware of Blair's true mission,[62] which was really to sound out Davis on the possibilities of negotiating a peace. Davis finally agreed to send a commission, as he thought, to Washington, consisting of Vice-President

57. Cobb to Davis, Jan. 6, 1865, Howell Cobb Papers, Duke Univ. Libr.

58. M.W. Phillips to Jefferson Davis, Richmond, Jan. 28, 1865, Confederate Mem'l. Literary Society.

59. John A. Campbell to John C. Breckinridge, Mar. 5, 1865, Campbell-Colston Papers, Univ. of N.C. Library.

60. Rowland, Dunbar, ed., *Jefferson Davis, Constitutionalist*, Jackson, Miss., 1923, VI, 458-461, Davis to Seddon, Feb. 1, 1865.

61. *O.R.N.*, Ser.II, Vol.3, 1190-1194.

62. Nicolay and Hay, X, 94, 95.

Alexander H. Stephens, Senator R.M.T. Hunter, and Assistant Secretary of War John A. Campbell, none of whom could be termed to be in close relationship with Davis, either personally or in principle.[63] After a few days' delay, and induced by a dispatch from General Grant[64] at Fortress Monroe, Lincoln and Seward made a hasty trip from Washington to meet the Southern representatives at Hampton Roads aboard the *River Queen* on the morning of February 3, 1865, with the idea of carrying on informal talks.[65] No clerks, secretaries, or witnesses attended, and nothing was written or read at the meeting, which was informal, calm, courteous, on both sides. Accounts of the meeting, however, are found in the memoirs of the various participants.[66] Campbell, who had hoped for some agreement on peace measures even if based on preservation of the Union,[67] was greatly disappointed in the outcome of the mission, which ended where it began, with no yielding on the part of either Lincoln or Davis.[68]

The Confederate President, having consistently devoted most of his attention and very real talents to the alarming military situation, did join in the attempted resuscitation of the Confederate spirit during February. Even such a vitriolic enemy as Edward A. Pollard, editor and historian, could on occasion appreciate the unperceived gifts of the President. In one of his last public appearances, Davis arrived unannounced at a public hall just after the Hampton Roads Conference. In a worn gray suit, wrote Pollard, the thin figure stalked into the hall. "It appeared that the animation of a great occasion had for once raised all that was best in Mr. Davis; and to look upon the shifting lights on the feeble, stricken face, and to hear the beautiful and choice words that dropped so easily from his lips, inspired a strange pity, a strange doubt, that this 'old man eloquent' was the weak and unfit President . . ." He held the audience an hour, speaking extemporaneously, and pausing frequently to recover his strength. There were tremendous cheers, "and a smile of strange sweetness came to his lips as if the welcome assured him that, decried as he was by the newspapers and pursued by the clamor of politicians, he had still a place in the hearts of his countrymen . . ." The tone of his address was that of "imperious unconquerable defiance to the enemy." But Pollard concluded:

63. Davis, *Rise and Fall of the Confederate Government*, *op.cit.*, II, 612-620.

64. Lincoln, *Collected Works*, VIII, 282.

65. *Ibid.*, VIII, 277-282.

66. Seward, Frederick, *Seward at Washington*, III, New York, 1891, 260-261; Campbell, John A., memo on Hampton Roads Conference, Campbell-Colston Papers, Southern Hist. Collection, Univ. of N.C.; Hunter, R.M.T., "The Peace Commission of 1865," Southern Hist. Soc. Papers, III, 170-171; Stephens, Alexander, *Constitutional View of the War Between the States*, Philadelphia, 1870, II, 619-623.

67. *Diary of Robert Kean*, ms. Univ. of Virginia Library, Feb. 18, 1865.

68. Lincoln, *Collected Works*, VIII, 284-285; S.S. Cox to H.N. Marble, Feb. 5, 1865, Manton Marble Papers, LC.

"There was no depth in the popular feeling thus excited; it was a spasmodic revival, or short fever of the public mind."[69]

To an audience at the African Church, Davis "emphatically asserted that none save the independence of the Confederacy could ever receive his sanction. He had embarked in this cause with a full knowledge of the tremendous odds against us, but with the approval of a just Providence which he conscientiously believed was on our side, and the united resolve of our people, he doubted not that victory would yet crown our labors. . . ."[70]

That Davis was not oblivious of the attacks upon him, is borne out by a letter he wrote on March 30 to Mrs. Howell Cobb: "Faction has done much to cloud our prospects and impair my power to serve the country." He thought that this was not the purpose of his detractors, and he cherished the hope that when his enemies realized their attacks injured not only the President but also the cause, of which he called himself "a zealous though feeble representative, they might alter their course, and make an earnest effort to repair the mischief done it."[71]

That usually accurate observer, General Gorgas, had commented some weeks earlier: "People are almost in a state of desperation, and but too ready to give up the cause." This was not from a lack of patriotism, but because "there is a sentiment of hopelessness abroad—a feeling that all our sacrifices tend to nothing, that our resources are wasted, in short, that there is no leadership." Hence, many were "ready to despair. . . . The President has alas! lost almost every vestige of the public confidence," Gorgas added. "Had we been successful," he thought, "his faults would have been overlooked, but adversity magnifies them." He ended by striking an unflinching note: "We cannot lose the cause, and the President will perhaps show his strength of character in sustaining it when others have lost all hope."[72]

Lee did all he could to strengthen General Johnston, whom he had again placed in command, but, as we have seen, his efforts met with little success. The desertion problem was no better and Lee now, in late February, blamed friends and families of soldiers at home "who appear to have a very bad effect upon the troops who remain and give rise to painful apprehension. . . ."[73]

One of Lee's officers wrote in February: "Truly, matters are becoming serious and exciting. If somebody doesn't arrest Sherman's march, where will he stop? They are trying to corner this old army, but like a brave lion brought to bay at last, it is determined to resist to the death, and if die it must, die game.

69. Pollard, Edward A., *Life of Jefferson Davis*, Philadelphia, 1869, 468-470.
70. Richmond *Dispatch*, Virginia State Library, Richmond, Feb. 7, 1865.
71. Rowland, *op.cit.*, VI, 524-525.
72. Gorgas, Josiah, *Diary*, University of Alabama, 1947, 172, Mar. 2, 1865.
73. Lee, *Wartime Papers*, 910, Lee to Breckinridge, Feb. 24, 1865.

We are to have some hard knocks, we are to experience much that is dispiriting, but if our men are true (and I really believe that most of them are) we will make our way successfully through the dark clouds that now surround us. *Our people must make up their minds to see Richmond go,* but must not lose spirit, must not give up."[74]

On March 2, Lee told the President he had proposed to Grant that they have an interview, but was not sanguine of results. "My belief is that he will consent to no terms, unless coupled with the condition of our return to the Union. Whether this will be acceptable to our people yet awhile I cannot say. . . ."[75] It had come about because of conversations between Longstreet and E.O.C. Ord over prisoner exchange. Lee proposed that he and Grant talk about submitting the subjects of controversy to a convention.[76] Grant replied on March 4 rather curtly that, "in regard to meeting you on the 6th instant, I would state that I have no authority to accede to your proposition for a conference on the subject proposed. Such authority is vested in the President of the United States alone. . . ."[77]

The officers of Lee's army seemed to be aware of their plight and the grave threats all around them. By March 5, a change for the worse in public sentiment was noted by at least one pessimistic officer who spoke of the increased talk of "*terms* and *reconstruction.*"[78]

The new Confederate General-in-Chief warned the new Secretary of War Breckinridge, March 9: "It must be apparent to every one that it is full of peril and requires prompt action . . . it seems almost impossible to maintain our present position with the means at the disposal of the Government. . . . Unless the men and animals can be subsisted, the army cannot be kept together, and our present lines must be abandoned. Nor can it be moved to any other position where it can operate to advantage without provisions to enable it to move in a body. . . . If the army can be maintained in an efficient condition, I do not regard the abandonment of our present position as necessarily fatal to our success. . . . While the military situation is not favourable, it is not worse than the superior numbers of resources of the enemy justified us in expecting from the beginning. Indeed, the legitimate military consequences of that superiority have been postponed longer than we had reason to anticipate. Everything in my opinion has depended and still depends upon the disposition and feelings of the people. . . ."[79]

74. Taylor, Walter H., *Four Years with General Lee,* New York, 1878, 43, notes for Feb. 20, 1865.
75. *Ibid.,* 911.
76. *Ibid.,* 911-912, Lee to Grant.
77. *O.R.,* I, xlvi, pt.2, 825.
78. *Ibid.,* 144.
79. Lee, *Wartime Papers,* 912-913, Lee to Breckinridge, Mar. 9, 1865.

The hammer, the anvil, and strangulation had done their work! From the spring of 1864, the Federal strategy had been clearly open for all to see, but not everyone had scrutinized it accurately. Grant and Meade had seized upon the Army of Northern Virginia and had tightened their grip in the desperate battles of the Wilderness, Spotsylvania, and Cold Harbor, and would tighten it still further in the battles to follow until the final victory at Appomattox. Although several of Grant's other campaigns had proved disappointing and an early movement against Mobile had largely gone awry, Sherman had performed his great thrust magnificently. In the West the Confederacy had found little ground for hope since the period preceding Vicksburg in 1863. The outer fortress walls of the Confederacy had been breached before 1864, and now the inner works were being carried. To the east and south on the Atlantic and Gulf coasts the blockade had stiffened until near the end it was perhaps the major element in garroting the South. Through the use of enclaves and invasions, all the ports of any significance to the South had been first sealed and then captured. To the west the Trans-Mississippi was, after 1863, at best a useless appendage, although it did divert some Confederate energies and resources.

10

Victory

THE EXULTATION of victory filled all loyal breasts as April covered the land with blossoms in 1865. The end that all believers in the Union regarded as inevitable had come. It could be no other way! The question among all men was still, "When would the South lay down its arms?" The dragging conflict had long since dissipated the optimistic dreams held by many Northerners in the fever after Sumter. The conflict they had hoped would be short, quick, and glorious had turned into nearly four years of agony and grief, but the endurance of harrowing anxiety and defeat had taught the people grim lessons in fortitude and intellectual realism. They knew that the Confederacy could endure but a few months longer. Mangled and suffering by the sword thrusts of Sherman in the Carolinas, lightning invasions on the Atlantic and Gulf coasts, and Union marches in the West, the Confederacy, manacled by the ever-tighter grip of the blockade, was stumbling to its doom. Cardinal attention was still fastened upon Richmond and Petersburg, where the growing strength of the blue ranks under Grant and Meade held an increasingly clear mastery of the area where the last real army of the South, feebler and more discouraged day by day, struggled to hold its ground.

In the wide domain once so proudly ruled by the Confederacy, the economic and social erosion had become ruinously destructive. Much land had been conquered or depleted. Many people were dead or in exile. Large districts had been lost or rendered unproductive, and what remained was insufficient and often could not be utilized. Yet the South largely retained its old principles and its fealty to its special concepts of sectional liberty and State rights. As so often in the history of English-speaking peoples, some long-embattled men and women had made the sad period of desperation and defeat their finest hour of spiritual renewal and philosophic resolution; so, now, they exhibited a spirit that their descendants could remember with respect and even an alloyed admiration. Their doctrines might be subject to question, to much revision, and even to condemnation, but the spirit of Dixieland had aspects and qualities that would be cherished along with the memory of Robert E. Lee.

Many at the North had, during the dark months and years, broadened their view of both the war and the peace. The President had been re-elected, re-inaugurated, and, without disturbance, would have four years to deal with the imminent tasks of pacification and reconstruction. For the moment, however, as blossom and leaf unfolded and showers began to ease, most eyes and ears were tuned to the sound of the guns southward. This was the spring of 1865.

[I]

By March, the Administration could distract its attention from the war and its multitudinous labors and prepare to resume the long-postponed tasks required by national recovery and growth, and by governmental and social reorganization. All too many responsibilities demanded action by the President, Congress, and the States.

Lincoln once more faced a cohort of office-seekers, including many Republican politicians clamorous for favors ever since the November election. As more and more of the South came under partial or full Northern control, traders, both honest and dishonest, lifted noisy demands for commercial permits. Important Cabinet positions, including the Secretaryships of State, of the Treasury, and of the Interior, had to be filled with circumspect care. Happily, the care-worn President had a brief interval—all too brief, as it soon appeared—to concentrate upon the most exigent labors. Fortunately for him and the country, Congress was not in session, and he was free from the criticisms, denunciations, exhibitions of jealous spleen, and ebullitions of malicious plotting that would otherwise have come from Capitol Hill. In his last Cabinet meeting, on April 14, Lincoln frankly remarked that he "thought it providential that this great rebellion was crushed just as the Congress had adjourned, and there were none of the disturbing elements of that body here to hinder and embarrass us. . . ."[1] The war had begun without the benefit or interference of Congress in the administration of the government, and now it was to end the same way.

Although the pressure of office-seekers was still almost intolerable, Lincoln now seemed a little more resigned to it, and more hopeful of the government's future than he had been before, with most Northerners sharing his sanguine outlook. While many citizens, and especially politicians, were pondering the future with concern, national confidence was growing steadily, giving rise to expressions of relief and to a certain exuberance. As historians of the war have said, it is impossible to determine just when the people realized that a trium-

1. Welles, Gideon, typescript of article, "Lincoln and Reconstruction in April, 1865," John Hay Library, Brown Univ., Providence, R.I.,

phant close was inevitable. The belief in imminent victory had been spreading since the fall of 1864, which had brought victories in Georgia, Tennessee, and the Shenandoah.

On Washington's birthday, 1865, the North had thrilled to the headlines, "Charleston evacuated!" The city where the rebellion started was once more in Union hands![2] The New York *Tribune* correspondent on the scene described the fires, explosions, and the destruction of stores, bridges, and warships. The national colors once more floated over Sumter, a shapeless mass of rubble in the harbor. No American heard the news without emotion.[3] At the same time dispatches from Admiral Porter's flagship, the *Malvern*, in Cape Fear River, confirmed that Fort Anderson had fallen. The way to Wilmington at last lay open; the public, however, did not know as they read the news on February 22 that the city had been evacuated that day.

New York, like other parts of the North, was in a festive, holiday mood under sunny skies, the air soft and springlike. "We never saw Broadway so utterly jammed with human beings," reported the *Tribune*. The shipping in the harbor was gaily dressed, and at noon, guns began firing from all the forts, while the chimes of Trinity deepened the clamor. Veterans of the War of 1812 paraded, and the armories turned out the proudest militia regiments to join in the procession. The Seventh led the way, its band playing patriotic airs while the crowd cheered. At night the most elaborate fireworks the city had yet seen lighted up the skies. A huge audience pressed into the Brooklyn Academy of Music to hear Wendell Phillips speak on "Our Country, Our Whole Country." Greeley had declared in a *Tribune* editorial that the fate of the rebellion hung by a thread which a single decisive Union victory could sever. Next day, February 23, another headline, "Fall of Wilmington," blazed in the New York press over Navy Department dispatches announcing that national forces had entered the last Confederate port of importance left open.[4] Then, day by day, the newspapers offered fresh tidings of Union advances. Dispatches from Sherman in the Carolinas, Terry outside Wilmington, and Sheridan in his last victories over the remnants of Early in the Shenandoah, were especially gratifying, for they were popular heroes.

But even with the thrill of victory abounding, some faint-hearts still strove for a negotiated peace. Horace Greeley would not forsake his dream of fashioning an end to bloodshed. He wrote S.L.M. Barlow, March 15, that he was willing to go to Richmond and talk with the Confederates if Lincoln "will indicate in confidence the most favorable terms" which he was prepared "to accord to the insurgents, stating what he must require and what he is ready

2. For description of the fall of Charleston, see Chap. 9, "The Final Triumph of Union Arms."
3. New York *Tribune*, Feb. 22, 1865.
4. *Ibid.*, Feb. 23, 1865.

to concede with regard to the Union, Emancipation, confiscation, amnesty, restoration to political equality in Congress, etc. . . ."[5]

But cheering crowds, parading troops, and pounding bands did not express the deep earnestness of the people. In Washington departments and bureaus the grim work of conducting the war kept desk-lamps burning from midnight until dawn. Countless details required attention. For example, Grant had objected to the President's liberation of prisoners after merely taking the oath of allegiance. Lincoln responded that he had freed about fifty men a day recently. This was a greater number than he liked, but they were names brought to him mainly by Border State Congressmen, and vouched for by various sponsors. The President argued that in only one or two instances had his trust been betrayed.[6] As if he intended continuing this policy of calculated leniency, on March 11 he issued a proclamation giving deserters sixty days within which they might be pardoned if they came back and reported. Wilful absentees might incur severe penalties.[7]

It was often Lincoln's habit to make a memorable statement on what was ostensibly some merely perfunctory occasion. Addressing the 14th Indiana Regiment, he pithily remarked: "I have always thought that all men should be free; but if any should be slaves, it should be first those who desire it for *themselves*, and secondly, those who *desire* it for *others.* Whenever [I] hear anyone arguing for slavery, I feel a strong impulse to see it tried on him personally." He went on to remind his listeners that if the Negro fought for the rebels, he could not at the same time "stay at home and make bread for them."[8] In fact, he tolerantly held the view that, as he quaintly put it, "We have to reach the bottom of the insurgent resources; and that they employ, or seriously think of employing, the slaves as soldiers, gives us glimpses of the bottom." Lincoln, of course, was more correct than he thought, as to the glimpse of the bottom —not merely the bottom of the immediate Southern resources of white manpower, but the bottom of the age-old Southern exploitation of black manpower in all departments of life and activity.[9]

On the surface, March appeared to offer the President a quiet month, but it actually proved busy and harassing. All the old problems remained, and were growing more urgent and complex, while the President's minor tasks also made increasing demands on his time and strength. On March 20, Grant telegraphed that he wished to see the President, and thought a rest would do him good. Lincoln replied that he had been thinking of such a visit.[10] In

5. Greeley to Barlow, Mar. 15, 1865, Barlow Papers, HEH.
6. Lincoln, *Collected Works,* VIII, 347-348, Mar. 9, 1865.
7. *Ibid.,* 349-350.
8. *Ibid.,* 361.
9. *Ibid.,* 362, March 17, 1865.
10. Lincoln, *Works,* VIII, 367.

consequence, on the afternoon of March 23, Lincoln, Mrs. Lincoln, Tad, a maid, and two bodyguards left on the *River Queen* for City Point, arriving at that vital Virginia base at nine on the evening of the next day. The President had been slightly ill on the trip. He did not even have a secretary with him, and Stanton for the interim seemed to be the unofficial Washington substitute for Lincoln, the two keeping in communication by wire.

One of Lincoln's motives for the trip was apparently to escape the hectic atmosphere of the capital and the pressure of trivial details, so that he might better concentrate his attention on the military climax soon to come in Virginia. Earlier Sherman had repelled Johnston's desperate attacks at Bentonville in North Carolina with ease, and on March 22, the able young cavalry commander, James Harrison Wilson, had led his Union forces into Alabama to threaten Selma and defeat Forrest's worn troopers. On the Gulf Coast, meanwhile, Union pressure entered upon a bolder phase as Canby began an energetic movement against Mobile.

All could see that great events impended on theVirginia battlefront, and, in fact, they began to disclose themselves on March 25, the morning after Lincoln's arrival. The weary President, looking unwell, boarded a special train from City Point to the Petersburg line. He toured the field of the recent engagement at Fort Stedman, viewing the burial of men slain in that abortive Confederate attack. The cars returning to City Point bore wounded soldiers.[11]

A few miles away from the point where Lincoln had surveyed the smoke-wreathed lines, but in the grip of a mood much darker and more perturbed, President Davis, Lee, and their Confederate associates faced an ominous future. No attempts to muster a transitory optimism could conceal the ugly realities of their plight. The most exhausting efforts had proved unavailing to check the steady decline in Southern strength and spirit during 1864; instead, almost everything had grown worse.[12]

There were ardent Southerners who held, or pretended to hold, a belief that some hope of success still remained. But shrewder or more practical men could not blind themselves to the harsh fact that not even a miracle could now save the sinking cause.

In January, 1865, Lee had written letters urging the use of Negroes as soldiers. Much as he disliked this measure, it now seemed unavoidable to him if he was not to overtax the white population.[13] Lee, therefore, after describing the Northern preponderance of strength, continued with a suggestion which many people considered ghastly: "I think, therefore, we must decide whether

11. *Lincoln Day by Day: A Chronology, 1809-1865*, Lincoln Sesquicentennial Commission, Washington, 1960, 322.

12. See the previous Chapter.

13. Lee to Andrew Hunter, "Lee's View on Enlisting the Negroes," Memoranda of the Civil War, *Harper's Monthly*, Vol. XXXVI, No. 4, Aug. 1888, 600-601.

slavery shall be extinguished by our enemies and the slaves used against us, or use them ourselves at the risk of the effects which may be produced upon our social institutions. . . ."[14] As early as February 20, one of Lee's staff-officers wrote: "Our people must make up their minds to see Richmond go. . . ."[15] And in Richmond itself, the laggard Confederate Congress, on March 13, finally completed passage of a measure approving the enrollment of Negroes for army service on a voluntary basis, involving the free action both of slaveholders and slaves. Davis signed this measure immediately after Lee had pressed him hard to give his assent. Lee was now more anxiously urging prompt action upon it. Negroes might not be made available in season for the spring campaign, but "no time should be lost in trying to collect all we can."[16]

Under the law of March 13, the Confederate Congress authorized the President to call upon slaveowners to seek volunteers of 18 to 45 in age among their Negroes. However, the new legislation did not require owners to volunteer the slaves, nor did it specifically give those slaves who volunteered to serve their freedom. It was nevertheless tacitly understood that the States would emancipate such slaves. Negro troops were to be willing to go as volunteers, and would receive the same pay, rations, and clothing as other troops. Recruiting thus began in the Richmond area amid considerable early excitement, and in the last weeks of the war a few Negro troops were seen parading in Richmond.[17]

A number of officers, all white, saw the opportunity for gaining a higher rank. By March 24, the Richmond *Sentinel* reported that enlistments were continuing.[18] On March 22, the Richmond *Dispatch* had begged Virginians to give the call their support, and reported that a devoted group of farmers in Roanoke County had offered to liberate any of their slaves who volunteered.[19]

Davis, however, later recorded that insufficient time remained to obtain any result from the enactment.[20] This was not the true explanation, for the underlying problem was lack of support by any considerable number of slaveholders. Davis frankly wrote Lee on April 1 that, "I have been laboring, without much progress, to advance the raising of negro troops . . . ,"[21] to which Lee replied that he had been willing to detach recruiting officers.[22]

In the War Department, on March 23, Robert Kean wrote the following

14. *Ibid.*
15. Taylor, Walter H., *Four Years with General Lee,* New York, 1878, 143.
16. Lee to Davis, Mar. 10, 1865, Lee Papers, Duke Univ. Libr.
17. *American Annual Cyclopaedia,* 1865, 194.
18. Richmond *Sentinel,* Mar. 24, 1865.
19. Richmond *Dispatch,* Mar. 22, 1865.
20. Davis, *The Rise and Fall of the Confederate Government,* New York, 1881, I, 518.
21. *O.R.,* I, xlvi, pt. 3, 1370.
22. Lee to Davis, Apr. 2, 1865, Lee Headquarters Papers, Virginia State Hist. Soc.

illuminating paragraph: "This measure was passed by a panic in the Congress and the Virginia Legislature, under all the pressure of the President indirectly, and General Lee directly, could bring to bear. My own judgment of the whole thing is that it is a colossal blunder, a dislocation of the foundations of society from which no practical results will be reaped by us. The enemy probably got four recruits under it to our one. . . ."[23]

The fact is that slaveowners simply did not respond. Robert Toombs, even stronger in disapproval, felt the Negro unfit to be a soldier or at least a Confederate soldier. He believed they would rapidly "abandon their flag. . . . In my opinion the worst calamity that could befall us would be to gain our independence by the valor of our slaves . . . instead of our own. . . . The day that the army of Virginia allows a negro regiment to enter their lines as soldiers they will be degraded, ruined, and disgraced."[24]

One of Lee's officers wrote General Ewell that Lee "directs me to . . . say that he regrets very much to learn that owners refuse to allow their slaves to enlist. He deems it of great moment that some of this force should be put in the field as soon as possible, believing that they will remove all doubts as to the expediency of this measure. He regrets it the more in the case of the owners about Richmond, inasmuch as the example would be extremely valuable, and the present posture of military affairs renders it almost certain that if we do not get these men, they will soon be in arms against us, and perhaps relieving white Federal soldiers from guard-duty in Richmond."[25]

Though of small consequence in the actual life of the Confederacy, this legislative admission that Negro troops were needed and the approving actions of some in recruiting them, revealed that powerful social stresses were at work in the Confederacy, operating under duress but nonetheless important.

By March 6 it had become evident in the War Department that plans were being made to evacuate Richmond.[26] Conditions in Richmond for the average citizen had declined from bad to worse. In addition to worrying about the future of the armies and his country, the ordinary citizen had many daily hardships to encounter. Prices had risen steadily. One Richmond minister, on March 27, reported beef at $15 a pound, bacon $20, meal $100 a bushel; potatoes were $100 a bushel, and even turnip greens $10 a peck. There was another problem—what to do when the Yankees arrived—a problem which became daily more anguishing. "If we should evacuate Richmond," wrote the Reverend Mr. Alexander Gustavus Brown, "I do not know what is to become of us.

23. Kean, Robert G.H., *Inside the Confederate Government*, New York, 1957, 204.

24. Robert Toombs, Washington, Ga., to "Dear Dudley," March 24, 1865 (probably Dudley Mann), Charles A. Dana Papers, LC.

25. Lt.-Col. Charles Marshall to Ewell, Mar. 30, 1865, George Washington Campbell Papers, LC.

26. Jones, John B., *A Rebel War Clerk's Diary*, Philadelphia, 1866, 512, Mar. 6, 1865.

I have made up my mind to stay here, and take the chances."[27]

It was evident to all that the fall of Richmond must herald the beginning of the end. Some had tried to pretend otherwise. Lee, for instance, in January, in testimony to the Joint Committee on the Condition of the Army, is said to have replied to the question, "Will the Fall of Richmond end the war?": "By no means, sir, by no means. In a military point of view I should be stronger after than before such an event, because it would enable me to make my plan of campaign and battle. From a moral and political point of view the abandonment or loss of Richmond would be a serious calamity, but when it has fallen I believe I can prolong the war for two years upon Virginia soil. Ever since the conflict began, I have been obliged to permit the enemy to make my plans for me, because compelled to defend the capital. . . ."[28]

But even Lee's ideas had apparently changed. Reporting to Davis March 26 on the failure at Fort Stedman, he wrote, "I fear now it will be impossible to prevent a junction between Grant and Sherman, nor do I deem it prudent that this army should maintain its position until the latter shall approach too near."[29]

The Richmond *Sentinel* printed, as late as April 1, 1865, the statement of one unconquerable Southerner who proclaimed gallantly, if unwisely: "We are very hopeful of the campaign which is opening, and trust that we are to reap a large advantage from the operations evidently near at hand. . . . As for ourselves, *nothing* could equal, in its horror, the dreadful calamity of Yankee domination of our land. Awful as have been the four years of conflict through which we have passed, they have been four years of joy compared with what they would have been with the heel of Lincoln on our necks."[30]

But far sooner than that writer was willing to admit, the tramp of Lincoln's soldiers would make the campaign of which he was so hopeful nothing more than the last stand of the few fanatical rebels who remained staunch in spirit though weak in strength.

[II]

With Grant's two huge armies, those of the Potomac and the James, stationed around Richmond and Petersburg, Lee could really do nothing except await the now almost certain end. At the same time, Grant, impatient as he really was, had good reasons for waiting. He believed, as did most everyone,

27. Letters of the Rev. Alexander Gustavus Brown, Virginia State Hist. Soc.
28. Clipping from the New Orleans *Democrat*, July 5, 1881, interview with former Confederate Senator Benjamin Hill, Alfred Roman Papers, LC.
29. Lee, *Wartime Papers*, *op.cit.*, 916-918.
30. Richmond *Sentinel*, April 1, 1865.

that the spring campaigning would close the war. It had been a severe winter, making roads impassable in the early Virginia spring. As Grant put it in his *Memoirs*, "It was necessary to wait until they had dried sufficiently to enable us to move the wagon trains and artillery necessary to the efficiency of any army operating in the enemy's country." Sheridan, with the cavalry in the Shenandoah, had to move his force down to Petersburg by a long circuitous route. As early as March first, Grant issued orders to keep a sharp lookout for any move by Lee.[31]

On March 3, Grant outlined his ideas to Meade,[32] proposing an attack, when rumor came that Lee was moving, but Lee was *not* moving. Therefore, Grant decided: "It is better for us to hold the enemy where he is than to force him South. . . . To drive the enemy from Richmond now would be to endanger the success of Sherman and Schofield." At the same time he warned, "It is well to have it understood where and how to attack suddenly if it should be found at any future time that the enemy are detaching heavily. My notion is that Petersburg will be evacuated simultaneously with such detaching as would justify an attack. . . ."[33]

To the west and north of the Petersburg-Richmond position in the Shenandoah, major warfare, army against army, had almost ceased. Sheridan's cavalry had a free hand in the Valley now, except for isolated local opposition. Jubal Early in the Waynesboro-Staunton area had what was called a division, though by March the infantry was well under 3,000 men. He had a few cavalry units left, but they had much too wide an area to watch. The hard winter had not helped. Morale was low, and Early himself came under severe criticism.

By March 27, Lee became convinced from all reports available that Grant was about to move. Furthermore, he was sure that Grant would move westward from his existing line now extended to the area of Five Forks and Dinwiddie Court House. No possibility of deception existed. If the Confederate lines were lengthened by the four miles that seemed required, they would be overstrained. The only troops that Lee could possibly find to move were Pickett's division of about 5,000, suffering as all were from exhaustion.[34] Upon learning of Federal troop movements westward on the 28th, Lee prepared to shift Pickett from his position north of the James to the Five Forks area. No real attempt would be made to cover the whole new extension of the lines, but

31. Grant, *Memoirs*, II, 427, 430.

32. Grant had secondary problems on his hands as well, such as attempting to have Meade confirmed as major-general in the regulars, and the continuing problem of both legal and illegal trade with the enemy. Grant to Henry Wilson, Jan. 23, 1865, and Grant to Elihu Washburne, Jan. 23, 1865, Meade Papers, Hist. Soc. of Pennsylvania.

33. Grant to Meade, City Point, Mar. 3, 1865, Meade Papers, *ut supra*.

34. Freeman, *Lee*, *op.cit.*, IV, 24-27; an excellent analysis of Lee's troop problem.

rather one to provide a movable force to meet the enemy thrust. Orders were sent out on the 29th for Pickett to move forward, collect his isolated units and join the cavalry on the extreme Confederate right. Fitzhugh Lee was in command of the hastily convoked cavalry units, numbering about 4,200. Lee next gave Pickett some help from the force on the far Confederate right, bringing his infantry to 6,400.[35]

As Pickett and the cavalry moved toward Five Forks on the night of March 29 and the morning of the 30th, the rain fell in blinding sheets.[36] Forces of both armies marched in the rain through the broken country with its narrow roads, the terrain broken in places by swamps studded with alder thickets, briars and stunted pines.[37] Despite the rain and the rough terrain Lee at this critical time kept fairly good intelligence. On March 28 he learned that Sheridan had reached Grant's left, and on the 29th that both Union infantry and cavalry were in motion.[38]

On the night of March 27, E.O.C. Ord's Army of the James, three divisions strong taken from two corps, began to march westward, reaching their position near Hatcher's Run on the morning of March 29. That morning Warren's Fifth Corps began its march. Other troops shifted position, and Sheridan's cavalry now reached Dinwiddie Court House.[39] Grant felt, "Everything looked favorable to the defeat of the enemy and the capture of Petersburg and Richmond, if the proper effort was made." And despite the rain, delays, and other impediments, great exertions were pressed, showing that the troops that had fought from the Rapidan to the James and Petersburg, and then engaged in a siege, now remained sufficiently resilient to mount another offensive drive. In fact, another move spurted on the left flank, resembling the movement Grant had carried out in the campaign of the preceding May and June.

At the same time, many shifts had been made in the corps and division commanders, and two armies were operating together. On the 31st, Sheridan pushed out from Dinwiddie Court House, while Pickett and the Confederates were moving toward Dinwiddie. In the restricted fighting that ensued Sheridan suffered a tactical defeat, and the Confederates drove to a point near the Court House. Pickett asserts that with a half hour of daylight they would have reached Dinwiddie; others declare that Pickett failed to push the drive and presently halted.[40] Grant had decided to extend his lines no farther, but to turn north toward the enemy, believing Southern lines were now thin enough to

35. See also reports of Confederate generals in *Lee Headquarters Papers,* Virginia State Hist. Soc.
36. Munford, Thomas T., "Five Forks," mss. article, Virginia State Hist. Soc.
37. *Ibid.*
38. *O.R.*, I, xlvi, pt. 3, 1363, Lee to Early, March 28, 1865, and Lee to Breckinridge, March 29.
39. *Ibid.*, pt.1, 52-53.
40. *Lee Headquarters Papers,* Virginia Hist. Soc.

permit his general offensive to succeed. Warren, with the Fifth Corps, was impeded by bad roads, darkness, rain, and mud, while an enemy attack had thrown him back severely. Later, Grant and others charged Warren with slowness, faulty alignment and failure to keep his troops together.[41] But now, every assertion relating to Warren is subject to so much controversy that historians conclude their examination with opposite opinions upon him and his actions. Details of the events of these days on the Petersburg front may be left to the specialist, for they require detailed explanations which render full narratives unwieldy.

By the night of March 31, Lee had on his right 10,600 cavalry and infantry to oppose more than 10,000 Union cavalry and as many as 43,000 infantry that could be called upon. On April 1, Lee told Davis, "The movement of Genl. Grant to Dinwiddie Court House seriously threatens our position, and diminishes our ability to maintain our present lines in front of Richmond and Petersburg. . . . It also renders it more difficult to withdraw from our position, cuts us off from the White Oak Road, and gives the enemy an advantageous point on our right and rear. . . ."[42] He feared the South Side and the Danville railroads would be cut, and therefore preparations should be made if it became necessary to evacuate positions on the James. Some critics feel that Lee should have retreated while he still had time, after the failure at Fort Stedman, near Petersburg.[43]

After hearing of the action at Dinwiddie Court House and the withdrawal of Pickett's men to Five Forks, he issued firm orders. To Pickett he wrote, April 1: "Hold Five Forks at all hazards. Protect road to Ford's Depot and prevent Union forces from striking the South-side Railroad. Regret exceedingly your forced withdrawal, and your inability to hold the advantage you had gained."[44]

At about 4 p.m. on April 1, Sheridan's attack, delivered by both cavalry and infantry, came later than he had intended, but through considerable confusion in orders, bridges being out, and difficulties over roads and numerous other impediments, Warren's Fifth Corps had been delayed. After some brief, ill-directed moves, with the cavalry striking on the left toward Five Forks and the infantry on the right, the attack finally succeeded in forcing the Confederates to fall back in confusion.

The Union actions, or lack of them, at Five Forks were no better nor worse than those of many others in battle, and can even be justified by the facts of

41. *O.R.*, I, xlvi, pt. 1, 53-54.

42. *Wartime Papers of R.E. Lee, op.cit.*, 922-923.

43. Livermore, Col. Thomas L., "The Generalship of the Appomattox Campaign," *Military Hist. Soc. of Mass. Papers*, VI, 474.

44. Pickett, La Salle Corbell, *Pickett and His Men*, Philadelphia, 1913, 386.

the situation and the orders Warren received. Grant and others later suggested that Warren's difficulty stemmed from peculiarities of temperament, or defects of personality.[45] At any rate, the sacrifice of one corps commander could not minimize the striking importance of the Union victory at Five Forks, won by both the cavalry and infantry. On April 1, a Union witness wrote: "Sheridan is a tiger, up with the front line always, and in the heat of battle. . . . All of us fought on our own hook. . . . I never saw a fight before where the victory was so well followed up. Indeed, I think I never saw a perfect victory before. . . ."[46]

One cavalry officer, Thomas J. Munford, in his lengthy analysis of Five Forks from the Confederate side, was critical in the extreme of Pickett, Rosser, and Fitzhugh Lee "talking" two miles back of the line of battle. He claimed his 1,200 "carbines" faced 12,000 infantry and 2,000 cavalry. "It was indeed a glorious target. But what could we do? A handful to a houseful! We could do nothing but shoot and run. At their first fire the smoke enveloped them completely and as soon as it drifted so that we could see them advancing again we poured into them our salute of death—then turned and scooted through the woods like a flock of wild turkeys. . . . Shells went shrieking and screeching through the air or dropped with a long, mellifluous *wh-o-o-o-m!* into the tops of the mourning pines. Soon came the great bursting fusilade of Pickett's whole line; then the roar of gallant Pegram's thunderous guns and the crashing of Torbert's ten thousand carbines gave volume to the tumultuous voice of battle. The earth trembled under the shocks of the thundering guns; rolling volumes of sulphurous smoke wreathed the trees in ghostly, trailing garments. The low sun showed faintly through the smoke-clouds like a pale moon and the woods were stifled in their sulphurous draperies. No enemy was in sight, because of the smoke, but the hellish din of war arose on every hand, the deadly balls spat against the boughs or whined like pettish voices above our heads. Occasionally a man crumbled down in his place and a little rivulet of blood trickled away on the ground. . . ."[47] The battle did not last long. In the rough, broken, boggy country, cut up by creeks, and covered with a heavy growth of briars and brambles, the Confederates were breaking up. Finally Pickett came

45. An immense secondary and primary literature exists on the Warren case. Among them are: Higginson, T.W., "Five Forks: The Case of General Warren," *Contemporaries*, Boston, 1899, 317-321; Catton, Bruce, "Sheridan at Five Forks," *The Journal of Southern History*, Vol.XXI, No.3, Aug. 1955, reprint; Stern, Philip Van Doren, *An End to Valor*, Boston, 1958, 129-152. The Warren Papers in the N.Y. State Library, Albany, contain countless important documents. Grant, *Memoirs*, II, 213-215, 313, 445. The Sheridan Papers in LC are limited in value due to the destruction by fire of most of his papers. *O.R.*, I, xlvi, pt. 1, has numerous reports pertaining to this.

46. Fowler, William, *Memorials of William Fowler*, New York, 1875, 129-131.

47. Munford, Thomas T., "Five Forks—The Waterloo of the Confederacy," mss., Virginia State Hist. Soc., Richmond.

galloping up. Everything was in confusion among his retreating men and the General had to stave off "utter rout."[48]

Lee told Breckinridge late on April 1 that Pickett's present position was not known, but painted a gloomy picture.[49] On April 2, Lee told Breckinridge, "I see no prospect of doing more than holding our position here till night. I am not certain that I can do that. If I can I shall withdraw to-night north of the Appomattox, and, if possible, it will be better to withdraw the whole line to-night from James River. . . . Our only chance, then, of concentrating our forces, is to do so near Danville railroad, which I shall endeavor to do at once. I advise that all preparation be made for leaving Richmond to-night. . . ."[50] The move to Dinwiddie Court House and the Battle of Five Forks disrupted all the Confederate plans.

Sheridan's pursuit of the Confederates continued well into the evening of April 1, before he took up secure positions. That night from the well-placed Federal guns in the Petersburg siege lines, shells pounded the Confederate trenches and forts, landing within the city itself. Grant had constantly alerted his forces to be ready when the crisis came—and here it was at Five Forks.

Even before the success was fully known, orders had been issued for an attack at 4 A.M. on April 2 by the Sixth, Ninth and Twenty-fourth Federal Corps, clearing the way for the Second Corps. Troops were not sanguine; they had been in the trenches too long, facing abattis, chevaux-de-frise, tangled telegraph wire, stakes driven in the ground at a forty-five degree angle, and other defensive gadgets in front of the formidable Confederate earth works. Enemy guns clearly swept the front, along which attack must come. Curt remarks were common, such as, "Well, good-bye, boys, that means death."[51]

Early morning fog shrouded the land, hiding the slight rises that supported Confederate entrenchments. It took some prodding and urging, and smothered oaths to launch the attack when the signal gun was finally heard. For a time the Federals advanced in the sil ence of the fog until the shots of the enemy pickets rapped out, followed immediately by the rolling surge of full musket fire. Enemy guns roared; but with mighty cheers the Yankees rushed ahead. Formations were lost, a few men shrank from the task, but in the main they rolled ahead. Tearing away the obstacles, leaping over some and smashing into others, the Federals vaulted over one parapet after another, scattering the thinned ranks of Confederate defenders. The Sixth Corps did not even stop there, some plowing on in pursuit of the fleeing Southerners.[52]

48. *Ibid.*
49. *O.R.*, I, xlvi, pt. 1, 1263-1264.
50. *Ibid.*
51. Stevens, Hazard, "The Storming of the Lines of Petersburg," MHSM, VI, 422.
52. *Ibid.*, 423-424.

Grant knew that Lee had now been forced to the breaking point, and that the risk had become materially slighter than it had been only a few days before.[53] Grant kept close control over activities at Petersburg on April 2, making sure that Lincoln was fully informed at City Point. The President in turn wired Stanton in Washington the results as their news reached headquarters. At 11 A.M. Lincoln informed Stanton: "Dispatches frequently coming in. All going fine. Parks, Wright, and Ord, extending from the Appomattox to Hatcher's Run, have all broken through the enemy's intrenched lines. . . ." At 2 P.M. the President relayed Grant's message of 10:45 A.M. to Washington: "Everything has been carried from the left of the Ninth Corps. The Sixth Corps alone captured more than 3,000 prisoners. The Second and Twenty-fourth Corps both captured forts, guns, and prisoners from the enemy. . . . We are now closing the works of the line immediately enveloping Petersburg. All looks remarkably well. . . ."[54]

By 4:30 Grant telegraphed Lincoln: "We are now up, and have a continuous line of troops, and in a few hours will be intrenched from the Appomattox, below Petersburg, to the river above. . . . All seems well with us, and everything quiet just now." Lincoln, grasping the magnitude of the day's operations, sent Grant the following message: "Allow me to tender to you and all with you the nation's grateful thanks for this additional and magnificent success."[55] Grant, however, was not going to be rash at such a time, but ordered a heavy bombardment early on April 3 to be followed by a 6 A.M. assault, "only if there is a good reason for believing the enemy is leaving."[56] But at 8:30 on the morning of April 3, Lincoln telegraphed Stanton: "This morning General Grant reports Petersburg evacuated, and he is confident Richmond also is. He is pushing forward to cut off, if possible, the retreating army. I start to him in a few minutes. . . ."[57]

While the message carried the essential news, the situation was not quite as simple as it seemed to indicate. The Sixth Corps under Wright penetrated the lines *en masse*, on the morning of April 2, as did two Twenty-fourth Corps divisions of Ord's command. Another division of Ord had forced the lines near Hatcher's Run. Ord and Wright moved to the right toward Petersburg to try to hold the enemy in. Parke with the Ninth and Humphreys with the Second moved ahead as well. Parke penetrated the main line but failed to carry the inner defenses. After considerable fighting, Gibbon seized two strong enclosed works, thus shortening the Federal attack line considerably, while other Fed-

53. *O.R.*, I, xlvi, pt. 3, 422.
54. *Ibid.*, 447, 466.
55. *Ibid.*, 447-449.
56. *Ibid.*, 458, Grant to Meade, Apr. 2, 1865, 7:40 P.M.
57. *Ibid.*, 508.

eral troops harassed and harried the broken Confederate units. Grant later learned that Lee had evacuated Petersburg on the night of April 2,[58] being fortunate to have kept the Federals out of town until darkness covered his retreat.[59]

From the news of the defeat at Five Forks onward, it was clear that the only course the Confederates could take was to delay at Petersburg until they could evacuate the city and salvage whatever supplies and guns they could. In one of several messages to the Secretary of War, Breckinridge, Lee wrote on April 2: "It is absolutely necessary that we should abandon our position tonight, or run the risk of being cut off in the morning. . . . It will be a difficult operation, but I hope not impracticable. . . . The troops will all be directed to Amelia Court House."[60] This would not be an orderly, organized withdrawal. Under such heavy Federal pressure, the Confederate units were too widely disposed on the long defense lines to be brought together. Lee recognized this, ordaining that Amelia Court House be the concentration point. It was then that he sent to President Davis a similar message: "I think it is absolutely necessary that we should abandon our position to-night. I have given all the necessary orders on the subject to the troops, and the operation, though difficult, I hope will be performed successfully. I have directed General Stevens to send an officer to Your Excellency to explain the routes to you by which the troops will be moved to Amelia Court House, and furnish you with a guide and any assistance that you may require for yourself."[61] Lee issued rather specific orders to his various commanders regarding routes to Amelia Court House, but in spite of his well-laid plans, the withdrawal did not go as smoothly as expected. As transportation was rapidly falling into chaos, the already long-standing supply problem became steadily worse.[62] In order to secure needed forage, for months Lee had been obliged to separate cavalry and artillery units at points too distant from the lines. In this crisis of supplies, arms orders became confused, or were not properly issued.

Reports of Lee's principal generals, forwarded later to their commander, including many not appearing in the *Official Records,* told the same doleful story of the breakdown of their positions at Petersburg and Richmond.[63]

On the morning of April 3, it was uncertain whether Lee's retreating army,

58. *O.R.*, I, xlvi, pt. 1, Grant's report, 54-55.

59. Meade, George G., *Life and Letters of General Meade,* II, 269, to his wife, Apr. 3.

60. *O.R.*, I, xlvi, pt. 1, 1265.

61. *Ibid.*, pt. 3, 1378.

62. For a good summation, see Vandiver, Frank, "The Food Supply of the Confederate Armies," *Tyler's Quarterly Historical and Genealogical Magazine,* Vol.XXVI, 77ff.

63. Taylor, Walter H., *Four Years with General Lee, op.cit.*, 150; Gordon, John B., *Reminiscences of the Civil War,* New York, 1903, 418-419.

which crossed the Appomattox River at Goode's Bridge during the night, or his Union pursuers, would be first to reach the Danville Road. Early on the morning of the 6th, Lee reached Amelia Court House, where he found not a morsel of food, and had to halt and scour the surrounding area for supplies—a fatal delay, for Sheridan's cavalry pushed ahead of him, and reached the railroad at Jetersville, where the Army of the Potomac began to concentrate. The avenue for the retreat of Lee's hungry and exhausted army lay on the narrow line between the Appomattox and James Rivers. When night was falling, the head of Lee's columns reached Appomattox Station, where, as the tired veterans lay down to rest, Custer's cavalry burst like a thunderbolt upon them. The scene was set for the last act in the great drama.[64]

[III]

The strains of "Dixie" echoed from the seven hills of Richmond as marching columns climbed the streets toward the capitol. But, alas, the oncoming troops wore blue, and the regimental band pouring forth the familiar notes preceded a Negro regiment. Cavalry thundered past at a furious gallop. Worn army horses labored up the incline, dragging heavy cannon. Through the smoke of the burning city, men caught glimpses of flaming walls. Now and then they heard the report of repeated explosions. They forced their way through an hysterical crowd of dancing, shouting Negroes, some of whom were busy plundering the rapidly burning shops of ham, shoes, flour, dry-goods, bolts of cloth, chairs, and even sofas. Some of the gratefully exalted freedmen called out "Saviors, our Saviors!" to the Yankee troops. As blue-clad horsemen dashed up to the City Hall, an officer threw open the doors. Above the capitol dome two soldiers had unfurled a tiny flag. One Richmond lady sank to her knees, and, as she wrote later, "the bitter, bitter tears came in a torrent."[65]

The heart of a nation and a people was being deeply torn that April Monday in 1865. The burning of the city and scenes of anguish might have been anticipated for months; perhaps for four years. But, however it might have been foreseen, the surrender was a shock to all. For some days, great events had been occurring, and more were anticipated. Since President Lincoln had arrived in City Point, he had been indulging in the role of military tourist, or observer, combining long postponed vacation hours with a half-anxious, half-

64. Dowdey & Manarin, eds., *The Wartime Papers of R.E. Lee,* Boston, 1961, 901.

65. Letters of Mrs. Mary A. Fontaine to Marie Burrows Sayre, Confederate Memorial Literary Society, Richmond; and others felt equally stricken. See Letters of Emmie Sublett (age 13), Confederate Memorial Literary Soc., Richmond.

relieved watch over the death throes of the Confederacy from his *River Queen* headquarters.[66] On March 26, he saw Sheridan's troopers from the Shenandoah cross the James to add dash and strength to the irresistible panoply under Grant, Meade, and Ord, about to hew through Lee's army and advance upon Richmond. That afternoon, he attended a review of Ord's Army of the James, an occasion marked by Mrs. Lincoln's disclosure of open pique over the President's courteous attention to Mrs. Ord—a minor incident that had unfortunate social sequels.

However, national leaders were dealing with serious problems. For two days an earnest conference occupied an able group on the *River Queen*. Lincoln, Grant, and Admiral Porter conferred with Sherman, newly arrived from the Carolinas. Their decisions were expected to influence the future of the nation, but no one can be certain just what was concluded.

Sources are limited on what was said at this conference (unlike Hampton Roads) for we must depend primarily on memoirs, and on Sherman's accounts which may be colored and exaggerated. Much later, Grant was to write carefully in his own *Memoirs* that Sherman "had met Mr. Lincoln at City Point while visiting there to confer with me about our final movement, and knew what Mr. Lincoln had said to the peace commissioners when he met them at Hampton Roads, to wit: that before he could enter into negotiations with them [the Confederate agents] they would have to agree to two points: one being that the Union should be preserved, and the other that slavery should be abolished; and if they were ready to concede these two points, he was almost ready to sign his name to a blank piece of paper and permit them to fill out the balance of the terms upon which we would live together . . ."[67] The subject was to come up a few weeks afterward in the dispute over Johnston's terms of surrender to Sherman, upon which Grant wrote that Sherman doubtless thought he was following the President's wishes. It should be noted, however, that Grant stated Sherman came to the conference primarily to discuss military movements with him.

Lincoln's secretaries also dismissed the President's action as "a hasty trip to confer with Grant."[68] Yet, informal discussions in the cabin of the *River Queen* gave Lincoln, Grant, Sherman, and Porter an opportunity for a frank exchange about the prospects of early and final victory. Porter and Sherman reported that the President expressed some liberal views on the restoration of State governments in the conquered South which did not seem altogether

66. George Merryweather to his parents in England, March 26, 1865, George Merryweather Letters, property of grandson, John Merryweather, now in Chicago Hist. Soc.

67. Grant, *Memoirs, op.cit.*, II, 514-515.

68. Nicolay and Hay, *Abraham Lincoln, op.cit.*, X, 215.

compatible with the guarded language which Lincoln used elsewhere. We may presume that their private opinions sometimes colored their recollections, though we may well believe that he repeated his willingness to be generous to the verge of prudence, and let them understand that he would not be displeased by the escape from the country of Davis and other rebel leaders.[69] After the conference Sherman hurried back to North Carolina, where Schofield had been left in charge.

Sherman modestly assured his father-in-law as March closed: "It is perfectly impossible for me in case of failure to divest myself of responsibility, as all from the President, Secretary-of-War, General Grant, etc. seem to vie with each other in contributing to my success," adding that Ewing need not fear he would commit a political mistake, for he well realized that he would imperil the government by any unwise concessions. He had repelled all political advances made, and would continue to do so.[70] He thought he had "a clear view of another step in the game," a statement as dubious as it was cloudy.[71]

Sherman's *Memoirs* give a full and naturally somewhat defensive account of the meeting with Lincoln. He recalled that he was received by Grant "most heartily" and that they discussed the situation fully. When he went aboard the *River Queen* with Grant, he found the President highly curious about the incidents of the great march, and quick to enjoy its more ludicrous aspects, such as the activities of the bummers, and their eager devices to collect food and forage when many Americans supposed the invaders to be starving. At the same time he expressed anxiety lest some misfortune should befall the army in North Carolina during Sherman's absence. Sherman assured him Schofield could handle anything that came up. Clearly the assemblage on March 27 had its cheerful social moments.

The next day, after talks with Meade and others, Grant, Sherman, and Porter returned to the *River Queen*, where a more discursive conversation was held on such military topics as Federal operations, and Lee's possible activities. Many expected a bloody battle, and Lincoln inquired anxiously if it could not be avoided. "During this interview," relates Sherman, "I inquired of the President if he was all ready for the end of the war. What was to be done with the rebel armies when defeated? And what should be done with the political leaders? . . . He said he was all ready; all he wanted of us was to defeat the opposing armies, and to get the men composing the Confederate armies back to their homes, at work on their farms and in their shops. As to Jeff. Davis, he was hardly at liberty to speak his mind fully, but intimated that he ought to

69. *Ibid.*, X, 215-216.
70. Howe, M.A. DeWolfe, ed., *Home Letters of General Sherman*, New York, 1909, 337-338.
71. *Ibid.*

clear out, 'escape the country,' only it would not do for him to say so openly. . . ." After Lincoln told an apropos story, Sherman remarked that he ". . . inferred that Mr. Lincoln wanted Davis to escape, 'unbeknown' to him."

Sherman made no notes, later using those of Admiral Porter, and with some confusion over the dates. He continued: "Mr. Lincoln was full and frank in his conversation, assuring me that in his mind he was all ready for the civil reorganization of affairs at the South as soon as the war was over; and he distinctly authorized me to assure Governor Vance and the people of North Carolina that, as soon as the rebel armies laid down their arms, and resumed their civil pursuits, they would at once be guaranteed all their rights as citizens of a common country; and that to avoid anarchy the State governments then in existence, with their civil functionaries, would be recognized by him as the government *de facto* till Congress could provide others . . . ." Grant does not mention this, nor does Porter; and Porter has no record of the last vital clause respecting final Congressional provision as an important part of the utterance thus somewhat hazily attributed to Lincoln.

Sherman also tells us: "I was more than ever impressed by his kindly nature, his deep and earnest sympathy with the afflictions of the whole people resulting from the war. . . . His earnest desire seemed to be to end the war speedily, without more bloodshed or devastation, and to restore all the men of both sections to their homes. . . ."[72]

The recollections written by Admiral Porter[73] in 1866, despite their gossipy and often inaccurate character, may also merit brief quotation. His statement that Lincoln visited City Point "with the most liberal views toward the rebels," partially confirms Sherman's account. He seems less clearly credible when he writes: "Mr. Lincoln did, in fact, arrange the (so-considered) liberal terms offered General Jos. Johnston, and, whatever may have been General Sherman's private views, I feel sure that he yielded to the wishes of the President in every respect. . . ."[74]

In another account, written to Isaac N. Arnold of Chicago, Sherman expressed himself cautiously upon this meeting with Lincoln, and his talk with him of the experience of the campaign. He also says that General Grant and himself explained their next moves to Lincoln, though various leaders often said that Grant never told Lincoln of his plans in advance. Lincoln is said to have deprecated the probable necessity of one more bloody battle. Of the second visit Sherman wrote: "I ought not and must not attempt to recall the words of that conversation. . . . Though I cannot attempt to recall the words

72. Sherman, *Memoirs*, *op.cit.*, II, 324-328.
73. *Ibid.*, 328-331, written in 1866.
74. *Ibid.*

spoken by any one of the persons present, on that occasion, I know we talked generally about what was to be done when Lee and Johnsons [*sic.*] armies were beaten and dispersed. . . ." Sherman recalls that Lincoln remarked that he hoped there would be no more bloodshed, that the men of the Rebel armies would be disarmed and sent back home, and "that he contemplated no revenge—no harsh measures—but quite the contrary, and trusted that their suffering and hardships in the war would make them now submissive to law—I cannot say that Mr. Lincoln or any body else used this language at the time, but I know I left his presence with the conviction that he had in his mind, or that his cabinet had, some plan of settlement, ready for application the moment Lee and Johnston were defeated. . . ."[75]

The conference of the President and his generals was the last quiet moment in national events. That same day, Lee wrote his daughter: "Genl. Grant is evidently preparing for something. . . ."[76] He was correct in a conjecture that sprang naturally from the expectation (which he had held all spring) of an advance by Grant.

On March 29 Lincoln asked Grant, as he had asked other generals for four years: "How do things look now?" And on the 30th the President told Stanton he felt he should be back in Washington, but disliked to leave without seeing nearer to the end of Grant's movement. Stanton did not object, and Seward came down for a day or two. But most of the time Lincoln was without his official family. By March 31, as the battle news from Petersburg came in, Lincoln seemed depressed, and on April 1 he walked the deck of the *River Queen* most of the night. One of his bodyguards wrote: "I have never seen suffering on the face of any man as was on his that night."[77]

Indeed, the last campaign against the Army of Northern Virginia had begun. For twelve days, as we have seen, Grant extended his lines to the westward, stretching Lee's to the breaking-point and beyond. Union troops moved in rainy weather against Lee's far right, tearing away one of the last mobile forces in the Confederate defenses. On April 2, observers of the Petersburg line watched the Federal masses break the enemy.

Perhaps twenty miles distant from Lincoln, the scene was quite different. In Richmond a congregation quietly gathered in Lee's church to hear the service, a scene that is indelibly imprinted in Civil War history.

Lee had told Breckinridge on April 2 that he despaired of doing more than hold his position at Petersburg until night, and that preparations should be

75. Sherman to Arnold, Nov. 28, 1872, Isaac N. Arnold Papers, Chicago Hist. Soc. Cf. Naroll, Raoul S., "Lincoln and the Sherman Peace Fiasco Another Fable?" *Journal of Southern History*, Vol.XX, No.4, Nov. 1954, 459-483.

76. *Wartime Papers of R.E. Lee, op.cit.*, 919.

77. Lincoln, *Works*, VIII, 376-377; *Lincoln Day by Day*, III, 323-324; Crook, William H., "Lincoln's Last Day," compiled by Margarite S. Gerry, *Harper's Monthly*, Vol. CXV, Sept., 1907, 520.

made to quit the capital. Life in the city during the most recent days had gone on much as before, with the clouds of war ever darker, but not yet oppressive. Southerners were familiar with St. Paul's Episcopal Church, where the Reverend Dr. Charles Minnigerode now lifted his last prayer for the President of the Confederacy.[78] The waiting concourse watched in awed suspense as a messenger from the War Department slipped down the aisle, and the President quietly walked out of the church.

As Davis himself said, "the congregation of St. Paul's was too refined to make a scene at anticipated danger."[79] Hastening to his office, Davis summoned the heads of departments and bureaus, and gave instructions for removing the government. The news spread rapidly and, as Davis proceeded from his office to his house, many personal friends ventured questions. "The affection and confidence of this noble people in the hour of disaster," he declared, "were more distressing to me than complacent and unjust censure would have been. . . ." Mrs. Davis had already left.[80]

One resident later recalled: "The hours I remained in Richmond on that melancholy Sunday, after leaving St. Paul's, were among the saddest of my life. I felt that our cause was the Lost Cause. Many of the scenes . . . were heart-rending. The bad news had spread with lightning speed all over town. . . . The men, generally, were on the street, and large numbers of the ladies stood in the doors and on the steps of their houses, many bathed in tears, making inquiries and giving utterance to woeful disappointment and anguish. . . ."[81]

It was a lovely spring Sunday "when delicate silks that look too fine at other times seem just to suit . . ." wrote one woman. "I have never seen a calmer or more peaceful Sabbath morning, and alas! never a more confused evening. . . ."[82] "Then Mr. Davis, oh, so bowed, and anxious, came. When he told us he feared Richmond must be evacuated by midnight, the truth was forced upon us. . . ."[83]

By afternoon of April 2, officials started leaving on the Richmond & Danville Railroad. Sixty midshipmen under Captain William H. Parker escorted what remained of the Confederate treasury.[84]

Secretary Mallory wrote of the final scene in Richmond: "As usual the

78. Note the minister's name is often misspelled Minnegerode. St. Paul's and the Richmond Civil War Centennial Committee confirm the correct spelling.

79. Davis, Varina, *Jefferson Davis, a Memoir by His Wife*, New York, 1890, II, 582-584.

80. *Ibid.* For other accounts of the scene in St. Paul's, see Longstreet, *From Manassas to Appomattox*, Philadelphia, 1896, 607, his wife's account; Bruce, H.W., "Some Reminiscences of the Second of April, 1865," Southern Historical Society Papers, IX, No.5, May 1881, 206-207.

81. Bruce, *op.cit.*, 206-207.

82. Letters of Mrs. Mary A. Fontaine to Mrs. Marie Burrows Sayre, Confederate Mem'l. Literary Society, Richmond, Apr. 30, 1865.

83. *Ibid.*

84. Hanna, A.J., *Flight into Oblivion*, Richmond, 1938, contains secondary account of the flight of the Confederate government.

President's face was closely scrutinized as he entered St. Paul's alone . . . but its expression varied not from the cold, stern sadness which four years of harrassing mental labour had stamped upon it. . . . the cold, calm eye, the sunken cheek, the compressed lip, were all . . . impenetrable. . . ." Dull, booming sounds of the distant guns could be heard.[85]

At the President's office, Davis explained to his Cabinet the necessity for evacuation, and each pursued his duties, including the transfer of important papers to the depot. Mallory saw Secretary Benjamin, impeccably dressed and calmly carrying his habitual cigar, walking to his office, and caught sight of Mayor Mayo, spotless in white cravat, ruffles, and waistcoat, busy with plans to protect the people. "The African church had, at an early hour, poured its crowded congregation into the streets; and American citizens of African descent were shaking hands and exchanging congratulations upon all sides. Many passed through the confused streets," writes Mallory, "with eager faces, parted lips, and nervous strides, gazing about for friends and helpers."[86]

The government train finally got under way about 11 P.M. Hundreds sought to leave on it, but only those whose services were essential to the government were allowed, some women excepted. The train moved off "in gloomy silence over the James River," continues Mallory. "A commanding view of the river-front of the city caught their sad and wistful gaze; and as the last flickering lights died away, many spoke with sad and philosophic frankness upon the hopes, achievements, errors, and tragic final collapse of the Confederate Cause, until all relapsed into silence."[87] But one man retained a sense of cheerful detachment. Even at the end, Benjamin's epicurean philosophy and inexhaustible good humor cropped out in well-informed discussion of other lost causes, and he munched his sandwich and puffed his cigar with unconquerable poise.[88]

Slowed by the bad roadbed, the train did not make the 140 miles to Danville, Virginia, until mid-afternoon April 3. Government operations were reorganized, and continued in Danville until the evening of April 10. No substantial evidence supports the assertions made later that the movement of the official train prevented the collection of supplies at Amelia Court House for Lee's retiring army. Davis denied that he or the president of the railroad, who was with him, knew anything about supply plans.[89]

85. Mallory, S.R., *Diary*, Southern Historical Collection, Univ. of N.C. Library. His story of the last days of the Confederacy is one of the best records, though apparently written sometime afterward.

86. *Ibid.*

87. *Ibid.*

88. *Ibid.*

89. Davis, Jefferson, *op.cit.*, II, 675-676.

A large crowd met the party at the Danville station as the train came in, "and the President was cordially greeted. There was none of the old, wild, Southern enthusiasm, however, and there was that in the cheers which told almost as much of sorrow as of joy. . . ."[90]

Elsewhere the scene was different. One Confederate soldier, moving through the falling city of Richmond, said: "the men, as usual, light-hearted and cheerful round the fire, though an empire was passing away around them. . . ."[91] As they renewed their march, a tremendous explosion took place toward the James, probably a gunboat going up; others followed which "told, in anything but a whisper, the desperate condition of things. . . ." Passing through the Richmond suburb of Rockets, the soldier found a different atmosphere. "The peculiar population of that suburb were gathered on the sidewalk; bold, dirty-looking women, who had evidently not been improved by four years' military association, dirtier-looking (if possible) children, and here and there skulking, scoundrelly looking men, who in the general ruin were sneaking from the holes they had been hiding in. . . ." The rebel soldier continued: "The great crowd, as we soon saw, were . . . pillaging the burning city. . . . The roaring and crackling of the burning houses, the trampling and snorting of our horses over the paved streets . . . wild sounds . . . through the cloud of smoke that hung like a pall around him, made a scene that beggars description. . . . the saddest of many of the sad sights of war—a city undergoing pillage at the hands of its own mob, while the standards of an empire were being taken from its capitol, and the tramp of a victorious enemy could be heard at its gates. . . ."[92]

War refugees, particularly in recent months, had gathered in Richmond, which, it was believed, held about 5,000 deserters. The passage of Confederate troops westward April 3 was hindered by the flames. "As we sat upon our horses on the high hill on which Manchester stood, . . . a suburb south of the James," wrote one observer, "we looked down upon the City of Richmond. By this time the fire appeared to be general. Some magazine or depot for the manufacture of ordnance stores was on fire about the centre of the city; it was marked by the peculiar blackness of smoke; from the middle of it would come the roar of bursting shells and boxes of . . . ammunition. . . . On our right was the navy yard at which were several steamers and gunboats . . . burning in the river, from which the cannon were thundering as the fire reached them. . . ."[93]

90. Mallory, *Diary*, *op.cit.*

91. Boykin, Edward M., *The Falling Flag, Evacuation of Richmond, Retreat, and Surrender at Appomattox*, New York, 1874, 9.

92. *Ibid.*, 11-12.

93. *Ibid.*, 15.

Most of the residents of Richmond remained in the city, along with many refugees from Petersburg and nearby towns. General Alexander wrote that on April 3, Irish, Germans, and Negroes—men, women and children—crowded the city, "carrying off bacon, corn, bedding, saddles, harness, and every variety of army stores . . ." Nearly every shop on Main Street was plundered.[94]

A Richmond lady, describing the night of April 2-3, relates: "All through that long, long night we worked and wept, and bade farewell, never thinking of sleep; in the distance we heard the shouts of the soldiers and mob as they ransacked stores; the rumblings of wagons, and beating of drums all mixed in a confused medley. Just before dawn explosions of gunboats and magazines shook the city, and glass was shattered, and new houses crumbled beneath the shocks. Involuntarily I closed the shutters, and then everything had become still as death, while immense fires stretched their arms on high all around me. I shuddered at the dreadful silence. Richmond burning and no alarm. . . . I watched those silent, awful fires; I felt that there was no effort to stop them, but all like myself were watching them, paralyzed and breathless. After a while the sun rose as you may have seen it, a great red ball veiled in a mist."[95]

Among the refugees who did leave Richmond were men in broadcloth—politicians, members of Congress, and prominent citizens, nearly all on foot, but a few in carriages. One observer thought the ladies generally calmer than the men.[96]

Another resident of Richmond was struck by the burning of government offices, all the major newspapers, and other business establishments. Most of the windows were broken in her house and a shell from an exploding ordnance depot entered the library.[97]

The first major fires had been set by order of Confederate authorities, though some officers opposed this needless loss. Mrs. LaSalle Corbell Pickett described the scene as a saturnalia, saying that some law-officers fled from the frenzied mob. Liquor added to the excitement.[98] General Ewell, commanding in Richmond, admitted destroying military stores, but maintained that in many instances the mobs set fire to business and other buildings.[99]

One family feared their large, convenient house would be taken over by the Yankees, but their free colored man, Peter, said: "Don't you be scared, Miss

94. Letter of April 3, 1865, E.P. Alexander Papers, Southern Hist. Coll., Univ. of N.C.

95. Letters of Mrs. Mary A. Fontaine, Confederate Mem'l. Literary Soc., Richmond, April 30, 1865.

96. Blackford, Lieut.-Col. W.W., *War Years With Jeb Stuart*, New York, 1945, 283.

97. *Diary of Miss Lelian M. Cook*, Virginia State Historical Society, Richmond.

98. Johnson, Rossiter, ed., *Campfire and Battlefield*, New York, 1896, containing article by Mrs. LaSalle Corbell Pickett, "The First United States Flag Raised in Richmond after the War," 453-454.

99. *O.R.*, I, xlvi, pt. 1, 1292-1295.

May. I done tell 'em you is a good Union woman." This of course aroused indignation, and the young girls could hardly be restrained from hanging out a Confederate flag.[100]

Thirteen-year-old Emmie Sublett told of Confederate troops passing through the city the night of April 2-3, with friends in the army dropping by to say farewell. The family hid their jewelry, even covering ten gold pieces with green to make them buttons. In the murky red light of the next morning the Yankees came, "and first of all placed the *horrible stars and stripes* (which seemed to be to me so many slashes) over our beloved capitol. O, the horrible wretches! I can't think of a name horrible enough to call them. It makes us fifty times more southern in our feelings to have them here; . . ." But the fiery teenager did admit that the Yankees "have behaved very well indeed. No private property has been touched, and no insults have been offered to any of the citizens. . . ." Emmie noted that the Richmond girls went around the streets coolly, thickly veiled and without noticing the Yankees. "It seems a dreary life for one who is just setting out in life. . . ."[101]

Youthful Emma Mordecai, who lived just outside the city, came in April 4 and wrote that Richmond "could no longer be recognized. Yankee officers on fine horses dashing down Broad St., and the sidewalks thronged with people I never saw before, and negro soldiers, drunk and sober. The Screamersville population looked truly joyous, and seemed to be delighted at the new order of things. . . ." She spoke of general rubble and streets strewn with fragments of paper. To her the city was "desecrated, desolate and defiled."[102]

While it was obvious most of the white population were proudly sensitive, all evidence indicates that the Union forces occupied Richmond in an orderly manner, and without giving offense. One woman reported shortly after the occupation that they could no longer afford to keep Negro servants. "We now see what idle lives they must have led. We love the colored people and shall always love them, yet believe they have kept many families poor. We all prefer German servants. . . ."[103]

Two small Federal cavalry guidons were raised over the Confederate capitol by Major Atherton H. Stevens, Jr., Fourth Massachusetts Volunteer Cavalry, and Lieut. Johnston S. de Peyster of New York raised a larger flag.[104]

General Godfrey Weitzel with troops of the Army of the James promptly

100. Papers of Emmie Crump Lightfoot, Confederate Memorial Literary Society, Richmond.

101. Letter of April 29, 1865, Letters of Emmie Sublett, Confederate Mem'l. Lit. Soc.

102. Letters of Emma Mordecai, Confed. Mem'l. Lit. Soc., Richmond, April 5, 1865.

103. Benetta Valentine to her brother, E.V. Valentine, April 21, 1865, Valentine Family Letters, Valentine Museum, Richmond.

104. Maj.-Gen. G. Weitzel to the Governor of New York, Nov. 5, 1865, *Battles and Leaders*, extra-illustrated ed., HEH; Langdon, Loomis L., "The Stars and Stripes in Richmond," *Century*, May-October, 1890, 308-309.

took charge, extinguishing fires and partially restoring order. However, by April 14, War Clerk Jones thought that Weitzel's rule became "more and more despotic daily. . . ."[105]

The brigade under Edward H. Ripley was ordered to lead the way in for the infantry. "The bands had arranged a succession of Union airs which had not been heard for years in the streets of the Confederate capital," wrote Ripley.[106] He described the "surging mob of Confederate stragglers, negroes, and released convicts" that seemed in full control from the moment Ewell crossed the James, burning bridges behind him. "The air was darkened by the thick tempest of black smoke and cinders which swept the streets, and, as we penetrated deeper into the city, the bands were nearly drowned by the crashing of the falling walls, the roar of the flames, and the terrific explosions of shells in the burning warehouses. Densely packed on either side of the street were thousands upon thousands of blacks, . . . They fell upon their knees, throwing their hands wildly in the air and shouted 'Glory to God! Glory to God! Massa Linkum am here! Massa Linkum am here!' while floods of tears poured down their wild faces. . . ." Ripley's brigade had immediate command of the city. Other troops were cleared out although there was some disorder from the Negro troops. Regiments went to work fighting the fires, primarily by blowing up and pulling down buildings in the flames' path. Prisoners were released, Confederates rounded up, streets were patrolled and order brought from chaos. "This was done well, as even Confederates admitted."[107]

Charles A. Dana arrived shortly to preserve as many Confederate records as he could. He wrote Stanton that, "The malignity of the thorough rebel here is humbled and silenced, but only seems the more intense on that account. . . . there is a great throng of people after victuals. Confederate money is useless and they have no other."[108]

Reporters came in with the troops, for the public at the North was avid for news from this strange capital of rebeldom. One leading journalist wrote: "There were swaying chimneys, tottering walls, streets impassable from piles of brick, stones, and rubbish. Capitol Square was filled with furniture, beds, clothing, crockery, chairs, tables, looking-glasses. Women were weeping, children crying. Men stood speechless, haggard, woebegone, gazing at the desolation. . . ."[109] The capitol several times caught fire from cinders. "If it had not been for the soldiers the whole city would have gone. . . ." Another reported:

105. Jones, *A Rebel War Clerk's Diary*, *op.cit.*, 357.
106. Eisenschiml, Otto, ed., *Vermont General; The Unusual War Experiences of Edward Hastings Ripley, 1862-1865*, New York, 1960, 301.
107. *Ibid.*, 296-306.
108. Dana to Stanton, April 6, 1865, Stanton Papers, LC.
109. Coffin, Charles Carleton, *The Boys of '61*, Boston, 1881, 508.

Scene in the House of Representatives, January 31, 1865, after Passage of the Thirteenth Amendment.

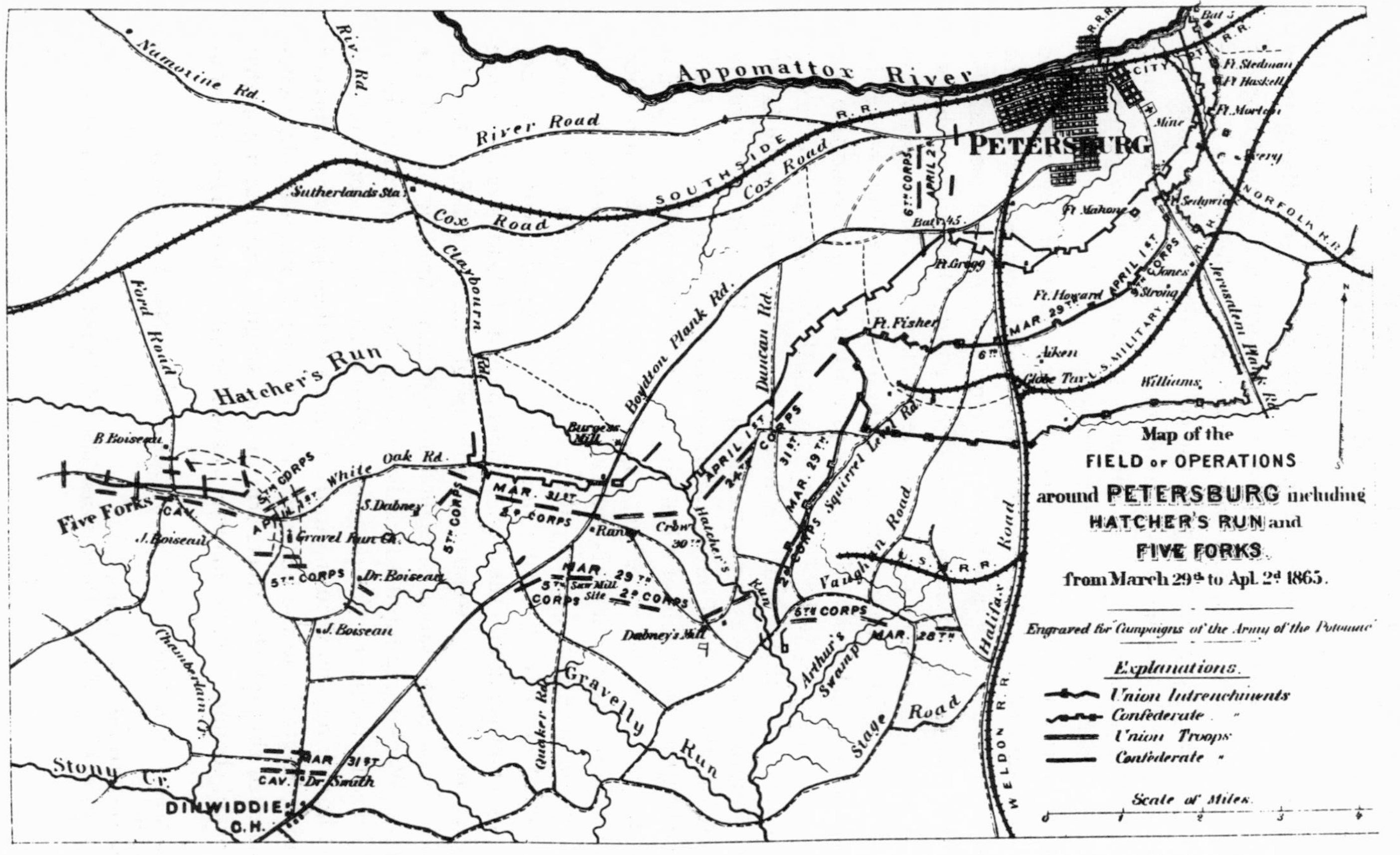

Map of Operations around Petersburg, March 29-April 2, 1865

"This town is the Rebellion; it is all that we have directly striven for; quitting it, the Confederate leaders have quitted their sheet-anchor, their roof-tree, their abiding hope. Its history is the epitome of the whole contest, and to us, shivering our thunderbolts against it for more than four years, Richmond is still a mystery. . . ."[110] However, "no people in their subjugation wear a better front than these brave old spirits, whose lives are not their own. Fire has ravaged their beautiful city, soldiers of the color of their servants guard the crossings and pace the pavement with bayoneted muskets. But gentlemen they are still, in every pace, and inch, and syllable,—such men as we were wont to call brothers and countrymen. . . ."[111]

Another Northern reporter was struck by the number of Negroes abroad and their exultant bearing. Not less than a thousand were promenading the State House grounds which they had never before been allowed to enter. One colored man was heard to exclaim, "We-uns kin go anywhar, jist anywhar we wanter. No passes!" A white citizen reported that three of his former slaves had told him they were a committee to inform him that the twenty-seven he had owned were free, but would continue to work for him on condition that they were *paid in greenbacks!* He took the news hard. Not a Negro in the city, it was reported, had failed to learn that he was free, and to count on the fact.[112]

In Washington there was the expected rejoicing. "Today is one long to be remembered in the annals of our country, for today we have occupied Richmond, the boasted stronghold of rebellion. . . ."[113] A large crowd assembled at the War Department and there were speeches by Stanton, Seward, Vice-President Johnson and others. News came in of rejoicing throughout the country, and on the night of April 3, there was a "grand illumination" all over Washington.[114] The news had come in about 10 A.M., April 3, with newspaper extras being sold throughout the city. "From one end of Pennsylvania Avenue to the other the air seemed to burn with the bright hues of the flag. The sky was shaken by a grand salute of eight hundred guns, fired by order of the Secretary of War—three hundred for Petersburg and five hundred for Richmond. Almost by magic the streets were crowded with hosts of people, talking, laughing, hurrahing, and shouting in the fullness of their joy. Men embraced one another, 'treated' one another, made up old quarrels, renewed old friendships, marched through the streets arm in arm, singing and chatting in that happy sort of abandon which characterizes our people when under the influ-

110. Townsend, George Alfred, *Campaigns of a Non-Combatant*, New York, 1866, 330.
111. *Ibid.*, 331.
112. New York *Tribune*, April 10, 1865.
113. Ms. Diary and Journal, David Homer Bates Collection, Stern Collection, Rare Book Room, LC.
114. *Ibid.*

ence of a great and universal happiness. The atmosphere was full of the intoxication of joy. . . ."[115]

Stanton read to the throng Grant's despatch telling of the capture of Richmond, and the fact that the city was burning. The War Secretary asked the crowd what they could reply. Some shouted "Let her burn!" "Burn it!" "Burn it!" and another, "Hold Richmond for the Northern mudsills!"[116] In fact, reporter Noah Brooks, said: "a more liquorish crowd was never seen in Washington than on that night."

In a remarkably few days, the Orange & Alexandria Railroad was opened and steamers were plying from Washington to Richmond. The Richmond post-office was opened by Federal authorities almost at once. These were outward tokens of restoration, though some deep scars of the war would remain for decades.

On April 2, Lincoln had spent the day inspecting lines and entrenchments. He also telegraphed to Stanton in Washington, Mrs. Lincoln, and Grant, and relayed messages from the General-in-Chief.

Monday, April 3, as Lee's disorganized and scattered troops were straggling toward Amelia Court House, as President Davis was traveling to Danville, and as Richmond was being occupied, President Lincoln went into Petersburg. He reviewed the passing troops, and conferred for an hour-and-a-half with Grant in a house vacated by a fleeing resident,[117] Grant having requested the meeting. The town was nearly deserted when the general and the President met. The correspondent of the New York *Tribune*, riding through Union lines at Petersburg on the morning of April 3, found the troops all astir, with knapsacks being slung, blankets rolled, and every preparation made for an immediate advance. Some units had occupied the town a few hours earlier, and a general fusillade was resounding, with bands playing "Hail, Columbia," "Yankee Doodle," "Kingdom's Coming," "We'll All Drink Stone Blind," and one striking up "Old Hundred." Although the enemy had removed his dead and wounded, many evidences of his heavy casualties were visible. The correspondent saw one dying Confederate, emaciated, half-clad, and pallid, with a wound in the side of his head red with clotted gore. Doors were closed and window-blinds shut in parts of the city not wrecked by the siege. But its whole eastern half showed how much shot and shell had been poured into it. Chimneys were smashed, windows splintered, walls toppled, porches knocked to bits, and even whole buildings obliterated. Before the war, Petersburg had been one of the neatest, most attractive Southern centers. Now it was an expanse of ruin.[118]

115. Brooks, Noah, *Washington in Lincoln's Time*, New York, 1895, 219.
116. *Ibid.*, 220.
117. Nicolay and Hay, *op.cit.*, X, 216.
118. New York *Tribune*, April 10, 1865.

It was here that Lincoln was said to have congratulated Grant, saying, "Do you know, General, that I have had a sort of sneaking idea for some days that you intended to do something like this?"[119] Grant was anxious that the Eastern armies should get the credit for vanquishing their long-time enemies. He wanted no bickering over the laurels and Lincoln agreed. The General is quoted as saying: "I had a feeling that it would be better to let Lee's old antagonists give his army the final blow and finish up the job. The Western armies have been very successful in their campaigns, and it is due to the Eastern armies to let them vanquish their old enemy single-handed. . . ."[120] Lincoln had informed Stanton of his plans to visit Grant. The Secretary expressed concern for the President's safety. Lincoln then told him of plans to go to Richmond, adding: "I will take care of myself. . . ."[121]

However, the truth is that Lincoln did not seem to take adequate good care of himself in his visits to Richmond on April 4 and 5. On the morning of April 4, the President started up the James on the *River Queen*, escorted by Admiral Porter's flagship, a transport, another small vessel and a tug. But, because of the obstructions in the river, the President went on in the twelve-oared barge of the Admiral. They landed, with no one to meet them, about a block above Libby Prison.

We still may wonder why Lincoln made such a hazardous trip so soon to the former enemy capital. Its propagandist value was no longer important. It is true he held some vital political talks, but was it necessary to go into Richmond to do this? Possibly the President was chiefly curious to see the now lifeless heart of the Confederacy. Perhaps he wished to demonstrate the restoration of a united country in which people could move about freely. His secretaries correctly wrote: "Never in the history of the world did the head of a mighty nation and the conqueror of a great rebellion enter the captured chief city of the insurgents in such humbleness and simplicity."[122]

Up the streets of Richmond the small party of ten armed sailors, a contraband guide, Admiral Porter, three officers and Lincoln, walked toward the capitol. The newly-freed Negroes crowded around, and continual risk was evident. The streets abounded with drunken rebels, liberated Negroes and onlookers. Confusion reigned and fires still blazed.[123]

Lincoln and his escort proceeded to the White House of the Confederacy, now used as General Weitzel's headquarters, which Davis had quitted less than forty-eight hours earlier. In the afternoon, the President took a drive about the

119. Grant, *Memoirs*, II, 459-460.
120. Coolidge, Louis A., *Ulysses S. Grant*, 2 vols., Boston, 1924, Vol.I, 193.
121. Lincoln, Works, VIII, *op.cit.*, 384-385.
122. Nicolay and Hay, *op.cit.*, X, 216-218.
123. Penrose, Major Charles B., "Lincoln's Visit to Richmond," *Century*, June, 1890, Vol. XL, No.2, 307.

city. A youthful Confederate girl, who wrote vividly of the fall of the city, stated: "You know Lincoln came to Richmond Tuesday the 4th and was paraded through the streets in a vehicle very much like an ambulance, only a little nicer, but *very common indeed,* attended by a bodyguard of about one hundred horsemen and dashing through the streets like the horses were wild. The 'monkey show' came right by here, but we wouldn't let them see us looking at them, so we ran in the parlor and peeped at them. . . ."[124]

During this first visit to Richmond Lincoln did see, upon his own request, John A. Campbell. Thus, for the third time during the Civil War, the former Associate Justice of the Supreme Court of the United States was to play a prominent, though controversial, part in national affairs. Twice before, as the intermediary between the Confederate commissioners and Seward during the crisis immediately preceding Sumter, and again at Hampton Roads in February, 1865, this highly-respected jurist had been involved. Even though he had been Assistant Secretary of War of the Confederacy, he had not fled Richmond.[125]

At their first meeting in Richmond, Campbell told the President that he was no official spokesman for Confederate leaders, but that obviously the war was over, "and all that remained to be done was to compose the country." Campbell said later: "I spoke to him particularly for Virginia, and urged him to consult and counsel with her public men and her citizens as to the restoration of peace, civil order, and the renewal of her relations as a member of the Union. . . ." Campbell informed Lincoln that prominent men in the state were ready to work for pacification. It must be remembered that at Hampton Roads Campbell had not been adamant in refusing Lincoln's terms for settlement. Of this new meeting he later made a brief record. Campbell declared that in referring to his remarks on Virginia, Lincoln "answered that my general principles were right; the trouble was how to apply them. . . ." The President wanted another talk with Campbell, and would stay in Richmond overnight.[126]

124. Letters of Emmie Sublett, *op.cit.*

125. As in so many events, controversy surrounds the identity of the men who attended two Lincoln-Campbell conferences, and the question of precisely what was said or meant. The following account is primarily based on Nicolay and Hay, *op.cit.*, X, 219-228; Connor, Henry G., *John Archibald Campbell,* Boston, 1920, 174-182; Letter of John A. Campbell to Horace Greeley, April 26, 1865, unsent, Southern Historical Collection, Univ, of N.C., Campbell-Colston Collection; Campbell, John A., "A View of the Confederacy from the Inside; a Letter from Judge John A. Campbell, July 20, 1865," *Century,* October, 1889, 952; Welles, *Diary,* II, 279; Lincoln, *Collected Works,* VIII, April 5, 1865, 386-387 (to Campbell); Lincoln to Grant, April 6, 1865, 388; Lincoln to Weitzel, April 6, 1865, 389; Lincoln telegram to Weitzel, April 12, 1865, 405; Lincoln to Weitzel, April 12, 405-408; *O.R.*, I, xlvi, pt.3, 655, 656, 657, 724. For worthy secondary accounts, see Randall-Current, *Last Full Measure,* New York, 1955, 346-347, 353-356; Hesseltine, William B., *Lincoln's Plan of Reconstruction,* 137-139.

126. Connor, *op.cit.*, 174-176.

Lincoln spent the night on the *Malvern* in the James; he saw Campbell again the morning of April 5. Again, the details and even the substance of who said what, and what was understood and not understood, is confused and debatable. Campbell and a lawyer, Gustavus Myers, saw the President and Weitzel. The President, now prepared, read and commented on a paper or memorandum. In this, as he had so often done, Lincoln called for restoration of national authority, and promised no retreat by the executive on the slavery question, and no cessation of hostilities short of an end to the war, plus the disbanding of all hostile forces. He stated that other propositions not inconsistent with the major points would be considered by the North. Lincoln said that confiscated property would be returned to the people of a State which should immediately withdraw its troops and halt its support of the rebels. Of course, that did not refer to slaves.[127]

Campbell said he did not believe there would be any opposition to the terms, and further stated: "Mr. Lincoln told me that he had been meditating a plan, but that he had not fixed upon it, and if he adopted it, would write to General Weitzel from City Point. This was to call the Virginia Legislature together, 'the very Legislature which has been sitting up yonder,' pointing to the Capitol, 'to vote the restoration of Virginia to the Union.' He said he had a government in Virginia—the Pierpont Government—but it 'had a very small margin,' and he was not 'disposed to increase it.' " There are many accounts, all of them after the event, as to what Lincoln said, or Campbell thought he said, and the nuances are important, though too lengthy to chronicle here.

Campbell later wrote to Greeley in an unsent letter: "My intercourse with President Lincoln both here and at Hampton Roads impressed me favorably and kindly to him. I believe that he felt a genuine sympathy for the bereavement, destitution, impoverishment, waste, and overturn that war had occasioned at the South. . . . "[128]

Campbell went on that Lincoln, in the conversation regarding the Virginia Legislature, "had expressed his object in desiring them to meet and to vote. . . ." Is this what Lincoln really said? Or did he, in exacting, carefully-chosen words, qualify the rôle of the Virginia Legislature? Certainly, at any rate, it was a departure in policy to suggest making use of the Virginia Legislature in any form.

Back at City Point on April 6, Lincoln wrote Weitzel the well-known statement: "It has been intimated to me that the gentlemen who have acted as the Legislature of Virginia, in support of the rebellion, may . . . now desire

127. Lincoln, *Collected Works*, VIII, 386-387.

128. John A. Campbell to Horace Greeley, April 26, 1865, Campbell-Colston Papers, Southern Historical Collection, Univ. of N.C.

to assemble at Richmond, and take measures to withdraw the Virginia troops, and other support from resistance to the general government. If they attempt it, give them permission and protection, until, if at all, they attempt some action hostile to the United States, in which case you will notify them and give them reasonable time to leave; and at the end of which time, arrest any who may remain. Allow Judge Campbell to see this, but do not make it public. . . ."[129]

Campbell gathered together a group of the legislators in Richmond, along with others, and issued a call for the legislature to meet. Lee surrendered April 9. On April 12, Lincoln wrote Weitzel calling the whole thing off. On April 14, Campbell and R.M.T. Hunter wired for permission to visit Lincoln. Thus, we have the second incident within a few days—the first involving Lincoln and Sherman, the second involving Lincoln and Campbell—in which confusion and misunderstanding abound.

Lincoln may not have placed high expectations upon the Virginia legislature, for the same day that he wrote Weitzel, April 6, he told Grant, "I do not think it very probable that anything will come of this; but I have thought best to notify you, so that if you should see signs, you may understand them. From our recent dispatches it seems that you are pretty effectually withdrawing the Virginia troops from opposition to the government . . ."[130]

In his letter of April 12 to Weitzel, Lincoln seems to take a tortuous dialectical approach in order to end the possibility that the Virginia Legislature would meet. He stated that Campbell "assumes, as appears to me, that I have called the insurgent Legislature of Virginia together, as the rightful Legislature of the State, to settle all differences with the United States. I have done no such thing. I spoke of them not as a Legislature, but as 'the gentlemen who have *acted* as the Legislature of Virginia in support of the rebellion.' I did this on purpose to exclude the assumption that I was recognizing them as a *rightful* body. I dealt with them as men who have power *de facto* to do a specific thing, to wit, 'to withdraw the Virginia troops, and other support from resistance to the General Government,' for which in the paper handed Judge Campbell I promised a specific equivalent, to wit, a remission to the people of the State, except in certain cases, of the confiscation of their property. I meant this and no more. Inasmuch, however, as Judge Campbell misconstrues this, and is still pressing for an armistice, contrary to the explicit statement of the paper I gave him; and particularly as Gen. Grant has since captured the Virginia troops, so that giving a consideration for their withdrawal is no longer applicable, let my letter to you, and the paper to Judge Campbell both be withdrawn or counter-

129. Lincoln, *Collected Works*, VIII, 389.
130. *Ibid.*, VIII, 388.

manded, and he be notified of it. Do not now allow them to assemble; but if any have come, allow them safe return to their homes. . . ."[131]

It may or may not be true that Campbell misconstrued Lincoln's full meaning, and it certainly was true that the surrender at Appomattox had taken the Virginia troops out of the war. But it also appears from his language and action that, after consultation with his Cabinet and its disapproval, Lincoln manoeuvered his course out of what had become an embarrassing situation.

It has long been assumed, and probably with a correct interpretation of the limited evidence available, that the Cabinet on April 11 was unanimous against the proposal of Lincoln to use the Virginia Legislature. Two days later, Welles had a talk with Lincoln in which the President said that as all Cabinet members had taken a view differing from his own, "he concluded he had perhaps made a mistake, and was ready to correct it if he had. . . ."[132] Stanton and Speed were the men most determined against the plan, while Dennison also was quite firm. Lincoln possibly said, as Welles reported, that "Their decisive opposition . . . was annoying him greatly . . ."[133] Welles pointed out to the President that the North had never recognized any of the Confederate "organizations."

Despite some intervals of anxiety, these days at the end of the war constituted a fairly happy interlude in the melancholy life of Lincoln, with plenty of good news, particularly from the military fronts. According to the New York *Tribune* correspondent, he returned to the capital much stronger "in body and soul" than he had left.[134] How could he fail to feel joyful on entering Richmond to behold Negroes, wild with delight, shouting, "Glory to God! Glory! Glory!"

On the other hand, the Campbell meeting had been a disappointment. Lincoln was indignant over accounts of it in the Richmond *Whig*, repeated in the Washington *Chronicle*. A paragraph appeared in Greeley's *Tribune*, on April 10, headed "Peace Rumors," which said: "R.M.T. Hunter and Judge Campbell were the leading spirits in the recent Richmond conference on peace." It added that they had admitted the hopelessness of their cause, the wickedness of a further waste of life in a fruitless struggle for independence, and were primarily anxious that such generous terms should be conceded by the government that continuance of the struggle would be impossible. "This and many other statements are afloat tonight, but beyond the fact that the President has returned with the deliberate purpose of issuing some sort of an address to the common masses of the South, all is sheer conjecture." Yet

131. *Ibid.*, VIII, 406-407.

132. Welles, *Diary*, *op.cit.*, II, 279-280.

133. Welles, Gideon, Typed Mss. of article, "Lincoln and Reconstruction," John Hay Library, Brown University.

134. New York *Tribune*, April 10, 1865.

Greeley, one of the foremost advocates of what he termed "magnanimity in victory," continued hopeful. On his editorial page of April 11, he declared: "We had hoped to print herewith the President's proclamation of amnesty and oblivion to the partisans of the baffled rebellion, and we do not yet despair of receiving it before we go to press." He went on to present a forcible argument against the indulgence of passion, and in behalf of a prompt restoration of the Union. In an editorial April 14 he wrote: "We entreat the President promptly to do and dare in the cause of magnanimity! The Southern mind is now open to kindness, and may be majestically affected by generosity." Thus, Lincoln's meeting with Campbell aroused the hopes of those who advocated generosity toward the South.

At 11 P.M. on April 8, the Lincoln party had left City Point for Washington. He had heard late on the 5th, after returning from Richmond, that Secretary Seward had fallen from his carriage and had suffered serious injuries. Mrs. Lincoln, Senator Sumner and others had come down from Washington for a visit to Richmond. Haunting the headquarters offices, Lincoln was keeping as close touch as possible on the progress of the Union armies as they sought to bring Lee to bay. He was intensely interested in the skirmishing near Amelia Court House, Sheridan's movements to cut Lee off from North Carolina, the engagement at Sayler's Creek April 6, and, of course, the question of how soon and in what way the war in Virginia would end.

On the 7th, Lincoln sent his well-known telegram to Grant: "Gen. Sheridan says 'If the thing is pressed I think that Lee will surrender.' Let the *thing* be pressed."[135]

Concerned over Seward's condition, Lincoln then turned back for the capitol and should have been content in knowing that his generals were pressing the "thing", indeed.

[IV]

"We have Lee's army pressed hard, his men scattering and going to their homes by thousands. He is endeavoring to reach Danville, where Jeff Davis and his Cabinet have gone. I shall press the pursuit to the end. Push Johnson [sic] at the same time and let us finish up this job at once." Thus, Grant wrote Sherman from Burkeville, Va., April 6, 1865.[136] Grant had been pressing since May of the previous year, and he was not about to stop.[137]

Now, however, had come the time to combine personal messages to Lee

135. Lincoln, *Collected Works*, VIII, 392.
136. *The History of America in Documents*, Rosenbach Company Catalogue, 1951, pt.1, 69-70.
137. For military events of the campaign from Richmond to Appomattox, see Chap.IX.

along with the use of military force against him. Appraising the losses to Lee's army at Sayler's Creek, in other fighting and in general attrition, Grant believed the situation of the Army of Northern Virginia utterly hopeless, and on April 7, opened correspondence with the Confederate general. From Farmville he wrote Lee that he regarded it his duty "to shift from myself the responsibility of any further effusion of blood, by asking of you the surrender of that portion of the C. S. Army known as the Army of Northern Virginia. . . ."[138]

Lee, in the field, read the communiqué, handed it to Longstreet, who read it and returned it, saying, "Not yet."[139] Lee formally replied to Grant: "Though not entertaining the opinion you express on the hopelessness of further resistance on the part of the Army of Northern Virginia, I reciprocate your desire to avoid useless effusion of blood, and therefore, before considering your proposition, ask the terms you will offer, on condition of its surrender. . . ."[140]

Grant had already received Lincoln's instructions of March 3 not to treat of anything but surrender, even if his tendency had been otherwise. He, therefore, sent Lee a firm and careful response on April 8 from Farmville: "I would say that, peace being my great desire, there is but one condition I would insist upon, namely that the men and officers surrendered shall be disqualified for taking up arms again against the Government of the United States until properly exchanged. . . ." He reiterated that any meeting would be for surrender. About midnight the same day, Grant received the reply, also carefully worded. Lee did not think the emergency was great enough for surrender, but he was interested in "restoration of peace." For this purpose he would be glad to talk with Grant.[141]

The verbal sparring of the two military leaders was worthy of diplomatic usage. Grant, on the morning of April 9, as his army nearly ringed Appomattox Court House, replied that he had no authority to treat on the subject of peace, but that he and the entire North desired peace. "By the South laying down their arms they will hasten that most desirable event, save thousands of human lives, and hundreds of millions of property not yet destroyed. . . ."[142]

After the war, Grant declared that "I saw clearly, especially after Sheridan had cut off the escape to Danville, that Lee must surrender or break and run into the mountains—break in all directions and leave us a dozen guerrilla bands to fight. My campaign was not Richmond, not the defeat of Lee in actual

138. *O.R.*, I, xlvi, pt.1, 56.
139. Longstreet, James, *From Manassas to Appomattox*, Philadelphia, 1896, 619.
140. *O.R.*, I, xlvi, pt.1, 56.
141. *Ibid.*, 56-57.
142. *Ibid.*

fight, but to remove him and his army out of the contest, and if possible, to have him use his influence in inducing the surrender of Johnston and the other isolated armies. . . ."[143]

Grant's staff secretary, Badeau, wrote a friend that, after the assault at Petersburg, "there was no pause, no hesitancy, no doubt what to do. He commanded Lee's army as much as he did ours; caused and knew beforehand every movement that Lee made, up to the actual surrender. . . . There was no let up; fighting and marching, and negotiating all at once. This accounts for the change in Lee's views; at the beginning of the correspondence you remember, he said he didn't agree with Grant that a surrender was inevitable, and he didn't think so till the very morning it occurred."[144]

The night of April 8 from Appomattox General Pickett wrote his wife: "It is finished. Oh, my beloved division! Thousands of them have gone to their eternal home, having given up their lives for the cause they knew to be just. The others, alas, heart-broken, crushed in spirit, are left to mourn its loss. Well, it is practically all over now. We have poured out our blood, and suffered untold hardships and privations, all in vain. And now, well—I must not forget, either, that God reigns. . . ."[145]

Learning of the condition of his army and the Union positions on the morning of April 9 in the Appomattox area, Lee requested a suspension of hostilities until terms of surrender could be arranged.[146] Later, Lee wrote Davis that "The apprehensions I expressed during the winter, of the moral condition of the Army of Northern Virginia, have been realized. . . ."[147] The disintegration of the rebel army had reached such a point that, on the 9th, Lee had only 7,892 effective infantry, and how truly effective even these were is dubious.

Many accounts exist of the last days of Lee's army and of what the General did and said.[148] A staff officer close to Lee related that on the morning of April 9 the General asked him, "Well, Colonel, what are we to do?" The officer replied that if they could abandon the trains, the army might escape. "Yes," said the General, "perhaps we could; but I have had a conference with these gentlemen around me, and they agree that the time has come for capitulation."

143. "Grant as a Critic," New York *Herald*, July 24, 1878, interview with Grant by John Russell Young.

144. Adam Badeau to James H. Wilson, May 27, 1865, J.H. Wilson Papers, LC.

145. Pickett, George E., *Soldier of the South: General Pickett's War Letters to His Wife*, ed. Arthur Inman, Boston, 1928, 128-133, letter of April 8, 1865.

146. *O.R.*, I, xlvi, pt.1, 1266, Lee's report; Ibid., 57, Grant's report.

147. Lee to Davis, April 20, 1865, *Wartime Papers of R.E. Lee*, 938-939.

148. Freeman, D.S., *R.E. Lee*, New York, 1935, IV, *passim*, for details and analysis.

"Well, sir," said the officer, "I can only speak for myself; to me any other fact is preferable. . . ." "Such is my individual way of thinking," interrupted the General. "But," added the officer, "of course, General, it is different with you. You have to think of these brave men and decide not only for yourself but for them." "Yes," he replied; "it would be useless and therefore cruel to provoke the further effusion of blood, and I have arranged to meet General Grant with a view to surrender, and wish you to accompany me."[149]

That morning of April 9, Lee was described "as calm and cool as at any time since he took command of the army, just as if the army was to pass in review before him. His face denoted great self-command and his dignity was conspicuously grand. He spoke out in his usual tone of voice, nor did it portray in the slightest the fierce conflict going on within. . . ."[150] The same soldier depicted Lee as clad in his best and newest uniform, with elegant cavalry boots, gold spurs, shining sword and accoutrements.

As for the army, another officer described the men as gathering as usual, on clear, cool, fresh mornings, around fires for breakfast. Noises from the distance of the approaching enemy seemed not to bother them. The responsibility lay with the officers.[151]

The final council-of-war held the night of the 8th, with what top officers were left, had come to the only conclusion possible. The absence of so many familiar names and faces was proof of the exhaustion of the Army of Northern Virginia. The discussion included the fate of the Southern people after surrender. There in the woods around the small fire, some spoke of the possibility of forcing a way through Grant's lines and saving a fragment of the army which would continue "a desultory warfare until the government at Washington should grow weary and grant to our people peace, and the safeguards of local self-government. . . ." But that was just chatter. As General Gordon later wrote: "If all that was said and felt at that meeting could be given, it would make a volume of measureless pathos. In no hour of the great war did General Lee's masterful characteristics appear to me so conspicuous as they did in that last council. . . ."[152] The conference did decide that they might attempt on the 9th to break through the Federals and ultimately join Joseph E. Johnston in North Carolina, but this was a forlorn hope and came to naught. General Gordon had a staff officer ask Lee where he should camp, to which Lee replied, "Yes, tell General Gordon that I should be glad for him to halt just beyond

149. Taylor, Walter H., *Four Years with General Lee*, New York, 1877, 151-152.
150. Transcript narrative of J.H. Sharp, 13th Virginia Artillery Battalion, Henry T. Sharp Papers, Southern Hist. Collection, Univ. of N.C.
151. Boykin, Edward M., *The Falling Flag*, 55-56.
152. Gordon, John B., *Reminiscences of the Civil War*, New York, 1904, 433-436.

the Tennessee line." Of course, that was 200 miles away, so Lee had had his grim joke.[153]

As General Grant's messenger was seen bringing news of the arrangement for the surrender, Longstreet is quoted by Gen. E.P. Alexander as saying to Lee: "General, unless he offers us honorable terms, come back and let us fight it out."[154] Alexander, admittedly overwrought, wanted to attempt to break out. He reported that Lee answered: "I appreciate that the surrender of this army is, indeed, the end of the Confederacy. But that result is now inevitable, and must be faced. And, as Christian men, we have no right to choose a course from pride or personal feelings. We have simply to see what we can do best for our country and people. Now, if I should adopt your suggestion and order this army to disperse, the men going homeward would be under no control, and moreover, would be without food. They are already demoralized by four years of war, and would supply their wants by violence and plunder. They would soon become little better than bands of robbers. A state of society would result, throughout the South, from which it would require years to recover. The enemy's cavalry, too, would pursue to catch at least the general officers, and would harass and devastate sections that otherwise they will never visit. Moreover, as to myself, I am too old to go to bushwhacking, and even if it were right to order the army to disperse, the only course for me to pursue would be to surrender myself to General Grant. . . ."[155]

The scene at the house of Wilbur McLean in Appomattox Court House on April 9, 1865, has been depicted many times in words, and often, though less accurately, in paintings, on the screen, and by television. No matter how familiar the scene, it will always conjure in the minds of millions of Americans historic memories and profound reflections. It will always inspire the imaginations of these millions to recreate a vivid vision of the impeccable Lee in his new uniform and the somewhat shoddy figure of Grant, who had been suffering from a severe headache for several days, and who looked half-sick in his shabby, field-worn private's uniform.

Many were to describe the physical and moral statuesqueness with which Lee loomed through these stormy hours. George Cary Eggleston wrote of the General at Amelia Court House as bearing a "heart-broken expression" on his face, and with "still sadder tones of voice."[156] "Lee's carriage no longer is erect; the troubles of those last days had already plowed great furrows in his forehead. His eyes were red as if with weeping; his cheeks sunken and haggard;

153. *Ibid.*, 436.
154. Alexander, E.P., *Military Memoirs of a Confederate*, New York, 1907, 609.
155. Alexander, E.P., "Lee at Appomattox," *Century*, April, 1902, 921-926.
156. Eggleston, George Cary, *A Rebel's Recollections*, with Introduction by David Donald, Bloomington, Ind., 1959, 130.

his face colorless. No one who looked upon him then, as he stood there in full view of the disastrous end, can ever forget the intense agony written upon his features. And yet he was calm, self-possessed, and deliberate. Failure and the sufferings of his men grieved him sorely, but they could not daunt him, and his moral greatness was never more manifest than during those last terrible days. . . ."[157]

It is well remembered that Grant and Lee chatted for a while, probably a bit awkwardly, about the weather, their Mexican War experiences, and several minor matters. Finally, Lee brought up the subject of their meeting. Grant wrote out the terms on field paper, on a little knobbed-legged table. Presently, Lee, sitting at the side of the room at a marble-topped table, rose and went over to read Grant's paper, which was addressed to General Lee:

"In accordance with the substance of my letter to you of the 8th instant, I propose to receive the surrender of the Army of Northern Virginia on the following terms, to wit: Rolls of all the officers and men to be made in duplicate, one copy to be given to an officer to be designated by me, the other to be retained by such officer or officers as you may designate. The officers to give their individual paroles not to take up arms against the Government of the United States until properly exchanged; and each company or regimental commander sign a like parole for the men of their commands. The arms, artillery, and public property to be parked and stacked, and turned over to the officers appointed by me to receive them. This will not embrace the side-arms of the officers, nor their private horses or baggage. This done, each officer and man will be allowed to return to his home, not to be disturbed by U. S. authority so long as they observe their paroles and the laws in force where they may reside. . . ." Lee accepted in writing.[158]

It all sounded so simple—just surrender and few details. Lee seemed satisfied with the terms that officers were to retain side arms and baggage. Turning to Grant, he explained that Confederate cavalrymen owned their own horses, which would be needed for plowing and planting, to which Grant replied that he would give orders to allow every man who claimed to own his horse or mule to take the animal with him. This was not put into the final terms, but Grant did carry out his word. During the copying of the documents,

157. *Ibid.*, 130-131.

158. *O.R.*, I, xlvi, pt.1, 57-58. Many and repetitious are the accounts of the scene of Lee's surrender. Among the more important original accounts are: Marshall, Charles, *An Aide-de-Camp of Lee*, ed., Sir Frederick Maurice, Boston, 1927, 268-275; Adam Badeau to Wilson, May 27, 1865 (typescript), J.B. Wilson Papers, LC; Pamphlet, "General Ely S. Parker's Narrative of Appomattox," Benjamin Harrison Papers, LC; "Lee's Surrender," endorsed by Grant as being accurate, Orville E. Babcock Papers, Chicago Hist. Soc.; "Grant as Critic," New York *Herald*, July 24, 1878; Grant, *Memoirs*, II, 483-496. For excellent secondary sources, see Freeman, *Lee*, IV, 117-148; Stern, Philip Van Doren, *An End to Valor*, Boston, 1958, 257-270; Catton, Bruce, *Grant Takes Command*, Boston, 1968, 404ff.

he arranged for supplying Lee with 25,000 rations. Grant signed his letter to Lee, stating the terms, and Lee signed a letter of acceptance to Grant. Thus, simply and briefly, without emotion or display, the war was ended.

General Lee, no longer in command of the Army of Northern Virginia or the remaining scattered remnants of other Confederate armies, stepped into the front yard of the McLean House. Union officers saluted by raising the hat; Lee returned the salute in like manner. Then, looking into the distance toward the encamped Confederates, he "smote the palms of his hands together three times, his arms extended to their full length. . . ."[159]

General Grant rode away toward his headquarters. Staff Officer Horace Porter asked the General if he did not think he should notify Washington of what had taken place. Grant exclaimed that he had forgotten it momentarily, and asking for note-paper, he wrote out a telegram while sitting on a roadside stone.[160]

As one Confederate artilleryman noted, many pathetic incidents occurred. Some men were crying, overcome by grief over the crushing defeat and their dread uncertainties, whether they should return home or try to join the effort to reach Johnston.[161] Others ran down the hillsides, wildly cheering, to express their relief.[162] Breaking ranks, many tearfully bade Lee goodbye.[163]

Staff-Officer Walter Taylor writes that no description could do the scene justice, as Lee returned to his army. "Cheeks bronzed by exposure in many campaigns, and withal begrimed with powder and dust, now blanched with deep emotion and suffered the silent tear; tongues that had so often carried dismay to the hearts of the enemy in that indescribable cheer which accompanied the charge, or that had so often made the air to resound with the paean of victory, refused utterance now; brave hearts failed that had never quailed in the presence of an enemy; but the firm and silent pressure of the hand told most eloquently of souls filled with admiration, love, and tender sympathy, for their beloved chief."[164]

One officer was seen to break his sword over his knee, others to rip their insignia from their collars.[165] "Men, we have fought through the war together;

159. Merritt, Maj.-Gen. Wesley, "Note on the Surrender of Lee," *Century*, April, 1902, 944.

160. Badeau, Adam, Letter to the Editors of Century Magazine, Sept. 2, 1885, Western Reserve Hist. Soc., Cleveland; Grant notebook with letter of W.D. Thomas, June 5, 1902, Rosenbach Foundation, Philadelphia.

161. Reminiscences of George W. Shreve, Virginia State Library, Richmond.

162. Boykin, *The Falling Flag, op.cit.*, 63.

163. Stinson, Thomas A., "War Reminiscences from 1862 to 1865," in *The War of the Sixties*, compiled by E.R. Hutchins, New York, 1912, 341.

164. Taylor, Walter, *Four Years . . . , op.cit.*, 153.

165. A Private, *Reminiscences of Lee and Gordon at Appomattox Courthouse*, Southern Hist. Soc. Papers, Vol.VIII, No.1, January 1880, 38-39.

I have done my best for you; my heart is too full to say more," Lee told Gordon's men.[166]

Federal soldiers, for the most part, treated the Confederates considerately. "Success had made them good-natured," said one Southerner. "Those we came in contact with were soldiers—fighting men—and, as is always the case, such appreciate their position and are too proud to bear themselves in any other way. . . . The effect of such conduct upon our men was of the best kind; the unexpected consideration shown by the officers and men of the United States army toward us; the heartiness with which a Yankee soldier would come up to a Confederate officer and say, 'We have been fighting one another for four years; give me a Confederate five dollar bill to remember you by,' had nothing in it offensive. . . ."[167] General Alexander wrote later, "In common with all of Grant's army, the officers and soldiers of our escort and company treated the paroled Confederates with a marked kindness which indicated a universal desire to replace our former hostility with special friendships. . . ."[168] Another soldier testified that the Union troops were very friendly, "in fact almost oppressively so. . . ."[169]

A Union veteran from the West drew the final scene in memorable paragraphs:

"Out of the dark pine woods, down the rock-strewn road, like a regiment of whirlwinds they come; Meade, bareheaded, leading them, his grave scholarly face flushed with radiance, both arms in the air and shouting with all his voice: 'It's all over, boys! Lee's surrendered! It's all over now! . . .' The men listen for a moment to the words of their leaders, and then up to the heavens goes such a shout as none of them will ever hear again. . . . The air is black with hats and boots, coats, knapsacks, shirts and cartridge-boxes, blankets and shelter tents, canteens and haver-sacks. They fall on each others' necks and laugh and cry by turns. Huge, lumbering, bearded men embrace and kiss like schoolgirls, then dance and sing and shout, stand on their heads and play at leapfrog with each other. . . . The standard bearers bring their war-worn colors to the center of the mass and unfurl their tattered beauties amid the redoubled shouts of the maddened crowd. The bands and drum corps seek the same center, and not a stone's throw apart, each for itself, a dozen bands and a hundred drums make discordant concert. . . . All the time from the hills around the deep-mouthed cannon give their harmless thunders, and at each hollow boom the vast concourse rings out its joy anew that murderous shot and shell

166. Lee, Fitzhugh, *General Lee*, New York, 1894, 377.
167. Boykin, *The Falling Flag . . , op.cit.*, 65.
168. Alexander, *Military Memoirs, op.cit.*, 614.
169. Haskell, John, *The Haskell Memoirs*, ed. Gilbert Govan and James W. Livingood, New York, 1960, 100.

no longer follow close the accustomed sound. But soon from the edges of the surging mass, here and there, with bowed heads and downcast eyes men walk slowly to the neighboring woods. Some sit down among the spreading roots and, with their heads buried in their hands, drink in the full cup of joy till their whole being feels the subtle influence of the sweet intoxication. Others in due and ancient form, on bended knees, breathe forth their gratitude and praise, while others still lie stretched among the little pines, and cry and sob and moan because their natures cannot contain the crowding joy. . . . For a brief moment, now and then, the clamor rounds itself into the grand swelling strains of 'Old Hundredth,' 'The Star-Spangled Banner' or 'Marching Along.' And the waving banners keep time to the solemn movement. . . ."[170]

In Chattanooga an artilleryman, destined to become one of the most eloquent church leaders of Chicago, recorded in his diary how he heard the news from a telegraph bulletin. Two hundred guns fired in rapid succession. There were the huzzahs of troops. "How the thought of peace and tranquility throbs in each soldier's breast when he thinks of the home and associates he left so reluctantly to follow the path of duty, soon to be restored to him. No wonder his spirits should be exuberant, aye, even intoxicated with delight. . . ."[171]

On Monday, April 10, Grant and Lee met again. Lee's aide relates that Grant wanted Lee to go and meet President Lincoln. He quotes Grant as saying, "If you and Mr. Lincoln will agree upon terms, your influence in the South will make the Southern people accept what you accept, and Mr. Lincoln's influence in the North will make reasonable people of the North accept what he accepts, and all my influence will be added to Mr. Lincoln's." Lee was apparently pleased, but said that as a Confederate soldier he could not meet Lincoln. He did not know what President Davis was going to do, so could not make terms.[172]

At this meeting, Lee held a friendly conversation with Meade and others. He told Meade that the years were telling on him, to which Meade replied: "Not years, but General Lee himself has made me gray."[173]

Meanwhile, Lee's aide, Charles Marshall, was composing the General Orders, No. 9. This, Lee's farewell to his men, was brief, stating that they had been compelled to yield. "You will take with you the satisfaction that proceeds from the consciousness of duty faithfully performed; and I earnestly pray that

170. Lee, Major Henry, "The Last Campaign of the Army of the Potomac from a Mud-Crusher's Point of View," California Commander Mollus, War Paper No.10, San Francisco, 1893, 8-10.

171. Jones, Jenkin Lloyd, *An Artilleryman's Diary*, Wisconsin History Commission, Madison, Wis., 1914, 321.

172. Marshall, *An Aide-de-Camp of Lee*, *op.cit.*, 274-275.

173. Gordon, *Reminiscences . . .* , *op.cit.*, 443.

a merciful God will extend to you his blessing and protection. With an increasing admiration of your constancy and devotion to your country, and a grateful remembrance of your kind and generous considerations for myself, I bid you all an affectionate farewell."[174]

On the morning of April 12 came the stacking of arms and colors. Rarely has there been such a scene! "Great memories arose," wrote Joshua L. Chamberlain, a Maine veteran. "Great thoughts went forward. We formed along the principal street . . . to face the last line of battle, and receive the last remnant of the arms and colors of that great army which ours had been created to confront for all that death can do for life. We were remnants also: Massachusetts, Maine, Michigan, Maryland, Pennsylvania, New York; veterans, and replaced veterans, cut to pieces, cut down, consolidated, divisions into brigades, regiments into one. . . ."[175]

General Gordon gathered the pitiful remains of his command, "wholly unfit for duty." "As my command, in worn-out shoes and ragged uniforms, but with proud mien, moved to the designated point to stack their arms and surrender their cherished battle-flags, they challenged the admiration of the brave victors." Gordon relates that the Union troops marshalled in line to salute their late foes, and that "when the proud and sensitive sons of Dixie came to a full realization of the truth, that the Confederacy was overthrown and their leader had been compelled to surrender his once invincible army, they could no longer control their emotions, and tears ran like water down their shrunken faces. The flags which they still carried were objects of undisguised affection. . . . Yielding to overpowering sentiment, these high-mettled men began to tear the flags from the staffs and hide them in their bosoms, as they wet them with burning tears . . . some of the Confederates . . . so depressed, so fearful as to the policy to be adopted by the civil authorities at Washington, that the future seemed to them shrouded in gloom. They knew that burnt homes, . . . poverty and ashes, would greet them on their return from the war. . . ."[176]

General Chamberlain, who ordered the final salute to the Confederates, wrote later that the moment affected him deeply. "Before us in proud humiliation stood the embodiment of manhood; men whom neither toils and sufferings, nor the fact of death, nor disaster, nor hopelessness could bend from their resolve; standing before us now, thin, worn, and famished, but erect and with eyes looking level into ours, waking memories that bound us together as no

174. Marshall, *An Aide-de-Camp of Lee*, *op.cit.*, 275-278; *O.R.* I, xlvi, pt. 1, 1267.
175. Chamberlain, Joshua L., *The Passing of the Armies*, New York, 1918, 258.
176. *Ibid.*, 447-448.

other bond . . . was not such manhood to be welcomed back into a Union so tested and assured?"[177]

"What visions thronged as we looked into each other's eyes! Here pass the men of Antietam, the Bloody Lane, the Sunken Road, the Cornfield, the Burnside Bridge. . . . The men who left six thousand companions around the bases of Culp's and Cemetery Hills at Gettysburg; the survivors of the terrible Wilderness, the Bloody Angle at Spotsylvania, the slaughter-pen of Cold Harbor, the whirlpool of Bethesda Church! . . . Here are the men of McGowan, Hunton, and Scales, who broke the Fifth Corps lines on the White Oak Road, and were so desperately driven back on that forlorn night of March 31st by my thrice-decimated brigade. . . ."

Lincoln spent the whole of April 9 aboard the *River Queen.* As the vessel steamed up the Potomac, the President diverted himself by reading, chiefly from Shakespeare, and by conversation on literary subjects. Some of his companions long remembered the feeling with which he recited the immortal lines from *Macbeth:*

> Duncan is in his grave;
> After life's fitful fever he sleeps well;
> Treason has done his worst: nor steel, nor poison,
> Malice domestic, foreign levy, nothing,
> Can touch him further.

He seemed in excellent health, though tired, with an outlook both philosophic and cheerful.[178] Passing Mount Vernon as the *River Queen* neared Washington, the President, probably inspired by a companion's remark, mused, "Springfield! How happy, four years hence, will I be to return there in peace and tranquility!"[179] Upon arrival in Washington, he visited the injured Secretary Seward, and received the news from Appomattox. Crowds in front of the White House called for Lincoln, and he briefly responded.

On the rainy morning of April 10, 1865, great booming noises shook the city, breaking windows in Lafayette Square. Five hundred guns fired in all. Quickly the crowds, as on a few days before when Richmond fell, formed again. Actually, a few newsmen and others up late had already heard the news, and sent it over the wires to the nation. The enthusiasm was not quite as great over the news from Appomattox as that of Richmond. Perhaps the mud dampened things, but slowly the implications of what had happened grew on the people.

177. Chamberlain, *op.cit.,* 260-261.
178. Chambrun, Marquis de, "Personal Recollections of Mr. Lincoln," *Scribner's,* XIII, No.1, January 1913, 34-35.
179. *Ibid.*

The Federal departments had the day off. Treasury employees gathered in the hall of their building singing "Old Hundredth" before marching across to the White House to serenade the breakfasting President with the "Star Spangled Banner." Impromptu processions sprang up everywhere, the whole converging on the White House, where the President, serenaded repeatedly, responded with brief sentences. When one of the larger processions appeared, young Tad Lincoln was seen waving a captured flag from a White House window. At this point, the President spoke briefly and promised them remarks at more length the next day, then asking the band to play that "captured" tune —"Dixie."[180]

Across the land the rejoicing was the same everywhere. In Chicago the people manifested a characteristic exuberance. On the stroke of midnight, one hundred guns were fired by the Dearborn Light Artillery, their echoes arousing the sleepers who had not left their beds at the stroke of the bell. Throughout the night the popular jubilation reigned unchecked, bonfires burned brightly, and cheers and laughter rose higher. At early dawn the streets were still crowded, and grew fuller and more joyously animated as the day wore on, with people giving no thought to business or meals in their abandonment to relief and exultation. Thousands of guns were fired, and a huge surge of fireworks poured upward in broad daylight, the more splendid pyrotechnical displays being reserved for evening. The people realized that the "four years of failure" had at last closed triumphantly, and felt that the menacing coils and fangs of the secession serpent had been crushed into dust. Thus the Chicago *Tribune*, on April 11, 1865, so often uncertain in the past but now so completely exultant, proclaimed.

New York diarist George Templeton Strong was aroused by the ringing of his doorbell on the night of April 9. A friend gave him the glad tidings of Appomattox. Unable to hold his hand steady, with wet eyes, he wrote the epitaph of the Army of Northern Virginia. "There is no such army any more. God be praised!" A hard rain dampened the celebration, but the guns kept firing all day.[181]

For at least three days after April 9, Washington was said to be "a little delirious," as it really had been since the fall of Richmond. Everyone celebrated and "The kind of celebration depended on the kind of person. . . ."[182]

Richmond, on Sunday night, heard volley after volley of artillery, as Federal troops celebrated the surrender of Lee. Emma Mordecai pathetically re-

180. Lincoln, *Works*, VIII, 393-394; Brooks, *Washington in Lincoln's Time*, *op.cit.*, 222-224.

181. Strong, George Templeton, *Diary of the Civil War*, ed. Allan Nevins, New York, 1962, 578-579.

182. Crook, William H., "Lincoln's Last Day," compiled and written down by Margaret Spalding Gerry, *Harper's Monthly*, Vol. CXV, Sept. 1907, 525.

corded that, for her circle, "this was agony piled on agony—Rose sat on the floor before the fire, weeping bitterly. . . . When Richmond fell I had given up all hope, so this was scarcely a new blow to me."[183]

Then a lightning bolt struck, and once more it was demonstrated that the unexpected, irrational, and fortuitous event has a larger place in history than the planned, expected, and rational occurrence.

183. Mordecai, Emma, *Diary*, Southern Hist. Coll., Univ. of N.C. Library.

11

Assassination of Lincoln

AMERICANS MAY reflect that it was perhaps fortunate for the future psychology of the nation, and for its national memories during long decades to come, that the war, which had filled four years with sullen rumblings and confused clamor, should end with a clap of thunder in the sudden murder of the Chief Magistrate, an event which caught the horrified attention of the civilized world, writing "finis" to America's agonizing years of violence and bloodshed, and lifting the dead President to a position where he would be apotheosized by later generations, the influence of his deeds and words deepened by the tragedy. The murder was clearly a sequel of the war, product of its senseless hatreds, fears, and cruelties. A fitting climax of the years of anger and butchery, it would help impress upon the American mind the terrible nature of the conflict. Although in its immediate results it was a long-felt disaster, its larger consequences were not so unhappy, for it seemed to give fuller meaning to the long contest, and enabled people to view their fallen Chief in a more heroic light, as William Cullen Bryant realized when he wrote in his elegiac poem that the assassination had placed Lincoln "among the sons of light."

The day after the informal serenades of April 10, Lincoln was apparently working on the remarks he had promised for that evening. He also presided, on April 11, over a Cabinet meeting devoted to the cotton problem, also talking for a time with Ben Butler on the position of the freedmen. Finally, that evening, he delivered to a great crowd on the White House lawn one of the most important addresses of his presidential years, for it dealt with the tasks of Reconstruction which the government must now assume. Since he knew that many who heard him were hostile to the plans that he believed should be followed, he was more intent upon speaking with care for the record (he read his remarks from script) than upon delivering a persuasive or eloquent plea, or upon paying tribute to people or chieftains, or upon hailing the victory. That very day Chief Justice Chase, after dining with a body of Maryland Radicals headed by Henry Winter Davis, had written a letter admonishing the

President that it would later be counted equally a crime and a folly if the freedmen in the lately rebellious States were left to the control of restored rebels who were "not likely to be either wise or just."[1]

By the victory being honored that night, Lincoln declared, "The reinauguration of the national authority—reconstruction—which has had a large share of thought from the first, is pressed much more closely upon our attention." The President admitted that "it is fraught with great difficulty," especially because of the fact that "there is no authorized organ for us to treat with. . . . We simply must begin with, and mould from, disorganized and discordant elements. Nor is it a small additional embarrassment that we, the loyal people, differ among ourselves as to the mode, manner, and means of reconstruction."[2]

Lincoln remarked that he was aware he had been censured for his Louisiana plan, and he defended it though admitting that other plans for Reconstruction were possible. He dismissed the question whether the lately rebellious States were in or out of the Union as a pernicious abstraction, declaring that the States were certainly out of their proper relation to the Union. Then he turned to a very practical and immediate problem, that of Louisiana, where he had been under heavy fire for his support of the new State government under Michael Hahn, based upon only ten percent of the voters.[3] Here Lincoln made the significant statements that the new government would be better if the electorate were larger, adding that, "It is also unsatisfactory to some that the elective franchise is not given to the colored man. I would myself prefer that it were now conferred on the very intelligent, and on those who serve our cause as soldiers. . . ." But, he declared, "The question is 'Will it be wiser to take it as it is, and help to improve it; or to reject, and disperse it?' 'Can Louisiana be brought into proper practical relation with the Union *sooner* by *sustaining*, or by *discarding* her new State Government?' . . ." He emphasized the advances toward Reconstruction of the Union already made, which included "giving the benefit of public schools equally to black and white." Lincoln went on: "Now, if we reject, and spurn them, we do our utmost to disorganize and disperse them. We in effect say to the white men, 'You are worthless, or worse—we will neither help you, nor be helped by you.' To the blacks we say, 'This cup of liberty which these, your old masters, hold to your lips, we will dash from you, and leave you to the chances of gathering the spilled and scattered contents in some vague and undefined when, where, and how.' " If this course, discouraging and paralyzing both white and black, has

1. Lincoln, *Collected Works,* VIII, 399.
2. *Ibid.*, 399-405.
3. Hahn had resigned March 4, upon election to the U.S. Senate.

"any tendency to bring Louisiana into proper practical relations with the Union, I have, so far, been unable to perceive it."

By sustaining the new government the Union would encourage the hearts and strengthen the arms of the 12,000 Unionists. The Negro also would be aided. And then, "What has been said of Louisiana will apply generally to other States. And yet, so great peculiarities pertain to each State; and such important and sudden changes occur in the same State; and withal, so new and unprecedented is the whole case, that no exclusive, and inflexible plan can safely be prescribed as to details and collaterals. . . ." While plans must be flexible, "Important principles may, and must, be inflexible . . ."[4]

As the journalist Noah Brooks described it, "Outside was a vast sea of faces, illuminated by the lights that burned in the festal array of the White House, and stretching far out into the misty darkness. It was a silent, intent, and perhaps surprised multitude. Within stood the tall, gaunt figure of the President, deeply thoughtful, intent upon the elucidation of the generous policy which should be pursued toward the South. That this was not the sort of speech which the multitude had expected is tolerably certain. In the hour of his triumph as the patriotic chief magistrate of a great people, Lincoln appeared to think only of the great problem then pressing upon the Government—a problem which would demand the highest statesmanship, the greatest wisdom, and the firmest generosity. . . ."[5]

The speech was bound to arouse much speculation and controversy and still does. Contemporaries could not agree whether Lincoln was moving closer to the Radicals or breaking with them. Most later historians feel that the lines were being drawn more sharply.[6]

For instance, Chief Justice Chase, in his long, rambling letter of April 11, told the President of his desire for Negro participation in the new State governments. In discussing Louisiana, Chase wrote: "I knew that many of our best men in and out of Congress had become thoroughly convinced of the impolicy and injustice of allowing representation in Congress to States which had been in rebellion and were not yet prepared to concede equal political rights to all loyal citizens. They felt that if such representation should be allowed and such states reinstated in all their former rights as loyal members of the Union, the colored population would be practically abandoned to the disposition of the white population, with every probability against them; and this, they believed would be equally unjust and dangerous. . . ."[7]

4. Lincoln, *Collected Works*, 399-405.
5. Brooks, Noah, *Washington in Lincoln's Time*, New York, 1895, 225-227.
6. For summations see Randall-Current, *Last Full Measure*, New York, 1955, 361-362, and Williams, T. Harry, *Lincoln and the Radicals*, Madison, 1941, 370-373.
7. Lincoln, *Collected Works*, VIII, 399-401, footnote.

The Marquis de Chambrun, who was a friend of Charles Sumner and sympathetic with Radical Republican ideas, heard Lincoln's speech. "I do not hesitate to say," he wrote later, "that the plan for reorganization was quite insufficient. On that day, Mr. Lincoln seemed to limit his view to the horizon of a material restoration; he did not seem to see that an entire moral and social transformation of the South was the only safeguard for a peaceful future. I only see in that enunciation of ideas an effort made to fathom the depths of public opinion, with a view perhaps to awake contradiction. . . . I do not in that speech find Mr. Lincoln's personal ideas expressed fully. . . ."[8]

The day after his speech of April 11 on practical Reconstruction, Lincoln discussed the subject with various persons, and mentioned the coming struggles. On this April 12, he telegraphed General Weitzel in Richmond, as we have seen, revoking the convocation of the Virginia legislature. On the 13th, he went over to the telegraph office and conferred with Stanton and Welles before a horseback ride out to the Soldiers' Home. He is said to have appeared weary and sad.[9] Stanton, on April 13, halted the manpower draft, curtailed a number of purchases, reduced the number of officers, and removed numerous military restrictions.

April 14, destined to be Lincoln's last day on earth, found him busier. His son Robert, who had been with the army, reached Washington in time for breakfast with the President. He had talks with Schuyler Colfax of Indiana and former Senator John P. Hale of New Hampshire, with members of Congress, and others. It was this day that Lincoln is said to have told several Cabinet members about his recurrent dream of being aboard a ship moving with great rapidity toward dim, indefinite shores—a dream which had several times presaged a great turning-point. As it had just occurred again, he thought some event of importance might be impending.[10] In near mid-afternoon, Lincoln lunched with Mrs. Lincoln, and in the afternoon saw various men on routine business. When Charles A. Dana informed him that the unprincipled Jacob Thompson, a Confederate agent recently busy in Canada, was in the United States preparing to sail for Europe, Lincoln made it clear that he should be allowed to leave.[11]

Late in the afternoon, the President and Mrs. Lincoln went for a drive, stopping at the Navy Yard to look at three monitors that had been damaged

8. Chambrun, Marquis de, "Personal Recollections of Mr. Lincoln," *Scribner's*, Jan. 1893, XIII, No.1, 36.

9. *Lincoln, Day by Day, op.cit.*, III, 328.

10. Lamon, Ward H., *Recollections*, 118-119; Seward, Frederick W., *Reminiscences*, New York, 1916, 255.

11. Dana, C.A., *Recollections of the Civil War*, New York, 1898, 172.

off Fort Fisher. He spoke happily to his wife of the time when they could return to Illinois to lead a quiet life. On his return to the White House, Lincoln found the genial Dick Oglesby, Governor of Illinois, and other home friends there. To Oglesby and others he read with warm appreciation several chapters from Petroleum V. Nasby's *War Papers*, which had appeared the previous year.[12]

Several items in the record of the morning are important and merit special mention. One is that Lincoln, visiting the Cipher Room of the War Department, told Thomas T. Eckert, who had ably organized and administered the United States telegraph system during the war, that he expected to go to the theatre that night, and invited him to go along, the President feeling that he would be a valuable guard. But Eckert declined the invitation, pleading that Secretary Stanton needed him for some special work. Another point of interest is that Lincoln wrote General James Van Alen, "I thank you for the assurance you give me that I shall be supported by conservative men like yourself in the efforts I may make to restore the Union so as to make it, to use your language, a Union of hearts and hands, as well as of States. . . ."[13] Van Alen had written him, incidentally, urging Lincoln, for the sake of his friends and the nation, to guard his life, and not expose himself to assassination.[14] Also on April 14, the President talked in mid-afternoon with Vice-President Johnson for the first time recorded since the inauguration.

But most important of all was the protracted Cabinet meeting at mid-day. Grant attended this meeting, and so did Frederick Seward, sitting in for his badly injured father. According to the younger Seward, the President had "an expression of visible relief and content upon his face." There was talk of what would happen to the leaders of the Confederacy. All agreed it was best to have as few "judicial proceedings" as possible. Yet could they go completely unpunished? Dennison, the Postmaster General, is quoted as asking the President, "I suppose, Mr. President, you would not be sorry to have them escape out of the country?" Mr. Lincoln replied slowly, "I should not be sorry to have them out of the country, but I should be for following them up pretty close, to make sure of their going."

Stanton came in late, and then Grant came and told of the surrender. Frederick Seward records that, "Kindly feelings toward the vanquished, and hearty desire to restore peace and safety at the South, with as little harm as possible to the feelings or the property of the inhabitants pervaded the whole

12. *Lincoln Day by Day*, III, 329-330.
13. Lincoln, *Collected Works*, VIII, 413.
14. *Ibid.*

discussion." Such questions arose as the proper identification of State authorities. Would Southern legislatures be continued in office? Should new elections be ordered by the General Government? Seward quotes the President as saying, "We can't undertake to run State governments in all these Southern States. Their people must do that,—though I reckon that at first some of them may do it badly." Stanton outlined his plan of Reconstruction. The Treasury, through the customs houses, should collect revenues. The War Department should occupy or destroy forts in the South, the Navy Department should seize navy yards, ships and ordnance, and in courts and other mechanisms the Federal authority should be reimposed. Violence or insurrection should be put down, but citizens should remain unmolested.[15]

Welles wanted a proclamation setting forth the plan to be pursued, and announcing that trade should be opened, while Stanton is said to have thought trade should not go beyond military lines. The President, glad that Congress was not in session, asked the Cabinet members to consider the issues, as they must soon begin to act. The question of Virginia and its government was discussed.[16]

Stanton, who was later to say that he proposed his plan "with a view of putting in a practical form the means of overcoming what seemed to be a difficulty in the mind of Mr. Lincoln as to the mode of reconstruction," prepared a rough draft form or "mode by which the authority and laws of the United States should be reestablished and governments recognized in the rebel States under the Federal authority, without any necessity whatever for the intervention of rebel organization or rebel aid. . . ."[17]

Secretary Usher of the Interior Department told his wife that the last Cabinet meeting was entirely harmonious, "and the President never appeared to better advantage. He was inspired with the hope that the war and strife was nearly over, and the meeting was assembled to consider the ways and means to restore to the troubled states government and security. He was full of charity to all and only thought of dealing with those who had led the people into the rebellion. . . ."[18]

Secretary McCulloch of the Treasury Department later recorded: "I never saw Mr. Lincoln so cheerful and happy as he was on the day of his death. The burden which had been weighing upon him for four long years, and which he had borne with heroic fortitude, had been lifted; . . . the Union was safe. The

15. Seward, Frederick W., *op.cit.*, 254-257.

16. Welles, *Diary*, New York, 1909, II, 281-282; Welles, *Lincoln and Reconstruction*, ms. in Welles Papers, LC.

17. Flower, Frank Abial, *Edwin McMasters Stanton*, 301-302. For good summations of this meeting, see Randall-Current, *op.cit.*, 362-364; Nicolay and Hay, *Lincoln*, X, 281-285.

18. John P. Usher to his wife, April 16, 1865, Miscellaneous Papers, LC.

weary look which his face had so long worn . . . had disappeared. It was bright and cheerful . . ."[19]

After supper on April 14, the fourth anniversary of the formal surrender of Fort Sumter, Lincoln talked with Schuyler Colfax of Indiana about a special session of Congress. Then he exchanged a few words with former Representative Isaac N. Arnold of Chicago, while climbing into his carriage to go to the theatre. Accompanied by Mrs. Lincoln, Miss Clara Harris, daughter of Senator Harris of New York, and Major Henry R. Rathbone, he was going to see Laura Keene in a performance of "Our American Cousin." The rest is one of the most tragic and thoroughly studied chapters of our American history.

It had long been clear to Lincoln himself, as to his friends and associates, that assassination was a possibility. Threats had been made upon his life before he left Springfield for Washington, and had thickened as the conflict proceeded. He had penetrated the meshes of an alleged conspiracy in Baltimore. He constantly received threatening letters, and thrust many into a special envelope. He said several times that in a country as free as the United States any man could kill the President who was ready to give up his own life in exchange. "If they kill me," he once remarked, "the next man will be just as bad for them." His attitude was not so much one of fatalism as of indifference. It was difficult for him to comprehend the vengeful malice that would find expression in so terrible a crime. Perhaps he felt that when tens of thousands were bravely giving up their lives for the country on the battlefield, he ought to possess the fortitude to face the possibility of his own murder. He walked to and from the War Department with complete freedom. On summer nights he rode out to the Soldiers' Home, his summer residence, with little or no escort. Once a bullet was fired through his hat as he rode. He sometimes drove to and fro in an open carriage. A striking illustration of the risks to which Lincoln was exposed may be found in the manuscript reminiscences of Robert Brewster Stanton. He had attended a military review where Lincoln was present. When it ended, he wrote, "our buggy was standing close to where the President's open barouche was waiting for him to enter for the return trip to the city." The buggy wheeled into line right behind the barouche, which it followed all the way into Washington and up to the White House gates. "Strange to say, there was no military or other [guard], which was remarkable considering the long miles through the country we had to go, the latter part of the distance after dark. But of this I am sure for this reason. The President's carriage was simply one of a long line of vehicles, before and after, and was frequently stopped by a line in front. On the back seat of the open barouche beside Mr. Lincoln was seated John Hay, his secretary. . . . We were driving

19. McCulloch, Hugh, *Men and Measures of Half-a-Century*, New York, 1888, 222.

quite fast, and Col. Corcoran's old war horse was most eager to go. As each jam occurred the President's carriage was obliged to stop, John Hay would turn around and put his hand up to warn us from running into the Presidential party. Several times our fiery steed could not stop quick enough, and his nose would push over the lowered top of the barouche and strike the President's back. We drove in this way to the very gate of the White House. . . . Remembering the many threats against Mr. Lincoln's life, and the manner of his death, it seems to me remarkable that on such a notable occasion the President of the United States had no military escort as Commander-in-chief of the Army to and from the great review."[20] Even in Europe, reported John Bigelow, plots were formed against him.[21]

Countless authors then and ever since record the events of Good Friday, April 14, 1865, and the following Saturday morning. Every nook and cranny of the assassination and of matters involved even remotely has been investigated. Even yet a few bits and pieces may be found. Some students have found discrepancies and raised legitimate questions. Others have carried their zeal so far as to find a possible conspiracy among anti-Lincoln Republican Radicals, and Secretary of War Stanton in especial has sometimes been vaguely implicated. Part of this historical research has admirable aspects, and within limits may be encouraged, but it has become increasingly frequent for some writers to strain the use of evidence, perhaps even for the sake of sensationalism. In fact, most of the modern writing on Lincoln's assassination is far from objective. Recent assassinations have only added to the legends, folklore, and fabrications of the events of April, 1865.

However, the consensus of serious historians is that the basic facts of the assassination are clear. Abraham Lincoln was shot in Ford's Theater in Washington shortly after 10 P.M., April 14, 1865, by the actor John Wilkes Booth. William H. Seward was viciously assaulted. It is known that Booth had collaborators, but that perhaps the role of one or two accused associates has been exaggerated, and that at least Mrs. Surratt and Dr. Mudd were falsely punished. It is generally agreed today that there was no plot made by President Jefferson Davis or anyone else in high position in the Confederacy to assassinate Lincoln, and that Booth and his array of miscreants acted on their own initiative. Most students agree that it was John Wilkes Booth who was killed in the Garrett barn in Virginia. Nothing in the flood of words written on the assassination seems really to contradict these general conclusions.

Much attention has properly been given to the emotions shown by the

20. Reminiscences in Civil War Times Section, 1861-1866, Manuscript Division, New York Public Library.

21. Holland, James Gilbert, *Life of Abraham Lincoln*, Springfield Mass., 1866, 517.

public and their response to the horror of the event. The pathos, the heartrending tragedy of such accounts affect all readers. Yet, a good many of the more popular writers never or seldom consider the deeper meanings of this event for the people both then and in the years to come. What impact did this first really major assassination of a political figure in this country truly make upon the national mind and heart? Violent deaths had previously attended duels, and many shootings or knifings had marked local political contests. But the assassination of Lincoln was the first deliberately plotted murder of a figure so eminent.

Further, the assassination of Lincoln needs to be regarded more closely as part of the fabric of its time. It is not an isolated episode, or a set eruption of violence upon a detached stage as in a melodrama. The psychological tensions of that spring of 1865 should properly be measured and weighed—the force of the interrelated series of blows upon emotions North and South produced by Sherman's great march, Appomattox, the fall of the Confederacy, and the disbandment of armies. These formed the background of the irresponsible crime—all contributing together to test the country's moral fortitude and inner faith in itself.

Part of the importance of the sad assassination chapter in American history is the severe test that it suddenly imposed upon the American government and people—a fourfold test, all the more gruelling because it came on the very heels of victory, when men were feeling the first sense of true relief and relaxation in years.

The first great question was whether the government could be transferred in such abrupt and harsh circumstances from one leader, fully tested, internationally admired, and popularly beloved by many (though not by all), to a much newer national leader, inexperienced, and mistrusted alike by some Northerners who did not relish his demagogic speeches in East Tennessee, and many Southerners who regarded him as a turncoat. Could such a transfer be effected without disturbance or disorder? The second question was whether the murder of the President could be viewed as the essentially senseless, impulsive and unanticipated crime that it was, and be cast into the gulf of malign fortuitous events, without any deepening of the long-felt hatred of many Northerners for the South, or the smouldering bitterness among Southerners against the North.

The third question, the most momentous of all, was whether the murder of so mild, magnanimous, and statesmanlike a leader, with the words "malice toward none and charity for all" so recently upon his lips, would divert national thought upon the problem of Reconstruction into sinister channels, and perhaps poison the politics of the country for years to come.

A relatively minor test now at hand, but one of importance to the dignity of the nation and to its sense of self-esteem, sprang from the necessity of conducting a careful inquiry into the antecedents of the assassination, including the possibility that it involved a conspiracy of a political or a sectional character; and along with this, the necessity of punishing the participants in any conspiracy in a strictly legal manner, after a just, dispassionate, and decorous trial. American judicial procedures, both State and national, had not escaped sharp censure at home and abroad, and now that the most heinous of all crimes had been perpetrated at the conclusion of a passionate and sanguinary civil conflict, the possibility of some form of judicial perversion seemed all too evident. The law should be vindicated with lofty dignity and decorum, untainted by prejudice, unsullied by violent antagonisms. Could the country give the principal accused participants in so foul a crime a fair trial, and a set of verdicts clearly judicious and just?

Here the nation did not emerge in so happy an aspect. Immediately identified, the foremost culprit was too rapidly removed from the scene to stand trial. John Wilkes Booth had been shot to death in the barn, or more properly tobacco-house, on the Garrett farm. Some details of his death remain controversial or obscure, but the primary fact was that Booth could not answer the charges against him.[22]

[I]

The trial of the seven men and one woman accused of conspiring with or assisting Booth in the assassination was, unfortunately, by no means so creditable to the country as the decorum with which Johnson entered upon his duties, or the courteous good feeling manifested by a majority of the Southern people and their leaders. It opened on May 9, 1865, in an improvised courtroom in the Washington Arsenal Penitentiary, only twenty-two days after the arrest of Mrs. Surratt.[23] Most of the accused had then been under arrest less than three weeks, or but a little more. Almost penniless, generally friendless, and held practically incommunicado in solitary confinement, they were pitiably helpless in preparing their defense. During the trial the seven men wore handcuffs

22. Many summaries of the repulsive plotting against Lincoln, his murder, and the subsequent pursuit and arraignment of those held guilty have been written, among which may be named: Roscoe, Theodore, *The Web of Conspiracy*, Englewood Cliffs, N.J., 1959; Eisenschiml, Otto, *Why Was Lincoln Murdered?*, Boston, 1939; Stern, Philip Van Doren, *The Man Who Killed Lincoln*, Cleveland, 1939; Kunhardt, Dorothy Meserve, and Philip B. Kunhardt, Jr., *Twenty Days*, New York, 1965. These are, however, only a few of the numerous secondary sources.

23. Roscoe, *op.cit.*, 431. The accused were; John Wilkes Booth, George A. Atzerodt, Mrs. Mary E. Surratt, Edward Spangler, John Surratt, Lewis Payne, Dr. Samuel A. Mudd, David E. Herold, Michael O'Laughlin.

fixed to a stiff metal bar, and ankle shackles with ball and chain. Much of the time they were forced to wear hoods. Gen. John F. Hartranft was in charge of the prisoners.

The tribunal was not a civil court, but a military commission hastily assembled on the theory that the slaying of the Commander-in-Chief of the armed forces of the country was a military crime. Although Secretary of War Stanton unhesitatingly supported the propriety of a military trial, President Johnson, to his credit, felt serious doubts. Before giving his approval, he asked Attorney-General James Speed for an opinion. Speed decided that the conspirators not only could, but should, be tried before a military tribunal, an opinion that unhappily was not published until after the trial opened.[24] The tribunal included three major-generals, David Hunter, Lew Wallace, and August V. Kautz, with four brigadier-generals and several lesser officers. Not one of them had received a sound legal training, or possessed any experience of a judicial character. Those who knew David Hunter, the presiding officer, regarded him as a stern military martinet. A descendant on his mother's side from a signer of the Declaration of Independence, and a graduate of West Point in the Class of 1822, Hunter had first come into wide public notice when, on superseding John C. Frémont in Missouri in 1861, he had annulled Frémont's agreement with Sterling Price for the suppression of guerrilla activity. He was a disciplinarian with a rigid conception of patriotic duty.[25] He had served in Kansas in 1860 when that State was full of animosities, and had later shown a special zeal for the liberation of slaves and the organization of Negro regiments. Lincoln had negatived one of his orders in the spring of 1862 as transcending his due authority. He could certainly not be termed a man of judicial temperament.[26] Neither could Lew Wallace, later celebrated as author of the somewhat melodramatic novel *Ben Hur*, but as yet best known for his service at Shiloh. One of the brigadiers on the Commission, Gen. T. M. Harris, later wrote a small book, *The Assassination of Lincoln: A History of the Great Conspiracy*, marked by prejudiced references to some of the defendants.[27]

The chief prosecutor was Joseph Holt, whom Lincoln had appointed Judge Advocate-General of the Army in the autumn of 1862, with the duty of taking, revising, and getting recorded the proceedings of all courts martial and military commissions. He had been an attorney in Kentucky and Mississippi, and had served briefly as Postmaster-General and Secretary of War. Associated with him in the prosecution were two striking figures. One was Henry Law-

24. *Ibid.*, 432.
25. Cullum, G.W., *Biographical Register, 1809-1892*, New York, 1868, *passim.*
26. Roscoe, *op.cit.*, 463.
27. *Ibid.*, 434.

rence Burnett who had been prominent in the trials of various Middle-Western Copperheads, and who was not especially active in the preparation of evidence against the alleged conspirators.[28] The other was a veteran Ohio politician and stump-speaker, John A. Bingham, who had climbed into Congress in 1854, the year of the Kansas-Nebraska Act. He had gained a reputation as a master of partisan speech, clever retort, and loose rhetoric, stuffed with historical allusions. Later he was to play a loud and self-confident part in the impeachment of President Johnson. In the conspiracy trials, according to one careful student, his role was "to bully the defense witnesses," and to assert in his summary of the evidence that "the rebellion was simply a criminal conspiracy and a gigantic assassination," in which Jefferson Davis was "as clearly proven guilty as John Wilkes Booth, by whose hand Jefferson Davis inflicted the mortal wound upon President Lincoln."[29] Such extravagance of speech was all too typical of Bingham, but a great deal of loose talk and writing was inescapably part of the hysteria of the time. The report of the assassination in even the temperate New York *Tribune* termed the assassin "the murderous emissary of the slave power," and stated without substantiation that "Booth's papers in his trunk fully prove a plot," and that the trunk contained the uniform of a rebel colonel—though Booth had never entered the Southern forces.[30]

The conspirators were tried under a blanket indictment drawn in the loosest terms. Not one of the accused was informed of the right to employ counsel. Several, including Mrs. Surratt and Dr. Mudd, made approaches to lawyers which were rebuffed.[31] All this was too obviously in contravention of Anglo-Saxon principles and precedents to be long tolerated, and various public-spirited men took appropriate remedial action. After vexatious delays and impediments had been overcome, a panel of defenders was finally assembled. It included the Hon. Reverdy Johnson of Baltimore, who had shown his courage as a devoted Unionist in a State full of secessionists, and had held that secession was treason. Long a Whig, though later a Democrat, and a member of the United States Senate from 1845, he had supported the War with Mexico, but opposed any annexation of Mexican territory. From his service in the Dred Scott case down to his support of Andrew Johnson's Southern policy, he showed himself a man of principle. He had been Attorney-General under Taylor, and later became minister to Great Britain under Johnson. In short, he was a man of character, moral valor, and intellectual distinction. He was supported by Thomas Ewing, Jr., another man of sterling character and re-

28. Burnett, Alfred, "Assassination of President Lincoln," *History of the Ohio Society of New York*, 1906, passim.
29. Pitman, Benn, *Assassination of President Lincoln*, Cincinnati, 1865, 351, 380.
30. New York *Tribune*, April 19, 1865.
31. Roscoe, *op.cit.*, Chap.XXII, offers the best general account.

cord, who had been one of President Taylor's secretaries for a time, after which he had practised law in Leavenworth, Kansas, with his foster-brother William Tecumseh Sherman and Daniel McCook. Early in the war, Ewing was named the first chief justice of the Kansas Supreme Court. Taking a command with the Kansas cavalry, he was appointed a brigadier-general of United States volunteers early in 1863. In the autumn of 1864, he commanded in St. Louis at the time of Sterling Price's invasion. His record and connections ensured that he would be treated with a respect greater than Hunter and others accorded Reverdy Johnson.[32] But counsel for the defense labored under serious difficulties. They had to prepare their cases and write their briefs while the trial was proceeding, and were given no opportunity before it began to confer with the accused, conduct investigations, or consult law libraries. While thus busy, moreover, they had to seek out friendly witnesses, whom it was very hard to find. The atmosphere and temper of the trial have been sharply criticized by a number of respected persons. Representative J. A. Rogers of New Jersey, a member of the House Judiciary Committee, later commented: "Since the trial of Cranbourne in 1690, no prisoner has ever been tried in irons before a legitimate court anywhere that English is spoken."[33] New fetters appeared. Henry R. Douglas, who had been a member of Stonewall Jackson's staff in Virginia, and who watched the proceedings closely from the room where he was held prisoner, opening into the courtroom, tells us that in its defiance of every principle of law and justice, the tribunal went beyond any rival since the days of the infamous Jeffreys.[34]

In vigorous yet restrained language, Douglas declared:

> If justice ever sat with unbandaged, bloodshot eyes, she did on this occasion. The temper, the expressions, the manners, the atmosphere pervading the Court made it an unprecedented spectacle. The Commission illustrated the very spirit and body of the times; and passion decided everything. Of judicial decorum, fairness, calmness, there was absolutely none. Even the Judge Advocates, of whom it can be said, their quality of mercy was not strained, were sometimes compelled to interfere for the appearance of judicial decency. Counsel for the prisoners must have had a hard time to submit in patience to their daily trials. I suppose there is no case on record where a distinguished attorney was compelled to submit to such indignities as General Hunter and several of his Court put upon the venerable Reverdy Johnson. Although the Court was organized to convict, the trial need not have been such a shameless farce. As Judge Elbert H. Gary, before whom the Chicago anarchists were tried in 1886, said, 'The end, however desirable its attainment, excuses no irregular means

32. *Ibid.*, 342.
33. *House of Representatives Report*, No. 104.
34. Douglas, Henry R., *I Rode with Stonewall*, Chapel Hill, 1940, 342.

in the administration of justice.' Lewis Payne, and all the men in the conspiracy with Booth, merited death, and would have been convicted in any court in the land. The Majesty of the Law could have avenged a President's death—as it did in the case of Charles J. Guiteau, the assassin of President Garfield; and the record of the trial would have been open for inspection of the world. The grief of the nation at the death of the gentle and merciful Lincoln would have had no touch of shame; it was due to his memory that in avenging his death passion should not depose reason. The administration of justice should not be degraded, and no unnecessary blood should be spilled at his grave. The range and character of the investigation indicated why a military commission and not a civil court was selected to try the murders.

So wrote Douglas. But, as he adds, another object, hardly secondary, was in view. This disreputable and deplorable object was to connect the Confederate government in some fashion with the conspiracy.

The charge and specifications levelled against the prisoners asserted that the principal figures, Herold, Atzerodt, Lewis Payne, Mrs. Mary E. Surratt, Dr. Samuel Mudd, and others "had conferred with, confederated with, and conspired together with John Wilkes Booth, Jefferson Davis, . . . Jacob Thompson, Clement C. Clay, and others" to kill President Lincoln, a statement made without qualification, just as the subsequent proceedings showed that it was presented without any shred of real evidence. Thompson, one of the leading planners of the outrageous attempt to set fire to New York hotels, was capable of infamous acts; C. C. Clay was by no means a man of elevated character. But neither of them had conspired with Booth, and Jefferson Davis would have shrunk with horror from assassination, or indeed any lesser crime of violence. Yet, besides making this foul charge, the Military Commission took pains to fill its proceedings with allegations upon the funds used by Booth and others intended to suggest that the Confederate Government had financed the conspiracy; and it also brought into its proceedings inflammatory testimony upon the maltreatment of Union prisoners in Confederate prisons.[35] As the trial went on, its cruel and unjust character became more evident. Representative Rogers of New Jersey did not exaggerate when he wrote later, in a report published by the House, that the persons alleged to have been incited to murder by Jefferson Davis were "held in constrainment and in pain, with their heads buried in a sort of sack, devised to prevent their seeing." He adds that "in this plight they were brought out from dark cells to be charged with having listened to incitements by Davis," and they pleaded not guilty.[36] When witnesses for the defense appeared, they were compelled to undergo cross-examination while facing the glowering hostility of the grim officers of the

35. Pitman, Benn, *op.cit.*, 18, and *passim.*
36. *House of Representatives Report* No. 104, 32.

Commission, and were not permitted even a questioning glance at the defense attorneys.[37]

For a time it appeared possible that the trial would be held *in camera*, under the strictest cloak of secrecy. The chief Army officers would have preferred this, but some of the generals saw the possible value of publicity in bringing themselves popular notice and praise.[38] Judge Advocate-General Holt favored a secret trial. But Secretary Stanton perceived that public opinion would regard any furtiveness or concealment with suspicion and resentment. On May 10, he said that he thought that the charges and specifications should go to the Associated Press, with a summary of the proceedings of the day, but asked Holt's assistant, General Burnett, to consult the Advocate-General upon the subject. Holt opposed any publication of the charges, and at first deemed that a very brief synopsis of the proceedings would suffice. But on fuller consideration, comprehending more clearly his responsibility, he gave way. The press obtained not only the charges, but a full synopsis of the proceedings, and next day the doors of the trial room were thrown open. Great crowds gathered at the penitentiary gates, and the demand for tickets was insatiable.[39] Yet, when the leading defense counsel, Senator Reverdy Johnson, attended the trial in order to make a plea for Mrs. Surratt as a citizen of Maryland, he was received with hostile objections and subjected to such insult that he drew himself up indignantly, shut his dispatch case, and withdrew.[40]

The trial of Mrs. Surratt excited especial interest because she stoutly protested her innocence, and bore herself with dignity in the most trying circumstances. A number of witnesses, some of them Catholic clergymen (for she was a Roman Catholic), and including also several colored people of transparent honesty, testified to her character, Christian piety, and readiness to befriend Union soldiers during the war. She had clearly been a Confederate sympathizer, but no substantial evidence was offered that she had participated in any murder plot. The most effective government witness testified only that he had boarded for a time at Mrs. Surratt's house; that on April 22 she had asked him to tell J. Wilkes Booth that she wished to see him "on private business;" and that several days before the assassination she sent him to the National Hotel to see Booth "for the purpose of obtaining his buggy."[41] This was quite inconclusive. Weichmann, who testified that he met Herold at Mrs. Surratt's, also declared: "During the whole time I have known her, her character, so far as I could judge, was exemplary and ladylike in every particular, and her conduct

37. Roscoe, *op.cit.*, 442.
38. *Ibid.*, 443.
39. *Ibid.*, 444.
40. Pitman, *op.cit.*, 316; Roscoe, *op.cit.*, 446-447.
41. Pitman, *op.cit.*, 113ff.

was in a religious and moral sense altogether exemplary."[42] One boarder, who testified that he had seen Wilkes Booth three or four times at Mrs. Surratt's house, said that Booth came to see her son, John Surratt.[43] Gen. Lafayette C. Baker, a notorious fabricator of evidence in trials, later alleged that Mrs. Surratt had made a confession of guilt to him after the trial, but his word is flimsy. Equally trivial, on the other side, is the sworn statement of Lewis Payne to Gen. Hartranft that Mrs. Surratt was innocent of the murder of the President, or any knowledge thereof. The one safe assertion is that guilt was not proved.[44]

On June 30, the Military Commission pronounced sentence. Mrs. Surratt, David E. Herold, and Lewis Payne were to be hanged. Samuel B. Arnold, Dr. Samuel Mudd, and Michael O'Laughlin were to be imprisoned for life at hard labor. Edward Spangler was to get six years' imprisonment at hard labor. In due course, these sentences were carried out. Mudd and Spangler were confined on the Dry Tortugas. John Surratt, after hiding for a time in Canada, went first to England and then to Rome, where he enlisted in the Pontifical Zouaves. Public sentiment generally approved of the verdicts. But the hanging of Mrs. Surratt by no means closed her case, for long after she was in her grave many judicious men believed that, although she had been a Confederate sympathizer, she had not participated in the plot against Lincoln.[45] The story of Dr. Mudd was also to have a dramatic sequel.

Indeed, so many facets of the trial and execution of the conspirators were open to question, that the dubiously legalized excesses of the case have been widely investigated and in most instances harshly criticized by historians and legal scholars. The record and many pronouncements upon it, some learned and many amateurish, have become a well-known body of evidence and attempted judgments. It is a deeply deplorable fact that part of this body of material later had to be scrutinized for possible use in the cases of assassination that have all too frequently horrified the American people during the period of more than a century since Lincoln was murdered.

[II]

The South was in utter confusion; rebel troops still held the field, and a perplexing disarray confronted the former tailor of East Tennessee. Johnson also had to play his part in helping to guide and express the sweeping public

42. *Ibid.*, 115.
43. *Ibid.*, 122-123.
44. Roscoe, *op.cit.*, 492.
45. *Ibid.*, Chs. XXIII-XXV.

response to the assassination; a wave of emotion, a manifestation of grief on a nationwide scale that made maximum demands upon his composure and his power of expressing sympathy with a stricken and bewildered people. In the days and weeks following the dreadful murder, the nation, rendered highly sensitive and emotional by the staggering events of the war, slowly and half-incredulously began to comprehend this final tragedy and to measure its manifold consequences.

The wave of sorrow that overspread the North, universal and heartfelt, was heightened by the sense of contrast with the jubilant victory cries which resounded only a few days before. People wept in the streets; crowded meetings and church services in every city, town and hamlet expressed poignant distress, and emblems of mourning appeared everywhere. The greatest writers of the republic spoke with an eloquence worthy of the sad occasion. Millions read Emerson's restrained but sensitive tribute, William Cullen Bryant's stately lines, "O slow to smile and swift to spare, gentle and merciful and just," and, in due course, Walt Whitman's greatest poem, "When Lilacs Last in the Dooryard Bloom'd," with a grateful feeling that, as so often before in the history of the English-speaking nations, the exalted bards and prophets of the land had fulfilled their mission. Manifestations of sorrow were prolonged as the funeral train moved from Washington to New York, and thence across the country, pausing again and again for processions with bands playing dirges, and mourners filing past the hearse. As in ancient Egypt, wrote Henry J. Raymond in the *Times*, in every house there seemed one dead.[46]

The Southern response to Lincoln's assassination was naturally less emotional than that of the North. It ran a wide gamut of emotion, from deep mourning and regret at one extremity, through callous indifference, to relief and rejoicing at the other extreme. Although many thoughtful people realized that the future lot of the defeated Southern people might be more troubled and unhappy now that a President, well known to be patient and conscientious, had been assassinated, others were willing to await events in a mood of perplexity and submission to the repeated blows of fate. One of the most creditable responses to the news of the murder came from the headquarters of Gen. Joseph E. Johnston, who was then intent upon negotiating the surrender of his army to Sherman.[47] As he wrote in his memoirs, he told Sherman that the deplorable event was in his opinion the greatest possible calamity to the South.[48] According to Sherman, he was even more explicit. "The perspiration came out in large drops on his forehead, and he did not attempt to conceal his

46. New York *Times*, Apr. 7, 1865.
47. For summary, see *Abraham Lincoln Quarterly*, Vol. VII, Sept., 1952, 111-127.
48. Johnston, Joseph E., *Narrative of Military Operations*, New York, 1874, 402.

distress. He denounced the act as a disgrace to the age, and hoped that I did not charge it to the Confederate Government."[49]

Jefferson Davis, then in flight, had an opportunity to place himself in a happy aspect with Americans of the time and with posterity by some similar declaration. But his actual utterance was somewhat cold. Speaking to Mallory, the Confederate Secretary of the Navy, he is quoted as remarking, "Certainly I have no special regard for Mr. Lincoln, but there are a great many men of whose end I would rather hear than his; I fear it will be disastrous to our people, and I regret it deeply."[50] In his later book, Davis spoke of the event as sad and portending evil. "For an enemy so relentless in the war for our subjugation, we could not be expected to mourn; yet, in view of its political consequences, it could not be regarded otherwise than as a great misfortune to the South. He had power over the Northern people, and was without personal malignity toward the people of the South; his successor was without power in the North, and the embodiment of malignity toward the Southern people, perhaps the more so because he had betrayed and deserted them in the hour of their need. . . ." Nothing of leniency was to be expected from the "renegade" who succeeded Lincoln.[51]

The Confederate Vice-President, Alexander H. Stephens, was more deeply touched. Confined at Fort Warren in Boston Harbor, he later wrote in his journal that the fate of the South would have been much different had Lincoln been spared.[52] When June 1, 1865, was fixed as a fast-day and day of mourning for Lincoln, Stephens requested the corporal attending him to bring nothing but a cup of hot coffee and a roll.[53] He also related in his diary that he had passed a restless night, with dreams and visions. "My whole consciousness, since I heard of President Lincoln's assassination, seems nothing but a horrid dream." Even more touching was the statement made by the vitriolic Louis T. Wigfall, a former Senator of both the United States and the Confederacy, who told some officers, on hearing the news, that he was damned sorry. "It is the greatest misfortune that could have befallen the South at this time. I knew Abe Lincoln, and with all his faults, he had a kind heart."[54]

One Confederate diarist, the Louisiana girl Sarah Morgan Dawson, condemned Booth's act in her diary as a foul murder, adding "and I hardly dare pray God to bless us, with the crepe hanging over the way."[55] Mrs. C. C. Clay of Alabama records that "a kind of horror" overcame her husband. This former

49. Sherman, *Memoirs, op. cit.*, II, 348.
50. Mallory, S.R., *Diary*, Southern Hist. Coll., Univ. of N.C. Library.
51. Davis, Jefferson, *Rise and Fall, op.cit.*, II, 683-684.
52. Avary, Myrta L., *Recollections of Alexander H. Stephens*, New York, 1910, 401.
53. *Ibid.*, 142-143.
54. Abbott, Martin, *op.cit.*, 113.
55. Dawson, Sarah Morgan, *A Confederate Girl's Diary*, ed. James I. Robertson, Jr., Bloomington, 1960, 437.

Senator was soon to be confined at Fortress Monroe. When he heard the news of the assassination confirmed, he exclaimed, "God help us! It is the worst blow that has yet been struck at the South."[56] Eliza Frances Andrew notes in her wartime *Diary of a Georgia Girl* that wise Southerners were gravely silent. She deemed the murder a terrible blow to the South, placing the "vulgar renegade" Johnson in authority, and enabling Yankees to charge the Confederacy with a crime actually committed by an irresponsible man.[57] It is doubtless true that the great majority of the Southerners who expressed their opinions publicly denounced the assassination, though of course sometimes with mixed motives.[58] Mass meetings to express regret were held not only in New Orleans, Nashville, and Savannah, where the Union banner waved, but in other cities, and one of the most generous of all estimates of Lincoln, appearing in the Galveston *Daily News* of April 27, was widely reprinted in Texas.[59]

On the whole, the reception of the news of the murder, North and South, was creditable to American minds and hearts. Few gave way to an ignoble burst of resentment. General Sherman watched closely the effect upon the army in the field near the capital of North Carolina, for he feared that some foolish man or woman in Raleigh might drop some utterance that would madden the troops, and that the city would suffer a fate worse than that of Columbia. But the Southerners behaved well, and his veterans refused to indulge in a single display of anger. In a special field order, Sherman seized the opportunity to denounce "any exhibition of wild passions in murder, violence, and guerrilla warfare."[60]

From Fort Warren in Boston Harbor, imprisoned Confederate officers, including Ewell, wrote Grant, April 16, that "of all the misfortunes which could befall the Southern people or any Southern man, by far the greatest . . . would be prevalence of the idea that they could entertain any other than feelings of unqualified abhorrence and indignation for the assassination of the President of the United States. No language can adequately express the shock produced upon myself. . . ." Ewell and all the other generals confined with him united in condemning 'the occurrence of this appalling crime" and deploring any tendency in the public mind "to connect the South and southern men with it."[61] Ben Crampton, a prisoner at Fort Delaware, wrote that he had not met any officers in the barracks who approved the act of the assassin. "For my

56. Clay-Clopton, Mrs. Virginia, *A Belle of the Fifties: Memoirs of Mrs. Clay of Alabama*, ed. by Ada Sterling, New York, 1905, 245.

57. Andrews, Eliza Frances, *The War-time Journal of a Georgia Girl, 1864-1865*, New York, 1908, 172-173.

58. Abbott, Martin, op.cit., 117.

59. *Ibid.*, 126-127.

60. Sherman, *Memoirs*, II, 350-351.

61. "Confederate Officers," in Civil War Centennial Display, National Archives, (Ewell and others to Grant, Apr. 16, 1865).

part," he declared, "I think it is a most unfortunate affair, particularly at this time." "If the worst comes," he asserted, he would much prefer Lincoln to Andrew Johnson.[62]

[III]

The transfer of national authority to a new Administration headed by Andrew Johnson was effected quietly, decorously, and with an elevated dignity creditable to the republic.

As soon as Lincoln died on April 15, 1865, four of the seven Cabinet members, in a formal message, called on Andrew Johnson to assume the office of President.[63] "The emergency of the Government," they wrote, "demands that you should immediately qualify according to the requirements of the Constitution, and enter upon the duties of the President of the United States . . ."

At shortly after 10 A.M. in the Kirkwood Hotel in Washington, Chief Justice Chase, standing in the presence of the Cabinet (with of course the exception of the injured Seward) and several members of Congress, administered the oath of office. Chase had just written friends that he feared Lincoln was so anxious for the restoration of the Union "that he will not care sufficiently about the basis of representation."[64] He had been delighted, when he wrote to Lincoln on April 12, that the President in his Reconstruction speech of the 11th had expressed a wish that the very intelligent Negroes, and those who had been in the armed services, should be allowed to vote, although the Chief Justice was sorry that he was not yet ready for universal or at least equal suffrage. At first eager to talk with Johnson about universal suffrage in Reconstruction, on second thought he had been reluctant to call on him lest his talk do more harm than good.[65] On his way to the Kirkwood House he picked up Secretary Hugh McCulloch of the Treasury and Attorney-General Speed. In his diary Chase briefly describes the ensuing scene. "The Vice-President solemnly repeated the oath after me. He was now the successor to Mr. Lincoln. I said to him, 'May God guide, support, and bless you in your arduous duties.' The others came forward and tendered their congratulations."[66]

As Secretary McCulloch recorded, the ceremony was simple; "the circumstances were painful and alarming" after the night of horrors. Fear of additional violence gripped the gathering, and rumors were omnipresent, but there

62. Capt. Ben Crampton to his sister, April, 1865, Ben Crampton Papers, Maryland Hist. Soc.

63. *American Annual Cyclopaedia*, 1865, 800; Stryker, Lloyd Paul, *Andrew Johnson, A Study in Courage*, New York, 1930, 195.

64. Chase, Salmon, *Inside Lincoln's Cabinet*, ed. David Donald, New York, 1954, 262.

65. *Ibid.*, 266.

66. *Ibid.*

was to be no interregnum. The Government was without an official head for only about twelve hours. "The conduct of Mr. Johnson favorably impressed those who were present when the oath was administered to him," McCulloch wrote. "He was grief-stricken like the rest, and he seemed to be oppressed by the suddenness of the call upon him to become President of the great nation which had been deprived by an assassin of its tried and honored chief; but he was nevertheless calm and self-possessed . . . He appeared to be relieved when he was assured that, while we felt it to be our duty to place our resignations in his hands, he should have the benefit of such services as we could render until he saw fit to dispense with them. Our conference with him was short, but when we left him, the unfavorable impression which had been made upon us by the reports of his unfortunate speech when he took the Vice-President's chair had undergone a considerable change. We all felt as we left him, not entirely relieved of apprehensions, but at least hopeful that he would prove to be a popular and judicious President. . . ."[67]

Secretary Usher, head of the Interior Department, wrote his wife that Johnson was not exalted but subdued and he had every reason to hope that his Administration would be successful. "In the murder of Lincoln the rebels have killed their best friend, they may expect in the President a rigid inforcement of the law and the leaders but little mercy. . . ."[68]

Johnson's statement upon taking office, his sole approach to an inaugural address, was, quite properly, devoted in the main to a careful acknowledgment of duty. After admitting that he was almost overwhelmed by the assassination, he went on, "I feel incompetent to perform duties so important and responsible as those which have been so unexpectedly thrown upon me." As for his policies, he declared that they must be left for development as the Administration progressed. The message or declaration must be made by the acts as they transpire. The only assurance that he could now give for the future is "by reference to the past." He spoke of his long efforts to ameliorate and alleviate the condition of the masses. "Toil, and an honest advocacy of the great principles of free government, have been my lot. The duties have been mine—the consequences are God's. . . . I feel that in the end the Government will triumph, and that these great principles will be permanently established . . ."[69] Some men wondered about his failure to mention the last President, and his pious generalization, "the duties have been mine, the consequences are God's" —a statement too conventional, oratorical, and ill-developed to have any real meaning.

67. McCulloch, Hugh, *Men and Measures of Half-a-Century*, *op.cit.*, 375-376.
68. John P. Usher to his wife, Apr. 16, 1865, Personal Papers, Miscellaneous, "U" Box, LC.
69. *American Annual Cyclopaedia*, 800.

Johnson, a man now fifty-seven, sprung from the plebeian background that he so often stressed—his father a poor immigrant, a casual laborer, from England—had risen slowly but far. First, a "bound-out" worker, then a humble and illiterate tailor, then a local politician who, by dint of strong convictions, unresting activity and a rough but sincere eloquence, reached a seat in Congress, he could well call himself a champion of the common people of East Tennessee; a hard-working, self-respecting population passionately devoted to freedom and instinctively hostile to all class pretensions of superiority based upon money or birth. His character, opinions, and early rise can be best understood by some thoughtful use of Charles Kingsley's classic novels, *Yeast*, and *Alton Locke*.

With the aid of his devoted wife, Eliza McCardle, herself at first illiterate, but a woman of great ability and fine spirit, Johnson had learned to read, and had provided himself with books. He had then steeped himself not only in some masters of British eloquence, but in the writings of the fathers of the republic. By the time Lincoln made him military governor of Tennessee, he knew the works of our best early statesmen almost as well as did the Lincoln of the Cooper Union address. As befitted a tailor, he dressed with neat distinction; and as befitted a rising popular leader, he carried himself with dignity, his firm chin, piercing eyes, and evident pride in his climb from lowly beginnings adding to his air of distinction. He was a man of action as well as of stiff and unyielding adherence to his beliefs, and in his difficult position as governor of the much-divided, tempestuous State of Tennessee, he upheld the principles of emancipation and the Union, as enunciated by Lincoln, with a firmness and vigor that were worthy of comparison with the course of such greater States executives as John A. Andrew of Massachusetts, Curtin of Pennsylvania, and Oliver P. Morton, Governor of Indiana.

In taking office as President, he neither said nor did anything that would arouse sectional feeling or partisan emotions. The immediate questions in the public mind concerned the opinions of the new President, and the plans he would follow in the reorganization and reconstruction of the Union. Delegations from various States, and eager individuals hastened to propound these questions to Johnson, and present their officious views. But he was too shrewd to be stampeded.

Inevitably, much distrust of the new President and apprehension concerning his probable course of action appeared. It was obvious that as Vice-President he had not been intimate with the President, nor privy to the operations of the Administration, except on a limited scale. Vice-Presidents of that era had far less influence and importance than they were to achieve a century later;

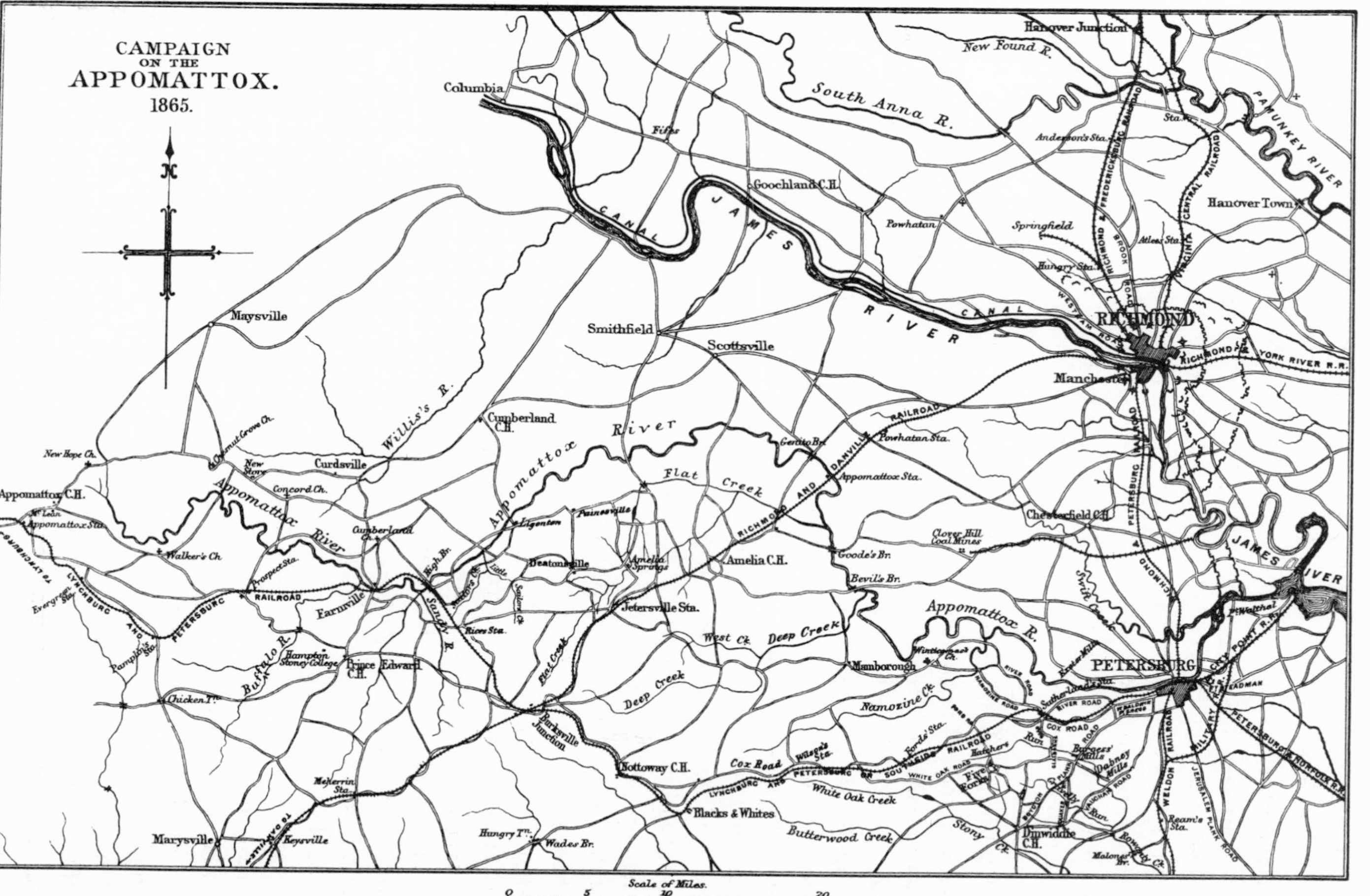

Map of the Campaign on the Appomattox, 1865

even then many men still felt that the office was a thankless position. But, though such samplings of opinion as are available perhaps offer an inaccurate indication of the public judgment, it is clear that many people felt a hesitant mood, not so much of opposition or hostility, as of perplexity and uncertainty.

Even among the Radicals, many of whom felt erroneously cocksure that Johnson was on their side, some men were waiting before deciding on the new President. Carl Schurz, for instance, wrote a friend in German, "Lincoln indeed was not the enlightened mind who could instantly grasp the whole tendency of a period, but through close observation and slow decision he always at last came to the right view. Besides, he was definite and inflexible. Johnson, I fear is a narrower mind. He is not devoid of talent but we shall have to see whether he possesses clearness and decision . . ."[70] The prominent Democrat S.L.M. Barlow could observe in late April, "I hope Mr. Johnson's policy will be such as to give us a speedy peace with all its attendant blessings and a Government of law, and his friends here all believe that he will secure these things." After all, Johnson was a Democrat![71]

General Halleck, whose letters often display more discernment than do some of his acts or his historical image, wrote his confidant, the intellectual Francis Lieber, April 16, "Matters here are settling down more calmly today. The new President has quietly entered upon his duties, and the great governmental machinery, notwithstanding the fearful shock, is working firmly and regularly in its accustomed channels. No cabinet changes will be made for the present, and all will work harmoniously. This sad event may have the effect to open the eyes of all to the danger of the times and the absolute need of a strong and firm policy, but not a cruel one towards our unscrupulous enemies. But our greatest danger is that popular demagogues may take advantage of the present excitement to do things which we shall all wish undone . . ." Two days later Halleck wrote again, "I have known President Johnson for some three years and have had considerable intercourse with him. I like him very much, and think he will make a firm and judicious chief magistrate. He was the only civil-military governor of a rebel state who gave us no trouble and who had the good sense to always act right. This speaks volumes for him. . . . Probably his policy will not be as lenient towards rebels as that of Mr. Lincoln, but, perhaps after all, it may be the better."[72]

The Peace Democrat, James A. Bayard, wrote Barlow that while he would

70. Schurz to Frederick Altheus, June 25, 1865, Carl Schurz Papers, State Historical Society of Wisconsin, (translated from German.)

71. Barlow to T.J. Barnett, Apr. 28, 1865, S.L.M. Barlow Papers, HEH.

72. Halleck, to Lieber, April 16 and 18, 1865, Lieber Collection, HEH.

not prejudge Johnson, "I have more fears than hopes as to his course. . . ." On the other hand, Montgomery Blair, an opponent of the Radicals, informed Barlow: "In my view of the matter, the Democracy, if they are true to their own principles, must sustain Andrew Johnson. . . . There is no issue now in our politics but reconstruction."[73]

Ben Wade, as Chairman of the Committee on the Conduct of the War, a body controlled by the Radical Republicans, had written the President on April 15 that they had just returned from Richmond, where they had seen and heard much which they wished to impart to him at once.[74]

Although a few eccentrics or bitter Copperheads braved the peril of assault to express hostility to the memory of Lincoln, some Radical Republicans, who remembered the Wade-Davis Manifesto and felt alarmed by the Hampton Roads Conference and the speech of April 11, betrayed their mean-hearted satisfaction that the way now lay open for such measures as Thad Stevens, Ben Wade and Sumner were known to demand. Representative George W. Julian of Indiana, then a prime Radical, spent most of the afternoon of the day of Lincoln's murder at a political caucus held to consider "the necessity for a new Cabinet, and a line of policy less conciliatory than that of Mr. Lincoln;" and while everybody was shocked at the murder, the feeling was universal, Julian wrote later, "that the accession of Johnson to the Presidency would prove a godsend to the country." He added that, "aside from his known tenderness to the rebels, Lincoln's last public avowal, only three days before his death, of adherence to the plan of reconstruction he had announced in December, 1863, was highly repugnant to the extremists in Congress." The Radical leaders believed that Johnson was now ready to follow a very different course of action.[75]

In response to Wade's request, the President on April 16 met the Committee on the Conduct of the War in the Treasury Department. Julian relates that an illuminating colloquy took place: "He received us with decided cordiality, and Mr. Wade said to him: 'Johnson, we have faith in you. By the gods, there will be no trouble now in running the government!' The President thanked him, and went on to define his well-remembered policy at that time. 'I hold,' he said, 'that robbery is a crime; rape is a crime; murder is a crime; treason is a crime, and the crime must be punished. Treason must be made infamous, and traitors must be impoverished.' "[76] It is possible that the Radicals, in their desire to control Johnson, had misunderstood their man, or that in the sad aftermath of

73. James A. Bayard to Barlow, Apr. 18, 1865, S.L.M. Barlow Papers, HEH.
74. M. Blair to Barlow, Apr. 18, 1865, S.L.M. Barlow Papers, HEH.
75. Julian, George W., *Political Recollections*, Chicago, 1884, 225.
76. *Ibid.*, 260-261.

Andrew Johnson

the assassination Johnson was reacting from his first deep emotions. But it is clear that the Radicals were placing the President under the heaviest pressure. The impetuous and strong-tempered Zach Chandler of Michigan wrote his wife on April 23, "As there is to be a struggle for the supremacy in the future, much depends upon the formation of the Cabinet of Mr. Johnson. The Blairs are trying their utmost to get control and to turn out Stanton, while we want to clean out the whole Blair tribe. . . . Johnson is *right.* He now thinks just as we do and desires to carry out radical measures and punish treason and traitors, but much depends upon his surroundings. Preston King eats and sleeps with Johnson and is all right except upon Seward. But he stands by Seward and is not right upon that point. Had Mr. Lincoln's policy been carried out, we should have had Jeff Davis, Toombs, etc., back in the Senate at the next session of Congress, but now their chances to stretch hemp are better than for the Senate of the U. S. So mote it be. I have had several conferences with Mr. Johnson and *all* were satisfactory, [he] having been associated with us on the Committee on the Conduct of the War. Our relations *were* perhaps as intimate as any others, but after the 4th of March trouble the Blairs rushed in and took possession, and what the result may be God knows. . . ." In another letter, also dated April 23, Chandler informed his wife, "The Blairs are making a desperate effort to control President Johnson; but thus far I think without success. This morning I called upon the President and found Mr. Blair there. He and I took up Sherman's surrender and the President listened for half-an-hour when B. left *and then* the President took hold of the matter and condemned it worse than I did. . . . We are running our Committee on the Conduct of the War every day. . . ."[77]

Montgomery Blair also told of this meeting with the President and Chandler. He accused Stanton of hoping "to get hold of Johnson as he did of Lincoln by making himself a leader in attacking and denouncing the supposed rival of Johnson's for the succession as he did with Lincoln in attacking McClellan. . . . It is plainly an attempt to take advantage of a blunder of Sherman to recommend themselves (Stanton and Halleck) to Johnson as the great antagonists of the Copperhead Candidate, as they already call him, for Succession. I met Chandler of Michigan, one of Stanton's satellites, at Johnson's room on Sunday morning, and he said to Johnson a lady had just told me I ought not to complain of Sherman's doings. It was a providential blunder as it destroyed the Copperhead candidate for the Presidency. . . ."[78]

One of the most penetrating comments on the consequences of the assassination was made by the journalist Noah Brooks in a newspaper letter from

77. Chandler to his wife, Apr. 23, 1865, Zachariah Chandler Papers, LC.
78. M. Blair to Barlow, Washington, April 28, 1865, S.L.M. Barlow Papers, HEH.

Washington, dated April 27, 1865, and headed "A Radical President."[79] "The radicals in Washington," he wrote, "appeared to think that they have drawn an elephant in the new President. When the late President was alive, they omitted no opportunity for criticism, and no chance which promised success to an attack was neglected. Now that the radicals have their President, however, they are not altogether satisfied. . . . Lincoln used to say that the responsibilities of office had the effect to make men conservative, and Johnson's friends begin to fear that such will be the result upon him. There are now several little cliques of the ultra men who are attempting to get control of Johnson just as some such men tried to get control of President Lincoln when he came into office. It remains to be seen into whose hands Johnson will fall, or whether he will, like Lincoln, offend and anger those who are thereby to be made his opponents by refusing to be controlled by any. Certain it is, however, that the men who are near the new President and who have any designs upon him are those whom we are wont to call radical; they will at least nominally have the control of the administration. It will afford us, who have stood by the former president against captious criticism and ill-natured attacks, some sort of satisfaction to see how they will manage matters with their former champion, who is radical if nothing else. Many think that if Seward should recover and stay in the Cabinet, he will virtually control Johnson. Seward is sagacious and sound, but Preston King would like his place and is at work to secure it. It should not be understood that any new feud is likely to arise from the sudden change in the presidency." Rather, he saw a continuation of the old feud which had almost resulted at one time in a drastic reconstruction of the Cabinet, intended to eject the moderate Seward and to place Chase and the extremists in control. He realized that these feuds might become much more intense.[80]

To a delegation from New Hampshire, the President talked of the trial and suffering of the war, but said he could not forecast his future policy. However, "The American people must be taught to know and understand that treason is a crime. . . . It must not be regarded as a mere difference of political opinion. It must not be excused as an unsuccessful rebellion, to be overlooked and forgiven. It is a crime before which all other crimes sink into insignificance; and in saying this it must not be considered that I am influenced by angry or revengeful feelings. Of course, a careful discrimination must be observed, for thousands have been involved in this rebellion who are only technically guilty of the crime of treason. They have been deluded and deceived and have been

79. The letter caption probably had a question-mark, "A Radical President?"—but the question-mark dropped out.

80. Brooks, Noah, mss., LC.

made the victims of the more intelligent, artful, and designing men, the instigators of this monstrous rebellion. The number of this latter class is comparatively small. The former may stand acquitted of the crime of treason—the latter never; the full penalty of their crimes should be visited upon them. To the others I would accord amnesty, leniency and mercy . . ."[81]

Saturday, April 22, a group of citizens of Indiana, led by Governor Morton, called upon Johnson in the Treasury building offices. Indiana Republicans held Johnson in considerable esteem because of his rôle in Tennessee, and the cordial amity between him and Morton. The Governor addressed the President, declaring in severely combative tones, "Each rebel is politically and criminally responsible for his action, without regard to the number who may have united with him. Nor is there any power to punish rebels collectively by reducing a State to a territorial condition, or declaring its municipal character forfeited. . . ." He called for support of the loyal elements in the rebel States and declared suffrage should be intrusted only to them.[82]

Johnson, in his reply, once more denounced treason and called for the punishment and impoverishment of traitors. However, going further, he expressed a cautionary fealty to the doctrine of State integrity and the rights of the States, saying emphatically: "Some are satisfied with the idea that the States are to be lost in territorial and other divisions—are to lose their character as States. But their life-breath has only been suspended, and it is a high constitutional obligation we have to secure each of these States in the possession and enjoyment of a republican form of Government. A State may be in the Government with a peculiar institution, and, by the operation of rebellion, lose that feature. But it was a State when it went into rebellion, and when it comes out without the institution it is still a State. I hold it as a solemn obligation in any one of these States where the rebel armies have been driven back or expelled—I care not how small the number of Union men, if enough to man the ship of State—I hold it, I say, a high duty to protect and secure to them a republican form of government. . . . If a State is to be nursed until it again gets strength, it must be nursed by its friends, and not smothered by its enemies. Now permit me to remark that, while I have opposed dissolution and disintegration on the one hand, on the other I have opposed consolidation—or the centralization of power in the hands of a few. . . ."[83] This was a refreshing statement indeed to those who wished to retain the old balance of government, and to follow in the moderate path of the resolute but magnanimous Lincoln.

A Negro delegation which called at this time told the President, "The

81. *American Annual Cyclopedia*, 1865, 800-801.
82. Foulke, William Dudley, *Life of Oliver P. Morton*, Indianapolis, 1877, I, 440-441.
83. *American Annual Cyclopedia*, 1865, 801-802.

colored American asks but two things. He asks, after proving his devotion to his country in responding to her call in the hour of her sorest trial, and after demonstrating, upon many hotly-contested battlefields, his manhood and valor, that he have, first, complete emancipation, and secondly, full equality before American law. Your past history, as connected with the rebellion, gives us full assurance that in your hands our cause shall receive no detriment, and that our liberty and rights will be fully protected and sustained."

Johnson made a friendly reply. He declared that the Negroes would find in his and their past history the guaranty of his future conduct toward them. "Where the colored people know me best, they have confidence in me. No man can charge me with having proved false to the promises I have made to any class of the people in my public life. . . ." He added the generous statement that, although it was hard for the Negro to understand that they had friends on the south side of the line, "they have, and they are as faithful and staunch as any north of the line . . ."[84] This was refreshing, too, and breathed the very spirit of Lincoln.

Johnson received other delegations, and to a South Carolina group later on he said, "The policy, now that the rebellion is suppressed, is not to restore the State through military rule, but by the people." Thus, within a few weeks of Lincoln's death, the new President had publicly demonstrated that he repudiated one of the most brutal and evil Radical ideas, that the former Confederate states were no longer part of the Union. The schism between Johnson and the Radicals is generally dated later by most students, but the incipient division, with portents of future conflict, was at least visible within days of his ascendancy.

On Sunday, April 16, the Cabinet had met and Stanton brought up his draft of a Reconstruction plan, much the same that he had presented to Lincoln only two days before, though with some changes. That evening at the War Department, Stanton read his document to Welles and a number of Congressmen. Secretary Welles wrote that Senator Sumner interrupted and "requested Mr. Stanton to stop, until he could understand whether any provision was made for enfranchising the colored man. Unless the black man was given the right to vote, Mr. Sumner said his freedom was a mockery." Stanton replied that differences existed among their friends on this subject, and it would be unwise in his judgment to press the proposal just then. Thereupon Sumner blustered that "he would not proceed a step unless the black man had his rights. . . ."[85] But apparently Stanton held to his objection.

The general welcome given Andrew Johnson on his accession, outside of

84. *Ibid.*, 801-802.

85. Welles, Gideon, "Lincoln on Reconstruction," typescript, John Hay Library, Brown Univ., Providence, R.I.

the politically prejudiced men, pleased many observers. "He grows steadily in public confidence and esteem," commented the New York *Tribune* on April 22. Old stories were recalled of the sad but brave persistence with which, after never enjoying the advantage of a school for a single day, he had obtained an education by his unwearied exertions and the assistance of his devoted wife. It became widely realized that he had never practised law because, after his election to the Legislature, he had insisted upon remaining in the public service. Men began to perceive that he possessed some rare qualifications for his vast responsibilities. In the Reconstruction struggles now at hand he could never be attacked as "Yankee," for he was a Southerner born and bred. Indeed, he had never lived in a free State until he helped make Tennessee free, though he had held a few slaves. The poor whites of the South would regard him as a natural ally. Since he had always voted against protective tariffs, again a prospective issue, it would be hard to make anybody believe that he favored special favors to industry or trade. He knew the rebellion, its leaders and their objects as few men did. Having never manifested any special regard for the colored people, he could not be taunted as a "nigger-lover." He had nevertheless shown that he was not antagonistic to the black folk.

Yet Johnson faced an angrier crisis, and more difficult problems than perhaps any other successor to the Presidency would have to meet until Vice-President Harry Truman suddenly succeeded Franklin D. Roosevelt.

Prompt action upon Reconstruction was plainly needed. The Southern people were anxiously awaiting some announcement of terms, and the Northerners were eagerly awaiting the opportunity to resume a more normal life. While the planting season at the South was rapidly expiring, enterprises there remained disorganized and apprehensive. Many former Confederates were not certain that they could safely return to their families. Numerous freedmen were still deserting plantations where they were needed, and fleeing to towns where they were idle. A typical news dispatch of April 13, 1865, from Raleigh, N. C., declared, "Great anxiety prevails everywhere among the people. The State is thoroughly impoverished, and distress and starvation must overtake them unless an immediate cessation of hostilities affords the opportunity to plant a crop during the present spring. Days, even hours, are now more precious than gold to those who must depend upon this year's crop for support for themselves and families."[86]

One of the first problems of the Johnson Administration was to bring about the surrender of other Confederate forces in the field, especially that of Joe Johnston in North Carolina, and also to effect the capture of the fleeing

86. New York *Tribune*, April 27, 1865.

Confederate government and its complete dissolution. By April 15, Sherman was advancing from Goldsboro, N. C., and his cavalry held Chapel Hill and Durham Station. Johnston was pulling back on roads from Hillsboro to Greensboro. Halleck, shortly to be in command of the armies around Richmond and in southern Virginia, blocked Johnston to the North. Stoneman's cavalry was to the West. On April 14 Johnston had written Sherman regarding "a temporary suspension of active operations . . . the object being to permit the civil authorities to enter into the needful arrangements to terminate the existing war. . . ."[87]

Sherman at once replied from Raleigh that he was empowered "to arrange with Johnston any terms for the suspension of hostilities . . . and would be willing to confer with him for that object. . . ." Already, it is evident that Sherman was going further than Grant had done at Appomattox and certainly his reply showed a marked departure from the policy indicated in Grant's letters to Lee, calling for surrender alone. Sherman did add, "I undertake to abide by the same terms and conditions as were made by General Grant . . ."[88] Altogether, his message was less firm and decisive than Grant's communication to Lee.

On the 15th, Stanton telegraphed Sherman of Lincoln's assassination. Sherman had assured Grant and Stanton the previous day that he would adhere to the terms that Grant had given Lee, and be careful not to "complicate any points of civil policy. . . ."[89] But it became clear within a few days that he would "complicate" the civil policy of the government a great deal.

In a conference at Greensboro, N. C., with Davis, Breckinridge, Mallory, and Reagan, Johnston persuaded Davis to outline a proposal for a meeting to discuss the terms of an armistice. Johnston signed his letter and sent it, as we have noted, to Sherman on April 14.[90] Then Sherman and Johnston met at the Bennett house near Durham Station on April 17 in what would prove a monotonous and controversial conference. At the outset, Sherman informed the Confederate general of the assassination, news which elicited from Johnston the statement that this was a national calamity, which we have already quoted. Later, Johnston wrote that Sherman added, "in a manner that carried conviction of sincerity," that he earnestly wished to protect the South from such devastation as the prolongation of the war would make inevitable; and, as a means of hastening its termination so far as the armies they commanded could be helpful, "he offered me such terms as those given to General

87. *O.R.*, I, xlvii, pt. 3, 206-207.
88. *Ibid.*, 207.
89. *Ibid.*, 221.
90. Johnston, Joseph E., *Narrative of Military Operations*, *op.cit.*, 399; Mallory, *Diary*, *op.cit.*, April 14.

Lee. . . ."[91] In this Sherman was undoubtedly taking the correct course, and following the example of Grant. He was later to declare, it seems quite correctly, that he had not received Lincoln's instructions of March 3 to Grant suggesting that no conference be held with the enemy except for "capitulation."[92] Nevertheless, Sherman began by demanding that Johnston accept the same terms as Lee. Johnston refused, pointing to the difference in relative positions as a reason why such a capitulation would not be justified. Johnston tells us in his autobiography that he intimated to Sherman that "instead of a partial suspension of hostilities, we might, as other generals had done, arrange the terms of a permanent peace. . . ."[93] Johnston and Sherman proceeded to discuss possible terms and, according to Johnston, agreed on most points, except that Sherman did not consent to an amnesty for President Davis and officers of his Cabinet.

Before daybreak on April 18, the Confederate Cabinet members, Breckinridge and Reagan, met with Johnston. After Reagan wrote down the terms discussed the previous day, Johnston and Breckinridge then met with Sherman, who listened to Reagan's record, and then made his own written list of the terms, which differed from Johnston's only in being fuller. When the generals signed, a copy was sent to both Presidents. Davis approved these terms within a few days.[94]

Thus it appears, and the conclusion is not really contradicted by Sherman's later comments, that the meeting at the Bennett house produced not only a talk on army surrender, but a discussion of the nature of the final peace, involving negotiations between the two warring peoples. This discussion went to such lengths that it was submitted to the Confederate President as well as to Washington! After all, Davis had not been consulted as to Lee's surrender at Appomattox, even though it had been a political and not merely a military event, so that the Durham Station arrangements would have amounted to a peace treaty between the Union and the Confederates, involving the future of the nation.

Sherman's accounts of this transaction actually do not differ substantially from the account here given, except that they assign to Sherman a larger rôle than appears in Johnston's own records. In his formal report, written with bitter overtones, Sherman called the talks frank and soldierlike. Sherman said that Johnston admitted the terms given Lee were "magnanimous and all that

91. Johnston, *ut supra*, 134.

92. Lincoln, *Collected Works*, VIII, 330-331. The message to Grant is in Lincoln's script, though signed by Stanton.

93. Johnston, *Narrative*, *op.cit.*, 403.

94. *Ibid.*, 404-407; Johnston to "My Dear Maury," March 21, 1879, Chicago Hist. Soc., J.E. Johnston Papers; Letter Mar. 30, 1868, Western Reserve Hist. Soc., Cleveland.

he could ask, but he did want some general concession that would enable him to allay the natural anxieties of his followers, and enable him to maintain control over them" until they could be returned to the area of their homes, thereby saving North Carolina the devastation that would be inevitable if he dispersed his troops then and there without providing for their urgent wants, and subjecting them to possible pursuit as they scattered over the broad State. He also wished to have some general provision made to alleviate the fate of all the Confederate armies that remained. Sherman tells us that, "I never made any concession as to his own army, or assumed to deal finally and authoritatively in regard to any other, but it did seem to me that there was present a chance for peace that might be deemed valuable to the Government of the United States. . . ."[95]

In their second talk on the 18th, Sherman says Johnston satisfied him as to the power of the Confederate general to disband other forces than his own. Sherman went on to explain that his consent to Johnston's points was based upon Lincoln's message of 1864, his proclamation of amnesty, Grant's terms to Lee, the invitation to the Virginia legislature, and "a firm belief that I had been fighting to re-establish the Constitution of the United States;" and finally, but not least, upon the universal desire to close a war which was now without means of organized resistance. These, he declared, were the leading facts that "induced me to pen the 'memorandum' of April 18."[96]

Sherman elaborated his testimony when he spoke to the Joint Committee on the Conduct of the War, stating: "I had had frequent correspondence with the late President of the United States, with the Secretary of War, with General Halleck, and with General Grant; and the general impression left upon my mind was that if a settlement could be made consistent with the Constitution of the United States, the laws of Congress, and the proclamation of the President, they would be not only willing but pleased thus to terminate the war by one single stroke of the pen. . . ."[97]

In the discussion of April 18, Sherman testifies that the points raised included: the question whether the States were to be dissevered; the question whether their people were to be denied representation in Congress, so that, as some Southern extremists put it, they might become slaves to the people of the North. Understandably, but unwisely, the impulsive Sherman states that he answered "No; we desire that you shall regain your position as citizens of the United States, free and equal to us in all respects, and with representations, upon the condition of submission to the lawful authority of the United States

95. *O.R.*, I, xlvii, pt. 1, 31-32.
96. *Ibid.*, 33.
97. *Report of the Joint Committee on the Conduct of the War*, Washington, 1865, Vol.III, 3-4.

as defined by the Constitution, the United States courts, and the authorities of the United States supported by those courts." It seems strange that by the time he gave his testimony, Sherman had not realized that these questions were beyond his province to decide on or even discuss.[98] To the Committee Sherman reported that he had rejected Reagan's memorandum "at once." But the record hardly supports this statement. He told the Committee that the talk went on in the conference at the Bennett place. "There was universal assent that slavery was dead as anything could be; that it was one of the issues of the war long since determined. . . . As to reconstruction, I told them [the Confederates] I did not know what the views of the administration were. Mr. Lincoln, up to that time, had in letters and by telegrams to me, encouraged me, by all the words that could be used in general terms, to believe in not only his willingness but his desire that I should make terms with civil authorities, governors, and legislators, even as far back as 1863. . . ."[99] In the light of all we now know, this later statement seems extreme. There is no firm evidence that Lincoln wished Sherman to make such terms, and the idea that he did stands in opposition to all known evidence.

In time, the supposition grew that Lincoln had told Sherman what to do concerning peace during their conference on the *River Queen* in late March. Neither Grant nor Lincoln, nor Admiral Porter, indicates that this was true, and Sherman himself never said so. In his Committee testimony, Sherman admitted that the talk about terms contained "Nothing definite; it was simply a matter of general conversation; nothing specific and definite." His official report does not mention the conference. In fact, in this report Sherman states, "Up to that hour I had never received one word of instruction, advice or counsel as to 'plan of policy' of Government looking to a restoration of peace in the rebel States of the South. . . ."[100] In a long letter to Lincoln's friend, Isaac N. Arnold, however, Sherman describes the *River Queen* meetings at length. Most of the discussion there concerned military plans. Sherman admits that he ought not to attempt reproducing the words of that conversation. "I know we talked generally," he wrote, "about what was to be done when Lee and Johnston's armies were beaten and dispersed." On this point Lincoln was very full, and said that he wanted the rebels disarmed and sent home. Lincoln also declared that he contemplated no revenge or harsh measures, but quite the contrary, and that the suffering and hardships of the Southern people in the war should make them now submissive to law. Sherman tells us that "I cannot say that Mr. Lincoln or anybody else used this language at the time, but I know

98. *Ibid.*, 4.
99. *Ibid.*, 5.
100. *O.R.*, I, xlvii, pt. 1, 33.

I left his presence with the conviction that he had in his mind, or that his Cabinet had, some plan of settlement, ready for application the moment Lee and Johnston were defeated. . . ."[101]

It is clear that Sherman and his defenders do not say that Lincoln had dictated the controversial terms. In fact, it is clear that the Confederates had a more specific role than did Lincoln. But Sherman, over and over again, says his terms were within the spirit of what he thought Lincoln wanted.[102] It would be tedious and needless to extend any treatment of this controversy. We may merely note that in his later *Memoirs* Sherman stated that Lincoln, speaking fully and frankly, assured him "that in his mind he was all ready for the civil reorganization of affairs at the South as soon as the war was over; and he distinctly authorized me to assure Governor Vance and people of North Carolina that, as soon as the rebel armies laid down their arms, and resumed their civil pursuits, they would at once be guaranteed all their rights as citizens of a common country; and that to avoid anarchy the State governments then in existence, with their civil functionaries, would be recognized by him as the government *de facto* till Congress could provide others. . . ."[103] This is as close to being specific as Sherman came about the talks with Lincoln.

What about these terms? The "Memorandum or basis of agreement" arranged was between Joseph E. Johnston, "commanding the Confederate Army," and Sherman. First, the existing status of armies in the field was to be maintained until further notice was given by either commanding general. Second, the existing Confederate armies were to disband and be conducted to their various State capitals where they would deposit arms and public property in the arsenal. Each officer and man would execute and file an agreement to terminate martial activities, and to abide by the action of both State and Federal authority. Available arms would be used to maintain order within the State. In the third place, the Federal executive would recognize the several State governments as soon as their officers and legislatures would take the oaths prescribed by the Constitution of the United States. Wherever conflicting State governments arose from the war, the question of legitimacy would be submitted to the Federal Supreme Court. In the fourth place, the Federal courts were to be re-established. As a fifth part of the agreement, the people and inhabitants of all the States were to be guaranteed, so far as the Executive could do so, their political rights and franchises, as well as their rights of person and property, as defined by the Constitution of the United States and

101. Sherman to Arnold, Nov. 28, 1872, Isaac N. Arnold Papers, Chicago Hist. Soc.

102. Naroll, R.S., "Lincoln and the Sherman Peace Fiasco Another Fable?", *Journal of Southern History*, Vol.XX, No.4, Nov., 1954, 459-483; Lewis, Lloyd, *Sherman, Fighting Prophet*, New York, 1932, 536ff.

103. Sherman, *Memoirs, op.cit.*, II, 327.

of the States respectively. The sixth article of agreement was that the authorities of the United States would not disturb any of the people "by reason of the late war so long as they live in peace and quiet, abstain from acts of armed hostility, and obey the laws in existence at the place of their residences." Not only was the war to cease, but it was to be followed by a general executive amnesty on condition that the Confederate armies disbanded, their arms were scattered, and peaceful pursuits were resumed by the officers and men of these forces. Not being fully empowered by their respective principals to fulfil these terms, the parties to the agreement pledged themselves, individually and officially, to obtain promptly the necessary authority and to execute the above programs. A comparison of this document, as drawn by Sherman, with the provisions listed by Reagan, Postmaster-General of the Confederacy, reveals no substantial or even minor difference. Sherman's document was somewhat longer and fuller in wording, that is all.[104]

So many points here given vary from the known policies of Lincoln, and show such political naiveté, that the whole document may easily be questioned. First of all, it is labeled both a "memorandum" and "basis of Agreement." Both principles admitted they were not fully empowered to make such an agreement, and would have to submit it to their governments.The document thus virtually recognized the Confederate government and its President, something Lincoln had never done and no responsible officer could be expected to do now. The military commanders concerned had gone too far. Lincoln had always opposed an "armistice," which is what the first provisions really implied. To send the Southern armies home with their arms appeared an open invitation to guerrilla tactics, to which Sherman and Lincoln were implacably opposed. The soldiers would await action of both State and Federal authorities and yet Sherman's plan carried a seeming recognition of the existing Confederate State governments, until their officials took the oath of allegiance. These Confederate State governments might also come into collision with Union governments already set up in several States. Parts of the agreement seemed to concede a recognition of the validity of the Confederate State governments. There could be little quarrel with the idea of re-establishing Federal courts, providing that citizens were in a state of peace. But the guarantee of political, personal and property rights could be interpreted as a re-imposition of the rights of slavery, and sometimes was, although the memorandum did not mention slavery. At this point, Sherman departed more than ever from Lincoln, who had never retreated from his determination that slavery must die. No grant of amnesty was specifically extended, but was given a broad applica-

104. *O.R.*, I, xlviii, pt. 3, 243-244; Ms. "Synopsis of the Agreement between Generals Johnston and Sherman," Western Reserve Hist. Soc., Cleveland.

tion. Although nothing was said about Confederate debts, the agreement might have been interpreted as allowing their possible recognition as valid.

In short, little was here stated that Lincoln or any Federal government could have accepted as it stood without abrogating the Administration's war aims. Although we can never know, from Lincoln's many statements and actions it seems clear that he would have done just as Johnson did in rejecting this almost puerile document.

Sherman manifested enthusiasm in sending this agreement to Washington, stating that, if approved by the President, it would produce peace from the Potomac to the Rio Grande. He boldly informed Grant or Halleck, "if you will get the President to simply indorse the copy and commission me to carry out the terms, I will follow them to the conclusion. . . ."[105] Thus a field commander was asking the President to give him authority to carry out terms to which the President had never agreed.[106]

The subsequent results of this controversial episode belong primarily to the personal biography of Sherman, but are important to history at large because of their effect on the relations of Sherman with Stanton, Andrew Johnson, Halleck and others, and because the terms, when revealed to the whole nation, had a striking effect on public sentiment, both North and South.

As Sherman later wrote in his official report, he felt certain that Lincoln would have assented to the agreement had he lived. To many it seems more probable that Lincoln would have been emphatic in his rejection of it. On April 24, a messenger with dispatches arrived at Sherman's headquarters and with him, to everyone's surprise, came General Grant. Sherman was ordered to give Johnston forty-eight hours' notice to accept surrender on the terms which prevailed at Appomattox, or hostilities would be resumed.[107]

Grant told Stanton at the time that Sherman was not surprised by this repudiation of his arrangement, but rather expected it.[108] Sherman then resumed his negotiations with Johnston on grounds comprehending the surrender of his army alone, on the same terms that Grant had given Lee. While remaining at headquarters, Grant did not humiliate Sherman by joining in the talks at the Bennett house. On the afternoon of April 26 the terms were signed.

Sherman went to Hilton Head, where on May 2 he saw in the New York papers of April 28 a dispatch of the 27th from Stanton to General Dix, and a

105. *O.R.*,I, xlviii, pt. 3, 243, Sherman to Grant or Halleck, Apr. 18, 1865.

106. For able, though controversial, secondary accounts, see Naroll, *op.cit.;* Barrett, John G., *Sherman's March Through the Carolinas*, Chapel Hill, 1956, 226ff.; Lewis, *op.cit.*, 526-572; Randall-Current, *op.cit.*, 352-353.

107. *O.R.*,I, xlvii, pt. 1, 34.

108. *Ibid.*, 293.

dispatch of Halleck's. Halleck had told Stanton April 26 from Richmond that Meade, Sheridan and Wright were acting under orders not to consider any truce, or any orders of Sherman suspending hostilities. Their troops were ordered to push forward.[109] Halleck further urged other commanders to ignore the truce. Sherman on May 7 telegraphed Halleck, "After your dispatch to Mr. Stanton of April 26 I cannot have any friendly intercourse with you. I will come to City Point tomorrow, and march with my troops and I prefer we should not meet. . . ."[110] Halleck replied, "You have not had during the war, nor have you now, a warmer friend and admirer than myself. If, in carrying out what I knew to be the wishes of the War Dept. in regard to your armistice, I used language which has given you offense, it was unintentional and I deeply regret it. If fully aware of the circumstances under which I acted, I am certain you would not attribute to me any improper motives. It is my wish to continue to regard and receive you as a personal friend. With this statement, I leave the matter in your hands. . . ."[111] Actually, Sherman and Halleck had been quite friendly, but now Sherman was hotly repulsing a presumed slur upon his actions. He accused Halleck of going beyond the due limits of his authority and intimated that Stanton was guilty of offenses which he left vaguely undefined. Even in his official report he wrote that Stanton's attitude was "too much," adding: "I turn from the subject with feelings too strong for words, and merely record that so much mischief was never before embraced in so small a space as in the newspaper paragraph headed 'Sherman's truce disregarded,' authenticated as 'official' by Mr. Secretary Stanton, and published in the New York papers of April 28. . . ."[112]

Sherman apparently let loose to anyone who would listen. Admiral John A. Dahlgren was a sympathetic listener. On May 3, Dahlgren wrote that the General exploded "instanter" and "said Halleck had not been under fire once, that he could whip him and the Army of the Potomac; . . . All the little dogs are loose on Sherman. How they bark! He is a great sinner against the mass of respectable mediocrities,—the fossils, and the smooth trimmers . . ." The Admiral felt Sherman was "in a magnificent passion. . . ."[113]

Sherman later wrote Schofield of snubbing Stanton at the Grand Review by refusing to shake hands; "the matter being more than official, a personal insult, and, I have resented it and shall continue to do so. No man I don't care who he is shall insult me publicly or arraign my motives. . . .[114]

109. *Ibid.*, 311.
110. Sherman to Halleck, May 7, 1865, Sherman Papers, HEH.
111. Halleck to Sherman, May 9, 1865, Richmond, Nicholson Collection, HEH.
112. *O.R.*,I, xlvii, pt. 1, 38.
113. Dahlgren, M.V., *Memoir of Admiral John A.Dahlgren*, Boston, 1882, 510-511.
114. Sherman to Schofield, May 28, 1865, Sherman Papers, HEH.

The dispatch of Stanton to Dix which so deeply pained and irritated Sherman described his terms to Johnston, adding that after he had entered into this so-called "basis for peace," with the rebel general, in the presence of the rebel general Breckinridge, a Cabinet meeting was held at which the President, Grant, Stanton, and the entire Cabinet disapproved the terms. Grant was sent South.[115]

Grant at the time wrote that he read the agreement carefully before submitting it to the President and Stanton, "and felt satisfied that it could not possibly be approved. . . ." The Cabinet meeting, as Grant informed Sherman late in April, resulted in "a disapproval by the President of the basic terms laid down, in a disapproval of the negotiations altogether, except for the surrender of the Army commanded by Johnston . . . the rebels know well the terms upon which they can have peace and just when negotiations can commence, namely: when they lay down their arms and submit to the laws of the United States. Mr. Lincoln gave them full assurance of what he would do, I believe, in his conference with commissioners met in Hampton Roads. . . ."[116]

Sherman had to explain the situation to commanders under him. To General Thomas he wrote that his terms had been misconstrued, and that Johnston had asked him to help "to prevent his army and people breaking up into Guerrilla Bands . . . But the more I reflect the more satisfied I am that my dealing with the people of the South magnanimously will restore 4/5 of them at once to the condition of good citizens, leaving us only to deal with the remainder. . . ."[117]

Stanton wrote Grant on April 25: "The arrangement between Sherman and Johnston meets with universal disapprobation. No one of any class or shade of opinion approves it. I have not known as much surprise and discontent at anything that has happened during the war. . . . The hope of the country is that you may repair the misfortune occasioned by Sherman's negotiations." Grant did take some remedial steps, but vestiges of ill-feeling persisted.

Beyond much doubt, Sherman acted upon an impulse of generous good will for the Southern people, and a humane desire to halt the spilling of blood. His intentions had been completely honest, patriotic and high-minded. The President had dealt with him fairly; though he may have felt, as we must, that it is difficult to understand how Sherman could have been so misled by his own inclinations and by the opposing generals.

One glimpse into the reasons which inspired Sherman's course is perhaps afforded by a letter he wrote to Chase on May 6: "I am not yet prepared to

115. *O.R.*, I, xlviii, pt. 3, 285-286.
116. Grant to Sherman, April 21, 1865, J.P. Morgan Library, New York.
117. *Battles and Leaders,* Extra-illustrated ed., HEH, Vol.XVII, Sherman to Thomas, May 2, 1865.

receive the Negro on terms of political equality," he declared, "for the reasons that it will arouse passions and prejudices at the North, which, superadded to the causes yet dormant at the South, might rekindle the war whose fires are now dying out, and by skillful management might be kept down. . . . I, who have felt the past war as bitterly and keenly as any man could, confess myself afraid of a new war, and a new war is bound to result from the action you suggest of giving to the enfranchised Negroes so large a share in the delicate task of putting the Southern States in practical working relations with the general Government. . . ." [118] One difficulty was that Sherman apparently overestimated his own powers of "skillful management." Later he told a fellow officer: "I believe if the South had been promptly allowed some approximate representation as a concession to principle, they would have been so impressed with the honesty and fairness of the thing that a fair proportion would have acted from the beginning with the republican party."[119]

Not a few men were deeply disconcerted by Sherman's action. A Union officer from Virginia wrote: "I hope Sherman will be relieved for offering such terms to Johnston. What Gen. Grant gave Lee is sufficient for traitors, and they ought not to have as good since the murder of Mr. Lincoln."[120]

Montgomery Blair could not understand the occurrence; "It is the most incomprehensible thing that Sherman should have committed such a *faux pas*. He talked altogether in a different vein and was too much disposed to severity, I thought, when he met the President and Grant at City Point lately. . . ."[121]

The able and temperate Jacob D. Cox was highly resentful of the course taken by Stanton and Halleck. He particularly emphasized the fact that Stanton's dispatch did not mention that the memorandum had no binding force without the approval of the President, and sharply termed the Stanton account "ignorant, biased and very prejudicial to Sherman."[122]

We may also hazard a guess that Sherman's personal attacks upon Stanton and Halleck were perhaps his way of giving vent to his chagrin and vexation, although the central target of his wrath and disappointment was the rejection of his plan by everyone in Washington, including Grant and the President.

During the long halt or pause of Sherman's army, and as news of the capture of Richmond and surrender of Lee came in, rumor upon rumor swept the Union forces in North Carolina and the civilians of the area, reaching the

118. *O.R.*, I, xlvii, pt. 3, 410-411, Sherman to Chase, May 6, 1865.

119. Sherman to Maj. Willard Warner, Jan. 18, 1866, William T. Sherman Papers, Illinois State Hist. Libr., Springfield.

120. John M. Berry to Barlow, April 27, 1865, S.L.M. Barlow Papers, HEH.

121. M. Blair to Barlow, Apr. 26, 1865, S.L.M. Barlow Papers, HEH.

122. Cox, Jacob D., *Military Reminiscences of the Civil War*, New York, 1900, II, 495-508.

credulous ears of many excited men and especially influencing them in predicting new troop movements—half of them suggesting a direct march home by way of Richmond, and half of them a fresh offensive against Joe Johnston.[123] The news of Lincoln's assassination struck many suspicious soldiers as possibly another hoax.[124] When it was confirmed, some Union soldiers angrily forgot the truce, seized their arms and forgetful of orders, and heedless of officers, advanced to the front. "A single gun might have opened a conflict involving the whole army, in which no quarter would have been asked or given." But as wiser counsels prevailed, the hotheads went reluctantly to the rear.[125]

The North Carolinians were reported in "pitiable condition," but Northern soldiers came to the aid of at least those who professed Union leanings.[126] The Confederate soldiers were in equally pitiable plight. They had a full share of manly hardihood, and of devotion to what they deemed their convictions; by their valor as soldiers they had won general esteem and admiration. In their butternut jeans, which by courtesy were known as a uniform, and their broad-brimmed, gray, slouchy hats, wrote the historian Headley, "they looked anything but soldierly. . . . Yet amid all these hardships and discouragements they were courageous, self-reliant, even hopeful. . . ."[127] When news of Johnston's final surrender came, many of them were utterly dejected. "They scarcely had anything to say all day," wrote one man in his diary.[128] A Union veteran wrote, however, that when the birds awoke him with the day, "I never heard them sing so sweetly, and never saw them flit about so merrily." He added that "the green groves in which we were camped, had a peculiar beauty and freshness, and as the sun rose above the [Raleigh] steeples, it seemed as if we could float right up with it."[129]

A young refugee in Hillsboro made a spirited entry in her diary: "Gen. Johnston *has surrendered his army!* We have no army now—we have been overpowered—outnumbered, but thank God we have not been whipped—Did I ever think to live to see this day: After all the misery and anguish of the four past years—Think of all our sacrifices—of broken hearts, and desolated homes —of our *noble, glorious dead*—, and say for what? *Reconstruction!* how the very word galls—Can we ever live in peace with the desecrators of our homes

123. Capt. Robinson to Charlie Abbott, William Culbertson Robinson Papers, Illinois State Hist. Soc., and courtesy of Ralph G. Newman, Apr. 25, 1865, Holly Springs, N.C.
124. *Ibid.*
125. Headley, F.Y., *Marching through Georgia*, Chicago, 1890, 427.
126. Robinson Papers, Illinois State Historical Society.
127. Headley, *op.cit.*, 433.
128. Porter, Albert Quincy, Mississippi Archives, Jackson, Miss.
129. Loring Armstrong to G.F. Cram, Elmhurst, Ill., April 28, 1865, and to his mother on same date, Armstrong Letters in private collection, Oak Park, Ill.

and the murderers of our fathers, brothers and sons—*Never*—We are bound to rise again—My God, is it thy will that we should be *Conquered?* . . ."[130]

General Johnston had to telegraph to what remaining Southern governors he could reach: "The disaster in Virginia; the capture of all our workshops for the preparation of ammunition and repairing of arms; the improbability of recruiting our little army, opposed by more than ten times its number; or of supplying it except by robbing our own citizens, destroyed all hope of successful war. I have therefore made a military convention with General Sherman to terminate hostilities in North and South Carolina, Georgia and Florida. I made this convention to spare the blood of the gallant little army committed to me, to prevent further sufferings of our people by the devastation and ruin inevitable from the marches of invading armies, and to avoid the evils of waging hopeless war."[131]

The collapse and surrender of other Confederate pockets may be briefly dismissed, but their resistance had an emotional significance, and the memory of the stand they made affected the future of the district and section. A lamentable amount of confusion often appeared. As late as April 26, a Louisiana cavalryman sent his wife word from Alabama that his detachment had just received glorious news to the effect that Lee had fought a great battle with Grant and had killed a great number of Yankees; also that Grant had asked for an armistice, to which Lee had agreed. He reported the further "news" that since the death of Lincoln a hundred thousand of Grant's army had deserted. To cap the climax, intelligence had come that Johnston and Beauregard had whipped Sherman badly.[132] Just how could such preposterous canards circulate in the defeated West?

A Yankee soldier, furious over Lincoln's death, wrote of the dire abuse of Northern prisoners at Andersonville, while in Macon, Ga., Confederates were being paroled at a great pace.[133] By May 6, this Yankee found that in Augusta, Ga., the Northern and Southern soldiers already were mingling freely, smoking and chatting. Another Yankee in Georgia, near Columbus, described a jubilee meeting of Negro camp-followers.[134]

A few miles north of Mobile, the Confederate General Dick Taylor met E.R.S. Canby of the Union forces on April 30, and within a few minutes agreed on a truce. When news shortly came in of Johnston's surrender, Canby and

130. Diary of Elizabeth Collier, Southern Hist. Coll., Univ. of N.C. Library.

131. J.E.Johnston, Greensboro, N.C., to Govs. Brown, McGrath, and Milton, Apr. 30, 1865, HEH Miscellaneous.

132. Edwin Leet letter to his wife of Apr. 26, 1865, Edwin Leet Letters, Louisiana State Univ., Dept. of Archives.

133. Gilpin, E.N., Diary, LC.

134. Mitchell, C.D., Extract from *Field Notes of the Civil War*, ms. LC.

Taylor met again on May 4 to make their agreement official. Taylor dated his surrender May 8, when paroles were accepted at Citronelle, Ala., some forty miles north of Mobile. The terms were identical with those of Appomattox, although Taylor retained control of railroads and steamers to expedite the task of returning troops home. Many farewells were delivered. General Forrest issued his in the tone that might have been expected: "That we are beaten is a self-evident fact, and any further resistance on our part would be justly regarded as the very height of folly and rashness . . . The cause for which you have so long and so manfully struggled, and for which you have braved dangers, endured privations and sufferings, and made so many sacrifices, is today hopeless. The Government which we sought to establish and perpetuate is at an end . . . Fully realizing and feeling that such is the case, it is your duty and mine to . . . submit to the 'powers that be,' and to aid in restoring peace and establishing law and order throughout the land . . . Civil war, such as you have just passed through, naturally engenders feelings of animosity, hatred, and revenge. It is our duty to divest ourselves of all such feelings toward those with whom we have so long contested, and heretofore so widely but honestly differed . . . Whatever your responsibilities may be to Government, to society, or to individuals, meet them like men . . . You have been good soldiers, you can be good citizens. . . ."[135]

Elsewhere, rebels were laying down their arms in small batches and units from Florida to Missouri. Facing a hopeless situation, despite some demands that he continue the fight, E. Kirby-Smith beyond the Mississippi surrendered his forces on May 26 when General Buckner brought the summons approved by General Osterhaus in New Orleans;[136] and Smith signed the terms on June 2. Finally, out near lonely Fort Towson in Indian Territory, just north of the Texas line, Brigadier-General Stand Watie, three-quarters Cherokee, surrendered his ragtail remnant, the last significant Confederate land detachment to yield. On July 4, the spectacular cavalry raider, Jo Shelby, led his men across the Rio Grande to inflict new losses in final adventurous blows before allowing their flags and guidons to sink beneath the waters.

At last, all the gray hosts were gone—hosts that had numbered in all perhaps three-quarters of a million or more. No precise figure is possible. They had made a record of gallant devotion, self-sacrificing valor, and intelligently directed effort and ability that commanded the admiration of a host of historians, orators, and poets who later chronicled their deeds.

While the Southern army was collapsing, the Confederate government was in flight. Following its departure from Richmond by train, Davis had set up

135. *O.R.*, I, xlix, pt. 2, 1289-1290.
136. *O.R.*, I, xlviii, pt. 2, 600-601.

the semblance of a capital in Danville, Va., with headquarters in a Main Street mansion. Official word of Lee's surrender did not arrive in Danville until the afternoon of Monday, April 10. The government would have to shift again. As rumors were rife in the North[137] as to Davis's whereabouts, and as Lincoln hinted he would not mind if the Confederate President got away, the ever more diminished Southern government left for Greensboro, N.C. When the news from Appomattox had come in, at first those who read the message were mute, comprehending the solemnity of the hour, and the gravity of the trials facing them. Then, disconsolate, resigned to suffering, but still resolute in spirit, they turned to the responsibilities just ahead. Trudging through darkness, rain, and mud, the disorganized Confederate government boarded the cars, leaving behind disgruntled civilians and soldiers who could not board the train. On its way to Greensboro the train narrowly missed being taken by Federal cavalry. Arriving at that town, the refugees could not find adequate accommodations. A bed was found for the unwell President, but others had to adjust themselves to a "dilapidated passenger-car."[138] The Secretary of the Treasury, Trenholm, who was very ill, was cared for in a fine private home. Despite this, Greensboro was an hospitable exception in the long and somewhat aimless trek of the fleeing Confederate "government."

The "Confederate treasure," as it is called, of some $500,000 under a naval guard, stayed only a day in Greensboro and then went on, eventually arriving at Washington, Ga.[139] Here the funds from Richmond banks were deposited in vaults, and the rest paid out for various expenses and to soldiers. Mrs. Davis joined her husband near Dublin, Ga.

Davis had written his wife from Charlotte on April 23 that the issue before him was very painful, for he must choose between "the long night of oppression" certain to follow the return of the South to the Union, and the carnage and suffering to ensue if resistance continued, such resistance certain to be useless unless the people rose *en masse.* "I think my judgment is undisturbed by any pride of opinion," wrote this proud, self-willed man. "I have prayed to our Heavenly Father to give me wisdom and fortitude equal to the demands

137. Mallory, S.R., *Diary*, Southern Hist. Coll., Univ. of N.C. Library.

138. *Ibid.*

139. Hanna, A.J., *Flight Into Oblivion*, Richmond, 1938. For other accounts, see Mallory, S.R., *op.cit.*, Reagan, John H., "Flight and Capture of Jefferson Davis," *Annals of the War*, Philadelphia, 1879, 147-159; Harrison, Burton K., "The Capture of Jefferson Davis," *Century*, Vol.XXVII, No.1, Nov., 1883, 130ff.; Wood, Capt. John Taylor, C.S.N., *Diary*, Southern Hist. Coll., Univ. of N.C.; Davis to Reagan, Aug. 9 and Aug. 21, 1877, Davis-Reagan Papers, Dallas Hist. Soc., Texas; Davis, Jefferson, *Rise and Fall of the Confederate Government, op.cit.*, II, 675ff. This is only a small part of the rather large body of material available on the flight. For a reasonable explanation of the so-called "Confederate treasure" see Hanna, *op.cit.*, 90-92, 115-116, 264-265; Stutler, Boyd, "The Last Confederate Payroll," *Civil War History*, Vol. VII, No. 2, June, 1961, 201-204.

of the position in which Providence has placed me. I have sacrificed so much for the cause of the Confederacy that I can measure my ability to make any further sacrifice required, and am assured there is but one to which I am not equal—My wife and my children." He was anxious only to see them saved from ignominy or want. "For myself," he concluded, "it may be that a devoted band of Cavalry will cling to me, and that I can force my way across the Mississippi, and if nothing can be done there which it will be proper to do, then I can go to Mexico, and have the world from which to choose a location. Dear Wife, this is not the fate to which I invited [you] when the future was rosecolored to us both; but I know you will bear it even better than myself, and that, of us two I alone will ever look back reproachfully on my past career. . . . Farewell, my dear, there may be better things in store for us than are now in view, but my love is all I have to offer, and that has the value of a thing long possessed, and sure not to be lost. . . ."[140]

Near dawn of May 10, not far from Irwinville, Ga., the career of Davis as President of the Confederacy ended. His capture had been almost certain, and was merely a matter of time. A rather shabby dispute followed among Northerners at once over the question whether Davis had been disguised as a woman in trying to escape,[141] and over the disposal of credit among claimants for the distinction of seizing the fugitives. All this history may well ignore. The all-sufficient fact is that Davis and many other Confederate leaders were finally in Union hands. Vice-President Stephens was arrested at his home, Liberty Hall, in Crawfordville, Ga. Davis, after being delivered to General James Harrison Wilson at Macon, Ga., was taken by sea to Norfolk, Va. Then came his detention in the famous casemate-cell in Fortress Monroe, part of the time in irons, followed by efforts of leading Federal editors and others to improve his lot, and discussion of a trial. By the summer of 1866 Davis and his family were allowed rooms at Fortress Monroe. The ridiculous supposition that possibly Davis had something to do with Lincoln's assassination was dropped. Finally, in May, 1867, Davis was taken to Richmond for a hearing on the question of a pardon. He had refused to request one, but it proved to be wise

140. Rowland, Dunbar, *Jefferson Davis, Constitutionalist*, Jackson, Miss., 1923, VI, 560-561.

141. Davis, Varina, *Jefferson Davis*, II, 641; Davis, *Rise and Fall, op.cit.*, II, 701-702; Harrison, Burton K., "The Capture of Jefferson Davis," *op.cit.*, 142-143; Reagan, "Flight and Capture of Jefferson Davis," *op.cit.*, 156-158; Diary of John Taylor Wood, Southern Hist. Coll., Univ. of N.C.; letters of Davis to Reagan, Aug. 9 and Aug. 21, 1877, in Davis-Reagan Papers, Dallas Hist. Soc.; Walthall, Major W.T., "The True Story of the Capture of Jefferson Davis," *Southern Historical Society Papers*, Vol.V, no.3, Mar. 1878, 118-121; Hanna, *op.cit.*, 100-102; Wilson, James Harrison, *Under the Old Flag*, New York, 1912, II, 297-337; *O.R.*, I, xlix, pt. 1, 370-380, for Wilson's report, and 534-539 for report of Lt.-Col. Benjamin D. Prichard, 4th Mich. Cavalry, ranking officer present at the capture; Wilson, James Harrison, "Pursuit and Capture of Jefferson Davis," *Century*, Feb. 1890, 591; Stedman, William P., "Pursuit and Capture of Jefferson Davis by an Eyewitness," *Century*, Feb. 1890, 594-596, and other sources too numerous to list.

for the Federal government to free him, a particularly politic move, in the early days of Reconstruction.

It was clear that the President, as well as the people, desired the nation's return to peaceful pursuits and a normal frame of mind as rapidly as possible. On May 10, the same day Davis was taken in Georgia, Johnson proclaimed that "armed resistance to the authority of this Government in the said insurrectionary States may be regarded as virtually at an end." Another step which displayed his sagacious anxiety to promote the nation's future and its steady return to prosperity and growth, was his May 22nd proclamation that on July 1, 1865, all seaports, with the exception of four in Texas, were to be open to commerce, and that civilian trade in all parts of the country east of the Mississippi was to be resumed with no limitations except for contraband of war. These proclamations were issued even before Confederate forces west of the Mississippi had actually surrendered.[142] On May 27, the President also ordered the discharge of all persons imprisoned by military authorities, with but few exceptions.

142. Richardson, James D., *Messages and Papers of the Presidents*, 1897, VII, 3504-3512.

12

Martial Demobilization

I read last night of the Grand Review
In Washington's chiefest avenue,
Two hundred thousand men in blue,
    I think they said that was the number—
Till I seemed to hear their tramping feet,
The bugle blast and the drum's quick beat,
The clatter of hoofs on the stony street,
The cheers of people who came to greet. . . .
Till I fell in a revery, sad and sweet,
    And then to a fitful slumber.

And I saw a phantom army come,
With never a sound of fife or drum,
But keeping time to a throbbing hum,
    Of wailing and lamentation;
The martyred heroes of Malvern Hill,
Of Gettysburg and Chancellorsville. . . .

SO WROTE Bret Harte after the Grand Review of the returning armies of the North on May 23rd and May 24th, 1865. The same note of lamentation that he sounded over the more than half-a-million men lost as mortal casualties of the sad conflict was sounded by Henry Howard Brownell in a still more comprehensive poem published in the *Atlantic Monthly*, a requiem deeply appealing in its vision of a spiritual review of the dead heroes held on celestial ground under Lincoln's august eye. Henry Mills Alden (later editor of *Harper's Magazine*), called this poem "certainly the greatest of the many called forth by the war."[1] Overly sentimental, perhaps, to the modern ear, it struck just the right contemporary note of loss mingled with hope, recalling most vividly to that generation the glory, and the tragedy, and the promise.

1. Brownell, H.H., in *Harper's History of the Rebellion*, April, 1865, 789.

The colors ripple o'erhead,
The drums roll up to the sky,
And with martial time and tread
The regiments all pass by—
The ranks of our faithful Dead,
Meeting their President's eye.

With a soldier's quiet pride
They smile o'er the perished pain,
For their anguish was not vain—
'For thee, O Father, we died!
And we did not die in vain.'

March on, your last brave mile!
Salute him, Star and Lace!
Form round him rank and file,
And look on the kind, rough face;
But the quaint and homely smile
Has a glory and a grace
It never had known erewhile—
Never, in time and space. . . .

Their task completed, the Volunteer Armies of the Union gathered in Washington more than 200,000 strong on the bright, sunny spring days of May 23 and 24, 1865. For the first time since the death of the President in April, the capital seemed really alive again. The war was over, even though the Trans-Mississippi Confederacy did not formally surrender until May 26. The new President was gripping the reins and a wholly novel chapter of national history was being opened, but before this new series of events could unfold, the armies must march once more, duly ordered by Stanton and Grant.

Down Pennsylvania Avenue they came—on the first day the Army of the Potomac. Nearly continuous lines of grandstands, bleachers, and seats had been erected from the Capitol to the White House. The city swarmed with visitors, the schools were dismissed, and the jubilant populace donned gay attire to welcome home the victors. Viewers perched on lamp posts and crowded windows and roofs along the route. Near the White House special covered stands had been erected for the President, the Cabinet, Generals, diplomats, the press, and just commonplace politicians. One special stand, built at his own expense by a Boston gentleman, was reserved for the use of those who could not march—the crippled and the convalescent. Outlying parts of the city were nearly deserted.

The flags waved everywhere, some faded and in shreds. A few staffs bore no banners, for they had been entirely shot away. Bands blared; the cheering and the weeping were fervent; school children, dressed in white, strewed flowers and sang patriotic songs, while some held aloft such signs as: "The Public Schools of Washington Welcome the Heroes of the Republic." The parade included celebrities, too. The onlookers knew their names and faces, and had their favorite generals, heading corps, divisions, and even brigades.

In front of President Johnson, Secretary of War Stanton, and General Grant, the cavalry clattered past for a full hour. Some disappointment was expressed that the popular Phil Sheridan did not lead the horse troops of the Army of the Potomac, but he was already in the South with occupation forces. One critical observer stated that Sheridan's absence was due primarily to his reluctance to appear under Meade's command.[2] His nonappearance had a partial compensation when, near the reviewing stand, the bugle sounded "Charge" and the cavalry of George Armstrong Custer, each man wearing a red kerchief, thundered past with their youthful, blonde-haired leader in the van. His horse even managed to seize attention by running away briefly until the spectacular Custer reined him in.[3]

The engineer corps appeared with its cumbersome implements of service, including pontoons; the brigades of infantry were accompanied by six ambulances each; and the Zouaves marched proudly in gaudy uniform. The Irish brigade had sprigs of green in their hats; the Ninth Corps excelled in marching precision; many one-armed soldiers found places, each with a wreath over his empty sleeve. The youthfulness of the generals as they took their places in the reviewing stand impressed the watchers. As Sherman joined them, even louder cheers arose. The conqueror of Georgia and the Carolinas saluted the President and then pointedly declined the proffered hand of Secretary Stanton, for the controversy over Johnston's surrender terms was fresh, and Sherman had a nature that nursed old grudges.

The second day, May 24, furnished a contrast: at 11 A.M. Sherman and Howard led forth the soldiers of the West in their first review, before thousands of onlookers. The Western men, wearing their field uniforms, no matter how faded and camp-worn, were taller, strode in a long loose type of swinging step, and were said to have "magnificent physiques."

It was not merely an extraordinary pageant or a gigantic spectacle, such as

2. Wainwright, Charles S., *A Diary of Battle*, ed. Allan Nevins, New York, 1962, 525. Wesley Merritt led the cavalry of the Army of the Potomac.

3. There are many ample descriptions of the Grand Review, some with conflicting details. Brooks, Noah, *Washington in Lincoln's Time*, ed. Herbert Mitgang, New York, 1958, 271-283. For another description of Custer see Papers of Albert H. Prescott, personal notes for May 23, 1865, mss. HEH; newspaper reports such as New York *Tribune*, May 24, 25, 1865, and New York *Herald*, May 24, 25 and 27, 1865.

Libby Prison in 1865, after the Release of Union Prisoners

would probably never be seen again; it was the spectacular expression of "a deep, glorious, solemn sentiment," all patriots feeling deep pride in the "youthful strength of a republic tried and found stead-fast."[4]

Now the volunteer army had to be disbanded, dispersed—a task that could not wait. Four days after the surrender of Lee, the War Department directed that all recruiting and drafting in all States be discontinued. Thus, the machinery of army mobilization was thrown into reverse. By April 28, orders had been issued for reducing expenses of "the Military Establishment," and expenditures were cut as rapidly as was prudent. Purchases of horses, mules, wagons, and much forage were halted, ocean and river transports not required to bring troops home were disposed of, and all requisitions for railroad construction and transportation were stopped. The Commissary-General, and the Chief of Ordnance cut down on buying guns and supplies, and reduced production at government arsenals; engineers ceased work on field and other fortifications; all bureaus, in fact, were to curtail operations sharply, except those needed to maintain the regular army and to aid in disbanding the volunteer force. In addition, the number of general and staff officers was to be reduced, and military restrictions upon trade and commerce were to be removed, "so far as might be consistent with the public safety."[5]

After a conference of not more than an hour-and-a-half, Stanton and Grant on May 11 approved orders, only about a page-and-a-half in length, formulating plans for demobilization of the Union army. Thus was begun what Ida M. Tarbell called "the greatest feat in handling men which this or any government has ever performed."[6]

For months the War Department would be as active as during hostilities. On May 1, 1865, the volunteers in the army totaled 1,034,064. By August 7, 1865, in something over two months of processing, 640,806 troops had been mustered out. By November 15, 1865, nearly four-fifths of the total, or 800,963, had been demobilized. On July 19 the final regiment of the Army of the Potomac was sent home from Washington and by August 1 the last of Sherman's regiments left Louisville. A year later, on November 1, 1866, the army had still left in service only 11,043 volunteer soldiers, of whom 8,756 were U. S. Colored Troops.

General Grant felt the collapse of resistance "rendered a large part of our military force unnecessary," because by July, 1865, it was apparent that the necessity of surrender was being accepted by the South without any apprecia-

4. *Harper's Weekly*, June 10, 1865.
5. *O.R.* III, iv, 1263, 1280-1281; v, 509-510.
6. *Ibid.*, 1-3; Tarbell, Ida M., "Disbanding the Union Army," *McClure's Magazine*, March, 1901, 408.

ble reaction. The Regular Federal Army remained, and although it was over three times as large as the pre-Civil War Army, it was a long way from the million under arms in May, 1865. By fall of 1866, the aggregate strength was set at 54,302, a number below the maximum of 75,382 authorized by Congress. During the last year of the war the Army had cost the United States over a billion dollars; two years later that cost was under a hundred million.[7]

The Federal Navy began its gradual reduction of forces used on blockade duty even before the army started demobilization. After the fall of Fort Fisher in North Carolina in January and Wilmington in late February, 1865, steps were taken to cut down naval forces. This reduction was accentuated after Charleston, Mobile, and Galveston were taken over by the Union. The main purpose of the cutbacks seems to have been to reduce expenses. Commanders were ordered to send north purchased vessels needing extensive repairs and naval stores no longer required. Around May 1, squadrons in home waters were reduced by half, and near the end of May even greater cuts were made. The Potomac Flotilla and the Mississippi Squadron were discontinued, so that from a fleet of 471 vessels on blockade duty alone, in January, 1865, there remained only thirty steamers and receiving ships of the blockaders by mid-July.

The total Union Navy had 530 vessels with 2,000 guns in commission at the start of 1865, and was reduced to 117 with 830 guns by December of that year. Foreign squadrons were re-established in European, Brazilian, and East Indian waters, and a new one set up for the West Indies. The Pacific squadron had never been discontinued.

As for manpower, the Navy had grown from 7,600 in 1861 to 51,500, plus 16,880 artisans and laborers in the navy yards, with a like number employed in private shipyards under government contract. By December, 1865, these numbers were substantially reduced to 12,128 men.

The renowned ironclad vessels, mainly monitors, which had proved, according to Secretary Welles, "so formidable in war, but unsuited for active service in peace," were now laid aside, "ready to be brought forward at any time for active duty should circumstances require." Since March 4, 1861, of a total of 418 vessels purchased at a cost of nearly eighteen-and-a-half million dollars, some 340 had been sold by December 1865 for a mere five-and-one-half million.[8]

Thus the demobilization of men and material was accomplished without

7. Oberholtzer, Ellis Paxson, *A History of the United States Since the Civil War*, Vol. I, New York, 1917, 26; *O.R.*, III, v, 1033.

8. Welles, Report, Dec. 4, 1865, *Cong. Globe*, 39th Cong., 1st. Sess., Appendix, 19-23; Richardson, James D., *A Compilation of the Messages and Papers of the Presidents*, New York, 1887, Vol. VII, 3561.

severe disruption, and the world viewed with mixed emotions the return of the war-weary veterans to peacetime civilian life.

No separate reviews, however, were held by certain other elements in the long stormy struggle, who well merited the salutes and homage of crowded streets and cheering people—the women, who, as resolute wives and mothers, unwearied workers, and nurses, had sustained and comforted the fighters; the worn files of unpaid men who had enlisted in the Sanitary and Christian Commissions; the humble trudging Negroes who had donned the uniforms of the Republic and risked obloquy and bullets in order to wield bayonets and trench-shovels. Silent and nameless in their devotion, they fittingly melted away into the throngs of patriotic citizens returning to their habitual labors and duties. But the nation would never forget them or their priceless services —never cease to reverence their memory.

13

Mobilization for Peace

[I]

MUCH MORE thoughtful planning and effort were involved in demobilizing the American people from their widely varied war efforts, and in reorganizing their thinking, energies and resources to meet the multitudinous problems of peace, than were expended in merely disbanding the armies and selling unneeded parts of the naval armada. The fact that these exigent tasks were accomplished with speed and efficiency contributed immeasurably to post-war economic stability and growth. A disorderly and delayed dispersal of the armies, while guerrilla activities continued, and coastal trade remained weak and inadequate to help meet the nation's commercial needs, would have resulted in sufficiently widespread friction and bitterness to cripple all American activities for decades. Meanwhile, the morale of the nation might have suffered heavily from years of internal dissension and uncertainty.

If we can imagine the possibility of the type of civil war known at times in various parts of Europe, where the sinking flames of internal conflict were blown into a more destructive blaze by neighboring countries pursuing malevolent or greedy aims, and where the victorious as well as the vanquished elements in the population were forced to live in close proximity while their passionate hatreds and increasingly disparate cultural and economic systems generated a succession of angry new collisions, then we can better picture the malign possibilities facing the weary, bewildered people, North and South, in 1865.

Fortunately, the background of the conflict was American, not European; and still more fortunately, both Northerners and Southerners had long been committed to the fundamental Anglo-Saxon principle of compromise, and were at last ready to turn to mutual concessions to readjust their differences. Another important fact was that the successful North had suffered no crippling injuries, either material or moral, except for human casualties. Few of its areas had been invaded, and it was gaining tremendously in economic strength through development of its resources, and full organization of its manpower to meet the demands of the conflict. Fortunately, also the defeated Confederacy had been seeking not to overthrow the United States, but simply to vindicate what it believed to be the right of secession.

With the opening of the West and its accompanying railroad expansion, broad areas all the way to the Pacific became available to absorb the expanding population of the older States, ready to receive the great flood of immigration about to come. For the most part, too, the victorious North was sufficiently separated geographically from the South so that the defeated Confederates were not obliged to live in neighborhoods with their victors. Above all, the veterans of the North, the West, and the borderland returned home to a civilian economy full of enterprise and growth.

The dual strength of the American economy, its ability to carry on a great war, and at the same time achieve a growth in wealth, business enterprise, and cultural vigor that impressed the world, enabled the nation to quickly bridge the gap from the war era to the post-war period now opening. The Northern stamina and resilience so evident throughout the conflict were undiminished, and now served equally well in peace. The whole nation moved valiantly forward, bringing even defeated sections to at least partial recovery.

Clearly great new developments would have taken place in the 1860's, in spite of the war,[1] for American ingenuity and business genius were definitely manifesting themselves at the outset of the industrial revolution. Railroads would have gone racing over the prairies, mountains, and deserts. Petroleum, still largely a novelty, was becoming a popular topic of conversation; new processes in iron-making were evolving, and Bessemer steel would soon be introduced. The emergence of iron vessels entirely powered by steam would have been certain; telegraph and cable wires would have extended communication both within and without the country; business capital would have proliferated; immigration would have surged forward; new inventions would have abounded; expansion westward was as natural as the passage of time. These and many other striking new changes would have taken place. Indeed, these and many other marvelous changes did appear! But it is a certainty that the war altered and helped reshape some of these developments.

Numerous observers both anticipated and reported these progressive trends at the time.[2] The influential *American Railroad Journal* early in 1865, optimistically believing that peace was at hand, declared: "We may . . . look forward to a brilliant future, when our present difficulties are settled, and an advance in all our material interests, at a rate hitherto unknown. . . ."[3]

1. See Chapter 7, "The Great Boom" in Nevins, *The War for the Union: The Organized War.*
2. Nevins, Allan, *The Emergence of Modern America,* 290.
3. *American Railroad Journal,* Jan. 7, 1865.

The *Scientific American*, at the start of 1865, pronounced: "There is nothing more illustrative of the national energy and genius than the indomitable spirit exhibited under adverse circumstances. If in any other country than our beloved America, faction should arise and threaten the national existence, the plow would stand idle in the furrow, the threads of the loom swing listless from the frames, and anvils clink only to the sharpening of swords. The arts have not languished with us though the war still goes on. . . ."[4]

Later in the year, the New York *Tribune* stated: "The country may be compared to a great ant-hill, of which the swarming inhabitants rapidly and wisely repair damages, and speedily return to the work of provision. . . . There is no suspicion of insolvency. There is no fear of depreciation. There is confidence everywhere among a people proverbially sharp and suspicious in all matters of money. . . ."[5] For example, in early spring before the war ended, when there was a temporary drop in the health of the economy, financial circles remained optimistic. Creditors had never before been so accommodating.[6]

The perceptive economist, Sir S. Morton Peto, who observed much of this near-phenomena, wrote: "Even under all the effects of Civil War—with a population diverted from her labour fields, with her commerce impeded, and the country labouring under a burden of taxation, rendered the more onerous because it could only be applied to a section of the population—even under all these disadvantages, America is shown to have progressed. I have already observed that there is nothing to correspond with this in the records of history." He continued: "Throughout the war the nation gave evidence of rapidly increasing wealth . . . America, which in so many respects has shown herself superior to ordinary rules, has, in regard to the effects of the war, shown that the heaviest and most costly conflict can be borne not only without exhaustion, but even with an increase of national prosperity. . . . In my travel through the United States in the autumn of last year, (1865) the abundant resources of the country . . . struck me most forcibly . . . the key to everything else . . . was the wonderful elasticity of the *resources of the United States.*"[7]

A usually conservative and often pessimistic financial publication wrote in

4. *Scientific American*, Jan. 2, 1865.

5. New York *Tribune*, Sept. 28, 1865.

6. *Merchants Magazine and Commercial Review*, Vol. XLII, April, 1865, 288; New York *Independent*, March 30, June 15, 1865.

7. Peto, Sir S. Morton, *The Resources and Prospects of America*, London, 1866, 391-392, 395. Sir Morton's book is undoubtedly significant, being the observations of a British capitalist, or perhaps the observations of a group of capitalists and investors. Peto led a junket of British gentlemen interested in investment on a tour of the United States in late 1865. Expenses were charged to the Atlantic & Great Western Railroad. His book, published in 1866, caused quite a stir and might well be interpreted as a brochure on the glories of the United States, extolling it as a fine ground for investment. See Jenks, Leland Hamilton, *The Migration of British Capital to 1875*, Thomas Nelson & Sons, Ltd., London, Knopf edition, 1963, 258-259.

July, 1865: "[It is] with a feeling of relief that we perceive ourselves almost upon the eve of the last change from the abnormal to the normal, from the day of battles and proclamations to those of legislation and law. The probable flow of capital, the rate of interest, the signs of future movements, all these soon may be within the compass of practical experience and scientific knowledge, and not as of late totally subject to the chances of war or official caprice. And when the drama is ended, and the dawn of peace and constitutional government ripens into bright morning, the mists of deficit revenues, national poverty and repudiation . . . will disappear."[8]

Senator John Sherman of Ohio wrote his brother, General William T. Sherman, "The truth is, the close of the war with our resources unimpaired gives an elevation, a scope to the ideas of leading capitalists, far higher than anything ever undertaken in this country before. They talk of millions as confidently as formerly of thousands. . . . Our manufactures are yet in their infancy, but soon I expect to see, under the stimulus of a great demand and the protection of our tariff, locomotive and machine shops worthy of the name."[9]

These predictions were perhaps excessive in their optimism, but such an outlook reflected the thinking and hopes of the vast majority of the populace, at least in the North.

[II]

Thanks to the dual strength of the Northern economy the vast majority of returning Union veterans slipped back into old familiar niches, or found new ones with a minimum of trouble and confusion. For instance, perceptive specialized journals of economics have very little to say about demobilization in general.[10] Inevitably, a few weak spots and some pockets of temporary unemployment appeared, particularly in the cities. While many men returned to former jobs or kindred trades, four years had witnessed numerous changes in business, and often old-time jobs were no longer open. Furthermore, many of the youngest veterans had never been gainfully employed before the war, so jobs had to be found for them. Many simply returned to the farm to help ease the wartime load of those left at home, while countless able and venturesome men set out for the West.

Newspapers and other journals continued to urge businessmen to find

8. *Merchants' Magazine and Commercial Review*, Vol. LIII, July, 1863, 53.

9. Nevins, *The Emergence of Modern America*, 31-33; *The Sherman Letters, Correspondence between General and Senator Sherman from 1837 to 1891*, edited by Rachel Sherman Thorndike, London, 1894, 258.

10. *Merchants' Magazine*, 1865-1866, *passim.*, hardly mentions the problem of the returning soldiers in either its articles or in monthly summaries of the economic situation; see also *Prairie Farmer*, 1865-1866, *passim; American Railroad Journal*, 1865-1866, *passim.*

places for the "heroes." In late July in New York, thousands of men were reported "out of work" during the slack season, though the reliability of such reports is hard to verify. In August, 1865, a meeting was held in New York by the "Discharged Soldiers and Sailors' Employment Agency" on Canal Street, where a large number of veterans gathered "for the purpose of forming an association that might urge their claims upon the community with greater force than individuals were capable of doing."[11] In some areas employers were reluctant or refused to hire the one-armed or one-legged men, or rejected crippled veterans entirely, a fact reported by the Sanitary Commission in Philadelphia.[12] The Pension Act of July 14, 1862, which was revised in 1864, provided pensions for veterans disabled by wounds or disease contracted while in line of duty.[13] As yet no pension was provided for mere service in the Union forces.

The majority of the enlisted men seemed to have little trouble fitting into the post-war picture. They were young, adaptable and most of them had not tied themselves down to any single trade or locality. In addition, a large number of them were as yet unmarried. Very often the veterans received the somewhat preferential treatment which most people believed to be their just due, often at the expense of men who had not seen service.[14]

Officers of high rank, especially former West Pointers, found a world of opportunity awaiting them in both national and local politics, in Federal jobs, in engineering, particularly in railroad operation, and in construction work of all kinds, while many veterans continued to serve in the regular Army. It was apparent that the promotional value of having been an officer of any rank in the war far outweighed in value whatever ground had been lost to the men who had stayed at home. Generally the people at home wished to assist the returning soldiers, even after the glitter had worn thin and become tarnished. Moreover, many a veteran would not forget his service "comrade" when it came to setting up a new business.

Officers in the lower echelons apparently did encounter some difficulties, in many instances finding it impossible to return to their pre-war occupations for a variety of reasons. On the other hand, they were often content to take positions which at first glance seemed to be a step down for a captain or major who had commanded fighting men. Sir Morton Peto may have exaggerated the situation slightly in writing that by the end of 1865 no one was without employment; but he did feel that one reason the veterans did not overcrowd the

11. New York *Tribune*, July 22, Aug. 21, 1865.
12. Maxwell, William Quentin, *Lincoln's Fifth Wheel*, New York, 1956, 287.
13. *Congressional Globe*, 37th Cong., 2nd Sess., Appendix, 405-406.
14. Rogers, Joseph, *The Development of the North Since the Civil War*, Vol. XVIII, and Barrie, George, *The History of North America*, Philadelphia, 1906, 33.

country was *"because their several occupations afforded them superior rewards for their labour."* He recalls having visited a printing establishment in Chicago where the owner had employed 47 former soldiers as compositors. One man was a major, another a captain, a third a lieutenant, and another an ex-sergeant. After all, it was explained, the employees received four dollars for every dollar they had received in the army. This employer had kept jobs open for those who had joined the colors. Sir Morton further concluded: "This was the means by which a reign of terror from disbanded soldiers was prevented in America at the conclusion of the Civil War." If there had been no employment for the people, anarchy would have reigned throughout the country. "How entirely inconsistent was all this," wrote Peto, "with our European notions of the consequences of military success!"[15]

What sort of a world did these veterans and their families face in the summer of 1865? While the conclusion of the war had been imminent for some months, no one was really ready for the actual event, especially with the sudden shock of the assassination.

While most of the veterans arrived home in fairly wholesome estate, physical and moral, and were easily absorbed into the civilian body, and while business made its readjustment to peace with a minimum of disruption, a great civil war of four-years' length could not but leave a heritage of profound social consequences, even though some of them might lie beneath the surface.

A myriad of novel social and psychological reactions had arisen from the endlessly varied tensions and passions of the long and feverish war; how deeply penetrating and masterful they were is a question no one can really answer. One commentator of the time spoke of a "certain public frenzy" that characterized the nation's thought and action in the tumultuous year 1865 as the period opened, finding expression in "enormous speculations, losses, and consequent frauds; an increase of crime, a curious and tragic recklessness in the management of railroads and steamers; a fury of extravagance at public watering-places . . . all observable the first months of peace." This ungoverned emotionalism was attributed to several causes, such as sudden fictitious wealth from large issues of paper money; the rapid and wonderful development of America's new Golconda Petroleum; the fact that war inevitably erodes old standards of public morals; the thirst for excitement during the war which had now to be satisfied with new sensations. "The public must have its startling [headlines], its exclamation points, its heavy type; and if there are no battles in Georgia or Virginia to authorize their use, a murder, or a defalcation, or a riot

15. Peto, *op.cit.*, 387, 404, 405.

must suffice. . . ." The theory was enunciated that "a great civil commotion is always followed by a deranged state of society." Perhaps all the above phenomena can be explained as part of the natural readjustment that had to take place before society could settle down to a new "normal condition." The "momentum" of a war is hard to stop or alter.[16]

For one memorable instance, the Fourth of July celebration at the North in 1865 seemed bigger, more frantic and raucous than ever; the country was letting off steam. General Grant appeared at Albany; a cornerstone was laid for the soldiers' monument at Gettysburg Cemetery; a gigantic parade enlivened New York City, and mobilized thousands of happy marchers celebrated elsewhere, while private homes and public buildings displayed "illuminations" emblazoned with patriotic slogans. "There never will be another such Fourth of July—whence it behooved us to make the most of this. There can never be another on which we shall for the first time celebrate at once the Salvation and the Emancipation of the Republic. . . ."[17] After the holiday, Greeley's *Tribune* commented, "The newspapers from all parts of the land are bringing us depressing tidings of homicides, of houses burned, of gunners killed by their own guns, of broken bones, of casualties in dreadful profusion and variety. We are the most impetuously festive people in the World. . . . Upon other days of the year the railway companies conspire with reckless switch-tenders to help the community upon its way to another and a calmer world; but upon the Fourth of July, we, ourselves, mount the locomotive and rush rapturously into the jaws of destruction. Dreadful bells fright us from our propriety; inopportune explosions communicate the mania to our horses; fireworks stimulate in the evening the frenzies of the morning; cocktails, smashes, juleps, slings, and punches keep up the conflagration; great crowds of jostling men, of weary women and of frightened and feverish children eating what they should not eat, drinking what they should not drink, standing where they should not stand, and moving on when safety required them to remain stationary."[18] Additional excitement was contributed on July 14 when Barnum's famous Museum in New York burned down, permitting the escape of a black bear from the menagerie into Wall Street.[19]

Beyond question, the year 1865 beheld an increase in both public and private laxity and corruption. Growth unshackled by the war, in addition to widespread confusion and the overthrow of many old standards, created new uncertainty and instability. Numerous established classes of society in many

16. Curtis, George William, *Harper's Weekly*, Sept. 2, 1865, 546.
17. New York *Tribune*, July 6, 9, 1865.
18. *Ibid.*, July 10, 1865.
19. *Ibid.*, July 14, 1865.

areas were being remoulded. What William Sumner later called the "cake of custom" had been broken in many spheres of conduct and business. Excessive speculation in both financial and personal activities was visible on every hand, and in every community. Men were becoming addicted to taking "chances."[20]

The underlying soundness of the people was coupled with a tendency that has usually been discernible in America in times of sharp crisis or profound change. Even when expected, as peace was in 1865, the majority of the population is seldom quite prepared for the alterations in the national life that such a shift brings about. A sudden feeling of vacancy, or insecurity, overtakes people as they suddenly realize how much of their lives will be altered in color, texture, and feeling. So it was in 1865. The multitudes North and South rushed into their new state of peace with a kind of startled frenzy, which endured until they felt a new serenity in the lifting of a long-sustained load of general anxiety and private sorrow. Yet there remained the new life, new enlarged opportunities for most, new jobs for others, along with national problems such as a new President, the fate of the freed slaves, what would happen in the South, and a host of other difficulties. Just as they had not been prepared for the end of the war, so were they unprepared for the reopening of peace, in a totally free society.[21]

[III]

The returned war veteran faced the harassing consequences of the conflict in the inexorable rise of the costs of living which outpaced all increases in wages, and the same grinding difficulties met by all veterans and civilians during the war years. Clearly, the inescapable inflation was endured by the people with much belt-tightening and some real distress, but happily it did not reach such calamitous depths as in England in the trough of depression or in Germany in the years of wild inflation after the first World War.[22]

By mid-1866, "the chief obstacle to the restoration of [the United States] . . . to its former prosperity, the obstacle which must be removed as soon as practicable, is the high rate of prices upon all the necessities of life."[23] It was of comparatively small consequence that colossal fortunes were amassed, and

20. For analysis of this trend, see Nevins, Allan, *The Emergence of Modern America*, Chap. VII, "The Moral Collapse in Government and Business, 1865-1873," p. 179: "Corruption had been far from unknown before the war; yet the impetus which the conflict gave to evil tendencies was alarming."

21. *Ibid.*, 190-191.

22. *Ibid.*, 225-227.

23. *Merchants' Magazine*, Vol. LV, July, 1866, 61-62.

that many people seemed able to make extravagant exhibitions of wealth, while others suffered hardship. The nation, compelled to pay exorbitantly for whatever necessities were eaten and worn, was fast becoming truly impoverished. The burden of inflation fell primarily on laborers and mechanics in the cities, and especially on "female operatives" and seamstresses. The war had diverted some private building, population in urban centers continued to swell, and there was a scarcity of dwellings in some areas. It was believed that property value would soon be enhanced twofold. For instance, in Massachusetts in 1868 nine more males were living in every hundred houses than had dwelt there in 1860, most of these being heads of families.[24]

Sir Morton Peto showed his characteristic sympathy and effervescence when he declared that the feature of the people that struck him most forcibly was "the absence of pauperism." In comparison with some areas of Europe, like southern Italy, perhaps he was right; at least when he emphasized the fact that in America "You see no rags, you meet no beggars." And he certainly made a telling observation when he stated, "Every one has the means before him of improving his position." He was also generally correct in asserting that "the wealth of America is diffused;" that is, it was well distributed, without areas of sore congestion. Though perhaps not true quite to the extent he implied, this was a statement reasonably sound respecting the roomy nation. He felt that the British had not fully appreciated "the American character . . . its energy, its enterprise, its independent spirit."[25]

Deeply affecting the price structure in postwar days was the excessive issuance of greenbacks and other paper money, the heavy taxation, the difficulties of readjustment from war production to the manufacture and use of civilian goods, the necessity of helping markets to re-arrange themselves. One critic explained the principal reasons why the British observers saw no beggars in the United States; incomes were larger and those who did feel the pinch of necessity practiced retrenchment and economy. Little absolute want existed; "The poor of the United States were not then and are not now identical as a class with the poor of Great Britain and Europe. In the United States, poverty, as a general fact, means simply deprivation of comforts and luxuries, and rarely, if ever, implies a want of necessities or a possibility of starvation . . ."[26] People kept up appearances in the majority of instances.

Within a year after the war, however, the long-anticipated economic trends

24. New York *Tribune*, Sept. 28, 1865; Wells, David A., "The Recent Financial, Industrial and Commercial Experiences of the U.S.," *Cobden Club Essays*, 2nd Series, 1871-72, London, 1872, 483-484.

25. Peto, *op.cit.*, 386-387, 389-390.

26. Wells, David A., "The Recent Financial, Industrial . . . ," *op.cit.*, 482.

resumed their course as affecting the life of the average worker. The situation was again becoming normal, although not all features of the return to normal economic life were entirely pleasant for everyone.

[IV]

A brief fall in economic activity appeared in March, 1865, as similar declines had occurred in previous wartime springs. The premium on gold dropped, the prices of commodities were depressed, a tighter money-market appeared, and an increase took place in mercantile failures. But this relapse had no lasting importance, except to prick some of the gold and silver-mining bubbles and increase the transfer of capital to government securities. One authoritative periodical declared that it made "people a little more careful for a few months."[27] Another factor in the decline was that, since the fall of Atlanta in the autumn of 1864, people had been anticipating peace, and now came the Northern victories of early 1865. These affected commercial transactions, as did "the rapid absorption of nearly $160,000,000 by the Government, mainly through the seven-thirty loans. . . ."[28]

By April the situation and economic factors remained in general unchanged. *Merchant's Magazine* recorded that "events of the most important historical character have since come to pass. . . . but none of them had any perceptible effect upon prices. . . . The daily life of the people is seen to throb with a pulse as regular as though it were passing through the most placid and peaceful portion of its history."[29] In other times far less striking occurrences had caused great cataclysms in trade and commerce; but nothing of the kind now happened in the Federal Union, which had apparently become somewhat inured to transient turbulence. Currency was the main agency used in moving Western Produce to coastal markets in the usual spring trade along the Atlantic; and in making government purchases. Subscriptions to the seven-thirty loan were termed "colossal" in May and the loan attracted more and more capital. Little concern was felt over the withdrawal of capital from industry for the loan, for expert opinion believed that would be replaced by foreign capital. In one day $40,000,000 was subscribed, and during the month ending May 14, 1865, subscriptions reached $300,000,000.[30]

The record of the prices of gold at New York is a primary barometer in

27. *Merchants' Magazine and Commercial Review*, Vol. LII, April, 1862, "Commercial Chronicle and Review," 287.
28. *Ibid.*, 288.
29. *Ibid.*, May, 1865, 380.
30. *Ibid.*, June, 1865, 444-445.

judging the financial conditions of these post-war days. From a high point in July, 1864, of 276-285, gold had dropped fairly steadily to a figure in May, 1865, of 128½-131¾. In the summer of 1865 a small rise occurred, with the price remaining in the mid-140s for the rest of the year and showing a firm post-war stability.[31] Another gauge used at that time was that of "treasure," i.e. gold especially held by the banks and the Sub-Treasury. By an early date in 1866, the condition in respect to this treasure was "one of unusual strength. The supply of gold held at the close of 1865 being thirteen million dollars larger than at the same period of any of the last seven years . . . ," declared the *Merchants' Magazine and Commercial Review.*[32]

The responsible *Merchants' Magazine* in the last half of 1865 mentions numerous factors affecting capital and the market such as Mexican complications, the exodus of Negroes from the South, state tax laws, greenback issues, the opening of communication with the South, as well as the changing political and economic scene. But there is no emphasis on the impact of demobilization.

By September, 1865, even fewer stirring events took place, and commercial activity seemed more stable. "It is less spasmodic in its modes of manifestations," stated the *Merchants' Magazine and Commercial Review.*[33] Economic activity was not lessened, however, and observers noted "we have the slower but infinitely more extensive, though less attractive, operations of a legitimate foreign commerce and domestic traffic." Crops were good this summer and fall of 1865, except for wheat, and a normal peacetime economy was taking hold. This did not mean, however, an unvarying market; "Change, incessant change, is the order of the day,"[34] declared the *Merchants' Magazine.*

Violent agitations affected the prices of many commodities except gold, such as the great politico-economic forces of the time, including the tariff, the expansion and contraction of the currency, the activities of the newly-reopened South, the emergence of hoarded capital at home as well as foreign capital. Leading price increases in all textiles, whiskey, and other liquors, played a part in the general shake-up.[35]

The clamor for resumption of specie payments was increasing in some circles and was certain to continue. The New York *Tribune* was one of the leaders in calling for resumption.[36]

That American finances were in a relatively healthy state is testified by Sir Morton Peto, who states that one of the most remarkable features of the war

31. *Annual Cyclopaedia*, 1865, Vol. V, New York, 1865, 346-347.
32. *Merchants' Magazine*, Vol. LIV, Feb. 1866, 98.
33. *Ibid.*, Vol. LIII, Sept. 1865, 224.
34. *Ibid.*, Oct. 1865, 306.
35. *Ibid.*, Vol. LIV, Feb. 1866, 123 and *passim.*
36. New York *Tribune*, October 23, 1865.

was "the marvellous sustentation of credit in the North, throughout the whole period of the rebellion."[37]

A favorable response by capital to the ending of the war was a cardinal necessity. Peto deplored the fact that when the Civil War threatened, British capital was diverted from the North, and loans were made to Austria, Greece, Turkey, and Egypt, not to mention the Confederacy. He felt that this was a gross mistake, for, as he wrote, what could those countries pay Britain "compared with what America can pay us, where in the course of a few months, the army has been restored to a peace establishment, and the navy has been converted into a commercial marine?" He urged putting British money into securities of a country now at peace rather than where countries "are perpetually threatening their neighbors, . . ." Knowing that considerable amounts of German capital had come into the North during the war, Peto deplored the fact that British capitalists did not take similar action. The fear that filibustering enterprises might be undertaken by some Americans worried the British economist, but he felt that the chances of this could be mitigated by a healthy American economy and affording "them no excuse for taking up arms in illegitimate and piratical enterprises."[38]

British capital certainly responded.[39] However, in the sixties railroads were the main interest of British capital in the United States. A flurried eruption of articles, pamphlets and short books appeared in Britain during the latter part of the war and just after the close, all intended to influence the foreign market.[40] However, balance of payments during the war and the immediate post-war years was adverse to the United States.[41] There seems to have been no major outflow of capital during the war, despite reports to the contrary.[42]

On the Federal level, President Johnson, like Lincoln, appears to have taken very little interest in finance, and possessed little experience in such matters. Financial affairs were left pretty much to the new Secretary of the Treasury, Hugh McCulloch, who had the support of many influential men, despite significant opposition to his policy of elimating greenbacks from the currency.[43]

37. Peto, *op. cit.*, 3-4.

38. *Ibid.*, 392-393, 401-403.

39. Jenks, Leland Hamilton, *The Migration of British Capital to 1875*, London, 1963, 426.

40. Hazard, R.G., *Our Resources, a Series of Articles on the Financial and Political Condition of the United States*, London, 1864, *passim.*; Walker, George, *op.cit.*, *passim.*

41. Simon, Matthew, "The United States Balance of Payments, 1861-1900," *Trends in the American Economy in the Nineteenth Century*, *op. cit.*, 699-700.

42. *Historical Statistics of the United States*, *op.cit.*, 563.

43. Sherman, John, *Recollections of the Forty Years in the House, Senate and Cabinet*, Chicago, 1895, I, 384; McCulloch, Hugh, *Men and Measures of Half-a-Century*, New York, 1888, 377; Dunning, William Archibald, *Reconstruction, Political and Economic, 1865-1877*, New York, 136-137.

The war had been costly, especially when wartime disbursements were compared with the expeditures of the government in the pre-war years, and national deficits worried many. Total wartime costs were estimated to be over three billion dollars for both Army and Navy.[44]

Although taxation was undoubtedly burdensome, some patriotic businessmen "not only *endured*, but welcomed the burdens which the great war effort imposed upon them."[45] The diffuse and overlapping wartime taxes were considered a primary cause of the increase in prices and of reductions in production and consumption, according to the Federal Revenue Commissioners in their report for 1866. The government levied and collected from eight to fifteen percent, and even twenty percent, on most finished industrial products.[46] Thus, careful revision downward was needed to release the national economy from unnecessary and repressive restrictions.

Secretary of the Treasury McCulloch managed to reduce internal taxes, but made little progress in cutting tariffs.[47] Yet, despite the wide array of facts demonstrating both the strength and weakness in the financial situation, both of private citizens and of the government, it was undoubtedly the venturesome spirit, the expansive and confident drive for new sources of wealth, that carried the nation forward in many original and exciting fields of activity. Demobilized war veterans, along with countless other citizens, now flung themselves into a new and highly competitive, though more impersonally strenuous struggle, mobilizing themselves into corporations for personal gain.

[V]

The disbanding of the Northern military power brought considerably more with it than just the return of a million men to civilian life. The already badly stricken American carrying-trade was reduced to sad levels by 1865. The loss of scope and vigor in the nation's merchant marine had begun long before the Civil War. Restrictions and injuries brought about by the exigencies of the conflict hastened and intensified that decline to an almost disastrous extent.[48] Of the fifteen lines of sea-going steamers out of New York before the war, only three survived the conflict—one to Panama, one to Maine, and one to Cuba.

44. Dewey, Davis Rich, *Financial History of the United States*, New York, 1934, 299, 329-332, for an accurate general summary; "Report of the Secretary of the Treasury," December 4, 1865, *Cong. Globe*, 39th Cong., 1st Sess., Appendix, 39.

45. *Report of the United States Revenue Commission*, Treasury Dept., Washington, 1866, 19.

46. *Ibid.*, 19-20.

47. Dewey, *op.cit.*, 332, 340, 343, 395; Dunning, *op.cit.*, 136-142, for summaries.

48. Wells, David A., *Our Merchant Marine, How it Rose, Increased, Became Great, Declined and Decayed*, New York, 1890, 20-21.

During the war, it was estimated that some 600 American vessels transferred to the British flag alone, and that trade between the North and Europe was placed almost wholly in the hands of foreigners, while trade to South America and the Far East was in nearly as disadvantageous a situation.[49] A leading trade journal stated in February, 1865: "It is a well known and not very agreeable fact, that our foreign commerce has, during the last four years, been conducted almost entirely under foreign flags . . . and unless some radical measures are taken, even the return of peace will not be attended with the immediate return of our lost commerce."[50] The writer further noted the obvious fact that if you multiply the means of communication, you increase trade. He also called upon the government to use surplus naval ships as mail packets to all parts of the world. Others were likewise alarmed; the *Scientific American* in 1864 had bemoaned the fact that, "the American ocean-carrying-trade has been almost destroyed for want of fast steamers: for if we had a sufficient number of these they would bid defiance to the *Alabama* and all its conquerors, and would have maintained our ocean trade in its integrity."[51] Editors of another publication, writing in 1863, lamented: "In a war like the present, of course every interest must suffer, and yet it seems strange that two or three privateers should have been able to almost destroy our shipping interests."[52] Certainly the highly publicized Confederate raiders had caused some destruction and much consternation in the American merchant fleet sailing to foreign shores. The coastal fleet also had been sadly depleted by the needs of the blockade, cutting off most shipping south of Maryland. All of these factors increased maritime debilitation in the late sixties.

The Union Navy had actually preserved a considerable portion of the merchant marine by its construction, purchase, and leasing of vessels for various war purposes, as the army had done by its active management of its transports. The return of these vessels to private ownership at very reasonable prices was a great boon to the entire merchant marine. Men trained in the shipyards during the war turned to the new ship-construction in 1865, although rising wages hampered their activities. "The demand for steamships is more active than it ever was," stated *Harper's Weekly* in the fall of 1865.[53]

The war was not yet fully over when the coastal trade, then a major part of the entire marine business, began to revive, with passenger and freight vessels leaving for Charleston and other ports. This trade was especially welcome to New York. "The close of the war, and the release of many new and

49. *Ibid.*
50. *American Railroad Journal*, Feb. 4, 1865.
51. *Scientific American*, Jan. 2, 1864, Vol. X, No. I, 9.
52. *Merchants' Magazine*, Dec., 1863, 435-439.
53. *Harper's Weekly*, Oct. 7, 1865.

finely equipped steamers from government service, have given our enterprising merchants ample opportunity to resume this great trade . . . and they have embarked in the business with an enterprise and energy that demonstrate their ability to successfully carry it on, and in a manner never before attempted. . . ." Vessels were also being constructed in New York for the French and Pacific trade.[54] Plans were well afoot, also, for American carriers on the North Atlantic,[55] and coastal trade made a startling recovery, enhanced to a very appreciable extent by the American Navy's sale of vessels.[56]

Among other valuable assets dumped on the general market by the government at the close of the war were horses and mules, frequent sales being held in major cities.[57]

Of transcendent importance in restoring the country as a whole was the improvement in communications by the telegraph. Telegraphic connections were rapidly completed so that by early June, 1865, New York again had a direct rapid communication link with New Orleans, Charleston and other principal Southern cities.[58] In the middle of 1865, when the *Great Eastern* began laying a cable across the Atlantic, widespread disappointment was felt when it broke after about two-thirds of the line had been laid. Early attempts before the war in 1857 and 1858 had failed, and a seemingly successful second effort in 1858 had operated less than a month. The failure in 1865, however, found compensation in 1866 when a very effective cable linked Europe in almost magical proximity with the eastern coast of the United States, and thence even with the Pacific.

The story of the swift spread of our railroads with the efficiency of a great spinning-machine, is a subject too large to explore in this study of the closing of the great conflict. Moreover, the expansion of the railroads is well known. Railroad construction which had been getting into full stride just before the war had added a new dimension to war itself. Everyone foresaw that they would be for decades by far the principal commercial carriers of the expanding inland domain of the continent.

Capital was still absorbed in railroad financing during and after the war, many plans being laid for new truck- and branch-lines, with fresh tunnels, renovated equipment, and novel methods of operation.[59]

The efficiency and experience gained by railroad management and operation during the war was an invaluable legacy. The rapid movement of such

54. New York *Tribune*, July 4, 1865.
55. *Harper's Weekly*, Oct. 7, 1865.
56. Wells, *op.cit.*, 23.
57. New York *Tribune*, July 18, 1865.
58. New York *Herald*, June 4, 1865.
59. *Historical Statistics of the U.S.*, *op.cit.*, 427.

large bodies of troops as Hooker's two corps from Virginia to the proximity of Chattanooga in the fall of 1863, shipment of Schofield's corps from the West to the East in 1864, and the steady transfer of smaller bodies of men, taught lessons in logistics that could be well applied to commercial activities. Huge quantities of supplies, picked up in various places, and moved about, involved new methods of freight handling that in peace would have taken years to learn. Skillful modes of repairing damaged track and equipment had been mastered of necessity, while need for uniform gauges, standard time, and a rapid interchange of cars, was emphasized by the war. In short, the country's railroad management had learned how to operate great lines swiftly and efficiently.

Wartime tests of equipment in service proved that new, larger, and more durable rolling-stock was needed. Iron rails were soon to be replaced by steel rails, the first being rolled by the Bessemer process in Chicago in May, 1865. In 1867, the Baldwin locomotive works, the nation's largest, were producing twelve steam engines of 25 to 38 tons apiece each month.[60] The use of horse-drawn street railroads, steadily developing before and during the war, was quickly enlarged in immediate postwar years.

Southern railroads, on the other hand, were in appalling condition by the end of the war. Whatever rolling stock still remained in use was worn and battered, many lines were heavily disrupted and almost all at least partially wrecked. Recovery took time, but the market for railroad equipment of all kinds was extremely high, and Northern capital soon became available to the dilapidated railroads of the South, as well as to the opening of the new West.[61]

[VI]

One of the principal sources of the general economic optimism prevalent in 1865 was a belief in the "Fountains of Wealth." The New York *Tribune* commented in October, 1865, upon the "tide of returning prosperity which now rolls across the country" and added, "we must not forget that wonderful legacy of nature to which we fell heirs at the beginning of the war; we mean the Petroleum fields." "Prince Petroleum," had become a recognized potentate creating a whole new industry which would soon dominate many others.[62]

Oil had created frenzied excitement and speculation during the last years of the war, but with peace, oil prices went down along with the value of oil stock. The New York *Tribune* warned its readers that well-managed money

60. Oberholtzer, Ellis Paxson, *A History of the United States Since the Civil War*, I, 240; Clark, Victor S., *History of Manufactures in the U.S.*, New York, 1929, II, 74.

61. Black, Robert C., III, *The Railroads of the Confederacy*, Chapel Hill, 1952, 289-293.

62. New York *Tribune*, July 12, Oct. 6, 1865.

should seek refuge in United States Securities, where it was safe, and should keep clear of speculations, particularly oil speculations. For two months after the war ordinary oil stocks were not worth carrying to market, but, during this time the oil regions had not been idle. Speculators, stated the *Tribune*, had been banished, but "the borers have been unremittingly at work." New wells appeared in the Pennsylvania fields, while others increased their output.[63]

By June, 1865, the oil fever appeared to have subsided, and no longer was there talk of paying off the national debt with petroleum profits, for immense sums of money had been lost through reckless over-speculation. Millions of dollars represented in paper shares, were swept out of existence.

Scientific American declared that "Nothing in the history of this country, if we except the furor that followed the opening of the gold fields of California, has caused so much excitement in business circles as the rapid development of the petroleum oil interests. There are oil stock exchanges, oil stock journals, and all the other appliances of regular commercial and financial operations. Oil cities even have sprung into existence, and speculation is running up to fever heat. . . ." Although many companies were substantial, caution in investing was advised to avoid losses.[64] A few speculators would get control of a patch of land in the oil region, and then try to sell a prodigious amount of stock, giving rich commissions for the sales. Productive value of the land may or may not have been hypothetical. "The stock speculative fever is now raging throughout the whole community to alarming degree—and when the reaction comes on, many an unfortunate dupe will suffer a most prostrating debility."[65] And the break in the oil bubble came in 1865. Abandoned wells and discarded machinery stood dolefully in the Pennsylvania fields.

But the market slowly rose as people made increased use of petroleum as an illuminant. The attractions which oil held for speculators and inventors would not cease to attract venturesome men and bold pioneers even though life in the oil fields was rough. One observer of the miracle of the Oil Creek branch of the Allegheny River stated: "A perplexing maze of derricks is woven thickly along both sides of the stream, from the banks to the bases of the hills. Engine-houses, shanties, offices, tanks, groceries, taverns, embryo villages, give the whole valley an air of activity which surrounds the machine-shops and manufacturies of large cities. . . . Men on horseback and men on foot—hundreds of them throng the crooked ways or linger besides the derricks. . . ."[66] But although destructive fires and disastrous accidents were still common-

63. *Ibid.*, June 27, 1865; *Merchants' Magazine and Commercial Review*, Vol. 53, July 1865, 49; *Scientific American*, Jan. 2, 1865, Vol. XII, No. 1, 19.

64. *Scientific American*, Jan. 2, 1865, p. 8.

65. *Ibid.*

66. *Ibid.*, Mar. 25, 1865, 192.

place, the observer noted that speculation and recklessness were less serious.[67] The land value and the oil itself represented actual value, and these were soon to rise. The search for oil continued across the country from Pennsylvania until oil became a world-commodity, a vital force in the wartime and post-war scene.[68]

Meanwhile, the mineral fields of the West still beckoned men imperiously. The appetite for iron, the developing use of steel, the demand for railroads, ships, and a thousand other needed products and implements indicated that mining would face vigorous expansion and command a bright future. For example, although the precise statistics can be disputed, the production of gold and silver in the West in the year 1866 was said to exceed in value all the gold and silver in the national treasury plus all banks throughout the country.[69]

From the famous Comstock lode of Nevada, with its fluctuations at the close of the war, great fortunes were made and lost. A fall of fifty percent or a rise of two hundred percent in the market value of a large mine within the space of six months was a common occurrence.[70]

Industry and manufacturing in the North perhaps encountered the greatest post-war economic adjustment in all its facets, while in the South it had to undergo complete reconstruction. The sudden termination of war contracts was at first a severe blow to a number of manufacturing fields but most areas made the readjustment rather easily. Naturally those industries connected with armament were particularly hard hit, though there was still a demand for weapons in the post-war domestic life. And in spite of a large government surplus of gunpowder, companies like Remington, Sharp & Colt, and Winchester survived and prospered, while others, equally famous, disappeared.[71]

The famous muzzle-loading repeating Spencer rifle, known as the "Horizontal Shot-Tower" developed by tool-maker Christopher Miner Spencer now became a legend,[72] and Spencer turned to other interests.

As to industry in general, the war produced no startling changes in the location of industrial centers. During the immediate post-war years, New England continued to be a mighty, diversified manufacturing area. Textiles were restored to their near-normal balance as soon as cotton became available

67. *Ibid.*, Jan. 2, 1865, 19.

68. *Ibid.*, Jan. 2, 1865, 19; good summation is found in Oberholtzer, *op.cit.*, 249-266.

69. Browne, J. Ross and James W. Taylor, *Reports upon the Mineral Resources of the United States*, Washington, 1867, 9.

70. Browne and Taylor, *op.cit.*, 35.

71. Edwards, William B., *Civil War Guns*, Harrisburg, 1962, 158, 195-196; Winchester was really a war-born concern, taking its name in 1866 from the New Haven Arms Company. It had manufactured the well-liked Henry rifle, most of them sold privately to soldiers. Winchester went on to become a name familiar to all. Sharps and Colt also had a successful post-war career.

72. *Ibid.*, 156-157; Buckeridge, J.O., *Lincoln's Choice*, Harrisburg, Pa., 1956, *passim.*

in quantity once more. Manufacturing was stimulated in the mid-Atlantic and Great Lakes states. Philadelphia remained the leading center of manufacturing. Industries in upper New York State, Cincinnati, St. Louis and Chicago continued to develop after the war. The most accurate figures available show that the country's manufacturing product rose between 1860 and 1870 about 52 percent, nearly twice as rapidly as the population.[73]

Records were set in the great majority of industries during the five years after the war, the market for most products remaining high, sustained by some wartime shortages, demands of returning soldiers with their new activities, immigration, rebuilding in the South, and the westward movement. Because of lack of shipping, local needs and energies, the war had broken down whatever dependence had existed upon European manufacturing and had stimulated national industry. This was possible because the nation found it could simultaneously support a great war and a burgeoning civilian economy too.[74]

Feeling the stimulus of the Civil War, "iron and steel industries at once entered upon a period of extraordinary development." Blast-furnace procedures were revolutionized by more powerful blowing engines and improved hot-blast stoves, by larger furnaces, general use of bituminous coke and richer and purer ores, mainly from the Lake Superior region.[75]

Steel manufacture was in its infancy, but rapidly expanding into wider fields of usage. Production of all kinds of crude steel in the United States trebled from 1863 to 1866, the Bessemer process, invented in England in 1856, having at last begun to dominate steel-making.[76]

In other fields of manufacture changes were equally startling, some of them resulting from the influences of war. Development of machinery for making shoes and ready-made clothing persisted. Demand was tremendous, and while these innovations were bound to emerge sooner or later, the war certainly accelerated the production of daily necessities. Thus, Northern industry, generally immune to wartime damage, moved into the late sixties in a very healthy and energetic condition, with markets available, and capital, manpower and brains ample.

[VII]

The problems in the South were many. The war-torn section had a long, hard path to traverse before economic restoration and readjustment to peace

73. Clark, Victor S., *History of Manufactures in the United States*, *op.cit.*, II, 145-153, for summary.

74. For a summation see Nevins, *Emergence of Modern America*, Chap. II.

75. Swank, James M., *Notes and Comments on Industrial, Economic, Political, and Historical Subjects, American Iron and Steel Association from 1872 to 1897*, Philadelphia, 1897, 145-146.

76. Swank, James M., *History of the Manufacture of Iron in All Ages*, Philadelphia, 1892, 511.

would be complete. Conditions varied widely from Texas to Virginia; the states faced dissimilar problems, and the political aspects of Reconstruction were naturally affected by numerous economic difficulties. Most assuredly conditions were dismal enough, but it is easy to exaggerate their grimness.

The New York *Tribune*, for example, regarded the "bugaboos" of "Southern industry" as greatly exaggerated. It criticized journals that alleged the Negroes refused to work; that masters refused or were unable to employ them; that fields were standing idle and that danger of general famine threatened the section. These, declared the *Tribune*, "are gross and misleading exaggerations; while stories of Negroes crowding into the cities to die of famine, vice, exposure, and pestilence, are even worse. . . ." The *Tribune* contended that many Negroes stayed peaceably on the farm and plantation and went to work not for cash, but for a share of the crop. For the most part, except when they dealt with severe or unkind masters, the Negroes accepted employment with their former owners. The *Tribune* felt that the South would necessarily remain poor for the foreseeable future and should not revert to its old ways of buying luxuries from the North on credit. Meanwhile, it thought that crops were inevitably suffering for want of teams, livestock, and fences.[77]

While no one can give any accurate figures on the number of displaced Negroes who had left the plantation slave home to follow the armies or those who had gathered in the city, it does seem clear that the total of the uprooted came nowhere near the four-million Negroes who had been held in slavery.

Southern buyers in New York City did not lag far behind the Western customers in numbers during the early fall of 1865. "Notwithstanding all that has been said about the poverty of the South, purchasers from that section are arriving here in droves," declared *Harper's Weekly*, "and all seem able to pay for what they want." Of course, it added, "merchants are not over-anxious to sell on credit to the men who made the rebellion an excuse for cheating their Northern creditors. But everyone is willing to sell for cash; and this, or cotton, which amounts to the same thing, Southern buyers seem to possess to an amount entirely unexpected." Even in areas overrun by Sherman, trade was brisk, with cash and cotton abundant. No longer did buyers emphasize the luxury-trade of silks, laces, wines, and jewels. Now it was coarse dry goods and essential farm implements that they demanded. Furthermore, "The white trash, for the first time in history, are making themselves felt in the market," in place of rice planters and slaves who had vanished.[78] A bale of cotton in 1865 would buy fifteen barrels of flour instead of five. Another factor affecting trade was the large emigration from North to South by enterprising businessmen.

77. New York *Tribune*, July 4, 1865.
78. *Harper's Weekly*, Sept. 16, 1865.

Coastal passenger steamers before the war did a light trade, but now, at much higher passage fares, the steamers were full. The same fact was true respecting railroads running south through Ohio and Kentucky. Mechanics such as masons, carpenters, and bricklayers, were now commanding good wages. The work of common day-laborers was still assigned mainly to Negroes, and skilled labor was in such demand that a worker's market appeared. The need for rebuilding in the South was tremendous—and some of the people had the means for it in the form of cotton.

The year 1865 was a fairly good crop year, although yields were spotty. Wheat production fell below expectation in quality. However, as one authority put it, "So vast is the extent of the country . . . , and so varied its climate, that with our abundant and constantly multiplying means of communication, a deficiency of a particular crop in one section is readily made up by its excess, or at least abundance, in another."[79]

It was to cotton, however, that many minds turned even before the end of hostilities. Within a few days of Johnston's surrender Grant told commanders Schofield and Gilmore in the South: "Give every facility and encouragement to getting to market cotton and other Southern products. Let there be no seizure of private property or searching after Confederate cotton. The finances of the Country demand that all articles of export should be got to market as early as possible."[80]

Little new cotton was put in because planting time came just as the South was in the throes of surrender. Some planters, although late, did plow up young corn and plant cotton instead, hoping for a late frost.[81] Nevertheless, since cotton is a crop that does not deteriorate materially when stored for a reasonable length of time, it was not surprising that a large amount of old cotton came out of storage in time to make a good market.

[VIII]

The sudden surplus of manpower and energy released by the end of the war found an outlet apart from the normal life of the nation—in a great Westward surge. The press promoted this movement, enjoining returning soldiers to "turn their faces westward and colonize the public lands. Thanks to the beneficient policy of the Homestead Law, land is open to all. . . ."[82]

Many looked upon the American West as the nation's greatest resource. Sir

79. *American Annual Cyclopaedia*, 1865, 2-9.
80. Grant to Schofield and Gilmore, Ms., May 29, 1865, Ohio State Museum, Columbus.
81. New York *Tribune*, July 4, 1865.
82. New York *Tribune*, July 11, 1865.

Morton Peto, among others, felt that the resources of the United States were inexhaustible, and would insure prosperity.

Federal land policy offered advantages to the ex-soldier as well as to everyone else. The Homestead Act of May 20, 1862, made possible the ownership of a quarter section of land free-of-charge, except for filing fees, for any head of family who was over 21 and a citizen. An act of March 21, 1864, made it possible for men in the service whose family or a member of his family was residing on the land to make an affidavit to his commanding officer rather than having him file personally at the district land office.[83]

A new belt of wheat-farming had developed in Ohio, running west through Iowa, Missouri, Kansas, Nebraska, and Minnesota, enticing a host of veterans to rush there in time to prepare a crop for harvest in 1865. Others went into Wisconsin and Michigan, and this movement kept its momentum as it reached farther and farther into the West.

Western land, indeed, opened a new world of opportunity to the excess manpower, North and South, after the war. Without it, the absorption of thousands into the normal stream of life would have been much more difficult, or perhaps even impossible without severe economic dislocation.

83. *Congressional Globe*, 38th Cong., 1st Sess., Appendix, 149-150.

14

Toward a Mature Nation

FROM THE flame and ashes of the Civil War emerged, not instantaneously as in the Oriental fable, but slowly and gradually, a phoenix-like apparition—a new country, in the main a creation of evolution rather than revolution, its golden wings and feathers mingled with more familiar and time-tested adjuncts of flight and splendor.

The shock of the conflict had obscured the old gnomic sentiments on the irresistible destiny of the nation; had banished the idea that a shining new chariot could and would replace the heavy-laboring wagon of the past. The long years, seemingly endless, of loss, grief, and almost intolerable strain, had discouraged aspiration in thought and reflection.

Now succeeded a sense of release and relief. It was tinged with less exultation than men had anticipated; rather, it expressed simply a deep sense of happiness that the American people had regained their former sense of grandeur and beauty in their country—the sense that James Russell Lowell expressed in his exclamation, "Ours once more!"

As we have indicated, the changes of the Civil War period, like those which had overswept the country during the War of 1812, and the war with Mexico, sprang largely from internal forces that were not directly connected with the war itself. These included the westward movement that had marked American development from the infancy of New England in Plymouth, of Virginia and the Carolinas in Jamestown; they included the march of invention and technology from the time of Eli Whitney and Fulton and their ever-heightened application; they included also the diffusion of population, the increased productivity of agriculture, mining, and industry, and the accumulation of capital.

Such a war, like the classic Greek tragedy, which in some aspects it closely resembled, had a purgative value, clearing the mind of the nation, as it cleansed the bosom of the people of old prejudices, misunderstandings, and passions which would have yielded to no less powerful and painful a medicine.

The question whether the war was inevitable can never be settled, for our conclusion depends upon the positing and evaluation of too many mutable facts and forces. It is essentially a useless question, for its study involves too many vague and imponderable factors to permit of an answer. What is certain is that, inevitable or not, the war had become in the long period from Jackson to Buchanan a spiritual necessity for the healthy future of the American people. Once it was ended, the country could dismiss the ghastly struggle into its past, with a sense that it had been a necessity even if a cruel one, as other countries had been compelled to dismiss even more costly and anguishing wars as an integral incident of growth and reorientation. It could face the coming centuries with a lightened heart and fuller sense of freedom. This emotional gain might seem imponderable, but was actually far weightier than any ponderable result from the conflict. It was not to be expressed in statistics nor ledger balances; not, alas, in any music that came out of the war, nor in any major contemporary literary productions. Apart from a handful of verses—Herman Melville's "March into Virginia;" Walt Whitman's "When Lilacs Last in the Dooryard Bloomed," "Come Up from the Fields, Father," and "Cavalry Crossing a Ford;" H. H. Brownell's stanzas as quoted in Chapter 13; and Lowell's "Commemoration Ode"—a few bits of fiction, like Thomas Nelson Page's "Burial of the Guns", J. W. DeForest's *Miss Ravenel's Conversion from Secession to Loyalty,* and Ambrose Bierce's short tales—and Whitman's vivid prose recollections of ardors and endurances—the major literary performances inspired by the war were some of Lincoln's best letters (such as those to J. B. Conkling or Erastus Corning) and the President's Second Inaugural Address and his words at Gettysburg.

The republic emerged from the struggle, as men enjoying a little perspective of time later realized, in the grip of some heady new impulses of vast extent and irresistible force. One lay in the truly titanic impulse given to all enterprise in America by the rapid extension of the railroad and the telegraph throughout the ontinent; another lay in the discovery in every scenic reach, from the gold mines of Nevada to the oil fountains of Pennsylvania, of incalculable natural wealth; still another lay in the more and more unshakable confidence of the civilized world in the permanence of American institutions. Less obvious, but of enormous forcefulness, was the impetus to development lent by the availability of huge quantities of stored capital, which could no longer find a profitable employment in Europe, or safe investment in Asia, Africa, and other uneasy lands. This was added to the huge accumulations of capital already to be found in America in the hands of millionaires, mechanics, and all the intermediate men of property in the country. Of great significance in connection with this tidal flow of dollars and sterling was the fact that it could be used in America by groups which E.L. Godkin correctly termed, "the shrewdest and most indomitable speculators the world has ever seen."

All these forces in combination inevitably created an eager hunger for labor, attracting as by a gigantic magnet an inflow of workers, ranging from the skilled artisans of Britain and Germany to the uninstructed throng of pigtailed Chinese whose incourse excited alarm on the Pacific Coast. The importance of this avid national hunger for labor was the greater because the abolition of slavery had removed from America a great body of manual workers equipped for servile tasks, but without higher social ambition. And as immigration thus poured in, the throngs from the Shannon to the Vistula fed swelling towns and cities in another germinal movement the war had encouraged—that of urbanization. These six forces: first, the explosive expansion of communications; second, the discovery of new treasures of natural resources; third, the growing confidence of the civilized world in the perpetuity of the American political system and its social institutions; fourth, the accumulation of capital ready to be poured into the New World; fifth, the demand for labor; and sixth, the irresistible progress of urbanization, the movement of an always-mobile people from rural environments to the towns and cities, were creating a new America.

As a new and far-stronger nation thus emerged from the war, students at home and abroad searched earnestly for means of identifying the basic ideas and characteristics of the American people which might be deemed responsible for their irresistible and headlong emergence into a position of power, dominating the New World and gradually but surely outstripping nations and alliances of the Old World. These students recognized the error of Lord Macaulay in his famous letter predicting a future time of dire trial and turmoil for America. They measured the shortcomings of Tocqueville in his masterly book, *Democracy in America*, laying altogether too heavy an emphasis upon the egalitarian element in American life; they were ready to discount sharply the criticisms of men abroad and at home who had exaggerated the defects and shortcomings contributed to American society by the heavy immigration of the mid-century era. A surer and far more interesting analysis of the central force of American growth and character was supplied by E.L. Godkin, who, anticipating Frederick Jackson Turner, declared that the vigor and power of American life, unique in its philosophy and ideology, were rather to be connected with what he called "the frontier spirit" and cast of thought in America, as the frontier had moved westward from the Atlantic to the Rockies, and was still moving onward. The temper of pragmatic individualism in America had been partly inherited, and partly nurtured by environment as the pioneer folk engrossed their energies in dealing with raw nature and savage beasts and peoples. Godkin saw that the frontier was not so much conquered by the pioneer as made effective by conquering the pioneer, and imparting its tone and ethos to American life.

Probably the greatest single change in American civilization in the war period, directly connected with the conflict, was the replacement of an unorganized nation by a highly organized society—organized, that is, on a national scale. Various students had remarked before the war that the United States made organization an important goal and had striven toward it with marked success. But they perceived that organization was to a large extent local and regional in character, not yet national. The South, in especial, which was rural and in large part crudely developed, had been in 1860-61 as yet ineffectively organized.

Still lagging behind in this regard when Southern cannon opened against Sumter, the United States had frantically to pull itself together, raise armies East and West which ultimately reached nearly a million in numbers, to move them to the fighting fronts, and to throw them into battle; at the same time collecting a colossal and, for the New World, a totally unprecedented sum of money, about four billions of dollars. Meanwhile, it had to take steps to maintain the devotion and ardor of its people; it had, by gigantic industrial effort, to provide its armies with weapons and ammunition, ships and other armaments; it had to build and sustain railroads in campaign areas behind the lines; it had to furnish pontoon bridges, balloons, telegraphs and hospitals with the latest equipment; for the first time it had to make Herculean exertions in the field of welfare; to pay pensions to disabled and ill veterans; to maintain the families of soldiers called to the front; and to take care of widows, orphans and other dependents. All this required a degree of organization that the country had never before contemplated.

Even the South had its special achievements in the field of organization, such as the work of the Mining and Nitre Bureau, the Quartermaster's Office, and other services of supply. The growth of organization in the South would be better understood if prompt and comprehensive attention had been given to the subject in Southern memoirs and monographic histories, and if records of the bureaus mentioned had been better preserved. The unfortunate nature of the gap left by neglect of the subject is briefly noted by Douglas Freeman in his volume, *The South to Posterity: An Introduction to the Writing of Confederate History.* Unhappily, only by groping among manuscript letters, autobiographies, and in the 128 volumes of the *Official Records of the Union and Confederate Armies,* can some of the requisite information be obtained. Meanwhile, one of the saddest chapters of Southern history is the counter-record of disorganization written by the overwhelming array of refugees, including fighters, prisoners, deserters, demobilized veterans, and displaced Negroes who, by hundreds of thousands, swept back and forth during the war over the whole terrain between the Canadian line and the Gulf. At times, as when Sherman ordered noncombatants out of Atlanta, and Beauregard bade much of the civil population leave Charleston, a whole city seemed to join the despairing concourse of refugees.

The war, beginning so suddenly and unexpectedly for many, and conducted with innumerable mischances and startling developments unforeseen even by the most astute, proved far more protracted than anyone had expected. At the outset, many men had predicted that it would end within weeks. Numerous Southerners had expected and even boasted that secession would bring about a process of negotiation between Northerners and Southerners that would end in the grant to the seceding States of terms for a continuance of national life in a renovated Union, in which the States would find guarantees of a better position and a more amicable nation. Many Northerners, underrating Southern fighting-power, had believed that a few battles might decide the contest and bring peace. Instead, the war proved a contest not in valor, quickly mobilized bodies of troops, or strategic skill, so much as a contest in Spartan endurance—as did the first World War. The requirement of stoicism, which tried national and sectional character to the utmost, tested the institutions of the two peoples even more searchingly.

Most important of all, the prolonged duration of the conflict produced results in the thought, feeling and practises of the people proportionate to its length and multi-faceted force. At its end, Americans who looked about for its consequences, good and bad, found plenty of both. Some were elementary and superficial, such as the firm knotting of the Union tie, and the shattering of the many glaring myths which had marked Southern thought and conduct. And some of the most striking and obvious of the elementary consequences were written into the new Thirteenth, Fourteenth, and Fifteenth Amendments to the Constitution, which in effect constituted the terms of a treaty of peace between North and South, and had all the effect of a far-reaching and adamantine compact.

One prime result was a better understanding by the people of the nation of the true character of the huge American continent, so variegated, so radiantly beautiful, so well-stored with aesthetic as well as economic wealth. By tens and hundreds of thousands, American farm-boys, mill-hands and clerks had moved across prairie, mountain, lake or coastal beaches, from Iowa grain fields or Indiana prairies to the Carolina headlands; those who remained home had read of these diverse geographic expanses in thousands of newspaper columns.

How rich in new experiences of nature was this war! Many a Yankee or Western lad had fancied he knew all about nature. Nevertheless, he would never forget the totally new rapture he felt as he and his comrades broke camp one frosty morning on a long march; as he experienced with clearer senses than ever before the warming light of the sunshine, and saw with sharper vision than in past days the beauty of the dawn, throwing rose-tints into the trees overhead; as he happily felt the comradeship of lines of young men falling in unison into light, springy step. In many a Grand Army gathering he would later recall with delight the youthful exertions of campaigning as in some novel countryside he strode down a dew-spangled slope, or, turning another of nature's pages, inhaled the unaccustomed perfume of pine boughs stretching over tansy-beds in the Great Smokies. He might recall a glimpse of distant goldenrod-clad vistas in Virginia, Ohio, or Tennessee; or, as recruits met a more laborious challenge, the fatigue of city volunteers in struggling through the viscid dampness of sloughs of gumbo mud in Missouri that gripped their army brogans like the hydras of Asia Minor clinging to Xenophon's exhausted Greeks; or the delight of hungry marchers as, in the gleam of new campfires, they sensed the sound and aroma of saltpork frying in a treasured camp-pan over a glowing trench.

For the first time, thousands of troops realized that the long panhandle of Virginia stretched northward over stony crags and dales almost to the gleam of the Great Lakes. But it was not the new land alone, from the chugging steamers on the Yazoo and the moss-draped oaks of Florida to the sandy capes above Wilmington that were a novel revelation to millions of Americans. New continents in psychology and manners were also explored as troops gained a better understanding of the land and its natural life; the wandering armies achieved a fuller comprehension of the intellectual, emotional, and aesthetic variegations of life in a population which could produce a fiery Rhett at one extreme of thought, and a morosely egotistical Sumner at the other. The war, to hundreds of thousands, unlocked an understanding of the intellectual, psychological, and artistic wealth of talent increasingly available to the people of the land, and of their ever-growing achievements.

Another profoundly important moral sequel of the Civil War, which originated during the conflict, was the enlargement and liberalization of attitudes toward the Negro, both North and South. No reflective American could doubt that, as Reconstruction began, the problem of race relations was not only still one of the greatest, but the most urgent, that the country faced. No thoughtful man who had seen anything of plantation life or freedmen's camps could doubt that both sections would have sooner or later to discharge old prejudices and antiquated varieties of ignorance. It was plain, also, after Appomattox and the new Amendments, that this complicated and difficult problem, full of social, economic and political implications, would have to be solved on a national basis, overriding local, sectional and political limitations; and that a solution would have to make use of the latest scientific findings in every sphere, dispelling the dark miasmas of ignorance and prejudice. The most important, tenacious, and morally and socially mischievous of the many expressions of stupidity and bias was the belief held widely in the North, and almost universally in the South and borderland, that the Negro required a special position and treatment because of congenital inferiority; because he was, as even a friend put it, "lower in the scale of development than the white man, his inferiority being rooted and inherent." This postulate respecting Negro inferiority was reinforced by a misreading of Darwin and writers on anthropology. It was reinforced also by a historical sensitivity of many Southerners. They had cultivated the myth that women held a specially exalted status in Southern society and thought. It was natural for many to believe that this myth justified the South in throwing special protections about women, and that loyalty to the heroic memories of the Southern people called for a perpetuation of the myth as one relic of the Confederacy that could be preserved. This attitude played its part in the erection of a defensive shield even around such a flagrant wrong to all people of the South—both white and black—as lynching. Yet, here and there in the South, the war was quickly followed, if not accompanied, by a change in racial attitudes, and by the emergence in some areas of individuals and groups demanding "a reasonable and responsible program of action." Ferments were at work which were to bring forward such courageous men as John Spencer Bassett of Trinity College, later Duke University in North Carolina, and Andrew Sledd, a Methodist minister and teacher of Latin at Emory College in Georgia.

It is not strange that the *Atlantic Monthly* from 1900 through 1905 should publish seventy-two articles dealing with the race problem. But it is strange that only one of the seventy-two articles should depart from the "Southern" point of view in its treatment. This was the article by Andrew Sledd in the *Atlantic* for July, 1902, entitled, "The Negro, Another View." As Henry W. Warnock writes, it not only repudiated the natural-inferiority assumption but implied, in a caustic account of the intolerable condition of the Negroes, that black people should be treated courteously on the streets, and allowed to use waiting-rooms, restaurants, and hotels on the same basis as white people.

The Civil War had brought the country emancipation from slavery, an institution deeply harmful to the white and the black alike, and the 14th Amendment had brought the beginnings of a too-long-deferred acceptance of the principle of equality. But America had fallen in important respects behind

Russia. When Tzar Alexander II freed the serfs, or land-ascribed peasants, in 1861, the serfs were granted sharply limited allotments of land. Serf-emancipation was but part of a larger program of legal and consequently social equality, to which the Tzar, in assuming his throne as the Crimean War ended, had announced the adherence of his government. That program deserved American study, both countries being rich in numerous varieties of class-consciousness and tyranny.

The Southern type of slavery, and the segregation on which it was based, tended, as Frederick Olmsted had observed, to bring Negroes toward equality with domestic animals. But wartime experience had done more to implant the beginnings of a new order than many at first realized. The United States had a complex society that was certain to become more and more pluralistic. In this society, equality must be religious, political and racial. Wartime experience had taught some previously doubtful or indifferent men much-needed lessons on the benefits the Negroes could give the country through their warm appreciation for music, which some developed into a passion; through their social responsiveness to friendly people of all kinds, and through their emotional spontaneity. Many Northerners came to believe that, although the retarding effects of servitude might last for a number of years, they could be alleviated or largely abolished by education. Hence, the zeal with which many Abolitionists flung themselves into educational work both under and outside the Freedmen's Bureau.

A significant myth exploded by the war was the belief of great numbers of men, North and South, that abolition of slavery would in effect mean the destruction or confiscation of a great part of the wealth of the Southern people. On the contrary, within a quarter-century it was abundantly evident that the Southern people prospered much more generously and completely from the labor of the liberated Negroes as freedmen than it could ever have prospered from their assistance as slaves. As men looked about them in 1865 and later, the fact became plain that the abolition of slavery, while terminating an infectious national malignancy, did not reduce the wealth or income of the South. This fact was irrefutably evident by 1884, the year of Cleveland's election, when a Republican alarmist of the South, a prominent Southern plantation owner, wrote in the *Nation* that even if such a step as the restoration of slavery would be tolerable to the North, it would be overwhelmingly defeated if put to popular vote in the South. For "the labor of the Negro, once held as property by a small class, has now become a source of profit to a much larger one, and generally one that never owned, or would have owned one under the old system, or would ever have been the employer of labor at all; a class, too, in whose hands the labor of the Negro, since emancipation, has been much more profitable than to his former owners. Those and others equally interested in Negro freedom would trample any effort at curtailment of freedom under foot at the polls."

The Negro's eagerness for education was pathetic. Although the hopes of some white workers were inflated and patronizing, other men under General Rufus Saxton held realistic ideas. As education increased the number of well-informed Americans, especially in the cities, responsiveness to the Negro and sympathy with his elevation increased. During the war, 178,185 Negroes are recorded as having served in Union armies. They served well, making good soldiers, on the march, in camp, and in battle. They were somewhat more dependent upon white officers than the white troops, but in other respects not essentially different. One entire corps, General Weitzel's Twenty-fifth Corps, was all black, except for its officers.

As succeeding generations after Appomattox studied the history of the war, they had to conclude that in valor the two sides were equally matched. If it was a Northern statesman who extolled the fighters who gave "the last full measure of devotion," it was a Southern poet who, with a heart too full after the death of Pelham to bear the sound of a funeral dirge played by a band, exclaimed: "The living are brave and noble, but the dead were the bravest of all." It is impossible to read unmoved the long lists of soldier-dead in newspaper columns or regimental histories, each with its curt line, "Killed in Battle at Gettysburg," or "Died from Wounds at Dallas, Ga.," and there comes at once to mind John Masefield's challenging lines written of World War I, "The Sinister Spirit said, 'It had to be.' But still, the Spirit of Pity whispered, 'Why?' "

The war more or less directly affected every one of the 35,000,000 men, women, and children in the two sections, Northern and Southern, of the United States. It happily exploded many suppositions that Americans had long held and dreaded as probable results of a stubborn conflict. For example, it totally failed to leave the country a heritage of military ideas, traditions, and impulses, which some had feared. It did not in the least "militarize" the people as various pacifists had anticipated. The best proof of this fact did not lie in the fact that it failed to lead to adventures in foreign conquest, overseas interventions, or filibustering forays, which would have been totally uncharacteristic of the American character. Proof rather lay in the fact that, when Reconstruction came, although one broad course of policy in treating the defeated and restless Southern States was certainly open and many thought inviting, the policy of holding these States in subjugation as territories policed to maintain peace and protect the freedmen in their new rights was never adopted, and was barely approached by the Military Reconstruction Act. On the contrary, the opposed policy was chosen of readmitting the Southern States, while the army was being disbanded, to equal membership in the Union. The military policy would have been a death-knell for the political system which the American people, under wise leadership, had inaugurated in 1789, and which had since then been the admiration of the civilized world. The peaceful policy proved an unassailable success to both North and South, to black and white alike, and vindicated the whole purpose of the founders of the Republic and the men who, from Hamilton and Jefferson to Lincoln, had maintained it. The spirit of the republic in the year of victory was good. It was not boastful or arrogant, for repeated checks and defeats had taught lessons of humility. No outburst of militaristic feeling occurred. Wendell Phillips declared in a speech in Boston that the old farming and reading republic was at an end, and that a strong military and predatory nation might take its place; but he was completely mistaken.

The prevalent foreign criticism of American civilization for decades had been that the republic was the land of the commonplace, and that its democracy inevitably gave emphasis to a code favoring the mediocre average—that its life tended to be dull. One foreign visitor after another touched this chord of criticism, until James Russell Lowell voiced American resentment in his essay "On a Certain Condescension in Foreigners." But Americans were not wont to give way either to bursts of petulance or displays of braggadocio. Their characteristic mood was that of Walt Whitman's "Song of the Banner at Daybreak," a mystical chant over a banner of effort and labor, not of war. His vision was of a land ever higher, stronger, and broader. Americans were well aware that what their land most lacked was high excellence, and distinction.

The United States in the year of Appomattox was a country without a single true university, without any art gallery of wide scope and true eminence, with but few museums of merit in any field (although Natural History was beginning to assert its claims to attention), and with no well-organized library that would satisfy both general students and specialists. The colleges in the State of North Carolina did not offer a single course in English literature worthy of the name. The many and glaring cultural deficiencies of the country were just beginning to receive the attention they demanded. New books were much too few in number, and too poor. The *American Publisher's Circular* listed only 681 works issued in the United States in the second half of 1865 (July 6 through December); and the New York *Nation* thought that only about 140 of them were really substantial books. More distressing than quantitative poverty, however, was the poor quality of American letters during this half-year. The only important volumes of poetry were Walt Whitman's *Drum Taps,* which included "When Lilacs Last in the Dooryard Bloomed," commonly esteemed his greatest single poem; and H.H. Brownell's small book of war verse, which Theodore Roosevelt later praised for its spirited celebrations of the "River Fight" before New Orleans, and the "Bay Fight" before Mobile. In literary criticism Richard Grant White produced some studies of Shakespeare that merited attention. Various chronicles of the war came out, but the writer was correct who asserted that to call them histories would be an abuse of the language. One novel of quality appeared, Elizabeth Stoddard's *Two Men*, and one estimable work of theology, Horace Bushnell's *Vicarious Sacrifice*. In general, however, the crowning year of the war was relatively barren in American letters.

Thoughtful Americans knew well that the pursuit of distinction by production of highly superior works of art, music, and letters, is still more eagerly competitive in democratic than aristocratic societies, other avenues to preëminence being closed. They knew that in a young and struggling and long-impoverished country, the principal prerequisites to the production of real excellence included time, leisure, accumulations of materials of study, the collection of high models, and the clash of active minds in a stimulating environment. They knew that, young and strenuously preoccupied with imperative material tasks as the United States had been, it was already yielding to the world's gaze examples of high excellence, with gleams of distinction that held rare qualities of inspiration. They knew that every year added to the list. One of the many touches of distinction that began to appear in the American scene lay in the vigorous estate of the American Oriental Society, under a president, S. Wells Williams, who stood as high as any other scholar in the world in opening a knowledge of China, the Chinese language, and Chinese letters to the Occident. He had accompanied Commodore Perry as interpreter on his expedition of 1853-54 to Japan; had become secretary and interpreter to the American Legation in China, remaining at that post until 1876; had helped negotiate important treaties; and had become professor of the Chinese language and literature in Yale (1877), writing books of preëminent merit on China and her culture.

The generation of men which read with excited astonishment about the revelations of the ancient past, made by Schliemann in his excavations at the sites of Troy and Mycenae, found equal astonishment and excitement in the revelation of wonders in the Far West as Othniel Charles Marsh built up palaeonto-logical collections in Washington and at Yale of equal significance to the extension of human knowledge.

America had long been a nation of dauntless explorers, and inventive pragmatists. Much of distinction in American life now logically found varied practical expressions, and the mechanical field admitted as high endeavors as any area of the arts and letters. Distinction was given a striking new opening, for example, when the Civil War called young Henry M. Leland, an ardent volunteer in the excitement after Sumter, into government service as a machinist in the Crompton Works in Worcester, Mass., making the Blanchard lathe for turning gun-stocks. In Eli Whitney's day in America, uniformity of machine parts had been brought to the one-hundred-thirty-second part of an inch, after which much filing was required to make machine-joints even.

This would not do. By the labors of artisans such as Leland, precision of machine tools—the cutters, borers, and milling-machines which made the parts of a final mechanism before they were assembled—was steadily improved until uniformity was brought to one-half-thousandth part of an inch. No truer artist was to be found in any land than Blanchard, the lathe-maker, or Leland, the finisher of gauges, jigs, cutters, borers, and other tools that contributed to the development of what men in time called "American industry," preëminent for the combination of delicacy, precision, and adaptability to quantity-manufacture. No truer artists existed in the world than Joseph R. Brown, a clockmaker by origin, who in 1851 introduced the Vernier Caliper, able to make measurements to one-thousandth of an inch.

For all the general poverty of the American cultural scene by the end of the war, it had some aspects of undeniable distinction. Among scholars and writers of high international repute in 1865, the roster included Henry C. Lea, who, already known for his historical articles, published his volume, *Superstition and Force,* in 1866; Frances Parkman, who brought out his *Pioneers of France in the New World* in 1865, and Adolf F. Bandelier, who knew more about Mexican antiquities than any other scholar in Europe or the Americas. A.F. Hall, who had spent years in England studying Sanskrit, Hindustani and Indian jurisprudence, was equally distinguished; Charles F. Peirce, mathematician and philosopher, would have done honor to any country. So would the greatest champion of scientific studies in America, Louis Agassiz, who was laboring along a wide front, his activities respected abroad as well as at home. We find Emerson writing in his journal for March 26, 1864, in the grimmest days of the war, that Agassiz had just returned to Boston from a lecture tour, having created a Natural History Society in Chicago for which 19 persons had subscribed $4,500. Agassiz, with equal enterprise, also took steps to create the Harvard University Museum where he was a pioneer who loved to embark upon costly undertakings with no apparent means of carrying them through —usually with success. William James later summed up his career as that of "a leader who lived from month to month and year to year with no relation to prudence, but on the whole, achieved his aims, studied the geology and fauna of our continent, trained a generation of scientists, founded one of the chief museums of the world, gave a new impetus to scientific education in America, and died the idol of the public."

Another heartening fact was that, with the triumphant close of the war, the American people began to realize that they had larger destinies than those of a purely national character. In 1865 they learned that Mazzini had written the London agent of the Sanitary Commission that the United States had done more in four years for the cause of Republicanism than had been accomplished in Europe in fifty years of discussion. Mazzini added that her task had hitherto been that of self-realization, of vindicating within her own boundaries the ideals that she had erected before herself, the abolition of slavery being her last main achievement. Now she faced a larger body of duties, for the republic must turn from responsibilities that were merely American to purposes of a cosmopolitan and international character. Mazzini hoped she would now assume the leadership in the stern battle rising in all lands between tyranny and liberty, between privilege and equality, furnishing sympathy, moral encouragement, and the support of a successful, enduring, republican society, consistent in all its aims.

The sense of Americans in 1865 that they stood at the close of one era and the beginning of another, a sense which gave millions a new hopefulness and a more convinced belief in the national destiny, was confirmed and strengthened by the evident fact that the perspective of all mankind had been sharply and decisively revolutionized by Union victory in the war. To multitudes the world lost its constricted and limited appearance, and wore a new freshness. It was suddenly evident to the American people that the United States had swiftly and unexpectedly, but undeniably, become one of the principal world powers, with a new set of responsibilities, challenges, and opportunities.

BIBLIOGRAPHY

MANUSCRIPT SOURCES

The author specially thanks Mrs. Pierre Jay for access to the papers of Robert Gould Shaw, and Robert D. Meade for use of the Judah P. Benjamin Papers, as well as Mrs. August Belmont for use of the August Belmont Papers. He thanks E. B. Long, and many others who have supplied transcripts of valuable documents.

In this list, and in the footnote citations throughout the text, the following abbreviations have been employed:

ASA – Alabama State Archives
CHS – Chicago Historical Society
CMLS – Confederate Memorial Literary Society
CUL – Columbia University Library
DU – Duke University
HEH – Henry E. Huntington Library
HSP – Historical Society of Pennsylvania
IHS – Illinois State Historical Society
KHS – Kansas Historical Society
LC – Library of Congress
LSU – Louisiana State University Library
MHS – Massachusetts Historical Society
NA – National Archives
NYHS – New York Historical Society
NYPL – New York Public Library
OHS – Ohio Historical Society
UCLA – University of California, Los Angeles
UNC – University of North Carolina Library
VHS – Virginia Historical Society

MANUSCRIPT COLLECTIONS

Alcorn, James L. Papers, UNC
Allan, Col. William Collection, UNC
Andrew, John A. Papers, MHS
Armstrong-Loring Papers, Private Collection, Oak Park, Ill.
Atwater, M.B., Ms. Reminiscences, State Hist. Soc. of Wisconsin
Babcock, Orville Papers, CHS
Banks, General Nathaniel P. Papers, LC
Barlow, S.L.M. Papers, HEH
Barney, Hiram Papers, HEH
Bates, David Homer Papers, Stern Collection, LC
Belmont, August Papers (Mrs. August Belmont, New York)
Benjamin, Judah P. Papers (Courtesy Robert D. Meade)
Blair-Lee Papers, Princeton University Library
Boynton, H.B. Papers, NYPL
Brayman, Mason Papers, CHS

British Foreign Office Correspondence, London
Broadhead, James O. Papers, Missouri Historical Society
Brooks, Noah Papers, LC
Brown, Campbell Collection, UNC
Brown, Rev. Gustavus Papers, VHS
Bryant, William Cullen Papers, NYPL
Buchanan, James Papers, HSP
Campbell-Colston Papers, UNC
Chandler, Zachariah Papers, LC
Chase, Salmon P. Collection, HSP
Clay, Clement Papers, LC
Collier, Elizabeth, Diary, UNC
Comstock Papers, LC
Connolly, Major James Austin, Letters, IHS
Coppet, Andre de Collection, Princeton University Library
Cram, George F. Papers, Armstrong Collection, Elmhurst, Ill.
Crampton, Capt. Ben Papers, Maryland Hist. Soc., Baltimore
Curry, J.L.M. Papers, ASA; LC
Dana, Charles A. Papers, LC
Davidson, James I. Papers, ASA
Davis, David Papers, IHS
Davis, Henry Winter Papers, Eleutherian Mills Hagley Foundation, Wilmington, Del.
Davis, Jefferson Papers, DU; CMLS, Richmond
Davis-Reagan Papers, Dallas Hist. Soc.
De Bow, J.D.B. Papers, DU
De Leon, T.C. Papers, South Caroliniana Library
Dodge, Grenville M. Papers, Iowa State Hist. Soc.
Dodge, Theodore A. Papers, LC
Doolittle Papers, State Hist. Soc. of Wisconsin
DuPont, H.A. Papers, Eleutherian Mills Hagley Foundation, Wilmington, Del.
Eldredge Collection, HEH
Eustis, George Papers, LC
Forbes Papers, MHS
Fox, G.V. Papers, NYHS
Gale-Polk Papers, UNC
Gardiner, E.C. Papers, HSP
Garland, Hamlin Papers, UCLA
Gay, S.H. Papers, CUL
Gettysburg College Civil War Papers, Gettysburg, Pa.
Gilpin, E.N., Diary, LC
Gladstone Papers, British Museum
Grant, Ulysses S. Papers, IHS; OHS, Columbus, O.
Grant-Halleck Papers, Eldredge Collection, HEH
Grant Notebook, Rosenbach Foundation, Philadelphia
Harding, Sidney, Ms. Diary, LSU
Harrington, George Papers, Missouri Hist. Soc.
Harrison, Benjamin Papers, LC
Hatch, O.M. Papers, IHS
Hay, John Papers, IHS
Heintzelman, Samuel P., Ms. Diary, LC
Hill, D.H. Papers, VHS
Historical Records Survey, Civil War Letters, Records of Middle Tenn.

Hotchkiss, Maj. Jed. Manuscript and Map Collection, LC
House Executive Documents, Washington, D.C.
Howard, Oliver Otis Papers, Bowdoin College Library
Jones, Joseph Russell Papers, CHS
Judge Advocate General Record Books, NA
Keitt, Laurence M. Papers, DU
King, Rufus and Mary Papers, Indiana Univ. Library
LeDuc, William G., Memoirs, HEH
Lee, Robert E. Papers, LC; VHS
Leet, Edwin Papers, LSU
Letcher, John Papers, VHS
Lieber, Francis Papers, HEH
Lightfoot, Emmie Crump, Letters, CMLS
Lincoln, Robert Todd Papers, LC
Long, E.B. Collection Civil War Letters and Mss., Oak Park, Ill.
Mackall Papers, UNC
Madigan, Thomas F., Catalogue of Papers
Mallory, S.R., Diary, UNC
Manipault, Arthur M., Ms. Memoirs, UNC
Marble, Manton Papers, LC
McClernand, Gen. John A. Papers, IHS
McKee, R.M. Papers, ASA
Meade, Gen. George G. Papers, HSP
Meigs, Montgomery C. Papers, LC
Memminger, C.G. Papers, UNC
Meredith, Roy Papers, HSP
Military Historical Society of Massachusetts Papers, Boston
Miller, T.D., Letterbook, C.S.A. Agent, LSU
Moody, Joseph E., Mss. Palmer Collection, Western Reserve Hist. Assoc.
Mordecai, Emma Papers, CMLS
Morgan, E.D. Papers, NYHS, State Library
Morrill, Lot M. Papers, Univ. of Maine, Brunswick, Maine
Morris-Sidley Papers, LSU
Murdock, Eugene C., Ms. "Patriotism Limited," OHS
Nicolay and Hay Papers, IHS
Oral History Collections, CUL
Palfrey, John C. Papers, Military Hist. Soc. of Mass., Boston
Palmer, John M. Papers, IHS
Palmer Collection Civil War Papers, Western Reserve Hist. Soc.
Papers Relating to Treaty of Washington, LC
Parsons, Lewis B. Papers, IHS
Pemberton, John C. Papers, NYPL
Pettus, J.J. Papers, Alabama and Mississippi State Archives
Pickens-Bonham Papers, LC (Petitions of S.C. Negroes)
Pickett, George E. Papers, DU
Porter, Albert Quincy, Diary, Mississippi Archives, Jackson, Miss.
Prescott, Albert H. Papers, HEH
Provost-Marshal General's Records, NA
Quartermaster General's Miscellaneous Letters, LC
Rawlins, John A. Papers, CHS
Records of Relief Commission, CHS
Register of Letters Received, War Records, NA

Reynolds, T.C. Papers, LC
Robinson, Capt. William Culbertson Papers, IHS
Rosecrans, Gen. William S. Papers, UCLA
Royal Engineers Professional Papers, British War Office, London
St. John, Gen. I.M. Papers, NA
Schurz, Carl Papers, State Hist. Soc. of Wisconsin
Secretary of the Interior Reports, Washington
Secretary of the Navy Reports, Washington
Seward, William H. Papers, LC; Univ. of Rochester, N.Y.
Sharp, Henry T. Papers, UNC
Shaw, Robert Gould Papers (Property of Mrs. Pierre Jay)
Sherman, William T. Papers, LC; (Nicholson Collection) HEH; IHS; J.P. Morgan Library, New York; Houghton Library, Harvard Univ.
Shreve, George W., Ms. Reminiscences, Virginia State Library, Richmond
Smith, E. Kirby Papers, UNC
Smith, W.H. Papers, OHS
Southern Historical Collection, UNC
Southern Historical Society Papers, NA
Special Agents' Reports and Correspondence, *Censuses of 1860*, NA
Stanton, Edwin M. Papers, LC
Stearns, George L. Papers, KHS
Stephens, Alexander H. Papers, Manhattanville College, N.Y.
Stiles, Joseph Clay Papers, HEH
Sublett, Emmie Papers, CMLS
Tarbell, Ida Collection, Allegheny College
Trescot, William H. Papers, South Caroliniana Library
Trumbull, Lyman Papers, LC
Valentine Family Letters, Valentine Museum, Richmond, Va.
War Papers (1893), San Francisco Archives
Washburne, Elihu Papers, LC
Welles, Gideon Papers, LC; Brown Univ., Providence, R.I.
Wigfall, Louis T. Papers, Univ. of Texas Library
Wilson, J.H. Papers, LC
Wise, Henry A. Papers, UNC
Wood, Capt. John Taylor, Diary, UNC
Woodman, Horatio Papers, MHS
Yancey, William L. Papers, ASA

NEWSPAPERS AND PERIODICALS

Abraham Lincoln Quarterly
Agricultural History
Alabama Historical Quarterly
Alabama Review
Albany *Evening Journal*
Albany *Evening Journal Almanac*
American Historical Review
American Iron and Steel Association Reports
American Journal of Pharmacy
American Pharmaceutical Association Proceedings
American Railroad Journal
Army and Navy Gazette

Atlanta *Daily Herald*
Atlantic Monthly
Bankers' Magazine
Belvidere, Illinois *Daily Review*
Boston *Advertiser*
Boston Board of Trade—Annual Reports
Boston *Commonwealth*
Boston *Transcript*
Bugle Horn of Liberty (Georgia)
Bulletin of Business Historical Society
Century Magazine
Charleston *Courier*
Charleston *News*
Chicago *Morning Post*
Chicago *Tribune*
Cincinnati Chamber of Commerce and Merchants Exchange Annual Reports
Cincinnati *Commercial*
Cincinnati *Daily Gazette*
Civil War History
Commercial and Financial Chronicle
Confederate Inflation Charts
Congressional *Globe*
Contemporaries, Boston
The Country Gentleman
Cultivator Magazine
Genesee Farmer
Harper's Weekly Magazine
Harrisburg, Pa. *Daily Telegraph*
Hartford *Press*
Hartford *Times*
Historical Statistics of the United States, Washington, D.C.
Hunt's Merchant's Magazine and Commercial Review
L'Indépendence Belge
Journal des Débats, Paris
Journal of the Congress of the Confederate States of America, Washington, D.C.
Journal of Negro History
Journal of the Royal United Service Institution
Journal of Southern History
Kansas Historical Quarterly
Le Pays, Paris
Frank Leslie's Illustrated Newspaper
Lincoln Herald
Lincoln Lore
Abraham Lincoln Quarterly
London Daily News
London Illustrated News
London Saturday Review
London *Times*
Louisiana State Historical Quarterly
Massachusetts Historical Society *Proceedings*
Massachusetts *Ploughshare*
McClure's Magazine

Military Surgeon
Mississippi Historical Society Publications, *Centenary Series*
Mississippi Valley Historical Review
Mississippian, Jackson, Miss.
Missouri Historical Review
Montana, the Magazine of Western History
Montgomery *Advertiser*
National Almanac
New England Farmer
New Orleans *Democrat*
New York *Evening Post*
New York *Herald*
New York History
New York *Independent*
New York Journal of Commerce
New York *Nation*
New York *Tribune*
New York *Tribune Almanac*
North American Review
Norwich, Conn. *Aurora*
Ohio Archeological and Historical Quarterly
Pennsylvania Magazine of History and Biography
Philadelphia *Weekly Times*
The Portfolio (Juvenile Publication of Charleston, S.C.)
Prairie Farmer
Public Personnel Review
Punch (London), 1861–1865
Register of Officers and Agents, Civil, Military and Naval, in the Services of the U.S. 1865, Washington (1861–1870, published biennially)
Richmond *Age*
Richmond *Dispatch*
Richmond *Enquirer*
Richmond *Examiner*
Richmond *Record of News, History and Literature*
Richmond *Sentinel*
Richmond *Whig*
Rural Annual, Rochester, N.Y.
Sacramento *Daily Union*
St. Louis *Globe-Democrat*
Scientific American
Selma, Alabama *Daily Reporter*
Selma, Alabama *Dispatch*
Smith and Barrow's Monthly Magazine (Richmond)
Southern Cultivator
Southern Field and Fireside (Augusta)
Southwestern Historical Quarterly
Southern Literary Messenger
Southern Monthly (Memphis)
Southern Planter
Southern Presbyterian Review
Southern Sentinel (Alexandria, La.)

Tennessee Historical Quarterly
Toronto *Globe*
Transactions of the American Medical Association, Philadelphia
Tyler's Quarterly Historical and Genealogical Magazine
United States Naval Institute Proceedings
Virginia Magazine
Washington *Morning Chronicle*
Washington *National Intelligencer*
Washington *National Republican*
Wilmington *Messenger*
Wisconsin Magazine of History
Yale Review

BOOKS

Abbot, H.L., *Memoir of Andrew Atkinson Humphreys*, Nat'l. Acad. Sci. *Biog. Memoirs* (New York, 1865)
Abbott, Lyman, ed., *Henry Ward Beecher* (New York, 1883)
Abrams, A.S., *A Full and Detailed History of the Siege of Vicksburg* (Atlanta, 1863)
Adams, Charles Francis, *Charles Francis Adams, 1835–1915: An Autobiography* (Cambridge, 1916)
Adams, Charles Francis, *Richard Henry Dana: a Biography* (2 vols., Boston, 1891)
Adams, Charles Francis, Jr., *Charles Francis Adams* (Boston, 1900)
Adams, Ephraim D., ed., *Great Britain and the American Civil War* (2 vols., Gloucester, Mass., 1957)
Adams, George W., *Doctors in Blue* (New York, 1952)
Adams, Henry, *The Education of Henry Adams: an Autobiography* (Boston, 1918; 1961)
Agassiz, Elizabeth C., *Louis Agassiz, His Life and Correspondence* (2 vols., Boston, 1885)
Agassiz, George R., ed., *Meade's Headquarters, 1863–1865* (Boston, 1922)
Ages of United States Volunteer Soldiers—a Report (New York, 1866)
Aid Societies in the Civil War (Special volume of pamphlets bound together in the Newberry Library, Chicago)
Alexander, De Alva Stanwood, *A Political History of the State of New York* (New York, 1906–1909)
Alexander, Edward Porter, *Military Memoirs of a Confederate* (New York, 1907)
Ambler, Charles H., *Francis H. Pierpont: Union War Governor of Virginia* (Chapel Hill, 1937)
American Annual Cyclopaedia (New York, 1862–1875)
Ames, Blanche Butler, ed., *Chronicles from the Nineteenth Century: Family Letters of Blanche and Adelbert Ames* (Clinton, Mass., 1957)
Ammen, Daniel, *The Atlantic Coast* (New York, 1883–1885)
An English Merchant, *Two Months in the Confederate States* (London, 1865)
Andreano, Ralph, ed., *The Economic Impact of the American Civil War* (Cambridge, Mass., 1962)
Andreas, A.T., *History of Chicago* (Chicago, 1884–1886)
Andrews, Eliza Frances, *The Wartime Journal of a Georgia Girl, 1864–1865* (New York, 1908)
Andrews, J. Cutler, *The North Reports the Civil War* (Pittsburgh, 1955)
Annual Messages of Governors (Richmond, 1863)
Annual Reports of the Sanitary Company of the New York Police Department (New York, 1862)
Aptheker, Herbert, *A Documentary History of the Negro People in the United States* (2 vols., New York, 1968)
Arkansas Civil War Centennial Commission, *Arkansas and the Civil War* (Pamphlet, Little Rock, 1961)
Armstrong, William M., *E.L. Godkin and American Foreign Policy* (New York, 1957)
Association for Improving the Condition of the Poor; Report (New York, 1865)
Atkins, Gordon, *Health, Housing and Poverty in New York City* (Ann Arbor, 1947)

Avary, Myrta L., ed., *A Virginia Girl in the Civil War* (New York, 1903)
Avary, Myrta L., *Recollections of Alexander H. Stephens* (New York, 1910)
Ayer, Col. I. Winslow, *The Great Treason Plot in the North During the War* (Chicago, 1895)

Badeau, Adam, *Military History of Ulysses S. Grant* (3 vols., New York, 1868–1881)
Baker, George E., ed., *The Works of William H. Seward* (5 vols., New York, 1853–1884)
Baker, L.W., *History of the Ninth Massachusetts Battery* (South Farmington, Mass., 1888)
Bancroft, Frederic, *Life of William H. Seward* (2 vols., New York, 1900)
Bancroft, Frederic, ed., *Speeches, Correspondence, and Political Papers of Carl Schurz* (6 vols., New York, 1913)
Barksdale, Richard, *Cornerstones of Confederate Collecting* (Charlottesville, Va., 1952)
Barnard, Harry, *Rutherford B. Hayes and His America* (Indianapolis, 1954)
Barnes, Thurlow Weed, *Life of Thurlow Weed: Memoir by His Grandson* (2 vols., Boston, 1884)
Barrett, John G., *Sherman's March Through the Carolinas* (Chapel Hill, 1956)
Barrie, George, *The History of North America* (Philadelphia, 1906)
Barrus, Clara, *Life and Letters of John Burroughs* (Boston, 1925)
Bartlett, Irving H., *Wendell Phillips* (Boston, 1961)
Barton, William E., *Lincoln at Gettysburg* (Indianapolis, 1930)
Barton, William E., *Life of Clara Barton* (2 vols., Boston, 1922)
Basso, Hamilton, *Beauregard, the Great Creole* (New York, 1933)
Bates, David Homer, *Lincoln in the Telegraph Office* (New York, 1907)
Bates, Ralph S., *Scientific Societies in the United States* (New York, 1951)
Baxter, James P., *The Introduction of the Ironclad Warship* (Cambridge, Mass., 1933)
Baxter, James P., *Orville H. Browning: Lincoln's Friend and Critic* (Bloomington, 1957)
Beale, Howard K., ed., *The Diary of Edward Bates* (Washington, 1933)
Bearss, Edwin C., *Decision in Mississippi* (Jackson, Miss., 1962)
Belden, Thomas Graham and Marva Robins Belden, *So Fell the Angels* (Boston, 1956)
Bell, Herbert C.F., *Lord Palmerston* (2 vols., London, 1936)
Bellows, Henry W., *Historical Sketch of the Union League Club of New York* (New York, 1879)
Belmont, August, *Letters, Speeches, and Addresses of August Belmont* (New York, 1890)
Bemis, Samuel Flagg, *A Diplomatic History of the United States* (New York, 1936)
Bemis, Samuel Flagg, *The American Secretaries of State and Their Diplomacy* (10 vols., New York, 1928; 1958)
Bennett, A.J., *Story of the First Massachusetts Light Battery* (Boston, 1886)
Bentley, George R., *A History of the Freedmen's Bureau* (Philadelphia, 1955)
Bernard, Montague, *A Historical Account of the Neutrality of Great Britain During the American Civil War* (London, 1870)
Bernath, Stuart L., *Squall Across the Atlantic* (Los Angeles, 1970)
Bettersworth, John Knox, *Confederate Mississippi* (Baton Rouge, 1943)
Bickham, William D., *Rosecrans's Campaign* (Cincinnati, 1863)
Bidwell, Percy W. and John I. Falconer, *History of Agriculture in the Northern United States* (Washington, 1925)
Bierce, Ambrose, *Battle Sketches* (London, 1930)
Bigelow, Maj. John, Jr., *The Principles of Strategy* (New York, 1891)
Bigelow, John, ed., *Letters and Literary Memorials of Samuel J. Tilden* (New York, 1908)
Bigelow, John, *The Life of Samuel J. Tilden* (2 vols., New York, 1895)
Bill, A.H., *The Beleaguered City: Richmond, 1861–1865* (New York, 1946)
Billings, John D., *History of the Tenth Massachusetts Battery of Light Artillery* (Boston, 1881)
Billington, Ray Allen, *America's Frontier Heritage* (New York, 1966)
Binney, C.C., *Life of Horace Binney* (Philadelphia, 1903)
Binney, Horace, *The Privilege of the Writ of Habeas Corpus Under the Constitution* (Philadelphia, 1862)

Bishop, Joseph Bucklin, *A Chronicle of One Hundred and Fifty Years, the Chamber of Commerce of the State of New York, 1768–1918* (New York, 1913)
Black, Robert C., III, *The Railroads of the Confederacy* (Chapel Hill, 1952)
Blackford, William W., *War Years with Jeb Stuart* (New York, 1945)
Blaine, James G., *Twenty Years of Congress: From Lincoln to Garfield* (2 vols., Norwich, Conn., 1884–1886)
Blair, Montgomery, *Revolutionary Schemes of the Abolitionists* (Baltimore, 1863)
Blake, Henry N., *Three Years in the Army of the Potomac* (Boston, 1865)
Blake, Robert, *Disraeli* (New York, 1967)
Blochman, Lawrence G., *Doctor Squibb* (New York, 1958)
Boatner, M.M., *Civil War Dictionary* (New York, 1959)
Bodart, Gaston, *Losses of Life in Modern War* (London, 1916)
Bokum, Herman, *Wanderings North and South: the Testimony of a Refugee from East Tennessee* (Philadelphia, 1863)
Bolles, Albert S., *Industrial History of the United States* (Norwich, Conn., 1879)
Borcke, Heros Von, *Memoirs of the Confederate War for Independence* (Edinburgh, 1866)
Borthwick, J.D., *Three Years in California* (Edinburgh, 1857)
Bosson, C.P., *History of the 42d Massachusetts Volunteers* (Boston, 1886)
Boston Board of Trade, *Tenth Annual Report for 1863* (Boston, 1864)
Botkin, Benjamin A., ed., *Lay My Burden Down: A Folk History of Slavery* (Chicago, 1945)
Boulding, Kenneth F., *The Organizational Revolution* (New York, 1953)
Boutwell, George S., *Reminiscences of Sixty Years in Public Affairs* (New York, 1902)
Bowen, James Lorenzo, *History of the Thirty-seventh Regiment Massachusetts Volunteers* (Holyoke, Mass., 1884)
Bowers, Claude G., *The Tragic Era; The Revolution After Lincoln* (Cambridge, 1929)
Boykin, Edward M., *The Falling Flag: Evacuation of Richmond and Surrender at Appomattox* (New York, 1874)
Boykin, Edward C., *Ghost Ship of the Confederacy* (New York, 1957)
Boynton, H.V., *Sherman's Historical Raid* (Cincinnati, 1875)
Boynton, H.V., compiler, *Dedication of the Chickamauga and Chattanooga National Military Park* (Washington, 1896)
Boynton, Percy H., ed., *Poems of the Civil War* (New York, 1918)
Bradford, Gamaliel, *Confederate Portraits* (Boston, 1914)
Bradford, Gamaliel, *Union Portraits* (Boston, 1916)
Bradford, Gamaliel, *Lee the American* (Boston, 1927)
Bradlee, F.B.C., *Blockade Running During the Civil War* (Salem, Mass., 1925)
Bradley, Joseph F., *The Rôle of Trade Associations and Professional Business Societies in America* (University Park, Pa., 1965)
Bragg, J.D., *Louisiana in the Confederacy* (Baton Rouge, 1941)
Brigance, William N., *Jeremiah Sullivan Black, a Defender of the Constitution and the Ten Commandments* (Philadelphia, 1934)
Brigham, Johnson, *James Harlan* (Iowa City, 1913)
Brinley, Thomas, *Migration and Economic Growth: a Study of Great Britain and the Atlantic Economy* (Cambridge, 1954)
Brodie, Fawn M., *Thaddeus Stevens: Scourge of the South* (New York, 1959)
Brooks, Noah, *Washington in Lincoln's Time* (New York, 1895); ed., Herbert Mitgang (New York, 1958)
Brooks, Robert P., *Conscription in the Confederate States of America, 1862–1865* (Athens, Ga., 1917)
Brooks, Van Wyck, *Makers and Finders: A History of the Writer in America, 1800–1915* (5 vols., New York, 1936–1952)
Bross, William, *Biographical Sketch of the Late B.J. Sweet and History of Camp Douglas* (pamphlet, Chicago, 1878)

Brown, Dee A., *Grierson's Raid* (Urbana, 1954)
Brown, Ernest Francis, *Raymond of the Times* (New York, 1951)
Browne, Francis, *The Every-Day Life of Abraham Lincoln* (Chicago, 1913)
Browne, J. Ross and James W. Taylor, *Report upon the Mineral Resources of the United States* (Washington, 1867)
Browning, Orville H., *Diary*, ed., T.C. Pease and James G. Randall (Springfield, Ill., 1925–1933)
Brownlow, W.G., *Sketches of the Rise, Progress, and Decline of Secession* (Philadelphia, 1862)
Bruce, Kathleen, *Virginia Iron Manufacture in the Slave Era* (New York, 1930)
Bruce, Robert V., *Lincoln and the Tools of War* (Indianapolis, 1956)
Bryan, George S., *The Great American Myth: The True Story of Lincoln's Murder* (New York, 1940)
Bryan, Thomas Conn, *Confederate Georgia* (Athens, Ga., 1953)
Bryant, Sir Arthur, *Years of Victory* (New York, 1945)
Buck, Irving, *Cleburne and His Command* (Jackson, Tenn., 1959)
Buckeridge, J.O., *Lincoln's Choice* (Harrisburg, Pa., 1956)
Buckmaster, Henrietta, pseud. (Henrietta Henkle), *Let My People Go* (New York, 1941)
Buell, Augustus, *The Cannoneer* (Washington, 1890)
Ballard, F. Lauriston, *A Few Appropriate Remarks: Abraham Lincoln and the Widow Bixby* (New Brunswick, N.J., 1946)
Bulloch, James D., *The Secret Service of the Confederate States in Europe* (New York, 1959; London, 1883)
Burgess, John W., *Reminiscences of an American Scholar* (New York, 1934)
Burn, James Dawson, *Three Years among the Working Classes in the United States During the War* (London, 1865)
Burne, Col. Alfred H., *Lee, Grant and Sherman* (New York, 1939)
Burr, Anna Robeson, *Dr. S. Weir Mitchell, His Life and Letters* (New York, 1929)
Burrow, James P., *American Medical Association, Voice of American Medicine* (Baltimore, 1963)
Burtis, Mary E., *Moncure Conway, 1832–1907* (New Brunswick, Me., 1952)
Burton, Theodore E., *John Sherman* (Boston, 1906)
Butler, Benjamin F., *Autobiography* [*Butler's Book*] (Boston, 1892)
Butler, Pierce, *Judah P. Benjamin* (Philadelphia, 1907)
Byers, S.H.M., *With Fire and Sword* (New York, 1911)

Cadwallader, Sylvanus C., *Three Years With Grant*, ed., Benjamin P. Thomas (New York, 1955)
Cain, Marvin R., *Lincoln's Attorney-General, Edward Bates of Missouri* (Columbia, Mo., 1965)
Capers, Gerald M., *The Biography of a River Town: Memphis, Its Heroic Age* (Chapel Hill, 1939)
Capers, H.D., *The Life and Times of C.G. Memminger* (Richmond, 1893)
Cappon, Lester J., *Virginia Newspapers, 1921–1935, a Bibliography* (New York, 1936)
Carmon, Harry J. and Rembard H. Lytkin, *Lincoln and the Patronage* (New York, 1943)
Carpenter, John A., *Sword and Olive Branch* (Pittsburgh, 1964)
Carr, Clark E., *My Day and Generation* (Chicago, 1908)
Carr, William H.A., *The DuPonts of Delaware* (New York, 1964)
Carter, Robert and Walter, *War Letters from the Battlefront, 1861–1865* (Ms. Notebooks, HEH)
Carter, W.C., *History of the First Regiment of Tennessee Volunteer Cavalry* (Knoxville, 1902)
Caskey, Willie M., *Secession and Restoration of Louisiana* (University, La., 1938)
Casson, Herbert N., *Romance of Steel* (New York, 1907)
Catton, Bruce, *Grant Moves South* (Boston, 1960)
Catton, Bruce, *Grant Takes Command* (Boston, 1968)
Catton, Bruce, *Mr. Lincoln's Army* (Garden City, 1951)
Catton, Bruce, *Glory Road* (Garden City, 1952)
Catton, Bruce, *A Stillness at Appomattox* (Garden City, 1954)
Catton, Bruce, *U.S. Grant and the American Military Tradition* (Boston, 1954)
Chadwick, J.W., *Henry W. Bellows; His Life and Character* (New York, 1882)
Chamberlain, Joshua L., *The Passing of the Armies* (New York, 1915)

Chambers, William N., *Old Bullion Benton* (Boston, 1956)
Chandler, William E., *The Soldier's Right to Vote* (Washington, 1864)
Channing, Edward, *History of the United States* (Vol. VI), *War for Southern Independence* (New York, 1925)
Chase, Philip H., *Confederate Treasury Notes* (Philadelphia, 1947)
Chase, Salmon P., *Diary and Correspondence of Salmon P. Chase* (Washington, 1903)
Chesnut, Mary Boykin, *A Diary from Dixie* (Boston, 1949; 1st ed. 1905)
Church, William Conant, *Grant* (New York, 1897)
Civil War Centennial Commission, *Tennesseans in the Civil War* (Nashville, 1964)
Civil War Naval Chronology (Washington and Philadelphia, 1907)
Claiborne, John F.H., ed., Life and Correspondence of John A. Quitman (2 vols., New York, 1860)
Clapham, John Harold, *An Economic History of Modern Britain* (Cambridge, Eng., 1930–1938)
Clark, Victor S., *History of Manufactures in the U.S.* (New York, 1929)
Clarke, Grace J., *George W. Julian* (Indianapolis, 1923)
Clay, Victor S., *History of Manufactures in the United States, 1607–1860* (New York, 1929)
Clay-Clopton, Mrs. Virginia, ed., Ada Sterling *A Belle of the Fifties; Memoirs of Mrs. Clay of Alabama* (New York, 1905)
Cleaves, Freeman, *Meade of Gettysburg* (Norman, Okla., 1960)
Cleaves, Freeman, *Rock of Chickamauga; the Life of General George H. Thomas* (Norman, Okla., 1948)
Cleveland, Henry, *Alexander H. Stephens, in Public and Private* (Philadelphia, 1866)
Clews, Henry, *Twenty-eight Years in Wall Street* (New York, 1887)
Cobden Club Essays (London, 1872)
Cochran, Hamilton, *Blockade Runners of the Confederacy* (New York, 1958)
Cochran, Thomas and William Miller, *The Age of Enterprise* (New York, 1942)
Coddington, Edwin B., *The Gettysburg Campaign: A Study in Command* (New York, 1968)
Coffin, Charles Carleton, *Marching to Victory* (New York, 1889)
Coffin, Charles Carleton, *The Boys of '61* (Boston, 1881)
Coit, Margaret L., *John C. Calhoun* (Boston, 1950)
Cole, Arthur Charles, *The Irrepressible Conflict* (New York, 1938)
Cole, Arthur Charles, *The Era of the Civil War, 1849–1870* (Springfield, Ill., 1919)
Cole, Arthur Harrison, *The American Wool Manufacture* (Cambridge, Mass., 1926)
Coleman, Ann Mary Butler, *The Life of John J. Crittenden*, ed. by his daughter, Mrs. Chapman Coleman (Philadelphia, 1871)
Colyer, Vincent, *Report of the Services Rendered by the Freed People to the U.S. Army in North Carolina in the Spring of 1862* (New York, 1864)
Commager, Henry S., *Theodore Parker* (Boston, 1936)
A Committee of the Regiment, *The Story of the Fifty-fifth Regiment, Illinois Volunteer Infantry* (Clinton, Mass., 1887)
Commons, John R. and others, eds., *A Documentary History of American Industrial Society* (10 vols., New York, 1910–1911)
Commons, John R. and others, eds., *History of Labor in the United States* (4 vols., New York, 1918–1935)
Comte de Paris, *History of the Civil War in America* (Philadelphia, 1875–1888)
Conger, A.L., *The Rise of U.S. Grant* (New York, 1931)
Connolly, Major James Austin, *Diary* (Springfield, 1928)
Connor, Henry G., *John Archibald Campbell, Associate Justice of the United States Supreme Court, 1853–1861* (Boston, 1920)
Conrad, Earl, *The Governor and His Lady: the Story of William Henry Seward and His Wife Frances* (New York, 1960)
Conway, Moncure, *Addresses and Reprints* (New York, 1908)
Conway, Moncure, *Autobiography: Memories and Experiences* (Boston, 1904)
Conyngham, Capt. David P., *Sherman's March Through the South* (New York, 1865)

Cook, Sir Edward, *Delane of the Times* (New York, 1916)
Cooke, John Esten, *Wearing of the Gray* (New York, 1867); new ed., Philip Van Doren Stern (Bloomington, 1959)
Coolidge, Louis A., *Ulysses S. Grant* (2 vols., Boston, 1924)
Copeland, Melvin T., *The Cotton Manufacturing Industry of the United States* (Cambridge, Mass., 1912)
Cornish, Dudley T., *The Sable Arm: Negro Troops in the Army, 1861–1865* (New York, 1956)
Cortissoz, Royal, *The Life of Whitelaw Reid* (2 vols., New York, 1921)
Coulson, Thomas, *Joseph Henry: His Life and Work* (Princeton, 1950)
Coulter, E. Merton, *The Confederate States of America, 1861–1865* (Baton Rouge, 1950)
Coulter, E. Merton, *William G. Brownlow, Fighting Parson* (Chapel Hill, 1937)
Coulter, E. Merton, *The Civil War and Readjustment in Kentucky* (Chapel Hill, 1926)
Courtney, W.L., *Life of John Stuart Mill* (London, 1889)
Cox, Jacob Dolson, *Military Reminiscences of the Civil War* (New York, 1900)
Cox, Jacob Dolson, *Atlanta* (New York, 1882)
Cox, Jacob Dolson, *March to the Sea, Franklin and Nashville* (New York, 1882)
Cox, Jacob Dolson, *The Battle of Franklin, Tennessee* (New York, 1897)
Cox, Lawanda and John H., *Politics, Principle and Prejudice, 1865–1866* (London, 1963)
Cox, Samuel S., *Three Decades of Federal Legislation* (Providence, 1885)
Cramer, Jesse G., ed., *Letters of U.S. Grant to His Father and His Youngest Sister* (New York, 1912)
Crane, Stephen, *The Red Badge of Courage* (New York, 1896)
Craven, Avery, *The Coming of the Civil War* (New York, 1942; 1947)
Craven, Avery, *Repressible Conflict* (University, La., 1939)
Craven, Avery, *Civil War in the Making* (Baton Rouge, 1959)
Craven, Avery, *Edmund Ruffin, Southerner* (New York, 1932)
Crippen, Lee F., *Simon Cameron: Ante-Bellum Years* (Oxford, Ohio, 1942)
Croffut, W.A., ed., *Fifty Years in Camp and Field, Diary of Major-General Ethan Allen Hitchcock, U.S.A.* (New York, 1909)
Crownishield, Benjamin W., *A History of the First Massachusetts Cavalry* (Boston, 1891)
Crownover, Sims, *The Battle of Franklin* (reprint, Nashville, 1955)
Cruises of the Sumter and the Alabama: Log (London, 1864)
Cudworth, Warren Handel, *History of the First Regiment Massachusetts Infantry* (Boston, 1866)
Cullum, G.W., *Biographical Register of the Officers and Graduates of the U.S. Military Academy, at West Point, N.Y.* (New York, 1868)
Cumming, Kate, *Kate: the Journal of a Confederate Nurse*, ed., Richard Harwell (Baton Rouge, 1959)
Cunningham, Edward, *The Port Hudson Campaign, 1862–1863* (Baton Rouge, 1963)
Cunningham, H.H., *Doctors in Gray* (Baton Rouge, 1958)
Current, Richard N., *Pine Logs and Politics* (New York, 1950)
Current, Richard N., *The Lincoln Nobody Knows* (New York, 1958)
Current, Richard N., *Old Thad Stevens, a Story of Ambition* (Madison, 1942)
Curti, Merle E., *The Growth of American Thought* (New York, 1943)
Curtis, George T., *The Life of Daniel Webster* (2 vols., New York, 1870)
Curtis, George William, *From the Easy Chair* (New York, 1892–1894)
Curtis, George William, ed., *The Correspondence of John Lothrop Motley* (2 vols., New York, 1889)
Curtis, Newton Martin, *From Bull Run to Chancellorsville* (New York, 1906)

Daggett, Stewart, *Railroad Reorganization* (New York, 1966)
Dahlgren, M.V., *Memoir of Admiral John A. Dahlgren* (Boston, 1882)
Dana, Charles A., *Recollections of the Civil War* (New York, 1898)
Dasent, A.I., *John Delane, 1817–1879, ed. The Times* (London, 1908)
Davis, Burke, *Jeb Stuart, the Last Cavalier* (New York, 1957)
Davis, Burke, *Gray Fox: Robert E. Lee and the Civil War* (New York, 1956)
Davis, Burke, *To Appomattox; Nine April Days, 1865* (New York, 1959)

Davis, Capt. C.H., *Life of Charles Henry Davis, Rear-Admiral, 1807–1877* (New York, 1899)
Davis, Charles E., Jr., *Three Years in the Army; the Thirteenth Massachusetts Volunteers* (Boston, 1894)
Davis, Jefferson, *The Rise and Fall of the Confederate Government* (New York, 1881)
Davis, Rebecca Blain Harding, *Bits of Gossip* (New York, 1904)
Davis, Reuben, *Recollections of Mississippi and Mississippians* (Heston, Miss., 1889)
Davis, Varina Howell, *Jefferson Davis . . . A Memoir by His Wife* (New York, 1890)
Dawson, Sarah M., *A Confederate Girl's Diary*, ed., James I. Robertson, Jr. (Bloomington, 1960)
De Chenal, Francois, *The American Army in the War of Secession* (Ft. Leavenworth, 1894)
DeForest, John William, *A Volunteer's Adventures* (London, 1946)
DeLeon, T.C., *Four Years in Rebel Capitals* (Mobile, 1890)
Dennett, Tyler, *Lincoln and the Civil War, in the Diaries and Letters of John Hay* (New York, 1939)
Dennett, Tyler, *John Hay: From Poetry to Politics* (New York, 1933)
De Trobriand, Regis, *Four Years with the Army of the Potomac* (Boston, 1889)
Detroit *Post* and *Tribune*, *Zachariah Chandler* (New York, 1880)
Dew, Charles B., *Ironmaker to the Confederacy: Joseph R. Anderson and the Tredegar Iron Works* (New Haven, 1966)
Dewey, Davis R., *Financial History of the United States* (New York, 1903; 1934)
Dicey, Edward, *Six Months in the Federal States* (2 vols., London, 1863)
Dix, Morgan, ed., *Memoirs of John Adams Dix* (2 vols., New York, 1883)
Dodd, Dorothy, *Henry J. Raymond and the New York Times* (New York, 1936)
Dodd, Ira S., *The Song of the Rappahannock* (New York, 1898)
Dodd, William E., *Robert J. Walker, Imperialist* (Chicago, 1914)
Dodge, Maj. Gen. Grenville M., *The Battle of Atlanta* (Council Bluffs, 1911)
Dodge, Maj. Gen. Grenville M., *Personal Recollections of President Abraham Lincoln, Gen. Ulysses S. Grant and Gen. William T. Sherman* (Glendale, Calif., 1914)
Donald, David, ed., *Inside Lincoln's Cabinet: the Civil War Diaries of Salmon P. Chase* (New York, 1954)
Donald, David, *Charles Sumner and the Coming of the Civil War* (New York, 1960)
Donald, Henderson H., *The Negro Freedman* (New York, 1952)
Dorfman, Joseph, *The Economic Mind in American Civilization, 1606–1918* (3 vols., New York, 1949)
Dorris, Jonathan Truman, *Pardon and Amnesty Under Lincoln and Johnson* (Chapel Hill, 1953)
Dorsey, Sarah A., *Recollections of Henry Watkins Allen* (New York, 1866)
Doubleday, Abner, *Chancellorsville and Gettysburg, Campaigns of the Civil War* (New York, 1882)
Dowd, Clement, *Life of Zebulon B. Vance* (Charlotte, N.C., 1897)
Dowdey, Clifford, *Experiment in Rebellion* (Garden City, 1946)
Dowdey, Clifford, *Death of a Nation* (New York, 1958)
Dowdey, Clifford, *Lee's Last Campaign* (Boston, 1960)
Dowdey, Clifford and Louis H. Manarin, eds., *The Wartime Papers of Robert E. Lee* (Boston, 1961)
Downey, Fairfax, *Storming of the Gates: Chattanooga, 1863* (New York, 1963)
Duberman, Martin B., *Charles Francis Adams* (New York, 1961)
DuBois, James T. and G.S. Mathews, *Galusha A. Grow, Father of the Homestead Law* (Boston, 1917)
DuBose, J.W., *Life and Times of William Lowndes Yancey* (Birmingham, 1892)
Duke, Basil W., *A History of Morgan's Cavalry* (Bloomington, 1961)
Dulles, Foster R., *Labor in America* (New York, 1949)
Dumond, Dwight L., ed., *Letters of James Gillespie Birney* (New York, 1938)
Dumond, Dwight L., *Antislavery Origins of the Civil War in the United States* (Ann Arbor, 1939)
Dunbar, Seymour, *A History of Travel in America* (4 vols., New York, 1915)
Duncan, Capt. Louis C., *The Medical Department of the U.S. Army in the Civil War*
Dunning, William Archibald, *Reconstruction, Political and Economic,* (New York, 1907)
DuPont, H.A., *Rear-Admiral Samuel Francis DuPont* (New York, 1926)
Dupuy, Richard E. and Trevor N. Dupuy, *The Compact History of the Civil War* (New York, 1960)
Durden, Robert F., *James Shepherd Pike: Republicanism and the American Negro, 1850–1882* (Durham, 1957)
Dutton, William S., *DuPont, One Hundred and Forty Years* (New York, 1942)

Dyer, Brainerd, *Zachary Taylor* (Baton Rouge, 1946)
Dyer, Frederick H., *A Compendium of the War of the Rebellion* (Des Moines, 1908)
Dyer, John P., *The Gallant Hood* (Indianapolis, 1950)
Dyer, John P., *"Fightin' Joe" Wheeler* (University, La., 1941)

Early, Jubal A., *Autobiographical Sketch and Narrative of the War Between the States* (Philadelphia, 1912); new ed. titled *War Memoirs . . .*, with introduction by Frank E. Vandiver (Bloomington, 1960)
Eaton, Clement, *A History of the Southern Confederacy* (New York, 1954)
Eaton, John and Ethel O. Mason, *Grant, Lincoln, and the Freedmen* (New York, 1907)
Eckenrode, H.J. *George B. McClellan, the Man Who Saved the Union* (Chapel Hill, 1941)
Eckenrode, H.J. and Bryan Conrad, *James Longstreet, Lee's War Horse* (Chapel Hill, 1936)
Edwards, William B., *Civil War Guns* (Harrisburg, 1962)
Eggleston, George Cary, *A Rebel's Recollections* (Bloomington, 1959)
Eisenschiml, Otto, ed., *Vermont General: The Unusual War Experiences of Edward Hastings Ripley, 1862–1865* (New York, 1960)
Eisenchiml, Otto, *Why Was Lincoln Murdered?* (Boston, 1939)
Elliott, Charles W., *Winfield Scott: the Soldier and the Man* (New York, 1937)
Emilio, Louis F., *History of the Fifty-fourth Regiment of Massachusetts Volunteer Infantry, 1863–1865* (Boston, 1891)
Evarts, Sherman, ed., *Arguments and Speeches of William Maxwell Evarts* (3 vols., New York, 1919)
Everhart, William G., *Vicksburg National Military Park, Mississippi* (Washington, 1954)

Fahrney, Ralph R., *Horace Greeley and the Tribune in the Civil War* (Cedar Rapids, 1936)
Falls, Cyril, *A Hundred Years of War* (London, 1954)
Farley, Porter, *Reminiscences of the 140th Regiment New York Volunteers* (Rochester, N.Y., 1944)
Farragut, Loyall, *The Life of David Glasgow Farragut* (New York, 1907)
Ferleger, Herbert R., *David A. Wells and the American Revenue System* (New York, 1942)
Fessenden, Francis, *Life and Public Services of William Pitt Fessenden, United States Senator from Maine, 1854–1864* (Boston, 1907)
Field, E.A., *Record of the Life of David Dudley Field* (Denver, 1931)
Field, Maunsell, *Memories of Many Men and of Some Women* (London, 1874)
Fielder, Herbert, *Sketch of the Life and Times and Speeches of Joseph E. Brown* (Springfield, Mass., 1883)
Fishbein, Morris, *A History of the American Medical Association* (Philadelphia, 1947)
Fisher, Sidney G., *The True Daniel Webster* (Philadelphia, 1911)
Fite, Emerson Davis, *Social and Industrial Conditions in the North During the Civil War* (New York, 1930; 1963)
Fladelander, Betty L., *James Gillespie Birney; Slaveholder to Abolitionist* (Ithaca, N.Y., 1955)
Fleming, W.L., *The South in the Building of the Nation* (Richmond, 1909–1913)
Fleming, W.L., *The Freedmen's Savings Bank* (Chapel Hill, 1927)
Fleming, W.L., *Civil War and Reconstruction in Alabama* (New York, 1905)
Flick, Alexander C., *Samuel Jones Tilden* (2 vols., New York, 1895)
Flippin, Percy S., *Herschel V. Johnson of Georgia* (Richmond, 1931)
Flower, Frank A., *Edwin McMasters Stanton* (Akron, 1905)
Foner, Philip S., *History of the Labor Movement in the United States* (New York, 1947)
Foote, Henry S., *Casket of Reminiscences* (Washington, 1874)
Foote, Shelby, *The Civil War* (New York, 1958)
Ford, James, *History of the Civil War* (New York, 1917)
Ford, Worthington C., ed., *A Cycle of Adams Letters* (2 vols., Boston, 1920)
Ford, Worthington C., ed., *Letters of Henry Adams* (Boston, 1930–1938)
Ford, Worthington C., ed., *War Letters of John Chipman Gray* (Boston, 1927)
Formby, John, *The American Civil War* (New York, 1910)

Foth, Joseph Henry, *Trade Associations, Their Services to Industry* (New York, 1930)
Foulke, William Dudley, *Life of Oliver P. Morton* (Indianapolis, 1877)
Fowler, Dorothy Canfield, *The Cabinet Politician: the Postmasters-General, 1829–1909* (New York, 1943)
Fowler, William W., *Ten Years in Wall Street* (Hartford, 1870)
Fowler, William W., *Memorials of William Fowler* (New York, 1875)
Fox, William F., *Regimental Losses in the American Civil War* (Albany, 1889)
Franklin, John H., *The Diary of James T. Ayers, Civil War Recruiter* (Springfield, 1947)
Freeman, Cleaves, *Meade of Gettysburg*, (Norman, Okla., 1960)
Freeman, Douglas Southall, *Robert E. Lee, A Biography* (4 vols., New York, 1934–1935)
Freeman, Douglas Southall, *Lee's Lieutenants* (New York, 1946)
Freeman, Douglas Southall, *Lee's Dispatches* (New York, 1915; 1957)
Freidel, Frank, *Francis Lieber, Nineteenth-Century Liberal* (Baton Rouge, 1947)
Freidel, Frank, ed., *Union Pamphlets of the Civil War* (Boston, 1967)
Fremantle, Lt. Col. James Arthur Lyon, *Three Months in the Southern States, April–June, 1863* (New York, 1864), new ed. by Walter Lord, titled *The Fremantle Diary* (Boston, 1954)
Frothingham, Paul R., *Edward Everett: Orator and Statesman* (Boston, 1925)
Fry, James B., *New York and the Conscription of 1863* (New York, 1885)
Fry, James B., *Military Miscellanies* (New York, 1889)
Fuess, Claude, *Carl Schurz, Reformer, 1829–1906* (Port Washington, N.Y., 1963)
Fuess, Claude, *Daniel Webster* (2 vols. Boston, 1930)
Fuller, J.F.C., *The Generalship of Ulysses S. Grant* (New York, 1919; 1958)
Fuller, J.F.C., *Grant and Lee* (London, 1933; Bloomington, 1957)

Gabriel, Ralph H., *The Course of American Democratic Thought* (New York, 1940)
Gallman, Robert E., *Trends in the Size Distribution of Wealth in the 19th Century* (New York, 1969)
Gardner, John W., *Self-Renewal: The Individual and the Innovative Society* (New York, 1864)
Gates, Paul W., *Agriculture and the Civil War* (New York, 1965)
Gates, Paul W., *The Farmer's Age* (New York, 1960)
Gerrish, Theodore, *Army Life, a Private's Reminiscences of the Civil War* (Portland, Me., 1882)
Gibson, John M., *Those 163 Days* (New York, 1961)
Giddens, Paul H., *The Birth of the Oil Industry* (New York, 1939)
Gilchrist, David T. and W. David Lewis, eds., *Economic Change in the Civil War Era* (Greenville, Del., 1965)
Gilder, Rosamond, *Letters of Richard Watson Gilder* (Boston, 1916)
Gilmore, James Robert, *Personal Recollections of Abraham Lincoln and the Civil War* (London, 1899)
Godkin, Edwin Lawrence, *Unforeseen Tendencies of Democracy* (Westminster, England, 1903)
Goodrich, Lloyd, *The Graphic Art of Winslow Homer* (New York, 1968)
Gordon, John B., *Reminiscences of the Civil War* (New York, 1903)
Gorham, George C., *Life and Public Services of Edwin M. Stanton* (2 vols., Boston, 1899)
Gosnell, Harpur A., ed., *Rebel Raider: . . . Raphael Semmes's Cruise in the C.S.S. Sumter* (Chapel Hill, 1948)
Gosnell, H. Allen, *Guns on the Western Waters* (Baton Rouge, 1949)
Govan, Gilbert E., ed., *The Haskell Memoirs* (New York, 1960)
Govan, Gilbert E., *The Chattanooga Country 1540–1951* (New York, 1952)
Govan, Gilbert E. and James W. Livingood, *A Different Valor: the Story of Gen. Joseph E. Johnston, C.S.A.* (New York, 1956)
Graham, Matthew John, *The Ninth Regiment New York Volunteers* (New York, 1900)
Grant, Ulysses S., *Personal Memoirs of U.S. Grant* (New York, 1885)
Gray, John Chipman, *War Letters, 1862–1865, of John Chipman Gray . . . and John Codman Ropes . . . with portraits* (Boston, 1927)
Gray, Wood, *The Hidden Civil War: the Story of the Copperheads* (New York, 1942)
Greeley, Horace, *The American Conflict* (Hartford, 1867)

Greeley, Horace, *Recollections of a Busy Life* (New York, 1868)
Green, Fletcher M., ed., *I Rode with Stonewall* (Chapel Hill, 1940)
Greene, F.V., *The Mississippi* (New York, 1882)
Grodinsky, Julius, *Jay Gould: His Business Career* (Philadelphia, 1957)
Grossman, Jonathan, *William Sylvis, Pioneer of American Labor* (New York, 1945)
Guernsey, Alfred H. and Henry M. Alden, *Harper's History of the Civil War* (Chicago, 1894–1896)

Hagood, Johnson, *Memoirs of the War of Secession* (Columbia, S.C., 1910)
Hague, Parthenia Antoinette, *A Blockaded Family in Alabama During the Civil War* (Boston, 1888)
Hale, William H., *Horace Greeley, Voice of the People* (New York, 1950)
Hall, Clifton R., *Andrew Johnson, Military Governor of Tennessee* (Princeton, 1916)
Hall, Newman, *A Reply to the Pro-Slavery Wail* (London, 1868)
Hamilton, Holman, *Zachary Taylor* (2 vols., Indianapolis, 1941–1951)
Hamlin, Charles E., *The Life and Times of Hannibal Hamlin* (Cambridge, Mass., 1899)
Hammond, Bray, *Banks and Politics in America* (Princeton, 1957)
Hammond, M.B., *The Cotton Industry* (New York, 1897)
Handlin, Oscar, *Boston's Immigrants* (Cambridge, 1941)
Handlin, Oscar, ed. with others, *Harvard Guide to American History* (Cambridge, 1954)
Hanna, A.J., *Flight Into Oblivion* (Richmond, 1938)
Hannaford, Ebenezer, *The Story of a Regiment* (Cincinnati, 1868)
Hansen, Marcus Lee, *The Immigrant in American History* (Cambridge, 1940)
Harlow, Ralph V., *Gerrit Smith: Philanthropist . . .* (New York, 1939)
Harper, Ida H., *The Life and Work of Susan B. Anthony* (2 vols., Indianapolis, 1898–1908)
Harper, Robert S., *Lincoln and the Press* (New York, 1951)
Harper's Pictorial History of the Rebellion (New York, 1866)
Harrington, Fred H., *Fighting Politician: Major-General N.P. Banks* (Philadelphia, 1948)
Hart, Albert B., ed., *Salmon Portland Chase* (Boston, 1899)
Harwell, Richard B., *Cornerstones of Confederate Collecting* (Charlottesville, Va., 1952)
Haskell, Franklin A., *The Battle of Gettysburg* (Boston, 1898); new ed. by Bruce Catton (Boston, 1958)
Hassler, Warren W., Jr., *General George B. McClellan* (Baton Rouge, 1957)
Haupt, Herman, *Reminiscences* (Milwaukee, 1901)
Hay, Mrs. John, ed., *Letters of John Hay and Extracts from his Diary* (3 vols., Washington, 1908), selected by Henry Adams
Hay, Thomas R., *Hood's Tennessee Campaign* (New York, 1929)
Hayes, Rutherford B., *Diary and Letters*, ed., Charles R. Williams (Columbus, Ohio, 1922–1926)
Hazard, R.G., *Our Resources* (London, 1864)
Hebert, Walter H., *Fighting Joe Hooker* (Indianapolis, 1944)
Hedley, F.Y., *Marching Through Georgia: Pen Pictures of Every-day Life in Gen. Sherman's Army* (Chicago, 1890)
Henderson, G.F.R., *The Science of War* (London, 1910)
Henderson, G.F.R., *The Civil War: A Soldier's View*, ed., Jay Luvaas (Chicago, 1958)
Hendrick, Burton J., *The Life of Andrew Carnegie* (2 vols., Boston, 1932)
Hendrick, Burton J., *Statesmen of the Lost Cause* (Boston, 1939)
Henry, Robert S., *"First with the Most" Forrest* (Indianapolis, 1944)
Henry, Robert S., ed., *As They Saw Forrest* (Jackson, Tenn., 1956)
Hertz, Emanuel, *Abraham Lincoln: A New Portrait* (New York, 1931)
Hesseltine, William B., *Ulysses S. Grant, Politician* (New York, 1935)
Hesseltine, William B., *Lincoln and the War Governors* (New York, 1949)
Hesseltine, William B., *Lincoln's Plan of Reconstruction* (Tuscaloosa, 1960)
Hibben, Paxton, *Henry Ward Beecher, an American Portrait* (New York, 1927)
Higginson, Mary T., ed., *Letters and Journals of T.W. Higginson* (Boston, 1921)
Higginson, Thomas Wentworth, *Army Life in a Black Regiment* (Boston, 1870)

Hill, Louise Biles, *Joseph E. Brown and the Confederacy* (Chapel Hill, 1939)
Hinman, Walter F., *The Story of the Sherman Brigade* (Alliance, Ohio, 1897)
Historical Statistics of the United States (Washington, 1949)
History of the DuPont Company's Relations with the U.S. Government (Wilmington, 1928)
Hoar, George F., *Autobiography of Seventy Years* (2 vols., New York, 1903)
Hobart-Hampden, Augustus Charles, *Hobart Pasha*, ed., Horace Kephart (New York, 1915)
Hobart-Hampden, Augustus Charles, *Sketches from My Life* (New York, 1887)
Hobson, J.A., *Cobden, the International Man* (New York, 1919)
Hodges, W.R., *The Western Sanitary Commission* (St. Louis, 1906)
Hoehling, A.A., *Last Train from Atlanta* (New York, 1958)
Holbrook, Stewart H., *Yankee Exodus* (New York, 1950)
Holland, Cecil F., *Morgan and His Raiders* (New York, 1942)
Holland, James Gilbert, *Life of Abraham Lincoln* (Springfield, Mass., 1866)
Holst, Hermann E. Von, *Constitutional and Political History of the United States* (9 vols., Chicago, 1889–1892)
Holzman, Robert S., *Stormy Ben Butler* (New York, 1954)
Hood, John Bell, *Advance and Retreat* (New Orleans, 1880); new ed. by Richard N. Current, 1959
Hooker, Richard, *The Story of an Independent Newspaper* (New York, 1924)
Hopkins, Owen J., *Under the Flag of the Nation*, ed., Otto F. Bond (Columbus, O., 1961)
Horan, James D., *Mathew Brady: Historian with a Camera* (New York, 1955)
Horgan, Paul, *Songs After Lincoln* (New York, 1960; 1965)
Horn, Stanley F., *The Decisive Battle of Nashville* (Baton Rouge, 1956)
Horn, Stanley F., *The Army of Tennessee* (Norman, Okla., 1953)
Horner, Harlan H., *Lincoln and Greeley* (Urbana, 1953)
Howard, Leon, *Victorian Knight Errant; A Study of the Early Literary Career of James Russell Lowell* (Berkeley, 1952)
Howard, Oliver O., *Autobiography* (2 vols., New York, 1907)
Howe, Caleb, *The Supplies for the Confederate Army* (Boston, 1904)
Howe, M.A. DeWolfe, *The Life and Letters of George Bancroft* (New York, 1908)
Howe, M.A. DeWolfe, *Justice Oliver Wendell Holmes* (Cambridge, 1957)
Howe, M.A. DeWolfe, ed., *Marching with Sherman* (New Haven, 1927)
Howe, M.A. DeWolfe, ed., *Home Letters of General Sherman* (New York, 1909)
Hubbard, Charles Eustis, *The Campaign of the Forty-fifth Regiment, Massachusetts Volunteer Militia* (Boston, 1882)
Hughes, Sarah F., ed., *Letters and Recollections of John Murray Forbes* (2 vols., Boston, 1899)
Hume, John F., *The Abolitionists* (New York, 1905)
Humphreys, A.A., *The Virginia Campaign, 1864 and 1865* (New York, 1883)
Humphreys, H.A., *Andrew Atkinson Humphreys, a Biography* (Philadelphia, 1924)
Hungerford, Edward, *Men of Erie* (New York, 1946)
Hunt, Gaillard, *Israel, Elihu, and Cadwallader Washburn* (New York, 1925)
Hunter, Louis C., *Steamboats on the Western Rivers* (Cambridge, 1949)
Hutchins, E.R., ed., *The War of the Sixties* (New York, 1912)
Hutchinson, William T., ed., *The Marcus W. Jernegan Essays* (Chicago, 1937)
Hutchinson, William T., *Cyrus Hall McCormick* (2 vols., New York, 1930–35)
Hyde, Thomas W., *Following the Greek Cross* (Boston, 1894)

Illinois Commandery, *Military Essays and Recollections* (Chicago, 1894)
Illinois Infantry, *Military History and Reminiscences of the Thirteenth Regiment of Illinois Volunteer Infantry* (Chicago, 1892)
Inman, Arthur C., ed., *Soldier of the South: General Pickett's War Letters to His Wife* (Boston, 1928)
Irwin, Richard B., *History of the Nineteenth Army Corps* (New York, 1892)
Isely, Jeter A., *Horace Greeley and the Republican Party* (Princeton, 1947)

Jackson, W. Turrentine, *Treasure Hill: Portrait of a Silver-Mining Camp* (Tucson, 1963)
James, Marquis, *The Raven: A Biography of Sam Houston* (London, 1929)
Jarrell, Hampton M., *Wade Hampton and the Negro* (Columbia, S.C., 1949)
Jellison, Charles A., *Fessenden of Maine* (Syracuse, 1962)
Jenks, Leland Hamilton, *The Migration of British Capital to 1875* (London, 1963)
Johnson, Allen, *Stephen A. Douglas* (New York, 1908)
Johnson, Allen and Dumas Malone, eds., *Dictionary of American Biography* (New York, 1928–1944)
Johnson, Ludwell H., *Red River Campaign* (Baltimore, 1958)
Johnson, R.U., and Buel, C.C., *Battles and Leaders* (New York, 1887–1888)
Johnson, Richard W., *Memoir of Major-General George H. Thomas* (Philadelphia, 1881)
Johnson, Rossiter, *Campfire and Battlefield* (New York, 1896)
Johnston, John, *The Defense of Charleston Harbor* (Charleston, 1890)
Johnston, Joseph E., *Narrative of Military Operations* (New York, 1874)
Johnston, Richard M. and William H. Browne, *Life of Alexander H. Stephens* (Philadelphia, 1878)
Jones, Archer, *Confederate Strategy from Shiloh to Vicksburg* (Baton Rouge, 1961)
Jones, George R., *Joseph Russell Jones* (Chicago, 1964)
Jones, Jenkins L., *An Artilleryman's Diary* (Madison, 1914)
Jones, John Beauchamp, *A Rebel War Clerk's Diary* (2 vols., New York, 1866; 1935; 1958)
Jones, Maldwyn Allen, *American Immigration* (Chicago, 1961)
Jones, Rufus M., ed., *The Record of a Quaker Conscience: Cyrus Pringle's Diary* (New York, 1918)
Jordan, Donaldson and Edwin J. Pratt, *Europe and the American Civil War* (Boston, 1931)
Josephson, Matthew, *The Robber Barons: the Great American Capitalists* (New York, 1934)
Julian, George W., *Political Recollections* (Chicago, 1884)

Kamm, Samuel R., *The Civil War Career of Thomas A. Scott* (Philadelphia, 1940)
Kean, Robert Garlick Hill, *Inside the Confederate Government: the Diary of R.G. Hill Kean*, ed. Edward Younger (New York, 1957)
Kellogg, John A., *Capture and Escape* (Madison, 1908)
Kennedy, Joseph A., *Population of the U.S. in 1860* (Washington, 1864)
Ketring, Ruth A., *Clay of Alabama: Two Generations in Politics* (Duke Univ. Ph.D. Thesis, 1934)
Kibler, Lillian A., *Benjamin F. Perry, South Carolina Unionist* (Durham, 1946)
King, Willard L., *Lincoln's Manager David Davis* (Cambridge, 1960)
Kirke, Edmund (pseud. J.R. Gilmore), *Among the Pines* (New York, 1862)
Kirkland, Edward C., *Men, Cities, Transportation: A Study in New England History* (Cambridge, 1948)
Kirkland, Edward C., *Business in the Gilded Age* (Madison, Wis., 1952)
Kirkland, Edward C., *Dream and Thought in the Business Community, 1860–1900* (Ithaca, N.Y., 1956)
Klement, Frank L., *The Copperheads in the Middle West* (Chicago, 1960)
Knox, Dudley W., *A History of the U.S. Navy* (New York, 1936)
Koerner, Gustave, *Memoirs* (2 vols., Cedar Rapids, 1909)
Korn, Bertram W., *American Jewry and the Civil War* (Philadelphia, 1951)
Korngold, Ralph, *Two Friends of Man* (Boston, 1950)
Kriedberg, Marvin A. and Merton G. Henry, *History of Military Mobilization in the U.S. Army, 1775–1945* (Washington, 1955)
Kunhardt, Philip B., Jr., *Twenty Days* (New York, 1965)

Lamers, William E., *The Edge of Glory: a Biography of General William S. Rosecrans, U.S.A.* (New York, 1961)
Lamon, Ward Hill, *Recollections of Lincoln* (Washington, 1911)
Lane, Wheaton J., *Commodore Vanderbilt* (New York, 1942)
Larkin, Oliver W., *Art and Life in America* (New York, 1949)
Larson, Henrietta M., *Jay Cooke: Private Banker* (Cambridge, 1936)
Laugel, Auguste, *The United States During the Civil War*, ed. Allan Nevins (Bloomington, 1961)

Leach, Jack F., *Conscription in the United States* (Rutland, Vt., 1952)
Lebergott, Stanley, *Trends in American Economy in the Nineteenth Century* (New York, 1964)
LeConte, Joseph, *'Ware Sherman: A Journal of Three Months' Personal Experience in the Last Days of the Confederacy* (Berkeley, Calif., 1937)
Lee, Fitzhugh, *General Lee* (New York, 1894)
Lee, Robert E., Jr., *Recollections and Letters of General Lee* (New York, 1904; 1924)
Lee, William, *The Currency of the Confederate States of America* (Washington, 1875)
Leech, Margaret, *Reveille in Washington* (New York, 1941)
Lefler, Hugh T., *North Carolina History Told by Contemporaries* (Chapel Hill, 1956)
Lerwill, Leonard L., *Personnel Replacement System in the U.S. Army* (Washington, 1954)
Letterman, Jonathan, *Medical Recollections of the Army of the Potomac* (New York, 1866)
Lewis, Charles Lee, *David Glasgow Farragut, Our First Admiral* (Annapolis, 1943)
Lewis, Lloyd and Henry Justin Smith, *Chicago: The History of Its Reputation* (New York, 1929)
Lewis, Lloyd, *Captain Sam Grant* (Boston, 1950)
Lewis, Lloyd, *Sherman, Fighting Prophet* (New York, 1932)
Liddell Hart, B.H., *Sherman, Soldier, Realist, American* (New York, 1929)
Lincoln, Abraham, *Collected Works* (New York, 1886)
Lindsey, David, *"Sunset" Cox, Irrepressible Democrat* (Detroit, 1959)
Livermore, Col. Thomas L., *Numbers and Losses in the Civil War in America* (Boston, 1901)
Livermore, Col. Thomas L., *Sketches of Some of the Federal and Confederate Commanders* (Boston, 1895)
Livermore, Col. Thomas L., *Days and Events, 1860–1866* (Boston, 1920)
Lloyd, Arthur Y., *The Slavery Controversy, 1831–1860* (Chapel Hill, 1939)
Locke, Alain, *The Negro and His Music* (New York, 1969)
Lodge, Henry C., *Daniel Webster* (Boston, 1883)
Lomask, Milton, *Andrew Johnson: President on Trial* (New York, 1960)
Long, A.L., *Memoirs of Robert E. Lee* (New York, 1886)
Longstreet, James, *From Manassas to Appomattox: Memories* (Philadelphia, 1896; new ed., Bloomington, 1960)
Lonn, Ella, *Foreigners in the Union Army and Navy* (Baton Rouge, 1951)
Lonn, Ella, *Foreigners in the Confederacy* (Chapel Hill, 1940)
Lonn, Ella, *Desertion During the Civil War* (New York, 1928)
Lord, Francis A., *Civil War Collector's Encyclopedia* (Harrisburg, 1963)
Lord, John, *History of the Twenty-second Massachusetts Infantry* (Boston, 1887)
Lord, Walter, ed., *The Fremantle Diary* (Boston, 1954)
Lossing, Benson J., *The Pictorial Field Book of the Civil War* (Hartford, 1881)
Lossing, Benson J., *The Civil War in America* (3 vols., Hartford, 1868)
Lurie, Edward, *Louis Agassiz* (Chicago, 1960)
Luthin, Reinhard H., *Lincoln and the Patronage* (New York, 1943)
Luvaas, Jay, *The Military Legacy of the Civil War* (Chicago, 1959)
Lyman, Theodore, *Meade's Headquarters* (Boston, 1922)
Lyons, Capt. W.F., *Brigadier-General Thomas Francis Meagher* (New York, 1870)
Lytle, Andrew Nelson, *Bedford Forrest and His Critter Company* (New York, 1931)

Mabee, Carleton, *Black Freedom* (New York, 1970)
Macartney, Clarence E., *Grant and His Generals* (New York, 1953)
Macartney, Clarence E., *Mr. Lincoln's Admirals* (New York, 1956)
MacGill, Caroline E., and others under direction B.H. Meyer, *History of Transportation in the United States* (Washington, 1917)
Mack, Edward C., *Peter Cooper, Citizen of New York* (New York, 1949)
Magee, E.F., *History of the 72d Indiana Volunteer Infantry* (Lafayette, Ind., 1882)
Magnus, Philip, *Gladstone* (New York, 1954)

Mann, Albert W., *The Campaign of the Forty-fifth Regiment Massachusetts Volunteer Militia* (Boston, 1882)
Marshall, Charles, *An Aide-de-Camp of Lee*, ed. Sir Frederick Maurice (Boston, 1927)
Marshall, Helen E., *Dorothea Dix: Forgotten Samaritan* (Chapel Hill, 1937)
Marshall, Jessie Ames, ed., *Private and Official Correspondence of General Benjamin F. Butler* (5 vols., Norwood, Mass., 1917)
Martin, Robert F., *National Income in the United States* (New York, 1939)
Marwick, Arthur, *The Deluge* (London, 1965)
Massachusetts Soldiers' Relief Association (Washington, 1863)
Massey, Mary Elizabeth, *Bonnet Brigade* (New York, 1966)
Massey, Mary Elizabeth, *Refugee Life in the Confederacy* (Baton Rouge, 1964)
Mathews, Lois K., *The Expansion of New England, 1620–1865* (Boston, 1909)
Maurice, Sir Frederick, *Robert E. Lee, the Soldier* (Boston, 1925)
Maurice, Sir Frederick, *Statesmen and Soldiers of the Civil War* (Boston, 1926)
Maxwell, William Q., *Lincoln's Fifth Wheel* (New York, 1956)
Mayer, George H., *The Republican Party, 1854–1964* (New York, 1964)
McCaleb, Walter F., ed., *Memoirs of John F. Reagan* (New York, 1906; 1936)
McClellan, George B., *McClellan's Own Story* (New York, 1887)
McClellan, H.B., *The Life and Campaigns of Major-General J.E.B. Stuart* (Boston, 1885)
McClure, Alexander K., *Lincoln and Men of War-Times* (Philadelphia, 1892)
McClure, Alexander K., *Recollections of Half a Century* (Philadelphia, 1902)
McCulloch, Hugh, *Men and Measures of Half-a-Century* (New York, 1888)
McDonald, Cornelia, *A Diary with Reminiscences of the War and Refugee Life in the Shenandoah Valley, 1860–1865* (Nashville, 1935)
McGuire, Judith White, *Diary of a Southern Refugee* (New York, 1867)
McIlvane, Mabel, *Reminiscences of Chicago During the Civil War* (Chicago, 1914)
McKaye, James, *The Mastership and Its Fruits: The Emancipated Slave Face to Face with His Old Master* (New York, 1864)
McKim, James M., *The Freedman of South Carolina* (Philadelphia, 1862)
McKim, Randolph H., *A Soldier's Recollections; Leaves from the Diary of a Young Confederate* (New York, 1910)
McKitrick, Eric L., *Andrew Johnson and Reconstruction* (Chicago, 1960)
McMaster, John Bach, *History of the People of the United States During Lincoln's Administration* (New York, 1927)
McNamara, Daniel George, *The History of the Ninth Regiment Massachusetts Volunteer Infantry* (Boston, 1899)
McPherson, Edward, *The Political History of the United States of America During the Great Rebellion* (Washington, 1864–1865)
McWhitney, Grady, *Braxton Bragg and Confederate Defeat* (New York, 1969)
Meade, George G., *The Life and Letters of George Gordon Meade* (New York, 1913)
Meade, Robert D., *Judah P. Benjamin and the American Civil War* (Chicago, 1944)
Mearns, David C. and Lloyd A. Dunlap, *Long Remembered, the Gettysburg Address* (Washington, 1963)
Medberry, James K., *Men and Mysteries of Wall Street* (Boston, 1879)
Medical and Surgical History of the War of the Rebellion, ed. Surgical-General's Office (Washington, 1875)
Meigs, William M., *The Life of Thomas Hart Benton* (Philadelphia, 1904)
Melville, Herman, *The Works of Herman Melville* (London, 1924)
Mende, Elsie Porter and H.G. Pearson, *An American Soldier and Diplomat* (New York, 1927)
Meneely, Alexander Howard, *The War Department, 1861* (New York, 1928)
Mercier, Alfred, *Biographie de Pierre Soulé, Sénateur à Washington* (Paris, 1948)
Meredith, Roy, ed., *Mr. Lincoln's General: U.S. Grant* (New York, 1959)
Meredith, Roy, *Mr. Lincoln's Camera Man, Mathew B. Brady* (New York, 1946)

Merriam, George S., *Life and Times of Samuel Bowles* (New York, 1885)
Merrill, James M., *The Rebel Shore: The Story of Union Sea Power in the Civil War* (Boston, 1957)
Michie, Peter S., *General McClellan* (New York, 1901)
Michie, Peter S., *Life and Letters of Emory Upton* (New York, 1885)
Miers, Earl Schenck, ed., *Lincoln Day by Day; a Chronology, 1809–1865* (Washington, 1960)
Miers, Earl Schenck, *Web of Victory; Grant at Vicksburg* (New York, 1955)
Miers, Earl Schenck, *The General Who Marched to Hell, William Tecumseh Sherman* (New York, 1951)
Miers, Earl Schenck and Richard A. Brown, *Gettysburg* (New Brunswick, N.J., 1948)
Mill, John Stuart, *Political Economy* (London, 1847)
Mills, John Harrison, *Chronicles of the Twenty-first Regiment, New York State Volunteers* (Buffalo, 1867)
Milton, George F., *The Eve of Conflict: Stephen A. Douglas* (Boston, 1934)
Milton, George F., *Abraham Lincoln and the Fifth Column* (New York, 1942)
Milton, George F., *The Age of Hate, Andrew Johnson and the Radicals* (New York, 1930)
Mitchell, Broadus, *William Gregg, Factory Master* (Chapel Hill, 1928)
Mitchell, Broadus, *Frederick Law Olmsted, a Critic of the Old South* (Baltimore, 1924)
Mitchell, Dr. Silas Weir, *Catalogue of the Scientific and Literary Work of S. Weir Mitchell* (New York, 1852)
Mitchell, Stewart, *Horatio Seymour of New York* (Cambridge, 1938)
Mitchell, Wesley Clair, *Gold Prices, and Wages under the Greenback Standard* (Berkeley, 1908)
Mitchell, Wesley Clair, *History of the Greenbacks* (Chicago, 1903)
Monoghan, Jay, *Diplomat in Carpet Slippers* (Indianapolis, 1945)
Monoghan, Jay, *Civil War on the Western Border, 1854–1865* (Boston, 1955)
Montgomery, James S., *The Shaping of a Battle: Gettysburg* (Philadelphia, 1959)
Montross, Lynn, *War Through the Ages* (New York, 1944)
Moore, Albert Burton, *Conscription and Conflict in the Confederacy* (New York, 1924)
Moore, Frank, ed., *The Rebellion Record: A Diary of American Events* (New York, 1861ff)
Morford, Henry, *Days of Shoddy: The Great Rebellion* (Philadelphia, 1863)
Morgan, James M., *Recollections of a Rebel Reefer* (London, 1918)
Morrell, Daniel J., *The Manufacture of Railroad Iron, 1866* (Philadelphia, 1866)
Morrow, Curtis H., *Politico-Military Secret Societies of the Northwest* (Worcester, Mass., 1929)
Moss, Rev. Lemuel, *Annals of the U.S. Christian Commission* (Philadelphia, 1868)
Mott, Frank L., *A History of the American Magazines, American Journalism* (Cambridge, 1950)
Munroe, James Phinney, *Life of Francis Amosa Walker* (New York, 1923)
Murrell, William, *A History of American Graphic Humor* (New York, 1933–1938)
Muzzey, David S., *James G. Blaine* (New York, 1934)
Myers, Margaret G., *The New York Money Market* (New York, 1931)

Nason, Elias and Thomas Russell, *The Life and Public Services of Henry Wilson* (Philadelphia, 1876)
Naylor, Emmett Hay, *Trade Associations, Their Organization and Management* (New York, 1921)
Nevins, Allan, *The Evening Post, a Century of Journalism* (New York, 1922)
Nevins, Allan, *The Emergence of Modern America, 1865–1878* (New York, 1927)
Nevins, Allan, ed., *The Diary of Philip Hone* (2 vols., New York, 1927)
Nevins, Allan, ed., *The Diary of the Civil War*, by George Templeton Strong (New York, 1962)
Nevins, Allan, ed., *Selected Papers of Abram S. Hewitt* (New York, 1935)
Nevins, Allan, *Abram S. Hewitt with Some Account of Peter Cooper* (New York, 1935)
Nevins, Allan, *Hamilton Fish* (New York, 1936)
Nevins, Allan, *John D. Rockefeller: The Heroic Age of American Enterprise* (New York, 1940)
Nevins, Allan, *Ordeal of the Union, 1847–1857* (New York, 1947)
Nevins, Allan, *The Emergence of Lincoln* (New York, 1950)
Nevins, Allan, *Study in Power: John D. Rockefeller* (New York, 1953)
Nevins, Allan, *Frémont, Pathmaker of the West* (New York, 1955)
Nevins, Allan, *The War for the Union: The Improvised War, 1861–1862* (New York, 1959)

Nevins, Allan, *The War for the Union: War Becomes Revolution, 1862–1863* (New York, 1960)
Nevins, Allan, *The Origins of the Land-Grant Colleges and State Universities* (Washington, 1962)
Nevins, Allan, James I. Robertson, Jr., and Bell I. Wiley, eds., *Civil War Books: A Critical Bibliography* (2 vols., Baton Rouge, 1969)
Nevins, Allan, *The War for the Union: The Organized War, 1863–1864* (New York, 1971)
Nevins, Allan, *The War for the Union: The Organized War to Victory, 1864–1865* (New York, 1971)
Newell, Joseph Keith, *"Ours," Annals of the 10th Regiment Massachusetts Volunteers* (Springfield, Mass., 1875)
Newman, Bertram, *Edmund Burke* (London, 1827)
Newman, Ralph G. and E.B. Long, *Civil War Digest* (New York, 1956)
Newton, Lord, *Lord Lyons; a Record of British Diplomacy* (London, 1913)
Nichols, Edward J., *Toward Gettysburg: a Biography of Gen. John F. Reynolds* (University Park, Pa., 1958)
Nichols, George W., *The Story of the Great March* (New York, 1865)
Nichols, James L., *Confederate Engineers* (Tuscaloosa, 1957)
Nichols, Roy F., *Franklin Pierce: Young Hickory* (Philadelphia, 1931; 1958)
Nicolay & Hay, eds., *Collected Works of Abraham Lincoln* (New York, 1886)
Nicolay, Helen, *Lincoln's Secretary: A Biography of John G. Nicolay* (New York, 1949)
Nye, Russell B., *George Bancroft* (New York, 1944)
Nye, Russell B., *William Lloyd Garrison and the Humanitarian Reformers* (Boston, 1955)
Nye, Russell B., *Fettered Freedom* (E. Lansing, Mich., 1949)

Oberholtzer, Ellis Paxson, *Jay Cooke, Financier of the Civil War* (2 vols., Philadelphia, 1907)
Oberholtzer, Ellis Paxson, *A History of the United States Since the Civil War* (New York, 1917)
Oliphant, Mary C. Simms and others, eds., *The Letters of William Gilmore Simms* (2 vols., Columbia, S.C., 1952–1956)
Olmsted, Frederick L., *A Journey in the Back Country* (New York, 1860)
O'Neill, Edward H., *Biography by Americans, 1658–1936* (Philadelphia, 1939)
Osterweis, Rollin G., *Judah P. Benjamin* (New York, 1933)
Overdyke, William Darrell, *The Know-Nothing Party in the South* (Baton Rouge, 1950)
Owsley, Frank Lawrence, *King Cotton Diplomacy* (Chicago, 1931; 1959)
Owsley, Frank Lawrence, *State Rights in the Confederacy* (Gloucester, 1925; 1961)

Paine, Albert B., *Thomas Nast: His Period and His Pictures* (New York, 1904)
Palmer, George T., *A Conscientious Turncoat: the Story of John M. Palmer, 1817–1900* (New Haven, 1941)
Parker, John Lord, *History of the Twenty-second Massachusetts Infantry* (Boston, 1887)
Parker, Theodore, *Collected Works* (Centenary ed., 15 vols., Boston, 1907–13)
Parker, Capt. Thomas H., *51st Pennsylvania Volunteers* (Philadelphia, 1869)
Parker, William B., *The Life and Public Services of Justin Smith Morrill* (Boston, 1924)
Parks, Joseph H., *General Edmund Kirby Smith*, CSA (Baton Rouge, 1954)
Parrington, Vernon L., *Main Currents in American Thought* (3 vols., New York, 1927–1930)
Parsons, Gen. Lewis B., *Reports to the War Department* (Washington, 1867)
Parsons, Gen. Lewis B., *In Memoriam General Lewis Baldwin Parsons* (private, 1909)
Parton, James, *General Butler in New Orleans* (New York, 1864; 1892)
Patrick, Rembert W., *Jefferson Davis and His Cabinet* (Baton Rouge, 1944)
Patrick, Rembert W., *The Fall of Richmond* (Baton Rouge, 1960)
Patterson, A.W., *The Code Duello* (Richmond, 1927)
Patton, James W., *Unionism and Reconstruction in Tennessee, 1860–1869* (Chapel Hill, 1934)
Paullin, Charles O., *Atlas of the Historical Geography of the United States* (New York, 1932)
Pearce, Raymond J., Jr., *Benjamin H. Hill, Secession and Reconstruction* (Chicago, 1928)
Pearson, Henry G., *The Life of John A. Andrew* (Boston, 1904)
Pearson, Henry G., *An American Railroad Builder, John Murray Forbes* (Boston, 1911)

Pearson, Henry G., *James S. Wadsworth of Geneseo* (New York, 1913)
Pellet, Elias P., *A History of the 114th New York State Volunteers* (Norwich, N.Y., 1866)
Pember, Phoebe Y., *A Southern Woman's Story* (New York, 1879)
Pemberton, John C., Jr., *Pemberton: Defender of Vicksburg* (Chapel Hill, 1942)
Pepper, George W., *Personal Recollections of Sherman's Campaigns in Georgia and the Carolinas* (Zanesville, 1866)
Percy, William A., *Lanterns on the Levee, Recollections of a Planter's Son* (New York, 1950)
Perkins, Jacob R., *Trails, Rails and War, The Life of Gen. G.M. Dodge* (Indianapolis, 1929)
Peto, Sir S. Morton, *The Resources and Prospects of America* (London, 1866)
Phelps, Mary M., *Kate Chase, Dominant Daughter* (New York, 1935)
Phillips, Ulrich B., *The Life of Robert Toombs* (New York, 1913)
Phillips, Wendell, *Speeches, Lectures and Letters* (2 vols., Boston, 1863–1891)
Piatt, Donn, *Memories of Men Who Saved the Union* (New York, 1887)
Pickard, Samuel T., *Life and Letters of John G. Whittier* (2 vols., Boston, 1894; 1907)
Pickett, La Salle C., *The Heart of a Soldier* (New York, 1913)
Pickett, La Salle C., *Pickett and His Men* (Philadelphia, 1913)
Pierce, Edward L., *Memoirs and Letters of Charles A. Sumner* (4 vols., Boston, 1877–1893)
Pitman, Benn, *Assassination of President Lincoln, 1865* (Cincinnati, 1865)
Pleasants, Samuel A., *Fernando Wood of New York* (New York, 1948)
Plum, William R., *The Military Telegraph During the Civil War . . .* (Chicago, 1882)
Polk, William M., *Leonidas Polk: Bishop and General* (New York, 1915)
Pollard, Edward A., *Life of Jefferson Davis* (Philadelphia, 1869)
Pollard, Edward A., *The Lost Cause* (New York, 1967)
Pollard, John A., *John Greenleaf Whittier, Friend of Man* (Boston, 1949)
Polley, J.B., *Hood's Texas Brigade* (New York, 1910)
Poore, Benjamin Perley, *Reminiscences of Sixty Years in the National Metropolis* (New York, 1886)
Porter, David D., *Incidents and Anecdotes of the Civil War* (New York, 1885)
Porter, Horace, *Campaigning with Grant* (New York, 1897)
Porter, Kirk H. and Donald B. Johnson, eds., *National Party Platforms* (Urbana, 1966)
Potter, David M., *People of Plenty* (Chicago, 1954)
Pound, Roscoe, *The Lawyer from Antiquity to Modern Times* (St. Paul, 1953)
Powell, William H., *Fifth Army Corps of the Army of the Potomac* (New York, 1896)
Powers, George W., *The Story of the Thirty-eighth Regiment of Massachusetts Volunteers* (Cambridge, 1866)
Pratt, Fletcher, *Stanton: Lincoln's Secretary of War* (New York, 1953)
Proceedings of the American Pharmaceutical Association (Cincinnati, 1864)
Pryor, Mrs. Roger A., *Reminiscences of Peace and War* (New York, 1904)
Putnam, George Haven, *Some Memories of the Civil War* (New York, 1924)
Putnam, George Haven, *A Memoir of George Palmer Putnam* (New York, 1903)
Putnam, Sallie A., *In Richmond During the Confederacy* (New York, 1961)

Quaife, Milo M., ed., *From the Cannon's Mouth; Civil War Letters of Gen. Alphous S. Williams* (Detroit, 1959)
Quarles, Benjamin, *The Negro in the Civil War* (Boston, 1953)
Quarles, Benjamin, *Frederick Douglass* (Washington, 1948)
Quint, Alonzo H., *The Record of the Second Massachusetts Infantry* (Boston, 1867)

Radcliffe, George L.P., *Governor Thomas H. Hicks of Maryland and the Civil War* (Baltimore, 1901)
Rains, Col. George W., *History of the Confederate Powder Works* (Augusta, 1882)
Ramsdell, Charles W., *Behind the Lines in the Southern Confederacy* (Baton Rouge, 1944)
Ranck, James B., *Albert Gallatin Brown* (New York, 1937)
Randall, James G., *Lincoln the President* (New York, 1945)

Randall, James G., *Last Full Measure* (New York, 1955)
Randall, James G., *Civil War and Reconstruction* (Boston, 1953)
Randall, James G., *Constitutional Problems under Lincoln* (Urbana, 1951)
Rawley, James A., *Turning Points of the Civil War* (Lincoln, Neb., 1966)
Reid, John C., *The Brothers' War* (Boston, 1905)
Reid, Whitelaw, *Ohio in the War* (Cincinnati, 1868)
Renouvin, Mélange Pierre, *Études d'Histoire de Relations Internationales* (Paris, 1966)
Rhodes, James Ford, *History of the United States* (New York, 1917; 1928)
Richards, Laura E. and Maude H. Elliott, *Julia Ward Howe* (2 vols., Boston, 1915)
Richardson, Albert D., *A Personal History of U.S. Grant* (Hartford, 1868)
Richardson, E. Ramsey, *Little Aleck: a Life of Alexander H. Stephens* (Indianapolis, 1932)
Richardson, James D., *Messages and Papers of Jefferson Davis and the Confederacy . . .* with Introd. by Allan Nevins (New York, 1966)
Richardson, James D., *Messages and Papers of the Presidents, 1789–1902* (New York, 1903)
Richardson, Leon B., *William E. Chandler, Republican* (New York, 1940)
Riddle, Albert G., *Recollections of War Times* (New York, 1895)
Riddle, Albert G., *Life of Benjamin F. Wade* (Cleveland, 1887)
Rippey, J. Fred, *The United States and Mexico* (New York, 1931)
Risch, Erma, *Quartermaster Support of the Army: a History of the Corps, 1775–1939* (Washington, 1962)
Roberts, Walter Adolphe, *Semmes of the Alabama* (Indianapolis, 1938)
Robinson, Johan, *The Accumulation of Capital* (London, 1956)
Robinson, Solon, *Selected Writings*, ed. Herbert Anthony Keller (Indianapolis, 1935–1936)
Robinson, William M., *The Confederate Privateers* (New Haven, 1928)
Robinton, M.T., *An Introduction to Papers of the New York Prize Court, 1861–1865* (New York, 1945)
Roeder, Ralph, *Juarez and His Mexico* (New York, 1947)
Rogers, Joseph, *The Development of the North Since the Civil War* (Philadelphia, c. 1906)
Roman, Alfred, *The Military Operations of General Beauregard* (New York, 1884)
Ropes, John Codman, *The Story of the Civil War* (New York, 1933)
Roscoe, Theodore, *The Web of Conspiracy* (Englewood Cliffs, N.J., 1959)
Rose, Willie Lee, *Rehearsal for Reconstruction* (Indianapolis, 1964)
Roseboom, Eugene, *History of Presidential Elections* (New York, 1947; 1964)
Rosenbach Company Catalogue, *The History of America in Documents* (Philadelphia, 1951)
Rosewater, Victor, *History of Cooperative News-Gathering in the United States* (New York, 1930)
Ross, Ishbel, *First Lady of the South* (New York, 1958)
Ross, Ishbel, *Angel of the Battlefield* (New York, 1956)
Rowland, Dunbar, *Jefferson Davis, Constitutionalist* (10 vols., Jackson, Miss., 1923)
Russell, William Howard, *My Diary North and South* (New York, 1863)

Sage, Leland L., *William Boyd Allison: A Study in Practical Politics* (Iowa City, 1956)
Sala, George Augustus, *My Diary in America . . .* (London, 1865)
Sala, George Augustus, *America Revisited* (3 vols., London, 1883)
Salter, William, *The Life of James W. Grimes* (New York, 1876)
Samuels, Ernest, *The Young Henry Adams* (Cambridge, 1948)
Samuels, Ernest, *Henry Adams: the Middle Years* (Cambridge, 1958)
Schafer, Joseph, *Carl Schurz, Militant Liberal* (Evansville, Wis., 1930)
Schafer, Joseph, ed., *Intimate Letters of Carl Schurz* (Madison, 1928)
Scherer, James A.B., *Cotton as a World Power* (New York, 1916)
Schiebert, Captain Justus, *Seven Months in the Rebel States During the North American War, 1863* (Tuscaloosa, 1958)
Schiebert, Captain Justus, *Mit Schwert und Feder: Erinnerungen aus Meinen Leben* (Berlin, 1902)
Schmidt, Louis B., *Readings in the Economic History of American Agriculture* (New York, 1925)
Schofield, John M., *Forty-Six Years in the Army* (New York, 1897)

Schouler, James, *History of the United States* (Washington, 1880–1913)

Schuckers, J.W., *The Life and Public Services of Salmon Portland Chase* (New York, 1874)

Schurz, Carl, *Reminiscences* (New York, 1907)

Schwab, J.C., *The Confederate States of America, 1861–1865; a Financial and Industrial History* (New York, 1901; 1968)

Scott, Winfield, *Memoirs of Lieut.-General Scott* (2 vols., New York, 1864)

Scudder, Horace E., *James Russell Lowell.*(2 vols., Boston, 1901)

Sears, Louis M., *John Slidell* (Durham, 1925)

Segal, Charles M., ed., *Conversations with Lincoln* (New York, 1961)

Seitz, Don C., *Braxton Bragg, General of the Confederacy* (Columbia, S.C., 1924)

Seitz, Don C., *Horace Greeley, Founder of the New York Tribune* (Indianapolis, 1926)

Seitz, Don C., *The James Gordon Bennetts, Father and Son, Proprietors of the New York Herald* (Indianapolis, 1928)

Semmes, Raphael, *Memoirs of Service Afloat During the War Between the States* (Baltimore, 1869)

Seward, Frederick W., *Reminiscences of a War-time Statesman and Diplomat* (New York, 1916)

Seward, Frederick W., *Seward at Washington, 1861–1872* (New York, 1891)

Seward, Frederick W., ed., *William H. Seward: an Autobiography* (3 vols., New York, 1891)

Shannon, Frederick A., *Organization and Administration of the Union Army, 1861–1865* (Cleveland, 1928)

Shannon, Frederick A., *The Farmer's Last Frontier, Agriculture, 1860–1897* (New York, 1945)

Sharkey, Robert P., *Money, Class, and Party* (Baltimore, 1959)

Sheridan, Philip, *Personal Memoirs* (New York, 1888)

Sherman, John, *Memoirs* (New York, 1875)

Sherman, John, *John Sherman's Recollections of Forty Years in the House, Senate and Cabinet* (Chicago, 1895)

Sherwin, Oscar, *Prophet of Liberty: Life and Times of Wendell Phillips* (New York, 1958)

Shotwell, Walter Gaston, *The Civil War in America* (London, 1923)

Shryock, Richard H., *The Development of Modern Medicine* (New York, 1947)

Sievers, Harry, *Benjamin Harrison, Hoosier Warrior* (2 vols., Chicago, 1952)

Silver, David, *Lincoln's Supreme Court* (Urbana, 1957)

Silver, David, *The Supreme Court During the Civil War* (Urbana, 1956)

Simms, Henry H., *A Decade of Sectional Controversy, 1851–1861* (Chapel Hill, 1942)

Simon, John Y., *The Papers of Ulysses S. Grant* (Carbondale, Ill., 1967–1969)

Skipper, O.C., *J.D.B. DeBow, Magazinist of the Old South* (Athens, Ga., 1958)

Smith, Charles William, *Roger B. Taney, Jacksonian Jurist* (Chapel Hill, 1936)

Smith, Daniel E., and others, eds., *Mason Smith Family Letters 1860–1868* (Columbia, S.C., 1950)

Smith, Donnal V., *Chase and Civil War Politics* (Columbus, O., 1931)

Smith, Rev. Edward P., *Incidents of the U.S. Christian Commission* (Philadelphia, 1869)

Smith, Rev. Edward P., *Christian Work on the Battle-Field* (London, 1870)

Smith, Elbert B., *Magnificent Missourian* (Philadelphia, 1958)

Smith, Elbert B., *The Death of Slavery* (Chicago, 1967)

Smith, Frank E., *The Yazoo* (New York, 1954)

Smith, George Winston, *Medicines for the Union Army* (Madison, Wis., 1962)

Smith, Theodore Clarke, *The Life and Letters of James Abram Garfield* (2 vols., New Haven, 1925)

Smith, William E., *The Francis Preston Blair Family in Politics* (New York, 1933)

Soley, James R., *The Blockade and the Cruisers* (New York, 1883)

Soley, James R., *Admiral Porter* (New York, 1903)

Sorrel, G. Moxley, *Recollections of a Confederate Staff Officer* (New York, 1905)

Sparks, David S., ed., *Inside Lincoln's Army: The Diary of Marsena Rudolph Patrick* (New York, 1964)

Speed, James (grandson), *James Speed: a Personality* (privately printed, Morton, 1914)

Spiller, Robert E. and others, eds., *Literary History of the United States and Supplement* (New York, 1948)

Sprout, H. and M., *The Rise of American Naval Power* (Princeton, 1942)

Sprunt, James, *Cape Fear Chronicles* (Raleigh, 1914)
Stackpole, Edward J., *They Met at Gettysburg* (Harrisburg, 1956)
Stampp, Kenneth M., *Indiana Politics During the Civil War* (Indianapolis, 1949)
Stanton, H.S., *Random Recollections* (New York, 1881)
Stanwood, Edward, *A History of the Presidency from 1788 to 1897* (Boston, 1912)
Steere, Edward, *The Wilderness Campaign* (Harrisburg, 1960)
Steiner, Bernard C., *Life of Reverdy Johnson* (Baltimore, 1914)
Steiner, Bernard C., *Life of Henry Winter Davis* (Baltimore, 1916)
Steiner, Bernard C., *Life of Roger Brooke Taney* (Baltimore, 1914)
Stephens, Alexander H., *The War Between the States* (2 vols., Philadelphia, 1868)
Stephens, Alexander H., *A Constitutional View of the Late War Between the States* (Philadelphia, 1870)
Stern, Philip Van Doren, *The Man Who Killed Lincoln* (Cleveland, 1939)
Stern, Philip Van Doren, *The Assassination of President Lincoln* (New York, 1954)
Stern, Philip Van Doren, *An End to Valor; the Last Days of the Civil War* (Boston, 1958)
Steward, T.G., *The Colored Regulars in the U.S. Army* (New York, 1969)
Stewart, George R., *Pickett's Charge* (Boston, 1959)
Stiles, Robert, *Four Years Under Marse Robert* (New York, 1904)
Stille, C.J., *History of the U.S. Sanitary Commission* (Philadelphia, 1866)
Stoddard, Henry L., *Horace Greeley: Printer, Editor, Crusader* (New York, 1946)
Storey, Moorfield and Edward W. Emerson, *Ebenezer Rockwood Hoar . . . a Memoir* (Boston, 1911)
Stowe, Charles E. and Lyman B. Stowe, *Harriet Beecher Stowe: the Story of Her Life* (Boston, 1911)
Stowe, Harriet Beecher, *The Lives and Deeds of Our Self-made Men* (Boston, 1889)
Strode, Hudson, *Jefferson Davis: Confederate President* (New York, 1959)
Strode, Hudson, *Jefferson Davis, Private Letters . . .* (New York, 1966)
Strode, Hudson, *Jefferson Davis, Tragic Hero* (New York, 1964)
Strong, George Templeton, *The Diary of the Civil War*, ed. Allan Nevins (New York, 1962)
Struik, Dirk J., *Yankee Science in the Making* (Boston, 1948)
Stryker, Lloyd Paul, *Andrew Johnson: A Study in Courage* (New York, 1929)
Swanberg, W.A., *Sickles the Incredible* (New York, 1956)
Swank, James M., *Notes and Comments on Industrial, Economic, Political and Historical Subjects; American Iron and Steel Association from 1872 to 1897* (Philadelphia, 1897)
Swank, James M., *History of the Manufacture of Iron in All Ages* (Philadelphia, 1892)
Swiggett, Howard, *The Rebel Raider: A Life of John Hunt Morgan* (Garden City, 1937)
Swinton, William, *Campaigns of the Army of the Potomac* (New York, 1882)
Swisher, Carl B., *Roger B. Taney* (New York, 1935)
Symonds, H.C., *Report of a Commissary of Subsistence* (New York, 1888)

Tate, Allan, *Jefferson Davis: His Rise and Fall* (New York, 1929)
Tatum, Georgia Lee, *Disloyalty in the Confederacy* (Chapel Hill, 1934)
Taylor, Emerson G., *Gouverneur Kemble Warren: Life and Letters* (Boston, 1932)
Taylor, George R., *The Transportation Revolution, 1815–1860* (New York, 1951)
Taylor, Richard, *Destruction and Reconstruction* (New York, 1879)
Taylor, Thomas E., *Running the Blockade* (London, 1896)
Taylor, Walter H., *Four Years with General Lee* (New York, 1877)
Temperley, Harold and Lillian M. Penson, *Foundations of British Foreign Policy* (Cambridge, 1938)
Terrell, John Upton, *The United States Department of Agriculture* (New York, 1966)
Tharp, Louise H., *Adventurous Alliance: the Story of the Agassiz Family* (Boston, 1959)
Thayer, William R., *The Life and Letters of John Hay* (2 vols., Boston, 1915)
Thomas, Benjamin P., *Abraham Lincoln* (New York, 1952)
Thomas, Benjamin P., *Russo-American Relations, 1815–1867* (Baltimore, 1930)
Thomas, Lately, *The First President Johnson* (New York, 1968)

Thompson, Robert L., *Wiring a Continent: The History of the Telegraph Industry in the United States, 1832–1866* (Princeton, 1947)
Thompson, R.M. and R. Wainwright, eds., *Confidential Correspondence of Gustavus Vasa Fox* . . . (2 vols., New York, 1918–1919)
Thompson, S.B., *Confederate Purchasing Operations Abroad* (Chapel Hill, 1935)
Thorndike, Rachel Sherman, *The Sherman Letters: Correspondence Between General and Senator Sherman from 1837 to 1891* (London, 1894)
Ticknor, George, *Life, Letters and Journals of George Ticknor* (Boston, 1876)
Tilburg, Frederick, *Handbook on Gettysburg* (National Park System, Gettysburg)
Todd, Helen, *A Man Named Grant* (Boston, 1940)
Todd, Richard C., *Confederate Finance* (Athens, Ga., 1954)
Todd, William, *The Seventy-ninth Highlanders, New York Volunteers* (Albany, 1886)
Towne, Marvin W. and Wayne Rasmussen, *Trends in American Economy in the Nineteenth Century* (Princeton, 1960)
Townsend, George A., *Campaigns of a Non-Combatant* (New York, 1866)
Trent, William P., *William Gilmore Simms* (Boston, 1892)
Trevelyan, George M., *The Life of John Bright* (Boston, 1913)
Trimble, Bruce R., *Chief Justice Waite* (Princeton, 1938)
Trowbridge, J.T., *A Picture of the Desolated States* (Hartford, 1868)
True, Frederick W., *A History of the First Half-Century of the National Academy of Sciences, 1863–1913* (Washington, 1913)
Tucker, Glenn, *Chickamauga: Bloody Battle in the West* (Indianapolis, 1961)
Tucker, Glenn, *Zeb Vance, Champion of Personal Freedom* (Indianapolis, 1966)
Tupper, Henry Allen, *A Thanksgiving Discourse* . . . (Macon, Ga., 1862)
Turner, Carol, *Life of Turner* (Urbana, 1911)
Turner, Frederick Jackson, *The Frontier in American History* (New York, 1920)
Turner, George E., *Victory Rode the Rails* (Indianapolis, 1953)
Tyler, William S., ed., *Recollections of the Civil War . . . by Mason W. Tyler* (New York, 1912)

Upton, Emory, *The Military Policy of the United States* (Washington, 1912)

Vallandigham, James L., *A Life of Clement L. Vallandigham* (Baltimore, 1872)
Van Deusen, Glyndon G., *Horace Greeley: Nineteenth-Century Crusader* (Philadelphia, 1953)
Van Deusen, Glyndon G., *William Henry Seward* (New York, 1967)
Van Deusen, Glyndon G., *Thurlow Weed: Wizard of the Lobby* (Boston, 1947)
Vandiver, Frank E., *Ploughshares into Swords: Josiah Gorgas and Confederate Ordnance* (Austin, 1952)
Vandiver, Frank E., *Rebel Brass; the Confederate Command System* (Baton Rouge, 1956)
Vandiver, Frank E., ed., *Confederate Blockade Running Through Bermuda* (Austin, 1947)
Vandiver, Frank E., *Jubal's Raid* (New York, 1960)
Van Horne, Thomas B., *History of the Army of the Cumberland* (Cincinnati, 1875)
Van Horne, Thomas B., *The Life of Major-General George H. Thomas* (New York, 1882)
Van Oss, S.F., *American Railroads as Investments* (New York, 1893)
Van Tyne, Claude H., ed., *The Letters of Daniel Webster* . . . (New York, 1902)
Villard, Henry, *Memoirs of Henry Villard* . . . (2 vols., Boston, 1904)
Villiers, Brougham, and W.H. Chesson, *Anglo-American Relations, 1861–1865* (London, 1919)

Wainwright, Col. Charles S., *A Diary of Battle*, ed. Allan Nevins (New York, 1962)
Walcott, Charles Folsom, *History of the Twenty-first Regiment Massachusetts Volunteers* (Boston, 1882)
Walker, Francis A., *History of the Second Army Corps* (New York, 1891)
Walker, George, *The Wealth, Resources and Public Debt of the United States* (London, 1865)
Walker, Peter F., *Vicksburg: A People at War, 1860–1865* (Chapel Hill, 1960)
Wall, Joseph F., *Henry Watterson, Reconstructed Rebel* (New York, 1956)

Wallace, Irving, *The Fabulous Showman* (New York, 1959)
Wallace, Sarah A., and F.E. Gillespie, eds., *The Journal of Benjamin Moran* (Chicago, 1948–1949)
Wallace, Lew, *Lew Wallace: An Autobiography* (New York, 1906)
Wallace, Willard M., *Soul of the Lion: A Biography of General Joshua L. Chamberlain* (New York, 1960)
Walpole, Spencer, *The Life of Lord John Russell* (London, 1899)
Ward, A.W. and G.P. Gooch, eds., *The Cambridge History of British Foreign Policy, 1783–1919* (Cambridge, 1922–1923)
Warden, Robert B., *An Account of the Private Life and Public Services of Salmon P. Chase* (Cincinnati, 1874)
Ware, Capt. Eugene F., *The Indian War of 1864* (Lincoln, Neb., 1960)
Ware, Norman, *The Industrial Worker, 1840–1860* (Boston, 1924)
Warmoth, Henry C., *War, Politics, and Reconstruction* (New York, 1930)
Warner, Ezra J., *Generals in Blue* (Baton Rouge, 1964)
Warren, Charles, *A History of the American Bar* (Boston, 1911)
Warren, Louis A., *Lincoln's Gettysburg Declaration* (Fort Wayne, 1964)
Watkins, S.R., *"Co. Aytch," Maury Gray's First Tennessee Regiment* (Nashville, 1882)
Watts, John, *The Facts of the Cotton Famine* (London, 1866)
Wealthy Citizens of New York (New York, 1845)
Weber, Thomas, *The Northern Railroads in the Civil War, 1861–1865* (New York, 1862)
Weed, Thurlow and Harriet A. Weed, eds., *Life of Thurlow Weed* (2 vols., Boston, 1884)
Weigley, Russell F., *Quartermaster-General of the Union Army: a Biography of M.C. Meigs* (New York, 1959)
Weiss, John, *Life and Correspondence of Theodore Parker* (2 vols., New York, 1864)
Welles, Gideon, *Diary of Gideon Welles, Secretary of the Navy . . .* (Boston, 1911)
Wellman, Manly Wade, *Giant in Gray: a Biography of Wade Hampton of South Carolina* (New York, 1949)
Wells, David A., *Our Burden and Our Strength* (Norwich, Conn., 1864)
Wells, David A., *The Recent Financial, Industrial and Commercial Experiences of the United States . . .* (New York, 1872)
Wells, David A., *Our Merchant Marine, How It Rose, Increased, Became Great, Declined and Decayed* (New York, 1890)
Wells, H.G., Introduction to *The Outline of History* (New York, 1927)
Wells, Capt. James M., *With Touch of Elbow* (Philadelphia, 1909)
Werner, M. R., *Barnum* (New York, 1923; 1926)
West, Benjamin F., *Lincoln's Scapegoat General: a Life of Benjamin F. Butler, 1818–1893* (Boston, 1965)
West, Richard S., Jr., *Gideon Welles: Lincoln's Navy Department* (Indianapolis, 1943)
West, Richard S., Jr., *The Second Admiral: a Life of David Dixon Porter* (New York, 1937)
Wharton, Vernon L., *The Negro in Mississippi, 1865–1890* (Chapel Hill, 1947)
White, Andrew D., *Autobiography* (2 vols., New York, 1905–1907)
White, Horace, *The Life of Lyman Trumbull* (Boston, 1913)
White, Laura A., *Robert Barnwell Rhett; Father of Secession* (New York, 1931)
White, Leonard D., *The Jacksonians* (New York, 1956)
Whitman, Walt, *Specimen Days in America* (London, 1932)
Whitman, Walt, *The Wound Dresser* (Boston, 1898)
Wiley, Bell, *The Life of Johnny Reb* (Indianapolis, 1943)
Wiley, Bell, *The Life of Billy Yank* (Indianapolis, 1952)
Wiley, Bell, *Southern Negroes, 1861–1865* (New York, 1938)
Wiley, Bell, ed., *This Infernal War: Confederate Letters of Sgt. Edwin H. Fay* (Austin, 1958)
Wiley, Bell, ed., *Fourteen Hundred and 91 Days in the Confederate Army: a Journal Kept by W.W. Heartsill, for Four Years, One Month, and One Day* (Marshall, Tex., 1876)

Wilkerson, Frank, *Recollections of a Private Soldier . . .* (New York, 1887)

Williams, Charles Richard, ed., *Diary and Letters of Rutherford B. Hayes* (5 vols., Columbus, O., 1922–1926)

Williams, Charles Richard, *The Life of Rutherford Birchard Hayes . . .* (2 vols., Boston, 1914)

Williams, Kenneth P., *Lincoln Finds a General* (New York, 1959)

Williams, T. Harry, *Lincoln and the Radicals* (Madison, 1941)

Williams, T. Harry, *Hayes of the Twenty-third; the Civil War Volunteer Officer* (New York, 1965)

Williams, T. Harry, *P.G.T. Beauregard: Napoleon in Gray* (Baton Rouge, 1955)

Williamson, Harold F., ed., *The Growth of the American Economy* (New York, 1951)

Willson, Beckles, *John Slidell and the Confederates in Paris* (New York, 1932)

Wilson, Forrest, *Crusader in Crinoline, the Life of Harriet Beecher Stowe* (Philadelphia, 1941)

Wilson, James G., *The Life and Public Services of Ulysses Simpson Grant* (New York, 1885)

Wilson, James Harrison, *Under the Old Flag* (2 vols., New York, 1912)

Wilson, James Harrison, *The Life of Charles A. Dana* (New York, 1907)

Wilson, James Harrison, *Life and Service of William Farrar Smith* (Wilmington, 1904)

Winks, Robin, *Canada and the United States: the Civil War Years* (Baltimore, 1960)

Winslow, Col. I., *The Great Treason Plot in the North* (Chicago, 1895)

Winston, Robert W., *Andrew Johnson, Plebeian and Patriot* (New York, 1928)

Winthrop, Robert C., Jr., *Memoir of Robert C. Winthrop* (Boston, 1897)

Wise, Jennings, C., *The Long Arm of Lee* (New York, 1959)

Wise, John S., *The End of an Era* (Boston, 1899; 1902)

Wistar, Isaac Jones, *Autobiography of Isaac Jones Wistar, 1827–1905 . . .* (New York, 1914; Philadelphia, 1937)

Wolseley, Viscount Garnet Joseph, *The American Civil War, an English View*, ed., James A. Rawley (Charlottesville, 1964)

Woodward, W.E., *Meet General Grant* (New York, 1928)

Woolfolk, George R., *The Cotton Regency: the Northern Merchants and Reconstruction* (New York, 1958)

Worthington, George, *Doctors in Blue* (New York, 1952)

Wright, Edward N., *Conscientious Objectors in the Civil War* (Philadelphia, 1931)

Wright, Lt. Howard C., *Port Hudson, Its History from an Interior Point of View* (Baton Rouge, 1861)

Wyeth, John A., *Life of General Nathan Bedford Forrest* (New York, 1899)

Yates, Richard E., *The Confederacy and Zeb Vance* (Tuscaloosa, 1958)

Yearns, Wilfred Buck, *The Confederate Congress* (Atlanta, 1960)

Yeatman, James E., *Report on the Condition of the Freedmen of the Mississippi to Western Sanitary Commission, 1863* (St. Louis, 1864)

INDEX